BY ANTHONY PAGDEN

The Enlightenment: And Why It Still Matters

Worlds at War: The 2,500-Year Struggle Between East and West

Peoples and Empires: A Short History of European Migration, Exploration, and Conquest, from Greece to the Present

The Idea of Europe: From Antiquity to the European Union

Facing Each Other: The World's Perception of Europe and Europe's Perception of the World

Spanish Imperialism and the Political Imagination: Studies in European and Spanish-American Social and Political Theory 1513–1830

Lords of All the World: Ideologies of Empire in Spain, Britain and France c. 1500–c. 1800

European Encounters with the New World: From Renaissance to Romanticism

The Languages of Political Theory in Early-Modern Europe

The Fall of Natural Man: The American Indian and the Origins of Comparative Ethnology

THE ENLIGHTENMENT

The ENLIGHTENMENT

AND WHY IT STILL MATTERS

Anthony Pagden

RANDOM HOUSE
NEW YORK

Published in the United States by Random House, an imprint of The Random House Publishing Group, a division of Random House, Inc., New York.

Random House and colophon are registered trademarks of Random House, Inc.

Library of Congress Cataloging-in-Publication Data
Pagden, Anthony.
The Enlightenment : and why it still matters / Anthony Pagden.
pages cm
Includes bibliographical references (pages) and index.
ISBN 978-1-4000-6068-9
eBook ISBN 978-0-679-64531-3
1. Enlightenment. I. Title.
B802.P26 2013
940.2'5—dc23 2012043848

Printed in the United States of America on acid-free paper

www.atrandom.com

2 4 6 8 9 7 5 3 1

First Edition

Book design by Christopher M. Zucker

For Giulia

Tu mihi sola places

PREFACE

There are many ideological divisions within the modern world. One of the most persistent, most troubling, and increasingly most divisive, however, is the struggle over the legacy of the Enlightenment. The "Enlightenment"—that period of European history between, roughly, the last decade of the seventeenth century and the first of the nineteenth—has had a far greater and more lasting impact on the formation of the modern world than any of the intellectual convulsions that preceded it. The Renaissance and the Reformation, although they too transformed the cultures of Europe, and subsequently the whole of Christianity, in irreversible ways, are for most people today simply periods in history. Not so the Enlightenment. If we regard ourselves as modern, if we are forward-thinking, if we are tolerant and generally open-minded, if stem-cell research does not frighten us but fundamentalist religious beliefs do, then we tend to think of ourselves as "enlightened." And in thinking this, we are in effect declaring ourselves to be the heirs, however distant, of a particular intellectual and cultural movement.

There has been much heated debate over just what the "Enlightenment" was, when and where it occurred, and whether it was one or many. Attempts have been made to divide it up into radical and conservative groups or to distinguish between different national varieties in which the level-headed and reasonable English or the solemn and philosophically serious Germans are generally set against the extreme, overhasty, and unduly literary French. Some of these distinctions have their origins in the eighteenth century itself. Some are simple speculative fantasy. But for all the clear differences that did exist within it, the Enlightenment has been identified with an exalted view of human rationality and of human benevolence, and with a belief, measured and at times skeptical, in progress and in the general human capacity for self-improvement. It has been broadly understood to stand for the claim that all individuals have the right to shape their own ends for themselves rather than let others do it for them and—what comes to much the same thing—to live their lives as best they can without help or hindrance from divine decrees. It has been seen as the source of most modern liberal, tolerant, undogmatic, and secular understandings of politics and as the intellectual origins of all modern forms of universalism, from a recognition of the essential unity of the human race and the evils of slavery and racism right through to the humanistic sentiments behind Médecins sans frontières. It is widely regarded as having been the intellectual origin of our still slowly emerging conviction that all human beings share the same basic rights and that women think and feel no differently from men or Africans from Asians. As an intellectual movement it also saw the beginning of those disciplines—economics, sociology, anthropology, political science, and certain kinds of moral philosophy—that dictate much of how we view, and attempt to control, our lives today. Modernity was the creature of a great many intellectual and scientific configurations, from the invention of the steam engine to the Internet, very little of which can be attributed to the Enlightenment (even if it was the eighteenth-century German philosopher Gottfried Wilhelm Leibniz who first devised the binary system on which the modern digital computer is based). What can be attributed to it, however, is the broadly secular, experimental, individualistic, and progressive intellectual world that ultimately made those innovations possible—a world in which the old and apparently unassailable forms of association, of belief and tradition, that had for centuries divided human beings into mutually suspicious and often brutally homicidal groups were slowly and painfully, but irreversibly, abandoned. This is not to say that without the Enlightenment modernity—however understood—would never have taken place, that without it we would all still be burning unbelievers or listening to hellfire sermons for our weekly entertainment. But it most certainly would not have taken place how and where it did.

It is to the Enlightenment that we also owe the modern conception of the global society. The world is, of course, still firmly divided into nation-states, many still struggling furiously with one another; to any mildly skeptical observer, the prospect of what the United Nations once optimistically referred to as "Our Global Community" must still seem a long way off. But the fact that most liberal-minded and educated persons now accept that peoples should be willing and able to cooperate across frontiers must be cause for hope.

Such "globalism" or "cosmopolitanism" is also an Enlightenment conception, and it is one of my main objectives in this book to describe how it became possible for an admittedly small number of European intellectuals to refer to themselves as ultimately not English, French, Dutch, Saxon, Spanish, or Neapolitan but "citizens of the world." Cosmopolitanism is an ancient creed, but before the eighteenth century it had been largely the refuge of a few dissenting and rootless outsiders, like Diogenes the Cynic, who first coined the term in the fifth century BCE; or it had been closely associated with empire (one of the greatest of the ancient cosmopolitans, Marcus Aurelius, was also one of the greatest of the Roman emperors); or else it had been a cloak for religious uniformity (in both Christianity and Islam there are no nations, only one people under God).

During the Enlightenment, however, the claim to be a "citizen of the world" acquired quite different meanings. It came to stand for a form of ecumenism open to all those who were prepared to live by certain minimal legal and moral codes. It became a way of combating the narrow tribalism that seemed to many to be the ultimate cause of so many of the ills of the world. It became a way of understanding human and international relations that might finally lead what the English utilitarian Jeremy Bentham called "the cabinet of mankind" to conclude that "universal and perpetual peace" that had eluded the species *Homo sapiens sapiens* since its creation. Today we may not have gone very far toward realizing these ambitions, but if there does exist some conception of universal justice, if even the most powerful states on occasion feel compelled to abide by the demands of international law, that we owe to the Enlightenment.

Not everyone sees it this way, however. Today many have grown suspicious of precisely those values and aspirations that are now closely identified with the "West"—itself an eighteenth-century coinage—of which the Enlightenment is seen as the most heinous representative. The past century and a half of Euro-American history has come to be regarded—and not without reason—as little more than a litany of war and oppression, colonization and exploitation. In the light of such a history, the airy, optimistic, ecumenical claims of the Enlightenment—or what is widely taken to be the Enlightenment—have come to look threadbare, if not hypocritical and presumptuous. It is the Enlightenment that is now accused of being responsible for a "Eurocentrism" that led inexorably to an implacable intolerance of everyone, and everything, that rose to challenge its rationalistic, reductive objectives, thus making it the midwife to modern imperialism and modern racism.

In one respect at least, these accusations are not entirely groundless. Although a great many of the claims made on its behalf can be found in many other cultures across the world, the Enlightenment was certainly a process confined to Europe and its overseas settler populations. It is also undeniable that the confidence that the Enlightenment helped to instill in the "West," a confidence that derived from a sense of independent intellectual achievement rather than from some supposedly superior understanding of God, did have a subsequent impact on nineteenth- and twentieth-century conceptions of the "civilizing mission." If, the argument went, we can free our own peoples from what the Marquis de Condorcet called "those sacred despots and foolish conquerors," then we must surely have an obligation to help all those others across the globe who are still suffering in darkness to do the same. In doing so, Condorcet added, "we would become for them . . . generous liberators." And if they were to show no sign of wishing to be liberated, then that could only be because their "priests and kings" had blinded them to everything they had to gain by following our example. In which case we might be justified, in Jean-Jacques Rousseau's infamous phrase, to "force them to be free." But none of the enlightened intellectuals of the eighteenth century—the *philosophes,* as the French usefully called them, a word that describes someone who is at once more and less than a "philosopher"—ever espoused such views. They were terrified by visions of a future dominated by a number of what they called "universal monarchies," which could only ever be, as Immanuel Kant said of them, the "graveyard of freedom" and a "soulless despotism." The line that supposedly leads from eighteenth-century rationalism and the apotheosis of modern science, via such atrocities as the massacres in the Belgian Congo and the Opium Wars in China, to the virtual domination of the world by the so-called Great Powers of Europe and the United States is an illusory one. The real source of so much of the undeniable injustice that the "West" has inflicted upon the "Rest"—not to mention upon itself—in the more recent past lies elsewhere: in the distorted forms of nationalism and "scientific" racism of the late nineteenth century, in the sense of omnipotence conferred by the new technologies of the Industrial Revolution, and in the resurgence of a (Protestant) Christian piety and evangelical fervor, which all of the *philosophes* would have abhorred.

There are also those who accuse the Enlightenment of having undermined ancient and tested systems of religious belief, of having set up reason over all other human faculties, of having reduced sentiment, sympathy, affection, and feeling to mere delusion and, in the process, of having destroyed all possibility of a consoling belief in an omniscient and benevolent deity. The world, they say, is not made up of individuals, as the *philosophes* and their followers naively supposed. Humans are not so much the creators of the social and political worlds they inhabit; they are their creatures. They live in complex cultures that have evolved over very long periods of time, all of which makes the Enlightenment belief in a scientifically intelligible "human nature" simply unsustainable. Certainly, they would argue, all humans should recognize each other as human and respect each other's chosen ways of doing things. But it is merely absurd to believe that such essentially diverse creatures could ever be brought, by reason alone, to agree upon so difficult an issue as how best to live their lives. Without the guidelines of tradition, without those systems of religious belief that all human societies possess and have always possessed, humans are lost. All those attempts—most of which have taken place in Europe or under the influence of the European Enlightenment—to employ coercion to bring about an entirely ethereal vision of a wholly new, ideal, rational world have only ever resulted in unimaginable horrors. Look at the French Revolution, the Russian Revolution, the Chinese Revolution, they say. Look, too, at the final outcome of National Socialism and of Fascism.

It is undeniably true that the Enlightenment was profoundly antireligious. There were unmistakably "enlightened figures," particularly in southern Europe, who were obviously sincere believers. The Italian Giambattista Vico (whom we shall meet again), in many respects one of the more radical figures of the century, was clearly one such—despite attempts to present him as a closet Spinozist and thus a deist, if not quite an atheist. So, too, was Benito Jerónimo Feijoo, perhaps the most obviously "enlightened" Spaniard of the period and also a Benedictine friar. A number of the other figures of the Enlightenment were in minor orders (although this was generally only a means of securing a reliable income), and as David Hume observed, in his day true atheists were very rare—even in Paris. But by and large, the major figures of the eighteenth century, if they were not exactly atheists, certainly had no time for the deities of any of the world's monotheistic religions. (They were generally more accommodating of polytheism.) To be "enlightened" meant, as Immanuel Kant famously put it, freeing the human mind from "the ball and chain of an everlasting permanent minority" that had been imposed upon it by the "dogmas and formulas" of, among other things, organized religion. Most of the *philosophes* would have agreed that it is a matter of choice—and inclination—if you think it desirable or not to believe in an afterlife to make up for the shortcomings of this one or in the existence of a kind-hearted deity to help you out in a tight spot. But what they also insisted upon was the need for a clear understanding of what it meant to hold such beliefs, above all the right of every individual to reject them with impunity, if he or she saw fit.

The familiar and often unquestioned claim that the Enlightenment was a movement concerned exclusively with enthroning reason over the passions and all other forms of human feeling or attachment is, however, simply false. The exercise of reason clearly did have a decisive role to play in the process of enlightenment. But to reduce a highly complex, nuanced, and often allusive intellectual project—and I shall argue that it was indeed a *project*—to what later came to be called the "empire of reason" is, as I hope to show, absurdly reductionist. It was, after all, David Hume—who must rank, with Kant, as the greatest of the eighteenth-century philosophers—who famously declared that "reason is and ought to be a slave of the passions and can never pretend to any other office but to serve and obey them." The Enlightenment was as much about rejecting the claims of reason and of rational choice as it was about upholding them.

The Enlightenment has also been accused of being the exclusive concern of a small coterie of intellectuals scattered across Europe. In part this, too, is true. But if the coterie was relatively small, the diffusion of its works was immense, from Stockholm to Naples, from Boston to Bombay. Its members wrote in a large number of different idioms—philosophical, economic, and anthropological treatises; plays, poems, novels, histories—and in some cases, such as Vico's *New Science* or Montesquieu's *Spirit of the Laws,* created works that defied all simple classification. They captured, in effect, all the literate public that then existed. They were also all concerned with reaching out far beyond the narrow professional circles to which their predecessors had been confined. As Hume complained, in the past all learning had been "shut up in Colleges and Cells, and secluded from the World and Good Company." It was his task, as he saw it, to free learning from its imprisonment and make it intelligible to what he called the "Conversible" part of mankind. Even Kant, who forged a philosophical language of quite remarkable complexity, hoped that at least the many articles that he wrote for the monthly German press would reach a readership beyond the university—and they clearly did. Many of the arguments of the *philosophes,* suitably simplified, reached even wider audiences through the relatively new medium of the press, and some of their works became, in their own way, best sellers. Jean-Jacques Rousseau's sentimental novel *Julie, or the New Héloïse,* was so popular that copies had to be rented out by the hour. But for all that, the Enlightenment was no popularist movement. Even Rousseau's devoted readership was made up of members of the new middle class, well off, educated, and literate. Indeed, most of the enlightened of eighteenth-century Europe were no less suspicious of the undisciplined enthusiasm and what Denis Diderot called the "wickedness, stupidity, inhumanity, unreason, and prejudice" of the masses than were their unenlightened contemporaries. Enlightenment was, as Kant argued, initially at least, suited only to the "*man of learning* addressing the entire *reading public,*" and in the eighteenth century the size of the "entire reading public," although on the rise, was still small indeed. Only in time, he believed, and with the kind of good government that the men of learning would finally persuade their leaders to adopt, would the rest of the public become capable of "enlightening itself." The Enlightenment was not, despite what some of its enemies claimed, a revolutionary movement. It was concerned with reform—and reform is inevitably a top-down process.

Today, most of what we have gained since the end of the Second World War we owe to its legacy. In a world still populated largely by corrupt, murderous, and far from enlightened regimes, this may not be very much. But for all their otherwise unenlightened behavior, in particular in the international arena, most of the world's more powerful states now pay lip service, if sometimes little more, to the claim that human rights and universal justice are truly universal, not merely—as the Ayatollah Khomeini once claimed—the cultural expression of western imperialism. We have an International Court of Justice and, since 1998, a Permanent International Criminal Court—even if some of the otherwise enlightened nations of the world refuse to accept its judgments. We have widely, if not universally, accepted agreements on climate change and global warming and what might be done about them. It is becoming increasingly difficult for those guilty of "crimes against humanity"—itself an Enlightenment conception—to escape censure, if not always punishment, as the fate of so many of the former warlords involved in the atrocities committed during the conflict in the Balkans during the 1990s has made clear. The World Bank and the IMF, for all the claims that they are little more than the agents of a new brand of "informal empire," seek to raise all nations, without meddling too much in their internal affairs, to the economic and thus social standards of those in the "developed" world. Phrases such as "international community" and "global governance" may not have much specific content, but the fact that they can be used at all, and command some degree of respect, would seem to be cause for hope. Most nations would broadly accept that different religions and different traditions should be tolerated, if for no other reason than that security and social well-being require a measure of regard for the things that are important to all peoples, however incomprehensible. But very few states would argue that where religious beliefs conflict with the secular laws of the state or with the values of the "international community," they might have some claim to be treated as worthy of special dispensation. International law—like the laws of most states—does not accept that forced marriages or honor killings are merely local customs, comparable to morris dancing and ten-pin bowling. Female circumcision—the subject of impassioned debate during the eighteenth century itself—is not looked upon as a matter of opinion but as the violation of a basic human right.

Without the Enlightenment, none of this would be true. This is why it is not only of professional interest to historians. It is why it still matters. And it is why it is important to understand just what it was.

This book is not intended to be a political tract, nor a moral homily. It is a work of history, an attempt, to borrow the words of the dying Hamlet to Horatio, the loyal humanist historian, to "report . . . my cause aright." But all history, if it is to be anything more than mere archaeology, must be a reflection of what the present owes to the past.

PARIS–LOS ANGELES–VENICE

SEPTEMBER 2012

ACKNOWLEDGMENTS

The initial idea for this book goes back much further than I care to remember. Along the way I have had assistance of different kinds from many different people. Much earlier versions were first aired as lectures at the University of Santiago de Compostela, while I was fortunate enough to be the holder of the Banco de Bilbao y Vizcaya visiting chair in philosophy and at the Seminario público de la Fundación Juan March in Madrid. On those occasions, as on many others, my friend José Maria Hernández was a patient and widely critical reader. Other attempts were given as the Priestley Lectures at the University of Toronto, the Solomon Katz Distinguished Lecture at the University of Washington, and the Verne Moore Lecture at the University of Rochester. Long conversations with Roberto Farneti also provided me with some understanding of the possible future of religion in the modern West.

I am, as always, indebted to my editors Will Murphy and Ben Steinberg at Random House, and Matthew Cotton at Oxford University Press, for their patience and careful pruning. I would also like to thank my agent, Andrew Wylie, above all for his patience and Scott Moyers, who took the time to read though some of the earlier chapters and whose comments helped me to see more clearly where I should have been going. Jeff New, Hayley Buckley, and Martin Schneider read through the entire manuscript with scrupulous care and saved me from several blunders and numerous infelicities.

I owe a very special debt to Peter Campbell, who read the entire book in an earlier draft, made extensive comments, and suggested numerous revisions from which the present version, has, I hope, benefited immeasurably. As always, my wife, Giulia Sissa, has put me right about more things than I can name. To her, as always, for her support, her generosity, her encouragement, her wisdom, and her love, I owe more than I can ever express or hope to repay.

CONTENTS

LIST OF ILLUSTRATIONS

THE ENLIGHTENMENT

INTRODUCTION

WHAT IS ENLIGHTENMENT?

I

IN 1794 MARIE-JEAN-ANTOINE-Nicolas de Caritat, marquis de Condorcet, sat in hiding in a tiny room in the house of Madame Vernet in the rue Servandoni in Paris. By the light of a candle, shaded so as not to reveal his whereabouts while the forces of the French Revolution closed in on him, he wrote a brief fragment of what was intended to be a much longer work, the *Sketch for a Historical Picture of the Progress of the Human Mind*. Condorcet was one of the great mathematicians of his or any other age, one of the creators of differential calculus, and the first person to attempt to predict the possible outcome of human decision-making by using mathematics, which makes him the forefather of modern political science. He was also a champion of equal rights for women and for all peoples of all races and an abolitionist who devised the world's first state education system. Like all men of his class in the eighteenth century, he was deeply involved in politics.[1] He had been an active supporter of the Revolution in its early stages, becoming the

Paris representative of the National Assembly in 1791 and then its secretary. Although a member of the Girodins, the more moderate of the two revolutionary parties, he continued until his death to see the Revolution as a force that had accelerated the normal course of history, and he looked upon the French constitution, as did its authors, as not merely a constitution for a new republican France but a constitution for humankind.[2] When, in December 1792, the National Assembly put the king, Louis XVI, on trial as a traitor, Condorcet supported the move, believing, like the Anglo-American radical Tom Paine—now a naturalized French citizen—that it would show the world that kings, too, could be held accountable for their crimes. But because, like all good liberals—like Paine, indeed—he rejected the idea that the state had the right to take human life, he passionately opposed the idea of his execution. This did not win him friends among the revolutionary hard-liners, and when in 1793 he voted against the new constitution proposed by the Jacobins, he was branded as a traitor and an enemy of the Revolution. A warrant for his arrest was issued on July 8, after which he went into hiding in the rue Servandoni. On March 25, 1794, sensing that the forces of the Terror were closing in on him and fearful that his continuing presence might prove dangerous to the good Madame Vernet, he fled Paris, taking with him only a volume of the poems of Horace. He seems to have spent the night of the 26th in the countryside around Clamart, some nine kilometers outside Paris, and on the 27th, exhausted, famished, and apparently wounded in one leg, he stopped at an inn and ordered an omelette. The innkeeper asked him how many eggs he wanted. "Twelve," replied Condorcet. He was immediately arrested and taken to Bourg-la Reine to await prosecution by the dreaded Revolutionary Tribunal. (Only aristocrats ever ate so many eggs at one sitting.)[3] Two days later, on March 29, 1794, he died in prison, under somewhat mysterious circumstances, the victim of what the conservative Anglo-Irish orator, philosopher, and political theorist Edmund Burke nicely called "the delusive plausibilities of moral politicians."[4]

Condorcet was one of the most prominent, distinguished, and widely loved victims of the revolutionary fury, yet for the enemies of the Enlightenment, on both the extreme left and the far right, he became one of the worst exponents of the confidence in human rationality that had supposedly made the Revolution possible. "That *philosophe* so dear to the Revolution," the arch-conservative Joseph de Maistre said of him, "who used his life to prepare the unhappiness of the present generation, graciously willing perfection to posterity."[5] Maximilien de Robespierre, the sanguineous theoretician of the Terror, thought no better of him. "A great geometrician," he called him after his death, "or so say the men of letters; a great man of letters in the opinion of the geometricians, and later a timid conspirator despised by all parties."[6]

Much of this hostility, and De Maistre's in particular, was not directed at Condorcet's mathematical writings, although his vision of a life regulated by the certainty of predication struck some—as it did the Romantic literary critic Charles-Augustin Sainte-Beuve—as a recipe for "universal mediocrity," in which there would be no place "for great virtues, for acts of heroism," a bright new world whose unfortunate citizens would all die of boredom. It was directed instead at the *Sketch,* which was his most accessible and would become his best-known work.[7]

As its somewhat provisional title makes clear, the *Sketch* is a universal history of mankind, divided into ten "epochs." It starts in prehistory with small wandering bands whose condition can only be inferred by "examining the intellectual and moral faculties and the physical constitution of man." It then takes the reader through the successive stages of human social evolution until it arrives at the current condition of the "enlightened nations of Europe." The final epoch lies in the future. It is here that all the promises of that period, which, like his contemporaries, Condorcet referred to as the "century of light" or the "century of philosophy" and we today call the Enlightenment, "would finally be realized." The natural sciences, he argued, which had achieved such astounding successes in the seventeenth century, are based upon one single and unwavering belief: that all the laws of the universe are "necessary and constant" throughout time. As humans are part of this universe, the study of their history, although it is unlikely to uncover laws as certain as those of physics, will at least allow the historian to "predict with great probability the events of the future." What, then, will the future bring? Given the conditions in which he was writing, Condorcet was perhaps being unduly optimistic. But he remained convinced that

> Our hopes for the future state of the human species may be summed up in three important points: the elimination of the inequality between nations; progress in equality within the same peoples; and finally the real perfection of mankind. All peoples should one day approach the state of civilization attained by the most enlightened, the most free, and the most free from prejudices, such as are the French and the Anglo-Americans.

Today we have grown wary of the word *civilization,* after the uses to which, in the nineteenth and twentieth centuries, it was put. But Condorcet understood it not as some undifferentiated cultural and political state that all peoples should be compelled to adopt but what he called an "equal diffusion of enlightenment," a condition in which all mankind would acquire

> the necessary enlightenment to conduct themselves in accordance with their own reason in the common affairs of life, and to maintain them, free of prejudices, so that they might know their rights and be at liberty to exercise them according to their own opinion and their conscience, where all might, through the development of their faculties, obtain the certain means to provide for their needs.

In 1794 these conditions clearly did not yet exist. But Condorcet assured his readers that the "progress which science and civilization" had made was such that there were "the strongest reasons to believe that nature has set no limit to our hopes." Even now, or so he thought, the principles behind the French constitution were shared by all enlightened beings across the world. Soon they would be shared by all mankind. Soon, what he called the "great religions of the Orient"—by which he meant not only Islam but also, and most especially, Christianity—which for so long had kept their cringing adherents trapped in a state of "slavery without hope and a perpetual infancy," would finally be revealed for the lies, tricks, and deceits that they were. When that day arrived, "The sun will rise only upon a world of free men who will recognize no master other than their own reason, where tyrants and slaves, priests and their stupid or hypocritical instruments, will exist only in history or in the theatre." When that day arrived, as he had told the doubtless skeptical members of the Académie française twelve years earlier, "We will have seen reason emerge victorious from that struggle, so long and so painful, [so] that at last we will be able to write: truth has triumphed; the human race is saved!"[8]

Some aspects of Condorcet's imaginary future can today sound uncomfortably like a precursor to the objectives of the civilizing missions that would flood so much of the world in the nineteenth century. Yet for all his belief in the goods that the inescapable forward march of western civilization would finally bring, he was also acutely aware of the depredations that that civilization, in its insatiable quest for "sugar and spices" in Africa, Asia, and America, and "our betrayals, our bloody contempt for men of a different color or belief, our insolence and our usurpations" had inflicted on "those vast lands."[9] But he firmly believed that now that the perpetrators themselves had thrown off the kings and priests who had been largely responsible for these horrors, these depredations would soon be only a distant memory, and the peoples of Africa and Asia (alas, it was already too late for the poor American Indians) would be waiting patiently for the day when they might become the "friends and disciples" of new, enlightened Europeans.

Condorcet's vision of the future, although challenged and derided, has had and continues to have a powerful hold over the imagination of the western world. It is, although he does not use the term, deeply cosmopolitan. Cosmopolitanism, like so much else in the western philosophical tradition, has been with us since antiquity. Diogenes the Cynic of the fourth century BCE, the man famous for living in a barrel and walking the streets of Athens at midday with a lighted lamp in search of an "honest man," was supposedly the first to declare, when asked from what city (*polis*) he came: "I am a citizen of the world [*kosmopolites*]."[10] Later the expression was taken up by the Stoics, who, as we shall see, were to play a transformative role in its subsequent history. For all the opprobrium directed against it in the nineteenth and twentieth centuries, when "cosmopolitanism" came to be cast as a form of immorality, a betrayal of every man's true and proper objects of loyalty, which was not to the world but to the nation, it has shown itself to be remarkably resilient. It has been the inspiration behind the League of Nations and the United Nations, behind the International Court of Justice and the beleaguered, but still enduring, belief in the possibility for a truly international law. Today it provides the theoretical foundations for the modern conceptions of "international justice," "geo-governance," "global civil society," and "Constitutional patriotism."[11] It has, as the Anglo-Ghanaian philosopher Kwame Anthony Appiah, himself an exemplary cosmopolitan, rightly says of it, "certainly proved a survivor."[12]

The version of cosmopolitanism that Condorcet was proposing, like Condorcet himself, was also unmistakably a creature of "the Enlightenment." To say that, however, is to beg a number of questions. For just what exactly the Enlightenment was has been the subject of irate and furious debates ever since the eighteenth century itself. No other intellectual movement, no other period in history, has attracted so much disagreement, so much intransigence, so much simple anger. The key terms of almost every modern conflict over how we are to define and understand "humanity"—modernism, postmodernism, universalism, imperialism, multiculturalism—ultimately refer back to some understanding of the Enlightenment. No topic of historical debate, none of the great controversies over the turning points in history or over the moment in which "modernity" is believed to have begun—not the Renaissance, nor the Reformation, not the Scientific Revolution nor the Industrial Revolution—has exercised anything like the hold that the Enlightenment does over the ideological divisions within the modern world.

The struggle over the identity of the Enlightenment was also a part of the Enlightenment itself. In December 1783 the *Berlinische Monatsschrift,* a widely read and generally progressive journal, published an article by a theologian and educational reformer named Johann Friedrich Zöllner. The article was on the desirability of purely civil marriages—a somewhat recondite topic. It might have passed unnoticed, and probably unread, if it had not been for a single footnote. "What is enlightenment?" Zöllner asked. "This question, which is almost as important as what is truth, should indeed be answered before one begins enlightening. And still I have never found it answered!"[13] It was perhaps the most significant footnote in the entire history of western thought—it was certainly the most widely discussed. Six years later, shortly before the outbreak of the French Revolution, the German poet and philosopher Christoph Martin Wieland—once described as the German Voltaire—while seated on the toilet and reaching for what he coyly calls a "maculature" (in other words, a piece of toilet paper), found, "not without a slight shudder of astonishment," that the sheet of "good white soft paper" he held in his hand had printed on it six questions, the first of which was: "What is enlightenment?"[14]

The debate that Zöllner had inadvertently begun seems to have been a uniquely German event. But the widespread diffusion of the term *Enlightenment—Aufklärung* in German, *Lumières* in French, *Ilustración* in Spanish, *Illuminismo* in Italian, *Oplysning* in Danish—and the confusion it aroused was by no means confined to the German-speaking lands (there was, as yet, no such place as Germany). In France, in England, in Spain, in Sweden, in Holland, in Italy, in Portugal people had been asking themselves similar questions since at least the middle of the century. Despite this, however, the answer was very far from being, as Wieland breezily claimed, "known to everyone." Condorcet himself, who was not beset by the intellectual anxiety that has afflicted modern historians, described it as a "disposition of minds." The Germans called it a *Denkart,* a frame of mind, and the French a *mentalité,* a view on the world. The great Jewish philosopher Moses Mendelssohn took it to be the theoretical part of education (culture being the "objective" part).[15] For the sometime Jesuit novice and Freemason Karl Leonhard Reinhold, it was the process of "making . . . rational men out of men who are capable of rationality."[16] For the Prussian jurist Ernst Ferdinand Klein it meant, rather more prosaically, the freedom of the press (something he seems to imagine, wistfully, that the Prussian king Frederick the Great had endorsed). For the radical and theologian Carl Friedrich Bahrdt it meant the "holiest, most important, most inviolable right of man," to "think for oneself."[17] It was a "pure insight," in the words of the nineteenth-century German philosopher Georg Wilhelm Friedrich Hegel, that seeped into men's thoughts like a "perfume" or—since Hegel was at best uncertain about its benefits—an "infection."[18] It may well be true, as the twentieth-century German philosopher (and author of what is still one of the most powerfully persuasive accounts of the Enlightenment) Ernst Cassirer said in 1932, that "the real philosophy of the Enlightenment is not simply the sum total of what its leading thinkers . . . [t]hought and taught," but a process, the "pulsation of the inner intellectual life," that consisted "less in the certain individual doctrines than in the form and manner of intellectual activity in general."[19] Whatever it was, it was certainly ubiquitous. Even a Scottish cleric on one of the remotest islands in Europe could protest to the urbane lowlander James Boswell that up there in *ultima Thule* he and his companions were "more enlightened" than Boswell might have supposed.[20]

Yet for all the questioning, and for all the massive historical industry that has grown up around the Enlightenment, we are still far from certain quite what all this means. What exactly was Wieland's light? What was its source? Are we talking about a philosophical project or a social movement—or a combination of both, or neither? Then there is a somewhat different question. Even if there were people throughout Europe (even in Scotland) who were proud to call themselves "enlightened," even if these people were conscious of living through something that might be called "the century of enlightenment" or of philosophy, even if they believed that it was a distinct and probably transformative moment in western history, did these terms—*enlightenment, philosophy,* and so on—mean the same thing to everyone everywhere? A number of historians have argued that, on close examination, there was so very little in common among, say, British or German philosophers, French *philosophes,* Italian historians, and Spanish political economists, beyond a dislike of bigotry and a certain conviviality, that it makes no real sense to talk about *the* Enlightenment. Instead we should, as the historian

J.G.A. Pocock has insisted, abandon the definite article altogether and instead talk only about "Enlightenments."[21]

It is certainly true that there were some very significant differences among what the enlightened in France, the German-speaking states, or Britain, not to mention in Spain, Portugal, Naples, Milan, Denmark, and Ireland, thought on almost every topic. The intellectual, moral, and affective hold over even the most independent minds of traditions, institutions, religions, and customs obviously varied immensely across Europe. The Italians, the Spanish, and the Portuguese were more cautious about what they said about established religion and monarchical government than either the French or the British (or most of the Germans). The French were more extreme in their impiety than the British, if only because the Catholic Church sought to exercise a far greater hold over what they could say than the more moderate Anglican Church, or even the Church of Scotland, did in Britain. The philosophers, essayists, historians, novelists, playwrights, poets—most escaped any simple description—who, on any account, made up what was called loosely "the republic of letters" were a very heterogeneous group. Some were clearly more radical than others, some were successful, others (often for good reasons) obscure. Some came from comfortable backgrounds, some—including two of the best known, Denis Diderot and Jean-Jacques Rousseau—were the children of artisans (although prosperous, educated ones); not a few were titled aristocrats, and some were in minor orders. No group so heterogeneous could ever be expected to agree upon everything, to speak with the same voice, or even to share a common intellectual stance.

Neither can the Enlightenment easily be described as a single, coherent movement any more than any other transformative moment in history. Like the Renaissance, the Reformation and the (much-contested) Scientific Revolution that preceded it, and the Industrial Revolution and the democratic and socialist revolutions that followed, it defies simple description. It was more than a revolution in customs or a project for moderate legal and political reform, as the great Italian historian Franco Venturi argued, although it was clearly also both of these things too.[22] It was more than a salon culture or even what the contemporary

German philosopher Jürgen Habermas has made famous as a "public space."[23] It was not only a new kind of book trade or an underground of racy, anti-establishment pamphleteers. All these things were, in their ways, highly significant developments in the culture of eighteenth-century Europe.[24] But to argue that any one of them, or even all of them together, constituted the Enlightenment is to empty the concept of much of its real philosophical content, and without that it is hard to see that the debate over its identity can be for us, its conscious or unwilling heirs, anything more than a merely antiquarian dispute. For the Enlightenment, as its proponents insisted time and again, was above all else a "century of *philosophy*." It is significant that Zöllner did not ask, "What is *the* Enlightenment?" He did not even ask, "What is an 'enlightener,'" an *Aufklärer,* or a philosopher, which might have been another way of phrasing the same question. Instead, he asked, "What is enlightenment?" He was not, that is, asking about a mental state, nor about a period in social or intellectual history, nor about the objectives of an intellectual fraternity. He was asking about the content of an intellectual process.

The modern use of this phrase, "the Enlightenment," also suggests a discrete moment in time—the "long" eighteenth century, as it is sometimes called—marked off by the quite distinct intellectual concerns we associate with the nineteenth century and above all with Romanticism. Needless to say, the *Aufklärer* themselves did not see it this way. They identified themselves and their objectives with the historical present; their concerns were with the historical future. They were conscious that they were living though a century of "light" or "philosophy." But they were also acutely aware that, as Kant famously said, although they lived in "an age of Enlightenment," it was "not yet an Enlightened age."[25] Kant himself did not, in fact, have a very high opinion of the present condition of humanity even within the cultivated and polite societies of Europe.

> We are still [he wrote as late as 1789] a civil minority. We are judged according to laws which we cannot know in their entirety

> and by books we do not understand. . . . This has placed us in such a condition of minority that if all constraint were to cease we would be unable to govern ourselves. . . . We have no power of judgment of our own. In the place of a natural conscience we have an artificial one, which is guided by the judgment of the learned, instead of custom and virtue we have mere observance.[26]

Yet if "we" were still a long way from true self-knowledge and intellectual independence, we were clearly making progress. And enlightenment, like philosophy (but, significantly, unlike theology), was always an open-ended process. No one, however enlightened he or she might be, could foresee exactly what the future might bring. But all assumed the existence of a steady advancement toward something like Condorcet's "Tenth Epoch"—for as Kant himself once remarked, "Whatever might be the highest degree of perfection at which humanity must stop, and however great a gulf must remain between the idea and its execution, no one can or should try to determine this, just because it is freedom that can go beyond every proposed boundary."[27] Whatever else we may also be discussing, "enlightenment" was a concern with the understanding of the historical evolution of the human mind. As the modern French philosopher Michel Foucault neatly summed it up: the question "What is enlightenment?" marked "the discrete entry into the history of thought of a question that modern philosophy has not been capable of answering, but that it has never managed to get rid of either."[28] And it was, he added, inescapably a question that "sought a difference: what difference does today introduce with respect to yesterday?"

Because enlightenment, as Foucault had seen, was so clearly about a continuing process, perhaps no previous or subsequent intellectual or cultural movement has been so keenly aware of its own place in history. In this the Enlightenment is unlike those two great periods of change that preceded it, the Renaissance and the Reformation—and of which, as we shall see, it was perceived as being in many significant respects a continuation. Many of those who lived during the fifteenth and sixteenth centuries spoke of themselves as experiencing "*a* Renaissance," that is, a rebirth of the values and styles that, in their perception, had lain buried since the collapse of the ancient world. But few, if any, had any real sense of "*the* Renaissance" as a historical period. They knew that things had changed, but they did not attribute to that any overwhelming historical significance. The same is broadly true of "the Reformation," which had been an attempt to reestablish what was imagined to be the primitive apostolic church that centuries of Roman corruption had perverted and debased. Undoubtedly some of the reformers and their historically conscious critics, such as the sixteenth-century Venetian Paolo Sarpi, were well aware that Christendom had been divided, perhaps even irrevocably, but they had very little sense that the actions and ideas of Luther and Calvin would eventually change European culture forever. Certainly that had never been any part of their intent. If the Renaissance and the Reformation now exist for us as clear and distinct periods in our pasts, ages of great cultural, intellectual, and moral change, this is largely because the "Enlightenment," so aware of its own historical identity, made them so and made them so precisely as antecedents to its own.

The Enlightenment was, as its exponents all insisted, like every philosophical movement also a *critical* one. In this sense it was the true beginning of modernity, as an open-ended, continuing progression, subject to constant scrutiny and reevaluation. It had, as we shall see, a very clear sense of the direction in which mankind was heading and why, but it never placed any limits on its future development. The objective was to arrive at Condorcet's "state of civilization," but when that had been attained there was to be no cease, no end to history.

Unlike either the Renaissance or the Reformation, the Enlightenment had begun not as an attempt to rescue some hallowed past but as an assault on the past in the name of the future. If a century could be described as "philosophical" merely because it rejected the wisdom of past centuries, wrote the mathematician and philosopher Jean-Baptiste d'Alembert, who had been Condorcet's teacher and whom we shall meet many times again, then the eighteenth would have to be called the "century of Philosophy par excellence."[29] It was a period that sought to overturn every intellectual assumption, every dogma, every "prejudice" (a favorite term) that had previously exercised any hold over the minds of men. "Our Age," declared Immanuel Kant in a famous passage in the first of his three great Critiques, the *Critique of Pure Reason* (itself, of course, a work of criticism),

> is the genuine age of criticism, and to which everything must submit. Religion through its holiness and legislation through its majesty, commonly seek to exempt themselves from it. But in this way they excite a just suspicion against themselves, and cannot lay claim to the unfeigned respect that reason grants only to that which has been able to withstand its free and public examination.[30]

It was the task of every enlightened being—as the Baron d'Holbach, one of the most radical and contentious figures of the eighteenth century, put it—to "attack at their source the prejudices of which the human race has been so long the victim."[31] For the members of what Kant called the "thinking section of the community" *not* to act, *not* to question, was to remain in a state of prolonged infantilism, and since humans are unable to remain literal children for all their individual lives, so the choice to remain intellectual children constitutes a self-imposed denial of their being. The writers of the Enlightenment were those who, in Condorcet's enthusiastic account, had attempted to "prove that they possess a truth which was independent of the dogmas of religion, of fundamentals, and of sects; that it was in the moral constitution of man that one had to seek for the foundations of his obligations, the origin of his ideas about justice and virtue."[32] These were the true "philosophers." They spoke in many different voices, wrote in many different languages, and used many different forms of expression, from poetry to biology. But for all that, and although not one of them ever used the word, they all contributed to a single "project."

II

The now much-quoted, and much-abused, phrase "the Enlightenment project" was probably coined some thirty years ago by the Scottish philosopher Alasdair MacIntyre (about whom I shall have more to say later). It was not meant to be complimentary. For MacIntyre, all that the Enlightenment project had aimed at was the application of the rational intellect to the murky reaches of the human mind, wherein lurked the menacing, disruptive forces of prejudice, religion, superstition, uncontrolled and unimagined emotions, everything that conspired to deprive the autonomous individual of self-knowledge and self-control. Enlightenment, as Wieland put it, meant having "enough light . . . that those who ought to see by it are neither blind nor jaundiced, nor through any other case, prevented from being able to see nor from wanting to see." It meant separating the true from the false, disentangling the entangled, dissolving the complex into its simple original components and then pursuing them back to their origins. Above all, it meant that "no representation or claim passed off by men as true is granted reprieve from unrestricted scrutiny." Only by this means would it finally be possible to diminish "the mass of mistakes and pernicious deceptions that darken human understanding."[33] The trouble with this, in MacIntyre's opinion, was that all the insistence on the primacy of reason and of "rational debate" had ever achieved was to have erased from men's minds what, since Aristotle, had been the main support for their entire moral, intellectual, and political lives: the concept of virtue. And it had given them nothing in return. Their intellectual "light" was, in fact, nothing other than moral darkness.[34]

MacIntyre, however, was not responsible for conjuring up this image of Enlightenment as the simple application of reason to the vast complexities of the human condition. This had been the work of the early Romantics, some of whom had grown up in the shadow of the Enlightenment. Eager to replace what they saw as the cold rationalism, soulless secularism, and bleak, rootless cosmopolitanism of the Enlightenment with a vivid attachment to home, hearth, and heart, they cast the entire philosophical culture of their predecessors as a relentless bid to impose upon all mankind the deadweight of what they significantly called the "Empire of Reason." What had once been looked upon as a means to liberty was now described as a form of enslavement; what had once sought to expose intellectual confusion and the deceptions perpetrated by religion and the uncritical adherence to custom was now seen as itself a form of deception. Human reason, it was now claimed, was at best a very imperfect instrument for understanding the human condition. And the kind of uncritical belief that the Enlightenment had supposedly placed in it had led to far worse forms of slavery than any that the past epochs of human history had dreamed up. As early as 1774 the German philosopher and historian Johann Gottfried Herder, once one of Kant's most devoted pupils and subsequently among his most determined and perceptive critics, had condemned what he called the much-vaunted "civilization" and "enlightenment" we get from "our Voltaire and Hume, Robertson and Iselin"—"classical ghosts of the twilight." Those who "rave on about our century's *light,* that is, about its *superficiality* and *unrestraint,* about its *warmth* in ideas and its *coldness* in *actions,* about its *seeming strength* and *freedom,* and about its real *weakness-unto-death* and *exhaustion* under *unbelief, despotism, and luxury*" had been under a delusion, and their entire project was a philosophical hoax.[35] From there it was an easy step to lay the ultimate blame for all the excesses of late-nineteenth-century positivism, the Industrial Revolution, and the horrors of modernity that had followed from them on the perverse ambitions of the "century of philosophy."

The Romantic characterization and condemnation of the Enlightenment inspired an indignant moral onslaught not merely on all forms of rationalism but also on the entire edifice of "western civilization." The depredations of the European empire-builders in the late nineteenth century and the overwhelming horrors of the first half of the twentieth only helped to deepen the view that all belief in the human capacity for amelioration through reason and understanding, any attempt at criticism, any belief in any species of universalism could only lead down the road that Europe itself had supposedly traveled, from the delusions of

Enlightenment to nationalism, imperialism, and pseudo-scientific racism to the mass mobilization of "scientific socialism" and finally, inexorably, to the gas chambers of Auschwitz.

Possibly the most extreme and the most influential version of this view is *Dialectic of Enlightenment,* a short, often perverse, but also immensely clever book first published in 1947. For its authors, Max Horkheimer and Theodor Adorno, both refugees from Nazi Germany living in New York, the great enemy was the technology of the modern world and the institutions that had made it possible, something that they believed they had witnessed in its most gruesome manifestation at first hand. All of this, as they understood it, had been made possible only by the Enlightenment. They had no quarrel with the Enlightenment's stated aim of "liberating men from fear and establishing their sovereignty." The tragedy, as they saw it, was that the Enlightenment had failed to achieve either of these goals. Instead, it had sought to detach myth from reason and then to enthrone reason as the only human good, and in the process Enlightenment itself had been transformed into a myth, "the myth that one can ever escape the mythic imagination."[36] The result had been a species of perverse self-deception that had brought all manner of atrocities in its train, and as a consequence the "fully enlightened earth radiates disaster triumphant." Deluded by the conviction that human beings could rise above their condition through reason, the Enlightenment had visited all kinds of horrors on the world in the attempt to make these beliefs fit with reality. All the intellectual revolutions of the nineteenth century, to which the Romantics themselves had unwittingly contributed, the rise of nationalism, the collapse of the human sciences created by "the inflexible Encyclopedists" into Positivism and racism—that "self-assertion of the bourgeois individual integrated within a barbaric collective"—and finally neo-Darwinism, eugenics, and the like; all of these and many more were, in Horkheimer and Adorno's view, but the inevitable outcome of the eighteenth-century bid to live by reason alone. Before the eighteenth century "only the poor and savages [had been] exposed to the fury of capitalist elements" (for the market, too, was the inevitable creation of the Enlightenment), but once Enlightenment had seized hold of the European imagination, authoritarianism and imperialism, that "most terrible form of the *ratio,*" in the gruesome new shape of Fascism and National Socialism, had been visited upon the whole world. "And it was the hand of philosophy that wrote it on the wall."[37]

Nor were Horkheimer and Adorno alone in seeing some kind of Enlightenment as responsible for the Holocaust. Much cruder versions of their thesis were in wide circulation in the aftermath of the Second World War, for surely something grander than simple human malevolence was needed to explain the seemingly inexplicable, the sheer horror of Auschwitz. In July 1946 Kurt Kauffmann, the lawyer charged with defending Ernst Kaltenbrunner, the highest-ranking SS officer to stand trial for crimes against humanity at Nuremberg, read to the court a long, rambling history of modern nihilism. Rationalism had come out of England, he claimed, to become the "state religion of France," and then "the French Revolution burst into flames and wrote the idea of emancipated human rights with flaming letters into the sky of Europe. . . . Sarcastic and scornful laughter at everything sacred went through the raving masses." Thereafter, "these ideas also conquered Germany; for Germany looked with amazement and awe toward France in this century. The manifestation of religion became a religion of pure humanity. The last step was taken by Kant, he drew the last consequence from the principle of free science." From there it was but one short step—taken by Hegel—to the ideological monstrosity that was Hitler's Reich. In Kauffmann's view, Kaltenbrunner had been little more than the victim of a deeply misguided historical process that had begun with the French Enlightenment.[38] Kauffmann's argument was dismissed by the president of the court as "completely unlikely to have any influence at all upon the minds of the Tribunal." It did not: Kaltenbrunner was found guilty and duly executed.

Some less picturesque versions of these claims, however, are still very much with us.

Postcolonialists and the more radical opponents of "globalization" have cast the Enlightenment, as Adorno and Horkheimer cast it, as the apotheosis of a rationalism that scorns difference and, in the name of science, devastates the environment; strips indigenous peoples of their moral dignity, legal rights, and if possible their cultural identities; and condemns more than two-thirds of the population of the world to penury and misery in order to supply the excessive wants of the other third. Empires may be no more, but the universal spirit of the Enlightenment that had made those of the nineteenth century so successful did not vanish with them. It merely changed its language. Enlightenment supposes, in the words of the English philosopher John Gray, a "universal emancipation and a universal civilization." But in reality this is merely another name for "western cultural imperialism."[39] The modern postcolonial heirs of the Enlightenment no longer rule in the name of "civilization," emancipation, self-determination, and all those other consoling terms deployed by the empire-builders of the nineteenth century to cloak their intentions; they do so now in the pursuit of "development," "democracy," "good governance," the "rule of law," and the like. Their agents were once national states; now they are international, global agencies: the IMF, the World Bank, and any number of apparently well-meaning but deluded international aid agencies. The project that had begun in the eighteenth century as a bid to free every individual from his or her dependence upon the rigid social and moral codes by which the powers, secular and religious, of the old regime had kept their subjects in check and to create a fit social world in which all human beings might flourish had, by the twentieth century, evolved into little more than the attempt by a self-convinced European elite to impose its own will and its own image upon the entire world. And it had done so because at its heart there lay the flawed assumption that all humans could and should decide how to live their lives by their rational abilities alone, independent of the communities, the religious beliefs, the customs, and the bonds of affection into which they had been born. Reason was a specifically European form of tyranny.

III

The belief that the Enlightenment was concerned with subjecting every aspect of human life to reason is not, of course, entirely groundless. Had this been so, such a belief would hardly have endured for so long. To be "enlightened" meant, as all insisted, to be critical, and criticism necessarily involves the use of reason. It was, as Kant argued in the most famous of the many replies that Zöllner received to his troubling question, reason that would allow the still infantile person to exit from its "self-incurred minority." Minority, he explained, was the "inability to make use of one's own understanding without the guidance of another." The term Kant used, *Unmündigkeit,* refers to the legal condition of both children and women, who in Roman—and contemporary German—law could not represent themselves before a court of law but required an adult male to do so for them.[40] What this minority meant, he explained, using the image of an early version of the walker, was to "step out of the leading reins of the cart to which they are tethered." The walker is intended to teach the infant how to walk. The walker provided by society, the Church, convention, and prejudice, however, gave only the illusion of learning; in reality it was meant to keep the child tethered for his entire life. And it was so easy, Kant reflected, so cozy to accept this condition. Most men (and all of the "fairer sex"—Kant is not very enlightened about women) live much as domestic animals or children do: "If I have a book that has understanding for me, a pastor who has a conscience for me, a doctor who judges my diet for me, and so forth, surely I do not need to trouble myself. I have no need to think, if only I can pay; others will take over the tedious business for me." Enlightenment would allow the individual to walk by himself. It would liberate him (and increasingly her) from the constraints that had been placed upon him. But to achieve this end, he had to question what his pastor, his doctor, the books he had read, even his ruler had to say. He had to cast aside all those "dogmas and formulas, those mechanical instruments for rational use (or rather misuse) of [mankind's] natural endowments," which were "the ball and chain of his permanent minority."[41] To do that, he had to *think* for himself. The motto of Kant's Enlightenment—and it was by no means only Kant's—was the Latin poet Horace's famous phrase *sapere aude*—"dare to know"—and knowing clearly required the use of reason.

But that, as I hope to show, was by no means the entire story.[42] For at the core of the "Enlightenment project" was an attempt to discover a new definition of nothing less than human nature itself. And this required far more than the simple application of unfettered reason. It required, first, an understanding of the "passions," in particular those passions that in the eighteenth century were referred to as "sentiments." It required a complete revaluation of the sources of human sociability and of the course of human history—a new understanding of the place of humanity in nature and in a nature conceived as independent of any divine regulator. It demanded a study of difference as well as similitude, in particular the differences displayed by the myriad peoples across the globe. It led, in the end, to the foundation of what in the eighteenth century came to be called the "science of man," something that would replace all the previous attempts, most notably those of the theologians, to understand what it meant to be human. The Enlightenment's objective was to describe and define humankind in all its immensely varied aspects in the same way, but with very different methods and different instruments, that the natural sciences, which had made such startling advances in the seventeenth century, sought to describe and define the natural world. As D'Alembert envisaged it, this science would resemble a series of "mappamundi based on different projections," a thread or a "chain" of truths—D'Alembert liked to mix his metaphors—that would guide mankind out of the labyrinth in which he had been imprisoned for centuries.[43] The project was to demonstrate the unassailable truth of two very basic claims, which have been a source of controversy ever since. The first was that although the human species is unique among animals, it shares nothing in common with the divinity (even supposing that a divinity were actually to exist). The "science of man" was to be, as the natural sciences had now become, resolutely secular. The second was that there exists a universal "human nature," which could be understood wherever it was found. There were very obvious and recognizable differences among Europeans, Asians, Africans, and Amerindians, but these were the outcome of environment, upbringing, and culture. None of these things was believed to be irrelevant or incidental, but neither were they a structural part of the human condition. From this it could be shown that all human beings shared a common disposition for a shared and universal social and political life in what would ultimately be called the "city of the world," the "cosmopolis."

The contemporary French philosopher Jean-François Lyotard, who first coined the term *postmodernism,* had understood all this. Human beings, he maintained, are essentially storytelling creatures, not so much *Homo sapiens* as *Homo fabulans,* and the stories they tell each other make up their conscious lives. All religions, all political systems, are stories, and the trouble with the entire history of western thought was, he complained in 1978, that it had been driven by what he called the "meta-narrative" (*grand récit*) of the Enlightenment. What this meta-narrative had sought to do was not to impose reason upon the unruly human personality but to create the—for Lyotard—impossible concept of a universal human identity, a universal human destiny, what he called the "cosmopolitical."[44] This was the story of the modern world that, or so he believed, the now-"postmodern" world was set to replace. It had, he claimed, been "anchored in the reader by centuries of humanism and the 'human sciences.' " Insofar as that had indeed been the true objective of the "century of philosophy," he was right. And this book is an attempt to explain how that came to be.

I

ALL COHERENCE GONE

I

IN 1835 THE LIBERAL aristocrat and sometime parliamentarian Alexis de Tocqueville sat down to record and analyze his impressions of the wholly unprecedented new society that was growing up across the Atlantic. He began by giving his French readers some idea of how the still-fledgling United States of America could have come to be the way it was: so evidently the child of Europe, so obviously the creature of the Enlightenment, yet also so very much, and in so many ways, unlike Europe and in so many ways dangerously unenlightened. The United States was, he believed, the perhaps unwitting beneficiary of a very remarkable European historical process that had begun in the sixteenth century, when the great religious reformers Martin Luther and John Calvin had "subjected to individual reason some of the dogmas of the ancient faith." For all their apparent modernity, however, both men—and Luther in particular—had remained "narrowly enclosed within the circle of religious ideas." A century later the English scientist, philosopher, essayist, and politician Francis Bacon and the French philosopher René Descartes had taken what Luther had begun out of the realm of religion and into "philosophy properly speaking, abolishing received formulas, destroying the empire of tradition and overthrowing received authority." In doing so they ushered in what ever since has been called the "Scientific Revolution." A century or so after that, the thinkers of what had come to be called "the Enlightenment" had "generalized the same principles, attempting to submit to the individual examination of each man, the object of his beliefs."[1] From this historical process the modern world, and with it that quintessential modern society the United States, had been born.

Tocqueville was looking back on a century that had produced two great and very different revolutions—the American and the French—that between them had, as he saw it, transformed the world forever. He was also writing when many of the more obvious attributes of the Enlightenment had been buried under the carnage of the Napoleonic Wars. But his brief history of the birth of the modern world, although striking in itself, was not altogether new. In 1759, more than half a century before Tocqueville wrote *Democracy in America* and in a radically different world, Jean-Baptiste Le Rond D'Alembert—to give him his full name—had come to very much the same conclusions. D'Alembert, the illegitimate son of the novelist and *salonnière* Claudine Guérin de Tencin and a wealthy artillery officer, Louis-Camus Destouches, was a mathematician, a philosopher, a musicologist, among other things, as well as the permanent secretary of the French Academy, and the editor, with Denis Diderot, of one of the Enlightenment's most characteristic products, that great multi-volume, multi-author attempt to capture all human knowledge from philosophy to hydrography: the *Encyclopédie.* He was witty, urbane, and, like most of the great writers of the Enlightenment, fiercely opposed to any kind of dogma. Unusually for a distinguished scientist and man of letters—who generally liked to adopt more serious poses—D'Alembert had himself painted by Maurice Quentin de La Tour in 1754 with a wry smile on his lips. He also had a strong sense of history, and he began his *Essay on the Elements of Philosophy* with a brief outline of the "human mind in the middle of the eighteenth century." Every century, D'Alembert explained, at its midpoint—at the moment, that is, when he was writing—attempts to throw off all that it has accumulated hitherto. Thus, in the middle of the fifteenth century the seizure of Constantinople by the Sultan Mehmed II in 1453 had led to the flight of Byzantine scholars to Italy, and with them had come "the Renaissance of Letters in the West." Then, in the middle of the sixteenth century, came the Reformers, Luther and Calvin—"sustained on one side and attacked on the other with that fervor which only the interests of God, rightly or badly understood, can inspire in man"—who between them had brought about the destruction of all the dogmatic certainties of religion. As the consequence of this series of events, "knowledge of all kinds, and enlightenment born out of this error and discord, cast itself on subjects which themselves seemed the most remote from these disputes." Then, in the middle of the seventeenth century, came Descartes, the founder of a new philosophy, and finally, in the middle of the eighteenth century, to judge by "the events which move us, or at least with which we have busied ourselves, by our customs, our works, even by our entertainments," there had come "a remarkable change in our ideas":

> The invention and application of new methods of philosophizing, a species of enthusiasm which accompanies every discovery, a certain exaltation of ideas which the spectacle of the universe produces in us: all of these have excited in men's minds a vivid excitation and exultation which, driven in every sense by its very nature, has swept all before it, like a river bursting its dams [and] has been carried along with a violence which has swept away all that stood in its way. . . . The slower men have been to throw off the yoke of opinion, the more, once they have broken with some, they then break with all the rest . . . and once they have taken the pains to retrace their steps, they look upon, and accept, a new system of ideas as a sort of reward for their courage and labor. Thus, from the principle of the profane [natural] sciences to the foundations of revelation, from metaphysics to matters of taste, from music to morals, from the scholastic disputes of the theologians to the objects of com-

> merce, from the rights of princes, to those of peoples, from the natural law to the arbitrary laws of nations—in a word, from the questions which touch us directly to those which affect us little, everything has been discussed, analyzed, and stirred up.

Not everything that had come out of this turmoil was entirely to be admired. D'Alembert was too skeptical, too ironic on the subject of human fallibility, to have believed that that was possible. A "new light on some objects, and a new obscurity on many others" had been "the fruit of this general effervescence of mind, just as the effect of the coming and going of the ocean is to carry some things to shore, and to take others away." But whatever, in the end, might prove to have been of lasting value in this "century of philosophy," the time had now come "to fix the object, the nature, and the limits of this revolution, whose advantages and inconveniences will be better known to posterity than they can be to us." This was to be the task of the *Encyclopédie,* which would provide the lasting record of all that was known and which would "do for our century and the following ones what . . . our ancestors failed to do for us."[2]

All of this may sound a little too much like an attempt to reduce history to the certainty of algebra, but it captures the sense of what all those who thought of themselves as the architects of the new enlightened modern world owed to the Renaissance and more directly to the Reformation, understood not as a religious revival but as a revolution that had effectively unseated all religion and to the rationalist philosophy that had grown out of it. For what separated this "century of philosophy" from the Renaissance and the Reformation that had preceded it was that now there could be no going back. Enlightenment was a continual process that might never be completed. But what all those who participated in it were certain of was that it could not now be reversed. As Condorcet told the Académie française in 1782, the huge progress the physical sciences had made now "assured the progress of the moral sciences," so that now they would "preserve us from a return to barbarism." It was a persistent theme. In this new enlightened era, in this "happy epoch," Condorcet assured his colleagues, "the human race will no longer return to the alternating periods of darkness and light, to which it seemed for so long nature had condemned us." Now truth had finally triumphed: "Humankind is saved!"[3]

D'Alembert and Tocqueville's brisk prehistory has, in broad outline, become the most widely repeated genealogy of the Enlightenment. The Renaissance prepared the ground for the Reformation, and without the Reformation the Scientific Revolution of the following century could never have taken place, and it was that revolution that had laid the foundations for the "century of philosophy" that was to follow.

True, historians have often questioned the appropriateness of speaking of a scientific revolution in the seventeenth century—there was, they argue, a significant shift perhaps, but hardly a *revolution*—pointing out that many of the old ways of thinking, not least the belief in the Christian God, survived into the seventeenth century and beyond. Sir Isaac Newton—the "last of the magicians," as the celebrated twentieth-century economist John Maynard Keynes once called him—wrote more about theology than he did about mathematics (but then, mathematics takes up very little space on the page). And not only theology. When Sotheby's auctioned Newton's personal papers in 1936, they revealed that he also had a vivid and credulous interest in astrology (at the time closely related to astronomy) and, more embarrassingly, with alchemy. To his dying day he had hoped to discover how to transmute lead into gold: a somewhat quixotic, if not simply perverse, ambition for the future "Warden and Master of the Mint."[4]

For all that, however—for all that no revolution can ever change everything—the great reordering of all modes of knowledge from astronomy to moral philosophy that assuredly did take place in the seventeenth century changed how and by what means the cosmos was understood, to a degree that was not matched until the advent of computer technology in the twentieth century and perhaps not even then. It clearly was not, however, as Tocqueville and D'Alembert would have us believe, the creation of only two men. To Bacon and Descartes we would have to add, among others, the Italian physicist Galileo Galilei, the French astronomer and mathematician Pierre Gassendi, Newton, and the philosophers John Locke and Thomas Hobbes. The Dutch humanist Hugo Grotius and the heretical Jewish philosopher Baruch Spinoza were also recognized to have played crucial roles. So, too, did the French Cartesian Nicholas Malebranche and the Huguenot encyclopedist Pierre Bayle.

What all of these thinkers of the seventeenth century had achieved, in their very different ways, was the systematic destruction of what in the eighteenth century came to be called "the system." When used pejoratively, as it generally was, this "system" was usually identified with theology and, more narrowly, with what had long been labeled "scholasticism." Originally scholasticism had been a vague term, describing innocuously only what was taught in the "schools"—that is, the universities of medieval Europe—*scholastic* and *schoolman* being simply other words for university professor. Professors, however, have always had a dubious press, and by the fifteenth century *scholasticism* had become a term of abuse, associated with bad Latin and tortuous reasoning. The scholastics were accused of frittering away their time, and that of their pupils, on abstruse questions whose answers, when there were any, could be of no interest to anyone outside the universities themselves. It is doubtful that there was ever a debate over how many angels could dance on the head of a pin, but that was the kind of subject that was widely said to be the staple of theological disputes. It was a caricature of what was, in reality, an imposing intellectual edifice. But like most caricatures, it was not entirely inaccurate. As D'Alembert said of the "schoolmen" after their influence had all but vanished, their "empty and scholastic questions were as little suited to instructing us as they were to making us good."[5]

The majority of the scholastics were theologians. Theology—the study (*logos*) of God (*theos*)—dealt with what were called "primary" or "first" causes, what became known, from the title of one of Aristotle's writings, as "Metaphysics," that is, all that was "beyond" or "after" physics—most obviously, the elucidation of the always obscure intentions of the deity itself. For this reason theology was held to be—by its practitioners at least—the "Mother of Sciences." Throughout the Middle Ages, and in some places as late as the eighteenth century, what today we would call moral philosophy, jurisprudence, epistemology, and psychology were studied as ancillary to theology, and most of the great theologians from the thirteenth century onward wrote on all of these subjects. Theology had begun, however, as an attempt to grasp the nature of the Christian God, through the scattered writing his adherents had left behind them. This had meant in the first place the Bible, in particular the New Testament. But since these writings offered little beyond a rudimentary ethics, Christian theologians had been forced to go elsewhere to find answers to the larger questions about the nature of the universe. Inevitably they had gone to Greek sources, the only ones they had, and in the process they transformed Christianity from what had been, in essence, a world-rejecting late Roman mystery cult into—to use a recent term—"Hellenized Judaism." Beginning in the thirteenth century with the encyclopedic writings of the great Dominican St. Thomas Aquinas, this heavily Hellenized theology became an all-embracing study of the natural world, and of mankind's exalted place within it. Aquinas, the "Angelic Doctor," an aristocratic Dominican from southern Italy, cousin to the Hohenstaufen, Holy, Roman, and Imperial, was fat and genial—so fat indeed that in later life he had a desk made for him with a space carved out of it to accommodate his belly. He was also probably the most original and influential thinker in Christendom in the years that separate St. Augustine, author of the first major work of Christian theology, *The City of God,* in the fifth century from John Locke and Thomas Hobbes in the seventeenth. "Thomism" was by no means the only school of theology, but it gradually came to predominate in the faculties of the universities of Europe, and today it is the semiofficial doctrine of the Catholic Church.

Scholasticism first came under attack from the humanists of the fifteenth century, who derided its mode of argument and the "barbarous" and jargon-ridden Latin in which it was written, and its entire metaphysical edifice was effectively demolished during the seventeenth. But its influence survived in many of the universities of Europe well into the eighteenth century, when it was still perceived as the most dangerous opponent of the "new philosophy" or, as the French *lumières* often called it, simply "philosophy." "Scholasticism," warned D'Alembert in the "Preliminary Discourse" to the *Encyclopédie,* "which included all the so-called Science of the centuries of ignorance, still hinders the progress of Philosophy in this first century of Enlightenment."[6]

The method employed by the scholastics was essentially what is called "hermeneutical." That is, their science consisted in the painstaking reading and rereading of a canon of supposedly authoritative texts, which by the sixteenth century had been expanded from the Bible to include the writings of the early Greek and Latin theologians, known as the "Church Fathers," and those of a select number of saints called "Doctors of the Church" (there are thirty-three of them to date), together with a canon of classical Greek, and some Roman, authors. By far the most important of these was Aristotle, whose authority throughout most of the Middle Ages was such that he was commonly referred to simply as "the Philosopher."

By the time the brilliantly precocious son of a renegade clergyman named Thomas Hobbes—who has a critical part to play in this story—came to study at Oxford in 1603, the scholastics had, he complained, reduced all philosophy to what he called scathingly "mere Aristotelity."[7] "The natural Philosophy of those Schools," he added later, "was rather a Dream than Science and set forth in senseless and insignificant Language." And it was not only "natural philosophy"—that is, the natural sciences—that was illusory. "I believe," he went on, "that scarce anything can be more absurdly said in natural Philosophy, than that which now is called *Aristotles Metaphysiques;* nor more repugnant to Government than much that hee hath said in his *Politiques;* not more ignorantly than a great part of the *Ethiques*."[8] (In 1683 Oxford repaid him for his contempt by ritually burning copies of his two major works, *Leviathan* and *De Cive.*)

For the great philosophers and natural scientists of the seventeenth century, the most urgent task was to dethrone scholastic Aristotelianism, which meant, in effect, to dethrone theology. Few, if any, of the men who set out to do this had any real quarrel with the study of God as such, as long as it was confined to the understanding of God—the *theos*—and made no claims to meddle in the means by which the operations of the natural world were understood or to dictate the terms by which humans should live their lives or organize their societies. Everything, they claimed, that belonged to natural sciences and to what in the eighteenth century would become the "human sciences" could only be understood on the basis of direct experience. On these matters neither God nor his theologians had anything to say. "Theologians, mind your own business," as the Italian jurist and renegade Protestant Alberico Gentili, who became Regius Professor of Civil Law at Oxford, told them as early as 1588. Centuries later, in 1833, the German philosopher Friedrich Schelling neatly summed up the whole process. "The history of modern European philosophy," he wrote, "is counted from the overthrow of scholasticism until the present time." It may have been an oversimplification, but it was, in essence, right. Gradually scholasticism came to be replaced, even in most of the universities of Europe, by what was often, and significantly, called "the mechanical philosophy," a philosophy grounded solely on irreducible and incontestable first principles and on direct experience—a philosophy that, in Schelling's words, had "erased as with a sponge" all that had preceded it.[9]

The revolution that brought this about changed forever the intellectual landscape of the western world. It opened up an immense potential for scientific knowledge. For by marginalizing theology it also undermined the idea that there could exist one single source of knowledge or one single source of authority. Almost every schoolchild knows the story of Galileo's confrontation with the Church over the heliocentric theory. Having come to the conclusion, on the basis of his own observations, that contrary to received opinion the Earth revolved around the Sun and not the Sun around the Earth, Galileo found himself in serious trouble with the Church authorities. Nothing theologically very much depended on the ancient Ptolemaic vision of the heavens, beyond the literal interpretation of a few stray phrases in the Bible. The Vatican's own astronomer had even confirmed Galileo's findings. But as Cardinal Roberto Bellarmino (now a saint and one of the Doctors of the Church), although in private he agreed with Galileo, pointed out, if the rulings of the Church were to be refuted by direct observation on this issue—even if it was not, as he recognized, a matter of faith—they might be refuted on others, which were. In 1633, after a long and bitter struggle, and in order to save himself from a heretic's death, Galileo agreed to recant his views. As he left the audience chamber, however, he remarked laconically under his breath, *"Eppur si muove"*—"And yet it moves." The story is certainly apocryphal. But its meaning is clear enough, and Galileo, perhaps because he was the most famous victim of the Inquisition, became also the most celebrated champion of the new science. No amount of clerical cant, no ancient tomes, not even the supposed word of God (not that God had had anything much to say on this particular matter) could alter the brute facts of existence. No matter what the Church—or churches, since the Protestants were just as wary of the challenges that empirical science posed to their authority as the Catholics—might think about the movement of the Earth, it would continue for eternity to revolve around the Sun.

II

As Tocqueville and D'Alembert had rightly seen, the historical origins of this astonishing transformation can be traced back to the Reformation. Anyone, however, familiar with the writings of either Luther or Calvin might question whether subjecting dogma to "individual reason" was what they really had in mind. If anything, the reverse was true. Far from being a rationalist, Luther was a Christian fundamentalist claiming divine inspiration, and his theology, which made a clear distinction between Law (*Gesetz*) and Gospel (*Evangelium*) left very little, if any, space for what he dismissively called "philosophy," much less for "individual reason." But it was not Luther's theology—or even that of his successor, John Calvin—that had set the seventeenth-century revolt against religion in motion. Calvin in particular, that arch-dogmatist and burner of heretics, had, as François-Marie Arouet (better known by his sobriquet Voltaire) put it, been "driven by theological hatred" quite as forcefully as any of his Catholic rivals. What had finally destroyed the power and credibility of the Catholic Church, indeed of any church, had been not the Reformation itself but the terrible Wars of Religion between the 1550s and the 1650s that the struggle over theological differences had brought in its wake.[10] As Voltaire noted, if anyone had told Luther at the time that "he would destroy the Roman religion throughout half of Europe, he would not have believed it; he went far further than he intended, as happens in all disputes and in almost all the affairs of men."[11]

The turmoil that followed Martin Luther's revolt against the Church in the 1520s left all of Christendom divided against itself. For the first time in their history the peoples of Europe began to fight one another not over dynastic claims, not for land or to defend the supposed rights of their rulers. They began to fight over beliefs. True, in the French Wars of Religion between 1562 and 1598, in the English Civil War (1642–51), in what the Spanish called the Dutch Revolt and the Dutch the Eighty Years' War between Spain and the Netherlands (1568–1648), which raged from northern Europe to the South China Seas, there was often more at stake than a conflict over the nature of God's grace or even the authority of the pope. As with most ideologies, Catholicism in its various forms, and the several shades of Protestantism by which it was confronted, enforced older divisions and armed dissident groups across the continent with new arguments to buttress old claims. But for all the cynicism and opportunism that any ideological conflict necessarily involves, what divided Europe, and turned so much of it into a killing field for over a century, was religion.

The worst and last of these conflagrations was what is now known as the Thirty Years' War. It began in 1618, when the Holy Roman Emperor, Matthias, was deposed and replaced (briefly) by the Protestant Frederick V of the Palatinate. It then spread to the whole of central and eastern Europe, drawing into its maw, at one time or another, all the major states of the continent, from Spain to Sweden. The huge armies that this war created left behind them vast tracts of Europe in smoldering ruins. Millions died in the carnage. The death toll has been calculated at 5.75 million, which, expressed as a percentage of the world's population, is considerably greater than that of the First World War.[12] Millions more perished from famine and disease. When it was finally over, a third of the population of central Europe was dead. As Voltaire remarked in astonishment on rereading his own description of all this butchery: "Is it the history of snakes and tigers which I have just written? No, it is that of men. Tigers and snakes do not treat their own kind in that manner."[13]

In 1644 the representatives of some two hundred Catholic and Protestant powers gathered in the northeastern German province of Westphalia to negotiate a settlement. Nearly four years later, after a great deal of squabbling, much of it over issues of protocol, on January 30 and again on October 24, 1648, a lasting agreement among the various representatives was finally reached. The "Peace of Westphalia," as it came to be known, was the first treaty among sovereign nations that succeeded in creating a lasting peace and not merely a temporary cease-fire, as all previous treaties had. It was also the first truly international gathering of European states and the first formally to recognize the existence of two new states, the United Netherlands, which had, in effect, established its independence from Spain forty years earlier, and the Swiss Confederation, which now became a sovereign republic, independent of the Habsburg Empire. Most important of all, however, the Peace of Westphalia identified "the grievances of religion" as being "for the most part the cause and occasion of the present war." Having done that, it established a clear dividing line between the public and the private, instituted a right to religious toleration, and drove confessional differences, and the papacy, from the world political stage forever. Unsurprisingly, the papacy was the only party to the conflict to refuse to endorse the treaty. It was, as Pope Innocent X said of it, mustering all the derogatory epithets he could think of, "null, void, invalid, iniquitous, unjust, damnable, reprobate, inane, empty of meaning and effect for all time."[14] But no one except his own bishops and a handful of the faithful were around to listen to him. Even their most Catholic Majesties, the kings of Spain and France, quietly accepted that in future religion would play no role in international politics. Henceforth, a formula began to be used in the monarchies of Europe to describe the relationship between Church and States: *cuius regio eius religio,* which translates roughly as whoever was king would decide what the religion should be in his kingdom. It was a neat, acceptable, and essentially secular solution to a problem that for nearly a century had littered the continent with corpses.[15]

The treaty did not achieve an immediate or indeed, in the end, a lasting peace. The fighting straggled on in Germany for a further nine years, and from 1648 until 1656 Poland and Lithuania were invaded by waves of Swedes and Russian and Ukrainian Cossacks who left as much as a third of the population dead. The Poles still refer to this as "the Deluge" and still look upon it as the worst calamity in their particularly calamitous history. Then, in 1650, followed the first Anglo-Dutch War (there were three of them in all), in 1660 the Anglo-Spanish War, in 1668 the French War of Devolution, in 1701 the War of the Spanish Succession, and so on.

None of these, however, were conflicts over religion. None were civil wars, the most bloody and the most devastating of all human conflicts. After 1648 the nations of Europe would never go to war with each other again because they disagreed over their understanding of God's intentions for mankind. (Perhaps the only exception, where confessional differences can still have all-too-bloody consequences, is Ireland. But in Ireland religion became an anticolonial cause, a way of ridding the country of a hated ruler that was not only Protestant but also English.) From 1648 the disordered, divided monarchies of Europe slowly began to transform themselves into the modern nation-states that most of them still are to this day. As the great liberal philosopher John Stuart Mill wrote in 1859, the Reformation, and the violence it unleashed upon Europe, had created a situation in which no faction could hope to emerge victorious:

> When the heat of the conflict was over, without giving victory to any party, and each church and sect was, therefore, reduced to limit its hopes to retaining possession of the grounds it already occupied; minorities seeing that they had no chance of becoming majorities were under the necessity of pleading to those whom they could not convert for permission to differ.

Toleration—or what today is called "negative toleration," the willingness to accept the continuing existence of those you *know* to be wrong—is, Mill knew, "admitted with tacit reserves" by "almost all religious persons" in "even the most tolerant countries."[16] It was not the recognition of error or any willingness to accept the possible validity of divergent opinions that had ultimately compelled the Christian churches in Europe to relinquish their hold over the judgment of the individual. It was defeat on the battlefield.

The Peace of Westphalia made possible the modern "Europe of Nations." It also drew a curtain across the continent, between a Catholic south and a predominantly Protestant north, which has remained until this day. Over time the north, which had once been poor, backward, and agrarian, would become rich, innovative, and urban, and the south, in particular Italy, Spain, and Portugal, which had for centuries been the most powerful, inventive, and wealthy regions of Europe, would gradually decline to become frail, impoverished shadows of their former selves, a position from which Italy only began to emerge in the nineteenth century and Spain and Portugal in the late twentieth. Only France, poised midway between the two and, although overwhelmingly Catholic, with a substantial Protestant population, maintained her status and her authority undiminished. It is no coincidence that the Enlightenment, although its impact on Catholic Europe has generally been underestimated, is most closely linked to France, the German-speaking lands, Britain and her American colonies. As Adam Smith told the readers of the influential *Edinburgh Review* in 1756 (with a good measure of exaggeration), although

> learning is cultivated in some degree in almost every part of Europe, it is in France and England only that it is cultivated with such success or reputation as to excite the attention of foreign nations. In Italy, the country in which it was first revived [during the Renaissance] it has been almost totally extinguished. In Spain, the country in which, after Italy, the first dawnings of modern genius appeared, it has been extinguished altogether.[17]

In Hobbes's view—and in this respect at least he was not untypical of the generation that had lived though the English Civil War—the Reformation and the struggles it had unleashed had all been the direct outcome of the sophistries of the schoolmen;[18] "the state religion," as his near-contemporary John Locke tartly put it, is "usually the state trouble."[19] Religious conflict had destroyed all faith in the certainty of the intellectual system that had hitherto sustained the authority of the Catholic Church and that could now no longer support the massive political, moral, and intellectual structures that it had once claimed to legislate. "It was the avowed intention of Mr. Hobbes," wrote Adam Smith in 1759, "to subject the conscience of man immediately to the civil and not to the ecclesiastical powers, whose turbulence and ambition, he had been taught, by the example of his own times, was the principal source of the disorders of society."[20] Europeans who had once lived in a world of theological certainty and who had, at least at the level of belief, all shared a common culture now found themselves adrift. And since theology had provided the basis not only of their understanding of their relationship with God but also of their moral and even their physical worlds, they were driven to reexamine not merely all the old certainties but, more significantly, all the older methods of inquiry.

Together with the collapse of the religious consensus, another kind of challenge to the old order arrived from overseas. From the late fifteenth century on, an ever-increasing body of information about hitherto unknown societies in Africa, Asia, and above all America began to reach Europe. Europeans came increasingly, in Locke's words, to "look abroad beyond the Smoak of their own Chimneys."[21] And there they found worlds that to many seemed not merely different but in so many significant ways exact inversions of what was known and accepted as normal in Europe. The wilder fantasies about America—that it was filled with un-aging virgins, cities of gold, fountains of eternal youth, Amazons and dog-headed men, rivers that flowed upstream, and women who urinated standing up—soon evaporated. The real facts of Amerindian ethnography remained, though, and they were startling enough. But it was not only the European confrontation with this new and startling "other" that launched a new inquiry into exactly what it meant to be human. For the very existence of the American continent—of which the ancients had had no knowledge and the very possibility of whose existence they had consistently denied—radically upset the long-cherished idea that their science and all that had been based upon it—which included most of the Christian conception of humanity—might be omniscient.

On March 18, 1523, the Italian humanist Pietro Pomponazzi was giving a lecture at the University of Padua on Aristotle's theories about geography and the earth sciences. He explained that Aristotle and his twelfth-century Arab commentator, Abû al-Walîd Muhammad ibn Rushd—known in the West as Averroës—had denied that there could be any life below the Antipodes. (St. Augustine, too, had mocked any such suggestion, by claiming that the inhabitants would have to live upside down, the rain falling away from them rather than on them.) "This, gentlemen," he told his audience, "is what Aristotle and Averroës think. But what should we today think?" He had, he went on, just received a letter from a Venetian friend describing a journey to the "southern hemisphere," where his friend had sailed "for three months and came across more than three hundred islands each separate from the next, which were not only inhabitable, but were also inhabited." (This friend was probably Antonio Pigafetta, who accompanied the Portuguese navigator Ferdinand Magellan on his circumnavigation of the globe between 1519 and 1522.)

Where, then, did this leave Aristotle and Averroës? "I am of the belief," replied Pomponazzi to his own question, "that where experience and reason [and by "reason" he meant what was written in the canonical texts] are in conflict, then we should hold to experience and abandon reason."

The "reason" of the ancients had denied that life could exist below the equator. The discovery of America had shown that it could. As Galileo was to say later: "One thousand Demosthenes and one thousand Aristotles may be routed by an average man who brings Nature in."[22] Nature, if only one could look at her directly, unblinded by theological dogmas, could tell you all you needed to know about herself. Science could do, should do, nothing else than hold up a mirror to Nature. By the first decade of the seventeenth century it was obvious to all that, between them, the destruction of a unified Christendom and the discovery of America had "brought Nature in" and in the process had left the philosophical consensus of Europe in disarray. Faced with such uncertainty, the only possible conclusion to which any reflective person could come was that there could be no certainty, no undisputed source of authority, in the world. The outcome was the creation of a new and fundamentally un-Christian metaphor, one in which authority was no longer provided by illumination or grace but by what the French essayist Michel de Montaigne, who had lived and suffered through the French Wars of Religion, famously called "that which is properly mine." Now everything that was known about the world, the rightness or wrongness of every act, had to be decided by the individual acting on his or her own. The English poet John Donne captured this poignantly, and somewhat despairingly, in 1611:

And new Philosophy calls all in doubt,
The Element of fire is quite put out;
The Sun is lost, and th'earth, and no man's wit
Can well direct him where to look for it.

'Tis all in peeces, all coherence gone;
All just supply, and all Relation:
Prince Subject, Father, Sonne, are things forgot,
For every man alone thinkes he hath got
Toe be a Phoenix, and that there can bee
None of that kinde, of which he is, but hee.[23]

To be a Phoenix was the task of every thinking person. To rise up out of the ashes of the old order, by his intellect alone, to recognize that he is alone of all his kind: that there is no he, but he—and as later, more enlightened, generations would add, no she, but she.

What Donne called this "new philosophy" began with a simple

question: "How can I know anything?" It was a question that an ancient school of philosophers called the Skeptics had put most forcibly. This question—and the need to find some kind of answer to it—was sometimes known as the "Challenge of Carneades," after one of its best-known exponents. Carneades of Cyrene was an orator of the second to first century BCE, an ex–professional boxer with a loud voice who claimed that if it were possible—as he frequently demonstrated it was—to argue just as forcibly for any case as against it, nothing of certainty could be known about the world. On one celebrated occasion in 155 BCE Carneades went to Rome on a diplomatic mission and delivered two public orations on successive days. On the first day he argued that there is a natural order in the cosmos guided by natural law and that civil society was a replica of this natural order. We use our reason to discover what this order is, and this, he concluded, is justice. On the second day he argued that there is no order in the cosmos. Indeed, the cosmos is nothing other than a collection of atoms. Since civil society does exist, however, it can only be a purely human creation. Reason serves to reach an agreement among human beings about what is just. Justice then is only what is possible and useful. On both occasions he was loudly cheered and carried in triumph around the city, by substantially the same audience. This led to Carneades' immediate expulsion in order to protect the morals of Roman youth. Skepticism has always been unwelcome to those claiming any kind of authority.

The first of the two antithetical positions described by Carneades was the one sustained by the Stoics; the second, that held by the Epicureans. We shall meet both of them again. Together with Skepticism, they had been the dominant schools of philosophy in the ancient world. With the rise of Christianity, however, Skepticism, and most forms of Epicureanism, had been largely silenced. For the Christians had no more liking for uncertainty than the Roman magistrates had, and besides, they had a ready answer to the question of knowledge. Everything any person knows comes to them from God. God is the only guarantor we need that what we have good reason to believe must in fact also be the case. Now, however, that centuries of conflict and the unsettling presence of hitherto unknown worlds across the ocean had shattered the certainty offered by the Church and the theologians, this easy assumption seemed no longer so obvious or uncontestable. Skepticism had returned, as seemingly the only tool with which to confront the universe.

Skepticism came in many forms, from the milder tendency to question all established authority to, at its most extreme, what is called Pyrrhonian skepticism (named after the Greek philosopher Pyrrho, c. 365–275 BCE), which claimed that no certain knowledge about the external world was available at all—which meant, as Pyrrho put it, that there could be no real difference between "yes" and "no."

Most of the philosophers of the seventeenth century hovered somewhere in between. Most were prepared to accept the evidence of their senses as possibly flawed and easily misled but nevertheless the only handle we have on reality. (This is known as "sensationalism.") Then there was the certainty of the knowing, reasoning person himself. What if, asked Descartes, "I have convinced myself that there is absolutely nothing in the world, no sky, no earth, no minds, no bodies. Does it follow from that that I, too, do not exist?" No, he answered—because "if *I* have convinced myself of something then I must certainly exist." From this he concluded "that this proposition I am, I exist, is necessarily true whenever it is put forward by me or conceived by my mind."[24] This form of reasoning, which was subsequently turned into the famous Latin phrase *Cogito ergo sum*—"I think, therefore I am"—became one of the touchstones of the new philosophy.

Not many Skeptics went so far as to doubt the existence of the world. But Descartes's point is much the same as both Montaigne's and John Donne's: The only things of which I can be certain must come directly from the individual in his or her immediate and direct contact with the external world. The implications for the traditional Christian view of the world of even a moderate form of this kind of skeptical reasoning could be devastating.

It would, however, be wrong to describe many of the philosophers of the seventeenth and eighteenth centuries as true skeptics. Some, such as Bishop Berkeley, who argued that things of themselves have no material existence independently of the person who perceives them and coined the phrase *Esse est percipi* ("To be is to be perceived"), certainly were, but many more—in particular, those we associate with the Scientific Revolution, such as Descartes, Hobbes, and Bacon—saw their task as the search for an *answer* to skepticism. And the answers they came up with provided the moderns—as they came to be known—with the instruments with which they were able to tear down the tottering metaphysical fortress of the "Mother of Sciences." In its place they erected a secular, autonomous method that took at its starting point only those propositions that were "clear and self-evident," in Descartes's famous phrase. All authority, and in particular the authority of the written word, whether ascribed to some venerated dead sage or even to God himself, was now to be utterly disregarded. This did not mean that some of the things that the ancients—or even the scholastic theologians—had written might not still be true. But they could no longer be taken to be true merely because those particular authors, secular or divine, had uttered them.

The Scientific Revolution, for all that subsequent historians have tried to diminish the violence of its break with the past, was a true "revolution" in the modern sense of the term. It was not, as so many previous ones had been—as the Reformation, for instance, had been intended to be—a turning back (this is, after all, what the word *revolution* had originally meant). This was not a reevaluation of a hallowed past of the kind we associate with the Renaissance, an attempt to purify what had become sullied through abuse. This was a radical, decisive, and irreparable break.

Above all, what the moderns had achieved was to have severed scientific inquiry forever from any reliance upon any prior condition, belief, custom, or authoritative text. They had made the "I" the center of all inquiries into the human condition. Starting from these premises, the writers of the Enlightenment set out to construct an entire program for social, intellectual, and moral reform, one that would ultimately transform not only those countries where it took effect but gradually the whole of Europe and finally the entire world.

III

This is the most widely repeated genealogy of "Enlightenment." Its authority derives, in large part, from the Enlightenment's own sense of its prehistory. Not only D'Alembert but also Voltaire, Diderot, Shaftesbury, and Kant—all of whom we shall meet again—and many more had similar conceptions of their origins. It is also obvious that all the great thinkers of the Enlightenment were indebted in a number of ways to the canon of seventeenth-century empirical philosophers and natural scientists—Newton, Galileo, Locke, Hobbes, Descartes, Spinoza—that we have already encountered. But as a genealogy it fails to capture what it was that made *the* Enlightenment so different from previous revolutions in thought and belief. It fails, too, to explain why the very idea of "Enlightenment" has had the profound influence it has had on almost every aspect of life in what in the eighteenth century first came to be called "the West." Today, no one but obscurantist religious fundamentalists question the basis of modern science. But almost everywhere people struggle with one another over what are, quite evidently, the legacies of the Enlightenment: over the universality of rights, over the status of women, over the respect and toleration that should be accorded to different religions, however seemingly implausible, and so on. They struggle, too, over what was the most important of all the claims of the Enlightenment, and the one from which so many of these other concerns derived: that all humans not only belong to a single "race" but also share a common identity and thus belong ultimately to a single global community—a "cosmopolis."

To understand fully what divides what we call the Enlightenment from its seventeenth-century origins, we have to look more closely at one particular piece of the great theological machine that had hitherto guaranteed the intellectual supremacy of the Catholic Church. The collapse of the ancient consensus that had followed in the aftermath of the Wars of Religion and the discovery of the Americas had shattered not so much a belief in the deity, nor the message to be found in the Gospels; it had not even, in any specific sense, demolished the arguments of the theologians themselves, insofar as these were concerned with strictly theological matters. What it had done was to deny any credence to the traditional Catholic conception of what was called the "law of nature," the *ius naturae* or *ius naturale*.

This requires some explanation. There were (for Christians) three distinct forms of law, ranked in order of perfection. At the top, there stood the divine or eternal law. This was known to God alone. It was, the scholastics liked to say, something like the blueprints an architect uses in the construction of a building. Insofar as it is intelligible to man at all, it comes only in the form of a revelation, which for Christians means the Decalogue and the Gospels. Religion, or at least the three religions that were recognized as such in early modern Europe—Christianity, Judaism, and Islam—were all, in the language of the Middle Ages, *leges*—that is, founded upon a law—and as such were distinguished from all other systems of belief, which were generally branded as undifferentiated "superstitions." Religion was, as Hobbes said of it, self-evidently "not philosophy but law."[25]

At the bottom of the hierarchy was the positive, or human, law. This last was the law enacted by human societies for their own governance. Positive laws are mandatory because they are decreed by the community or by the ruler or, alternately, by the legislature acting in the name of, and on behalf of, the community. They are purely human creations, and most are, in origin, simply conventional, or as it is sometimes called today, "merely morally permissible." It does not, for instance, matter to God or nature which side of the road you drive on. But the preservation of society demands that there be a law that requires everyone to drive on the same side.

Beneath this divine law and above the positive law was the law of nature. This was generally understood as the law that governed every action that occurred in the natural world. What this meant, however, when applied to the behavior of human beings, became the subject of violent, and ultimately irresolvable, dispute. "Natural law," said Diderot in the article he wrote on the subject for the *Encyclopédie* in 1755, was a term "used so frequently that there is scarcely anyone who is not convinced in his own mind that he knows just what it means."[26] Yet no two people could ever fully agree on what that was. For all its vagaries and uncertainties, however, the idea that there existed in nature—and was thus available to all rational beings, independently of their beliefs or the cultures to which they belonged—a set of rules by which all human conduct was ultimately judged would survive until the nineteenth century, when Hegel buried it under the weight of Idealism. Like so much else in western thought, the idea of a law of nature, of a common law for all humanity, was first suggested by Plato and then developed by Aristotle. It was what the ancient Stoics, who have a central role to play in this story, called the *koinos nomos*. It had then been refined and extended—overextended, many would say—by generations of commentators, until by the seventeenth century it had come to determine what distinguished good from evil, rational from irrational, and thus human from nonhuman. All positive laws were binding only so long as they were just, and to be just they had to be in accordance with, or at least not in violation of, natural law. No ruler, for instance, could pass a law requiring that his subjects practice cannibalism or human sacrifice (a real issue when it came to considering the possible significance of the behavior, or reported behavior, of the American Indians). Such a law would not, as the saying went, be binding "in the court of conscience."

Originally the natural law had meant simply the sum of all the behavior of all living creatures—human and nonhuman. It was, said the Roman jurist Ulpian in the third century CE, "not peculiar to the human race, but belongs to all animals," which made of it something nonrational—nothing more, indeed, than a brute instinct.[27] Ulpian conceded that humans might have more complex instincts than other animals, but in his view their moral and rational lives were untouched by nature. As a Christian he believed that the ultimate source of all moral conduct could be only God. Throughout the Middle Ages, however, the definition of the natural law underwent a radical transformation.[28] If for the Roman jurists it had been something that humans shared with the animal world, for the theologians it rapidly became precisely that which distinguished mankind from all other forms of life. Humankind may have been built to the same specifications as the rest of the universe, and the laws that govern human actions are part of the body of wider laws that govern all matter. But for the theologians man was also an exalted part of the creation; he was God's special concern, the only animal possessed of reason (and speech) and the ultimate link in what was known as the Great Chain of Being, which united all living beings to the Godhead itself. He was "the horizon," in the words of St. Thomas Aquinas, "the boundary-line of all things corporeal and incorporeal."[29]

It was Aquinas who provided the account of the natural law that was to become authoritative—doctrinal, indeed—until the seventeenth century. Law is one of the means (the other is Grace) by which God moves us to our ends or good. Animals also act toward their ends, but only by means of the instincts that God has implanted in them. At some level, humans also have a purely instinctual understanding of the natural law. (Their response to hunger, thirst, and the fear of death is not very different from that of other animals.) But they also "participate" in the Eternal Law through the rational comprehension of God's laws, and this is unique to them alone. This is what Aquinas understood by the natural law. It allows human beings to direct themselves, by their own understanding and volition, toward their ends.[30]

Rational creatures, he wrote,

> are subject to divine Providence in a very special way; being themselves made participators in Providence itself, in that they control their own actions and the actions of others. So they have a certain share in divine reason itself, deriving therefrom a natural inclination to such actions and ends as are fitting. This participation in the Eternal Law by rational creatures is called the Natural Law.

This raised the natural law from a basic instinct to the level of something that served as a bridge between the purely human and the divine. Natural Law was nothing less than "the impression of the Divine Light within us."[31] By defining it in this way, Aquinas had made it the basis of all further discussion of what it was to be "human."

Hovering uncomfortably between the natural and the positive laws was something called the "law of nations," the *ius gentium*. This had originally been the law used by the Romans in their dealing with the *gentes*—that is, non–Roman citizens. In a wider sense, however, it was taken to be what the second-century jurist Gaius called the law that "natural reason establishes among all men and is observed by all peoples alike."[32] This made it some kind of universal law that would apply beyond the limits of particular states. Yet no one could quite decide if this meant that it was, in effect, a part of the natural law or a positive law that, in the words of the Spanish theologian Francisco Suárez, "had been introduced . . . by the probable and common estimation of men."[33] Neither of these definitions was in any way satisfactory, and the struggle over the definition of the law of nations was to have a prolonged and powerful impact on all subsequent European legal thinking and on every subsequent attempt to imagine how a truly enlightened cosmopolitan world would be governed.[34]

Some version of Aquinas' definition of the Natural Law was to prove definitive until the entire conception was radically redescribed—as we shall see—in the seventeenth century. It was, however, only one part of a much larger project. Aquinas was very largely responsible for introducing the writings of Aristotle into Christian thought, and in particular what are known as Aristotle's moral triad—the *Nicomachean Ethics,* the *Politics,* and the *Economics* (although the last of these turned out not to be by Aristotle). It was Aquinas who Aristotelized Christianity—much as Augustine had Platonized it—and in the process he had ecclesiasticized "the Philosopher."[35] Aristotle, however, unlike Plato, had created an entire language of scientific description that ranged from the laws of motion to the human soul—the first, and in many respects also the last, great universal system of knowledge. It is ultimately to Aristotle that we owe the beginnings of almost all the modern natural sciences: physics, astronomy, biology, physiology, even meteorology and geology. To these he added logic, moral philosophy, and the science of politics. Other Greeks, and some Egyptians, had written on most of these subjects before Aristotle. But no one had attempted to link them together into a unified theory. By "Aristotelizing" rather than "Platonizing" the schematic Christian message, Aquinas and his followers provided Christianity with a perfectly coherent account of the entire universe. Furthermore, Aristotle's view of nature, and of humanity's place within it, owed nothing to a divinity, beyond the useful recognition—for the Christians—of the existence of an initial creative force in the universe, what he called the "unmoved mover."[36] This overcame the potentially embarrassing fact that the man who had laid the intellectual foundations of so much of Christian theology had been a pagan; it also made it possible for his Christian admirers to claim that he had recognized the existence of something resembling the Judeo-Christian God through natural reason alone.

Aristotle allowed Aquinas to give to the purely human, as distinct from the divine, elements of humanity a far greater importance than any of his predecessors had done. For St. Augustine, by far the most powerful and most influential of Aquinas' predecessors, life on earth, what he called the "Earthly City," had been a mere way station, a place of passage for the human soul on its journey to the afterlife. All that was redemptive in man—all that really mattered—came not from his or her own nature but from God's grace. For Aquinas, by contrast, the basic character of humanity was determined by nature. For Augustine, grace had erased human nature. For Aquinas, it perfected it. And the phrase *Gratia naturam non tollit, sed perficit* ("Grace does not erase nature, but it perfects it") became, as Descartes's *Cogito ergo sum* was to be for later generations, the summation of an entire system of thought.

What Aquinas meant by saying that the natural law was mankind's "participation in the Eternal Law" was that all rational persons could read in nature, as if it were a book on which God had written his will, regarding all "such actions and ends as are fitting" for all human beings.[37] Aquinas' "divinized natural law," as it has been called, had the effect of freeing humans, partially at least, from their dependency upon revelation.[38] Of course, you could still enter heaven only because of the sacrifice of Christ, and if you did not believe in that you were damned. As poor Aristotle himself says pitifully in Dante's great poem *The Divine Comedy,* in which he languishes in the second circle of Hell because he, like Plato, Cicero, Seneca, and the other "virtuous pagans," had, through no fault of his own, "before the Gospel lived . . . [and] served not God aright":

> *For these defects*
> *And for no other evil, we are lost,*
> *Only so far afflicted that we live*
> *Desiring without hope.*[39]

But while you lived on this earth, you belonged to a single natural order, and you had to conduct yourself in accordance with its laws. The presence of the natural law in all men also meant that there must exist a community of all men. All men were, so to speak, parts of a single, natural body, and the harmony of their movements resembled that of the heavenly spheres.

Aquinas' formulation of the natural law was one of the prime concerns—perhaps *the* prime concern—of his fifteenth- and sixteenth-century followers, called after him "Thomists," many of whose (usually prolix) writings the future architects of the Scientific Revolution would encounter in the classrooms of Oxford, Cambridge, and Paris in the early seventeenth century. The Thomists developed a very complex set of explanations that underpinned what had by then become the orthodox definition of humanity. But their basic claim was that natural law was made accessible to all humans, no matter what their origins, by means of what they called "first precepts" that had been inscribed in the minds of all human beings—hard-wired, so to speak—by God at the creation.

These were not simple instincts, such as animals (and humans) possessed. They constituted what were called "innate ideas" or "innate senses," which the great Scottish philosopher David Hume, who did not believe in them, would later define as "original and copied from no precedent perception."[40] They allowed humans to see the world God had created as it really was, which meant that they allowed the rational human animal to recognize God's existence and then to distinguish between good and evil and to act accordingly.

The first precepts of the natural law, although superior to mere instincts, were nonetheless very basic. They allowed you, for instance, to know that killing, theft, rape, incest, the eating of human flesh, and so on were all unnatural. They could be summed up in the commandment

"Do unto others as you would have others do unto you." They could not, however, offer much guidance about all the myriad codes of conduct, the habits and customs of which all societies are composed. They did not tell you, for instance, that having more than one wife is unnatural, as is defecating in public or belching after meals. They did not tell you that modesty and the wearing of clothes (covering one's "shameful parts," as the theologians coyly phrased it) was natural, as was offering hospitality to strangers. This was where reason came in. The rational mind, acting on the innate first precepts, could deduce what codes were natural and what were contrary to nature. The problem was that the further you traveled from the initial "innate" idea, the more precarious the process of deduction became. You could, therefore, only be certain that your particular deductions were correct if they coincided with those of your fellows. This "common persuasion," as it was called, was your sole guarantee, not because the community must always be right, but because, as God had created all men's minds alike, it followed that if any sufficiently large number of them were ultimately to come to conclusions radically different from those of their fellows, then it could only be because God had confused them. And that clearly was unthinkable. "Our intellect is from God," the great Spanish Thomist theologian Francisco de Vitoria explained to his students at the University of Salamanca in the mid–sixteenth century, "and if it were to have a natural inclination toward error or falsehood then this would have to be attributed to God."[41] Individual humans, and even entire communities, can be led astray by the Devil, by false prophets, or by malign rulers—this, for instance, was what had happened to the Jews and the Muslims. There was also a great deal of variety in the world; it was part of God's bounty. But there could exist no place on the planet where what was held to be not simply odd or eccentric but *unnatural* in Christendom was not also, in fact, contrary to natural law. It was remarks like this that led Hegel to the entirely reasonable assumption that all the natural law amounted to was a series of generalizations from existing traditions.[42]

Because it was rational in this way, because it defined humanity's place in the natural world itself, the natural law could not be otherwise.

God could create whatever kind of world he chose, a world in which crows were white and fire did not burn, but it would not be *this* world governed by *this* law of nature.[43] From being, in Aquinas' hands, a simple participation by humanity in the divine plan, the natural law had, by the sixteenth century, become an independent body of rational principles, immutable and transcendental.

The entire edifice was, as John Locke said of it, "props and buttresses, leaning on borrowed or begg'd foundations,"[44] and as John Stuart Mill was later to demonstrate, it was all based on a confusion between the descriptive laws of nature and the purely prescriptive laws of man.[45] If what we all see before us is a tree, it is unlikely that in some far-flung region of the world there are beings who think of it as a horse. But it does not follow from this that if in Paris raw fish is considered to be unfit for human consumption, then it will also be in Tokyo.

Yet so long as there seemed to exist a general consensus as to which—in Aquinas' terms—"actions and ends" were fitting for all humanity, such a vision of a single, if varied, law governing all human conduct seemed credible. Once, however, that consensus had collapsed, once entire continents were discovered to be filled with persons who had very different views as to the fitness of their actions and ends from those of the majority of Europeans, it rapidly began to seem parochial, when not absurd. In the world in which men might slaughter one another because of their differences of opinion over God's grace or the composition of the Eucharist—whether it should be made of leavened or unleavened bread—or where some men raised their hats as a sign of greeting and others turned their backs; in which some buried their dead as a sign of respect and others ate them; where there existed peoples for whom it "is considered polite to wipe their fingers when eating on their thighs, on their balls, or on the soles of their feet," or where it is "a sign of high breeding to bite the lice that has bitten them," or among whom "greeting consists of putting one's finger on the ground and then rising it heavenwards," or "where the women stand up to piss and the men squat down . . . where fathers have the responsibility of punishing the male children and the mothers the female," and so on and so on, the "natural law" came to be seen as nothing other than an elaborate device for transforming local preferences into divinely sanctioned universal decrees.

All of the examples I have just given—and there are many more of them, going on for page after page—are provided by Michel de Montaigne in an essay entitled "On habit: and on never easily changing a traditional law."[46] Montaigne had had a famous encounter at Rouen in 1561 with a group of Tupinamba "cannibals" brought back from the coasts of Brazil and put on display in an "Indian" village specially constructed for the purpose, so that the French king, Charles IX, who was visiting the city, might see for himself what strange creatures lived in his "New World." (As it turned out, there were not enough real Tupi to populate an entire village, so a number of protesting peasants were drafted, decked out in feather headdresses, and painted to make them look as "red" as possible.) We do not know what Charles made of the cannibals. But Montaigne was impressed by their dignity, their physique, and what he describes as their natural reason. (Why, they asked, did full-grown men, "bearded, strong, and bearing-arms," bow down before a child—Charles was only eleven years old at the time—why did the destitute, whom they had seen, "emaciated with poverty and hunger . . . put up with such injustice and not take the others by the throat or set fire to their houses?") These men were, Montaigne concluded, "barbarous only in that they have been hardly fashioned by the mind of man, still remaining close neighbours to their original state of nature." As for their cannibalism, which most Europeans looked upon as proof of their inhumanity, Montaigne came to the conclusion that it was better to eat someone who was dead, as he supposed the Tupinamba did, than someone who was still alive, "under the pretext of piety and religion," as both Catholic and Protestants had done in France.[47] (In 1725 Voltaire claimed to have had an identical encounter with a "savage from Mississippi," which had led him—with acknowledgment to Montaigne—to the same conclusion. We kill and slaughter our enemies, he observed, so as "to prepare food for crows and worms. . . . We respect the dead more than we do the living.")[48]

Altogether, these experiences of confessional violence and the disturbingly rational ways of exotic "others" had taught Montaigne—"the first Frenchman who dared to think," as the arch-materialist, triumphant atheist, and unrepentant gourmand Lucien Offray de la Mettrie said of him—that: "The laws of conscience which we say are born of nature, are born of custom; since man inwardly venerates the opinions and the manners approved and received about him, he cannot, without remorse, free himself from them nor apply himself to them without self-approbation."[49]

As the seventeenth-century French philosopher, mathematician, and physicist, inventor of the syringe and of a forerunner of the digital computer Blaise Pascal summed it up, all that the word *natural* meant was something that was generally accepted by one or another group of people. "Truth on this side of the Pyrenees," he wrote, is "error on the other side." (If, that is, you were French.) And if "nature" could no longer be relied upon to be consistent between France and Spain, who could know what might be natural in China or Ceylon? What evidence, asked Locke, was there that could persuade anyone who was "but moderately conversant with the History of Mankind" that there could exist a "practical Truth that is universally received without doubt or question, as it must be if innate? Justice, and the keeping of contracts is that which most men agree in." And these have nothing to do with any innate perception of the difference between right and wrong. Even thieves "keep Faith and rule of Justice one with another," and " 'tis without receiving these as the innate Laws of Nature. They practice them as Rules of convenience within their own Communities."[50] Wherever you looked, there were clearly no grounds for supposing, as Hobbes put it, that there had ever existed "right reason in the nature of things." Things were what you made of them. And those, he observed dryly, who "commonly . . . call for right reason to decide any controversy, do mean their own."[51]

One of the most important "first precepts" of the natural law was the premise on which first Aristotle, then Aquinas, and thereafter every political and social theorist until Hobbes constructed their claims about how human societies should be built: namely, that all humans are by their very nature social beings. For Aristotle this had been a quasi-biological principle. Like many other animals—bees and bears, for instance—humans could not live by themselves. They, too, were naturally sociable, but unlike other animals, they were made for a particular kind of social life. They were, Aristotle said, *zoa politika,* that is, literally animals made for life in what the Greeks called the *polis,* the city or the state. This did not mean that they were not also individuals. It meant only that no human being could fulfill his or her potential as a human in any space other than the *polis*. Only here was the practice of virtue possible. Actual human societies, however, were artificial creations, the expression of what the Greeks called *techne*—skill or art: the word from which *technology* derives. But *techne* was itself conceived not merely as an ability, a craft, or a skill but also as a form of knowledge, and as such it was an integral and defining component of what it was to be human. Thus there could never be a race of peoples who lived literally outside society—although, in the opinion of many, the average European peasant came pretty close. In the wilderness beyond the human community, said Aristotle, only "beasts and heroes" could survive. When William of Moerbeke translated Aristotle's *Politics* into Latin in about 1260, he transformed this into "beasts and saints," thus apparently Christianizing Aristotle's text. But the argument remained the same: only those who, by nature, were either so far above ordinary humanity as not to require virtue or so far below as not to be able to acquire it could make a life beyond the bonds of the social order.

The most important of the "primary precepts" of the law of nature thus became "Love thy neighbor as thyself" and "Do unto others as you would have others do unto you." (These are, of course, both biblical commandments. But it was crucial for the Thomists that divine revealed law had to be as accessible to reason as human law.[52] Christianity, although, as no human could ever understand fully the mind of God—it possessed a part that was accessible only to faith—was believed to be a preeminently *rational* religion.)

Neither Aristotle himself nor Aquinas wished to deny that societies could take many forms. But whereas they might differ across time and space (and Aristotle himself discussed at some length the merits and demerits of the various types that existed in his day), they had all to be *societies,* and the definitions as to what constituted a society were drawn very tightly. Any group of people whose ways of life did not fulfill the necessary criteria was all too likely to be classified as something less than human. It was, most famously, the fate that befell many American Indian groups and most Africans.

The destruction of this elaborate mechanism, which for over three centuries had been the bedrock on which all the ethical systems of Europe had rested, we owe in large part to two men: the English philosopher Thomas Hobbes and the Dutch humanist poet, historian, and jurist Hugo Grotius. Both cast long shadows over the Enlightenment, and Hobbes especially has perhaps had more influence on subsequent social and political thought than any other single writer. In one sense the Enlightenment can be seen as an attempt to broaden and humanize Hobbes's unpitying view of human nature and the inescapable conclusions to be drawn from it without slipping back into the constraining, if welcoming, embrace of the idea of a benign God.

There are marked differences between Hobbes and Grotius. Hobbes, for one thing, was intent on reaching as wide an audience as possible and with creating a wholly new philosophical language. He therefore wrote his longest, most ambitious work, *Leviathan,* in English rather than in Latin, and together with his near-contemporary John Locke, who had similar ambitions, was one of the first major thinkers to do so. Grotius, however, wrote wholly in Latin, and his major work, *On the Law of War and Peace,* was constructed as a traditional natural-law treatise, very much like those of his scholastic predecessors. It also seemed, with its long quotations and endless references to ancient and biblical history, far less threatening than *Leviathan*. Jean-Jacques Rousseau, who claimed to loathe Hobbes but who called Grotius the "master of all savants," recalled how, as a child, he would stand beside his father, who was a clockmaker, and watch him work while, "nourishing his soul with the most sublime of Truths," he read from "Tacitus, Plutarch, and Grotius," whose works lay in front of him, "mixed together with the tools of his trade." The image Rousseau is trying to convey is that of the sage artisan, the true "honest man." But the choice of authors was not arbitrary. Tacitus would have taught Rousseau *père* the principles of government, Plutarch the moral values of the ancient Roman state,

Grotius the basis of all social and judicial theory.[53] Yet for all the significant differences between Hobbes and Grotius, Rousseau also believed that, at least as far as their principles were concerned, "they are exactly the same: they only differ in their expression. They also differ in their methods. Hobbes relies on sophisms and Grotius on the poets; all the rest is the same."[54]

Even if saying that they were "exactly the same" was a typical Rousseauian exaggeration, there was one thing on which Hobbes and Grotius certainly agreed: the collapse of the consensus that had followed in the wake of the Reformation and the discovery of the peoples of America had demonstrated beyond any possible doubt that the Aristotelian conception of natural sociability was an illusion based, in Hobbes's words, on a "superficial view of human nature." True, all humans had some initial inclination to congregate together. But: "By nature," he wrote derisively of the cozy view that society was the ultimate expression of a natural human desire for companionship, "we are not looking for friends but for honour and advantage . . . if {men} meet for entertainment or fun, everyone usually takes most pleasure in the kind of amusing incident from which (such is the nature of the ridiculous) he may come away with a better idea of himself in comparison with someone else's embarrassment or weakness."[55] And if it was not the desire to get the better of their fellow creatures that drew them together, then it was fear:

> I mean by that word any anticipation of future evil. In my view, not only flight but distrust, suspicion, precaution and provisions against fear are all characteristics of men who are afraid. On going to bed they lock their doors; when going on a journey, they arm themselves because they are afraid of robbers. Countries guard their frontiers with fortresses, their cities with walls for fear of neighbouring countries.

This "mutual fear," as Hobbes put it, was the ultimate engine that drove humans not merely to congregate but ultimately to submit themselves to the necessary constraints of civil society. Man was, and would remain until restrained, a constant threat to himself: *Homo homini lupus*—"Man is a wolf to man," as Hobbes expressed it, borrowing a phrase from the Roman playwright Plautus.[56] In both Hobbes's and Grotius' view, the Aristotelian-Thomist theory of natural sociability rested upon a false ontology—a point to which I shall return—and an equally untenable teleology.

The "general inclination of mankind" was, said Hobbes in one of his most memorable phrases, "a perpetual and restless desire of power after power that ceaseth only in Death." There was no "ultimate good," as the Aristotelians had claimed, because the desires that drive all humankind can never be satisfied. "For there is no such *Finis ultimus* [ultimate aim]," he wrote, "no *summum Bonum* [greatest Good] as is spoken of in the Books of the old Moral Philosophers. Nor can a man any more live, whose Desires are at an end, than he whose senses and Imaginations are at a stand. Felicity is a continual progress of the desire from one object to another."[57] It was one of Hobbes's most radical claims. What he was in effect arguing was not only that humanity had no ultimate purpose to fulfill, save for remaining alive, but that "blessedness"—the "greatest Good" to which he refers—far from being the desirable state in which all the passions had been transcended, could only mean the destruction of all that was human, a form of death. From this devastatingly simple principle it was possible to construct a new conception of the natural law independent of any complex, and unverifiable, suppositions about the nature of human psychology.[58] If, in Hobbes's view, we could not suppose that the "law of nature" had been somehow hardwired in the human mind by God, we could know from simple observation that humans possessed a marked disposition to inflict harm on their fellows, and that, despite this, humans, like all living creatures, wished for one thing: to avoid death for as long as possible. True, there were individuals who for special reasons of their own—misguided fanaticism, for instance, or an illusion about what awaited them after death—might choose to embrace death. But for all the tempting images that the world's religions had conjured up about the afterlife, very few ever, in fact, did so. For Hobbes, the suicide bomber would have been a freak, an aberration, and quite probably mad.[59] The normal rational person always did his or her best to avoid the destruction of the body for as long as possible. This Hobbes described as a movement "as powerful as that by which a stone falls downwards." From which he concluded: "It is therefore not absurd, nor reprehensible, nor contrary to reason, if one makes every effort to defend his body and limbs from death and to preserve them. And what is not contrary to right reason, all agree is done justly and of Right."[60]

For Hobbes, the law of nature could, therefore, be torn from its elaborate metaphysical moorings and reduced to one simple, irrefutable, *right:* "The Right of nature, which Writers commonly call the *jus naturale,*" he declared, "is the Liberty each man hath, to use his own power, as he will himself, for the preservation of his own Nature; that is to say, of his own Life; and consequently, of doing any thing, which in his own Judgement and Reason, he shall conceive to be the aptest means thereunto." And again: "A Law of Nature [*Lex Naturalis*]" is a "Precept, or generall Rule, found out by Reason, by which a man is forbidden to do, that, which is destructive of his life, or taketh away the means of preserving the same; and to omit, that, by which he thinketh it may be best preserved."[61] That, and nothing more. (From this, Hobbes derived nineteen general "Laws of Nature dictating Peace." There were also clearly others, prohibiting those things which tended "to the destruction of particular men" as distinct from society as a whole, such as drunkenness, but that are "not necessary to be mentioned, nor are pertinent enough to this place.")[62]

In Grotius' not dissimilar version of this, the primary "precepts" of the law of nature became not the commandments "Love thy neighbor as thyself" and "Do unto others as you would have others do unto you," but instead: "It shall be permissible to defend one's own life and to shun that which threatens to prove injurious," and "It shall be permissible to acquire for oneself and to retain those things which are useful to life." Only these, in his view, were principles so fundamental that no one could disagree with them "without doing violence to himself."

The natural law that, in the hands of the scholastics, had once offered a complex argument for human sociability had now been reduced to one seemingly irrefutable principle on which all humans could be brought to agree, whatever they might be like in Iceland or the Antipodes. It had also been detached entirely from the divine law. "The law of nature is unchangeable," wrote Grotius, "even in the sense that it cannot be changed by God."[63] To which he added his famous—or infamous, depending on your point of view—claim that such a law would bind mankind, "though we should even grant, what without the greatest wickedness cannot be granted, that there is no God, or that he takes no care of human affairs."[64]

It is little wonder that Hobbes, at least, was condemned as an atheist, and as we shall see, his name became linked for most of the following century to a philosophy that looked only to man's narrow concern with his own survival—which, having deprived humans of their link to the divinity, had then reduced them to little more than rationalizing, maximizing, and—a key word—"selfish" automata.

But if humans are not naturally sociable, what explains the formation of societies? Hobbes's answer was simple self-interest. To explain how this worked, he employed a fable that was to have some far-reaching, if unintended, consequences for the subsequent history of the Enlightenment. If societies were artificial, man-made creations, they clearly had to have had a beginning, which meant that there had to have been a time before they existed. This came to be called the "state of nature." Hobbes did not invent it. Ever since the Greek poet Hesiod in the eighth century BCE, humans have provided themselves with mythical pre-social origins, and their genealogy has been an accepted means of establishing the legitimacy, or impugning the illegitimacy, of the kinds of societies they have created for themselves.[65] Hobbes's use of the myth was, however, different in significant ways. In the first place, most previous pre-social worlds had been imagined as idyllic states where mankind had lived a charmed, effortless, and eternal existence in the presence of the gods, or of God. In the Greek version men and the gods had dined at the same table, until one day Zeus got tired of having these lesser beings around and banished them to Earth. There Prometheus, who had taken pity on them, brought them the gift of fire in order to make their lives more bearable. For this Zeus had him chained to a rock and ordered that his liver should be pecked out each day by an eagle and then grow again each night. The Hebrew version of this—the expulsion of Adam and Eve from the Garden of Eden—involves an act of defiance on the part of the newly created humans. They are sinners, not mere victims. But the outcome is much the same. Banished from their original homes, they are now bound to roam the world, which they must make habitable for themselves using the one thing that the gods (or God) have left to them: their reason.

Hobbes turns this on its head. In his state of nature there are no gods, no celestial dinner tables, no garden "eastward of Eden" provided with all that mankind required to survive. Instead there is only unrelenting violence. In such a world, wrote Hobbes, in what is his most famous utterance and one of the most powerful sentences in the English language:

> there is no place for Industry; because the fruit thereof is uncertain; and consequently no Culture of the Earth; no Navigation, no use of the commodities that may be imported by Sea; no commodious Building; no Instruments of moving and removing such things as require much force; no Knowledge of the face of the Earth; no account of Time; no Arts; no Letters; no Society, and which is worst of all, continual fear and danger of violent death; and the life of man, solitary, poor, nasty, brutish, and short.[66]

But humans, even the most primitive of them, are not only passionate, bellicose, vicious creatures, they are also—some of the time—rational ones. They could see that a situation in which every individual was permitted to do precisely as he pleased was, ultimately, disastrous for all of them. To put an end to this situation, of this "war of all against all," primitive man had therefore come to the conclusion that it would be "necessary, to lay down this right to all things and be contented with so much liberty against other men, as he would allow other men against himself." To achieve this end, these early men had entered into a contract—or what Hobbes calls a "covenant"—with one another and by this means created civil society for themselves.

Society, then, was not natural; it was inescapably artificial. "For by Art," wrote Hobbes, "is created that great Leviathan called a COMMON-WEALTH or STATE (in latine CIVITAS) which is but an Artificiall Man."[67] And not everyone had made this move. There were, Hobbes believed, large numbers of humans roaming the earth who still lived in the state of nature. The American Indians, for instance, without being either beasts or heroes (much less saints), "dependeth on natural lust, have no government at all; and live at this day in that brutish manner, as I said before."[68]

From this initial move laws and the institutions of government had been created, and since neither government nor laws could be enforced over large areas, the world had eventually been divided into nations, each with its own rights and its own civil codes. This made the state a composite whole, created by human will, and thus crucially independent of the will, or even of the designs, of God. The sovereign had to be obeyed as the repository of the collective will and the power of judgment of the entire nation. His (or its) power was absolute so long as he did not infringe every human's natural right to self-protection and so long as he provided the protection against civil war and foreign invasion for which the covenant had been created. Such power necessarily held all men in awe. But there was nothing divine, nothing sacral, nothing remotely mysterious about it.

Whereas for Aristotle and his heirs the creation of the *polis* had been the fulfillment of an a priori plan on the part of nature (or the divinity), for Hobbes and Grotius it was nothing more than a rational calculation intended to ensure the continuation of the species. Social life was not, as it had been for Aristotle and the entire Thomist theological tradition, necessary for humans to fulfill their ends as humans. It was merely a condition of survival. And not all men had made that choice.

For Hobbes, the creation of civil society had made the world a safer place, but it had not done so, as Aristotle and the theologians had imagined, by transforming the very nature of man himself. It had done so by limiting mankind's natural inclination for destruction. Society does not change us. We remain at heart the same villainous creatures we were in the state of nature. By casting primitive man in this light,

Hobbes started a controversy that would last for well over a century and in some ways survives to this day.

In a Europe torn by ideological conflict and simultaneously in the process of rapid overseas expansion, these were powerful and compelling claims. Simply stated, Hobbes offered a solution to civil war—for, as he put it, "all such calamities as may be avoided by human industry, arise from war, but chiefly from civil war." If the right of self-protection was the basis for the natural law, he argued, then it followed that the role of the society was to uphold that right. To achieve that end the sovereign power—and for Hobbes it mattered little whether it was a king or a committee, a monarchy or a republic (the phrase he uses is "Man or Assembly of Men," and he repeats it again and again)—had to be undivided and unchallenged. As he put it, the subjects of the ruler had to surrender to him—or to them, or to it—not only their will but also their judgment.[69] He—or it—would not only act for them but also *think* for them, a claim that Kant said later he found "appalling."[70]

Hobbes and Grotius had succeeded in radically redescribing the law of nature without rejecting the idea that there might exist such a law altogether. They had left humans very much to their own devices, dependent now only upon their senses, their passion, and their reason to guide them. It was, as later generations were to discover, a profoundly unsettling vision of the human condition.

The seventeenth-century onslaught on scholasticism had been immensely convincing. The prose in which it had been written, that of Hobbes in particular, had been powerfully engaging, something that could not be said for the bulky tomes of the "schoolmen." There was also something direct and appealing about what has come to be called Hobbes's "realism," his refusal to consider anything of any relevance that could not be shown to be accessible to direct experience. Anthony Ashley Cooper, Earl of Shaftesbury (of whom more later), although he loathed the conclusions to which Hobbes had come, referred to him as "an able and witty philosopher of our nation."[71] The Scottish philosopher Francis Hutcheson, although he too could hardly stomach a philosophy that "over-look'd every thing which is *generous* or *kind* in mankind" nevertheless called Hobbes "that bold author [who] having carried on his inquiries in a singular manner, and without regard to authorities and having fallen into a way of speaking which was much more intelligible than that of the Schoolmen, soon became agreeable to many free wits of his age."[72] Even Diderot, who believed that Hobbes suffered from the failing of all "systematic philosophers" in distorting all the evidence he could find "to fit his hypothesis," acknowledged that "even his mistakes have contributed more to the advance of the human mind than a host of works strung together with commonplace knowledge."[73] But, he warned, "Take care not to go beyond his first principles, if you do not wish to follow him everywhere he cares to lead you." No one in the succeeding generation, no one perhaps until today, could ever quite avoid him. But neither, as we shall now see, were they ever so easily led as Diderot supposed.

2

BRINGING PITY BACK IN

I

THE SCHOLASTIC INTELLECTUAL landscape that Hobbes had apparently so devastated had not, however, been anything like as unfertile as he suggested. True, the Aristotelianism of the schools, when he first encountered it, was as arid an academic language as any to be found in any part of academia today. But the Thomist and Aristotelian conception of the law of nature allowed for many things that the Hobbesian (if not the Grotian) definitions did away with. For one thing, the scholastics had made their version of the natural law the basis for a universal moral and political code that demanded that all human beings be regarded in the same way, no matter what their culture or their beliefs. It also demanded that human beings respect each other because they share a common urge to "come together," and it required them to offer to each other, even to total strangers, help in times of need, to recognize "that amity among men is part of the natural law."[1] Finally, while Hobbes and Grotius had accepted the existence of only one natural right—the right to self-preservation—the scholastics had allowed for a wide range of them—among them the right of free access to all the lands on this earth and the right to be heard in any dispute—which are the direct antecedents of what later came to be described as "human rights."[2]

None of this, of course, played any part in Hobbes's, or even Grotius', drastically simplified account. (Grotius, it is true, did suggest that men had some obligations to their neighbors, but these were only expressed in terms of abstention from doing harm.) The Enlightenment, and in particular that portion with which I am concerned, was in part, as we shall now see, an attempt to recover something of this vision of a unified and essentially benign humanity, of a potentially cosmopolitan world, without also being obliged to accept the theologians' claim that this could only make sense as part of the larger plan of a well-meaning, if deeply inscrutable, deity.

By the early eighteenth century the political landscape of Europe, and of the world beyond, had changed dramatically since the end of the Thirty Years' War. Grotius' *On the Law of War and Peace* had been written in 1625. *Leviathan* first appeared in 1651, but the basic ideas concerning the law of nature were all to be found in the Latin treatise *De Cive,* the work by which Hobbes was best known outside England, which had been written sometime before 1641. It was, that is, the creation of the world that had been radically altered—or so it often seemed to contemporaries—by the Peace of Westphalia in 1648. Westphalia had not, as we have seen, put an end to internecine war within Europe. But it had begun a process that would lead slowly to the creation of what a number of writers would call the "Republic of Europe," a society of states held together by a shared, if not common, culture, a common legal system, and living—in admittedly uneasy alliance—with one another. It was a highly optimistic perception of the future of the western world, but it provided enough of a sense of security to the generations that grew up in the half century after 1648 to drive them to unpick the seemingly irrefutable account that Hobbes and the entire "mechanical philosophy" had provided of the origins of human sociability.

The main theoretical weakness of both the Hobbesian and Grotian conception of "the human," as so many of its critics from their day to this have pointed out, was that it required a highly reductionist view of the human personality as one motivated only by egotism.[3] Hobbes went to great lengths to remedy this, but his claim that the only thing that united all humans was their desire to remain alive for as long as possible seemed to many of his successors, as it did to David Hume, "to have proceeded from that love of simplicity which has been the source of much false reasoning in philosophy."[4] Hume's most significant contemporary critic and fellow Scot, Thomas Reid, although his notion of "common sense" in Hume's view merely "leads us back to innate ideas," agreed with him at least on this. "This love of simplicity," he wrote, "and of reducing things to a few principles, hath produced many a false system." The worst culprits, in his view, had been Descartes and "the greater Newton," who, in their assumptions as to the fundamental simplicity of the world, had "formed their notions of the unknown parts of nature, from those which they were acquainted, as the shepherd Tityrus formed his notion of the city of Rome from his country village."[5] (Reid also thought that Hume, Descartes, and Hobbes had overreached themselves by attempting to create "a system of human nature; an undertaking too vast for any one man, how great soever his genius and abilities may be.")[6]

Hobbes's understanding of the natural law had also, as Francis Hutcheson—"the never to be forgotten Hutcheson," as Adam Smith called him—who had been David Hume's friend and mentor, was perhaps the first to point out, not merely reduced the natural law to a single irrefutable principle, it had also reduced it to a right.[7] And although rights were clearly invaluable for defining the limits of the state, they could not really hope to account for all the variety of human experience. It seemed very much as if, by toppling the old Aristotelian idea of natural sociability, Hobbes had not merely demolished the Aristotelian-Thomist theological order; he had also banished any possibility of any mode of human interaction that was not based upon a crude calculation of interests. Hobbes in particular, although his whole argument rests upon a passion, seemed to many to have stripped the human personality of any capacity for love or tenderness or even simple fellow-feeling, leaving instead only fear. The bath was dry, and the baby had vanished.

A similar objection is to be found in the brief history of the evolution of the modern philosophical mind that D'Alembert provides in the "Preliminary Discourse" to the *Encyclopédie*. Here, however, the target is not Hobbes but Descartes, who for D'Alembert stands for the "mechanical philosophy" in its entirety—as he was to do for Schelling. Descartes is duly acknowledged, as Hutcheson had somewhat grudgingly acknowledged Hobbes, as the agent of liberation from scholasticism who "had shown sharp minds [*bons esprits*] how to lift the yoke of scholasticism, of opinion, of authority, in a word, of prejudices and barbarism." Alas, however, he had then proceeded to substitute for these false certitudes of his own. These were not evidently false, but they did exclude the possibility of future criticism, and enlightenment was a process of unrelenting critique. As a consequence, it also had the effect of sealing off the future. It was, D'Alembert regretfully concluded, a human weakness that when one prejudice is overthrown, it is generally replaced by another. "The uncertainty and the variety of the mind are such," he wrote, "that it always requires an opinion to which it can attach itself."[8]

In the somewhat more stable world that followed the end of the Thirty Years' War, a new need emerged for some deeper, more sympathetic account of humanity's basic instincts that did not rely upon simple egoism. It needed a philosophy that was independent, not merely of the inflexible and indemonstrable claims of the religious but also of every kind of dogmatic certainty—of "prejudices," in other words—a philosophy that would be responsive to the changing nature of the external world and above all to the ever-changing perceptions, passions, and beliefs of the human animal.

The first person to attempt something like this was the Saxon historian and jurist Samuel Pufendorf. Pufendorf—whose main work, *On the Law of Nature and Nations,* first appeared in 1671—is not well-known today. But although he, like Grotius, wrote in Latin and in a highly conventional academic manner, he became one of the most widely read and influential social, political, and moral theorists of the eighteenth century, so much so that Laurence Sterne, in his hugely popular comic novel *Tristram Shandy,* could refer to him as among the "best ethick writers" and assume that his by no means learned readers would know who he was. Rousseau, in two of the educational programs he wrote for influential friends, recommended that their children be given Pufendorf to read, "for it is right that an honest and intelligent man should understand the basis of good and evil, and the foundations on which the society of which he is a part is based."[9]

What Pufendorf seemed to offer was precisely what Rousseau and most of the other writers of the Enlightenment most needed—an escape from the bleak account provided by Hobbes and Grotius of the sources of human sociability—while at the same time accepting their basic premise that "man is so framed that he thinks of his own welfare before the welfare of others." Pufendorf's account of the origin of society is, in fact, roughly similar to both Grotius' and Hobbes's (to the extent that he lifted entire passages almost verbatim from the latter's *De Cive*).[10] He also agreed with his predecessors that the creation of the first societies out of the state of nature was an act, or acts, of will made by individual human beings and not the fulfillment of some divine plan. The crucial difference, however, was that whereas for both Grotius and Hobbes these societies, although they evolve technically, remain morally static, for Pufendorf they constitute moral persons, each being as a "single person with intelligence and will performing other actions peculiar to itself and separate from those of individuals."[11] By its own volition, mankind had brought into being not an artificial state but a "natural" one endowed with moral properties of its own.[12] This Pufendorf called "sociality" (*socialitas*). As Hutcheson observed with approval, "According to this view of Pufendorf's, even if social life apparently is not immediately and in itself natural to man, still it is rightly considered to be natural to man in a secondary sense."[13]

For Pufendorf and for all his successors, as we shall see, this implied a necessary inner consciousness of oneself. Pufendorf believed that an assault upon a person's identity as a person is as much a threat to his or her being as any physical assault upon his or her body:

> In addition to that love man has for his life, body, and things and because of which he cannot avoid rebelling against or fleeing from

> everything that tends to their destruction, we also find embedded in his mind a very delicate sense of self-esteem. And if anyone detracts from this in any way, he is usually no less, but in fact often more upset than if harm is done to his body or possessions.

Along with the knowledge that one day we must all die and the (for Pufendorf) natural recognition of the existence of God, this is what it means to be a person, as distinct from a dog. It is, in a sense, the definition of human as opposed to animal nature, and "human nature belongs equally to all men, and since one cannot lead a social life with someone by whom one is not esteemed at least as a man, it follows as a precept of the natural law that everybody must esteem and treat other men as his equals, or as men in the same sense that he is."[14]

By making this apparently self-evident claim, by appealing to every human being's "natural" instincts, their passions, or, as later generations would say, their "sentiments," Pufendorf had given to all humans the status of naturally moral creatures and, crucially for the turn that the entire discussion of the natural law would take in the eighteenth century, the image of beings who were, unlike Hobbesian men, naturally disposed to benevolence toward their fellow creatures.

It was, then, not Hobbesian fear, anger, and hatred but what Hegel would later characterize as "recognition," that "being for another" that drives human beings to form societies. Society was not the creation of a common agreement among terrified pugilists responding rationally and "selfishly" to a passion but the "natural" outcome of one passion responding to another. It was this that, for Pufendorf, gave the social world its moral qualities; unlike Hobbes's account, it did not leave men as they were but transformed their very being. As Rousseau, oversimplifying as always, put it, in a jotting for a future "History of Customs" (one of his many abandoned projects): "The error of most moralists" had always been to suppose that man is essentially a rational being. In fact, however: "Man is nothing but a sensitive [*sensible*] creature who consults only his passions in order to act, and whose reason serves only to palliate the idiocies which these induce him to make."[15]

Pufendorf himself—in common with the English and Scottish moralists of the early eighteenth century, Hutcheson, Richard Cumberland, and Shaftesbury—characterized his distance from Hobbes and Grotius in terms of the opposition between Epicureanism and Stoicism. "The basic premise from which I draw the law of nature," he wrote, in reply to the jurist Nicolaus Beckmann, one of the critics of *On the Law of Nature and Nations,* "stands in direct opposition to the theory of Hobbes. For I come very close to the reasonable theory of the Stoics, whereas Hobbes serves up a *rechauffé* of Epicurean theories."[16]

The contrast between these two ancient schools of philosophy, the Epicurean and Stoic, and the relationship of both to Skepticism were to become dominant features of late seventeenth- and early eighteenth-century social and political theory. We find them in Adam Smith and Francis Hutcheson, in Diderot and Rousseau, in Condorcet and Hume, in the Neapolitan Giambattista Vico and in Immanuel Kant; lecturing on all three schools of philosophy became a major component of university curricula throughout Europe. Skepticism we have already encountered. Stoicism and Epicureanism—the two philosophies expounded on succeeding days by Carneades in 155—were different, in that both created systems of knowledge about the entire universe. What mattered most about them, however, in particular to the writers of the eighteenth century, was their moral philosophy.

Epicurus (341–270 BCE) was a Greek philosopher who was celebrated, and much reviled, for establishing a school based upon the claim that the sole objective of human life should be the pursuit of pleasure. In about 306 he bought a house in Athens with a garden that became the headquarters of his school. Here he and his followers, who unusually—and shockingly for the ancient Greek world—included women, lived together as a family, bound by ties of friendship, ignoring the world outside, and rejecting any involvement in political life. Most of the more salacious stories about what took place in that garden were mere fantasy, but Epicureanism never succeeded in shedding its image as a philosophical justification for a life of simple hedonism. The Epicureans' insistence on the wholly material origins of the cosmos and their rejection of the existence of any effective deity or of any kind of human immortality also made them loathed by Christians.

In fact, most Epicureans were ascetics. The basic claim that men should always strive to avoid pain and cultivate pleasure led not to the conclusion that they should spend their lives in dissoluteness, because dissoluteness always brings with it pain, and the greater the initial pleasure the greater the subsequent pain. The truly rational, pleasure-seeking individual would, therefore, cultivate only those pleasures that had no downside to them, and this, in effect, could mean only the life of contemplation. Of course, only the Epicurean philosopher, immured behind his or her garden wall, could hope to achieve that. The rest of us, condemned to live our lives in the world outside, should, however, as far as possible, struggle to keep our pains to a minimum and enjoy as much of life as we can. Or as one of Kant's students, with the unlikely name of Mongrovius, claimed that Kant had said: "Those who reduce the principles of morality to physical sense are the Epicureans, and their principle is that of self-love, and rests upon the comfort and safety of our condition."[17] It was a fairly crude summary. But it reflects fairly accurately how many Stoically inclined thinkers during the eighteenth century, like Kant, regarded Epicureanism.

What Pufendorf meant, therefore, by saying that all Hobbes had done was to serve up "a *rechauffé* of Epicurean theories" was that Hobbes's philosophy rested on the claim that the calculation of pleasure and pain was the only thing that humans had in common, the only thing, in the end, that constituted their humanity. Hobbes also certainly shared, although he never explicitly said so, the Epicurean denial of the existence of an omniscient and providential deity, and, like Epicurus, he began his account of the human condition not with the cosmos but with the individual.

Accusing Hobbes in particular of "Epicureanism" was intended, in the first instance, as a slur and was something analogous to the charge of atheism to which he was also constantly subjected. But for all that—and for all that Hobbes's theory of the passions, for instance, is heavily indebted to Stoic sources—there is a sense in which Hobbesian egoism, or what Hume later called "the selfish philosophy," did have its origins in Epicurus' claim that "we say that pleasure is the beginning and the end of living happily."[18] "An Epicurean or a Hobbist," wrote Hume in his *Enquiry Concerning the Principles of Morals* of 1751,

> readily allows that there is such a thing as friendship in the world without hypocrisy or disguise; though he may attempt, by a philosophical chymistry, to resolve the elements of this passion, if I may so speak, into those of another, and explain every affection to be self-love, twisted and moulded, by a particular turn of imagination, into a variety of appearances.[19]

The Stoics, with whom Pufendorf allied himself, were represented—as Carneades had represented them—as the precise opposite of the Epicureans. They took their name from the *Stoa Poikile* ("painted porch") in Athens where Zeno of Citium, the founder of the school in about 323 BCE, held his outdoor lectures. In general the Stoics maintained that only virtue will lead to happiness. The Stoic sage lives a life guided only by reason. He also looks upon the world as a harmonious whole with a distinct and transcendental purpose. Unlike the Epicurean and unlike Hobbes (at least in this respect), the Stoic begins with the cosmos, not with the individual. He avoids all harmful or damaging emotions, and above all he seeks to see all the evil that might befall him as external to his being. Faced with even the most powerful emotions or the worst of troubles—or the greatest of pleasures—the Stoic wise man remains impassive. This is the doctrine of *ataraxia,* or freedom from anxiety and care, and, it should be said, of indifference—not only to one's own suffering or pleasure but also to that of others. At best it was, as Kant said, "ill-adapted to the forces of man"; at worst, in Condorcet's words, it was a mask behind which hid "the hard, the proud, and the unjust."[20] When we today speak of someone being "stoical," this is roughly what we mean. (We also mean much the same thing when we say that someone is being "philosophical," which is an indication of how central Stoic thinking has been to the western understanding of what "philosophy" is.)

Stoicism, however, was more than simple resignation. Too much attention has been paid to Stoic indifference and far too little to the social and political arguments of the Stoics, which were what attracted the thinkers of the Enlightenment. For Stoicism also embraced the notion that the natural world was a harmonious whole with a distinct and transcendental purpose. And at the core of this belief lay a claim that all human beings, no matter what their cultures or beliefs, share a common identity as humans. Like Aristotle, the Stoics accepted the presence of what were called "common notions," that is, a basic collection of notions or ideas that all men might be thought to accept, no matter what their creeds or cultural differences. Humans were also believed to be bound by a sentimental attachment to one another, which the Greeks called *oikeiosis,* the natural attachment we feel to what is "appropriate" or "akin" to oneself. Thus, my blood relatives, my family, my children are "appropriate" in this sense, and because of that I inevitably love them. I love them, however, not merely for my own sake, because they are the sole guarantee of my continuity. I love them because I *identify* with them. This, then, reaches out, in the truly wise person, to embrace first of all family and friends, then members of the same community or nation, and finally the whole of humanity. As the great Roman jurist Cicero put it: "From [parental love] there originates also a form of natural concern shared by humans among humans, that simply on account of that fact that he is human, one human should be thought to be not alien from another."[21] It was precisely this, as we shall see, that formed the basis of what later came to be called "cosmopolitanism."

Despite taking a violent dislike to one another, these ancient schools were not ever wholly distinct. Nor were they ever consistent. The Romans, who were responsible for developing the ideas of all three schools, also sometimes departed markedly from their Greek predecessors. Cicero, who loathed the Epicureans, is generally thought of as a Skeptic, but when it came to moral philosophy he was also a Stoic. Seneca, the playwright and moralist who was forced to commit suicide by the emperor Nero and whose works probably had more influence on the greatest of the Elizabethan and Jacobean dramatists, Shakespeare, Marlow, and Ben Jonson, than those of any other author, came during the eighteenth century to represent the height of Roman Stoic virtues. Yet even he was not untouched by Epicureanism. He was, said Diderot, who nevertheless venerated him, a "mitigated Stoic."

For all the confusions and conflations, however, in the late seventeenth and early eighteenth centuries the labels "Epicurean" and "Stoic" came to be used, as Pufendorf used them, to distinguish broadly between the Hobbesian "rationalists," on the one hand, and those like Pufendorf, on the other, who accorded a greater role to "sentiment" and moral autonomy in their attempts to describe what it was that most clearly defined human beings. In the admittedly schematic history of the western philosophical tradition provided by Shaftesbury, there never had been "any more than two real distinct philosophies, the one derived from Socrates and passing into the Academic, the Peripatetic, and Stoic; the other derived in reality from Democritus and passing into the Cyrenaic and Epicurean." Or as Diderot, in his article on "Stoicism" for the *Encyclopédie,* put it, "The Stoic sect was the last flowering of the sect of Socrates."

Not that many of the major figures of the Enlightenment were, in any formal sense, true Stoics. They were, if anything, eclectics: Stoics much of the time, but not infrequently Epicureans, and almost always Skeptics. That, as Diderot put it, was precisely what "Enlightenment" meant. The eclectic, he said uncompromisingly, "was the philosopher who trampled under foot prejudice, tradition, antiquity, universal agreement, authority—in a word everything which subjugates the mass of minds." He is the philosopher who "dares to think for himself, to go back to the clearest of all general principles, to examine them, discuss them, and to accept nothing save on his own experience and reason." Above all, he is what Diderot calls a "particular and domestic philosopher," one who is "less interested in being the instructor of the human race than its disciple, less interested in reforming others than in reforming himself, less interested in teaching the truth than in learning about it."[22] An eclectic and, of course, a critic.

But in this heady mix, it was the Stoic element that provided the basis of the understanding of human society, and it was Stoicism that led first to the creation of a science of man and thence to the birth of cosmopolitanism. Adam Smith's celebrated image of the "invisible hand," the idea that there exists a hidden mechanism by which nature regulates the market, is a reflection of Stoic ideas about the essential harmony of the natural world.[23] Immanuel Kant's famous "categorical imperative," the argument that we have a moral duty to treat all other human beings as ends in themselves and not merely as means, has clear affinities with the Stoic notion of virtue. Then there is that all-too-familiar figure the "noble savage," one of whom we shall encounter later, and who is, as Shaftesbury complained, nothing other than an exoticized version of the Stoic "nay-sayer"—the naturally wise man who questions all those things that are offered as certainties but that in his view do not correspond to the design of nature.

Pufendorf's bid to reintroduce a Stoic notion of sociability as a counter to both scholastic conceptions of innateness and the Hobbesian-Grotian vision of a humanity composed solely of calculating, self-regarding individuals was to have a long and lasting influence upon the Enlightenment. For Pufendorf had understood that the world of post-Reformation, post-Discovery Europe was one in which the older structures of learning could never be revived. Only the university theologians would struggle on, and even they with increasing difficulties, until well into the nineteenth century in the belief that the apparatus of Aristotelian and neo-Thomist psychology could be made to recapture the consensus it had once enjoyed. For the rest of Europe it was all too obvious that it was gone forever. This did not, however, mean that the possibility of *any* consensus had vanished along with it. As Hume later remarked, there were very few occasions on which the question "*What is that to me?* . . . is not pertinent." Yet had the scholastic view of man possessed the "infallible influence" the "Hobbists" and their like had attributed to it, it would have turned "into ridicule every composition, and almost every conversation, which contains any praise or censure of men and manners."[24] Starting from the "selfish hypothesis," we could, as Hobbes had done, offer fairly cogent arguments for why man should observe his sovereign's laws. But we could do little more.

Hobbes himself had not been concerned with anything more. But if, as Hume put it, we must "renounce the theory which accounts for every moral sentiment by the principle of self-love," and accept that humans must, in the end, be bound to one another by something deeper, more compelling, than the simple fear of extinction, the question then arose: What is it? The answer was neither fear nor reason but what in the eighteenth century was called "sentiment." To understand how this came about, however, we will have to look at another, and hitherto neglected, aspect of the story.

II

The entire scholastic theory of moral and political life rested, as we have seen, on the idea that our basic understanding of the law of nature was made up of certain "innate ideas" or "innate senses." Both Hobbes and Grotius had, implicitly at least, rejected this idea, or at least reduced it to one urge—it can hardly be called an "idea"—or "sense," so basic that no one could doubt that without it humanity would not have survived. Neither thinker, however, had attempted to tackle the question of innateness itself. The writer who did that, and to devastating and lasting effect, was John Locke.

In 1668 Locke was living at Exeter House, the London home of the powerful Whig statesman Anthony Ashley Cooper, First Earl of Shaftesbury. Locke had met Ashley in 1667 and subsequently become his physician, adviser, and friend. Ashley also appointed him as Secretary to the Board of Trade and Plantations and Secretary to the Lords Proprietors of the Carolinas (in which capacity he helped draft the constitutions for the Carolinas). One evening Locke had a conversation with "five or six friends meeting at my chamber." The subject was morality and revealed religion. Later he recorded that:

> After we had awhile puzzled ourselves, without coming any nearer a resolution of those doubts which perplexed us, it came into my thoughts that we took a wrong course; and that before we set ourselves upon inquiries of that nature, it was necessary to examine our own abilities, and see what objects our understandings were, or were not, fitted to deal with.[25]

The result of these reflections, published many years later in 1690, was *An Essay Concerning Human Understanding*. In it, said D'Alembert, Locke had done "nothing more" than present "mankind with a mirror in which his mind might gaze upon himself. In a word, he reduced metaphysics to what it really ought to be: the experimental physics of the mind."[26] Together with Hobbes's *Leviathan* and Newton's *Principia Mathematica* (although this very largely through popularized summaries and commentaries such as Voltaire's *Philosophical Letters* of 1778 and Francesco Algarotti's engaging *Newtonianism for Ladies* of 1737), the *Essay* was among the most widely read philosophical texts of the eighteenth century. The highly controversial utilitarian philosopher Claude-Adrien Helvétius (who as a young man had written a eulogistic poem, "Le Bonheur," in praise of Locke) may have been exaggerating when he said that one could count on the fingers of one hand all those who had not read, practiced, and admired what Locke had written on almost every conceivable subject. But it is certainly true that his influence and his fame, like Newton's, reached far beyond the learned circles for which he had written. Alexander Pope tells the story of a young English girl of good breeding who asked to have her portrait painted clutching a volume of Locke's works in one hand, to assure posterity that she had been more than simply a pretty face. In *The False Agnes* of 1759, a play by the (admittedly rather obscure) playwright Philippe Néricault Destouches, a girl feigns madness in order to get rid of an undesirable suitor. When the would-be lover finally leaves in despair, she demonstrates her sanity to the audience by summarizing the argument of *An Essay Concerning Human Understanding*.[27]

The reason for all this admiration is not hard to see. The *Essay* seemed to have swept away almost all previous attempts to account for how we come to understand the world. Like Descartes, Locke conceived the task of philosophy as one of preparing the intellectual ground for the natural scientists of his day, the "master-builders," as he called them, "whose mighty Designs" will leave "lasting Monuments to the Admiration of posterity." He saw himself as a humble "Under-Labourer in clearing the Ground a little, and removing some of the Rubbish that lies in the way to Knowledge."[28] And in his view, one of the most obtrusive bits of rubbish was the scholastic theory of innateness. At the very beginning of the first book of the *Essay,* he explained that he had set out to

> consider the discerning Faculties of a Man, as they are employ'd about the Objects which they have to do with: and I shall imagine I have not wholly misimploy'd my self in the Thoughts I shall have on this Occasion, if, in this Historical, plain Method I can give any Account of the Ways, whereby our Understandings come to attain those Notions of Things we have.[29]

Few historians of philosophy have paid much attention to this lengthy onslaught on the notion that there might exist no "innate Principles" or "innate Characters of the Mind which are to be Principles of Knowledge" beyond "a desire of Happiness and an aversion to Pain."[30] It has also generally been assumed that Locke's intended target in the first book of the *Essay* was Descartes, whose own "clear and simple" first principles, although far removed from scholastic "first precepts," were nevertheless also held to be innate. And so, in part, it was. But since the range of items under attack at the beginning of Book I goes far beyond Descartes's acceptance of what is sometimes called "dispositional" innateness, and crucially includes in its list of targets the Stoic "common notions," it is difficult to see how it could be so limited. And indeed, many of Locke's contemporaries and eighteenth-century successors believed that his objective had been to demolish not Descartes but instead the "scholastic" basis of the natural law. This is certainly how the great German philosopher and mathematician Gottfried Wilhelm Leibniz, who identified Locke's targets as Plato, the Schoolmen, St. Paul, the Stoics, and the fifteenth-century Italian Aristotelian Julius Caesar Scaliger, interpreted it in his long and admiring attempt to refute this part of the *Essay*.[31] David Hume, although he dismissed the entire question of innateness as a confusion over terms, also believed that Locke had been "betrayed into this question by the schoolmen."[32] So too did Anthony Ashley Cooper, the Third Earl of Shaftesbury, grandson of Locke's benefactor, who sneered that Locke (who had supervised his early education) had been lucky to have "so poor a spectre as the ghost of Aristotle to fight with. A ghost indeed! Since it is not in reality the Stagyrite [Aristotle] himself nor the original Peripatetic hypothesis, but the poor secondary tralatitious system of modern and barbarous Schoolmen which is the subject of his continual triumph."[33] So did Diderot, whose long and admiring article on Locke for the *Encyclopédie* is almost wholly concerned with this problem and credits Locke with having finally demonstrated "that there is no principle of speculation, no innate moral ideas."[34] Diderot's own highly controversial *Letter on the Blind* of 1749 (for which he spent three months in the prison at Vincennes) and *Letter on the Deaf and Dumb* of 1751 were both, at least in part, written to dispel any lingering belief anyone might still have in the possibility that innate senses might be the source of the ideas we form about the world.

Virtually all subsequent writers—except the theologians—agreed with Locke that the kind of complex structures grounded upon principles of innateness on which the scholastics had built their understanding of the natural law could no longer be sustained. All that we knew about the world, Locke insisted, we knew through our senses. Look, he said, at children. If the scholastic "primary precepts" existed, then one would expect to find some evidence of them in the very young. Yet there clearly was none at all. It was evident to anyone who had ever met and spoken with a child that the mind of the newborn was an "empty cabinet" or a "piece of white paper" on which the senses wrote all that they could about the world.[35] On this account, it was the sensations that created what Locke, not unproblematically, called "ideas," and these, in time and through association and reflection, evolved from the simple to the complex. What he called "judgment" could then lead the ever-agile human mind to move from a simple and direct experience of the world to such abstract notions as order, beauty, and liberty.[36]

True, all that "sensationalism" gave us was knowledge of what were called "secondary causes." But then, for all of the empiricists of the seventeenth century secondary causes were all that were available to the human mind. One of the central arguments of "the incomparable Mr. Newton" had been precisely that "we are to admit of no more causes of natural things than such as are both true and sufficient to explain their appearances."[37] We could never answer the supposedly "grand" questions: Why did the natural world evolve the way it did? Do our lives have any meaning? Is there an afterlife, and if there is, what form does it take? And so on. Nor should we try to answer them, because either they are simply unknowable—and thus at bottom without interest—or, as a good Christian such as Newton himself would argue, because only God had the answers. Even if humans could, as the theologians grandly supposed they had, come up with their own answers, they could never know if they were correct. There was simply nothing out there to test them against. One response to the obvious impenetrable mystery of the universe had been Skepticism. For Locke, however, Skepticism could lead only to despair. It was, he said "unpardonable, as well as Childish Peevishness, if we undervalue the Advantages of our Knowledge, and neglect to improve it to the ends for which it was given us, because there are some Things which are set out of the reach of it." If we could never know anything about primary causes, we could at least acquire a sufficient knowledge of "secondary" ones. We might not be able to answer the "why?" questions, but we could answer the "how?" ones. We could never, as Locke put it, "fathom all the depths of the Ocean." We will never have "Demonstration" and "Certainty." Instead, we have "Probability," and that "is sufficient to govern all our Concernments."[38] Anyone who preferred not to think about anything if he could not find answers to the "big" questions was, Locke said, like a man "who would not use his Legs, but sit still and perish, because he had no Wings to fly."[39] And the way to probable understanding was through our senses.

Lockean sensationalism turned out to be very persuasive, and the probability theory of knowledge perhaps even more so. But Locke's fierce and relentless onslaught against any kind of innateness was more difficult to accept in its entirety. And to many of even his most admiring readers—to Leibniz, for instance—he could sometimes seem like a false friend. For in getting rid of innateness altogether, Locke had apparently also threatened the idea that there might exist any *common* natural affinity among humans beyond the faculty of reason and the power of speech—indeed, in Locke's case, since he took it that animals also possessed some degree of reason and the capacities for communication, beyond the ability to form universals or "general Ideas."[40] For if we come into the world equipped only with the senses and the reason required to form ideas from them, then it seemed that there could be no principles of any kind that we could assume *a priori* to be shared by all mankind. As Voltaire told Frederick the Great in 1737, "Locke, the wisest metaphysician I know, in rightly challenging innate ideas, seems to believe that there can be no universal principle in the world."[41]

By the time Hobbes and Locke had finished with it, no one had any interest in rebuilding the scholastic edifice of the natural law. But most of the writers of the eighteenth century were equally unhappy with the idea that there could be nothing beyond the urge to survive and a capacity for abstraction that was natural to man as a species. Both scholastic innateness and Lockean sensationalism, complained Diderot, had been dreamed up "to reduce man to the condition of an oyster, or raise an oyster to the condition of a man."[42] Furthermore, as Francis Hutcheson had seen, the "fear of innate ideas" had driven many to abandon not merely the Aristotelian moral virtues and the idea of natural sociability, but with them an entire vocabulary, an entire way of characterizing the human personality, and that, as a consequence, "the old notions of natural affections and kind instincts, the 'common sense' [*sensus communis*], the *decorum* and *honestum* are almost banished out of our book of morals."[43]

Shaftesbury expressed the same fears. Like most of his generation, he was hostile to the Hobbesian image of man as a self-regarding rationalist. His real concern, however, was not Hobbes, because he believed that "Mr. Hobbes's character and base slavish principles in government took off all the poison of his philosophy." His real animosity was directed toward Locke. (Shaftesbury seems to have had no particularly warm feelings for his former tutor.) Shaftesbury took Lockean sensationalism to be a denial of the possibility of any kind of communality among human beings.

"It was Mr. Locke that struck the home blow," he wrote to his young protégé Michael Ainsworth in 1709:

> 'Twas Mr. Locke that struck at all the fundamentals, threw all order and virtue out of the world, and made the very ideas of these (which are the same as those of God) *unnatural* and without foundation in our minds. *Innate* is a word he poorly plays upon; the right word, though less used is *connatural*. For what has birth or progress of the foetus out of the womb to do in this case? The question is not about the time the *ideas* entered, or the moment that one body came out of the other, but whether the constitution of man be such that, being adult and grown up, at such or such a time . . . the idea and sense of order, administration, and a God, will not infallibly, inevitably, necessarily spring up in him.[44]

Shaftesbury had no time for the "philosophy of the Schools," which he described as a "choking weed . . . purely thorn or thistle." But his main concern—and he was not alone—was that by denying the existence of any kind of innate disposition Locke seemed to have made morality into a matter of mere local preference. In Shaftesbury's view this rendered the concept of the human itself untenable. "Even the species themselves," he complained, "were called into question, and more than called into question, flatly denied."[45] What Locke had left us with was a collection of distinct individuals with no particular reason to like, help, or even recognize each other. Yet, as Shaftsbury wrote in his notebook in Rotterdam in August 1698, "The end and design of nature in man is society, for wherefore are the natural affections towards children, relationships, fellowship and commerce but to that end?"[46]

There was plenty of evidence in the *Essay* to support Shaftesbury's understanding of Locke's main argument. Faced with the variety of customs and beliefs that existed in the world, and with which Locke, an avid reader of travelers' tales, was thoroughly familiar, it was hard for Locke to see how any coherence could be reached by means of reason alone. "He that will carefully peruse the History of Mankind," he wrote,

> and look abroad into the several Tribes of Men, and with indifferency survey their actions will be able to satisfy himself, That there

> is scarce that Principle of Morality to be named, or *Rule of Vertue* to be thought on . . . which is not, somewhere or other, *slighted* and condemned by the general Fashion of *whole Societies* of Men, governed by practical Opinions, and Rules of living quite opposite to others.[47]

Moral principles, he concluded, were dictated not by secure first principles but only by opinion. For Locke himself, however, it was not, as Shaftesbury had somewhat disingenuously supposed, a matter of mere indifference which opinion a person chose to follow. Some were clearly false, others true, but the truth or falsity of any moral understanding was not one that could be arrived at by claiming the existence of some kind of innate moral understanding, however rudimentary. Such certainty could only, in the end, be reached through divine command. Morality, for Locke, was not a question of applied psychology. It was a question of observance. But this conclusion was unlikely to be sympathetic to anyone not possessed of Locke's Calvinist conviction in the clarity of God's commands.

What was needed was a theory of the human mind that, while it dispensed with the vision of a natural law whose principles were innate, also provided some denser, richer account of the human person than one ruled wholly by sensation or guided only by unenlightened self-interest. To create such a theory, the writers of the eighteenth century turned away from the reasonable, rational principles, for both the "Hobbists" and their scholastic predecessors, of which the "natural law" had been composed. Instead they focused on "feelings," "sentiments," or "passions." Most held that the natural law, however defined, could only be, as Hume insisted, "more properly an act of the sensitive, than of the cognitive part of our natures."[48] The definitions offered by the "selfish philosophy" might provide the basis of a right. But since the self-interest that lay at the core of Hobbes's and Grotius' accounts was also, as Hume pointed out, "an *imaginary* interest known and avowed for such," it could not "be the origin of any passion or emotion."[49] For Hobbes it did not need to be, because rights were all that he was interested in. But for Hume, as for most of his contemporaries on both sides of the English Channel, any satisfactory account of human nature had to be one that would also yield a richer descriptive account of human sociability, precisely what Hume himself called a "human science."

III

The key figures in the move that will take us from Pufendorf to Hume; to Diderot, Rousseau, and Voltaire; to Montesquieu and Adam Smith, and finally—although then things begin to change—to Kant are Francis Hutcheson and Shaftesbury. Neither is much read today or is often accorded any significant place in the genealogy of the Enlightenment. But the writings of both were much discussed in their own lifetimes and had a considerable influence on a number of philosophical concerns in both France and Germany that lasted well into the nineteenth century.

Shaftesbury, in particular, is something of an enigmatic, elusive figure. He had, like his grandfather, the First Earl, been a Whig politician, but although he played an active part in Parliament, asthma, aggravated by the London fog, and then consumption had forced him to take refuge at first in Holland—which he, like Locke, for some reason believed to have a healthy climate. Then, as his health deteriorated, he rented a villa in Naples, where he died in 1713.

Shaftesbury was a benign and congenial, if not very profound, writer. He believed in toleration and the liberating force of education, disliked clerics and academics, abhorred intolerance and bigotry, and insisted that the only way to defeat fanaticism, or what in the eighteenth century was widely known as "enthusiasm," was not suppression but humor and wit. It was, he said, the "wisdom of some wise nations to let people be fools as much as they pleased and never to punish seriously what deserves only to be laughed at."[50] The "philosophical scoffer whose laughter contains more truth than do other people's cough and spittle," the German philosopher and historian Johann Gottfried von Herder called him—although he also remarked that Shaftesbury's vision of what constituted an enlightened, educated man derived largely from his own image of himself and from the court circles in which he moved.[51] Shaftesbury's many and varied writings have no obvious coherence. Some are essays, some letters, others dialogues. Shaftesbury himself, however, thought of them as constituting a single body of work, and in 1711, shortly before his death, he published all of them under the characteristically evasive title *Characteristics of Men, Manners, Opinions, Times.*

Despite the lack of any single philosophical position and despite the generally conversational tone of everything he wrote, Shaftesbury exercised a great fascination over many of the major and minor thinkers of the Enlightenment. Diderot began his literary career as the translator of Shaftesbury's *An Inquiry Concerning Virtue or Merit.* Hutcheson began his by defending him against the criticisms of the Dutch physician Bernard Mandeville. His theory of aesthetic "disinterestedness" had a profound impact on Kant and later on Schopenhauer, and the highly influential German historian of philosophy Karl Friedrich Stäudlin went so far, in his massive *History of Moral Philosophy* of 1822, as to dismiss all eighteenth-century French writers, with the possible exception of Rousseau, as entirely derivative of Shaftesbury.[52]

Like so many Germans at the beginning of the nineteenth century, Stäudlin was eager to throw off what he saw as the suffocating influence of those whom Herder had dismissed as French "literary types."[53] But although he was certainly not anything like as important as Stäudlin claimed, Shaftesbury did exercise a considerable influence over subsequent attempts to rework the idea of a coherent form of natural sociability that would be acceptable to a post-Hobbesian, post-Lockean world. "It is impossible," wrote the German jurist Johann Gottlieb Heineccius in 1738, "to set the sociability of our nature in a clearer and stronger light than my Lord Shaftesbury has done."[54] Herder too, despite his caustic comments on Shaftesbury's gentlemanly nature, classed him together with Plato, Rousseau, and Hume as one of those who had gone the furthest in demonstrating that "philosophy can be reconciled with humanity and politics, so that it also really serves the latter."[55] Hume himself listed both Shaftesbury and Hutcheson, along with Locke, Mandeville, and Joseph Butler (admittedly a curiously heterogeneous group), as those "late philosophers of *England,* who have put the science of man on a new footing," because "although they differ in many points among themselves, [they] seem all to agree in founding their accurate disquisitions of human nature entirely upon experience."[56]

Shaftesbury's rejection of both Hobbes and Locke clearly implied no desire to resurrect the older scholastic edifice of innate ideas. Like Pufendorf, he was prepared to acknowledge that humans had an "Affection towards private or Self-Good," since a creature who did not have any sense of self-preservation (or the desire to propagate the race) "would be injurious to the Species."[57] But he refused to accept that this could be adequate grounds for any further set of affections, much less a basis for sociability. It was, he said, "ridiculous to say there is any obligation on man to act sociably or honestly in a formed government, and not in that which is commonly called the state of nature." After all, both Hobbes's and Locke's accounts of the origins of civil society relied upon promises, themselves made "in the state of nature, and that which could make a promise obligatory in the state of nature must make all other acts of humanity as much our real duty and natural part."[58] What Shaftesbury meant to replace both Hobbesian egotism and scholastic innateness with—what was intended to bridge the gap between man as a "sensational" Lockean creature and man as a naturally sociable one—was what Hutcheson (but not Shaftesbury, who never uses the term) called a "moral sense." This was not what the scholastics had understood by a self-evident precept ("Do unto others as you would have others do unto you"), nor was it a clear and simple idea in the Cartesian sense ("It is impossible for the same thing to be and not be at the same time"). It was, like Pufendorf's *socialitas,* a measure of affective recognition, and it worked not through reason—although we have to use reason in order to assess what its implications might be—but through the imagination. For Shaftesbury, this was what he called the "natural affection" that all human beings supposedly have for their own kind. This alone was, and could only be, "innate." Or, "if you dislike the word 'innate,'" as he has the speaker Theocles say, in implicit response to Locke, in his dialogue *The Moralists, a Philosophical Rhapsody,* "let us change it, if you will for 'instinct,' and call instinct that which nature teaches, exclusive of art, culture or discipline."[59] The answer, then, was simple. What nature teaches is not, as the scholastics had claimed, a set of connections that allowed the brain to identify moral and cultural properties in the world in the same way as it registered physical ones. What it teaches is rather a kind of recognition of our common humanity—"species recognition," it is sometimes called. It was, said Hutcheson, speaking of the "moral sense," based simply on the assumption that "All Men have the same *Affections and Senses,*" and that "Most Men who have thought of human Actions, agree that the *publickly useful* are in the whole also *privately useful* to the Agent either in this Life or the next."[60] It was what Smith and Rousseau called "pity," Hume "sympathy," and Diderot "natural commiseration."[61] The prolonged western philosophical hostility toward feeling and the somewhat artificial distinction between reason and the passions pursued by the theologians—which Hume had done so much to demolish—had now been reversed.[62]

For Shaftesbury, as he had made abundantly clear in his letter to Ainsworth, the point was not how we acquire our ideas but how we evaluate them once we have acquired them. No human creature, Shaftesbury believed, could be indifferent "from the moment he comes to be try'd by sensible Objects . . . and receiving into his Mind the Images and Representations of Justice, Generosity, Gratitude, or other Virtue, shou'd have no *Liking* of these or *Dislike* of their Contrarys." There may indeed, he conceded, exist no "*real* Amiableness or Deformity in moral Acts," but there could not fail to be "*an imaginary one* of full force," and that the imaginary must have its origins in nature.[63] Moral properties become objects that we contemplate in very much the same way as we contemplate objects in the external world. Just as our perception of

> the species or images of bodies, colours and sounds are perpetually moving before our eyes and acting on our senses even when we sleep, so in the moral and intellectual kind [of objects], the form and images of things are no less active and incumbent upon our mind, at all seasons, and even when the real objects themselves are absent.[64]

Unlike the information that the other senses present to us, that provided by our "moral sense" or "natural affection" is of things that continue to exist even when we no longer have direct experience of them. As Hume expressed it, to extend our imaginative identification with the feelings of others requires "some circumstance in the present which strikes us in a lively manner." From this we may, if we are sufficiently aware and experienced, acquire a "lively notion of all the circumstances of that person whether past present or future; possible probable or certain."[65] My moral repugnance at, say, cruelty will, therefore, persist even when I am not actually witnessing an act of cruelty. Once I have had some experience of it, the mere *thought* of cruelty, which in the educated person will be heightened by reading or the theater, will leave forms and images in the mind that will be forever eradicable. It is on the basis of this that we all construct our ethical lives.[66]

Adam Smith, although he had his doubts about Shaftesbury's conception of virtue, would later make much the same claim at the very beginning of *The Theory of Moral Sentiments,* the great treatise on ethics he wrote some sixteen years before *The Wealth of Nations.*[67] Like Shaftesbury and Hume, Smith argued that what unites us to others is neither reason nor sensations but imagination. When "our brother is upon the rack," he said, as long as "we ourselves are at our ease, our senses will never inform us of what he suffers." It is

> by imagination only that we can form any conception of what are his sensations. Neither can that faculty help us to this in any other way, than by representing to us what would be our own, if we were in his case. It is the impressions of our own senses only, not those of his, which our imaginations copy. By the imagination we place ourselves in his situation, we conceive ourselves enduring all the same torments, we enter as it were into his body, and become in some measure the same person with him.[68]

This meant that my sympathy does not derive from any simple response to the outward display of emotions. Anger, for instance, is generally greeted with disgust or fear, unless we know the cause. I might feel some initial sympathy with someone I see crying in the street, because I know that tears are a sign of suffering. But my sympathy—or, as we would say today, empathy—will be limited. Most people will hurry on by rather than stop to help. After all, the person who is crying might be doing so precisely in order to arouse my sympathy. Beggars often act in this way. For this reason, Smith believed that I, the spectator, will only experience real sympathy for that person once I know *why* he or she is crying, because only then can I know how I might feel if I were to find myself in the same predicament. My imagination, that is, has to be governed, so to speak, by reason. "Even our sympathy with the grief or joy of another, before we are informed of the cause of either," he wrote, "is always extremely imperfect." "The compassion of the spectator must arise altogether from the consideration of what he himself would feel if he was reduced to the same unhappy situation, *and, what perhaps is impossible, was at the same time able to regard it with his present reason and judgment.*"[69]

This "sympathy" was not linked in the way that innate ideas were to any specific moral code. You could feel sympathy for those whose moral world was ultimately wholly unlike your own. All it provided was a passion that offered a minimum psychological principle on which to base a claim to human sociability, both within individual communities and, what is still more significant for my purposes, across them. "No quality of human nature is more remarkable," wrote Hume, "both in itself and in its consequences, than that propensity we have to sympathize with others, and to receive by communication their inclinations and sentiments, however different from, or even contrary, to our own."[70]

At the farthest end of Europe from Hume and (probably) in ignorance of what he had written, the Neapolitan philosopher and political economist Antonio Genovesi (the first man to hold a chair in economics in any university anywhere), in a little book he wrote for the instruction of schoolchildren, had come to not-dissimilar conclusions. The pain we feel, he wrote, when "confronted by the sufferings of others and the corresponding wish to help them," is proof that we possess an innate "love of our own species." "*Homo homini,*" he added, turning Hobbes's famous adage on its head, "*natura amicus*"—man is by nature the friend of man.[71] Even if we were prepared to accept that suffering and fear are the only things all humans have in common, as Hobbes had claimed—this, for Genovesi as for Smith, and as for Hume, was not merely a reason for action; it was also a shared experience. "No passion," as Hume said, "if well understood can be entirely indifferent to us; because there is none, of which every man has not, within him at least the seeds and first principles." We seem, he reflected, to have a concern even for those whose lives are remote from ours. Why else would we find, as we seem to, "the fates of states, provinces, or many individuals," even if we have nothing particular at stake in what happens to them, so "extremely interesting"? Why otherwise do we read newspapers? Why are we moved by reading poetry and by the lives of beings who are entirely imaginary? Although the passions aroused by reading great tragedies or accounts of the fate of remote millions "may not always be so strong and steady as to have great influence on our conduct and behaviour," we are seemingly incapable of remaining indifferent to them. I may not be able, or willing, to do anything about the victims of suicide bombers and—since my sympathies can also be aroused by the sufferings of the dead for whom I can do nothing (Hume's example is the cruelty of Nero and Tiberius)—the victims of the Holocaust, but this does not mean that the thought of them does not keep me awake at night. "The interest of society," Hume said, "appears to be the interest of every individual."[72] From here, as we shall see, it was only a short step to imagining the existence of a cosmopolitan world, made up of diverse peoples all united by this common interest, although the form it would take was still, as yet, vague and uncertain.

Although he would ultimately turn against its cosmopolitan implications, few had understood the operations of sympathy better than Jean-Jacques Rousseau.[73] Like most of his contemporaries, Rousseau acknowledged that Hobbes had seen "very clearly the defect of all modern definitions of natural right." Even though he was often represented, by Smith and Diderot among others, as "almost the inverse of . . . Hobbes," Rousseau in fact shared many of Hobbes's initial premises about the state of nature and was prepared to recognize that in his account of man's insatiable quest for power, "the principle of Hobbes is true up to a certain point." It was enough, he thought, to look at the behavior of children, who, he noted with some bitterness, "have only to desire to obtain what they wish, [and] think themselves masters of the universe," who "treat all men like slaves," and who, when denied anything, "take this rejection as an act of rebellion." The child is "a Despot; he is at once both the most vile of slaves and the most miserable of creatures."[74] So, one must assume, would have been the natural man. Evil was, after all, as Hobbes himself had said, a "robust child" (*puer robustus*). The phrase "up to a certain point" was, however, a telling one. For what Rousseau really objected to in Hobbes's bleakly realist account of the natural condition of humanity were the conclusions that he had drawn from it. For Hobbes, as we have seen, the only things that primitive men shared in common—other than the "perpetual and restless desire of power after power that ceaseth only in Death"—was fear, the desire to avoid suffering and death for as long as possible, and the rational ability—as well as the collective will—to do something about it. The natural aptitudes of Rousseau's primitive man similarly included the repugnance to pain and the power of reasoning (although not the collective will); crucially, however, he also possessed the capacity for imaginative suffering, something, Rousseau claims, that humans share with many of the higher mammals.[75]

Rousseau's true *bête noire,* however, was not so much "the Sophist Hobbes" as Bernard Mandeville, that "most extreme Detractor of human virtues."[76] Mandeville was a Dutch physician who lived in London and wrote scathing political and economic treatises, the most influential of them in rhyming doggerel. In one of these, *The Fable of the Bees,* originally issued as a sixpenny pamphlet in 1705 and then as a greatly expanded book nine years later with the significant and catchy subtitle *Private Vices, Public Benefits,* he argued that the natural, human, and "Hobbist" pursuit of personal gain was more certain to bring about the greater good of the entire society than any degree of moralizing could possibly do. The much-vaunted notion of "virtue" was, for Mandeville, the greatest single enemy of human material progress. For moral interference, by threatening the harmonious working of the natural order, could only prove disastrous in the long—and probably also in the short—run. Let human beings pursue their own naturally selfish ends, and nature's intricate mechanism of adjustment could be relied upon to translate this into a gain for all. It was a devastating, and devastatingly simple, thesis that seemingly punctured the gaseous, over-inflated balloon of early eighteenth-century moral piousness. *The Fable of the Bees* caused a public outrage and was condemned by a court in Middlesex as a "public nuisance." It has also exercised a continuing, if erratic, influence on the evolution of modern economic theory, through the great Austrian economist of the early twentieth century Joseph Schumpeter, to the prophet of modern libertarianism Friedrich von Hayek, who called Mandeville a "master mind."[77]

For Rousseau, Mandeville's main argument was unpalatable, even if, as Adam Smith shrewdly noted, his own vision of the "primitive state of mankind" and of mankind's progress out of it and Mandeville's had much in common.[78] But what most repelled him about the *Fable* was that, although Mandeville had recognized that man possessed, in Rousseau's words, an "innate repugnance at seeing his own kind suffer," he had been so blinded by his belief that self-interest was ultimately the only beneficial force within human society and must therefore have been the sole reason why men had created societies in the first place that he had failed to make the next obvious step in recognizing that

> from this single attribute flow all the social virtues he wants to deny men. Indeed, what are generosity, clemency, humanity if not pity applied to the weak or the guilty or the species in general? Even benevolence and friendship, properly understood, are the products of a steady pity focused on a particular object: for what else is it to wish that someone not suffer, than to wish that he be happy?[79]

It was not Rousseau alone who identified "pity"—a word that at the time had none of the patronizing inflection it has today—as the one universal, and universalizable, human emotion, but it was certainly this identification that, as the great twentieth-century French anthropologist Claude Lévi-Strauss recognized, had made possible the entire subsequent project of the "human sciences."[80] This is also what Adam Smith—despite disparaging comments about Rousseau being "more capable of feeling strongly than analysing accurately"—meant when he said of "sympathy" that "though its meaning was, perhaps, originally the same [as pity and compassion], [it] may now, however, without much impropriety, be made use of to denote our fellow-feeling with *any passion whatever*."[81] This did not, however, rule out reason altogether. Hume is quite clear about this. Reason may well be an "inactive principle" and "utterly impotent" as far as morals are concerned. It also clearly is, "and ought . . . to be"—in what is often thought of as Hume's most outrageous statement—"the slave of the passions and can never pretend to any other office but to serve and obey them."[82] But like every good slave, it can also be a very valuable instrument.

If anything could now stand as the definition of humanity, it was not reason or speech, as the ancients had insisted; it was not even, as Locke had claimed, the ability to form concepts, although all of these would have to be included in the general description of the species. It was the unique human ability to respond to the "sentiments," the passions and the feelings of others. And if that were the case, then a very different image of the human mind and the human personality arose from the ones that Hobbes and Locke and Grotius had created. It gave to humankind an identity independent of God, a reason for recognizing all peoples as of equal worth, and of embracing some kind of common good, without endowing them with immortal souls or thinking of them as pale, if identical, images of the divine. This is how Diderot summed it all up:

> Everything you conceive, everything you contemplate, will be good, great, elevated, and sublime, if it accords with the general and common interest. There is no quality essential to your species apart from that which you demand from your fellow-men to ensure your happiness and theirs. It is the measure of your conformity to all of them and of all of them to you which determines when you transgress the borders of your species and when you remain within them. Hence do not ever lose sight of it, or else you

> will find your comprehension of the notions of goodness, justice, humanity, and virtue grows dim. Say to yourself, "I am a man and I have no other inalienable *natural rights* except those of humanity."[83]

If we now ask where the law of nature may be found, the answer will be in what Diderot—not Rousseau—called the "general will."[84] And if you were to ask: "In what does the general will reside? Where can I consult it?" the answer would be: "In the principles of the prescribed laws of all civilized nations; in the social practices of savage and barbarous peoples," that is, in the collective practices of all humankind regardless of their condition, status, color, or beliefs. The shift from "selfishness" to "sentiment," from the calculation of interests to the awareness that all humans were bound together by bonds of mutual recognition, became the basis on which a new conception of the social and political order of the entire world would eventually be based. For the truly enlightened person, he or she who lived according to this new specification of the laws of nature, who could be moved imaginatively by "the fates of states, provinces, or many individuals," could not be anything other than a cosmopolitan. To demonstrate why that should be the case, however, required a great deal more understanding of the workings of the human mind and of human society than the bare definition of human sympathy had offered. It required the creation of entirely new forms of knowledge: the "human sciences." Those sciences that Condorcet described as "having been almost invented in our own days, whose ultimate objective was the good of mankind" would one day come to have "a place no less certain than that of the physical sciences."[85] But before that could be achieved, there still remained a good deal of what Locke had called "the Rubbish that lies in the way to Knowledge" to be disposed of. And for most of the philosophers of the Enlightenment, this included the still-lingering presence of the belief in the Judeo-Christian God.

3

THE FATHERLESS WORLD

I

THE DESTRUCTION OF THE intellectual unity of the Catholic world brought about by the Reformation, the theologically destabilizing impact of the revival of Skepticism that had followed, and the discovery of the Americas had dealt all the self-assured claims of the theologians a blow from which they would never fully recover. Faculties of theology would survive into the modern world, as they survive to this day. But theology had lost its standing as the "Mother of Sciences," and theologians would no longer be consulted as to the nature of the human condition or on the moral legitimacy of price controls or on the movements of the planets or on the laws of motion. The architects of the "scientific revolution" had successfully banished God as a source of causal explanation and replaced him with an impersonal nature whose law, as Grotius had put it, would still hold even if God did not exist. The existence of God, however, and the fact that he had created the universe, even if some questioned whether it might not have taken him rather longer than seven days, was rarely itself in doubt.

For all the charges of "atheism" and irreligion that were leveled against almost all the seventeenth-century empiricists, few had, in fact, been true unbelievers. True, Hobbes was routinely accused of being an atheist and, for all that he protested to the contrary, most probably was. His god, as Diderot slyly observed, "differed little from that of Spinoza," and Spinoza (who had been condemned by the rabbis of Amsterdam, in accordance with the Curse of Elisha, to be devoured by she-bears for his impiety) certainly harbored no illusions about the plausibility of the God of whom he had read in the Old and New Testaments.[1] Diderot's other claim about Hobbes's beliefs, that he "took aversion to God, to clergymen, to churches," is also certainly true.[2] When his friend John Selden lay dying and was uncertain, out of expediency rather than conviction, about whether to receive the last rites or not, Hobbes is said to have asked him, "Will you who have lived like a man now die like a woman?"[3] But even Hobbes, although he had pushed God to the margins, had not displaced him altogether. He looked upon the Church (if not religion itself) as one of the instruments by which the modern state, the great Leviathan, "held men in awe." In fact, most of the charges of "atheism" directed against both Hobbes and Spinoza were, as Voltaire remarked, also directed against just about anyone else who "rejected the jargon of the schools."[4] Throughout the seventeenth and eighteenth centuries, to call someone a "Hobbesian" or a "Spinozist" often meant very little more than that; it only rarely implied that the accused had any real understanding of what Hobbes or Spinoza had written—which is not to underestimate the very real and extensive influence of both.

No one, however, ever accused John Locke of atheism. Although much of "the Rubbish that lies in the way to Knowledge" of which he had successfully disposed had clearly emanated originally from the theologians, belief in the Christian God was never part of it. He was, in most respects, a staunch Calvinist and went to some lengths to ensure his nervous readers that his attack on innate ideas presented no threat "to either . . . the notion or proof of Spirits."[5] Newton, as we have seen, was a devout believer who wished to be thought of not only as a mathematician but also as a theologian;[6] Bacon seems to have been an unprotesting Anglican, although, as Lord Chancellor of England, he may have acted more out of wisdom than conviction; and Descartes made a determined, if ultimately unpersuasive, effort to shield the central Catholic doctrine of transubstantiation from his theory of atomism (or "corpuscularism"). Even Grotius' apparently scandalous argument that the natural law would be unchanged even if God did not exist did not, in fact, question the existence of God. It was, after all, only a counterfactual that "without the greatest wickedness cannot be granted." Nor was it particularly new. It had first been used, admittedly in a less blunt manner, by the fourteenth-century theologian Gregory of Rimini.[7]

Most of the major thinkers of the Enlightenment, however, distanced themselves not only from the claims made in the name of revealed religion and its self-appointed intermediaries: the majority of them also rejected the very idea of a deity at all, or rather of a deity who, at some remote period of historical time, had made his intentions known to man or took any interest in his affairs or was prepared to intervene on his behalf.

There were good practical, as well as theoretical, reasons for wishing to lay the terrifying myths of the Old Testament, and even much of the New, to rest. As Hobbes had seen more clearly than most, belief in a god not only limited the human imagination and the human capacity for reason and drove humans to commit unmentionable acts in his name; it also gave unlimited power to a priestly caste. Hobbes's response to this threat, as we have seen, was not to do away with the clergy altogether, much less with the idea of "God" it served, but to subordinate its power to that of the secular sovereign. It was the sovereign, that "Man or Assembly of men," or rather its laws, that would give meaning to every aspect of civil life. So long as the rule of law went unchallenged, there could be very little to fear from religious sects. What people chose to believe in their own homes could be of little interest to the state and posed very little danger to their fellow beings. This is why, in the famous frontispiece to *Leviathan* (which Hobbes had designed himself), the figure of the Leviathan consists of a body of faceless citizens resembling scales, topped by a human head wearing a crown and holding in one hand a sword and in the other a crosier. As Rousseau observed: "Of all the Christian authors, the philosopher, Hobbes, was the only one to have understood both the evil and its cure, who dared to propose that the two heads of the eagle be united and to restore political unity, without which neither state nor government will be well constituted." (What, however, poor Hobbes had apparently failed to see, in Rousseau's view, was that "Christianity was incompatible with his system, and that the interests of the priest would always be stronger than that of the State.")[8] In a somewhat similar, terser vein, and in a much-quoted phrase, Sir Robert Molesworth, who belonged to the same Whig circle as Shaftesbury, hoped that one day soon "the character of the priest will give place to that of the patriot."[9]

Many in the eighteenth century, however, did not share Hobbes's enthusiasm for an all-powerful state that controlled not only its subjects' wills but also their judgment. For them, no subjugation of the Church to Sovereign would be sufficient to check the power of the priesthood; worse, it would most likely become a double form of oppression. By the 1740s what the peoples of Europe most needed was not Hobbesian absolute sovereignty, under which much of the continent had been living for far too long, but free, liberal—as we would say—government, which had dispensed with religion altogether as a source of moral authority or at least deprived it of its more obviously murderous tendencies.

If the Peace of Westphalia had seemingly put an end to the horrors of religious conflict, at least within Europe, it had not erased it from memory. Over a century later it still lodged in the imagination, a reminder of what might yet engulf a world that was insufficiently vigilant in the defense of the separation of Church and State. As Anne-Robert-Jacques Turgot, economist, historian, and Controller-General of Finances from 1774 until 1776, warned Louis XVI in 1775, religious intolerance had once been responsible for, as he put it, placing "daggers into the hands of kings to butcher the people, and in the hands of the people to butcher kings." It would do so again if given the opportunity. "Here, Sire," he concluded, "is a great subject for reflection which princes should have constantly in their thoughts."[10] (Those who would too readily criticize the modern French authorities for their fierce defense of *laïcité* might do well to bear in mind the spectacle of, in Diderot's words, "one half of the nation bathing itself out of piety, in the blood of the other half.")[11] Clearly no one wished to see a return to the carnage and insecurity of the Wars of Religion. But religious conflict had had the advantage of keeping kings weak. In England it had led to the killing of one king and ultimately to a constitution that apparently had severely limited the power of all future ones. Across the rest of Europe, however, the resolution reached at Westphalia had placed in the hands of the state a hitherto unprecedented hold over the minds of its subjects. For Immanuel Kant, who was generally horrified by the conclusions to which Hobbes had come, "the self-incurred minority" from which all enlightened persons struggled to free themselves was most pernicious "in *religious matters*." For "that minority being the most harmful, is also the most disgraceful of all."[12]

There was also a theoretical concern. The empiricists of the seventeenth century had dismantled the main support for the notion that all humans moved according to a divinely inspired universal natural law. Having done that, they were content to leave God alone in his heaven and leave all those who cared to believe in the stories that the several religions had told about him to believe them as they might. They had no particular quarrel with the Christian views of the afterlife or even very much with the Christian account of the creation. There were a number of eighteenth-century writers who were happy to agree with them. Some even believed that by studying human nature they were, in some sense, advancing God's work; they certainly did not feel threatened by the possibility of his existence.[13] But most of the "sentimentalists" were acutely aware that by insisting upon the presence of some kind of intuitive bond between human beings, however minimal, they had opened a door—a small one, to be sure, but a door nonetheless—by which it might be possible to smuggle some kind of divine interventionism back in. For what, the Christian might ask, could ultimately be responsible for our "fellow-feeling" for one another and the "moral sense" other than God? Most eighteenth-century accounts of the operation of the sentiments were also, as we have seen, closely associated with ancient Stoicism, and there was an uncomfortable proximity between Stoicism and Christianity, if only because so much of Christian psychology and Christian ethics relies so heavily upon Stoic sources. It is also true that the Enlightenment was an exclusively European phenomenon, shared only with Europe's overseas settler populations, and it could never have arisen except in a broadly Christian world. It was, in a sense, a form of secularized Christianity. The most pure moral system, in the opinion of Jean D'Alembert, "with which natural enlightenment can inspire men," Christianity is also (as is its close neighbor Islam) a truly cosmopolitan faith.[14] There is a very obvious similarity between Stoic claims for the universality of humankind and St. Paul's message to the Colossians, the inhabitants of a city on the banks of the River Lycus in western Asia Minor, that the new Christian man—the man, as he put it, who had been "reborn" in Christ—had also been reborn into a world where "there cannot be Greek or Jew, circumcision and uncircumcision, barbarian, Scythian, bondman, freeman: but Christ is all and in all."[15] The Canadian philosopher Charles Taylor is certainly right in claiming that "what modern civilization has done, partly under the influence of Stoic natural law, partly under the influence of Christianity, has been to lift the parochial restrictions that surrounded [the] recognition of moral personality in earlier civilizations."[16] The task for the sentimentalists was to free the Stoic natural law from its association not with scholastic psychology—by now, in any case, a mere curiosity—not even from the broadly ethical message of Christianity, but from the founding myths of the Judeo-Christian account of humanity. The Skeptics of the seventeenth century had successfully undermined the credibility of theology. The theorists of the eighteenth hoped to undermine the credibility of God himself.

There was a further reason for this hostility to the Christian religion in particular. All of those who set out to create the new "science of man" based their arguments, to some degree, upon a history of the evolution of human society. Judeo-Christianity was similarly based upon a history, rooted, it need hardly be said, in the Old and New Testaments. It was divinely ordered, eschatological, and what St. Augustine had called the "operation of God" in time. The new "scientific" narratives of the eighteenth century, however, ran directly contrary to this vision of man as a fallen creature struggling with the legacy of Original Sin, redeemed by Christ's sacrifice, and thereafter moving forward inexorably to the end of human time in the Second Coming. In this new history humans are not burdened by sin. They are not the kind of plaything St. Augustine had imagined, dancing to the music of time conducted by an omniscient deity. They are free. They have their origins in the state of nature (about which more later) and their immediate end in what became known for the first time in the eighteenth century as "civilization." They progress; they improve. Their nature changes as their living conditions change.

II

The first task, then, was to discredit the stories of which the Old and New Testaments were composed. Taken at face value, these were evident fantasies dreamt up to explain the sheer unpredictability and seemingly gratuitous nastiness of life. In this they differed very little from the pagan stories that had preceded them and to which they often bore an uncomfortable similarity. Diderot had a great deal of sarcastic fun with the obvious parallels between pagan and Christian myths.[17] Why, he asked, does the story in which the Greek god Zeus, in the guise of a swan, descends on the mortal Leda in order to have sex with her make us laugh, but the story of the Annunciation in the Gospel does not? Just think of the folly, he went on: "One day, a young woman who habitually sleeps with her husband, receives a visit from a young man with a pigeon. Immediately afterward she becomes pregnant. Who, it is asked, is responsible for this child: the husband, the young man, or the pigeon? A priest who is present instantly replies: 'Clearly this is proof that it was the pigeon.' "[18] On the face of it, does this story seem any more credible than that of Leda? Diderot's point was that it is only widespread and generally unreflective belief that could persuade any reasonable person to accept either story as a statement of fact. Anyone who claimed to believe the myths of the ancients would be thought at best a madman. Yet millions take the stories in the Bible to be the literal truth without anyone doubting their sanity. The world's religions have been enforced not by reason or even by faith; they are the creations of convention and acceptance of that most damning of all eighteenth-century terms, prejudice. Once those conventions have changed or the society that upheld them has been swept away by some new creed, with new gods serving new masters, the old myths are revealed for the simple-minded and willfully deceptive storytelling they all really are. Mimeticism, the desire to imitate our fellows, to be and think like them, is the most powerful force known to any human society, and no one knew how to manipulate it to such good effect as the Christian Church.

Few were more convinced of this, and more systematically scathing about the tales to be found in the Bible, than Voltaire. Voltaire had spent much of the 1730s and 1740s shut up with his mistress Gabrielle-Émilie, Marquise du Châtelet, in her country house at Cirey-sur-Blaise. Madame du Châtelet was a brilliant mathematician and physicist; the translator of Newton's *Principia Mathematica,* to which she added her own "algebraical commentary"; and the author of, among other things, a treatise on happiness. She was strong-willed and independent in a way that Voltaire did not always like. When he suggested that she read Locke, she demanded that he read Leibniz. He called her the "Minerva of France" but also said of her, with characteristic bitchiness, that she was "a great man whose only fault was being a woman." Among their other pursuits, Voltaire and Madame du Châtelet spent their time together studying the Bible and biblical commentaries.[19] Like many well-off middle-class Frenchmen of his day, Voltaire had been educated by the Jesuits, and Jesuit education, although strong on theology, tended to avoid direct contact with the text of the Bible itself. Reading the Bible, as distinct from reading what carefully schooled interpreters had to say about it, was a largely Protestant activity. Direct exposure, in particular to what the English novelist Aldous Huxley once called the "bloodcurdling military history" of which the Old Testament is very largely composed, came as a great shock to them both. If the Holy

Ghost really was the author of the Old Testament, Voltaire commented archly, he certainly had not chosen a very edifying subject. "What horrors," he recorded, "seized us when we read the writings of the Hebrews together." The text seemed to be filled with "historical monstrosities which are repellent to nature and good sense"—of snakes that could speak, of cities consumed by fire and water, of women turned into pillars of salt, of men who sleep with their servants and sisters, and women who sleep with their fathers in order to repopulate the world. The wrathful and vengeful God portrayed in all these tales seemed to him to violate all "purity, chastity, good faith, justice, and universal reason." But the stories were not merely abhorrent; they were also derivative and contradictory. The Garden of Eden supposedly contained four rivers, but the sources of two of them, the Euphrates and the Nile, are in reality two thousand miles apart. So that Moses might wave his magic wand and part the waters of the Red Sea, God had sent his chosen people fleeing with all they owned from the vengeful, and unencumbered, Egyptians on a thirty-mile detour. Then there was the Ark, crammed with "fourteen elephants, fourteen camels, fourteen buffaloes, as many horses, elks, deer, serpents, ostriches"—over two thousand species and all the food required to feed them for ten months, loaded into a boat barely four hundred and fifty feet long. "Those who wrote this," Voltaire noted dryly, "were not great physicists—as you can see."

All of this was ridiculous enough. But it was only the prelude to the New Testament, the "child" of the old, the outpourings of the even less excusable "sect of the Nazarene." For Voltaire and Madame du Châtelet, Jesus is just another wandering prophet, one of the "large number of prophets without a mission who, not being priests, made a living by being inspired." The stories that had been concocted in his name had been written down years after his death by evangelists who could not agree on a single thing, and the stories they put about were absurd, fraudulent, and contradictory. "A child born of spirit," Voltaire remarked acidly, "is a truly astounding event; [but] an angel who informs Joseph of this prodigy in a dream is not a very decisive proof of the copulation of Mary with the Holy Spirit." The claim that the outcome of this copulation was the fulfillment of the prophecy of Isaiah was patently absurd, since Isaiah makes no mention of virgin birth—that was a deliberate mistranslation of a word that in fact means merely "young woman"—and the prophet's name was to have been not Jesus but Emmanuel.[20]

Although a touch less cruel and barbaric than the behavior attributed to the likes of Abraham, Isaac, and Jacob, Jesus has his own brand of petulance and injustice. He drives out devils from a man possessed and makes them enter into a herd of swine, who then drown themselves in the Lake of Tiberias. "We may suppose," remarked Voltaire, "that the owners of these swine, who were apparently not Jews, were not amused by this trick." And what does one make of a man-god who curses a fig tree because it will not produce figs for him in winter? Then, having repeatedly abused the Pharisees as "generations of vipers" and "whitened sepulchres," his followers the Apostles have "the nerve to tell us" that when the victims of all this verbal abuse finally take their revenge on Jesus and persuade a reluctant Roman governor to crucify him, God is so upset that, at his death, "the earth was covered with darkness at noon, when there was a full moon." Which, apart from being wholly unjust, was, as Voltaire remarked, "such a strange miracle." If the sheer improbability of all this were not enough to persuade any mildly critical reader that the Gospels are merely a collection of primitive tales, there was the fact that all of them clearly derived from the same source. For although the momentous events recorded in the Gospels, from the massacre of the Innocents to the Crucifixion, were supposed to have taken place under the eyes of a Roman governor in an admittedly remote Roman province, no Roman historian, not even one so "enlightened" as Josephus, who was himself a Jew and from a royal and priestly family, makes any mention of any of them or of the existence of Jesus.[21] And as for St. Paul, the true architect of Christianity, whose life as told in the Acts of the Apostles was a tissue of contradictions and obvious fabrications, what, asked Voltaire, would we think today of a man who demanded that we support both him and his wife, "while he judged us, punished us, and made no distinction between the innocent and guilty"? Cleary very little, certainly not enough to take what he had to say seriously.[22] And then, what possible grounds were there in any of these texts for the claims that the Church made on their behalf? As Paul-Henri Thiry, Baron d'Holbach, perhaps the most notorious "unbeliever" of his day, remarked in his *Critical History of Jesus Christ*—one of the earliest attempts, heavily polemical though it clearly was, to subject the Gospels to some kind of historical analysis—the "authority of these books which serve as the basis for the Christian religion is founded on nothing other than a council, that is, an assembly of priests and bishops. But these priests and bishops, judges and partisans in this affair in which they clearly have a vested interest, could they not be mistaken?" To this the answer given by the Church was always the same: a Council of the Church is infallible, "inspired by the Holy Spirit and . . . its decisions should be regarded as equivalent to those of God himself." But if you were then to ask on what basis the Church made such claims to infallibility, the answer was always a further appeal to the authority of the Gospels whose very authenticity they were asserting, "which is evidently a vicious circle."[23]

It was not, however, only the absurdity of the stories of which the Old and New Testaments were very largely made up, nor even the self-serving and ultimately risible arguments dreamed up in their defense, that caused the most indignation. So, too, did the teachings of Jesus himself. Some of these were unexceptional, simple moral principles. But they would have been self-evident to any reasonable person, no matter what their beliefs, and had no need of divine sanction and sacral intervention. Others, however, were not as evidently benign and ecumenical as they were often represented as being, even by nonbelievers. Holbach subjected the Sermon on the Mount to a withering critique that suggested that Jesus' true purpose had been to encourage stupidity, docility, and blind obedience, thus paving the way for the Church's stranglehold over the minds of its adherents.[24] For in the end, what was truly monstrous, as distinct from simply infantile and laughable, was the hideous wrongs, the damage and the bloodshed that the various churches had inflicted upon mankind in Jesus' name.

In 1770—in London, and under the suitably mocking pseudonym "Doctor Goodheart" so as to be out of harm's way—Voltaire published a small tract called *On Perpetual Peace,* a plea for universal religious toleration that consists for the most part of a similarly fierce condemnation of organized religion and of the patent absurdities of the stories on which Christianity and Judaism were based. At the center of this little book there is a discussion, supposed to take place in the presence of the emperor Marcus Aurelius, among a Christian, a Roman senator, and a "Jew of good sense," in which the Christian and the Jew attempt to explain to the emperor the claims of their respective religions. In this exchange it is the Christian, decidedly not of *bon sens,* who comes off by far the worst. Why, the senator asks him, "do you disturb the peace of the Empire? Why are you not content, like the Syrians, the Egyptians, and the Jews, to practice your rites in peace? Why, of all the sects, do you wish to annihilate all the others?" To this the Christian replies simply: "Because it is the only true one." He then tells the familiar story of how "his God" was born of a virgin Jewish mother from Judaea impregnated by "God" (who is, but is also not, the same god as the child of the mother), in a manger in the city of Bethlehem where they—because the virgin mother also has a human husband—had come to be counted in the census which the emperor Augustus had ordered. The senator listens to all of this with mounting incredulity and then remarks that even if it were possible to accept the truth of a story about virgin births and sort out the relationship between what appeared to be at least two, and possibly three, gods all rolled into one, it remained a fact that Augustus had never called a census of "all the world," and even if he had, he would not have conducted it in Judaea, which was a semi-independent kingdom, and that as subjects of King Herod "neither the mother nor the father of your god" would have been included, as they would not have been Roman citizens. As to the story—also offered up as proof of the divinity of Jesus—that "three kings or three philosophers came from the Orient to worship at the stable in which he was born" and that they had been guided there by a wandering star newly created for that purpose—had any such thing really taken place "we would have seen it, the whole earth would have talked about it, and our astronomers would have investigated such a strange phenomenon." But they did not. Challenged to produce some kind of proof of his preposterous assertions, the Christian replies that it is all written down in his sacred books, but that no unbeliever is allowed to read them. In the end, when the Jew has explained his own position—in terms that, while only slightly less ludicrous, are also far more reasonable—the emperor turns to the senator and remarks that, as far as he can ascertain, "both are equally deranged; but while the Empire has nothing to fear from the Jews, it has everything to dread from the Christians."

Marcus Aurelius, Voltaire remarked, "was not mistaken in his observation."[25] For despite the obvious nonsense in which it was dressed up by later generations of apologists, this new sect grew in audacity over time. A wandering prophet is transformed, with some help from Plato's metaphysics, into a god. "All superstitions come in crowds to inundate the Church. . . . This sect divides into a multitude of sects; at all times they battle, murder each other, slit each others' throats." "This, my very dear brethren," Voltaire concluded, "is the fruit of the tree of the cross of the gibbet which they deified. . . . This then was the reason why they dared to have God come to earth: to deliver Europe over to murder and brigandage for centuries!" All of these "Christian barbarities," he calculated, had resulted in 9,468,800 dead—and that took no account of those slaughtered by Muslims, Jews, and other fanatics from other, less well documented sects.[26] And this infinitesimally small collection of zealots perched on the edge of the Roman world in the first century BCE had the audacity to claim to speak for the entirety of humankind! "If there are about 16 hundred million people on the earth, as some scholars claim," Voltaire went on, "then the Holy Roman Catholic Universal Church accounts for scarcely sixty million of them, which is little more than a twenty-sixth part of the inhabitants of the known world." All of those remaining millions, all of Asia, Africa, and America, and about half of Europe, is thus condemned to be "the prey of the Devil so as to satisfy those holy words, 'For many are called but few are chosen.' "[27] And never believe those who tell you that these preposterous tales are necessary to keep the poor and ignorant masses in check, that "the common people need mysteries, that they must be deceived." For whatever may be the view of priests and kings, "the common people is not as idiotic as many think; it will accept without difficulty a wise and simple creed of a single God . . . such as all the sages of antiquity worshipped, and such as is accepted in China by all literate men," but not this farrago of nonsense.[28] If it appears to do so now, this is only because of the fear that the Church has, over the centuries, inculcated in it. "The only way to bring peace to mankind," he concluded, "was to destroy the dogmas which divide them, and to re-establish the truth which unites them. . . . This peace is not a chimera, it exists among honest men from China to Quebec."[29]

III

The image of God conjured up by both the Old and the New Testaments was patently absurd, grotesque in all its foundations, and murderous in its consequences.

But it was not the only one. For those who could not stomach the Judeo-Christian version of the divinity, there were other, more reasonable, more rational ones that still allowed for the presence of some kind of intelligible, discernible order in the universe but that still made human beings dependent upon a divine creator. In one of the most popular of these, God was a kind of celestial clockmaker.[30] Having created and then wound up the universe, he had absented himself—forever. He did not intervene in human affairs, he did not answer prayers—which were, in any case, vain claims for preferential treatment—he did not punish miscreants or reward the virtuous in this life, and there was no heaven or hell in which to do so in the next. God was merely an impersonal principle, the origin of life. He was always, however, assumed to be good and his creation perfect.

The idea owes its origins, as does so much in western philosophy, to Aristotle, who argued that as all matter is in motion and motion cannot be generated by itself, since that would lead to an infinite regress, there must exist a first principle that is infinite, without magnitude, and indivisible.[31] This thing is then identified with god (*ho theos*), which is described as "a living being, eternal, most good, so that life and duration continual and eternal belong to god."[32] Aquinas, unsurprisingly, made much of this and gave it as the first of his famous five proofs for the existence of God. For Christians, however, any attempt to attribute to this first principle any kind of benevolent interests, even at the moment of the creation, inevitably ran into the problem that had troubled theologians since the days of Epicurus: namely, what is known as "the problem of evil." If God is good and all-knowing and all-powerful, why does he allow so much purposeless suffering to exist? Is not, say, the death of a small child by cancer sufficient in itself to refute the possible existence of any deity that is both benevolent and omnipotent? (There was plenty of evidence for an impotent and malevolent deity, but conceptually that posed no difficulties.) As Holbach indignantly expressed it: "Who is the man, filled with good will and humanity, who does not wish, with all his heart, to make his fellow beings happy? If God surpasses in goodness every member of the human species, why does he not make use of his infinite power to make every one of them happy?"[33]

The conventional Christian answer to this, put very simply, depended upon the story of Original Sin and the concept of Free Will. Because of Adam's first sin, man was a doomed creature. But God had equipped him with Free Will. He did not have to act as his fallen nature inevitably dictated. All the evils that befell him were, therefore, of his own making. Very few in the eighteenth century were prepared to accept this as anything more than simply a means of restating the problem. If God were good, why on earth had he, as Voltaire scathingly put it, condemned Adam and all his progeny in perpetuity "for having swallowed an apple"? The whole story was, as the Socinians (one of the sects of the "Radical Reformation") and Unitarians rightly declared it to be, "the most absurd barbarism."[34] Even if we discard the story of the Fall, even if the deity is conceived to be a rather more dignified presence who does not intervene in nature, does not the simple existence of evil suggest that his creation is, at best, an imperfect one?

One immensely influential attempt to provide an answer came from the great German (Saxon) philosopher Gottfried Wilhelm Leibniz. Leibniz argued that the deity had provided an order in the universe that was ultimately beneficial to all his creatures, but since no one could grasp the whole, no one could hope to understand the place that individual events played in this grand design. What appeared to the present observer to be simply evil would, if that observer could see the whole of creation, inevitably turn out to have beneficial consequences. It is only our human inability to envision the whole of time and space that prevents us from understanding why the death of an innocent child might, in fact, be a good. On Leibniz's account, God had chosen which world to create from an infinite number of possible worlds that were present as ideas in his mind, and since he wills what is best, the world he actually created has the greatest possible number of compatible perfections. It was thus, in Leibniz's celebrated—and much-mocked—phrase, the "best of all possible worlds." Evil, which would seem to be an error, a blemish, in any perfect creation was, said Leibniz, borrowing a metaphor from St. Augustine, like a dark patch seen on a picture. From close up it appears to be nothing more than an ugly stain, but from a distance it adds beauty to the whole. Similarly, in a piece of music: "There are certain disorders in the parts which marvelously reveal the beauty of the whole, just as certain dissonances, when used correctly, render the harmony more beautiful."[35] Leibniz called this "theodicy."

For those like Adam Smith, who referred to God as "the great Director of the universe" and found the specter of a cosmos made up only of matter without consciousness—what he called, tellingly, the "very suspicion of a fatherless world"—an impossibly terrifying one, theodicy offered a means of warding off the "thought that all the unknown regions of infinite and incomprehensible space" should be filled with nothing but "endless misery and wretchedness." For what Smith called "this universal benevolence" from which his understanding of "sympathy" ultimately derived, which bound each human being to every other of his kind, would make no sense to anyone who was not at the same time convinced that "all the inhabitants of the universe, the meanest as well as the greatest," are under the immediate care and protection of a "great, benevolent, and all-wise Being, who directs all the movements of nature." If man had possessed that all-wise Being's eye-view and thus had been able to see "all the connexions and dependencies of things," he would easily grasp that "all the misfortunes which may befall himself, his friends, or his country [are] . . . necessary for the prosperity of the universe." Then he would not merely "submit with resignation" to whatever evil he saw around him but "ought sincerely and devoutly to have wished for [it]." This, however, would also seem to imply, at best, a form of fatalism, which, if taken literally, would make all attempts to improve the human condition not merely vain but, since Smith likens the human race to an army of foot soldiers and God to its "great Conductor," treasonous. Although he does insist that man is responsible for "the care of his own happiness, of that of his family, his friends and his country," quite how far this would be allowed to go before it countermanded the dictates of the "great Conductor" is not clear.[36]

What theodicy meant, as Smith clearly understood, was that if something unpleasant happens to me today, it will, at some point in the remote future (and possibly long after I am dead), turn out to be of some benefit to the cosmos as a whole. The father of the universe had set things up in such a way as to benefit all his human creation, past, present, and future. What it did not mean, therefore, is that if something unpleasant happens to me today, I only have to wait long enough and I will begin to see benefits in it for *me*. This, however, was inevitably how many interpreted it, and it proved to be immensely consoling for some, Jean-Jacques Rousseau among them. For others it seemed not only clearly indemonstrable but the emptiest kind of optimism.

In 1755 the vision of a deity who, far from caring for the well-being of his little platoon of dutiful soldiers, was impersonal and indifferent was given a helping hand by the deity himself. On the morning of November 1, Lisbon, the third-largest port in Europe after London and Amsterdam, a city that was as strictly orthodox as any in the Christian world, a city filled with churches and monasteries, was devastated by an earthquake, which was followed almost immediately by a gigantic tsunami and a series of fires that ranged largely unchecked for over five days. A large part of the city and the surrounding countryside were destroyed and as many as ninety thousand were killed. And all of this had taken place not just on any day, but on All Saints' Day, and not just at any time, but at around 9:40 in the morning, when a large proportion of the population was either attending or coming out of Mass. The righteous immediately seized upon the event as proof that God could, and did, smite down the sinner while he (or she) lived. What sins the people of Lisbon had been guilty of, and why they, rather than the residents of London or Paris, should have been singled out in this way, no one could say. The ways of God are, after all, inscrutable. For enlightened minds across Europe, however, the earthquake underlined what so many had believed since the great religious turmoils of the sixteenth and seventeenth centuries: that there was no God, that mankind was entirely alone in the world.

It was possibly this event more than any other that had convinced Voltaire of the vast absurdity of theodicy. He wrote a celebrated "Poem on the Disaster of Lisbon," which captures, in violent outrage, the sheer senselessness of all human suffering:

Oh, miserable mortals! Oh wretched earth!
Oh, dreadful assembly of all mankind!
Eternal sermon of useless sufferings!
Deluded philosophers who cry, "All is well,"
Hasten, contemplate these frightful ruins,
This wreck, these shreds, these wretched ashes of the dead;
These women and children heaped on one another,
These scattered members under broken marble;
One hundred thousand unfortunates devoured by the earth
Who, bleeding, lacerated, and still alive,
Buried under their roofs without aid in their anguish,
End their sad days!
In answer to the half-formed cries of their dying voices,
At the frightful sight of their smoking ashes,
Will you say: "This is the result of eternal laws
Directing the acts of a free and good God!"
Will you say, in seeing this mass of victims:
"God is revenged, their death is the price for their crimes?"
What crime, what error did these children,
Crushed and bloody on their mothers' breasts, commit?

Did Lisbon, which is no more, have more vices
Than London and Paris immersed in their pleasures?
Lisbon is destroyed, and they dance in Paris!

Three years later Voltaire attacked Leibnizian optimism again, this time in what has become probably the most widely known of all his works, the short novel *Candide, or Optimism,* which David Hume described to Adam Smith with relish as being "full of Sprightliness and, Impiety, and indeed a Satire upon Providence, under the Pretext of criticising the Leibnitian system."[37] Throughout the seemingly endless series of catastrophes that befall the novel's three main characters—the philosopher Pangloss, Candide himself, and his mistress Cunegund—Pangloss, his face half eaten away by syphilis, one buttock cut off, insists at every turn that, all appearances to the contrary, this world is nonetheless the "best of all possible worlds" and that in it "all is for the best." In the end, when the three have come to rest on the estate of a Turkish "dervish" and Candide finds himself married to the woman he has so long desired but now no longer wants, Pangloss observes that had he not undergone all the miseries he has had to endure, "you would not have been here to eat preserved citrons and pistachio nuts." To which Candide, like the good Epicurean he has become, makes his famously laconic retort: "Excellently observed, . . . but let us cultivate our garden."

But for all his furious debunking, even Voltaire, like so many others, could not quite accept the prospect of unqualified atheism and went to some lengths to defend the Chinese against the charge that, while they had a moral code (and an excellent one at that), they had no discernible religion. A universe that was made up only of matter struck him, as it did Smith and perhaps even Diderot (but not, as we shall see, Hume), as unacceptably bleak. Voltaire's religion—if it may be so called—like that of most of those who participated in that wide-ranging confraternity of the like-minded dubbed "the republic of letters," was some kind of deism—or, as he insisted, "theism."

Both terms were vague ones and covered a number of similar, overlapping beliefs. What all theists shared in common, however, besides a hostility to all organized religion, was the belief in some kind of creator, sometimes described as the "supreme Being," the "Great Architect," "the Universal Mind," or more frequently simply as the "Deity"—but rarely, if ever, as "God." "Theism," wrote Voltaire, "is embraced by the flower of humankind, by which I mean by decent [*honnêtes*] people from Peking to London, and from London to Philadelphia."[38] Theists do not know how God rewards or punishes, because they are never so "audacious as to flatter themselves that they know how God acts."[39] They believe that he exists, that he created all living beings, that he is just. But the role of even this much-reduced entity in human affairs was either negligible or nonexistent. He did not manifest himself in this world or pass judgment on his creation or favor one tribe over another. That "sordid, shameful Nauseous Idea of Deity," as Shaftesbury described it, which presided over the "vulgar Religion"—for Shaftesbury there could be no adjective more damning—in which he had been brought up, that anthropomorphic God who had first made his creatures frail and then punished them for failing to live up to his expectations was an insult both to human intelligence and to decent manners.[40]

The theists objected not only to the stories that the various religions of the world had told their faithful; they objected, too, to the claim that the believer had to accept unquestioningly whatever the person, or persons, to whom this God had supposedly entrusted his revelation chose to say. "As if our religion," protested Shaftesbury, "was a kind of magic, which depended not on the belief in a single supreme being, or as if the form and rational belief of such a being on philosophical grounds was an improper qualification for believing in anything further."[41] As Voltaire succinctly summed up the deist's and theist's position on immanence in the article on "laws" in his *Philosophical Dictionary* of 1764—a witty, alphabetically ordered summary of all useful human knowledge, laced with anecdote and invective:

> When Nature created our species she gave us certain instincts: self-love to preserve ourselves, benevolence for the preservation of others, the love which is common to all species, and the inexplicable gift of being able to combine more ideas than all the other

animals put together. Having thus given us our share, she said: "Now do the best you can."[42]

IV

Deism, or theism, dependent as it was on decency, good manners, and rational conversation, was clearly a creed only for the elite. No learned and reflective person could possibly require the support of religion, much less swallow the preposterous stories told in support of the Christian one. The theist or deist, declared Voltaire, "speaks the language which all people understand so long as they speak among themselves . . . from Peking to Cayenne [French Guiana], he counts all the wise as his brothers."[43]

The same, however, was not so obviously true of the uneducated, priest-harassed, and for the most part illiterate masses that made up most of the population of eighteenth-century Europe. Even the arch-cynic Bernard Mandeville was certain that, no matter how hard "philosophers and men of letters" may have attempted to disabuse their fellows of the claims of religion, "there never was an age or country in which the vulgar would ever come into the opinion that contradicted that fear, which all men are born with, of an invisible cause which meddles and interferes in human affairs."

Furthermore, even if they could, it might not be such a good idea. For even the most skeptical of the *philosophes* were prepared to accept that some kind of belief in a divine judge might serve a useful social purpose. As Mandeville shrewdly pointed out, if you can "make multitudes believe contrary to what they feel, or what contradicts a passion inherent in their nature. . . . If you humour that passion, and allow it to be just, you may regulate it as you please."[44] Regulated religion, in other words, was the best way to keep the multitude in check. This is what Rousseau, in *The Social Contract* of 1762, called a "civil religion" (although he was by no means the first to use the term). It did not matter if its theological content was true. What mattered was that it should contribute to the support of civil society. "Now it is very important for the state," wrote Rousseau, "that every citizen should have a religion which makes him love his duties; but the dogmas of this religion are of concern neither to the state nor to its member, unless those dogmas affect morality and the duties which he who profess it is bound to perform toward others." He was certain, however, that Christianity would not do this job, at least for the kind of society he had in mind, ruled by and in the interests of the General Will of all its members, because Christianity "preaches only servitude and dependence . . . Christians are made to be slaves; they know it and are hardly aroused by it. This short life has too little value in their eyes"; as the "*patria* of the Christian is not of this world," he was constantly drawn toward another, and often conflicting, source of loyalty.[45]

Like Hobbes, Rousseau looked upon religion as part of the law, not philosophy. Like many of his contemporaries, he was certain that most religious systems had been created to answer some very specific legal needs. The founders of states, those whom Rousseau calls "legislators," found themselves unable to communicate the laws they had created to the common people, because those "views which are very general and objects which are very remote are usually beyond their reach." Some, then, had resorted to the subterfuge of claiming that their laws were in fact the expression of divine wish. The legislator "puts into the mouth of the immortals that sublime reason which soars beyond the reach of common men, in order that he may win over by divine authority those whom human prudence could not move."[46] The teachings supposedly handed down to such beings as Moses or Jesus or Muhammad were in themselves valueless, when not merely obvious, or rather, they represented only the skillful manipulations by some highly gifted men of small (often very small) social groups in particular times and particular places. "In order to give a leader to a nation which until then had been ungovernable," Condorcet said of Muhammad, and might have said of Moses, "he began by raising up on the debris of their ancient cults, a more refined religion. Legislator, prophet, pontiff, judge, general, every means of subjugating men were in his hands, and he knew how to use them with ability, with grandeur."[47] Muhammad in particular, whose religion seemed to be more obviously tailored to the particular needs of his peoples than either Christianity or Judaism, was in general widely admired for these reasons. In Voltaire's play *Fanaticism, or Mahomet the Prophet* of 1742, which Adam Smith thought the best thing he had ever seen in the theater, Muhammad, although depicted as a somewhat unsavory figure, a scheming despot with strong sexual appetites, is also a brilliant tactician and passionately devoted to the future of the Arabs, whom he calls "this generous people, too long unknown."[48]

Religion, provided that it came with the right moral baggage, could, for similar reasons, be a useful ally in keeping the unruly and uneducated in check. Even Voltaire's attribution of a native common sense to the people was hardly consistent. They might be able to see through most of the silly stories they were told, but without an enduring fear of some kind of ever-watchful father figure, they could only rarely be trusted. It was, after all, Voltaire who was reputed to be the source of the famous quip that if God had not existed it would have been necessary to invent him, if only because, so long as his wife, his tailor, his lawyer, and his servants could be persuaded to believe in the threat of punishment in an afterlife, "I shall be cheated and robbed and cuckolded less often."[49]

If organized religion had grown up in response to a legal need, religious belief itself was believed to have arisen out of a need to explain the inexplicable. Small primitive societies struggling to survive had replaced an uncontrollable and unintelligible nature with anthropomorphic beings who might be placated, or bribed, into making life less intolerable. In the schematic history of religion that he inserted into the abbé Guillaume-Thomas-François Raynal's *History of the Two Indies* (of which more later), Diderot reflected that if nature had always satisfied man's needs, man would not have had to invent gods. As it was, when his fields were parched by the sun or swept away by floods, man "began to look for a cause for his misery." To explain the enigma of his existence, he had invented a large number of "different systems, all equally absurd," and "filled the universe with good and evil intelligence." From this early polytheism, the many had been reduced to two: this was Manichaeanism. The two were then reduced to one, resulting in monotheism. At this point canny men with political ambitions began to exploit all this human incredulity, claiming that "the right to rule had descended upon them from heaven." This, in turn, led to "sacred despotism, the most cruel and immoral of governments," in which

> one man, proud, evildoing, self-interested, and vicious, rules men with impunity in the name of God; where what is just is what pleases him and what is unjust is what displeases him—or the Supreme Being with whom he is in conversation and whom he makes speak in accordance with his own passions; where it is a crime to examine his commands, and an impiety to oppose him; where contradictory revelations are set up in place of conscience and reason, and reduced to silence by miracles or threats; where, finally, nations are denied any certain idea about the rights of man, or what is good and what is bad, since they look for the basis of their privileges and their duties in revelations which they can neither interpret nor reject.[50]

Some would have assumed that, in the middle of the eighteenth century, this now applied only to the well-established despotisms of Asia, to Turkey or to China. But Diderot does not name names, and it was not hard to see in this the image of the French king, who still claimed to rule by divine authority and who still believed that his touch could cure scrofula (an infection of the lymph nodes in the neck). Although the last French king to attempt to do this—to universal derision—was in fact Charles X in 1825, by the mid–eighteenth century this piece of royal magic had begun to seem faintly silly even to the incredulous. "In a time of ignorance," Voltaire wrote in his notebook, "a king must cure scrofula. Useless today."[51] Useless it certainly was, but it was a still-lingering evidence of the supposed privileged association between god and royalty. "That is why," Diderot warned, "it is important that in every country . . . sovereigns and those in authority, should be attached to no dogma, no sect, no religious cult."[52]

Most of the writers of the Enlightenment were also prepared to accept that, in a formative stage in human development, religion had had a crucial role to play in civilizing—or as the English said, "polishing"—

the otherwise rude, uncivil, unpolished human animal. It had helped to transform rough, wandering bands into nations. Religion, as the Marquis de Mirabeau—who may have been the first to coin the term *civilization*—noted, "is unquestionably the first and most useful brake upon humanity; it is the first resort of civilization, it preaches to us, and it reminds us ceaselessly of our brotherhood, and it softens our heart."[53]

Yet if religion could usefully serve to persuade primitive tribes to create reasonable, cohesive societies and to enforce laws that might otherwise have been incomprehensible to simple, untutored minds, it should over time, once its purpose had been served, have simply withered away. The fact that it had not—that, as Hume implied, the greatest of the Christian miracles was the survival of Christianity itself—suggested that it still fulfilled some vital social need. For many, religion seemed to be the only guarantee of the moral integrity of the social order. Without some form of Rousseau's "civil religion," without fear of an afterlife and of an eternal judge, what reason would anyone have to honor agreements or observe laws? To put it differently—in the most contentious form it could be put—could a society of atheists ever be a really just and moral one?

The question was by no means new. In 1682 a renegade Catholic convert to Calvinism named Pierre Bayle published a small book entitled *Diverse Thoughts on the Comet*. It was written in the aftermath of the appearance, on December 24, 1680, of a comet that had been visible in most of Europe and seems to have terrified all who saw it. Bayle's little book was—or so he claimed, at least—an attempt to reply to the many anguished requests he had received asking what the possible meaning of this apparition might be. It is an unusual work (all of Bayle's writings, however—and there are a great many of them—are highly unusual). It dealt with the history, nature, and possible implications for science, religion, and morality of the existence of comets. Were they followed by misfortunes? Did they ever reach the Earth, and what would happen if they did? Were they of miraculous origin? What impact did they have on people's behavior? And so on. What made the book an instant source of outrage, however, was the argument tucked away in section 113 (of 241), that "atheism does not necessarily lead to the corruption of morals." Since, in Bayle's view, religion, morality, and salvation are all independent, you did not need to believe in a god to be good, and it was therefore entirely possible for atheists to create a morally perfect society. Bayle is best known today as the author of a long, rambling, complex encyclopedia, the *Historical and Critical Dictionary,* one of the most widely read books of the early eighteenth century, part history, part literary criticism, part theology, part obscenity, one of whose articles had apparently prompted Leibniz to write his *Essays on Theodicy*. Although sufficiently heterodox to have had his works condemned by both by the Catholic Church in France and the Consistory of the Walloon Church in Rotterdam, Bayle was not—or at least not obviously—an atheist. He was not claiming that atheism could be justified. He was pretty certain that the atheist would still face a sticky end in the afterlife. What he was claiming was that religion and morality were independent. Humans, he pointed out, rarely acted on their beliefs—even those, such as the religious, who were professionally committed to doing so. Christians supposedly embraced an ethics of sexual restraint, yet the streets of Rome were awash with prostitutes. All that you required to be a good man while on this earth was to be a good citizen, and that required not the threat of a vindictive or vengeful deity but merely calculated self-interest.[54] It was an argument that made such an impact on Benjamin Franklin (Voltaire's brother in the Masonic lodge Les Trois Soeurs) that he wrote a series of articles in *The Pennsylvania Gazette* in defense of Bayle's thesis. The new United States, the world's first expressly secular political foundation, would, he hoped, demonstrate to the world at large that a society of unbelievers could be just as moral as a society of the devout.

Bayle's attempt to detach moral behavior from religion would continue to exercise a lasting fascination for the writers of the Enlightenment. Voltaire, although he found Bayle's writings long-winded and rejected his denial that there was any teleology in human history, said of him that he was "the greatest of the dialecticians who ever lived."[55] Leibniz called him "one of the most gifted men of our time, whose eloquence was as great as his acumen." David Hume lifted much of his argument against what he called Spinoza's "hideous hypothesis" that "there is only one substance . . . in the world; and that substance is perfectly simple and indivisible, and exists everywhere, without any local presence," from Bayle's *Dictionary*.[56] The physician Lucien Offray de la Mettrie, probably the most celebrated atheist of the day, was merely paraphrasing Bayle when he claimed that he did not, in fact, deny the existence of a "supreme being" but "as this existence does not prove the need for one religion any more than another, it is a theoretical truth which serves very little practical purpose. Since we can say after so much experience that religion does not imply perfect honesty, the same reasons allow us to think that atheism does not preclude it."[57] Religion, he concluded, was "only necessary for those who are incapable of feeling humanity."[58] So long as society was composed of truly civil beings, it was unlikely to require any kind of divine constraint, once the initial phase of barbarism was passed. After all, as he pointed out, it was not generally atheists who committed the worst atrocities against their fellow men but, as the Wars of Religion had amply demonstrated, devout religious believers of one persuasion or another. Spinoza, for instance, "the noblest and most loveable of the great philosophers," as Bertrand Russell called him, was the living proof of Bayle's point.[59] He had not only been an atheist, he had even taught atheism, yet he had taken no part in the "juridical assassination" of Jan van Barneveldt, Grand Pensionary of Holland, who in 1619 had been executed by Calvinist extremists, and "it was not he who tore the two de Witt brothers to pieces and then grilled and ate them." Mankind did not need the illusion that there existed a god—of any kind—who either watched over them or had provided for their use and benefit a naturally beneficent order. Neither did they need his rules and codes of conduct to assure their good behavior. The injunctions to be found in divine decree were in any case, insofar as they were of any significant value, also perfectly obvious to any truly civil persons. As the Roman emperor Julian "the Apostate" in the fourth century had asked the Christians, "Except for the commandment 'Thou shalt not worship other gods' and 'Remember the Sabbath day,' what nation is there which does *NOT* think it ought to keep the other commandments?"[60]

All that existed in the world, in particular all that was needed to live a decent, honest life, was wholly transparent to all humankind. The idea of a god like the Judeo-Christian one, who claimed that he had entrusted forms of knowledge that we all require for our survival and salvation to one tribe or, worse, to one man, who had in turn handed that over to a factious and secretive clerisy, could only be a tyrant. In Voltaire's short story "The Naïf" (*L'Ingénu*), a Canadian Indian is washed ashore on the coast of France; after having inadvertently violated the law, he winds up in a prison cell with a Jansenist called "Gordon," who painstakingly explains to him all the intricacies of the Christian faith and the squabbles among its various sects. "Stop," cries the astonished and increasingly indignant Indian, "it is an absurdity, an outrage to the human race, an assault on the infinite and Supreme Being, to say: 'there exists a truth which is essential for man and God has hidden it!' "[61] As D'Alembert remarked in a similar vein, the more we became aware of the existence of some kind of creator, by contemplating how remarkable we are, the more inexcusable it became to go searching for it in "the minute and trivial objects" of the kind of ritual observance that traditional religions demanded of their adherents.[62]

Voltaire was angry and irreverent and not infrequently extreme. Many of the major figures of the Enlightenment were inevitably more moderate, more cautious in their rejection of all social conventions based, directly or indirectly, on religion. Charles de Secondat, Baron de Montesquieu, although he claimed that it required only "the least reflection" for one to be cured of the atheism proposed by Pierre Bayle and was inclined to be more sympathetic to Christianity than many of the *philosophes,* nevertheless insisted that all one could ever know about the deity was that "he is an intelligent being who produced the order which we see in the world."[63] And he looked with horror upon the stultifying emptiness of conventional religion, of whatever kind, which he regarded as the main source of human fear, mistrust, and sexual misery—and which merely mirrored the prejudiced view of the world held by the believer.

Rousseau, whom Diderot once bitingly described as the most "honorable of the men of letters because of his supposed probity, the most dangerous because of his eloquence, the most adroit in his acts of vengeance, the most redoubtable in the multitude of his enthusiasms," sometimes comes across as an unsteady Calvinist.[64] But he seems to have been more attracted by Calvinism's social implications than by its theology, and if the scathing letter he wrote to Voltaire after reading his poem on the Lisbon earthquake is anything to go by, he certainly accepted Leibniz's optimism, at least as he believed it to apply to himself. He was undoubtedly more "religious" (as he himself said) than most of his "fellow *philosophes*." "I am," he told the archbishop of Paris, Christophe de Beaumont, with what he modestly described as "my customary frankness," "a Christian, and sincerely Christian, according to the doctrine of the Gospel." But he went on, perhaps incautiously: "I am a Christian not as a disciple of priests, but of Jesus Christ."[65] It was perhaps this disrespect for priests that led to the condemnation and burning of his treatise on education, *Émile*—a book, wrote D'Alembert, "filled with insights and smoke, with warmth and puerile details, with enlightenment and contradictions; in some places the work of a first-rate author, in others that of a child"—and his flight into exile to avoid imprisonment.[66] Since he was also passionately vindictive and was in later life burdened by an intense persecution complex, he harbored an insistent paranoid belief in the existence of an afterlife in which his enemies and detractors, real and imaginary, would be punished and he would receive his just reward. "Had I no other proof of the immortality of the soul," he wrote, "than the triumph of the wicked and the oppression of the just, then that alone would prevent me from doubting it."[67]

Diderot, although he may perhaps never quite have shed his belief in some kind of deity, had no belief in the Christian version and had very little time for Christian morality. It was not that the moral code to be found in the Gospels was in itself wrong—although clearly much of it was, in particular the parts that applied to such private matters as sexual behavior—it was that, "instead of enlightening, it offered an infinite multitude of obscurities and difficulties." Compared with what he called "natural religion," something any honest and virtuous person can grasp through reason alone, "Christianity is . . . nothing but an added burden, and thus no longer a blessing; it is indeed a difficult means of doing something which [by natural means] can be achieved very easily." It was also the case, as he pointed out, that whereas all the existing forms of religion had quite precise beginnings, "natural religion" had no recorded beginning, and thus "it will not end when all the others have passed away."[68] (Alas, however, there is no evidence that he ever said "Let us strangle the last king with the guts of the last priest." The saying seems to have been attributed to him in 1840, long after his death, by the reactionary literary historian Jean-François de La Harpe.) "Natural religion" was, on the most minimal account, "the knowledge of essential truths and the practice of important duties." It was, in other words, a form of Stoic wisdom grounded in the "sentimental" attachment that all human beings have for one another. It is all we require to lead good and useful lives, and it "leaves nothing essential or necessary to be provided by revelation."[69]

V

For all that the Enlightenment's onslaught on religion had banished any notion of a benign and caring deity or of a divine and omnipotent judge, there were, nonetheless, very few who were prepared to contemplate Smith's "fatherless world" entirely without flinching. David Hume, however, was certainly one of them. Although he often tried to hide the fact so as to protect himself from "the rage of both civil and religious factions," he was the most adamant, most concise, and most persuasive denier of the truth of any kind of religion and religiosity—those "sick men's dreams," as he called them—and he certainly believed in no kind of deity, rational or otherwise.[70] Yet even he doubted the existence of outright "atheists," those, that is, who believed only in the existence of pure matter, pure chance. According to Diderot, who was present at the time, once when Hume was at dinner with Holbach at his home in the rue Royale in Paris he voiced this doubt to his host. The baron gestured to his assembled guests. "Count how many we are here," he remarked (there were eighteen). "It is not too bad to be able to point out to you fifteen at once. The other three have yet to make up their minds."[71]

Holbach—who coined the term *anthropomorphism* to describe the tendency of humans to create gods in their own image—a self-styled materialist and a renowned opponent of the Church, was unusual in his vehemence. Wealthy, witty, and learned, he had dedicated most of his life and a considerable portion of his private fortune to publishing anonymous or pseudonymous publications aimed at dismantling all forms of religious belief. He was also host to probably the most popular salon in Paris and was known affectionately as "the leading *maître d'hôtel* of philosophy." The baron, observed André Morellet, economist, sardonic wit, and a frequent visitor, held "two dinner parties each week for ten, twelve, fifteen, or even twenty, men of letters, men of the world, men from other countries, and men who loved and cultivated the things of the mind" (but always men)—the "sheiks in the rue Royale," Hume called them—and among them all "there was plenty of good simple food, excellent wine and coffee, abundant discussion and never a quarrel."[72] The guests included Hume and Diderot; the diplomat, cultural critic, and tireless letter writer Friedrich Melchior von Grimm; D'Alembert and Rousseau; the historian Guillaume-Thomas-François Raynal; the arch-materialist and Diderot's intellectual opponent Claude-Adrien Helvétius; as well as, from time to time, Edward Gibbon, Adam Smith, Benjamin Franklin, Laurence Sterne, the chemist Joseph Priestley, and the Milanese utilitarian Cesare Beccaria. Rousseau, although he inevitably fell out with the baron and his coterie, as he did with everyone he ever met, drew on Holbach in his sentimental novel *Julie, or The New Héloïse,* as the model for Womar, an atheist who nevertheless embodies all the Christian virtues.

As Hume, Diderot, and Montesquieu all admitted, real atheists were hard to come by, even in Paris. (Alas, Diderot did not reveal the names of the fifteen.) But it is always difficult to know how much the denial of the possibility of true atheism in the mouths of such otherwise ardent enemies of religion as Voltaire is only a ploy, a defense against the forces of states whose very legitimacy depended on the alliance between king and God. Nearly every French intellectual had been censored or driven to publish his writings abroad or compelled to hide behind a pseudonym or had seen his books burned by the public executioner;

many had served time in prison for their views or, like both Voltaire and Rousseau, had found it prudent to flee the country. In his later years Voltaire went so far as to acquire a home at Ferney on the Franco-Swiss border, which would have allowed him, if need arose, to take refuge in Geneva at the first sign of trouble. D'Alembert—whom Hume called a "model of *virtuous* and *philosophical* character" and to whom he left £200, a not inconsiderable sum at the time, in his will—remained unrepentant and in Paris until the end and was rewarded for his impiety by being buried in an unmarked grave.[73]

If Hume continued to have his doubts after leaving Holbach's dining room and never once declared himself to be an atheist, it is very hard to see him as anything else. As he apparently told James Boswell shortly before his death, he had "never entertained any belief in religion" since, as a young man, he had begun to read Locke and the Christian rationalist Samuel Clarke—of whom it was said that no one had doubted God's existence until he had tried to prove it.[74] Boswell, gossipy and curious, visited Hume as he lay dying, convinced that, at the end, simple fear if nothing else would drive him into the awaiting arms of the deity. "I had," he wrote, "a strong curiosity to be satisfied if he persisted in disbelieving in a future state even when he had death before his eyes." He came away disappointed: "I was persuaded from what he now said, and from his manner of saying it that he did persist."

Some historians have argued that, leaving Hume aside, there was a profound difference, at least as far as religious belief and observance were concerned, between Britain and almost all of continental Europe. The English, despite having provided the Enlightenment with some of its most radical precursors—Bacon, Locke, Hobbes, Newton—are said to have taken a much more cautious view of the intellectual upheavals of the following century and to have been generally much less willing to shed their religious beliefs.[75] Edmund Burke's assertion that, unlike the revolutionary French, "ninety-nine in a hundred of the people in England" would prefer any of the "rust of superstition, with which the accumulated absurdity of the human kind might have crusted it over in the course of ages," to any brand of "impiety," was certainly exaggerated—most of what Burke had to say on religion was—but not entirely false.[76] Anglicanism, which was not as rusted over with superstition as Catholicism, at least in the opinion of its adherents, was, when compared with any of its Christian competitors, a moderate, tolerant faith and was never the threat to freedom of thought and conscience that Catholicism or Calvinism was throughout most of continental Europe. Hume may have been genuinely concerned, as he told Edward Gibbon, that "the prevalence of superstition in England" was likely to bring about the "fall of philosophy and the decay of taste."[77] But the Scottish divines who succeeded in preventing him from holding a chair in moral philosophy at the University of Edinburgh could not put him behind bars.

Between 1726 and 1728 Voltaire spent two years in virtual exile in England, following a conflict with the Chevalier de Rohan-Chabot and a characteristic miscarriage of *ancien régime* justice. (This episode led to Ezra Pound's quip that Samuel Johnson had been the most intelligent man in England in the eighteenth century, except "for the two years when Voltaire was there.") During that time he wrote a series of reflections on English life in letter form, which were first published in English in 1733 as *Philosophical Letters*. England, he noted, was "the land of sects." Yet: "An Englishman, as a free man, may go to Heaven by whatever road he chooses."[78] Anglicanism and Presbyterianism—"which is nothing but pure Calvinism as it was established in France and now exists in Geneva"—were the dominant sects. "But all the others are welcome and live well enough together, while most of their preachers detest each other with as much cordiality as a Jansenist damns a Jesuit." As this was a land where commerce had triumphed over fanaticism, the best place to witness the taming of religious strife was the Stock Exchange. "Enter the Stock Exchange in London," he wrote,

> a more respectable place than most courts, and there you will find gathered together representatives of all nations for the utility of mankind. The Jew, the Muslim and Christian treat each other as if they belonged to the same religion, and reserve the term "infidel" for bankrupts. The Presbyterian trusts the Anabaptist, the Anglican accepts the promises of the Quaker. On leaving these peaceful

> and free gatherings, some go to the synagogue, while others go drinking; one goes to be baptised in a great basin in the name of the Father, the Spirit and the Holy Ghost, another cuts off the foreskin of his son and mumbles over the infant words in Hebrew he does not understand, while a third goes to Church to await inspiration from God, with his hat on his head. And all are content.[79]

This greater tolerance, the presence of a cacophony of competing sects, made Christianity seem a less menacing intellectual presence than it was on the other side of the Channel. There were those in Britain, as there were throughout Europe, who might have declared themselves to be "enlightened" and yet at the same time loyal, if also sometimes heterodox, followers of some version of Christianity. The historian Edward Gibbon, after a lightning conversion to Catholicism and back again, remained for most of the rest of his life a staunch Anglican; so (probably) was Adam Smith's follower John Millar. So too were Lord Kames and the highly eccentric James Burnett, Lord Monboddo, who believed in the possible existence of human societies without speech and was convinced that somewhere in the world there must exist men with tails. Even Hume lacked the vehemence of his Parisian friends, who, in his view, sometimes "preached the tenets of atheism with the bigotry of dogmatists." It is unlikely, however, that there were many more of the truly devout among the intellectual elite in Britain than elsewhere in Europe or even America. "The Christian religion is almost extinguished throughout the whole of England," Diderot told his sometime mistress and lifelong correspondent Sophie Volland in October 1765 (admittedly on the somewhat biased evidence of Holbach, who had lived in London).[80] Even if he was referring only to the educated and enlightened elite, he was being unduly optimistic. But if, as he admitted, few of the English were outright atheists and those few "keep themselves hidden," the deists "were numberless." There was, too, in the British attitude toward religion a strong element of what Adam Smith called "prudence." A prudent man, Smith wrote, although "always sincere," is nevertheless not "always frank and open; and although he never tells any thing but the truth, he does not always think himself bound, when properly called upon, to tell the whole truth." Condorcet, who is said to have once remarked, "As for religion, I advise that we not speak about it," might have agreed with him.

The prudent man is either a mediocre hypocrite or the perfect English gentleman—depending on your taste—and, in Smith's view at least, much to be preferred to those

> of much more splendid talents and virtues; who, in all ages from that of Socrates and Aristippus to that of Dr. [Jonathan] Swift and Voltaire, and from that of Philip [of Macedon] and Alexander the Great, down to that of the great Czar Peter of Muscovy, [who] have too often distinguished themselves by their improper and even insolent contempt of the ordinary decorums of life and conversation.[81]

Such moderate caution, however, was more easily observed in London or Edinburgh than in Catholic Europe or Calvinist Geneva, with the ever-watchful eyes of the thought police fixed firmly on everyone. Even in Britain, however, most of the enlightened lived under constant suspicion. For all his prudence, Smith was accused of having said of Voltaire that he had done "more for the benefit of mankind than those grave philosophers whose books are read by a few only"; to have been, more plausibly, "not a Christian"; and since, in the minds of many, atheism and political radicalism were inseparable, to have "approached republicanism in his political principles." He was even, and most improbably, said to have spoken of Rousseau "with a kind of religious respect."[82]

On the whole, though, devout Christians—as distinct from those who merely kept up appearances for the sake of politeness—were looked upon with feelings that ranged from mild contempt to outright hostility. Smith once remarked of the cantankerous, obese, arch-conservative Samuel Johnson, a man he believed to be lacking in the "ordinary decorums of life and conversation": "I have seen that creature bolt up in the midst of mixed company; and without any previous notice fall on his knees behind a chair, repeat the Lord's Prayer and then return to his seat at table. . . . It is not hypocrisy, it is madness."[83]

Like most Enlightenment thinkers, however, what Smith most feared from religion was the real damage that could be inflicted by claims to private and personal inspiration. In the eighteenth century this was sometimes—although the word has many shades of meaning—called "enthusiasm," defined by Johnson in his famous *Dictionary* as "a vain belief of private revelation, a vain confidence of divine favour or communication."[84] It was, said Hume, a kind of frenzy in which "the fanatic madman delivers himself over, blindly and without reserve, to the supposed lapses of the spirit, and to inspiration from above."[85] The Christian martyrs so loathed by Montaigne had, in Shaftesbury's opinion, been just such creatures. It had, he wrote, been "more the misfortune indeed of mankind in general than of Christians in particular that some of the earlier Roman emperors were such monsters of tyranny," that they had unleashed a ferocious and bloody war of attrition "not on religious men merely, but on all who were suspected of worth or virtue." The joyous self-aggrandizing abnegation with which this had been greeted by its victims had tarnished the reputation of what was otherwise a respectful and politically compliant creed. Those times had now passed, and, thankfully, there was, "hardly now in the world so good a Christian . . . Who, if he happened to live at Constantinople or elsewhere under the protection of the Turks, would think it fitting or decent to give any disturbance to their mosque worship." Similarly, any "good Protestant" would consider anyone who would, "out of hatred of Romish idolatry," interrupt the priest during High Mass "with clamours or fall foul of his images and relics," no better than a "rank enthusiast."

But if good Christians no longer indulged in such behavior, there were many who were not so good who did. For its capacity to drive its adherents to commit the most atrocious crimes in its name made religion not merely foolish, unnecessary, and a delusion—it also made it, as centuries of internecine fighting had vividly demonstrated, highly destructive. Shaftesbury had seen in this brand of "enthusiasm," together with "superstition," the source of what he identified as "panic," named after the Greek god Pan, a deity who worked on the imagination and the groundless fears of his enemies, and who "is raised in a multitude and conveyed by aspect, or, as it were, by contact and sympathy." Panic was enthusiasm reinforced by the apparent inclination of all believers to insist that their assumptions about the Almighty and his wishes are the only true ones, and the rest not merely false but also sufficiently dangerous to deserve the kind of horrors that the organized churches of the world have inflicted upon their critics. This, which Shaftesbury called the "melancholy way of treating religion," was "that which according to my apprehension renders it so tragic and is the occasion of its acting in reality such dismal tragedies in the world." The only effective weapon against fanaticism was, in Shaftesbury's view, "pleasantness and good manners." This was a far more potent weapon than any "solemn attack." For this reason, if the world is to be rid of religious enthusiasts, "we can never use too much good humour or examine it [religion] with too much freedom and familiarity."[86] Shaftesbury was perhaps overly sanguine in his confidence that a good measure of politeness and quiet irony would finally see off most religious fanaticism. Beyond the drawing rooms of Whig London and the salons of Paris, much of Europe, let alone the rest of the world, even in the middle of the eighteenth century, was as riven with religious hatreds as it had ever been.

Across the ocean, in the nascent United States, religion was both more pervasive and of more social importance than it was perhaps anywhere in Europe—and it has remained so. As Alexis de Tocqueville had seen, religion in a truly democratic society was a necessary counterpart to "freedom," an effective device, as it had been in antiquity, that prevents the *demos* from "conceiving everything and forbids them to dare everything." It was also, or so he believed, a way of providing some kind of social cohesion in a society that, as he experienced it, was composed largely of isolated individuals. Tocqueville is duly respectful of Christian dogma, but he still sees it, as he saw all religions, as essentially civil. Its theological content was immaterial, as was its plausibility. Its purpose was to unite and constrain the always unstable and unpredictable *demos*.[87] Most of the founders of the United States, however, did not believe that they required any such limits to their own actions. They were unwilling to accept any kind of religion in which the deity played any direct role in human affairs, still less one that maintained that the only possible knowledge of humanity was to be found in a scripture and regulated by a clergy. Thomas Jefferson looked upon Jesus as a latter-day Socrates and as a Jewish "reformer," a "master workman," but also as one whose disciples "have disfigured and sophisticated his actions and precepts, from views of personal interests, so as to induce the thinking part of mankind to throw off the whole system in disgust."[88] Even John Adams, although in most other respects a devout Puritan, thought that the argument for Christ's divinity was an "awful blasphemy" in the "Enlightened age" in which he lived.[89]

Although it is perhaps true that very few educated people in the eighteenth century would have called themselves "atheists"—Holbach's guests were clearly exceptional—many were certain that if religion had any role to play in human life, it could only be limited to a very narrow private sphere. All religions, however seemingly insane, could be tolerated as long as their adherents kept to themselves and their beliefs had no social or political implications. "It does me no injury," wrote Jefferson in his *Notes on the State of Virginia,* "for my neighbour to say there are twenty gods, or no god. It neither picks my pocket nor breaks my leg." Jefferson was certainly no atheist or even a "French infidel," as he was frequently accused of being. His point was that belief played no role in the constitution of the state, that the "legitimate powers of government extend to such acts only as are injurious to others." It had been the Roman policy of permitting "free enquiry" that had ensured the very survival of Christianity, and it had been free inquiry that had given rise to the Reformation, which had "purged away" the corruptions of the Church. If the new United States failed to follow the same policy, "the present corruptions will be protected, and new ones encouraged."[90]

VI

Of course, not everyone saw it this way. A private religion might well turn out to be an impossible delusion. Sooner or later, most religious beliefs inevitably became matters of public concern. Could a Christian or a Muslim (or a even a Jew) quietly accept that others not merely rejected his (or her) view of how the cosmos worked, of how human beings ought to live their lives, but denied the entire premise on which those convictions were based, and still remain silent? Would he not, as had always in fact been the case in the past, seize every means, every opportunity to impose his creed upon the unbelievers and, if given the power, force his vision for humanity upon them? One of those who believed very firmly that the answer to all such questions could only be a resounding "yes" was La Mettrie. It must be said that La Mettrie did not give atheism a good name. He had a reputation for loose living and gluttony; was once said to have declared, only half jokingly, "you are what you eat"; was unduly sycophantic toward Frederick the Great, the ruler of Prussia, who had himself written a rather wooden "Poem on the Inexistence of God"; and was rumored to have died—exploded almost—at the French ambassador's table in Berlin, from an excess of *pâté de faisan aux truffes*.[91] He was, said Frederick, who delivered his funeral oration, "a good devil, a good doctor, and a very bad author." And it was not only the pious who detested him. "Dissolute, impudent, a buffoon, and a flatterer," Diderot called him, and "made for the life at court and the favors of the great. He died as he deserved, victim of his intemperance and his folly; he killed himself by the ignorance of all that he professed."[92] All that he professed included the commandments: "We shall be all body and ignore our souls. We shall not try to control what rules us. We shall not give orders to our sensations. We shall recognize their dominion and our slavery, convinced as we are that happiness in life lies there."[93] La Mettrie was a materialist—with the possible exception of Holbach, the most ardent materialist of the eighteenth century—whose objective was to demonstrate, on the basis of all he had learned as a doctor from direct encounter with the "guts of man and animals," that in every significant respect there was no real difference between humans and other animals. *The Natural History of the Soul,* published in 1745, had suggested, as Spinoza had done, though with rather less precision and in a language borrowed from contemporary medicine, that the "soul" was indistinguishable from the stuff of which the body was made. The title alone was inflammatory enough, since the soul (although the French word *âme* could also be understood to mean "spirit" or "mind"), because for the Christians it was immortal, could have no history. The book was immediately condemned to be burned by the public executioner, and La Mettrie fled to Holland. Today he is best remembered for a brief treatise called *Man a Machine,* published two years later. The title is an allusion to Descartes's famous distinction between humans—possessed of rational, if not immortal, souls—and all other animals, which Descartes had said were nothing more than animated machines. For La Mettrie, however, humans were no less mechanical than the supposedly "lesser animals"; all that distinguished them from brutes was a higher degree of competence that had been acquired over time. La Mettrie's evolutionism was not entirely new. But it was blunt, explicit, incautious, and deeply shocking. So, too, was his onslaught upon theology and the theologians.

What, however, made the book truly menacing was the way in which it turned Bayle's argument on its head. Bayle, as we saw, had claimed only that a society of atheists could be a perfectly virtuous one. La Mettrie argued that *only* a society of atheists, in which there was no taint of religion of any kind, could be a virtuous, and consequently happy, one. Like Mandeville, he assumed "virtue" to be an elaborate form of hypocrisy, potentially damaging and "foreign to the nature of our being," a mere device for holding the political community together. He was prepared to accept that some people clearly did get pleasure from being virtuous, but that was merely because it flattered their vanity, and there could be no significant difference between them and those who derived pleasure from being conventionally wicked.[94] "In a century as enlightened as ours," he declared emphatically, "it has finally been demonstrated . . . that there is only one life and only one happiness," and that is here on Earth. Only a world from which the "sacred poison" of religion and the cant of virtuousness had been thoroughly eliminated could ever hope to achieve that happiness. Only then would there be no more theological wars of the kind that had torn Europe apart in the preceding century and no more "soldiers of religion."

For the new "human scientists," the ultimate questions were whether the Christian, or any other, God could be known and whether through that knowledge it was possible to come to an understanding of what was always the main object of study, humankind. And here the universal answer was "no." Any idea of a deity, private or public, was inconsistent with any kind of true science—"science" as we understand it today and as it had come to be understood in the eighteenth century. As D'Alembert argued, the fact that we cannot prove the existence of Caesar by geometry does not mean that he did not exist. What, however, it does mean is that any properties that any god might be supposed to possess—unlike those attributed to Caesar—can have no place in any attempt to understand the operations of the human, or the natural, world.[95]

VII

Most of the attacks against religion in general, and Christianity in particular, had taken the form either of mockery of the stories on which it was based or a condemnation of the uses to which it had been put and the murderous consequences to which it had so often led. Few, however, had seriously addressed the defects in the fundamental tenets on which it was based. One of those who had was David Hume. Hume may have believed that the atheist "is only nominally so, and can never possibly be in earnest" (or he may only have said so in order to ward off his clerical critics). He also frequently alludes to "true religion," although this generally seems to mean little more than the practice of virtue, justice, and humanity, something that could plausibly be attributed to at least some portions of Jesus' teaching, although it could also just as easily be attributed to Socrates or Confucius.[96] For the most part, however, his onslaught on religion (and he wrote more about religion than on any other single topic except history) is the most sustained, and ultimately damning, of the entire century.[97] He was also keenly aware of how central the demonstration of the falsity of conventional religious beliefs was to his entire philosophical project. According to Adam Smith, as Hume lay dying he jokingly imagined what excuses he might offer Charon for allowing him a few more days on Earth. Having failed to persuade the ferryman of the Styx that he needed more time to revise his works for the public, he then, as a final plea asks him for a "a little patience," for:

> "I have been endeavouring to open the eyes of the public. If I live a few years longer, I may have the satisfaction of seeing the downfall of some of the prevailing systems of superstition." But Charon would then lose all temper and decency. "You loitering rogue, that will not happen these many hundred years. Do you fancy I will grant you a lease for so long a term? Get into the boat this instant, you lazy loitering rogue."[98]

Hume's target was not, however, as Voltaire and Diderot's had been, the demands that the Church made on faith. Ever since Aquinas, Catholic theologians had insisted that not only was the existence of some Supreme Being guaranteed by revelation, but that the truth of that revelation was fully in accordance with natural reasoning, to the extent that all non-Christians, if only they were sufficiently rational, could come to a fully "natural" understanding of the message of the Gospels. They could not, of course, have any knowledge of, nor share in, the benefits to be had from Christ's Passion, but in all other respects they were, so to speak, honorary Christians. Such people were often known as the "virtuous pagans," and they included among their number Socrates, Aristotle, Virgil, Cicero, and Seneca. For this reason, Dante (who was an enthusiastic Thomist), in his great poem *The Divine Comedy,* had placed them all—along with a number of more recent figures, including the great Muslim philosophers and scientists Abû al-Walîd Muhammad ibn Rushd ("Averroës") and Ibn Sînâ ("Avicenna")—in Limbo rather than in Hell. The fifteenth-century Italian humanist Marsilio Ficino even went so far to speak of "Holy Socrates" and, in what came close to being a parody of the Lord's Prayer, wrote, *Sancta Socrates ora pro nobis*" ("Holy Socrates, pray for us")—a phrase later repeated by Erasmus.

In the seventeenth and eighteenth centuries, as religion came more and more under attack, a stream of works began to appear with titles such as *The Obligations of Natural Religion, and the Truth and Certainty of the Christian Revelation,* and *Philosophical Principles of Natural Religion.* All of these were attempts to buttress the argument that there could be no essential conflict between religion and a rational, empirical understanding of the world—no conflict, in other words, between religion and science.

This was Hume's main concern. Voltaire and Diderot, even Holbach and Condorcet for the most part had only scoffed. Hume scoffed, too, but he also argued, and he argued to such good effect that, in his view at least, his arguments would be an "everlasting check to all kinds of superstitious delusion, and consequently will be useful as long as the world endures."[99] His first target was the fact that, no matter how rational it might claim its understanding of God to be, the Christian religion not only endorsed a series of miracles performed by Jesus—the resurrection of Lazarus, the multiplication of the loaves and fishes, the marriage at Cana, and so on—it was itself also founded upon a miracle: the resurrection of Christ. No amount of rationalizing could get around that, and no one who did not accept the resurrection as a historical fact could possibly claim to be a Christian.

Hume's struggle with the underlying principles of Christianity had begun when he was in his early twenties, in the village of La Flèche in Anjou. Hume had gone there in order, he said, to "maintain unimpaired my Independence and to regard every object as contemptible, except the Movement of my Talents in Literature." He remained there for the better part of three years. For a man who was already deeply skeptical about any conventional religious beliefs and one who would become perhaps the best-known unbeliever of the century, La Flèche was in some respects a curious place to choose, for the only thing that distinguished it from any other hamlet in the valley of the Loire was its Jesuit college, the Collège Royal Henry-Le-Grand, where both Descartes—who called it "one of the most famous schools in Europe"—and the philosopher and Minim friar Marin Mersenne had studied a century before. There, in the shadow of the castle overlooking "a great extent of fields and buildings," Hume had read French and other continental authors, especially the Oratorian philosopher Nicolas Malebranche, who had tried to reconcile Cartesian rationalism with Augustinian Christianity; the historian Jean-Baptiste Dubos; and Pierre Bayle. Later he recalled having gotten into an argument—by all accounts in fluent, if heavily accented, French—with one Jesuit, "of some parts and learning," over "some nonsensical miracle performed in their convent." The argument with which Hume "very much graveled" his opponent was the one he would use later in the tenth section, "On Miracles," of *An Enquiry Concerning Human Understanding* of 1748. The Jesuit observed that Hume's argument would work just as well against the Gospels themselves, in the belief, apparently, that that alone must count as a refutation. To which Hume responded laconically, "I thought proper to admit [this] as a sufficient answer."[100]

The argument goes like this. Reason always acts upon experience. However, there exist two kinds of experience: that which is certain, in the sense that there has been no known exception—the claim, for instance, that every living being will die—and that which is merely probable—that, for instance, in the northern hemisphere it is warmer in June than in December. In both cases we are drawing inferences from past experience. A cold June is perfectly in keeping with my own experience and the meteorological record—particularly if I live in Scotland. But if a dead man were to come to life, it would be contrary to all known forms of experience, "because that has never been observed in any age or country."[101] Now, miracles, because they are, by definition, transgressions of "a law of nature by a particular volition of the Deity," can only ever rely upon hearsay. And in this case the hearsay is, on internal evidence alone, deeply unreliable. Having first assured his readers that his target is not Christianity itself but those "dangerous friends, or disguised enemies of the Christian religion, who have undertaken to defend it by principles of human reason," in a passage of thinly veiled invective Hume launched into this description of the Old Testament:

> Here then we are first to consider a book, presented to us by a barbarous and ignorant people, written in an age when they were still more barbarous, and in all probability long after the facts

> which it relates, corroborated by no concurring testimony, and resembling those fabulous accounts, which every nation gives of its origin. Upon reading this book, we find it full of prodigies and miracles. It gives an account of a state of the world and of human nature entirely different from the present: Of our fall from that state: Of the age of man extended to near a thousand years; of the destruction of the world by a deluge: Of the arbitrary choice of one people, as the favourites of heaven; and that people the countrymen of the author: Of their deliverance from bondage by prodigies the most astonishing imaginable.

"I desire any one to lay his hand upon his heart," he concluded, "and after a serious consideration declare, whether he thinks that the falsehood of such a book, supported by such testimony, would be more extraordinary and miraculous than all the miracles it relates."

It was obvious that, when faced with such threadbare testimony as this, any attempt at a rational argument in defense of Christianity on the basis of miracles could only be a circular one. The only evidence for the truth of a revelation that defies all certain and probable experience is the revelation itself. And since that is to be found in a book filled with absurdities and written down by a remote Iron Age people who are themselves its intended beneficiaries, its veracity, Hume concluded sardonically, could only be accepted by one "conscious of a continued miracle in his own person which subverts all the principles of his understanding."[102] The same argument applied to prophecies, which for Hume were merely another kind of miracle. This demonstrated conclusively that "the truth of the Christian religion" is contrary to the "rules of just reasoning." The argument would, he believed, be "decisive" against all forms of miracles and "must at least silence the most arrogant bigotry and superstition."[103]

Having demolished any possible argument for divine intervention, Hume was left with the rather more troubling, because far more compelling, argument for design. This, which he calls the "the chief or sole argument for a divine existence," is the claim that the natural world is of such intricacy and coherence "that you think it extravagant to assign for its cause, either chance, or the blind and unguided force of nature."[104] It could, therefore, only be the creation of an intelligent being. The argument was considered to be very powerful in Hume's day, precisely because it was apparently entirely rational and, initially at least, avoided attributing any particular properties to the deity beyond supreme intelligence. Because it made no appeal to scripture, it served the needs of both Christians and theists, and it is still around in some places today, in a somewhat more attenuated version known as "intelligent design." To upset this idea, Diderot inserted into his *Letter on the Blind* of 1749 a fictional dialogue on the existence of God between Nicholas Saunderson, Lucasian Professor of Mathematics at Cambridge University from 1711 until his death in 1739, who had lost his sight due to smallpox at the age of 1, and a "very able minister," the Reverend Gervaise Holmes. With his usual gift for ventriloquism, Diderot claimed that only "a few fragments" of this exchange had survived and that he had merely set out to "translate [them] as best I can." Holmes begins by extolling the beauties of nature as proof of the existence of God. Saunderson, naturally, has never been able to see any of these. "If you want me to believe in God," he tells the minister, "you must make me touch him." Holmes tells him merely to touch his own person and he would see "the divinity in the admirable mechanism that are your organs." To this, Saunderson replies that they are "not so beautiful for me as they are for you." In any case, he fails to see how an "animal mechanism," no matter how beautiful, can be evidence of the existence of "a sovereign intelligence" at work in the world. Whenever we come up against something we do not understand, our response is to cry, "It's the work of God." It flatters our ego by making our ignorance universal. What humans required, in Saunderson's opinion, was "a little less arrogance and a little more philosophy." God is, in effect, an infinite regress. "When we come across a knot," says Saunderson, "which we cannot undo we should accept it for what it is, rather than turn to another being to untie it for us, whose existence thus presents us with another knot even more difficult to untie than the former." Ask an Indian why the world hangs in the air, and he will tell you that it is resting on the back of an elephant, and that the elephant is standing on a turtle. "But then, what is holding up the turtle? . . . You pity this Indian, but one could say to you, as to him: Mr. Holmes, my friend, confess your ignorance, and be so kind as not to inflict on me your own elephant and turtle."[105] It was this exchange more than anything else in the *Letter* that landed Diderot in prison at the Château de Vincennes. (He was released three months later on the intervention of Madame du Châtelet.)

Hume's deflation of the argument from design is similar to "Saunderson's." Like "Saunderson," he demonstrates that the argument from design is, in effect, circular. Once we abandon the idea that God has spoken directly to mankind through sacred texts and miracles, then all we are left with is what we can see of the world of nature itself. If we then suppose—as the Christians and the theists both did—that the proof of God's existence may be found in an examination of that world, and since there can be no place *outside* nature from which we can contemplate its existence, then all we are doing, in fact, is attributing to a God what we can actually see in the world.[106] Such a deity is what Hume, following Holbach, calls an "anthropomorphite." As Hume's mouthpiece the skeptic Philo, in his other great dissection of religious belief, *Dialogues Concerning Natural Religion* of 1751, points out, "We are led to infer by all the rules of analogy . . . that the Author of nature is somewhat similar to the mind of man; though possessed of much larger faculties, proportioned to the grandeur of the work which he has executed."[107] From this the believer, of whatever kind, then goes on to infer that God must be some grander, more intelligent, more powerful version of himself. Man, in other words, is not made in God's image; gods are always made in men's image. "The Apprehension of a universal Mind with power and knowledge," wrote Hutcheson, "is indeed an agreeable object of contemplation." But, he warned, "we form our idea of all intelligent natures with some resemblance or analogy with ourselves";[108] or, as Montesquieu said, speaking through the person of an imaginary Persian traveler named Rica: "When I see men creeping over an atom that is the earth which is merely a point in the universe, and immediately setting themselves up as models of Providence, I am unable to reconcile such extravagance with such smallness." From this he drew the famous observation that "if triangles had a god they would give him three sides."[109]

Furthermore, if we accept the presence of this original architect, or what Hume calls "intelligent principle," as the final cause of nature, then we are left with the task of explaining the existence of the architect himself, and so on. "Have we not the same reason," asks Philo, "to trace that ideal world [of the "Author of nature"] into another ideal world or new intelligent principle? But if we stop and go no farther; why go so far? Why not stop at the material world? How can we satisfy ourselves without going on *in infinitum*? After all what satisfaction is there in an infinite regression?"[110] If we ignore this advice and continue with the infinite regression, we will inevitably, as we are not ourselves infinite beings, find ourselves either throwing up our hands in despair or pleading, as all Christians ultimately must, not for a rational explanation of the universe but for faith. Do not question, just believe. And even if it were true that "there are few parts of the universe which seem not to serve some purpose, and the removal of which would not produce a visible defect and disorder in the whole"—and Hume is clear that even that is not consistently true—there would still be no obvious reason why random choice is not as good an explanation of the possible origin of what we see around us as some kind of designing power.[111] Is it not, after all, demands Philo, "as good sense to say, that the parts of the natural world fall into order of themselves, and by their own nature"?

There was another point. The presence, or otherwise, of an "intelligent principle" as the cause of the universe gets you nowhere unless you are then prepared to argue that that principle, architect, or designer has some kind of purpose. As Hume well knew, the real function of the argument from design was—and is—not to demonstrate the mere existence of an order in the world but to show that that order could only have been the work of the beneficent designer. A being, that is, with intent. This, however, was no more convincing than Leibniz's theodicy had been. For any supposition that the creator was in any way beneficent or had anything resembling morality on his (or her or its) mind when he created the universe was as directly contrary to our experience of the supposed creator's actual creation as miracles or divine decree. The same applied to the unverifiable claim that humans, unlike other animals, possessed a soul that was immortal, while our entire consciousness was limited to our short existence on this earth.

"What cruelty, what iniquity, what injustice in nature" could it be, Philo asks, "to confine thus all our concern, as well as all our knowledge, to the present life, if there be another scene still awaiting us, of infinitely greater consequence? Ought this barbarous deceit to be ascribed to a beneficent and wise being?" No, was the answer. It could be, in fact, nothing but a device dreamed up by those whose real purpose was "only to gain a livelihood and acquire power and riches in the world."[112]

In the end, as Philo protests, our entire experience of life, however we examine it, could point to only one possible, melancholy, conclusion: "The whole presents nothing but the idea of a blind nature, impregnated by a great vivifying principle and pouring forth from her lap, without discernment or parental care, her maimed and abortive children."

This brought Hume to the even more controversial argument on the relationship between religion and morality. For Hume, our moral life, our necessary willingness to respond to the "inclinations and sentiments," the desires and demands of others, is the natural outcome of the "sympathy" that all human beings possess by the simple virtue of their humanity. "Sympathy," as we have seen, is a passion; it is the urge to communicate and to "receive by communication" the "inclinations and sentiments of others," "however different from, or even contrary to our own" they might be.[113] As all human beings share a common nature, they all experience pleasure and pain in much the same way, and "we never remark any passion or principle in others of which, in some degree or other, we do not find a parallel in ourselves."[114] It would, therefore, seem obvious that all moral laws, and in particular all the laws of the state that serve to reinforce them, derive from a common understanding of what promotes happiness in general and what serves to avoid suffering. Moral laws, in Hume's view, can only be produced by human societies, not imposed upon them by a God who has dictated his wishes and intentions to us via some favored individual. The image of virtue, Hume maintained, is "our interested obligation," because our natural inclination to seek out "inward peace of mind, consciousness of integrity, a satisfactory review of our own conduct," together with our human desire to be loved and respected by those around us, make for a sufficient constraint upon our baser nature.[115] These things, since they all ultimately derive from "sympathy," are also passions and as such are the only source of human action. With these we have no need to fear the image of a vindictive father figure with a big stick and a vision of hell to keep us in line. "It is certain from experience," says Philo, "that the smallest grain of natural honesty and benevolence has more effect on men's conduct, than the most pompous views suggested by theological theories and systems."

For Hume, however, religion is not merely redundant, as it was for Bayle; it is positively malign. For religion tends to introduce into our natural human relationships, based as they are on a shared vision of happiness and misery, false conceptions of wickedness and equally false notions of good, or what Philo calls "the raising up of new frivolous species of merit," the creation of artificial crimes, and the "preposterous distribution which it makes of praise and blame."[116] Virtue is ascribed to such horrible practices as self-immolation and self-castigation. Hume, like Montaigne and Shaftesbury, looked upon Christian martyrdom as the Roman Stoics had done, with undisguised disgust. Similarly, the unthinking believer is all too happy to inflict pain and suffering on his fellow beings for crimes that are really only matters of personal conscience. One of these, and for Hume a crucial one, was suicide. The Christians had condemned suicide because their God had supposedly, in Hamlet's tortured words, "fixed his canon 'gainst self-slaughter." But there was nothing in the act itself that could possibly offend any rational conception of virtue. Hamlet, for all his introspection on other matters, here merely accepts as true something he has been told by someone claiming an authority superior to human reason. The threat of what might be awaiting us in that "undiscovered country, from whose bourn / No traveller returns" is likewise a fiction, another kind of miracle, conjured up to reinforce the power of the initial argument for God's omnipotence. But if we accept, with Hume, that morality is merely a question of usefulness to our fellow beings, then suicide cannot possibly be any kind of crime. For if a person chooses to take his own life, then "he does no harm to society." He only ceases to do good, "which if it be an injury is of the lowest kind." Furthermore, for someone who is, in some way, a burden to society, his leaving it "must not only be innocent but laudable."[117]

In the end, all that all the religions that had ever existed in the world seemed to have done for humans was to muddle, corrupt, and complicate their lives. They had brought not peace and morality and virtue, as their adherents claimed, but only turmoil, cruelty, and vice. As Philo triumphantly concluded, if the obvious rational arguments against the possible existence of a God were not enough, then we need only to consult the historical record: "If the religious spirit be ever mentioned in any historical narration, we are sure to meet afterwards with a detail of the miseries which attend to it. And no period of time can be happier or more prosperous, than those in which it is never heard of."[118]

Hume's demolition of religion was more assertive, better argued, more profound, and has been more long-lasting in its impact than that of any other philosopher besides Kant. But what Hume, unlike Kant, had done was to demonstrate that no religious belief could possibly exist—to use Kant's phrase—"within the limits of reason alone." Hume had shown that all the believer could now do was to seek refuge in feelings and unexamined subjective experiences, what in the eighteenth century came to be known as "pietism," the "feel-good" sentimentality and mass hysteria that informs so many of the varieties of religious belief that survive to this day. This departure of thought from religion into the realms of what he called "pure thinghood" had, complained Hegel, left only an emptiness, a "stain of unsatisfied longing."[119]

Hume was, however, fully prepared (or so he claimed) to acknowledge that "the whole frame of nature bespeaks an intelligent creator." Anything that resembled the worship of it could, however, only come from the blind surrender to "inspiration from above."[120] "Our most holy religion," he wrote, "is founded on *Faith* not on reason; and it is a sure method of exposing it to put it to such a trial as it is, by no means, fitted to endure."[121] (If he really believed this, one is tempted to ask, why had he himself done just that?) A similar position was taken at the end of the last century by the American paleontologist Stephen Jay Gould. He called it "non-overlapping magisteria," or NOMA. The idea is that science and religion constitute two quite distinct systems of knowledge—or "magisteria"—that operate by quite distinct rules of procedure.[122] On this account, it is perfectly possible to be a Christian *and* a rational empiricist. The two are simply incommensurable. Some within the Catholic and the Protestant churches have endorsed similar claims. These include the current pope, Benedict XVI, himself. But it is not a position that would have had much appeal to any of his predecessors, since it depends upon a statement, not an argument, and fails to explain how the same person is supposed to cross over from one "magisterium" to the other. In the end, as Hume half hints, to believe such a claim you have to be either very ignorant or very stupid—or, although Hume did not have that language, "bipolar."

In the eighteenth century, the suggestion that Christianity might be true even if it was utterly irrational was precisely what most churchmen did not want to hear. They did not wish to be told that their religion was effectively at odds with everything else they might know about themselves and the world around them—that it was, in effect, a form of rote observance and blind obedience. For all of that came dangerously close to being the mark not of a true religion—as they understood it—but of mere superstition, that "blind and terrified credulity," in Hume's own description, that had first driven mankind to concoct all manner of "ceremonies, observances, mortifications, sacrifices, presents" in order to appease imaginary beings, "unknown agents," whose "power and malevolence sets no limits."[123]

Not every enlightened thinker agreed with Hume, but most of those who still hoped to hang on to some vestige of the old system of beliefs would have accepted, as Hume himself somewhat disingenuously insisted, that if there was still a place for any kind of deity it could only be one of private devotion. This might even be an argument for the existence of theology, but it could never be confused with the new human sciences, any more than it should be with physics or astronomy.

The claims of Hume and Diderot, of D'Alembert and Voltaire, of Helvetius, Holbach, and Condorcet—to name only the most enduringly persuasive—had effectively discredited the idea that any kind of religious understanding might prove a true source of knowledge. "Those [studies] which pertain to revealed religion," said D'Alembert, were to be excluded from the domain of true knowledge, because, bound up as they were with the "ignorant subtlety of the barbarous centuries" and "concerned only with imaginary objects, speculations and disputes," they are absolutely foreign to the human sciences "by their object, by their character, and by the very species of conviction which they arouse in us." The "human sciences" are forms of knowledge that owe everything to observation, nothing to belief. Theology, by contrast, wrote D'Alembert, echoing Hume, owes everything to belief, to faith, which he defined, somewhat disingenuously, as "a species of sixth sense which the Creator grants or denies as he wills," and nothing to observation.[124] Even "natural religion" had no role to play in human understanding, other than to "warn us that it is in itself insufficient."[125]

Having thus wiped the slate clean of the very possibility that the natural world, and humanity's place within it, might be intelligible through revelation or any other species of religious experience, it still remained to be seen what form this new, purely *human* science would take.

4

THE SCIENCE OF MAN

I

THE NEW HUMAN SCIENTIST, the new enlightened man of learning, was a heroic figure. Free of prejudice, the burden of accumulated customs, and the slavish devotion to false beliefs, he was intellectual master of all he surveyed. D'Alembert imagined him meditating in his study:

> he assesses the men who have been placed on this earth, as witnesses, or judged as actors; he studies the moral universe as he does the physical, in the silence of prejudices; he follows the narratives of past writers with the same circumspection as he does the phenomena of nature; he observes the nuances which distinguish historical truth from historical probability, probability from fable. He recognizes the differing languages of simplicity, flattery, prevention, and hatred. . . . Enlightened by these rules which are as

> fine as they are certain, *it is mainly to understand the men amongst whom he lives, that he studies that which has been.*[1]

For D'Alembert, what he called "the great enigma of the world" was an immense labyrinth, from which we, who live within it, have no Ariadne's thread to guide us out. All we have are "pieces of a thread." The task of the human sciences is precisely to connect these pieces together so that they make what D'Alembert calls—mixing his metaphors—a single "chain of truths." This chain will allow us to emerge into a place from which the whole world, human and natural, will fall under a single gaze, "of which all the other truths would be nothing more than diverse translations."[2]

The urgent need for such a scientific understanding of "man" was not new. In 1683 Henri de Boulainvilliers, who had translated Spinoza's *Ethics* into French, had begun his treatise *On Man* with the claim that "the knowledge of ourselves is the most necessary and the most useful of the sciences we can acquire."[3] As yet, however, "man" was, he regretted, a relatively unknown quantity. Huge advances had been made in the seventeenth century in physics, astronomy, biology and anatomy, medicine, and chemistry. Human beings had learned more about how the world worked and the nature of the cosmos; they had traveled further and dug deeper in a hundred years than in all the previous two thousand. Yet they still knew precious little about themselves.

It became a frequently repeated and enduring complaint. "The most useful and yet the least advanced of all human knowledge," wrote Rousseau in 1754, in the preface to the *Discourse on the Origins of Inequality,* his own attempt to sketch a natural history of the human species, "seems to me to be that of man and I dare say that the inscription over the Temple at Delphi ["Know Thyself"] contains a precept which is more important and more difficult than all the weighty tomes of the moralists."[4] Yet of all the subjects of scientific inquiry, "man" remained, he lamented, the least studied. The eccentric Scot, Lord Kames—another of Hume's acquaintances—had much the same thought. "When we reflect on the different branches of human knowledge," he wrote in 1774, it might seem that of all the subjects human nature should be the best understood, precisely because "man" had ample opportunity in "his own passions and his own actions" to study it. But human nature, he added by way of a sobering understatement, although "an interesting subject, is seldom left to the investigation of philosophy."[5] This, then, was the project, and although D'Alembert was lyrical about what it might achieve for future generations, no one described it better, or more authoritatively, than his close friend David Hume.

In 1740 Hume published his *Treatise of Human Nature*. Like Locke's *Essay,* to which it owes rather more than a similarity in title, and Kant's *Critiques,* the *Treatise* is one of the works that changed the nature and the future direction of what we now call the philosophy of mind. Like many great and truly original thinkers, like Montesquieu—to whom we shall come shortly—and Giambattista Vico (who suggested that his readers could profitably spend their entire lives reading his *New Science*), Hume was fully aware of how important his work was. "My principles," he wrote, "are . . . so remote from all the vulgar Sentiments on this Subject, that were they to take place, they would produce almost a total Alteration in Philosophy."[6] In time that is very much what happened. At first, however, the *Treatise* failed to have the impact that its young author—he was barely twenty-six when he completed it—had hoped. It had, he wrote with characteristic self-irony, fallen "dead born from the press" and, he added wryly, "without reaching such distinction as even to excite a murmur from among the zealots."[7] Convinced that his failure had "proceeded more from the manner than the matter," he then "cast the first part of that work anew" in the *Enquiry Concerning Human Understanding*. This appeared in 1748, and was followed in 1751 by the *Enquiry Concerning the Principles of Morals,* which Hume believed to be "of all my writing, historical, philosophical or literary, incomparably the best." In his disappointment at the initial reaction to the *Treatise,* Hume was overstating the case. Despite his having, as he remarked, "castrated" the work by "cutting off its noble Parts,"[8] most significantly the essay "On Miracles," the *Treatise* certainly aroused sufficient murmurings among the bigots for them to deny its author the Chair of Ethics and Pneumatical Philosophy (Philosophy of Mind) at Edinburgh in 1745 and, six years later, the somewhat less controversial Chair of

Logic at Glasgow. He never tried again. The frontispiece of the *Treatise* carries a melancholy epithet from the Roman historian Tacitus: "Rare the happiness of times, when it is licit to think what you like and to say what you think." Like many of the great thinkers of continental Europe in the eighteenth century, with the exception of Kant, Hume never held any kind of academic post. (Not that that greatly concerned him. "There is nothing," he wrote in 1753, "to be learned from a Professor which is not to be met with in Books.")

At least in part because of this rejection, Hume became perhaps the first philosopher, essayist, or historian in Britain to earn a living from writing alone. For a brief period he was librarian to the Faculty of Advocates in Edinburgh, although he claims to have been paid little or nothing for his work and seems to have been dismissed for purchasing books that the Advocates deemed to be "improper." Later in life, like many of his contemporaries, he was granted a government pension, but for much of his career he lived from the sales of his books. This was no mean feat in an age before the introduction of royalties and copyright, when such a highly successful author as Rousseau could die in virtual poverty while his sentimental novel *Julie, or The New Héloïse,* was so popular that copies were being rented out by the hour.

Hume was always concerned—however disappointed he may have been in fact—that his works should reach the widest possible audience. The world, or at least what he called "the elegant part of Mankind, who are not immers'd in the animal Life," could, he believed, be divided into two groups: the "learned" and the "conversible"—by which he meant the average educated, intelligent, but nonspecialist reader. Alas, in the past all learning had been "shut up in Colleges and Cells, and secluded from the World and Good Company," and as a consequence "even philosophy" had gone "to wrack by this moping recluse method of study, and become as Chimerical in her Conclusions as she was unintelligible in her Stile and manner of Delivery." The "conversible," for their part, cut off from any more refined topics of conversation, found themselves reduced to "a continued Series of gossiping Stories and Idle Remarks." Hume's objective, then, was to bridge this gap, to create a "League betwixt the learned and conversible worlds."[9]

Neither the *Treatise* nor the *Enquiries* may have contributed very much to this enterprise. But they certainly reached well beyond the "Colleges and Cells." In December 1765 Diderot wrote to Sophie Volland telling her of how the Duc de Nivernais had gone to pay his respects to the Dauphin (the son of Louis XV), who was then on his deathbed "after a long and cruel infirmity whose pains he had suffered with a truly heroic resignation." The Dauphin was sitting up in bed and, much to the Duke's surprise, was reading "the philosophical works of Hume, works which you doubtless know and which are not renowned for their orthodoxy." The Dauphin had apparently told Hume himself that "the reading was most consoling to him, given the condition he was in."[10]

The Dauphin may have been a unique case, certainly among the members of the French royal family, but by the last decades of the century the *Treatise,* together with the two *Enquiries,* had become among the most widely read and influential philosophical works in Europe. It had been Hume, Kant said later, who "first interrupted my dogmatic slumber and gave my investigations in the field of speculative philosophy a quite new direction." That direction would lead him to the three great *Critiques,* which were to be his most enduring contribution to modern philosophy. When Jeremy Bentham, the father of Utilitarianism, read the *Treatise,* he felt, he recalled, "as if the scales had fallen from my eyes."[11] Kant may have been aroused to write what was to become the most powerful denunciation of empiricism ever written, and Bentham appears to have misunderstood Hume's concept of virtue. But for all that, Hume remains the single most influential proponent of a secular ethics based upon a "science of man" the Enlightenment ever produced.

For Hume, all science, even mathematics and "natural philosophy" (that is, what we today would call the natural sciences), because they "have a relation, greater or less, to human nature: and . . . are in some measure dependent on the science of Man." Instead, therefore, of "the tedious lingering method" of studying one segment of what was relevant to human nature at a time, which had only ever allowed us to take "now and then a castle or village on the frontier," the new human scientist would

> march up directly to the capital or centre of these sciences, to human nature itself; which being once masters of, we may every where else hope for an easy victory. From this station we may extend our conquests over all of those sciences, which more intimately concern human life. . . . There is no question of importance, whose decision is not compriz'd in the science of man; and there is none, which can be decided with any certainty, before we become acquainted with that science.[12]

Like Newton and Locke, Hume had no desire to search for what the theologians called "primary causes"—or what Hume would call "ultimate principles."[13] "Nothing," he wrote, "is more requisite of a true [philosopher] than to restrain the intemperate desire of searching into causes."[14] No philosopher, he said bluntly, who "would apply himself so earnestly to explaining the ultimate principles of the soul would show himself a great master in that very science of human nature which he pretends to explain, or very knowing in what is naturally satisfactory to the mind of man."[15] "Secondary causes," however, we could know. Or as the English poet Alexander Pope rather glibly phrased it:

> *What can we reason, but from what we know?*
> *[. . .]*
> *Know then thyself, presume not God to scan,*
> *The proper study of mankind is Man.*[16]

It was, in Hume's view, simply a defect "of all the sciences and all the arts, in which we can employ ourselves, whether they be such as are cultivated in the schools of philosophers or practiced in the shops of the meanest artisan," that none of them could ever hope to "go beyond experience, or establish any principles which are not founded on that authority."[17] We had no alternative but to live with that fact. Human beings could only acquire the kind of understanding their minds are equipped to acquire. That we could always imagine other kinds and could even pose questions to ourselves, incoherent though they might be, which in the nature of things had no answer, was simply a part of the human condition. These questions might, as D'Alembert put it, be real, but any attempt to answer them "is not useful for the progress of our understanding."[18]

The new human sciences could, therefore, make no pretense to the grandiosity, in any case pompous and illusory, of theology. They clearly also lacked its presumption to certainty. On the other hand, they had to avoid the temptation to descend into mere speculation. The moral philosophy of the ancients in particular—although like all philosophers of the eighteenth century Hume was in constant, sometimes acrimonious, conversation with them—was, he told George Cheyne (the otherwise forgotten author of a *Philosophical Principles of Natural Religion*) in 1734, "entirely Hypothetical and depending more upon Invention than Experience. Everyone consulted his Fancy in erecting Schemes of Virtue and Happiness, without regarding human Nature, upon which every moral Conclusion must depend."[19] The new "science of mankind" was to be a method, but it was also to constitute a body of knowledge. It would, as Shaftesbury had said of it, treat "man *as real man and as a human agent,*" not, as he had been for Descartes or Locke, "a watch or common machine."[20] To achieve that end it would have to bring together both the natural sciences and all those other forms of understanding, from poetry to philosophy, generally referred to as "letters." "This union of the arts and letters," declared Condorcet, in his inaugural speech as a member of the Académie française,

> is one of the features which should characterize this century in which, for the first time, the general system of the principles of our [forms of] knowledge has been discovered, and the truth has been reduced to an art, and, so to speak, to formulae; in which reason has at last discovered the route which it must follow, and seized the thread which will prevent it from ever being led astray.[21]

To achieve this end, it would have to be laid on a foundation of "experience and observation," just as the new natural sciences created during the previous century had been. The materials on which it would draw were to be found in the "records of wars, intrigues, factions, and revolutions" as well as the everyday lives, habits, and customs collected from past societies and from peoples across the world—for these, wrote Hume,

> are so many collections of experiments, by which the politician [political philosopher] or moral philosopher fixes the principles of his science, in the same manner as the physician or natural philosopher becomes acquainted with the nature of plants, minerals, and other external objects, by the experiments which he forms concerning them.[22]

Inevitably, the human sciences would lack the certainty of the Baconian natural sciences since, as Hume admitted, "in collecting its experiments, it cannot make them purposely, with premeditation."[23] The material with which the human scientist had to work, unlike that of the natural, was always some version of himself. The physicist could experiment; the "human scientist" could not, or at least only in a very limited sense. If the natural scientist wished to demonstrate, for instance, that there existed a maximum speed to which all falling bodies would attain, no matter what their weight, he could, as Galileo had done—more for dramatic effect than scientific demonstration—stand on top of the Leaning Tower of Pisa and drop off two weights, one of one pound, the other of ten, to demonstrate that, as all objects fall at the same speed no matter what their weight, they would both hit the ground at the same time. (According to Aristotle, the ten-pound weight should have fallen ten times as fast as the one-pound weight.) If, however, remarked Hume, the philosopher were to attempt "to clear up after the same manner any doubt in moral philosophy," he could only do so by placing himself "in the same case with that which I consider." In the study of humankind the object being observed and the subject doing the observing could only ever be the same person, or as Diderot—one of Hume's most fervent admirers—put it in 1751, in the *Letter on the Deaf and Dumb:* "It seems to me that one must be at once inside and outside oneself. One must perform the roles simultaneously of the observer and the machine that is being observed." But the moral philosopher had one advantage over the natural scientist. Since human society was a human artifice, humans might be thought to be in a particularly advantageous position to understand it.

Something like this had been suggested in much of the Renaissance literature on the dignity of man, and Hobbes, Leibniz, and Spinoza had all said similar things.[24] But the man who made the most of it was the Neapolitan Giambattista Vico. He called it his *verum ipsum factum*—"true because factual"—principle. "But in the night of thick darkness which envelops earliest antiquity," he had written,

> so remote from ourselves, there shines the eternal and never failing light of a truth beyond all question: that the world of civil society has certainly been made by men and that its principles are therefore to be found within the modifications of our own human mind. And this must give anyone who reflects upon it cause to marvel how the philosophers have all earnestly endeavoured to attain knowledge of the natural world which, since he made it, God alone knows, and have neglected to meditate upon this world of nations, or civil world, knowledge of which, *since men had made it, they could attain*.[25]

In style and approach, Hume and Diderot could hardly have been further removed from Vico, the embittered southern Catholic, the master of a prose style so dense that even his best-intentioned contemporaries despaired of ever understanding it. Vico was in almost all respects quite different from all the other major figures of the Enlightenment. He rarely left his native city of Naples, corresponded with no one beyond a small circle of close friends, and was largely ignored even by his better-known and better-connected Neapolitan contemporaries. He may have met Montesquieu, but if he did it made no lasting impression on him. He longed to hold a chair in jurisprudence, which was constantly denied him. (He became instead a professor of rhetoric, a much inferior position.) He was almost certainly what he outwardly seemed to be, a devout, if unorthodox, Christian. In the 1720s he fired off a long series of letters to members of the Roman clergy in an attempt to persuade them (apparently with success) that his major work the *New Science* was a refutation of the followers of both Hobbes and Bayle—that it was an antidote to the corruption of the times. It provided, he claimed, an irrefutable denial of the "Epicureanism" of both Descartes and Locke, and it had destroyed the jurisprudence of Grotius, Pufendorf, and the Englishman John Selden, because all three had ignored divine providence in their accounts of human history.[26]

For all that, however, Vico was also deeply contradictory. The *New Science* was meant to be entirely *new* (that is why he demanded of his long-suffering readers that they read it at least three times), and if it was intended to achieve any of the things he told the Roman clergy, then it was an attempt to do so by some very unorthodox means. Its very title is intended to be reminiscent of Francis Bacon's *Novum Organum* (or "New Instrument"), and if that were not enough, to make its objectives plain from the very beginning, the work was dedicated to "the academies of Europe which in this enlightened age have submitted not only the fables and vulgar traditions of pagan history, but also every authority of the most respected philosophers to the scrutiny of severe reason."[27] True, Vico insists repeatedly on the strategic role of Providence in human affairs—and roundly denounces Grotius, Pufendorf, and Selden, the "three princes of the doctrine of the natural law," for ignoring it. But for all his attempts to create what he called a "rational civil theology" that would allow the evolution of humankind to be described in terms that were both self-directed and somehow in keeping with the existence of a loving God's higher purposes, Vico never fully succeeded in detaching his account of Providence from what others would have called simply "nature." It is hardly surprising, then, that ever since his "rediscovery" in the nineteenth century by the French historian Jules Michelet, he has been looked upon as a closet Spinozist, a man who, like so many of the social theorists of the eighteenth century, was in effect, if not an atheist, then a deist and certainly someone who had no interest in promoting, in a different idiom, the traditional, providentialist Christian account of the past—and future—of the human race.[28]

Yet for all that—for all that they came from very different intellectual worlds; for all that Hume spoke essentially the same language as Hobbes, terse, ironic, conversational, and Vico wrote in a manner that, although highly idiosyncratic, was often all too reminiscent of the scholastics—both were struggling toward essentially the same objective.[29] Johann Gottfried von Herder (whom we shall meet again) placed Vico together with Montesquieu and the Scots Adam Ferguson, John Millar, and Adam Smith among others (although not Hume) as the man who "in this town [Naples] before others laid the foundation of a school of *human science* in the true sense of the word." By seeking "common first principles in physics, moral theory, law and the law of nations," in his "*New Science* he sought the principle of the *humanity of peoples*."[30] Similarly, the twentieth-century German philosopher Hans-Georg Gadamer (who pairs Vico with Shaftesbury) saw him as offering what he called the "self-understanding of the human sciences."[31]

The subject matter of these new human sciences was what Hume and all his contemporaries understood by that loose word *morals*. In the eighteenth century the term, although it was sometimes used—at least in English—as it is today as a variant on "ethics," was more often understood as a translation of the Latin word *mores,* meaning "custom" or "manners." (The most commonly used term in French was *moeurs* and in German *Sitten*.) It meant not only, as D'Alembert put it, "the duties which we all owe to our fellows" and which he believed to be "uniform among all peoples," not only the consciousness of good and evil, right and wrong (although by its very nature it must also include that); it meant everything that belongs to customs and habits, everything, in other words, which is distinctive to human beings as social creatures.[32] This, then, was the true subject matter of the new human science, and Hume's *Treatise,* as its subtitle declared, was "An *ATTEMPT* to introduce the experimental Method of Reasoning into *MORAL SUBJECTS*." "By moral causes," Hume explained,

> I mean all circumstances which are fitted to work on the mind as motives or reason, and which render a peculiar set of manners habitual to us. Of this kind are, the nature of government, the revolutions of public affairs, the plight or penury in which the people

> live, the situation of a nation with regard to its neighbours, and such like circumstances.[33]

For Hume, of course, without customs we would be "entirely ignorant of every matter of fact beyond what is immediately present to the memory and sense."[34] In short, "habits," "manners," "customs" are the stuff of which our worlds are made. Without custom we would not know that fire burns, that snow is cold, that we can drown in water, or that turnips are fit to eat. Above all, we would know nothing about the social world that human beings inhabit. "We must therefore," Hume concluded,

> glean up our experiments in this science from a cautious observation of human life, and take them as they appear in the common course of the world by men's behaviour in company, in affairs and in their pleasures. Where experiments of this kind are judiciously collected and compared, we may hope to establish on them a science, which will not be inferior in certainty and will be much superior in utility to any other of human comprehension.[35]

Hume was certainly not prepared, as Vico seems to have been, to dismiss the entire project of the natural sciences as another vain quest for "primary causes," but he shared Vico's broad insistence that as man was the architect of his own social world, it would only be by studying that world that we could acquire any understanding of the human mind. It was also central to what both writers called "Enlightenment": the need for human beings to possess a rational grasp of their shared world, based upon investigation and systematic observation.[36]

II

Like Descartes's *Treatise on Method* and Locke's *Essay Concerning Human Understanding,* Hume's *Treatise* was meant to provide the theoretical—or "abstract," as he called them—underpinnings for a new kind of knowledge. It was a "compleat system of the sciences built on foundations almost entirely new, and the only one upon which we can stand with any security."[37] But the human, like the natural, sciences were not only a set of theoretical principles; they also constituted a body of knowledge. How, then, was this new *human* scientist, once in possession of these abstract principles, to proceed? What materials was he to use, and to what conclusions could he hope to come? The natural sciences, although they were not what they would become in the following century, had already developed clearly determined methods of inquiry. The human sciences had none. Amid all the flux of human existence, however, one thing seemed certain. Although, like everything else in the universe, human beings change over time, although our identities, like the bodies we inhabit, cannot remain the same for very long, one thing all human beings clearly do possess is an unchanging nature.

As with so much else that is distinctive about European culture, this belief had been an intuition of the ancient world. Like all human groups, the Greeks had been fiercely ethnocentric. But they were unusual, if not unique, in having a single word—*anthropos*—with which to describe not merely Greeks but all human beings. Other peoples may have had similar terms, but they are not easy to identify, and most fail to distinguish very clearly among a people, a tribe, and the species as a whole. The Romans had inherited the same universal idea and created another word, or rather two—*homo,* "man," and *humanitas,* "humanity"—to describe the entire species, Roman and non-Roman. The coming of Christianity had reinforced this general classification into the idea that all of Eve's progeny not only possessed an immortal soul but also belonged, potentially at least, to a single community where, in St. Paul's words, "Christ is all and in all." The basic unity of the Christian world required that no distinction should be made between God's creatures on the basis of origin, nation, color, or any other physical property. The Hebrew account of the creation is—or at least was interpreted as being—the creation of the entire species and not, as is the case in so many creation myths, of one particular tribe. True, the Jews were God's people, but they were not the only one. God's purpose in creating Eve, and from Eve the entire race, declared St. Augustine, had been that "the human race should not merely be united in a society by natural likeness but should also be bound together by a kind of tie of kinship to form a harmonious unity."[38] This by no means implied equality of intelligence or skill or social standing. Some men might be free, some enslaved, some rulers, some ruled. But all humans, no matter what rank they occupied in this life, belonged to the same kind, the same large, extended family. All were the progeny of one man and one woman.

Certainly, no argument for the unity of the human race based upon the assumption of descent from a single pair (something that, by the eighteenth century, was known to be a biological impossibility) and upon divine intention was likely to find favor with most of the writers of the Enlightenment. But this, in itself, was no reason for denying that the authors of the Old Testament had at least been right in believing that, however varied actual human beings might be, they all shared a common identity as humans or, as Hume put it, as far "as observation reaches, there is no universal difference discernible in the human species."[39] And if the story of Adam and Eve was relegated to the realm of primitive myth along with Saturn and his sons, the image of humanity as a family survived. It was distance and time, not nature, as D'Alembert pointed out, that had eventually forced the human family to separate into different societies, "which then took the name of *States*."[40] Experience of one's own kind alone was sufficient grounds to assume that the basic dispositions of human nature were unlikely to vary much from one people to another. "It is universally acknowledged," insisted Hume, "that there is a great uniformity among the actions of men, in all nations and ages, and that human nature remains still the same, in its principles and operations." If any "traveller from a far country," he remarked acidly, should return home with stories of peoples "who were entirely divested of avarice, ambition or revenge; who knew no pleasure but friendship, generosity and public spirit," we would be no more inclined to believe him than if he had "stuffed his narration with stories of centaurs and dragons, miracles and prodigies."[41] Similarly, the distribution of human characteristics seems to have been discernible pretty much everywhere across the various peoples of the world, so that "stature and force of body, length of life, even courage and extent of genius, seem hitherto to have been naturally, in all ages, pretty much the same."[42]

Although there clearly did exist very obvious differences between a Frenchman, a Huron, an Indian, a Persian, and a Tahitian, these could only be attributed to extraneous circumstances, to upbringing, climate, and culture. They were not, in any sense, structural. "Study well the temper and actions of the French and English," wrote Hume in a much-quoted passage, "you cannot be much mistaken in transferring to the former most of the observations which you have made with regard to the latter. Mankind is so much the same in all times and places, that history informs us of nothing new or strange in this particular."[43]

All that distinguishes the wisest European from the most ignorant "savage" or "barbarian" is precisely the same as that which distinguishes one "civilized" people from another: it is custom, law, habit, and social expectations. These distinctions may, however, be very great indeed. In the remarkable "Dialogue" at the end of Hume's *An Enquiry Concerning the Principles of Morals,* the speaker, called "Palamedes," describes to an unnamed friend an imaginary country called "Fourli," whose inhabitants, although known to be paragons of civilization, nevertheless "have ways of thinking in many things, particularly in morals, diametrically opposite to ours." After Palamedes has recounted his experience of a number of these, his friend stops him in indignation. "Such barbarous and savage manners," he protests, "are not only incompatible with a civilized, intelligent people, such as you said these were; but are scarcely compatible with human nature. They exceed all we ever read of, among the MINGRELIANS [of Georgia] and TOPINAMBOUES [the Tupinamba of Brazil]." "Have a care, have a care!" Palamedes replies, and then reveals that all he had done was to describe "under these bizarre names" some of the most venerated customs of the ancient Greeks so as to convince his friend

> that fashion, vogue, custom, and law, were the chief foundation of all moral determinations. The Athenians, surely, were a civilized,

> intelligent people, if ever there was one; and yet their man of merit might, in this age, be held in horror and execration. The French are also, without doubt, a very civilized, intelligent people; and yet their man of merit might, with the Athenians, be an object of the highest contempt and ridicule, and even hatred. . . . What wide difference, therefore, in the sentiments of morals, must be found between civilized nations and barbarians, or between nations whose characters have little in common? How shall we pretend to fix a standard for judgments of this nature?[44]

Such arguments excluded the possibility of any distinction between peoples on grounds of race. Modern racism, understood as the claim that human groups differ from one another not only culturally and behaviorally but also genetically, is largely the product of the development of the biological sciences in the nineteenth century. This does not, however, mean that there did not exist before then forms of discrimination that shared at least some of the features to be found in the biological racism that we associate with Kant's correspondent Johann Friedrich Blumenbach—the first to attempt to classify humans by the shape of their skulls—and his heirs through to Charles Darwin's cousin Sir Francis Galton, and to the American eugenicists Charles Davenport and David Starr Jordan, president of Stanford, in the early years of the twentieth century.[45]

Perhaps the most influential attempt to account for the very obvious differences between peoples in some way other than by custom and culture was the theory of climates—or, to be more precise, since a significant number of factors other than climate were involved, "environment." This first makes its appearance in Aristotle, was embellished by the Greco-Roman historian Polybius, picked up by St. Thomas Aquinas, modified into a philosophy of history by the French political philosopher Jean Bodin in the sixteenth century, and elaborated into a full-scale theory of cultural differentiation by Montesquieu in the eighteenth. Crudely stated, this argued that those peoples—the Asians, the Africans, the American Indians, and their like—who lived in hot climes reacted to their environment by becoming lethargic and indolent.

Those who lived in the cold northern climes—the Goths, the Mongols, and others of their kind—went the other way, becoming hyperactive, aggressive, and uncouth. Only the Greeks, and in later versions Europeans generally, because they were poised midway between these two extremes, could achieve the necessary balance to remain free, in control of their passions, reflective, and morally active. And since civil life has always been the product of the mean, only they could create true civilizations.

The argument from climate, although it clearly persuaded D'Alembert that it had a sound empirical basis, offered at best an incomplete account of human difference, since, unlike the nineteenth-century concept of "race," it could only ever determine disposition.[46] Aristotle's lethargic Asians and uncivil northerners might well become perfectly balanced Greeks were they to take up residence in the Mediterranean—not perhaps within a single generation, but certainly within two. Environment may have been one element in determining "national character," but it could only operate in conjunction with a large number of others. And even in its most elaborate and refined form, the theory of climates could never quite escape from Voltaire's objection that you had only to glance at the populations of modern Greece and Egypt to see that "if there was irrefutably proof that climate influenced the character of men, government always had a far greater influence." If, asked Claude-Adrien Helvétius, whose *Essay on the Mind* was one of the most widely read philosophical works of the century, climate determined personal disposition, why were the Romans "so magnanimous, so audacious under a Republican government . . . today so soft and effeminate"? And why had the Persians and "those Asiatics who were so brave under the name of Elamites, become so cowardly and base by the time of Alexander"?[47] David Hume took much the same view. Soil and climate, after all, have remained unchanged throughout time, so far as we know. If human nature was determined by climate, then it should be unaffected by history, but, in fact, the "character of nation" is never the "same for a century together."[48] "I believe no-one," he remarked caustically, "attributes the difference of manners in WAPPING and St. JAMES's [poor and rich districts of London] to a difference of air or climate."[49] As even its most convinced advocate, Montesquieu, was ready to admit, under certain circumstances "the moral cause will destroy the physical." Thus, "slavery debases, weakens and destroys the spirit, while liberty shapes, elevates and fortifies it."[50]

The similarity in behavior and beliefs, customs and preferences among the differing members of what we today call "cultures," which had allowed Palamedes to dupe his friend into believing that the Greeks were no different from "savages and barbarians," was, Hume believed, yet another feature of the human personality that could be best explained by the operations of "sympathy." Sympathy is, as we have seen, a passion, a mode of communication between individuals, which we all possess by virtue of our very humanity. It makes it hard for all of us, even "men of the greatest judgment," to "follow their own reasons or inclination, in opposition to that of their friends and daily companions." It was to this, he believed, rather than to any unstable notion of "soil and climate," that "we ought to ascribe the great uniformity we may observe in the humours and turn of thinking of those of the same nation."[51] Montesquieu's contention that the Europeans were free because they were cold but energetic northerners, whereas the Asians were forever doomed to live under some kind of tyranny because they were hot and lethargic southerners, was similarly unsustainable. If, remarked Hume, it were true that northerners had always plundered southerners—and a familiarity with the history of the Mongols would suggest that it was not—then this had nothing to do with climate, and everything to do with poverty. In the past, at least, the north had invariably been poor, the south rich.

Not all the great thinkers of the Enlightenment were constantly as enlightened, or as consistent, on this issue as they might have seemed. Not even Hume. Despite his many claims that all humans were everywhere the same, in a notorious footnote to his essay on "National Characters" he was capable of reflecting that "I am apt to suspect that Negroes, and in general all other species of men (for there are four or five different kinds) to be naturally inferior to the whites. There never was a civilized nation of any other complexion than white or even any individual eminent in action or speculations."[52] If this claim were taken at face value, it would have made nonsense of the entire essay, since it distinguished not between Africans and the rest of mankind, but between "whites" and the rest of mankind. Similarly, Rousseau, who, despite sprinkling his pages liberally with the names of African, Asian, and American groups as examples of "natural" virtue, tended to treat all humans outside Europe as more or less indistinguishable, believed that "it would seem that the organization of the brain is less perfect at the two extremes [of the globe]. Neither the Negroes nor the Lapps have the same sense as the Europeans."[53] This would have to apply to the righteous "Hottentot" whose image adorns the frontispiece of Rousseau's *Discourse on the Origins of Inequality* and who, having taken a good, hard look at European civilization, prefers to return to the simplicity of his native jungles, thus making the virtuous "savage" virtuous only because of his intellectual inferiority. And if Rousseau wished his geography to be taken at all seriously, it would also have left very little of value beyond the northern and southern boundaries of Eurasia.

Then there is the still more notorious case of Kant's views on Africans, as expressed in his *Observations on the Feeling of the Beautiful and the Sublime* of 1764. This work belongs to Kant's "precritical phase," while he was still slumbering. He had, however, even by then read enough Hume to comment on the infamous footnote that "The Negroes of Africa have by nature no feeling that rises above the ridiculous" and that "among the hundreds and thousands of Blacks who have been transported elsewhere from their countries" and thus liberated from the supposedly deleterious effects of the African climate, not one of them, even among those who have been set free, "has ever been found who has accomplished something great in art or science or shown any other praiseworthy quality." Even those—and this, oddly, apparently applied also to the Indians—who had been driven "into northern regions," "have never been able to bring about in their progeny (such as the Creole *Negroes,* or the *Indians* under the name of gypsies) a sort that would be fit for farmers or manual laborers."[54] Nor could this be attributed to the Africans' disadvantageous upbringing, because among whites there were numerous examples of members of "the lowest rabble" who "rise up" and "through extraordinary gifts earn respect in the world."[55] As a people, then, the Africans, from the Sahara to the Cape, would seem to be naturally inferior to all others, and that inferiority would also seem to be one with the color of their skin and the shape of their faces: inherited, innate, immutable.

In *On the Different Races of Man,* written in 1775 and originally published as an advertisement for his course on physical geography, Kant softened these claims somewhat. The human genus, he argued, could only have one origin since, as the great French naturalist Georges-Louis Buffon (of whom more later) had pointed out, all humans, no matter what their race, could successfully interbreed with one another. But even though the species might have been fixed at its creation, varieties could arise within each species, in humans no less than in other animals, as a result of environmental factors.[56] On the basis of what he claimed to be observable behavior, Kant then divided humanity into four races and ordered them into depressingly predictable hierarchies, with the Europeans at the top and the Africans at the bottom. (He seems even to have been prepared to contemplate, on the grounds that Venetian and Tahitian nobles, "especially . . . the ladies," had an "altogether larger build than the common ones," the idea that it might be possible to breed "a naturally nobler sort of human being in which understanding, excellence and integrity would be hereditary.")[57] In his lecture notes on what he called "anthropology" and "physical geography" from the 1780s Kant goes so far as to claim that the "Americans and Negroes cannot govern themselves. Thus they serve only as slaves," and that whites are "the only ones who always progress towards perfection." All of this changed quite dramatically, however, in the final years of his life, when he argued powerfully against any kind of domination of one human group—the word *race* disappeared altogether—by another, denounced both slavery and European imperialism, and sought to embrace the entire world in the scope of what, as we shall see, he called the "cosmopolitan right."[58]

Lord Kames was another who had also begun his researches into the origins of mankind by wondering if the "inferiority of understanding of the Africans might not make of them a different species from the Whites." On "second thoughts," however, he rejected the idea. If the

"Negro" was seemingly inferior to the white, this was only because in Africa they "live on fruit and roots which need little culture: they need little clothing and they erect houses without trouble or art," while everywhere outside Africa they are "miserable slaves having no encouragement either to think or act." Human progress, he believed, was the outcome of the exercise of will, and "man never ripens in judgment nor in prudence but by exercising these powers."[59] In his homelands the African was prevented from ripening his judgment by nature; outside Africa he was prevented from doing so by others.

As Kames had seen and Kant seems somewhat reluctantly to have admitted, all humans could be dehumanized by their condition or occupation. Most of the Africans whom the Europeans encountered had been slaves, and ever since at least the time of Cicero slavery had been recognized as a condition that transformed humans into virtual beasts by robbing them of what Diderot called the "enjoyment in one's own mind." The slave, denied this feature of what it is to be a man, was thus reduced to a level lower even than that of a dog, for the dog is only an automaton, whereas the slave still retains some grasp on what, in the end, nothing can deprive him of: his consciousness. He alone *knows* that he is a slave. The possession of a fully developed sense of what it was to be human, while at the same time being deprived of humanity, meant that the African slave can have no cause for hope, no expectation, in Diderot's words, of "those happy times, those centuries of Enlightenment and of prosperity" that might one day allow even the most miserable European laborer to recover his identity to the full.[60] Little wonder, then, that he seemed "inferior to the whites" and apparently incapable of improving his condition. Aristotle, said Rousseau, had been right in claiming that there existed slaves by nature. His error was to have mistaken "the effect for the cause." "Slaves lose everything in their shackles, even the desire to escape. They love their servitude as the companions of Ulysses loved their brutishness. If, therefore there are slaves by nature, it is because they have once been slaves contrary to nature."[61] It was chance, the uncertainties of one's place of birth, that had placed the slave at the mercy of his dehumanizing master, not the slavish mind that was responsible for slavery. As Jacques-Pierre Brissot de Warville—

who, as one of the leaders of the Girondins, would lose his head during the Terror—claimed in 1776, "The ignorant and barbarous slave, born on the banks of the Bosporus, would be an enlightened Republican had he been born in Philadelphia."[62] Even an antirevolutionary and supporter of slavery like Pierre-Victor Malouet, a former commissaire of the island of Saint Dominque, could see that this was true, although for him it was precisely a reason for forbidding slaves to leave their master's home except "under the gaze of a vigilant police-force."[63] If they remained outside and unguarded for too long, he feared that they might begin to understand that their condition was not, as they were constantly being told, the burden that God had imposed upon them because of their debased and sinful nature. It was a purely human imposition, unjust and unnatural and, as such, could be reversed. Liberty, as the English Unitarian Richard Price phrased it, was the child of enlightenment, and enlightenment "is inseparable from knowledge and virtue." "Think of Greece," he continued, "formerly the seat of arts and science, but now, having lost liberty, a vile and wretched spot, a region of darkness, poverty and barbarity."[64]

III

What slavery had done to the Africans was not unlike what centuries of absolute, despotic monarchy and the intellectual tyranny of the Church had done to the Europeans, and, as Voltaire and Price had seen, centuries of Ottoman rule to the Egyptians and the Greeks. It had, in effect, marooned them in time (or, in the case of the Greeks and Egyptians, reversed the direction of history). And it was time, or rather history, and not climate or biology that divided one group of peoples, one race, from another. Neither the Africans nor the American Indians could be taken as evidence that there existed distinct races of men, insofar as their innate dispositions were concerned. Human nature was the same the world over. But it was not immutable. For all humans, unless constrained by external circumstances beyond their control, are evolutionary beings and thus, like the cosmos itself, in a state of constant movement. "What is our lifetime in comparison with the eternity of time?" asks the figure of Mademoiselle Julie de Lespinasse—the brilliant Parisian *salonnière* and the love of D'Alembert's life—caught up by the dizzying vision of the abyss of eternity, in Diderot's *D'Alembert's Dream*:

> Less than the drop that I have on the tip of my needle compared with unlimited space which surrounds me. . . . What do we know of the race of animals which have preceded us? What do we know of those who will follow our own? Everything changes, everything passes. It is only the whole which remains. The world begins and ends without cease; it is, at every moment, both at its beginning and its end: there has never been another, and there never will be another. In the immense ocean of matter, there is no single molecule which resembles another, nor one molecule that resembles itself for even an instant.[65]

Immobility, repose, was a mere abstraction, while movement was "a quality as real as length, width, and depth." "In this universe," wrote Diderot, the keen amateur chemist, "everything is in transition, or in a state of potential energy, or in both at once."[66] For Diderot, as for so many in the eighteenth century, it was both a startling revelation and the one great secret of all life, human and nonhuman. It was what linked humankind to the planet and made sense of all their collective actions. It explained the past and determined the future. Mademoiselle de Lespinasse's observations on the essential mutability of all matter reflected what had been one of the great achievements of the natural scientists of the eighteenth century: the systematic undermining of the earlier orthodoxy that, in accordance with the account of the creation provided in the Book of Genesis, all life had been created as perfect and must, therefore, be substantially unchanging. For why would anything which God had made and which he beheld to be "very good" need to change?

The writer who was, perhaps, most instrumental in upsetting this comforting notion was the great natural historian Georges-Louis

Leclerc, comte de Buffon, director of the royal gardens (the Jardins des Plantes) in Paris. Buffon, unlike most of the *philosophes,* was very much a man of the establishment.[67] Born into an aristocratic family and a favorite at court, he was dependent for his sumptuous lifestyle, and his prestige, upon royal patronage. (He looked, Hume once said of him, more like a Mareschal of France than a man of letters.)[68] Whereas many intellectuals of the day regarded a brief spell of imprisonment as a seal of approval, Buffon certainly had no wish to spend any time at the Château de Vincennes or to come under the scrutiny of Louis XIV's notorious secret police. Yet although he succeeded in steering clear of the censors and was duly cautious about his religious beliefs, or lack of them, his work was, in its own way, as subversive and as critical of the Christian vision of humankind as any of those of his contemporaries. The authorities at the Sorbonne (who were responsible for ensuring the religious orthodoxy of all books published in France) condemned his essentially materialistic account of the creation of the cosmos and the development of mankind. But persistent evasions, the vague promise of recantation, and Buffon's social standing and immense popularity finally led them in 1781 to abandon their attempts to have him condemned for impiety. His massive *Natural History,* which appeared in thirty-six volumes between 1749 and 1789, was, despite its subject matter, one of the most popular books of the eighteenth century. Although there were many, like Adam Smith, who liked it less for its scientific rigor than for its "agreeable, copious and natural eloquence"—it was Buffon who coined the phrase *le style c'est l'homme même* ("style is the man himself")—it had a significant impact on the future direction of the newly minted "science of man."[69] Its influence can be seen in Hume and Kames, in Diderot and Montesquieu, in Turgot and Voltaire, even in Condorcet—who had, nevertheless, opposed Buffon's election to the Académie française and, on his death, as president of the Académie delivered a eulogy filled with barbed comments about his scientific methods. D'Alembert called Buffon, significantly, the "rival of Plato and Lucretius," while Rousseau, although in the end he came to very different conclusions about the condition of "natural man," looked upon the *Natural History* as a precursor and a foundation for his own "historical study of morality." "M. Rousseau," wrote Johann Heinrich Formey, Perpetual Secretary of the Berlin Academy of Sciences, in 1756, "is in his field [*genre*] what M. de Buffon is in his: he handles men as that Philosopher handles Nature and the Universe."[70]

What was most damaging about Buffon's biology to the Church's ever-loosening hold over scientific understanding was his argument that the natural world itself existed in time. It changed. It had a past, a present, and presumably a future. Previous natural historians had limited themselves largely to classification. Even the most innovative, and certainly the best known, the Swede Carl Linnaeus, although he suggested that new breeds of animals and plants had evolved over time through hybridization, stuck firmly to the idea that the world of nature, and of man, was essentially the same as it had been on the seventh day of the Creation. Buffon used the fossil record and experimentation to argue not only that the biblical chronology for the creation of the world in 4004 BCE was woefully inaccurate (if not—although he was too cautious actually to say so—simply absurd) but also that nature itself was in a state of perpetual movement. In other words, it had a history that could, like the history of all things, be charted and understood. Crucially, too, that history, although it clearly had had a beginning and a future, had no foreseeable end.

What was true of all animal and plant life in general was also inescapably true of humankind, and it is really with "Man" that the *Natural History* is ultimately concerned. The eighth volume begins with the by now not unfamiliar complaint that "whatever interest we may have in knowing ourselves, I do not know if we are not better informed about everything that is not us." Humans are unlike other animals in being made up of two parts, one of which is "inextensive, immaterial, and immortal," the "other extensive, material, and mortal." Both are evolutionary, but whereas we share the second part—our bodies—with all other living beings, the first—our minds—are uniquely ours. Buffon did not, of course, say as much, but the Adam of the Book of Genesis would have been a hirsute, stumbling, bowed creature, more like the image derived from skeletal remains of *Australopithecus* than the languid, muscular young man who stretches out his hand toward God the

Father on the ceiling of the Sistine Chapel. The most significant form of human progress, however, is mental rather than corporeal, and it is brought about by the unique human ability to make comparisons—for "what is absolutely incomparable is utterly incomprehensible"—together with the capacity for speech and a natural sociability, of however rudimentary a kind.[71] Humans are also unlike other animals in that they alone are not merely aware of themselves; they are also aware of their own pasts (and possible futures). Animals, wrote Buffon, "possess an awareness of their present existence, but not of their past existence. They have sensations but lack the ability to compare them." Because of this they cannot, as humans can, form ideas, and their sense of existence is "less certain and less extensive than ours." Since they lack any sense of themselves ("they do not know they exist, although they feel it"), they can have "no idea of time, no knowledge of the past, and no notion of the future."[72] Humans, by contrast, possess an acute awareness of the past. They alone of all living beings know that they are going to die, and they alone can transmit the knowledge they have acquired during their brief individual existences from one generation to the next. They alone, therefore, are capable of perfectibility. This awareness of past time is also what allows them, however imperfectly, to direct the future. They can at least discern possible outcomes and act accordingly.[73] For Buffon, this ability to look both back and forward, as a feature of his own self-awareness, was a biological characteristic of "man." Humans also form societies. They are not alone in this; so, too, do bees and beavers. But unlike other gregarious animals, whose societies are always fixed in size and unchanging, human societies are constantly growing and changing. From the first small groupings, "which depend, so to speak, on nature," the inexorable growth of human populations drives their members into ever-larger communities, until finally they come to create the "great societies" and the "civilized [*policées*] societies" of the present day.[74] This, then, is the course of the irreversible progress of civilization. All humans will travel the same road. Some, the Europeans and the Asians, may have done so more rapidly than others. But it was time and the fortunate circumstances of their environment that were on their side, not nature.

Where a particular people stands in this process of evolution must therefore account for the vast differences among the different races of men and must consequently to some degree determine their mental and physical capabilities. The test of this hypothesis, as Buffon conceived it, was America. The New World, he believed, largely on the basis of the size of certain animals (pumas, horses, deer) that he supposed to be smaller versions of similar species to be found in Europe and Asia, was quite literally "new," or at least of more recent creation than the rest of the planet.

This implied (although it was not a conclusion that Buffon himself drew) that the continent was also inferior to Europe. It also suggested, by an obscure process of association, that if the Native Americans were inferior to Europeans (Buffon never said that they were, only that they were fewer in number), then the descendants of Europe's overseas settler populations in the Americas must be similarly inferior. This unwarranted assumption set off a furious debate, in both North and South America, that lasted well into the late nineteenth century and involved, at one time or another, almost every major thinker from Kant to Alexander von Humboldt to Hegel to Darwin to Marx.[75] Thomas Jefferson's *Notes on the State of Virginia* were originally written as a reply to Buffon, and when the book was published in 1785, Jefferson, then U.S. ambassador to Paris, arranged for a "seven-foot-tall" moose—or most of a moose—as well as the antlers of a deer, a caribou, an elk, and the skin of a panther to be sent over to France as empirical evidence that there were animals in America not merely as large as anything in Europe but, in the case of the moose, much larger. By the time they reached Paris, however, the moose, which Jefferson had hoped would be "stuffed, and placed on his legs in the King's Cabinet," was rotting, and Buffon was dying. Although the exhibits reached Buffon's longtime associate, the zoologist Louis-Jean-Marie d'Aubenton, Buffon himself seems never to have seen any of them.[76]

Most of the writers of the Enlightenment, Rousseau and Diderot in particular, would come to reject Buffon's materialism and the determinism that this involved. But his insistence on humanity's presence in time and on the human ability, however limited, to exercise a control over the future had a lasting impact on the development of the "human sciences." For it followed that if humans were evolutionary creatures, then so, too, were the cultural worlds they constructed for themselves. Like all organisms, these also moved from the simple to the complex or, in their case, from what was called "savagery"—a word that in the eighteenth century often meant little more than wild or uncultivated—to what would come to be called "civilization." In his *Philosophical Review of the Successive Advances of the Human Mind* of 1750, Anne-Robert-Jacques Turgot declared:

> Thus the present state of the world, marked as it is by these infinite variations in inequality, [has] spread out before us at one and the same time all the gradations from barbarism to refinement, thereby revealing to us at a single glance, as it were, the records and remains of all the steps taken by the human mind, a reflection of all the stages through which it has passed, and the history of all the ages.[77]

The new human science was to be precisely a record of these steps, an explanation of this progress. It was for this reason that D'Alembert's human scientist, meditating alone, "follows the narratives of past writers with the same circumspection as he does the phenomena of nature" and "studies that which has been" so that he will be able "to understand the men amongst whom he lives." The new human science was, in other words, to be a form of historical inquiry. For history, said Hume, was the sole means we had at our disposal that would allow us to "discover the constant and universal principles of human nature, by showing men in all varieties of circumstances and situations, and furnishing them with materials from which we may form our observations and become acquainted with the regular springs of human action."[78]

IV

It used to be argued that the eighteenth century was "unhistorical," an accusation that, as the twentieth-century German philosopher and historian Ernst Cassirer once remarked, had been "a battle cry coined by the Romantic Movement."[79] What the Romantics understood by "unhistorical" was the Enlightenment rejection of the past as the source of tradition and of the allegiance to kin, hearth, king, and religion. In this respect, at least, they were very largely right. Although there were many histories written during the period that, at least as far as their titles were concerned, resembled traditional national histories—Voltaire's *The Century of Louis XIV,* for instance, the Scottish historian William Robertson's *History of America* and *History of Scotland,* or, more tellingly perhaps, Hume's monumental *History of England*—few of these were intended to reinforce existing traditions or establish national identities in the way the great historical writings of the nineteenth century had been.[80] Most, and all the more important ones, were comparative studies of human actions and behavior. Their strategy was to employ the story of one particular people, or of one specific moment, to illustrate something about the history of the species as whole. D'Alembert, who had a lot to say about the writing of history, like Descartes, looked upon—and looked down upon—most of the history that had preceded him, with all its aimless erudition, its deplorable litany of the deeds of what Shaftesbury had called "the great butchers of mankind" as at best a form of entertainment, suitable perhaps for giving moral instruction for children, but of very little use for anything else. "The science of history," he wrote, "when it is not enlightened by Philosophy is the last of the human sciences."[81] When it is, however, it is the first. Although it is true that the kind of history written by the new human scientists frequently displaced, and sometimes even despised, the erudition that Edward Gibbon prized so highly, theirs was not, as D'Alembert's own assertions about the proper materials for any human science and Hume's critique of the overly speculative strategies of the ancients had made clear, the mere "let us imitate the botanists" Gibbon accused it of being.[82] The difference was not so much between "erudite" or "civil" on the one hand and philosophical history on the other, as between what the German poet and playwright Gotthold Ephraim Lessing in 1753 called "man in particular and man in general." To know "man in particular" was, he complained, merely to know "fools and scoundrels." The study of "man in general," however, was quite different. "Here he exhibits greatness and his divine origin. Consider what enterprises man accomplishes, how he daily extends the limits of his understanding, what wisdom prevails in his laws, what ambition inspires his monuments."[83]

The purpose of the "human sciences" was to know mankind as a species, and the best way to do that was through a detailed examination of their "manners," "customs," "*moeurs*." "You have employed philosophy to judge on manners," Edmund Burke told William Robertson, after having read his *History of America,* "and from manners you have drawn new resources for philosophy."[84] As Hume himself commented on his own project: "The only certain reason, by which nations can indulge their curiosity in researches concerning their remote origins, is to consider the languages, manners and customs of their ancestors and to compare them with those of their neighbouring nations."[85] It was this which made Hume, in the opinion of Herder—who was himself conscious of having created a new kind of philosophical history—not a "historian but a *philosopher* of British history."[86]

In form, the histories of Voltaire, Robertson, and Hume are conventional enough. But many of the "histories" written during the Enlightenment are of a very different kind. Giambattista Vico's *New Science* of 1725, for instance, was in some sense a history and was seen as such by its author. It was, Vico said of it, an "ideal eternal history" of mankind, made up precisely of "all those things which depend upon human will, as are all the histories of languages, of customs and the facts of the wars and the peace of peoples."[87] Montesquieu's *Spirit of the Laws* was similarly a form of history, drawing on a vast repertoire of past customs and laws to create a panoramic account of the evolution of all human culture, as was Turgot's *Philosophical Review* and Condorcet's *Sketch for a Historical Picture of the Progress of the Human Mind*.

So, too, was perhaps the most popular and widely read of them all: Voltaire's great universal history *An Essay on the Manners and Spirit of Nations*. This had been written to "satisfy a lady," Gabrielle-Émilie, Marquise du Châtelet, Newtonian and mathematician, whom we met in the last chapter and for whom history had appeared to be made up exclusively of "those fables which time had sanctified, are easy to repeat, and which ruined and weakened her mind." What she wanted to know about was precisely "the customs, the laws, the prejudices, the beliefs and the arts." It was "the spirit of mankind that she wished to contemplate." To meet these demands, Voltaire had written a new kind of narrative.[88] He had, he said, no desire to "accumulate an enormous multitude of facts," because they only ever canceled one another out. His objective was to collect the principal ones and use them to guide the reader, who could judge for himself "the extinction, the renaissance, and the progress of the human spirit and to acquaint him with the peoples [of the world] through the customs [*usages*] of those same peoples." It was, he added, the only method that "is suitable to a general history" and was the "one also adopted by a philosopher who has written the history of England"—David Hume, in other words.[89] Gabrielle died in 1749, before Voltaire had made much progress; in the end it took him thirty-four years, until just before his own death in 1778, to complete the task. The influence of the *Essay* can be seen in Gibbon and Robertson, in Turgot, in Condorcet, and in Hume himself.[90] It had earned him, said Lessing, who was otherwise Voltaire's fiercest critic, every right to boast—with the Roman poet Horace—that "I was the first to take these free steps through empty space."[91]

All of these histories, together with a large number of less-known works, were attempts to construct a "history of mankind," a history that the German philosopher Karl Werner in 1879, in describing Vico's *New Science,* called "philosophical historicism"—an account, as he explained, not of the simple facts of the past but of the *possibilities* that existed for human beings in time.[92] It was what in the eighteenth century came to be called a "philosophical" or "conjectural history." This, said Adam Smith's biographer Dugald Stewart, speaking of Smith's own *Dissertation on the Origin of Languages,* could best be described as a "specimen of a particular sort of inquiry, which so far as I know, is entirely of modern origins." Its purpose was to find an answer to the question "by what gradual steps that transition has been made from the first simple efforts of uncultivated nature to a state of things so wonderfully artificial and complicated."[93] The purpose of these histories was also, like all true social knowledge, not only descriptive—it was also emancipatory. In providing a proper scientific understanding of the origin and evolution of the human condition, they would, it was hoped, release man from his servitude to what was one of the eighteenth century's favorite words: *prejudice*.

The purpose behind his *Sketch for a Historical Picture of the Progress of the Human Mind,* Condorcet said, had been ultimately to reveal the "true nature of all our prejudices." Montesquieu's objective in *The Spirit of the Laws* had, he said, been to cure men of their prejudices. "I call prejudices," he wrote, "not what makes one unaware of certain things, but what makes one unaware of oneself."[94] The only way to achieve that, he claimed, was through an understanding of the principles that lay behind each people's "civil and political laws," their relationship to the physical aspect of the country to which they belonged, to its religion, to the "customs and manners" of its inhabitants, and to the relations that the laws themselves have with each other. And this in turn could only be understood historically, because "customs and manners," although they are, Montesquieu believed, determined originally by climatic and environmental factors, nevertheless grow and change over time, as do all other aspects of human life. "This," he concluded, "is what is called THE SPIRIT OF THE LAWS."[95] This, then, was to be the social, or "moral," equivalent of Buffon's biological evolutionism. As Jürgen Habermas phrased it, "Thinkers from Vico to Condorcet . . . shifted the teleology of nature into the dimension of history."[96] And what that history would reveal was that the final destiny of the species must be the creation of a universal, cosmopolitan civilization.

V

The procedures used in "conjectural" or "philosophical" history, as Kant explained at the end of one of his own contributions to the genre, the *Idea for a Universal History with a Cosmopolitan Purpose* of 1784, was not to "supersede the task of history proper, that of *empirical* composition." Rather, it was to provide "a notion of what a philosophical mind, well acquainted with history, might be able to attempt from a different angle." In Kant's view, the historian's position was like that of the earthbound observer of the heavens, for whom the planets seem to "sometimes move backwards, sometimes forwards, and sometimes not at all." The ideal viewpoint, the only one from which the regularity of the cosmos would be visible, would be that of the sun or what was sometimes called "the standpoint of Providence." Clearly this was unavailable to any mere mortal. But if it could not be acquired by direct personal experience, it could, in Kant's view, be achieved by reason and the imagination, drawing upon what could be known about the history of mankind's movement through time.[97] This was Kant's "different angle." Philosophical history is an attempt to make sense of the "free exercise of human will" by discovering in what might otherwise strike us as a "confused and fortuitous" series of human acts a regular progression of the "steadily advancing but slow development of man's original capacities." It does not do this, however, as traditional history would, by patiently enumerating the known facts about the past—what Kant refers to dismissively as details of "marriages, births, deaths"—precisely because these facts of human existence "seem to be subject to no rule in accordance with which their number could be determined in advance." The simple narrative of man's past deeds, which is the only kind of narrative available to the empirical historian, is merely a tale of purposeless actions.[98] But a history that sought to relate these actions to the larger purpose of nature—assuming that there was one—would be a history that would indeed be not merely a narrative of things past but also the grounds for a narrative of things future; it would, as Kant put it, be "designated as divinatory and yet natural."[99] The way in which it sets out to do this is by following what Kant calls "an *a priori* rule," which will allow the historian to "discover an aim of nature in this nonsensical course of human affairs; from which aim a history in accordance with a determinate plan of nature might nevertheless be possible even of creatures who do not behave in accordance with a plan of their own."[100]

In the opening remarks to *Conjectures on the Beginnings of Human History,* written in 1786 in response to Herder's *Philosophy of the History of*

Mankind, Kant compares such a history to "a movement of the power of the imagination accompanying reason and indulged in for the recreation and health of the mind." It is, he said half jokingly (if one can imagine Kant joking), something like a "mere pleasure trip," a journey made "on the wings of the power of imagination."

Such pleasure trips, however, had an entirely serious purpose. For while it "must not be ventured in the progression of the history of human actions, [it] may yet be attempted through conjecture about its *first beginnings,* insofar as *nature* makes them."[101] Kant's project here was, as he himself often points out, heavily indebted to Rousseau, whom he once referred to as the "Newton of the moral world," and in particular to the Rousseau of *A Discourse on the Origins of Inequality*.[102] Unlike Rousseau, however, Kant is quite unambiguous about his intentions. Since we cannot have been present at our beginning—otherwise we would have to have been our own creators—we may be permitted to fill in the gaps in our empirical knowledge by conjectures. Such conjectures, however, "must not be invented by fiction but can be taken from experience, if one presuppose that the latter in its first beginning was not better or worse than we encounter now." The potential conditions of life remain unchanged, since "nature . . . does not bring anything venturesome with it."[103] By reaching back from what we have experienced today, we may safely imagine what our remotest ancestors might have felt during these crucial stages of their development for which there is no historical record. "The progress of the human spirit," explained Condorcet, following much the same path entirely independently of either Kant (whom he had not read) or Rousseau (of whom he was suspicious),

> is subject to the same general laws which we can observe in the individual development of our faculties, for it is the consequence of that development, considered as it manifests itself in a great number of individuals gathered together in society. But the result which each instant presents depends upon that presented by previous incidents, and at the same time influences those times which will follow. This account is therefore historical.[104]

Humans are relentless and restless creatures, and although they may, as individuals, experience many setbacks in their long history, all the writers of the Enlightenment had no doubt that if, in Kant's words, "one looks to the vocation of the species," history was a narrative of "nothing but a progressing towards perfection."[105] As an individual you are at liberty to drop out, to live on your own desert island or, as Rousseau himself had done in the last weeks of his life, in a *cabane* in the wilderness—even if, in his case, the wilderness was the carefully nurtured gardens of the Marquis René-Louis de Girardin at Ermenonville, some twenty-eight miles outside Paris. For mankind as a whole, however, there could be no escape from time.

Like Rousseau's *A Discourse on the Origins of Inequality,* Kant's *Conjectures on the Beginnings of Human History* begins with a secularized (or at least unsacramentalized) version of the Book of Genesis, for as Rousseau said, trying perhaps to placate the more literalist Christians, although religion may "command that God himself" had drawn mankind out of the state of nature, it did not "prevent us from forming conjectures drawn solely from the nature of Man himself and the beings which surround him, concerning the future of Humankind, had it been left to itself."[106] In Kant's scheme (although not in Rousseau's), the event that in the Bible is described as a Fall and is brought about through disobedience is presented as the recognition of reason. For Vico, too, the Fall could only be understood as a cognitive experience. It was the expulsion from Eden that had launched mankind into history, but he had entered that history as a being wholly unlike the creature which he was eventually to become, as an idiot, a *stultus,* who carried with him from his prelapsarian condition only what Vico calls the "force of truth" (*vis veri*), the innate capacity to recognize the truth when it is presented to him. Thereafter his ascent was wholly a self-directed affair.

Kant's first pair, however, are more stripped down even than Vico's. He allows that they must have been capable not only of movement and an upright stance but also of both speech—"i.e. [to] speak according to connected words and concepts"—and consequently of thought, otherwise they could hardly have been described as human. (And with what other means could Eve have persuaded Adam to eat the forbidden fruit?) But even these are not in any sense innate, for Kant observed, as Locke had done, that had they been innate, "they would also be inherited, which, however, experience contradicts." Beside this ability to communicate with one another, they lived out their lives entirely by "instinct, that *voice of God* which all animals obey." Both Rousseau and Kant supposed that reason would first have made itself present by allowing man to "extend his knowledge of the means of nourishment beyond the limits of instinct." This he did "by comparing his usual diet with anything which a sense, other than that to which his instinct, was tied—for example, the sense of sight—represented as similar in character." As in Genesis this, too, constitutes a falling away of innocence—or rather of dependence upon the simple animal nature of the old Adam—and consequently a progress toward true humanity. Now, however, something occurs in Kant's history that has no place in the Old Testament narrative (nor in either Vico's or Rousseau's versions): reason joins forces with imagination, and together they "invent desires which not only lack any corresponding natural impulse, but which are even *at variance* with the latter." Humans, it would seem, had thus acquired the capacity to exercise their freedom with regard to nature or, as Kant puts it, to "cavil with the voice of nature." The consequences of this for the future of the race were quite as far-reaching as Eve's ploy with the apple. Man

> discovered in himself a faculty of choosing for himself a way of living and not being bound to a single one, as other animals are. Yet upon the momentary delight that this marked superiority might have awakened in him, anxiety and fright must have followed right away, concerning how he, who still did not know the hidden properties and remote effects of any thing, should deal with this newly-discovered faculty. He stood, as it were, on the brink of an abyss; for instead of the single objects of desire, to which instinct had up to now directed him, there opened up an infinity of them, and he did not know how to relate to the choice between them; and from this state of freedom, once he had tasted

> it, it was nevertheless wholly impossible for him to turn back again to that of servitude (under the dominion of instinct).[107]

Man thus becomes what he will forever be: a divided creature at war with himself. This is what will finally drive him to form societies and what will compel those societies steadily to perfect themselves, moving inexorably upward toward the cosmopolitan world that awaits them at the end of history. This conflict between choice and desire was not, however, the only challenge the fledgling human had to face. For now reason began to operate in ways that served not merely to extend this new range of possibilities; it also began to play upon the imagination. Kant puts the fig leaf from the Book of Genesis to a quite unexpected use. In the Bible, Adam and Eve are discovered by God sneaking around in the garden of Eden, wearing some very unusual garments, because having acquired reason (or as Genesis puts it, having acquired "a knowledge of good and evil"), "they knew that they [were] naked; and they sewed fig-leaves together, and made themselves aprons." In Kant's version, however, Adam and Eve use their skirts of fig leaves not to hide their shame but to extend their sexual pleasure by withdrawing the objects of their mutual desire from the senses. By so doing they avoided "the satiety which follows the satisfaction of a purely animal desire." Kant, who never married, had a low opinion of sex, believing it to be "a degradation of human nature" that made "of the loved person an Object of appetite." He also believed—hence his ingenious interpretation of the role of the fig leaves—that "sexuality is not an inclination which one human being has for another as such, but is an inclination for the *sex* of another." It is "her sex [which] is the object of [a man's] desires," not her person.[108] In his view, men at least were made for higher things. But he did not underestimate the importance of sexual desire as the earliest, and still perhaps the most powerful, of all human impulses.

Such is the cunning of nature. In the first instance these sexual games might seem to indicate "a consciousness of some rational control over the impulses." In fact, however, they did something else. They extended the possible range of those impulses to infinity. Once man finally emerges into history, this primitive indulgence of his sexual urges will have ensured that henceforth "his nature is not of the sort to call a halt anywhere in possession and enjoyment and to be satisfied."[109]

Just as in his famous essay of 1784, "An Answer to the Question: What Is Enlightenment?" Kant had likened the civil—but still unenlightened—man to a child who is unable to walk without the help of a walker, so early, pre-civil man, although he is now equipped with the desires that will henceforth prevent him from ever remaining satisfied with his present lot for very long, is described as being still "in a rude and purely animal existence," still guided only by "the leading-reins of instinct." How, then, does this entrapped, seemingly inescapably infantile being ever begin to leave the state into which he has been born? Kant's response is an appeal to what he sees, like Hobbes, as the basically conflictual nature of all human emotions. Like Hobbes, Kant accepts that humans are not naturally sociable, in any fully developed sense of the term. True, they would seem to have some initial inclination for social life, but they are very far from being the "social animals" that Aristotle, and Aristotle's Christian commentators, had made of them. Society is obviously an artificial creation, and in this regard, Kant wrote, in what is a truly startling phrase, "Man was not meant to be guided by instinct or equipped and instructed by innate knowledge; on the contrary, he was meant to produce everything out of himself." Now, although each individual "natural" man was instinctively gregarious enough to feel more human in society, he was also possessed of an equally strong urge "to *individualize* (isolate) himself because he simultaneously encounters in himself the unsociable property willing to direct everything so as to get his own way."[110] His first response on meeting others of his kind would, therefore, almost certainly have been less one of instinctive fellowship than of fear and suspicion. "By nature," Hobbes had remarked tersely, whenever we encounter others "we are not looking for friends but for honour or advantage from them."[111] However, this loathing and instinctive competitiveness does not for Kant, as it had for Hobbes, lead to the unremitting violence of the "war of all against all." For Kant had noticed, or simply borrowed from

Rousseau, a crucial stage in the story that was missing from all previous accounts of the origins of human society. Hobbes's primitive man wishes only to survive and to be free to act precisely as he chooses. Rousseau's "savage," like his Hobbesian predecessor, also needs food and a mate. But that is not enough. For Rousseau and for Kant, Hobbesian man is an impossible creature, if only because no human being can live by meat and sex alone. If he is truly human and not a mere beast, he will soon discover that he also requires something more.

In *A Discourse on the Origins of Inequality,* Rousseau, an attentive reader of Pufendorf, imagines that the crucial step toward true sociability had come about something like this. Humans had come so far as to form families (a natural, not a social, act) and to build some kind of shelter for themselves (presumably also natural: rabbits dig warrens, bees build hives, and so on); they would also seem to have managed (although Rousseau fails to explain how) to establish some kind of common settlement. Humans are not, after all, as Aristotle himself had noted, the only sociable creatures: so too are wolves and ants. Rousseau's question, however, was not how humans came to be *sociable* but how they came to be unequal. The answer (and once again it is a Hobbesian one) is competition. Not, however, a competition over resources, nor the "perpetual and restless desire of power after power," but the desire for esteem:

> They now began to gather in front of their huts or around a great tree. Song and dance, the true offspring of love and leisure, became the amusement, or rather the occupation, of the carefree men and women gathered there. Everyone then began to look at the rest and wished to be looked at in turn, and public esteem acquired a value. He who sang and danced the best, the handsomest, the strongest, the most adroit, became the most respected; and this was the first step towards inequality, and at the same time towards vice. From these first preferences was born, on the one hand, vanity and contempt, and on the other, shame and envy; and the fermentation caused by these new leavens in the end produced compositions which were to prove fatal to happiness and innocence.[112]

In this account, the "savage" lives in himself; sociable man, however, is capable of living only in the opinion of others and "derives the sentiment of his own existence solely from their judgement."[113] For Rousseau this, too, is the moment at which the species enters historical time. What for Buffon had been the essential distinction between the human and the animal became for Rousseau a distinction between the "savage" and civilized "human." The savage, like the animals by which he was surrounded (and with whom he existed in perfect harmony), lived quite literally from day to day. The savage imagination "paints no pictures; his heart yearns for nothing; his modest needs are readily supplied at hand; and he is so far from having enough knowledge for him to desire to acquire more knowledge, that he can have neither foresight nor curiosity."[114] This is why the "poor Carib," in a story Rousseau borrowed from the Dominican Jean-Baptiste du Tertre and Kant borrowed from Rousseau, having sold his hammock in the morning to the European settler, comes begging for it back in the evening. Civil beings have individual identities, which the savage, like other animals, lacks, and identities, like an awareness of the passage of time, depend upon the presence of others. On a desert island the solitary man is literally no one. It is the desire for sustained recognition, not protection, that creates civil life. In time this perception of inequality will result in the imposition of political and social inequality and the construction of the societies of the unfree in which Rousseau imagined himself to be living. Kant had a more detailed explanation for the formation of hierarchies and orders. But for both, what mattered was that humans became sociable, just as they will one day become enlightened, not from some innate instinct for sociability, but from the individual desire for recognition, something which required the constant presence of others. This led Kant to identify what he famously called the "unsocial sociability" of mankind, that is, "their tendency to come together in society coupled, however, with a continual resistance which constantly threaten to break this society up." It is this resistance, this conflict and unease, that awakens all man's powers and induces him to overcome his tendency to laziness. Through the desire for honor, power, or property, it drives him to seek status among his fellows, whom, says Kant, "he cannot *stand* yet cannot *leave alone*."[115]

From the attempt to resolve these conflicts derives the *just civil constitution* of the modern state, that "*pathologically* compelled agreement to form a society" whose effect was to transform men's wild inclinations so that they "have the most beneficial effect." In a famous passage Kant likens this to the development of trees in a forest: "Precisely because each of them seeks to take air and sun from the other, [they] are constrained to look for them above themselves, and thereby achieve a beautiful straight growth; whereas those in freedom and separated from one another, that put forth their branches as they like, grow stunted and awry."[116]

Kant was inclined to agree with Hobbes, as was Rousseau and Condorcet, that these early societies were likely to be rigid and authoritarian, monarchies rather than republics. Where they will—indeed must—differ from the societies Hobbes had imagined was that, although the citizen is denied the free action of his will, he does have the full right to exercise his judgment. In time, then, within this "hard shell" of limited civil freedom, "the germ on which nature has lavished most care—man's inclination and vocation to *think freely* . . . gradually reacts upon the mentality of the people, who thus become increasingly able to *act freely*." From this, in time, comes the impulse to Enlightenment, which will finally set mankind free. And what applies, for instance, to the law or the structure of government applies also to the way our beliefs are determined. This is why anything resembling a permanent religious convention, "which would bind itself by oath to a certain unalterable creed" in order to carry on an "unceasing guardianship over all of its members and by means of them over the people," even if it were to be backed up by "the supreme power, by imperial diets and by the most solemn peace treaties," would in effect be a conspiracy "to keep all further enlightenment away from the human race forever" and that could only ever be a "crime against human nature, whose original vocation lies precisely in such progress."[117]

For Rousseau, civil society had been a calamity. The happy, if ignorant and indolent, savage had been forced by the logic of his own humanity to surrender the most precious thing he had: his freedom. But for Kant there was nothing valuable in the primitive, cowlike freedom of these "carefree men and women," these eternally happy, forever unchanging "noble savages." Ever since Aristotle (at least) everyone who thought about the matter had been in broad agreement that "happiness" was the prime goal of all human activities. As Aristotle had phrased it: "There is some end of the things we do, which we desire for its own sake (everything else being desired for the sake of this) . . . clearly this must be the good and the chief good."[118] And what was this thing? The answer, self-evident and tautological, was happiness. We do not desire to be strong, or skillful, or amorous, or successful, or even simply good, for themselves. We desire these things because they make us happy. The Greek word Aristotle used—*eudaimonia*—indicated, however, much more than the simple gratification that the modern word *happiness* implies. It meant something closer to fulfillment (or, to use an ugly modern coinage, "human flourishing"), and the theologians had routinely translated it as "blessedness." It was, however, on any account universally taken to be humankind's supreme goal. Kant was prepared to accept this insofar as happiness was the "first end of nature." But all that meant was that it was a condition in which human instincts and desires somehow matched what Kant calls man's "empirical conditions." The bliss enjoyed by the inhabitants of the Golden Age or of the "Fortunate Isles" where, in the words of the Roman poet Horace, "the unploughed earth distributes the gifts of Ceres year by year, where the vine blossoms untouched by the pruning knife," or, in some accounts at least, of Tahiti is, in every version of it, merely a state of satiation, a condition in which no one could wish to ask for more.[119] But for humanity, not wishing for more can only ever be what Kant calls the "mere *idea* of a state." For, if we were ever to acquire the perfect control over nature that would be required to achieve such a condition, what we fondly imagine to be "happiness" would be impossible, simply because the "nature [of man] is not of the sort to call a halt anywhere in possession and enjoyment and be satisfied."[120] What, then asked Kant, if we were to suppose that, contrary to what all the moralists had been saying for centuries,

> the genuine end of providence were not this shadowy image of happiness, which each makes for himself, but rather the always proceeding and growing activity and culture that is put in play by it, whose greatest possible degree is only the product of a state constitution ordered in accordance with concepts of human right, and consequently something that can be a work of human beings themselves?

The answer was obvious, and as we shall see, the "state constitution" Kant had in mind will eventually turn out to be the fulfillment of man's "cosmopolitan right."[121] For "the end of the existence of nature itself must be sought beyond nature."[122]

Most of the conditions that are commonly thought of as "happy" would be better described as supine stupidity. All those famously "happy" people of the literary imagination, had they really existed, would only ever have been merely "purposeless" creatures who would have held up "the development of all natural capacities of human beings." If "the happy inhabitants of Tahiti"—we will come back to them—who had been described in such glowing terms by the French explorer Louis-Antoine de Bougainville in his famous account of 1769 had not been "visited" by those from "more cultured nations" and had they remained "for thousands of centuries in their tranquil indolence," they would never, in Kant's view, have been in a position to "give a satisfying answer to the question why they exist at all, and whether it would not have been just as good to have this island populated with happy sheep and cattle as with human beings who are happy merely to enjoy themselves."[123] Once, at the beginning of the world, we may all have lived briefly in "a harmless and secure condition of a protected childhood—from a garden, as it were, which provided for [man] without any effort on his part." And as humans move through history, they frequently, especially when times are hard, dream of a return to that condition. The literatures of the world are filled with such dreams. It is this, said Kant, that "makes tales of Robinson Crusoe and voyages to the South Seas so attractive." These, however, can only ever be the playthings of the idle who "seek value in *pleasure* alone."[124] But every true human being, however lazy, is possessed of what Kant called "restless reason" that, "irresistibly driving him on to develop his innate capacities, stands between him and that imagined seat of bliss."[125] The Tahitians and their like, the "New Hollanders or the Fuegians," creatures who "live an Arcadian, pastoral existence of perfect concord, self-sufficiency, and mutual love," must presumably lack "restless reason," and their talents would remain "hidden forever in a dormant state" and they themselves, "as good-natured as the sheep they tended, would scarcely render their existence more valuable than that of their animals. The end for which they were created, their rational nature, would be an unfilled void." They might be nice to know, but they would not, in the full sense of the word, be really human. Kant was fully convinced that, in fact, such peoples as Bougainville had described did not exist. But this did not make the assumption that they might be any less of a danger to the future progress of the human species.

The history of real humans is the history of a struggle for the self-knowing that will finally bring humanity to the condition Kant called Enlightenment, which is the only condition that will allow mankind to resolve the conflict that first made him civil and that will finally allow him to grow straight without the need to find his acts of will constantly obstructed. When that time has come, Kant claimed in the last of the great Critiques, *The Critique of the Power of Judgment* of 1790, humanity—or at least postlapsarian humanity—will have entered into what he calls a true state of culture, for culture is "the ultimate end that one has cause to ascribe to nature in regard to the human species."[126] That final move, however, lies in an imaginable, but as yet unattained, future. It also, as we shall see, requires a radical reordering, not only of every individual society but also of the relationship that currently exists among societies, so as to create what Kant called "a society of the citizens of the world."

VI

The problem with all of these accounts, and with Kant's in particular, is that they all give the impression of being a story that could not have been told in any other way. This, apparently, is the story of a creature who, in Kant's telling phrase, is meant "to produce everything out of himself" and who is destined from the beginning to "participate in no other happiness or perfection than that which he has procured for himself free from instinct and through his own reason."[127] It is, then, a story of freedom and therefore of progress—in Kant's case, toward Enlightenment; toward inequality in Rousseau's. Yet on the most depressing reading of both Kant and Rousseau, even of Condorcet, it would appear that mankind has never been able to choose otherwise. The cunning of nature has always driven him inexorably, no matter what his own individual choices may have been. Even the cosmopolitan state of the future—which will make the full possession of "culture" attainable—will largely be a process of nature's own devising. We cannot choose but to get better. Only in relation to our capacity to free ourselves from our "self-incurred immaturity" would we seem to have a choice. Yet even here Kant is recommending only a step that, since it must be one of the many on the way to culture, has already been prepared by nature. Far from being the rational, autonomous agent the critics of the "Enlightenment project" have imagined him to be, Kantian and Rousseauian man is little more than a peculiarly constituted component in the process of nature. Substitute "God" for "Nature," and you might have a depressingly familiar Calvinist view of ontology.

You might. And many have argued that all that Kant—indeed, the whole edifice of "Enlightenment"—had ever really done was to replace one form of historical determinism with another: that in the end there is not really anything very significant that separates Providence from the "cunning of nature" except the inscrutability of the former.

The difference, however, between the God-centered universe of the theologians and the nature-centered one of the Enlightenment lies in the understanding of how human choosing plays out in time. For the theologians, history had a known beginning. It had been set down in the Bible. It had a recorded middle, so to speak, through which all human beings were currently living, and it would have a known end—whose broad outlines were also known from scripture. Despite the presence of free will, humanity itself had, in fact, only a small role to play in this story. Vico knew this, hence his constant struggle to reconcile the concept of Providence with an adequate account of human agency. The Enlightenment account of humanity's emergence from the state of nature has a known—or at least a knowable—beginning. It exists in histories and in the accounts of the still-living peoples of the world who have yet to leave it—it has a middle through which our era is currently living. But it has any number of possible ends. Things could always have been otherwise. "For we are dealing," wrote Kant, "with beings that act freely, to whom it is true, what they ought to do may be dictated in advance, but of whom it may not be predicted what they *will* do."[128] The history of humankind was a necessarily unending process. "These observations," declared Condorcet at the beginning of the *Sketch,* "on what man has been, on what he is today leads directly to the means of ensuring and accelerating the new developments which he may still hope to make."[129]

For the philosophical historians of the Enlightenment, the presence in the modern world of so many different kinds of culture, so many different levels of "civilization," was clear enough proof of this. The Tahitians, the Ostiaks and the Samoyeds, the Mongols and the Chinese, all were instances of the outcome of differing human choices. Once the general pattern has been sketched out, it will be possible for the species as a whole, if not always for the individual, to discover how one should act in order to ensure the most satisfactory outcome. For humans possess the "capacity of foresight," which is of greater importance than all their other capacities because "it is the condition of all possible practice and the goal to which man directs the use of his powers." Kant's history, like Condorcet's and Rousseau's, is, therefore, "premonitory"—prophetic as well as predictive. It is, as Kant said of it, "a narrative of things imminent in future time, consequently . . . a possible representation *a priori* of events that are supposed to happen there."[130] Both Kant's *Idea for a Universal History with a Cosmopolitan Aim* and Condorcet's *Sketch for a Historical Picture of the Progress of the Human Mind* end with general outlines for a future state of mankind. (Condorcet's longer text, which was never completed, would have been overwhelmingly concerned with such prospects.) Rousseau's *Social Contract* is similarly a project for a future possible state, a means to provide for a creature who was born free but is now "everywhere in irons," the closest moral equivalent to the perfect equality of the state of nature.[131]

VII

All of the various histories that made up the new "science of man" began, inevitably, with an account of the very origins of human life. There was nothing new in this. The claim that any attempt to define humanity had to begin with what Dugald Stewart called "the first simple efforts of uncultivated nature" had been the basis of most origin myths, and had been around at least since Plato. But the theorists of the seventeenth century, Hobbes, Grotius, and Locke in particular, had given it a wholly new direction. If, as all three had argued, human society was not, as Aristotle and his followers had supposed, a product of nature but instead a purely human artifact that had been created by individuals not out of some blind response to an innate sense of sociability but primarily as a means of protection, then it had to have had some quite specific beginning. There had, that is, to have been a time before the creation of human society, a time they called "the state of nature."

For Hobbes, "the natural condition of humankind" had been, as we have seen, a condition of war of all against all. To many of his eighteenth-century readers, this bleak, historically undifferentiated account of the origin of the human condition seemed not merely perverse but also highly improbable. "One cannot suppose," objected Montesquieu, "that men fell from the sky or sprang armed from the earth much like the soldiers of Cadmus in order to be destroyed. That is not where the state of mankind is to be found."[132] One of the problems was that Hobbes is never very precise as to whether he intended his terse, sparse description of the state of nature to be a historically verifiable one or merely an alternative, as he put it in *Leviathan,* to an "inference made from the passions." He does refer to the "savage peoples in many places in America" as evidence that even if the state of war of all against all "was never generally so, all over the world . . . there are many places where they live so now."[133] And in the frontispiece to *De Cive* the figure of "Liberty" is shown as a bowed and miserable Brazilian in a grass skirt, holding a bow in one hand and a spear in the other, faced by a resplendent—upright and unmistakably European—figure of "Imperium" (power/authority) bearing the scales and sword of justice. This and a number of other scattered allusions to the peoples of the non-European world would clearly suggest that Hobbes had conceived his account of primitive humanity as having had some historical truth to it.[134] Nowhere, however, is there anything that approaches a fully developed description. Grotius' account has a little more ethnological and historical depth, which led Leibniz to claim that "his examples, which draw on all of history and [on] ancient records, seem to be adapted in an excellent way to establish rules which can serve even today."[135] But it, too, is sparsely functional. Locke's state of nature is an altogether far more complex and more plausible condition in which humans are said only to be in a state of liberty, in that no sovereign power yet exists, but they still possess some degree of sociability and mutual recognition and consequently live together in a "state of Peace, Good Will, Mutual Assistance and Preservation." This is the state in which he believed the American Indians of his own day lived, and it is the state in which our ancestors lived in the primitive, patriarchal times described in the Old Testament. It is certainly not identical with the state of war—"however some Men," he said, taking a shot at Hobbes, "have confounded them."[136] But Locke is as evasive as both Hobbes and Grotius about just how much historical or ethnographical plausibility his state of nature was supposed to possess.

The problem with all these accounts of mankind's pre-civil condition was that they were altogether too schematic, too lacking in detail, too elusive to provide any grounds for a truly scientific history. "The Philosophers," wrote Rousseau dismissively, "who have examined the foundations of society, have felt it necessary to go back to the state of nature, but none of them has ever got there."[137] Vico was very much of the same opinion. The real problem with the accounts dreamed up by Grotius, Pufendorf, and John Selden—those "jurisconsuls of mankind" as he called them—was that they had always imagined "whatever they themselves know to be as old as the world." Because of that, all they had ever done was to fantasize about what *they* would have been like had they been living in the state of nature.[138] Grotius' natural man was, so to speak, Grotius himself without the benefits of technology, while the "licentious and violent man of Thomas Hobbes" could never have possessed the capacity to enter into a civil contract in the first place and thus could never possibly be even the most remote of our ancestors.[139]

There were also those—in particular the Scot Adam Smith and Smith's contemporary and Hume's successor as librarian to the Faculty of Advocates, Adam Ferguson—who briskly dismissed the whole idea of a presocial state. "To treat the laws of nature which would take place in the state of nature," Smith remarked, "in reality serves no purpose. . . . As there is no such state existing."[140] Humans might have no natural inclination to live the kind of life that Aristotle and his followers thought of as "political," but some kind of society was as much part of their being as their inclination to love and hate. The whole procedure, complained Ferguson, derived from the illusion that "to imagine . . . a mere negation of all our virtues is sufficient description of man in his natural state."[141] In fact, early man, like his heirs, is "determined from the first age of his being to invent and contrive." Society is as much man's natural habitant as water is for the fish. "His mixed disposition to friendship or enmity," wrote Ferguson, "his reason, his use of language and articulate sounds, like the shape and erect position of his body are to be considered so many attributes of his nature: they are to be retained in his description as the wing and the paw are in that of the eagle and the lion."[142]

It was also clear to many that, even if early men had been anything like the creatures described by either Hobbes or Rousseau, they could never have come together in the way Hobbes described and entered into the sophisticated negotiations that would have been necessary to reach the agreements required in order to work out the conditions of the social contract. Similarly, as the French jurist and one of Rousseau's more excitable critics, Simon-Nicolas-Henri Linguet, complained, Rousseau's (and Cicero's) vision of simple savages being persuaded into sociability by skillful legislators—Lycurgus and Solon, Moses and Muhammad—would be to imagine that they were "celestial intelligences rather than men."[143] Even then—and this would also have applied to Hobbes's primitive men—they would have had to have been in possession of language, an instrument that must itself have been the creation of society. And language would not have been all they would have required. For how could these simple, rude creatures have been in a position to respond to the sophisticated arguments that a Solon would have required to persuade them to abandon their old, and unrestrained, ways for the greater collective good of civil society, if they were not already in full possession of the sentiments necessary for understanding them? "One cannot claim," Linguet concluded, "that society is the effect of sentiment of which it is itself the cause."[144]

Because of this evasiveness, some argued that the "state of nature" was never intended to be anything other than what the philosophers of science call a "thought experiment." It was, to use Hume's phrase, a "philosophical fiction," analogous to the "poetical fiction of the golden age."[145] On this account, it did not much matter whether any such primitive state actually existed or not. What mattered was that it *could* have done. It only required the reader to imagine what life would be like if the world had once been in a state of unregulated warfare for him or her to recognize instantly the overriding need to create some kind of binding agreement to bring about a condition of peace. The "state of nature" is a condition that we carry with us wherever we go. Once civil order breaks down—as Hobbes had seen it do with devastating results during the English Civil Wars—then we find ourselves plunged back into it. In Hobbes's view, we had only to leave the safety of our own homes to see the obvious truth of this. How else, he asked, could you explain the fact that anyone, "when taking a journey . . . armes himself and seeks to go well accompanied."[146]

But not all were convinced. If it was a "thought experiment"; if, as Rousseau says airily at the very beginning of his *Discourse on the Origins of Inequality,* we should "begin, therefore, by setting all the facts aside, for they do not affect the question"; if, as the American political philosopher Judith Shklar once nicely put it, its purpose, like all forms of

Utopia, which it closely resembles, was merely to "induce moral recognition in the reader," why go to such lengths to make it seem as if it really corresponded to an actual condition?[147] Why the constant allusions, in both Grotius and Locke, to America? Why had Rousseau pored over the accounts of the Dominican Jean-Baptiste du Tertre and François Corréal on the Caribs, and those of the German Peter Kolb on the "Hottentots" (the Khoikhoi of South Africa), to substantiate his claims about the "savage life"?[148]

The question of how exactly these "savages," with whom all the conjectural historians had begun their fables, actually lived out their lives had never been answered. "Savage man," Buffon had written, "is of all the animals the most remarkable [*singulier*], and the least known. . . . A savage, absolutely savage would be an intriguing spectacle for the philosopher."[149] Yet in 1749 no philosopher had ever seen a "savage," let alone one who was "absolutely savage." "The Philosophers, Metaphysicians and Jurists," protested the radical *philosophe* Nicolas-Antoine Boulanger, author of *Antiquity Revealed by Its Customs* over twenty years later, in "default of any history have sought to create [their natural men] through reason alone." What they needed was some firsthand observation of, as Boulanger put it, a "real human being in a real state."[150] By the late eighteenth century, the quest for such a being had become a scientific reality.

5

DISCOVERING MAN IN NATURE

I

IN 1772 AN ANONYMOUS two-volume history of European overseas expansion since the fifteenth century appeared in the booksellers of Paris. It was called—to give its full, somewhat long-winded title—the *Philosophical and Political History of the Settlements and Commerce of the Europeans in the Two Indies*. Although it was, in fact, printed in France (and dated 1770), it carried an Amsterdam imprint, which, since Holland was famous for imposing few restrictions on the publications of books, made it clear that its content was inflammatory. Its author, as everyone secretly knew, was an otherwise largely undistinguished (despite having been elected to the Royal Society in 1754) abbé named Guillaume-Thomas François Raynal, a contributor to the venerable literary gazette *Mercure de France* and the author of a history of the English Parliament, for which he had been lauded, improbably, by Edmund Burke as "one of the finest authors of the age."[1] The *History of the Two Indies* was to make him famous. It became the most powerful denunciation of European empire-building to have appeared during the Enlightenment—indeed, at any time before the late twentieth century—and the most exuberant defense of the values of the eighteenth-century commercial society—of which we shall hear more later—as the "new soul of the moral world." More than thirty editions of the French text, and some fifty versions in translation, were printed between 1770 and 1787. There were abbreviations, a *Spirit of Raynal,* even a *Raynal for the Young*. A translation into English appeared in 1776 and was to play a not-insignificant role in shaping the revolutionary ideals of some of the founders of the new United States, due in part perhaps to the excessively rosy picture Raynal painted of the English colonies in America in comparison with the Spanish and the French.[2]

Not all of this, however, was due to Raynal's own efforts. From all accounts the abbé was, at best, a tepid enemy of both French overseas expansion and what was universally agreed to be the evil it harbored within it—slavery. He went on to be one of the grand old men of the French Revolution, but by inclination he seems to have been a moderate who, in the words of Friedrich Melchior von Grimm, held views that were "more in accordance with established politics than with justice."[3] He was also far from being a great stylist, much less a ready wit.

And in 1776 he made what turned out to be for him the mistake of appealing to Diderot "to correct his style" in preparation for a second, expanded edition. Diderot accepted, but only because he saw in the *History* an opportunity to create quite a different work. He not only polished and sharpened Raynal's sometimes lackluster prose, he inserted long passages of his own: on the barbarism of slavery, the despotism of China, the unsettling effects of travel, and the potential for moral rejuvenation offered by the United States. "A warmed-up thing," Voltaire commented archly when he read it, "with declamations." Raynal was horrified. Diderot, he complained loudly and bitterly to all who would listen, had abused "the confidence which he had placed in him. The tyrannical conditions which he had imposed—all or nothing—had been a cause for just reproach, and the only thing that was instructive and important about the work was the part that he had written himself."[4]

Raynal's indignation was ill-placed, at least as far as the success of the book was concerned. If, as Diderot told Grimm, Raynal's work had finally become "the book that I love, and which kings and courtesans detest, the book which will give birth to Brutus," this was largely because of his own contributions to it.[5] He had also asked a number of his friends and former collaborators from the *Encyclopédie*—Jean-Joseph Pechméja, the otherwise obscure author of a didactic travel novel, *Télèphe*; Holbach; Jacques Paulze, the farmer-general of taxes (and father of the chemist Marie-Anne Pierrette Paulze); the abbé Martin; and Alexandre Deleyre, librarian to the Duke of Parma, among others—to add passages of their own, so that by the time the final version appeared in ten volumes in Geneva 1780, the *History* had been transformed into a mini-*Encyclopédie* of all the varied evils that European colonization had visited upon the world, and—what is often overlooked—all the good that an Enlightened, commerce-based approach to the "barbarous" and "savage" peoples of the world might still achieve.

In making his numerous additions and emendations to Raynal's original text, Diderot, however, had a further objective. For to his mind, one of the many disastrous consequences of European colonization had been the steady elimination of the "primitive" peoples of the world. Not that Diderot much cared for the life of savages, as he said repeatedly. But however personally unattractive he might have found them, he was acutely aware that the records of travels in America, the Pacific, Africa, and Asia had revealed the existence of ways of life quite unlike those of Europe, ways that were apparently untouched by either religion or law. The observation of such peoples had made it clear to Diderot at least "that social institutions derive neither from the needs of nature nor from the dogmas of religion." They were instead the creation of men, the "founders and legislators" of individual human societies. Vice and corruption were not the inescapable consequences of a fallen human nature but creatures of mankind's own making. The discovery of the savage had finally shown the story of the Fall to be what it really was: a tale dreamt up by the would-be rulers of mankind to persuade their victims of their own culpability for the unfreedom they are forced to suffer. For Diderot, as for Boulanger, "the life and customs of savages" constituted a kind of living archive, which every effort should be made to preserve. It was, he believed, "perhaps to this knowledge that we owe all the progress which moral philosophy has made amongst us." Hitherto moral philosophers had looked for the explanation of "the origins and foundations of all human society" among those peoples, present and past, with whom they were familiar. Taking as their norm "those who had only blindness for their guide and master, they described as mysterious, supernatural, or divine what was in fact only the work of time, ignorance, weakness, or folly." The new discoveries, he enthused, "have already brought great enlightenment." It was still, however, only a "dawning of a beautiful day for humanity," and whatever was to follow, it was obvious to him that "we can say that it is the ignorance of savages which has in some sense illuminated the civilized peoples of the world."[6]

Gathering information about these savages was, however, another matter. Today, the heirs to the "human scientist" of the eighteenth century, the anthropologist and the sociologist, even the political scientist, take it for granted that they will have to spend some time in what is called, impressionistically, "the field." They will have not only to visit the people they are studying; they also will have to live alongside them, sometimes for prolonged periods of time. "Fieldwork" provides some kind of a guarantee of their sincerity and the truth of whatever claims they may eventually make. Like the natural scientists whose working methods and aspirations they hope to emulate, they must be responsible for both collecting and evaluating their own data. Things were very different in the eighteenth century. Few of the practitioners of the new science of man saw any need to leave the quiet (and safety) of their studies. For all his enthusiasm for an accurate account of the savage life, even Diderot had no desire to participate in acquiring it. "The contemplative man," he wrote, "is a sedentary being; the traveler is either ignorant or a liar. He who has been granted genius as his lot, is contemptuous of the minute details of experience, and he who experiences is almost always without genius."[7] This lofty attitude, complained the pioneer Orientalist Abraham-Hyacinthe Anquetil-Duperron—who between 1754 and 1762 had done a great deal of traveling, most of it in perilous circumstances in India, in the hope of being able to "perfect the knowledge of mankind, and above all assure us of the inalienable rights of humanity"—had led Europeans, content with their "presumptuous science," to believe that a command of Latin and Greek was all they required to understand all the peoples of the world.[8] The result, he complained, was that all of them had been raised "in the knowledge of four or five hundred leagues of country; the rest of the globe is foreign to us."[9] Anquetil's own attempt to remedy this situation, the *Journey to India, 1754–1762,* was greeted by the *philosophe* and Neapolitan ambassador to France Ferdinando Galiani with the comment that while Anquetil was "exact [and] precise," he was also "incapable of creating any system, incapable of seeing what is useful and what not."[10]

Galiani had a point—and not only about Anquetil. Even when reliably authentic travel books were self-evidently written by travelers, the trouble with travelers was their dubious probity and their inevitable selectivity. Why, asked Shaftesbury—taking another dig at his old tutor, who had been an eager, and in his view uncritical, reader of travel literature—had Locke placed such trust in "barbarian" interlocutors? For

> the faith of the Indian denier may be as well questioned as the veracity of judgment of the relater; who cannot be supposed to know sufficiently the mysteries and secrets of those barbarians: whose language they but imperfectly know; to whom we good Christians have, by our little mercy, given sufficient reason to conceal many secrets from us.[11]

Most travel writers were also far from being dispassionate scientific observers. They all, as Rousseau pointed out, belonged to one of four categories—sailors, merchants, soldiers, or missionaries—and they all clearly had some very sharp axes to grind.[12] "I have spent my life reading accounts of travels," he complained, in the long section "On Journeys" that he inserted into *Émile,* "and I have never encountered two of them who gave me the same idea of the same people."[13] What such travelers saw and what they chose to record was, even if not necessarily entirely biased, certainly conditioned by their needs and what they took to be the possible interests of their readers.

As a result of this division of labor between travelers and armchair philosophers, there was a great deal of suspicion on the part of the latter about the source of their raw materials. Travelers, whatever the category to which they belonged, wrote for a public that was increasingly avid for every tidbit of possible information about distant lands. And what the public was most interested in was the lurid, the exotic, and where possible the erotic. "For in this race of authors," complained Shaftesbury, "he is ever complimented and of the first rank, who is able to speak of things the most unnatural and monstrous." And he sneered (once again) at "the credulous Mr. Locke's" willingness to believe "Indian barbarian stories of wild nations," fed to him by "travellers, learned authors! and men of truth! and great philosophers!"[14] Francis Hutcheson was equally repelled by what he called the "Absurdity of the *monstrous Taste,* which has possess'd both Readers and Writers of Travels." Travel writers, he complained, disregarded all that was inherently virtuous in mankind on the grounds that such things were "but *common Storys*—No need to travel to the Indies for what we see in Europe every day."[15] Travelers, and their reading public, were far more concerned with human sacrifices, cannibalism, incest, polygamy, and the like than they were in the humdrum business of family love. A fascination with "exciting *Horror* and making Men *Stare*" led inevitably to a more general failure to distinguish between what was truly universal, and thus worthy of study, and what simply amounted to mere, and frequently titillating, detail.

Travelers not only embellished and exaggerated; they also accumulated worthless or irrelevant data while failing to see what was significant about what they had under their very eyes. "The true features which distinguish the peoples of the world," complained Rousseau, "and which would strike any eyes made to see, almost always escape theirs."[16] To make matters worse, they also could, and frequently did, lie. After all, there was rarely if ever anyone to check up on what they said. Implausibility and inconsistency could find out the more exaggerated inventions. And the farther one traveled from home, the more the fantasies multiplied and the more difficult it became to verify anything any traveler had written.[17] As Kant wrote dismissively in 1785, "The knowledge which the new travels have disseminated about the manifoldness in the human species so far have contributed most to exciting the understanding to investigation on this point than to satisfying it."[18]

At the time, however, for all their many and obvious shortcomings and their philosophical ignorance, travelers offered the only available window onto a wider world. As the German naturalist Georg Forster, who accompanied Captain Cook on his second voyage to the Pacific and had a much-publicized dispute with Kant over his racial theories, observed in the preface he wrote in 1785 for the Swedish naturalist Anders Sparrman's *Voyage to the Cape of Good Hope:*

> Every authentic and well-written book of voyages and travels is, in fact, a treatise of experimental philosophy. . . . It is the modern philosophers chiefly, and the living instructors of our own times, who have mostly had recourse to these treasures as containing the best materials for the purpose of building their systems, or at least, as being best adapted to the support and confirmation of their doctrines.[19]

For Forster, however, it was clear that the truly successful human science should be one in which, as was the case with the natural sciences, the observer and the speculator could be combined in one and the same person. "The whole earth," wrote Rousseau, in one of those long notes he added to his *Discourse on the Origins of Inequality,*

> is covered with nations of whom we know only their names. . . . Imagine that a Montesquieu, a Buffon, a Diderot, a Duclos [historian and linguist], a D'Alembert, a Condillac [scientist, psychologist, and linguist], or men of this kind were to travel in order to instruct their fellow men, observing and writing as they know how, of Turkey, Egypt, Barbary, the Empire of Morocco, Guinea, the lands of the Kaffirs [southern Africa], the interior of Africa and its eastern seaboard, Malabar, Mongolia, the banks of the Gan-

> ges . . . suppose that on their return from these memorable journeys, these new Hercules wrote down at leisure the natural, moral, and political history of all they had seen, then we would see a new world arise from their pens, and we would learn to understand our own.[20]

These strictly sedentary heroes of the French Enlightenment remained, however, very largely at home. Montesquieu traveled extensively in Italy and the Low Countries (and as we shall see, may have had conversations with a Chinese émigré); Condillac made it as far as Parma. But except for Diderot, who spent four miserable months at the court of Catherine the Great at St. Petersburg, none of the rest ever got beyond the frontiers of western Europe. Rousseau himself, ever reluctant to follow the advice he was so eager to offer others, except for a brief and disastrous stay in England with Hume, never went farther from France than Italy and his native Switzerland.

The idea that a learned, informed traveler might somehow find in the world the raw materials out of which a new science of humanity could be developed remained, however, a powerful and enduring one. In 1800 Joseph-Marie Degérando, the author of a once immensely popular work on the influence of signs in the history of human thought, together with Roch-Ambroise Cucurron Sicard, the founder of an institution for deaf-mutes; Louis-François Jauffret, a teacher and writer of children's books; and Joseph de Maimieux, a somewhat eccentric German émigré and inventor of a "universal language" (a kind of early Esperanto), set up a society to practice what they called the new "general science of man." They named it the "Society for the Observers of Mankind." Its objective was to study, through the painstaking collection of empirical data from all over the world, "man" in "all his various psychical intellectual and moral aspects."[21] The society lasted for only three years, but during that time, and despite the relative obscurity of its founders, it counted among its members the botanist Antoine-Laurent de Jussieu; the celebrated anatomist, paleontologist, and zoologist Georges Cuvier; and the zoologist and politician Bernard Germain de Lacépède. It also attracted a large coterie of sympathizers, including the *ideologue* Destutt de Tracy; the physiologist Pierre-Jean-Georges Cabanis; the pioneer psychotherapist Philippe Pinel; Jean Itard, a doctor who was a leader in the field of otology (the treatment of diseases of the ear) and child psychology; the *médecin-philosophe* Jacques-Louis Moreau de la Sarthe; the French nobleman, navigator, and mathematician Louis-Antoine de Bougainville; and Constantin-Francois Volney, former habitué of Holbach and Condorcet, friend and correspondent of Thomas Jefferson, and one of the most widely read authors of the late eighteenth century, who contributed a list of "statistical questions for the use of travelers."[22]

Degérando's own contribution to this enterprise was a kind of handbook for savage-watchers. He called it *Considerations on the Various Methods to Follow in the Observation of Savage Peoples*. Degérando declared confidently, like so many before him, that "the time of systems is past." The study of mankind had become the true end of philosophy, and the "science of man" had become a "natural science, a science of observation and the most noble of them all." The new "traveler-philosopher," the *voyageur-philosophe,* traveled in space in order to travel in time. "The islands he reaches," enthused Degérando, "are for him the cradle of human society. The peoples whom our ignorant vanity despises are revealed to him like ancient and majestic monuments from the origins of time." For Degérando, distances in space became distances in time. This new breed of traveler to the remoter regions of the globe, like every "human scientist," was yet another kind of "philosopher-historian." "The traveler-philosopher," wrote Degérando,

> who sails to the farthest corners of the globe, travels, in fact, along the road of time. He travels in the past. Every step he takes is a century passed. The islands he reaches are for him the cradle of human society. The peoples whom our ignorant vanity despises are revealed to him like ancient and majestic monuments from the origins of time, monuments which are a thousand times more worthy of our admiration and respect than the famous pyramids which line the banks of the Nile.

The pyramids, in his view, were nothing more than witnesses to "the frivolous ambition and transitory power of a few individuals whose names are barely known to us, whereas those others [the savages] tread in the step of our own ancestors and the first history of the world."[23]

II

The Society for the Observers of Mankind had been founded when the persistent demand for an informed account of the "ways and lives of savages" had already found expression in the evolution of a remarkable contemporary phenomenon: the scientific voyage. Beginning in the mid-eighteenth century, an astonishing number of voyages of exploration left from various parts of Europe to every region of the globe. In 1735–36 the astronomer Louis Godin sailed to Peru, in the company of Charles de la Condamine, to test Newton's hypothesis about the shape of the globe (that it was oval rather than spherical). La Condamine himself made several further voyages to Africa and the Near East and between 1743 and 1744 traveled the length of the Amazon in a voyage sponsored jointly by the governments of France and Spain. Between 1750 and 1754 the astronomer Nicolas Le Caille sailed into the southern hemisphere to measure the arc of the meridian. He identified and named thirteen of the eighty-eight southern constellations and in 1751 founded an observatory on the Cape of Good Hope. Between 1767 and 1769 Louis-Antoine de Bougainville—of whom we shall hear a great deal more later—circumnavigated the globe in what was to become one of the most famous voyages of the century. He was followed by Captain James Cook, who made three voyages into the Pacific between 1768 and 1779, the accounts of which were among the most popular reading material of the late eighteenth century and made Cook an international celebrity. In 1785 Jean-François de Lapérouse set off to verify and complete Cook's finding in the Pacific but vanished in the vicinity of the Solomon Islands in 1788. In 1789 the Italian-born navigator Alessandro Malaspina was sent by Charles IV of Spain—"in the wake of Messrs

Cook and La Pérouse"—to discover the Northwest Passage, to chart all the possessions still claimed, futilely, by the Spanish Crown (including the entire western seaboard of the United States) and to prove to the world at large that Spain was every bit as enlightened a nation as France and Britain. "The new Argonauts," Voltaire called them. Together with others of their generation, the botanist Sir Joseph Banks, the naturalists Johann Reinhold and Georg Forster, the Spanish astronomer Antonio de Ulloa, and the Swedish naturalist Anders Sparrman, they were the originators of a scientific tradition that ran, through the great German polymath and explorer Alexander von Humboldt at the end of the century, to Charles Darwin in the middle of the following one.

The objectives of these expeditions were always multiple. La Condamine went to chart the course of the Amazon and, where possible, to observe its native populations, few of which had had any previous contact with Europeans.[24] Bougainville had gone partly to circumnavigate the globe (because no Frenchmen had yet done so), to look for new species of plants and examine as many as possible, to chart "the lands lying between the Indies and western shores of America," and to find a useable sea route to China (a part of the project that he abandoned early in the voyage).[25] Cook had gone initially to observe the transit of Venus, a means of measuring the distance of the Earth from the Sun, and subsequently in search of the illusory Northwest Passage, which, it was hoped, would provide a suitable shipping lane between the Pacific and the Atlantic Oceans.

Most of the instructions issued for these expeditions also included a specific commission to observe and record the customs and habits of whatever peoples they might encounter. As Cook's editor John Douglas, in his preface to the official account of Cook's third (and final) voyage to the Pacific, expressed it, the islands Cook had visited were "a fit soil from whence a careful observer could collect facts for forming a judgement, how far human nature will be apt to degenerate, and in what respects it can ever be able to excel." The "enlightened" scientific expedition of the eighteenth century, quite apart from whatever other benefits it might provide its sponsors, had seemingly offered an unprecedented opportunity to reach deep into the collective past of the species. The "buried contents of Herculaneum," Douglas went on, were certainly worthy of attention, but all they did was to "exhibit proof of Roman magnificence," of which, it might be said, there was already proof enough. By comparison, "the novelties of the Society or Sandwich Islands [Hawaii] seem better calculated to engage the attention of the studious of our times," because only they could reveal something about the human condition we truly did not know.[26]

The quest for the untrammeled, uncorrupted specimens of "human nature" had, of course, been going on for some time. The earliest examples of "natural men" had been the American Indians. It had been they who had provided Montaigne with much of the material he had used to cast doubt on the civility and humanity of his Christian contemporaries, both Catholic and Protestant, and to suggest that, after all, "barbarian" might be nothing more than a word we use to describe what is unfamiliar to us. American Indians had also, as we have seen, made brief, if significant, appearances in all the earlier stories about the state of nature, in Hobbes and Locke, in Grotius and Pufendorf. Much of the ethnographical detail used by these writers, scanty though it was, had come from a number of familiar accounts: the Calvinist missionary Jean de Léry's description of the Tupinamba of Brazil (Montaigne's main source), Pierre-François-Xavier de Charlevoix's histories of Canada and of the island of Saint-Domingue, the Jesuit José de Acosta's *Natural History of the Indies*, and the *History of the Incas of Peru* by Garcilaso de la Vega, called "El Inca," the classically educated son of a Spaniard and an Inca princess who drew a flattering and wildly idealized picture of the Incas as latter-day Spartans or Romans.

The most enduringly influential of them all, however, was *New Voyages of M. the Baron de Lahontan in North America* of 1702. Louis-Armand de Lom d'Arce, to give him his true name, had lived for ten years in Canada as a soldier of fortune and, on his own account, had spent a great deal of that time in the company of the Algonquin, the Huron, and the Iroquois. In December 1693 he had fled to Europe under somewhat mysterious circumstances and from then on had wandered around Europe in search of employment and refuge from the French. He appeared in 1702 in Holland, "a spy by profession," and subsequently in

England, where he tried to persuade the British authorities to invade New France. Finally, in 1707, he turned up in Hanover, where he seems to have sustained a somewhat precarious existence on the periphery of the court until his death in April 1716.

Some of the qualities Lahontan ascribed to his "savages" were familiar enough from previous writers: they share everything in common and never quarrel for whatever reason among themselves; they know no jealousy; their marriages can be dissolved at the wish of either party, male or female. They are unfailingly courteous, even with their enemies, and their rhetorical skills are unsurpassed by anything in the modern world.[27] They also maintain, claimed Lahontan, "that no man should be deprived of the privileges of reason, because it is the most noble faculty with which God has enriched him." For this reason they reject Christianity, no matter how hard the Jesuits try to convert them, because, they declare, it is "not subject to the judgment of reason" and is consequently riddled with absurdities and contradictions.[28] Lahontan's anticlericalism, his picaresque life, and his apparently intimate knowledge of the lives of the Indians—together with the fact that, unlike most other writers on the subject, he was not a missionary, and although he had once been a soldier he was intensely critical of the French colonists—lent credibility to a work that was, in many respects, far from credible. Not everyone believed him. But Voltaire, Rousseau, Diderot, and Jefferson, to name a few, were all indebted to him. So too was Leibniz, who believed that his description of the life of those "savage neighbors of New France and New England" had finally "upset the too-universal political maxims of Aristotle and Hobbes." They had shown that "entire peoples" can live with one another, "without magistrates and without quarrels," and their "roughness" had demonstrated "that it is not so much necessity as the inclination to advance to a better [condition], and to arrive at felicity through mutual assistance, which is the foundation of societies and states."[29] Even the "pre-critical" Kant, who, as we have seen, excoriated the Africans and had only amused disdain for the Japanese and Chinese, claimed on Lahontan's authority that "among all savages there is no people which demonstrates such a sublime character of mind as that of North America." These, he said, were the kind of men to whom "Lycurgus gave laws . . . and if a law-giver were to arise among the six nations [of the Iroquois], one would see a Spartan republic arise in the new world."[30]

By the second half of the eighteenth century, however, any idealized image of the Amerindian as heroic or noble (or even "good") savage had largely evaporated, to be replaced by the vision of a corrupted, despondent victim of European oppression. Thomas Jefferson represented the Indians of Virginia as the living embodiment of man's natural desire for liberty and—silently borrowing Lahontan's description of the Huron—possessed of the poetic and oratorical skills sufficient to "challenge the whole orations of Demosthenes and Cicero."[31] But even he found them often far from edifying.

It had been to their "eradicable shame," wrote Bougainville, that the ambition of the Europeans had been to destroy the Amerindians, rather than study and understand them. Bougainville had spent three years, between 1756 and 1759, in Canada as captain of dragoons and aide-de-camp to General Louis-Joseph de Montcalm—who was destined to die in September 1759 while attempting vainly to prevent Quebec from falling into the hands of the British. While waiting for the British to attack, in the bitter Canadian winter, Bougainville had had ample time to observe, and admire, the courage and robustness of the American Indians. Had the Indians been left alone, he lamented, "the accounts of successive travelers [to America] might have become annals from which one could have discovered man in nature and in the influence of him of progressive civilization."[32] As it was, no such account had ever been attempted, and successive generations of Europeans had only corrupted or destroyed every vestige of the ancient Indian past to have survived.

III

Bougainville's experience of the Iroquois, and of what they might have represented for the new "science of man," made a striking impression on him. Seven years later he carried this vision of mankind in its infancy with him when he made his own sustained attempt to "discover man in nature"—not, this time, in America but in the Pacific. Here, it was hoped, in the vast uncharted waters that lay between America and Asia, might still be found the kind of simple, pre-civil peoples the Amerindians had once been. Driven by these expectations, the social theorists of the Enlightenment came to see in the Pacific a new frontier, a new "new world" where true specimens of uncorrupted natural man might at last be found. In 1756 Charles de Brosses, disciple of Buffon, friend of Diderot, president for life of the *parlement* of Burgundy, a powerful advocate for the already tentative French proposals for an exploration of the Pacific—and the man who gave the word *fetish* to the languages of Europe—published a widely read compilation of all the voyages hitherto undertaken into the "southern Seas." What he called the "Australians" (by which he meant the inhabitants of the South Pacific in general) were, he claimed, so isolated "from the rest of the universe" and so "deprived of all the resources offered by proximity and understanding with other humans" that by observing them the moderns might be able to "retrace the habits and the lives of the most ancient inhabitants of the universe."[33] De Brosses's *History of the Journeys to the Southern Lands* was sufficiently compelling to persuade Bougainville, then still in Canada, to attempt his own exploration of the Pacific.[34] It was also read with attention by the botanist and future president of the Royal Society Sir Joseph Banks, who would later accompany Cook on his first voyage and, as we shall see, leave his own particular mark on the history of the discovery of "natural man."

Bougainville, who introduced the bougainvillea to Europe and gave the plant his name—"my sole hope of fame," he wrote later, "rests on a flower"—was the perfect image of the "traveler-philosopher." "A true Frenchman" was how Diderot described him—not without irony—"balancing a treatise on integral and differential calculus on one side, with a voyage round the world on the other." (Bougainville's *Treatise on Integral Calculus* had earned him election to the Royal Society in 1755 and a somewhat inflated reputation as a geometrician.) He possessed, Diderot continued, all the necessary skills, "philosophy, courage, and veracity . . . a real desire to see, to be enlightened, to learn, a knowledge of calculus, mechanics, geometry, astronomy . . . and natural history."[35]

Diderot's brief sketch of the man owed not a little to Bougainville's own estimation of his skills and experience. His knowledge of the world, in all its diversity, the large number of places he had visited, and the various peoples among whom he had lived had, he declared sourly, prevented him from giving himself up to that "spirit of the system so common today and so little in keeping with true philosophy." He reviled, he went on—taking direct aim at Rousseau—that "class of lazy and arrogant writers"

> who in the obscurity of their studies philosophize interminably about the world and its inhabitants and imperiously submit all of nature to their imaginings . . . who having seen nothing for themselves, write and dogmatize solely on the basis of the observations made by those same travelers to whom they deny the ability to see and think.[36]

It was to provide an alternative to Rousseau's unstable, solipsistic imaginings that, on the morning of November 15, 1766, Bougainville left the French port of Brest in command of a frigate named *La Boudeuse* ("The Sulky Girl"). In February of the following year *La Boudeuse,* having joined up with a supply ship named *L'Étoile* off Rio de Janeiro, headed out into the Pacific. On the morning of April 2, 1768 they came across a deeply wooded, mountainous island. It turned out to have a perfect climate (untroubled, Bougainville noticed immediately, by the ferocious insects that infest most tropical paradises) and seemingly an abundance of food that required no cultivation. It was also inhabited by a people who, on first acquaintance, seemed to be happy, peaceful, and trustful and who paddled out in droves in long, garishly colored canoes, waving and singing, to greet the bizarre interlopers. "The number of their canoes around the ships was so great," recorded Bougainville, "that amid all that throng and noise we had difficulty in mooring. . . . They all came crying 'tayo' which means 'friend,' and they offered us a thousand signs of friendships," together with "coconuts, bananas . . . and other fruits of the land . . . all of which were delicious to us."

In exchange, all they asked for were "nails and earrings."[37] (At the time Bougainville seems to have shown no surprise at this apparently bizarre combination.) They showered Bougainville and his crew with flower petals and, somewhat to Bougainville's dismay, attempted to clamber aboard the ships. They were, he said of them in awe, beautiful—more beautiful, indeed, than anyone to be seen in Europe. "The men are six feet or more," he wrote, "and better proportioned and better made than any I have ever encountered; no painter could find a finer model for a Hercules or a Mars." Nothing in their coloring, he added, really distinguished them from Europeans, and if they were to live "a little less in the open air and in the light of the sun they would be as white as us." All of them, even the old, he noted in some astonishment, had "the most beautiful teeth in the world"—no small virtue in the eighteenth century, when few people over the age of thirty could count many of their own.[38] (Two years later Sir Joseph Banks remarked, in much the same tone of surprise, that their breath was "entirely free from any disagreeable smell.")

But it was not the men, nor their teeth, that really caught Bougainville's attention, and that of his crew. It was the women. All of them, Bougainville enthused, fulfilled all the requirements of a natural, unadorned beauty—a common theme at a time when costume and cosmetics, hats and shoes had reached the wildest extremes of fantasy. They were in their appearance, as in their behavior, entirely "natural," and the contours of their bodies in particular had "not been disfigured by fifteen years of torture"—a reference to the constraining corsets into which most of the wealthier women in Europe were strapped.

Not only did they not wear corsets. Most of them wore nothing at all, "for the men and old people who accompanied them had removed the loin-cloths with which they were normally covered." He observed shrewdly, however, that for all this display of apparent sexual availability, the women nevertheless seemed to him "somewhat embarrassed." Perhaps, he reflected, "either because nature has everywhere embellished their sex with a native timidity, or because even in this land where the freedom of the Age of Gold still reigns, women everywhere seem not to want what they most desire."[39] The men, on the other hand, knew precisely what the Frenchmen wanted. "They pressed us to choose a woman and to come on shore with her; and their gestures, which were nothing less than unequivocal, denoted in what manner we should form an acquaintance with her." Keeping his crew, who had not seen a woman for six months, at their posts proved to be a nearly impossible task; so, too, Bougainville admitted coyly, was keeping "command of ourselves." In spite of all his attempts to maintain discipline, and the women at a safe distance,

> a young girl came on board and placed herself upon the quarter-deck near one of the hatchways, which was open in order to give air to those who were heaving at the capstan below. The girl carelessly dropped a cloth which covered her, and appeared to everyone who saw her as Venus when she showed herself to the Phrygian shepherd [Paris], having indeed the celestial form of that goddess. Both sailors and soldiers tried hard to get to the hatchway, and the captain never heaved to with more alacrity than on that occasion.

On stepping ashore, Bougainville even thought that he heard Greek being spoken, or more exactly the word *eros,* which, he later explained unnecessarily to La Condamine, "means Love."[40] Although, as it turned out, they were not Greeks, or even Greek speakers; they, like the mythic Greeks of the Golden Age, lived only "in the tranquillity and the pleasure of the senses." "Their sole passion is love," he wrote, "sweet indolence, and the concern to please their most serious occupation." Yet despite all this apparent promiscuity, jealousy seemed to be unknown among them, "and all are encouraged to follow the inclinations of their hearts or the law of their senses, and are publicly applauded for doing so. The air they breathe, their songs, their dances, which are almost always accompanied with lascivious gestures, all speak at every moment of the pleasures of love."

Thereafter Bougainville's powers of description failed him. To do these people justice, he wrote, he would need the pen of François

Fénelon—the author, significantly, of the popular imaginary utopian voyage *The Adventures of Telemachus, Son of Ulysses*—or the palette of the Rococo painter François Boucher, whom Diderot once dismissed, for all his lush surfaces and louche subjects, as having "everything except the truth."[41] "One might think oneself," Bougainville declared, "in the Elysian Fields," and he renamed their home "The New Cythera," after the island off the Peloponnese on which Venus had been born. Its inhabitants, he noted, called it "Tahiti."[42]

In 1769 Bougainville returned to France to a hero's welcome and two years later published a highly detailed account of his experiences, *The Voyage Around the World by the Frigate La Boudeuse and the Supply-ship L'Étoile; in 1766, 1767, 1768 and 1769*. Despite its off-puttingly pedestrian title and, as Diderot later complained, its author's inclination to bury his more intriguing descriptive passages beneath a mound of scientific and navigational details, the book established Tahiti as an exotic—and erotic—paradise. Bougainville's account of the Tahitians seemed, as no other description of a "primitive" people had before, to provide proof that somewhere in the world it was possible to live wholly fulfilled lives beyond the reach of religious dogma, laws, or social conventions, without warfare and hardship. The Polynesians appeared to be evidence that this was how "natural," "primitive" man had indeed lived before the creation of civil society.

Bougainville's experience was repeated with, if anything, even greater gusto by Sir Joseph Banks, when he accompanied Captain Cook into the same waters on his first voyage in 1768. Banks described Tahiti as "the truest picture of Arcadia of which we were going to be kings, that the imagination can form."[43] (Banks's vision of himself as a future "king" suggests, however, that to his mind even Arcadia was not exempt from colonization.) The women were all exquisite beauties, whose bodies—with which they were very generous—were such that they "might even defy the imitation of the chisel of a Phidias or the Pencil of an Apelles." Not only were they not bowed under, as Europeans were, by the obligation to "Plow, Sow, Harrow, Reap, Thrash, Grind, Knead and Bake" to earn their daily bread, their perfect forms were "little aided by their dress, nor squeezed as our women are by cincture."

Instead, they were draped only in loose natural folds, as the ancient Greeks had been. "I have nowhere," he claimed, "seen such elegant women . . . such as the Grecians were from whose model the Venus of the Medicis was copied." On this "Island of Sensuality," he enthused, bodies and souls "are modelled into the utmost perfection, for that soft science Idleness, the father of Love, reigns here in almost unmolested ease."[44]

Even before he had returned to London, Banks had become celebrated for his lascivious, and vividly described, relations with Purea or "Oberea," whom he assumed to be the queen of Tahiti—and a fitting consort for his "king." Purea, famous for her tattooed buttocks, her "pinked bum," and her "painted breech," organized a public act of copulation for his amusement, which became the subject of a furious controversy as to whether, as seems most likely, the event was Purea's idea or if it was a common Tahitian "custom," as Cook himself suggests.[45] While Banks slept with her, the "Queen of Tahiti" also arranged for the theft of his trousers, his silver-frogged waistcoat, and his pistol.[46]

The records of Bougainville and Cook's expeditions rapidly transformed the "south Seas" not merely into the resting place of the last "natural man" but also into what Charles, Prince of Nassau-Sieger, who had shipped as a passenger on *La Boudeuse,* called the home of those happy nations that did "not even know the odious names of 'shame' and 'scandal,' " where Europeans might go to enjoy a brief respite from the religious and civil constraints they knew at home.[47] Banks, Bougainville, and the botanist and surgeon of *La Boudeuse,* Philibert Commerson, who in 1770 had written a long and scurrilous account (subsequently repudiated by Bougainville) of his own experiences of Tahiti in the *Mercure de France,* all recorded similar sentiments.

Most of these early impressions of the Tahitians and of the Polynesians from elsewhere in the Pacific were soon discovered to be either misleading or simply false. All Polynesians were, in fact, property owners, even if their understanding of possession did not always coincide with that of the Europeans. The social order of Polynesian society was also strictly hierarchical, a fact that Bougainville himself, having first described the Tahitians as all living in perfect equality, later went on to correct. The dedication of the women to "sweet indolence and the concern to please" was real enough, but it derived from a set of social practices and expectations no less rigid than those which in France compelled women to behave in quite other ways. Far from being hedonistic free thinkers, the Polynesians regulated their lives by rigid social laws and possessed deeply held religious beliefs. *Taboo,* after all, is a Polynesian word. Their famous promiscuity was, in Cook's view, not the spontaneous expression of a free and natural people—Cook had no time for such fantasies—but the sordid and demeaning consequence of "a commerce with Europeans." (Some modern anthropologists have agreed with him.) It was we "civilized Christians," he wrote in disgust, who were ultimately responsible for introducing among them "wants and perhaps diseases, which they never before knew, and which serve only to disturb that happy tranquillity they and their fore Fathers had injoy'ed." If anyone, he complained bitterly—if inconsistently—"denies the truth of this assertion let him tell me what the Natives of the whole extent of America have gained by the commerce they have had with Europeans."[48] It also became clear, in particular after the death of the Frenchman Marc-Joseph-Marion du Fresne in New Zealand in 1772, the slaughter of twelve of the companions of Lapérouse on Samoa, and Captain Cook's celebrated and much-debated murder in Kealakekua Bay in Hawaii on February 14, 1779, that the Polynesians were also intensely warlike. "No person," wrote Lapérouse, in ironic allusion to the concept of civilization as a process of corruption, "can imagine the Indians of the South Seas to be in a savage state. On the contrary they must have made very great progress in civilization, and I believe them to be as corrupt as the circumstances in which they are placed will allow them to be."

Despite these grim appraisals, the vision of Tahiti as a kind of earthly paradise, the modern version of the "Fortunate Isles," with breadfruit and coconuts in place of wheat and grapes, turned out to be immensely popular. The first edition of Captains James Cook's and James King's *A Voyage to the Pacific Ocean* of 1784 sold out in three days. By far the most popular, however, were the accounts of the voyages of Cook, and of his predecessors Wallis and Carteret, which the Admiralty commissioned from John Hawkesworth—minor playwright and librettist, editor of Swift, and, ironically, the English translator of Fénelon, whose powers of description Bougainville had wished he had. For this account Hawkesworth was supposedly paid £6,000, the largest sum for a literary work of the entire century. Compared with Commerson's, Banks's, and Bougainville's accounts of Tahiti, Hawkesworth's *Account of the Voyages undertaken by the Order of His Present Majesty for making Discoveries in the Southern Hemisphere of 1773*—not a title calculated to attract the salacious—seems very tepid stuff. Yet it unleashed in England a torrent of moral outrage at what one critic called "stronger excitements to vicious indulgences than the most intriguing French Novel could present to their imaginations."[49] "Hume or Voltaire," spluttered John Wesley, the founder of Methodism, might be prepared to believe the lurid tales of "men and women coupling together in the face of the sun, and in the sight of scores of people . . . but I cannot."[50] Satirists had a field day, in particular with Banks's adventures with "Queen" Oberea. "One page of *Hawkesworth* in the cool retreat," wrote the anonymous author of *An Epistle from M. Banks, Voyager, Monster-Hunter and Amoroso to Oberea, Queen of Otaheite,*

> *Fires the bright maid with more than mortal heat;*
> *She sinks at once into the lover's arms*
> *Nor deems it vice to prostitute her charms*
> *"I'll do," she cries, "what Queens have done before";*
> *And sinks,* from principle, *a common whore."*[51]

All of this hardly damaged the book's popularity with the general public. It became the most popular work of the entire century, overshadowing such best sellers as Samuel Richardson's two "sentimental" novels, *Pamela* and *Clarissa*. The notoriety, however, turned out to be too much for poor Hawkesworth, who had been awarded an honorary doctorate by the Archbishop of Canterbury in recognition of his stern defense of Christian morality and saw himself as a dutiful hack rather than the avant-garde of the new literary fascination with the erotic.[52] "You are *lawful game,*" shrieked the London newspaper the *Public Adver-*

tiser, "and ought to be *hunted* by every friend of Virtue." And hunted he was. On November 16, 1773, when his book was less than a year old, exhausted, he died of shame.

Although all of these accounts were lapped up by a public ever eager for just the kind of stories Shaftesbury had deplored as "things the most unnatural and monstrous," they also fed a serious scientific concern with tracing the origins of humankind. Bougainville's *Journey Around the World,* the official accounts of Cook's three voyages, the various accounts provided by Banks, by Johann Reinhold and Georg Forster, and by the Swedish naturalist Anders Sparrman, made of the Polynesians the kind of human laboratory that De Brosses and others had been hoping for.

IV

Bougainville and Cook carried back to Europe a greater knowledge of the extent and nature of the South Pacific than had ever been available before. They returned with data, with calculations and charts, with specimens of minerals and plants.[53] Both also returned with people, two real "primitives," living human specimens of the earliest ages of mankind.

Bringing back human samples from the rim of the world was nothing new. Looking directly on the face of the "Other" had always been far more rewarding than merely gazing at whatever bric-a-brac the explorer had been able to buy or steal. The Polynesians who accompanied Bougainville and Cook, however, were no mere exotica, as so many of their predecessors had been and so many other successors would be. They were objects of serious anthropological study and—although the evidence for this is all circumstantial—were probably looked upon as potential ambassadors, interlocutors in a future dialogue between "civilized" scientific Europeans and noble, if also useful, savages. They were both free to move about as they wished, and no attempt was made to convert either to Christianity. Both, too, seem to have come of their own free will.

When, in April 1769, Bougainville—"this new Robinson Crusoe," as he was sardonically called by one Parisian—arrived in Paris, he was accompanied by a Tahitian man he called Aotourou.[54] Aotourou had come aboard *L'Étoile* as soon as it arrived in Tahiti, had spent the night, and then had come and gone as he pleased for the remainder of Bougainville's stay on the island. He had chosen to leave with the French fleet entirely of his own accord, in order to visit the place called "France," although he can have had no idea of how far this was from his home, nor how long it would take him to get there.

Poor Aotourou, however, belonged to a group who were small in stature, with close-curled hair, "and whose features and colour did not differ much from those of the Mulattoes," and his appearance was quite unlike the Hercules and Mars Bougainville had described in his book. Bougainville complained that he was constantly being pestered by the *beau monde* of Paris, who, said Bougainville sardonically, "passed for learned" to know why it was that "from an island where the men are generally so beautiful I should have chosen some one so ugly." To which he replied with irritation, "I repeat once and for all that I did not choose him, he chose me."[55]

Despite his unpromising looks, Aotourou became something of a celebrity in Paris. He was feted by the duchesse de Choiseul and was a regular visitor to the Opera (the only feature of European life, Bougainville tells us, that really appealed to him), which he attended on his own, where he preferred to sit in the corridor rather than in the box provided for him. He was paraded in the Gardens of the Tuileries; presented to the king and the dukes of Provence, Artois, and Berry; and introduced to various salons, where he was met, and scrutinized, by the leading scientists and philosophers of the day, by De Bosses and D'Alembert, by Buffon and La Condamine (who generally had a dim opinion of most savages, and who later wrote an account of his visit), by Diderot, Helvétius, and Holbach, among others. His skull was carefully examined for signs of smallpox, and when none was found he was vaccinated at the suggestion of the king—vaccination, on which La Condamine had written a treatise in 1754, was one of the few, if only, medical innovations before the late nineteenth century to have been of any discernible benefit.

He was also subjected to numerous experiments into his linguistic and cognitive abilities, by La Condamine himself and by the phoneticist Jacob Rodrigue Péreire, who was asked by Bougainville to examine his palate. For although Bougainville claimed that Aotourou made up in intelligence for all that he lacked in looks, what seems to have most intrigued those Parisians whom Bougainville described contemptuously as "habitual *persifleurs*" was that, despite having spent nearly a year aboard *L'Étoile* and eight months in Paris, poor Aotourou had never succeeded in learning more than a few words of French. If after a similar amount of time, asked the "habitual *persifleurs,*" the English, Germans, and Italians could "converse passably" in French, why couldn't a Tahitian? Péreire came to the conclusion that the answer was to be found in Aotourou's inability to pronounce most French consonants and all French nasal vowels. Tahitian, a language to which Bougainville attributes the very high poetic and musical quality that all "savage" speech supposedly possessed, was too mellifluous for its speaker to adapt to the harsher sounds of French (which, Bougainville thought, might have made it easier for Aotourou to learn Spanish or Italian).[56]

In Bougainville's opinion, however, the true reason for Aotourou's failure was more cognitive than physiological. "Having a world of ideas," he wrote, "on the one hand relative only to the simplest and the most restricted of societies, and on the other to needs limited to the smallest possible number," Aotourou, when confronted with the demands of French society, had had to "create, so to speak, in a mind as indolent as his body, first a world of ideas, before being able to adapt them to the words in our language which corresponded to them."[57] Although Bougainville does not stress the point, Aotourou's failure was living proof of the contemporary assumption, derived ultimately from Locke, that individual words in any language related directly to objects in the external world. If you lacked the word, then clearly you lacked any knowledge of the thing.[58] The art of lying, says Voltaire's Inca princess Alzire, drawing on this same assumption, "is an art of Europe, not made for me."[59] It is not that she cannot grasp what lying is. She simply does not have the terms with which to do it. It was this argument that lay behind those frequent claims that, as Montaigne had said of his cannibals, "they have no terms for governor or political superior. . . . Among them you hear no words for treachery, lying, cheating, avarice, envy, backbiting," which in this respect, at least, clearly demonstrated their superiority to the torturing, burning Christians who had transformed France during his lifetime into a slaughterhouse.[60]

Charles de la Condamine took a very different view. "All the languages of South America of which I have had some understanding," he wrote,

> lack the terms with which to express abstract and universal ideas, evident proof of the slight progress which the minds of these peoples have made. *Time, duration, space, being, substance, matter, body,* all these words and many others have no equivalent in their languages. It is possible to render the names, not only of metaphysical entities, but also moral ones, in these languages only imperfectly and by means of long periphrases. There are no words which correspond to *virtue, justice, liberty, recognition, ingratitude.*[61]

Montaigne's lexicon, like Alzire's (and that of countless others), had been generally positive (although Montaigne was ironic and allusive about even this; one of the terms his cannibals lack is *forgiveness*). La Condamine's is wholly negative. But the underlying assumption was the same in both. As man in his original condition is one with nature, he responds directly to the data he finds around him. His language is transparent and immediate. "Savage" languages—as numerous travelers claimed to have observed—lack the abstractions and universals with which civilized men do their thinking. If the "Eskimos" famously have hundreds of different words for "snow" (in fact they do not) and the Algonquin multiple words for "tree" (and, according to Herder, the Singhalese "twenty sorts of names" for "woman," and the Arabs four hundred for "misery"), this is not because either the Eskimos or the

Algonquin have a more intimate and imaginative relationship with nature, or the Singhalese and the Arabs a more highly developed interest in women or a more powerful sense of misery, than the Europeans. It is only because they lack the universal abstractions *snow, tree,* and so on.[62] In their worlds, "snow falling" and "snow on one's igloo" are simply two different kinds of stuff, as—for the Algonquin—are oaks and maples. The languages of "savages" are made up solely of words for things. In contrast, the languages of civil man, said the great Jewish philosopher Moses Mendelssohn in 1764, store ideas, judgments, sensations, and "rational information."[63]

In this respect "savage" languages were clearly defective. But if they were poor in abstract terms, they were rich in metaphor; for of all the forms of speech, it is metaphor and complex compound nouns that most closely approximate to the original composite image that strikes the eye or the ear. Since "primitive" languages were thought, in this way, to share something with the original harmony between man and the natural world, they were also believed to be able to capture entire images with a single word. The first languages, as Rousseau put it, "give to each word the sense of an entire proposition."[64] Thus—or so the philosopher and mathematician Pierre-Louis Moreau de Maupertuis, best known as the man who determined that the world was oblate (flat at the poles) rather than prolate, or egg-shaped, claimed in 1756—"a savage whose language is not yet formed can compound and express at the same time, pronoun, verb, noun, proper name, substantive and adjective and thus say in a single word: 'I have killed a great bear.' "[65] Aotourou's language, therefore, had placed him, as ineluctably as had the social and moral codes of his society, at the infancy of the world, at the point from which all peoples, all civilizations, have their origins. As we shall see, this was turned by Diderot into a reflection upon the mistaken ways in which civil man has constructed his own social and moral universe.

Aotourou was returned to Tahiti in March 1770. He went, as Bougainville phrased it, "enriched with knowledge" and carrying gifts from the duchesse de Choiseul of seeds, animals, and tools, the advance guard of a French bid to create a new trading empire in the Pacific.

"What better way," reflected Bougainville, "of securing a fruitful and peaceful alliance with these peoples." "Let us hope to God," he added, "that the need and the zeal that have inspired us do not turn out to be disastrous for the brave Aotourou." His fears were well founded. The return journey, which was paid for by the now-bankrupt Bougainville, was long and arduous, and Aotourou died en route of measles, against which there was, at that time, no vaccine.[66]

When Cook returned from his second voyage to the Pacific in 1774, he also brought back with him a "natural man," a native of Huahine in the Sandwich Islands called Mai or Omai. Although Cook seems to have had a low opinion of his intellect, based largely on his failure to be impressed by the splendors of London, Omai, like Aotourou, also became a celebrity. He had his portrait painted, together with Banks and the Swedish naturalist Daniel Carl Solander, by the court painter William Parry, and by Sir Joshua Reynolds, in which he appears dressed in a belted version of a toga and in the traditional pose of the Roman orator. He was presented to the king and queen at Kew and is said to have knelt before the king saying, "How do King Tosh"? What poor, mad George III made of that is not recorded. He was taken to the House of Lords, to which he apparently made a speech, and went shooting on the north Yorkshire moors. He was dressed in Highland costume—something of a novelty at the time—criticized the coiffure of Georgina, Duchess of Devonshire; admired mousetraps; and spent some time unsuccessfully trying to make nails. (Nails became a Polynesian obsession—there is no metal in Polynesia—and it was the theft of the *Discovery*'s cutter for its nails that led to Cook's murder in Hawaii in 1779.) He was also given a sword to wear and dined with almost everyone of note in London, from the Lords Sandwich and Fife to the musician Charles Burney (who heard him sing a Polynesian love song and declared it to be a "mere confused rumbling of uncouth sounds"). He was given English lessons by the abolitionist and social reformer Granville Sharp as a "preliminary step" in bringing "the diffusion of Christian light over a new race of men." Although Omai managed to find time in his busy social schedule for only fifteen lessons, Granville claimed to have taught him "every combination of vowels and consonants that letters are capable of." He also tried to persuade him of the "divine truths of our religion and the several duties which it enjoins." For all his devout Christianity, Sharp was as sincere a believer in equal rights for men and women as he was in equality between the races, and many years later, in Sierra Leone, he recorded a conversation he had had with Omai on the injustices involved in polygamy. Sharp had been explaining to Omai the Ten Commandments. He had no difficulty with the first six, but when he came to the seventh, "Thou shalt not commit adultery," Omai stopped him.

> "Adultery! What that? What That?" "Not to commit adultery," I said, "is that, if a man has got one wife, he must not take another wife, or any other woman." "Ohh!" says he, "two wives—very good; three wives—very, very good." "No, Mr. Omai," I said, "not so, that would be contrary to the first principle of the law of nature." "First principle of the law of nature," said he, "what that? What that?" "*The first principle of the law of nature,*" I said, "is that *no man must do anything that he would not like done to himself.*" . . . For the women have the same passions and feelings, and love toward the men, that we have toward the women: and we ought, therefore to regulate our behaviour toward them by our own feelings of what we should like and expect of faithful love and duty from them toward ourselves."
>
> Omai was silent for a while. Then he moved to a nearby table.
>
> There was an ink-stand on the table, with several pens in it. He took one pen and laid it on the table, saying, "There lies Lord S——" (a Nobleman with whom he was well-acquainted, and in whose family he had spent some time); and then he took another pen and laid it close by the side of the former pen, saying, "and there lies Miss W——" (who was an accomplished young woman in many respects, but unhappily for herself, she lived in a state of adultery with that Nobleman); and then he took a third pen, and placing it on the table at a considerable distance from the other two pens, as far as his right arm could extend, and at the same time leaning his head upon his left hand, supported by his elbow

on the table, in pensive posture, he said, "and there lie Lady S——, and cry!"

"It was plain," concluded Sharp after this little demonstration, "that he thoroughly understood the force of the argument from the law of liberty, when it is applied to regulate, by our own feelings, the proper conduct and behaviour which we owe to other persons," and that "there was no need to explain the rights of women any further."[67]

Despite the comic turn of speech that Sharp attributed to him, when she met Omai, the novelist Fanny Burney, author of *Evelina or a Young Lady's Entry into the World,* said of him that his manners were so extremely graceful "that you would have thought he came from some foreign court." Samuel Johnson, who, although generally unimpressed, when not disgusted, by "savages," whether they came from Polynesia or the highlands of Scotland, had a similar reaction when he dined with him one evening at the home of Lord Mulgrave in Streatham. In the flickering, uncertain light of the candles, he could not make out clearly who was Omai and who his host, and "there was so little of the savage in Omai, that I was afraid to speak to either, lest I should mistake one for other."[68]

Omai was also the object of more detailed scientific scrutiny. He had his skull examined to ascertain "what faculties were strong and what less vigorous in his mind." He was found to be exceptionally "amative" and "combative and destructive" and to have a "very large Individuality" and extraordinary "Philoprogenitiveness"—apparently this meant that he missed his family—as well as "considerable self-esteem" and extraordinary "Ideality and wonder." His wit, however, despite the ingenious way in which he had demonstrated his understanding of the "law of liberty," remained "undiscovered."[69]

Omai was shipped home by Cook on his third and last voyage in 1776. He took with him a curious assembly of presents, including a suit of armor from Lord Sandwich that had been made especially for him by the armorers of the Tower of London, a hand organ, some firearms (much to Cook's misgivings), and a mechanical Punch and Judy show. On finally reaching Huahine on October 13, 1777, Omai took his leave of Cook on the deck of the *Resolution* and went weeping all the way to shore. As he put out to sea, Cook wrote in his journal: "It was no small satisfaction to reflect, that we had brought him safe back to the very spot from which he was taken." "And yet," he continued with foreboding, "such is the strange nature of human affairs, that it is probable that we left him in a less desirable situation than he was in before his connection with us."

What became of Omai after his return we cannot know for sure, since, as Cook somewhat wistfully concluded, that was a matter for "the future navigators of this ocean; with whom it cannot be a principal object of curiosity to trace the future fortunes of our traveller."[70] When, however, William Bligh visited the island on the ill-fated *Bounty* in 1788, he discovered that Omai had died in 1779.

V

Both Omai and Aotourou left behind them a number of imaginary personae. Omai served as a stock figure in several satirical attacks upon the morals of the court and became the subject of a pantomime, *Omai, or a Trip Round the World*—improbably, but significantly, described by the *Ramblers' Magazine* as "a school for the history of Man"—which played to packed houses in 1785. ("King Tosh" himself came to several performances.) In the last scene, a huge painting by the designer Philip James de Loutherbourg, *The Apotheosis of Captain James Cook,* was lowered onto the stage while the chorus chanted:

The Hero of Macedon ran o'er the World;
Yet nothing but death *could he give.*
'Twas George's Command and the Sail was unfurl'd
And Cook taught mankind how to live.
He came *and he* saw, *not conquer, but save;*
The Caesar of Britain was he;
Who scorn'd the Ambition of making a Slave
While the Britains themselves are so free.[71]

The allusions to Alexander the Great and Julius Caesar are perhaps a little confused, but the message was unambiguous: in the new British Empire, where science had replaced slavery and commerce had replaced conquest, the "savage," far from being dispossessed and destroyed as he had been in the Americas, would now be uplifted and enlightened—and *saved.*

It was, however, the semifictionalized person of Aotourou who was to make the most enduring impression on the European vision of the earliest condition of mankind.

In 1772 Diderot was commissioned to write a review of Bougainville's *Voyage Around the World* for Grimm's *Correspondence littéraire*. This subsequently grew into what became (although it was never published during his lifetime) the most widely read representation of the so-called good (*bon*)—or as the English insisted, "noble"—savage: the *Supplement to Bougainville's Journey*. Diderot's evocation of "primitives" has generally been taken to be something even more literary and fantastical than either Bougainville's or Banks's. But although the *Supplement* is ironic and elusive, it was also clearly a part of what Diderot's first editor and biographer, Jacques-André Naigeon, identified as his project to create a natural and experimental history of man, a history that would explore the conflict between the apparent homogeneity of the physical makeup of the species and the huge diversity of behavior of which its individual members were capable.[72] Its purpose was to provide what Diderot himself referred to as the "preliminary notion of mankind" that had to precede all moral and aesthetic judgment.[73]

Human nature, Diderot was convinced, was everywhere the same, but human identity, like the material substance of the planet itself, changes over time. The modern world had confronted this dilemma—or rather, it had attempted to erase the essential instability of the human personality—by setting up rules and regulations, moral standards and religious injunctions that would supposedly be true for all human beings at all times and all places. The result, as he had himself experienced at the hands of an overbearing father and now an estranged and bitter wife, was misery, violence, and despair, as individuals struggled to constrain their natural inclinations and desires to comply with artificial demands that had been devised to serve the needs, and qualm the fears, of others. In Bougainville's account of Tahiti, Diderot seemed to have found the image of a society that, with a little imaginative input, could be made to demonstrate the failure of "civilized" man to live the kind of life for which nature had intended him.

The subject on which Diderot focuses to make this point—the subject for which Tahiti was best known—is, of course, sexual relations and the distorted way in which European society has, as he put it, "attached certain moral ideas to physical actions which do not accord with them." The *Supplement* is, like so many of Diderot's writings, highly ambiguous, involving two set pieces—a long condemnatory oration aimed at European civilization by an old Tahitian—called "The Old Man's Farewells"—and an extended conversation between Aotourou—now simplified to "Orou"—and Bougainville's chaplain, both of which are said to be unpublished fragments from Bougainville's journal. These are then linked together by passages of dialogue between two characters called simply "A" and "B." At one level the *Supplement* is offered as an elaboration of a number of events and characters that appear in Bougainville's own text. At another, however, it is also, obviously a work of fiction that has clear links with two of Diderot's best-known stories, *This Is Not a Story* and *Madame de la Carlière,* characters from both of which are mentioned ironically, by "A," as if they were real people. (It also includes a sly dig at Raynal. "An excellent work," remarks "A," of the *History of the Two Indies,* "and one so different in tone from his previous writings that the abbé is suspected of having commissioned it from other hands.")[74]

In Diderot's hands Orou indeed becomes, as Shaftesbury would have complained, the very image of the Stoic "nay-sayer"—although, as we shall see, he will in the end come to some very un-Stoical conclusions. Like the itinerant Persians, Uzbek and Rica, of Montesquieu's immensely popular epistolary novel *The Persian Letters* and so many other fictional visitors to Europe, Orou is a curious, often baffled outsider whose role is to subject all the conventions, assumptions, and beliefs, all the prejudices and habits of mind of European society to withering criticism. Unlike the real Aotourou and Omai, who were for the most part as impersonal and as mute as the exhibits in a museum, Orou is eloquent, caustic, angry, and indignant by turns. He is not there to be questioned, examined, dressed up, exhibited, and taught a foreign tongue; it is he who questions, and before his withering gaze all that is accepted in Europe as "natural" is shown to be merely conventional, tyrannical, and self-denying, when it is not simply foolish.

In Diderot's version of the story, Bougainville's chaplain takes up lodgings with Orou before he leaves Tahiti. In accordance with the—by now famous—Tahitian laws of hospitality, Orou begins by offering his witless guest in succession his three daughters and his wife as sexual companions. Each time the chaplain refuses. Orou, offended, asks why. The chaplain answers by trying to explain the moral sanctions imposed upon him by his religion. Orou listens patiently and points out that not only are most of these obviously contrary to natural human inclination, they are in most cases more often ignored than observed. Of this, the chaplain himself turns out to be the living proof: "He was young, agitated, vexed. He averted his eyes from the lovely supplicants and then gazed at them again. He raised his hands and eyes to the heavens." Night after night he goes through the same tribulations. Night after night he finally succumbs to one woman after another, while crying out, "But my religion! But my holy vows!" thus demonstrating what Orou (and Diderot) had maintained all along, that Christian moral rules correspond in no way to human passions.[75]

For the chaplain, his moral inhibitions are sanctioned by religion and law and are enforced by magistrates and priests. For Orou, religion, at least as a system of moral constraints, can have no real place in nature, since all of nature's rules are transparent, self-evident, and self-evidently beneficial to all. Only a madman would wish to transgress them.

The real enemy of the customs and social order of the civilized world, as viewed by the kings and clergy who sought to control it, was desire. "Desire," as Diderot wrote in the *Elements of Physiology* of 1778, "is the offspring of the organism, the offspring of happiness and unhappiness, of good living and of evil living."[76] What the Europeans had tried to do for centuries was to suppress desire or to sublimate it in such things as the semierotic fantasies of the lives of the saints and martyrs. All that had achieved, claimed Diderot, in an image to which he would return again and again, was to create an artificial person who is forever at war with the natural one. The brief history of nearly all our misery, says the character named "B," comes down to this: "Once upon a time there was a natural man: inside him was introduced an artificial one, and within his breast a civil war broke out which will last for the whole of his life."[77] What separates the Tahitians from the Frenchmen who will one day transform their world into an image of their own is not, in the end, their simplicity or their innate goodness (in Diderot's account they are neither particularly simple nor especially good) but their capacity for self-understanding, for being both "the observer and the machine that is being observed."[78] Diderot makes the point with a story. A young woman called Jeanne Barret had shipped as Commerson's valet on *La Boudeuse,* in the guise of a man and under the name of Jean Baré. Throughout the voyage and despite what had struck some of the crew as an obsessive insistence on privacy, she had succeeded in passing herself off as a young man. On landing on Tahiti, however, the Tahitian men joyfully set upon her, eager, as Diderot puts it (echoing Bougainville himself), "to receive her in the proper Tahitian manner." (Later she married a French naval officer and became the first Frenchwoman to circumnavigate the globe.)[79]

The point of this little story, which in Bougainville's telling ends with the ironic observation that "if the two ships had been wrecked upon some desert island in that vast ocean, Baré's fate would have been very remarkable,"[80] is that because Europeans pay more attention to the outer person than the inner, they are more easily deceived by clothing than the Tahitians. The "savage," who is in direct contact with "nature," can see through to the true person beneath. (In fact, if François Vivez, the surgeon on the *Étoile,* is to be believed, the Tahitians pursued every faintly effeminate member of Bougainville's crew, insisting that they were all women in disguise.)[81] There was a further, and more serious point. The natural Tahitians, unlike the "civilized" Europeans, can recognize instantly differences in gender, because they recognize women for what they truly are: lovers, mothers, companions, friends. The Europeans, however, concerned only with the bonds—and bonds are what they are—of marriage, see them merely as objects of property. Having done that, they then assume that personal relations must be made to have the endurance and constancy of things. The Christian idea of marriage as something permanent and indissoluble and the laws and the sanctions that sustain it are a misreading not only of the nature of pleasure but also of human affections, both of which are necessarily transient. "The only solid objection to divorce," Diderot told Catherine the Great of Russia, who indulged a similar passion for inconstancy, was the problem of how to educate children.[82] Otherwise all humans, men and women, should be allowed to choose as many partners as they wished. "Don't you see," asks Orou,

> that in your country you have confused something which cannot feel or desire or will; which one takes or leaves, keep or sells, without it suffering or complaining, with a very different thing that cannot be exchanged or acquired: which does have freedom, will, desire: which has the ability to give itself up or hold itself back forever; which complains and suffers; and which can never be an article of exchange unless its character is forgotten and violence is done to its nature. Such rules are contrary to the general order of things. What could seem more ridiculous than a precept which forbids any change of our affections, which commands that we show constancy of which we are not capable, which violates the nature and liberty of male and female alike in chaining them to one another for the whole of their lives. What could be more absurd than a fidelity restricting the most capricious of our pleasures to a single individual; than a vow of immutability taken by two beings of flesh and blood under a sky that does not remain fixed for an instant, beneath caverns poised on the edge of collapse, under a cliff crumbling into dust, at the foot of a tree shedding its bark, beneath a quivering stone?

The one thing that should be constant, however, is precisely the rules that govern human behavior. These have always to be explicable in terms of "nature"; they have, that is, to be capable of being universalized and thus fully intelligible to one such as Orou who has no knowledge of the society that first created them. The rules that govern the society in which the chaplain lives, however, emerge, as he struggles to explain them, as arbitrary, unfounded, and obscure. They are based not upon nature and reason but upon unexamined prejudice. Prejudice had frozen the European capacity for passion and desire.[83] It had turned the women for the most part into frustrated harridans and quite literally unmanned the men. Charles-Félix-Pierre Fesche, a volunteer on board the *Boudeuse,* came to much the same conclusion after witnessing the Europeans' first encounter with the Tahitians. A woman, accompanied by an "old man and several of her compatriots," had been enticed "by the welcoming gestures of some of the Frenchmen" to come aboard the *Boudeuse.* In the canoe that had brought her to the ship, she had been draped in some kind of "veil." As soon as she reached the deck she let this drop, "following the ways (*usages*) of her country which the corruption of our customs (*moeurs*) have destroyed amongst us." What "paintbrush," enthused Fesche, "could describe the marvels revealed by the happy descent of that inopportune veil"? The crew could barely contain themselves. "We fell about in ecstasy," he recorded, "a sweet and gentle warmth overwhelmed our senses; we boiled." But decency, "that monster which so often struggles with the will of men," apparently rendered the unfortunate crew impotent. Despite several attempts by "this new Venus" to persuade the French to behave like men or, as Fesche somewhat prudishly puts it, to "perform a sacrifice to Venus," the apparently awestruck sailors, for all their pent-up lust, could not be induced "to transgress the bounds of decency, and of the prejudices established amongst us." Indignant, she picked up her "veil" and departed.[84] In France, Fesche reflected, all the inhibitions summed up by the word *decency* were the necessary condition of social survival, a part of the world that no one could imagine to have been constructed in any other way. In the Pacific it was merely a foolish unexamined prejudice.

The same refusal to see that any law, any custom, that does not correspond to the inescapable volatility of the entire cosmos cannot be "natural" also underlies the problems that the Tahitians appear to have had with the French language. Like Aotourou, Orou finds it hard to grasp what the chaplain is trying to say (not, it must be said, that the wretched man is given any very good arguments). Unlike Aotourou, however, Orou's linguistic difficulties derive not from any inability to understand French (in which he seems to be strikingly, and impeccably, eloquent) but rather from a refusal to concede to the linguistic trickery that allows the Europeans to fabricate a set of social and moral laws based on mere names for which there exist no corresponding things in nature. The law has become the law not because it corresponds to some dictate of nature, or some obvious need, but merely because at some point some authority codified it as such. Orou is, he declares, hardly surprised—although he is outraged—on hearing of the shame and disgrace that European society hands out to those who transgress its sexual rules:

> As soon as it's permitted to settle an idea of justice and property according to one's fancy, to ascribe or strike out traits of things as if they were arbitrary, to attribute or deny good and evil to actions on no other grounds than whim, each person blames, accuses, suspects another, everyone tramples upon each other, becomes envious, jealous, deceitful, distressed, secretive, covert, spying upon one another to take him or her by surprise; everyone quarrels and lies.[85]

Orou knows that the main goal of all human beings is happiness and that happiness derives from pleasure. Pleasure, as Diderot understands it, is not, however, the kind of hedonism that La Mettrie had urged upon his readers but what Diderot called "moral pleasure." This was, he said in the article he wrote on the subject for the *Encyclopédie,* "a feeling of the soul which makes us happy." Pleasure is the "only movement by which nature guides matter" and consequently the behavior of human beings. The Tahitians recognize the truth of this. They have built for themselves a society that reflects the essential instability and changeability of the human condition, instead of trying to overcome it by means of artificial rules and regulations, fantastical religious injunctions, and those "prejudices" born of long and unquestioned habit.

For all that, however, Diderot's Tahitians are not the indolent, unreflective perpetual children that Kant (among others) represented them as being, not, as he observed caustically, unlike the offspring of "rich parents and the sons of princes."[86] When the chaplain complains that there can be little space for maternal or paternal feeling in a society where a couple stay together only as long as they wish and where a woman may take as many sexual partners as she chooses, Orou replies emphatically that in place of such sentiments, "we've another which is altogether more energetic and durable: self-interest." For Buffon, the objective of natural man had merely been to live and be idle, and even the *ataraxia* of the Stoic "comes nowhere close to his profound indifference for all other objects." Diderot, by contrast, makes his natural man into something like an energetic "Spinozist," a utilitarian for whom self-interest is the source of a moral principle. So long as we desire and love, we value. So long as we value, we are following our own self-interests. The moment desire ceases, then it becomes no longer in our interest to pursue what had once been its objects. That is the way mankind (and not just men, I should add: in Diderot's Tahiti the women have just as much freedom to pursue pleasure as do the men) is *in nature*. "Look candidly into your conscience," demands Orou,

> and leave behind that sanctimonious bluster always foaming from the lips of your comrades but never to be found deep in their hearts; tell me if there's any country in the world in which a father, unless held back by shame, wouldn't rather lose his child, or a husband his wife, than accept the loss of his fortune and the comforts of his life. You can be sure that whenever a man is as attentive to his fellow creatures as to his bed, health, or peace of mind, his hut, harvests, or fields, he will do his utmost to ensure their welfare. It's here that you will see tears shed over the bed of a sick child, and mothers nursed though illness. It's here that we prize a fruitful woman, a nubile girl, an adolescent boy. It's here that we take an interest in their upbringing, because in preserving them our fortune grows, while with their loss it is diminished.[87]

To achieve this kind of "happiness and perfection" we have to understand desire for what it is, the ultimate reflection of our own love of self. This does not mean, as the uncomprehending chaplain supposes, that the Tahitians are no different from the French peasants who would "wear out their wives to spare their horses" or that the sorrow they feel for the suffering of those sick children or ailing mothers is any the less genuine. The love that Orou's utilitarian ethic engenders is indeed far more heartfelt, far more sincere, than anything the chaplain might be capable of, precisely because it is self-knowing. The chaplain loves because his vows demand that he do so. Orou loves because nature tells him to.

Diderot's Tahiti, like Hobbes's and Rousseau's own evocations of pre-civil man, is a thought experiment. Unlike either Hobbes's or Rousseau's savages, however, Diderot's Tahitians do not belong to any kind of state of nature. They live instead "in a kind of society which is half civilized [*policé*], half savage." Tahiti is a supposedly real reflection of the colony that Diderot dreamed, half ironically, in his ferocious onslaught on Helvétius' *On Man* of 1775—and believed might perhaps be constructed on the island of Lampedusa in the Mediterranean. The legislators of antiquity, he wrote, had had nothing from which to build their civilizations but the state of nature. Little wonder, then, that they had all gone so badly wrong. But was it not perhaps possible, wondered Diderot, that

> a modern legislator, more enlightened that they, might found a colony in some remote corner of the world, and would perhaps discover, between the savage state and our wonderful civilized state, an environment which would retard the progress of the child of Prometheus, and protect him from the Vulture, and which would fix civilized man between the infancy of the savage and our present decrepitude?

Were such a society ever to come into being, it would be the place where the only true and lasting "happiness of the species resides."[88]

The trouble is, however, that—as Diderot knew as well as Kant—for the species there never can be any lasting happiness. "The destiny which controls the world," as he admitted to his friend Grimm, "wishes that all should pass. The happiest condition of man, or of a state (as with all else), must have its day."[89] Orou may be a good Spinozist and a good utilitarian *avant la lettre*. But even his degree of self-knowledge will not allow him to escape the consequences of what "B" calls the "historical sketch of all our miseries." This, as the "Old Man" who is given the speech of farewell to Bougainville knows, will become the true tragedy of the Frenchman's visit. "Weep, wretched natives of Tahiti, weep," he implores his countrymen. "But let it be for the coming and not the leaving of these ambitious, wicked men."[90] For now the Tahitians have been "infected"—literally, since a new mixed race is about to come into being, the offspring of the tireless sex between Bougainville's crew and the women of Tahiti; a race that is already launched on the journey that will take it inexorably toward civil society. In the Old Man's tirade against the Europeans, this is described as Bougainville's crime. But even if the Europeans had never set foot on the island, the logic of human evolution would have taken them there all the same. All that Bougainville had done was to accelerate the process. "It seems to me," says "B,"

> that as soon as physical forces, such as the need to overcome the infertility of the soil, have brought man's ingenuity into play, the momentum drives him well beyond his immediate objective, so that when his need has elapsed he comes to be swept into the great ocean of fantasy from which he cannot pull out. May the happy Tahitian stop where he is! I can see that, except in this remote corner of the globe, there has never been any morality and perhaps never will be.

But stop is precisely what the Tahitians cannot do. Civilization is a learning process, and since all human beings, like the universe itself, are in constant movement, it is also inevitable. "All civilized peoples,"

Diderot declared, "had once been savages, and if left to their natural impulses all savage peoples are destined to become civilized." Diderot accused Bougainville of having "cried out against Hobbesianism at home but then carried it with him from nation to nation." Yet he also knew that sooner or later the Tahitians would have got there by themselves. They live in an arrested state, one so fragile that, on Diderot's paraphrasing of Bougainville, it required only the presence of the European, and European goods, to transform them into thieves. The Tahitian could easily understand the superiority of iron nails over rope and wood, and given the chance they would have been able to see the advantages of firearms over bows and spears. The mere recognition of their usefulness will change the simple "savage" life forever. And there could be no doubt that, once introduced to them, the Tahitians will also want all those other, less practical goods the Europeans crave. The desire for acquisition is a human urge almost as strong as sex. As the English poet William Cowper asked, in addressing Omai, now back home on Huahine:

Thee, gentle savage! Whom no love of thee
Or thine, but curiosity, perhaps
Or else vain glory, prompted us to draw
Forth from thy nature bow'rs to show thee here
With what superior skill we can abuse
The gifts of Providence, and squander life.
The dream is past; and thou hast found again
Thy cocoas and bananas, palms and yams,
Thy homestall thatch'd with leaves. But hast thou found
Their former charms? And having seen our states,
Our palaces, our ladies, and our pomp,
Our equipage, our gardens, and our sports,
And heard our music; are thy simple friends
Thy simple fare, and all plain delights,
As dear to thee as once? And have thy joys
Lost nothing by comparison with ours?[91]

The lure of civilization was inescapable. You might, like Rousseau, rail against it. You might fend it off for a while. But once seen it could never be forgotten.

Diderot's Tahiti was not intended to be a permanent retreat for civilized man. It was meant to be a lesson. "What shall we do?" asks "A," at the very end of the *Supplement,* "Return to nature? Submit to laws?" To which "B" replies, "We must speak out against senseless laws until they're reformed and, in the meantime, abide by them." In fact, we have no choice. Civilization is a one-way journey. The belief, which the "good savage" literature of the eighteenth century did so much to foster, that there was some viable alternative to the hideously imperfect societies in which human beings are currently divided is simply an illusion. If we are, as "B" says, to "improve the laws," we have to understand on what basis those laws have been built. That, and that alone, is something about which the "customs and habits" of "savages" may have much to teach us. Diderot's evocation of Tahiti, moralizing, ironic, and reflective by turns, is not, as it has been so often represented, the vision of a better, more desirable world. It is the image of a people at the very beginning of the process that will carry them inexorably toward civilization, and the main concern of Diderot's "natural and experimental history of man," as of all the various versions of the "science of man," was precisely to understand, and through understanding perhaps also control, the civilizing process.

6

THE DEFENSE OF CIVILIZATION

I

"YES, M. ROUSSEAU," Diderot wrote angrily to Sophie Volland in 1776, "I prefer refined vice under a suit of silk, than stupid ferocity beneath an animal skin."[1] The savage condition may well have been a state of true innocence and, equally surely, civilization was—reversing Hobbes's dictum—the "state of war and crime." But, Diderot added, "that the savage state is preferable to the civilized state. That I deny!"[2] If Diderot admired the stoicism that the savage—Tahitian, Canadian Indian, or those legendary Indian "Brahmanes" who could watch the sun with one eye closed from dawn to dusk without moving—seemed to possess, he also shuddered at the conditions that made it necessary.[3] For all his sympathy for the plight of the enslaved African and the persecuted Amerindians, and his professed admiration for the Hottentots (who he supposed had only one testicle), Diderot had little sympathy for what Voltaire scoffingly called "the nostalgia for the Neolithic."[4] He knew what a life of squalor, disease, and deprivation in fact lay behind all the expurgated, eroticized versions of the savage life, and he had no desire to shed the arts and sciences, any more than he had a desire to shed his clothes. The "savage," for all his other merits, could have "no knowledge of generosity or knowledge of those other virtues which have developed over a long time among civilized nations through the refinement of custom [*moral*]."[5] From his writing desk he could see very clearly that even within Europe, beset as it was by a miserable populace concerned exclusively with survival and the restrictive power of established religion, "the progress of enlightenment is limited." But he also knew that beyond the frontiers of the civilized world no enlightenment was possible at all. For, in the end, the attainment of a true "civilization" was all that "Enlightenment" was about. The two words were indissolubly linked, and both were the creations of the eighteenth century.[6] Both, however, were equally slippery terms. "Civilization," as John Stuart Mill observed in 1836, had by the time that he was writing acquired two rather different meanings. It could stand for the advancement along "the road to perfection," the pursuit of a "happier, nobler, wiser" existence. Or it could imply merely a distinction between a "wealthy and powerful nation" and "savages and barbarians." Disaggregating the two, however, as he admitted, was difficult. The present era, he believed—and this reached back to at least the middle of the eighteenth century—was "pre-eminently the era of civilization."[7] It was an era in which the "advanced" peoples of the world lived in the certainty that all life must change and, with effort, might also change for the better. Civilization was the outcome of our collective efforts to improve ourselves—what we loosely call "progress." Because of this it was also—and crucially—a "civil" life, which meant, among other things, that it was a life lived in cities, a life where suits of silk were serviceable garments. Our entire political and social vocabulary derives from this fact. *Civil, civility, citizen, civilization* all come from the Latin *civitas*. Originally the word referred to the community, or what would later come to be called "the state," rather than the urban space itself.[8] (For that there was another Latin term, *urbs,* from which we derive such related notions as *urban, urbane,* and *urbanity*.) But the community could never easily be separated from the physical location in which the civil existence was carried out, so that in all the modern vernacular languages that emerged out of Latin, they eventually became, if not synonymous, then certainly interdependent. For cities incontestably threw peoples together in ways that the scattered villages of the countryside never did. Civilization, said the economist and "Physiocrat" Victor de Riqueti, Marquis de Mirabeau (who may well have coined the term) in 1756, in an immensely popular book tellingly entitled *The Friend of Man,* was a process of the "softening of customs, urbanity, politeness, and the spread of understanding so that the niceties are observed."[9] Such things, as he knew, could only be acquired in cities.

In the Eurasian world, where they first developed, cities have always been thought of as engines of economic growth, freedom, creativity, even love. They may be the source of the rise of liberal democracy in the West, and if modern economists are to be believed, cities may also "make us smarter."[10] Certainly, many in the eighteenth century thought that they did. "Do you mean by savages," asked Voltaire archly, "those rustics living in huts with their mates and a few animals . . . knowing nothing except the land which feeds them, having few ideas and consequently few expressions?" Enslaved to their masters and their priests, such savages "can be found everywhere in Europe." "The people of Canada and the Kafirs [of South Africa]," and the "supposed savages of America," are in their sophistication, their good sense, and their moral awareness, he added, "infinitely superior to our own."[11] Nothing, it would seem, could match the obtuseness of the average French peasant. Rusticity, no less than savagery, made men stupid, sluggish, and resistant to change.

Like Voltaire, Diderot was appalled by what Rousseau had applauded, by the absence of the arts and sciences among such peoples, and by what the Neapolitan critic Francescantonio Grimaldi described as "the mask which makes [everyone] like his fellow" that all "savages" seemed to wear.[12] In such societies there was, as Adam Smith noted, not merely no diversity of labor, there was barely any diversity of any kind; there a man might be at once a producer, a statesman, a judge, and a warrior.[13] As Smith's famous remark that the African king, the "absolute master of the loves and liberties of ten thousand naked savages," was never any better off than the "industrious and frugal [European] peasant" made plain, the only possible society of equals was not the community of semiangelic beings of "M. Rousseau's" imagination but merely one in which all men lived equally miserable lives.[14]

If Orou had taught the chaplain anything, it was, despite his own insistence on the need always to follow the voice of nature, that nature, in effect, rarely ever spoke with the same voice. For the "savage," irreproachable though he may be, is "good" because his faculties are still inert. In the—perhaps fortunate—circumstances in which he finds himself, he has never had to exercise judgment. Savages were not exactly stupid, but their wisdom certainly did not lead to true happiness and was, in any case, useless to any civilized being, except as a point of reference. In 1751 the formidable Françoise de Graffigny, novelist and playwright, had published a highly successful epistolary novel called *Letters from a Peruvian Woman,* loosely modeled, like so many other such epistolary novels, on Montesquieu's *Persian Letters* of 1721. This claimed to be the correspondence of an Inca princess named Zelia, who is abducted and then taken to France. From there she writes a series of letters to her fiancé back in Peru that provide a scathing satire on French society and in particular on the status of women under the *ancien régime.* In 1751 Turgot wrote to Graffigny, in what he claimed to be the unfamiliar and "perhaps slightly ridiculous" role of critic, offering some tart observations on Zelia's assertions as to the supposed superiority of "savage"—in this case Peruvian—society over the French. It is true, he admitted, that "barbarous peoples" do enjoy certain advantages over civilized ones and that "our too arbitrary institutions have all too often made us forget nature, that we have been deceived by our own creations . . . that the savage, who does not know how to consult nature, knows, however, how to follow it." But following is all he knew how to do. The virtue of savages did not come from the exercise of will or judgment. It derived simply from following, blindly and unquestioningly, the most basic of human instincts. Actively to prefer such a life, as Zelia claims to do, was, Turgot suggested, "a ridiculous declamation."[15]

For Turgot, as for Diderot, true happiness was not inert unselfcritical innocence; it was, as it would be for Kant, the product of the exercise of mind. A vicious person or one who does not—as neither the child nor the savage properly can—know the distinction between good and evil cannot be truly "happy," however content or satisfied he or she may be. What Diderot saw in Bougainville's Tahiti, in all the supposed good or noble "savages," was merely an exemplum of what mankind had once been. The Tahitians are in a position to offer a powerful critique of the civilized man's social and above all his (and her) sexual mores, because, as they have never experienced what civilized man has experienced, they are able to stand outside the whole process of human understanding. The attacks of both the Old Man and Orou on the world Bougainville has brought with him are given all the high-flown eloquence for which "savages" were supposedly famous. But they are also dogmatic and undifferentiated. Just as savages, in Turgot's words, did not know how to "consult nature" (as opposed to simply following it), so they did not know how to argue, reflect, or compare. All they did was pontificate. And in the world that Diderot—if not Rousseau—wished to inhabit, conversation, not unironic assertion, was the most desirable mode of communication. They did not even, if John Stuart Mill is to be believed, "find much pleasure in each other's society."[16]

Enlightenment did not imply regression to some earlier condition, however free from the woes of the modern condition it might seem or actually be. It meant advancement. Crucially, it meant the resolution of the perennial struggle between Diderot's natural and artificial men. And the only way to achieve that was through the self-understanding that can come only through action. Tahiti was indeed a pleasure garden, a place of imaginary bliss. To Diderot it might be turned—contorted, one might say—into a mirror of the moral failings of the world of silk suits. But it could never have offered anything like a real objective for humanity. Humankind's true end was civilization, and because they are the products of reflective action, civilizations are inevitably plural, dynamic, and complex. They are also inescapable. Even Rousseau knew that. As an individual you could return to the state of nature—or at least something close to it—to those uncomfortable places Rousseau professed to prefer to Paris: Swiss alpine villages, Canadian forests, modern-day fantasies of ancient Greece or Rome. Humanity as a species, however, had no such option. But then, as Kant, an acutely critical reader of Rousseau, pointed out: "Rousseau did not ultimately wish that the human being *go* back to the state of nature, but rather that it should *look* back upon the state of nature."[17]

"Among animals," observed Kant, "the individual attains [its ends] immediately; among men only the species over the passage of generations, but in the end, through the species, the individual does so also." Mankind went through three stages: the cultivated, the civilized, and what he called the "moralized." And where are we now? he asked. To which the answer was: "(A) in the highest degree cultivated; (B) only half civilized; (C) hardly moral at all. . . . We are refined and polite, but without civic spirit." We had no grounds for complacency. True progress was a never-ending struggle for improvement. Humans were never intended to remain still, satisfied, complacent, happy with what they had and could do. That was what was wrong with those "noble" savages. Any people that has seemingly "arrived at its goal and lives in simple joyfulness," Kant wrote, is merely "superfluous," which is why the poor Tahitians would never be able to give an answer to the question of "why they exist at all and whether it would not have been just as good to have this island populated with happy sheep and cattle as with human beings who are happy merely enjoying themselves." Some might even say that "the world would lose nothing if Tahiti were simply swallowed up." Luckily for the Tahitians, however, their island had been visited by more "cultured nations," which might, much as Kant despised their rapacious ways, have the unintended merit of returning them to their true purpose.[18]

II

Savages stood on the threshold of a complex history. They existed at the very beginning of human time. It was that, as we have seen, that made them so fascinating. The final phase of that history was civilization. The narrative that provided the basis for the new human science was measured in terms of stages, in a sequence of crucial and transformative moments.[19] In the hands of the Scots, of Adam Smith and the historian William Robertson, of Lord Kames and the jurist John Millar and Adam Ferguson, this has been called the "Four-Stages Theory." But the theory seems to have originated with Pufendorf and was far more broadly European.[20] A history of humanity that went from hunter-gatherers to commerce, from savagery to civilization, provides the organizing principle behind Condorcet's *Sketch* and the writings of the ancient historian and chancellor of the Paris *parlement* Antoine-Yves Goguet—one of the first to suggest that the origins of urban civilization were to be found in Egypt and Mesopotamia, not Greece—the Huguenot Antoine Court de Gébelin, author of *The Primitive World Analysed and Compared with the Modern* and a follower of Franz Anton Mesmer (who may have died while experimenting on himself with electricity); and the Milanese Gianrinaldo Carli—to name only a few.

In all of these works, much more was at stake than mere subsistence. For, at each stage of this conjectural or "philosophical" history, not only do humans become better organized (as well as better fed); they become increasingly able to communicate with each other and, as a consequence, their societies become increasingly complex, increasingly "civilized." For the entire history of civilization, as the historians of humanity repeated again and again, was a progression from the simple to the complex. This basic insight was, like so many others about the identity of the species, an ancient one. But in its modern form it owed a great deal to Montesquieu.

In the *Spirit of the Laws* Montesquieu divided all the peoples of the world into three broad categories, in accordance with their ability to form civil societies or, as he put it, to "unite together" (*se réunir*). The simplest were the "savages"—a term that, in common with many eighteenth-century authors, he understood primarily in the botanical sense, as something as yet uncultivated. They are described as "small nations" that had "been unable to unite together." For the most part they were hunter-gatherers—those, that is, who lived only off what the land provided for them. His examples were the Tupi peoples of Brazil, but the Polynesians belonged in the same category. Then came the "barbarians," seminomadic pastoralists who, although they had been able to "unite together," had not yet developed the capacity for civil association. (Montesquieu's example is, somewhat puzzlingly, the Manchus.)[21] Finally there is "civilized man," who alone is capable of creating fully civil communities. It was a simple but compelling system of classification, to which nearly all the social theorists of the Enlightenment were ultimately indebted and around which Rousseau claimed that he had intended to write an entire moral history of mankind—although, as with so many of his more grandiose projects, he never found the time to do so. What Montesquieu had described was what John Stuart Mill would later identify as something like a law of human progress: the move from the individual to the mass. Civilization was essentially a process of aggregation and cooperation—the working out in time of the "sympathy" that bound all human beings inexorably to one another. It was cooperation that had allowed mankind to flourish and had prevented "lions and tigers from long ago extirpating the race of men." And it was their underdeveloped ability to cooperate that "makes all savage communities poor and feeble."[22]

Montesquieu's "savages" were unable to "unite together" because of some accident of terrain or climate, or what Edward Gibbon called their "supine indolence" and, significantly, their "carelessness of futurity"—but never from choice or from some vaguely intuitive understanding of the perils of any larger existence.[23] Far from being the predominantly peaceful communities that Rousseau and his many followers down to the mid-twentieth century would have us believe, such peoples were, in fact, particularly bloodthirsty. The actual wars they fought among themselves may have been, as Konrad Lorenz and others insisted in the 1960s and 1970s, largely ritualized. But by night, and always by surprise, they raided their neighbors' villages, killing everyone they could find, to the extent that some groups in North America and Australia were wiped out altogether. The ferocity of pre-civil man was evident, however, even in the eighteenth century. No people, wrote Kant, are more senselessly cruel than those "from the so-called state of nature." Warfare in itself had often served mankind well in the past (something to which I shall return), but "the scenes of unprovoked cruelty in the ritual murders of Tofoa, New Zealand, and the Navigator

Islands [Samoa] and the never-ending cruelty . . . in the wide wastes of northwestern America" were, in Kant's view, merely the senseless expression of the darker instincts of our purely animal natures "from which indeed no human being derives the least benefit."[24]

There was a further aspect of the hunter-gatherers' condition that impeded the development of civil society. It occupied a great deal of space. Nomadic peoples live in "great open spaces," and while, in Kant's opinion, this did not, as so many Europeans supposed, deprive them of their natural rights in the lands across which they roamed, it was the way of life "doubtless the most contrary to a civil constitution," precisely because the "great deal of space required in order to secure sustenance and clothing for themselves" made such people estranged from one another, and thus potentially hostile to one another.[25]

The lives of savages were not only bleak and brutish and likely to be short; they were also relentlessly repetitious. Faced with the constant prospect of extermination, dwindling resources, and an ever-increasing population and unable to provide food for anything larger than a single family, they began to look for a more sustainable, less precarious means of survival. The answer was pastoralism. "The most natural contrivance they could think of," wrote Smith, "would be to tame some of those wild animals they caught, and by affording them better food than what they could get elsewhere they would induce them to continue about their land and multiply their kind."[26] Herding, however, although it may not require much cooperation (or exertion), does require some, and unlike hunting and gathering, it cannot easily be confined to a single family. These pastoralists—Smith identifies them with not only the "Tartars" but also the "Arabians"—had thus been compelled to "unite together," at least to some limited degree. For Smith, the pastoral age had been the one in which "the inequality of fortune first begins to take place," and that inequality—the unfortunate, perhaps, but inevitable feature of all civilized life—"introduced among men a degree of authority and subordination which could not possibly exist before." With that came "some degree of that civil government which is indispensably necessary for its own preservation."[27] For all their primitivism, these "barbarians" had thus emerged, stumbling still, into history.[28] But it was not only the first flickering of civil government that distinguished pastoral barbarians from their savage predecessors. The move from hunting and gathering to herding also brought with it a significant change in the human personality. "Society within families," as Condorcet put it, "became gentler without becoming less intimate." This, in turn, led to the consolidation of a human social disposition that was to become the source of all subsequent reflection on the relationships not within groups but between them: hospitality.

A sense of reciprocity had already existed among "savages," but it had been sparse and erratic. Among pastoral peoples, Condorcet believed, "it acquired a more pronounced, more solemn character. . . . It provided more frequent occasions to exercise reciprocity from person to person, from family to family, from people to people." This, which Condorcet tellingly calls "an act of humanity," subsequently became a "social duty" bound by rules.[29] It was the most significant of the steps that man had made on his journey to civilization. For this "act of humanity" demanded for the first time that peoples from widely different communities recognize each other not only as French or Dowayo or Cherokee or Alyawara but also as *humans.* It was the real beginning of a *universal* human sociability. Hospitality became a semisacred practice among all people everywhere. The word itself derives from the Latin *hospes,* which, although generally rendered as "guest," literally means "guest-master."[30] (There is also a saying in Sanskrit that "the guest is god.") The "other," the "foreigner," once admitted to your home, acquires a special position that gives him or her a measure of purely moral authority over you—the host.

Violations of the laws of hospitality could, therefore, have dire consequences, as the people of the biblical city of Sodom discovered to their cost. (Mistreatment of strangers had been their true crime, not "sodomy," which did not come to mean what it does today until the eleventh century.) A violation of not the right but the corresponding duty of hospitality had been the initial cause of the Trojan War. (The guest may be a god, but he is not entitled to run off with his host's wife.) Hospitality, wrote Diderot, "is the most certain indication of the instinct and destination of man for sociability." It was evidence that, however hostile human groups might be toward one another, they nevertheless possessed a capacity for sociability across whatever national, cultural, and religious differences might separate them. "Born of natural commiseration," he wrote in one of the passages he inserted into Raynal's *History of the Two Indies,* "hospitality was universal in the earliest times. This was almost the sole link between nations; it was the seed of the most ancient, most revered, and most durable friendships between families separated by immense regions."[31] And it was, as we shall see, from the concept of hospitality that the possibility of a future world city would eventually arise.

At some point in this process, although no one could ever quite decide when, came the invention of language. In the seventeenth century a great debate had arisen as to the origin of language and the seemingly unanswerable question as to whether language was the creature of society or society the creature of language. It proved to be a long and passionate, but ultimately fruitless, debate, so much so that when the Linguistic Society of Paris was created in 1866, its bylaws forbade any further discussion of the subject. For Condillac and Vico, for Rousseau and Smith, for Maupertuis and Herder, and for all other lesser eighteenth-century theorists who turned to the history of language for some insight into the evolution of human society, one thing, however, seemed clear: the first languages had originated in cries, and cries are the outcome of the passions, of the need to reach out and to be noticed by others. "The *drive to communicate,*" observed Kant, "must have been what first moved him [man], when he was still alone, to make his existence known towards living beings outside himself." The same urge, he thought, could still be seen in children, "thoughtless people," and the religious, who "disturb the thinking part of the commonwealth with humming, shouting, whistling, singing, and other noisy pastimes." These, together with "religious devotions," were activities that, as far as he could see, had "no other motive than that they want to make their existence known far and wide."[32]

For Rousseau, the first manifestations of this "drive to communicate" must have taken place in the south, which, with its "gentle climates and fat and fertile lands," must also have been the first part of the globe to be inhabited. There a young man and a young woman first met over a well or by a river and said to one another, "Love me" (*Aimez-moi*). In the more inhospitable regions of the north, where "passions are born of need, and the languages, sad daughters of necessity, reflect their austere origins," the first words were likely to have been not a plea for love but a cry for help: *Aidez-moi*. "Love me" and "Help me" conjure up, in their simple immediacy, the full range of human sentiments. Rousseau's little fable was not, perhaps, meant to be taken literally. But what it revealed, to his mind, was that if language was in this way the creation of passions, then it could not be "at all of domestic origin." After all, one has no need to call on the members of one's family for assistance, and one takes their love for granted (or at least Rousseau did). Which is why, he claimed, American savages hardly speak at all, "except outside their homes."[33] In their huts they communicated only with gestures and signs—something that perhaps says more about Rousseau's own relationship with his illiterate and long-suffering companion Thérèse Levasseur than about the Algonquin. Whatever else it was, however, language was clearly a collective enterprise. As Condorcet put it, the invention of the bow had been "the work of a man of genius: the formation of language that of an entire society. . . . It was born out of reflections, out of the observations which are made to all men and from the habits which they contract in the heart of their common life."[34] At some later point there came, too, the invention of a script. Together, these two "arbitrary signs of speech and writing," in Turgot's words, "have made of all the individual stores of knowledge a common treasure house which each generation transmits to another, an inheritance which is always being enlarged by the discoveries of each age."[35] In this way, it might seem, humankind had finally succeeded in transcending the condition of time. The river, to reuse Heraclitus' famous metaphor, might never be the same twice, but it now carried with it an ever-increasing cargo of knowledge that, rather than change inexorably with each ebb and flow, would accumulate steadily over the centuries, bearing the human race ever closer to the state of perfection.

Language was the first true social bond, but so long as these early communities, whether hunter-gatherers or pastoralists, remained wanderers, they still lacked anything that resembled a civil code. In this pre-civil condition, all that men had to guide them were customs, the records of earlier practices as transmitted from generation to generation by, as Montesquieu put it, the "old men who remember past things": words, that is, not laws.[36] And, as we shall see, one of the crucial markers that defined civilizations was the presence of true laws, consensual, changeable, and above all secular.

Then came agriculture. This involved a far more dramatic and significant change than the move from hunting and gathering to pastoralism. Compared with other animals, humans are weak and defenseless, "in a much more helpless and destitute condition," as Adam Smith put it, "with regard to the comfort and support of life." But man had also "received from the bounty of nature reason, ingenuity, art, contrivance and the capacity of improvement."[37] Pastoralism had required at least one cognitive act: that the herder "observe that animals can multiply and that they might thereby offer a more durable resource" than simply killing and eating them.[38] Putting the soil to some productive use, however, demanded nothing less than the transformation of nature itself. With the invention of agriculture humans had unlocked nature's potential, and in doing so they had, in effect, become creative, technological beings. In a widely quoted section in the *Second Treatise on Government* of 1689–90, John Locke had argued that a person only acquired rights of ownership in a thing when he had "mixed his *Labour* with; and joined to it something that is his own."[39] In the case of land, this mixing of labor meant cultivation. Although initially a somewhat contentious claim, this became in time—not least because it was the work of Locke—the most widely accepted definition of the right to property. The first man, argued Rousseau, "who after enclosing a piece of ground, took it into his head to say *this is mine* and found a people simple enough to believe him, was the real founder of civil society."[40] For Locke, the necessary act was cultivation; for Rousseau, crucially, it was verbal, little more than a simple confidence trick. But for both, the acquisition of property, and consequently the recognition of thine and mine, had marked mankind's final departure from the state of nature. As Rousseau wrote approvingly, "According to the axiom of the wise Locke, 'where there is no Property there is no Injustice.' "[41] This was hardly Locke's point, but it nicely emphasized the distance that separated communal life from ownership. (Some form of these distinctions is still in use today. But we now know a great deal more about the economies of early, "primitive" peoples. Human prehistory is far messier, and the division between the three stages by no means as clear cut as all the eighteenth-century accounts imply. Hunters might also be pastoralists and, more often, horticulturalists. Hunter-gatherers, pastoralists, and agriculturalists also lived together for long periods of time, and many hunter-gatherer groups, rather than move to the next "stage," did far better for themselves by raiding the animals and crops of their more vulnerable pastoralist and agriculturalist neighbors.)

The invention of agriculture was the first act of what we call technology. The Greek word *techne* not only described a form of knowledge (*logos*), as we have seen; it is also the abstract form of *tikto,* to "generate" or "engender." Men, like the gods, were the *teknotes,* the creators, and what they made, the *tekna,* were their creations. The simple act of cultivation thus marked the beginning not only of humans' independence *from* nature but of their long struggle to make themselves masters *of* nature. It was the beginning of the belief upon which, although it has been constantly challenged down through the centuries, the whole of modern society now rests: that nature exists, as the great astronomer Nicolaus Copernicus put it bluntly, "for our use," *propter nos.*

More prosaically, this newfound mastery over the natural world also demanded the "division of lands" or, as it was sometimes called, the "creation of nations," since unlike hunting and pastoralism, agriculture, and the property rights it had created, could not easily be pursued without also establishing boundaries between one piece of territory and another. The hunter could, whenever he chose, pick up his bow, take his family, and move; even the shepherd could, as Condorcet phrased it, "drive his flocks before him." But the agriculturalist is necessarily and inescapably "attached to the land he cultivates." The shepherd faced with the threat of conquest could simply leave. The farmer had no choice but to remain "and work for his [new] masters."[42] This dependency had led inevitably to the creation of societies and the formulation of civil laws. What had once been mere customs, the received wisdom of past ages, derived ultimately, in some cases, from the utterances of a deity, were now slowly replaced by laws, which, although their origins were still to be found in common practices, were made public and became subject to interpretation and thus to change. As Kant imagined, there must have existed long periods of warfare between the two groups, as those "nations of nomadic herdsmen, which recognize only God as the master," continued "to swarm around the town-dwellers and farmers who are governed by a human master or civil authority." That conflict had survived into the modern world, in which what Kant and others believed to be the last remaining pastoral peoples, the Arabs and the Turks—both "barbarians" in Montesquieu's sense of the word—driven on by a body of laws that recognized "only God as master," had swarmed first over Greece and then into eastern Europe, regions that, although God-fearing enough, were bound not by divine decree but by a fully civil code.

It was the agriculturalists who were also responsible for the creation of cities, since only agriculture can, in Turgot's words, "sustain more men than are necessary in order to cultivate." And as the "inhabitants of cities . . . were cleverer than those of the countryside, they brought the latter into subjection."[43] That or, as Kant supposed, the lure of the "increasing luxury of the town-dwellers" and the "seductive arts" of their women, who, Kant imagines, must have offered a welcome alternative to the "dingy maids of the deserts," then drew the pastoralists steadily into the "glittering misery of the towns."[44] In this state too, women went from being mere objects of male gratification and the necessary instruments of procreation, to be discarded once their usefulness had expired, to acquiring, in Diderot's account of this transformation, a heightened "physical pleasure, a more noble sentiment." Marriage became no longer the random coupling it had once been, and the rituals of courtship that now emerged gave women not only some reason to care for themselves but also "some measure of dignity."[45]

Surplus, and the eventual domination over those who produced it, created leisure, and the fruits of leisure in the agricultural state are not indolence, as in the savage state, but the creation of the sciences and the arts. This is why Rousseau, who deplored the whole process, looked upon them as "garlands of flowers around the iron chains by which [men] are weighed down." No one could doubt—he declared, with an evident sneer on his face—that it was these that had ultimately been responsible for transforming primitive mankind into "what are called civilized peoples." For Rousseau, this had involved the loss of that "sentiment of that original freedom for which they seemed to have been born."[46] For others, however, it could only have been an immense gain.

This transformation of the human landscape resulted in the creation of one further thing: money. Agricultural societies could not remain self-sufficient for long. As their capacities expanded, so too did their needs. And these could only be satisfied through exchange with others. To make this possible, men invented a usable means of balancing a transaction. Money, however, was a mark of civilization for another, more important reason than the merely instrumental one that the economists had ascribed to it. Money had, in Locke's authoritative account, been introduced "by the tacit Agreement of man." These early agriculturalists, finding themselves in need of "enlarging" their possession, "had agreed that *a little piece of yellow Metal,* which would keep without wasting or decay, should be worth a great piece of Flesh or a whole heap of Corn."[47] Without money there could be no real society, at least not as Locke and his followers understood it. Locke's much-quoted phrase "In the beginning all the world was America," which is often taken to describe the state of nature in its entirety, meant only that "no such thing as Money was anywhere known."[48] Money was a "sign," and thus a form of language, and like language or the use of mathematical symbols, its creation could only be a collective enterprise. It spoke to cooperation, coordination, and a degree of social harmony. Sometime in the fifth century BCE the Socratic philosopher Aristippus was shipwrecked on the coast of Rhodes. When he came ashore he saw geometrical figures—another form of language—drawn in the sand, and cried out to his companions: "Let us be of good hope, for indeed I see the traces of men."[49] Centuries later Montesquieu picked up the story but turned these geometrical figures into money. "If you were alone," he wrote, "and happen to come by some accident to the land of an unknown people, and if you see a piece of money, you know that you have reached a civilized nation."[50] Money, language, and the development of the arts and sciences went hand in hand.

The invention of money made the produce of the land mobile. More important, it created the necessary condition for the division of labor and commerce. The first of these—"the greatest improvement in the production of the powers of labour," as Smith called it—was to make individual societies immeasurably more diversified and wealthier; the second was to transform not merely the entire world but, with time, human nature itself.[51] Or so, at least, it was hoped.

Commerce shared something, at least as far as its future possibilities were conceived, with what we today call "globalization." The very first sentence of Raynal's *History of the Two Indies* reads: "There has never been any event as interesting for human kind in general, and for the peoples of Europe in particular, than the discovery of the New World and the passage to the Indies by way of the Cape of Good Hope"—a passage picked up and repeated (without acknowledgment) by Adam Smith in *The Wealth of Nations,* who significantly changed "interesting" to "greatest and most important."[52] Between them, Columbus and Vasco da Gama—the one unknowingly, the other intentionally—had thrown a net over the entire globe. For optimists, such as Joseph Mandrillon, who had spent some time in the United States and had corresponded with both Washington and Adams, if only cursorily, before ending up beneath the guillotine in 1794, Columbus's true destiny had been not to bring the Europeans to America, not to find gold or conquer, not even to trade in any mundane sense of the word, but "to open new routes across the oceans . . . to create links of fraternity between the two worlds."[53] Smith, whose view of the role of commerce in the broader process of Enlightenment is a good deal less uncritical than that of many, was still far from certain what the possible outcome of all of this might be. So far, the effects of bringing together "the most distant parts of the world" would seem to have been, on balance, beneficial, at least "in their general tendency." But the fate of the wretched inhabitants of the "East and West Indies," who had found that any gain they might have gotten from commerce was "sunk and lost in the dreadful misfortunes" that the rapacious Europeans had been permitted, by "the superiority of force," to inflict "with impunity . . . in those remote countries," made him pause to reflect: "What benefits or what misfortunes to mankind may hereafter result from those great events no human wisdom can foresee."[54]

Diderot, more trusting in his own wisdom, was not so skeptical. Despite his own, still fiercer, diatribes against the behavior of the Europeans overseas, he saw in commerce, as had Mirabeau (and as indeed, ultimately, had Smith), a means of transforming the culture of the entire globe. "The rise and fall of empires is now no more," he declared ingenuously, in one of the more lyrical passages that he inserted into Raynal's *History*. Gone were the malign tyrants and the antique warrior cults that had been the driving force behind the nations of antiquity. Now, in this modern world, it would be impossible to find a man such as Alexander the Great, before whom it could be said that "the earth fell silent":

> The fanaticism of religion and the spirit of conquest are no longer what they once were. . . . A war among commercial nations is a fire that destroys them all. The time is not far off when the sanctions of rulers will extend to the individual transactions between the subjects of different nations, and when bankruptcy, whose impact may be felt at such immense distances, will become affairs of state . . . and the annals of all peoples will need to be written by commercial philosophers as they were once written by historical orators.[55]

A world community was on its way, and commerce was the engine that, by harnessing human needs—and human greed—would bring it about. To some it seemed as if the great trading nations of northern Europe, Britain and Holland, had really created a transition from the older society of rank, veneration, courtly snobbery, and violence to one of prosperity, a transition that had led to the English being dubbed, by the jurist and Tory politician Sir William Blackstone, with perhaps unintended irony, "a polite and commercial people." Certainly it seemed so to Voltaire. In England, he claimed, even the sons and brothers of the grandest in the land were perfectly happy to go into "trade," whereas in France, Parisian merchants were routinely snubbed by provincial nobodies whose "names happened to end in *Ac* or *Ille*." Worse still, the merchants themselves "so often spoke with contempt of their own profession" that they blushed to admit that that was indeed what they were. Yet, he asked, what was better and "more useful to the state, the powdered seigneur who knows at precisely what time the king rises, and what time he goes to bed, and who gives himself airs playing the slave in the antechamber of a minister, or a merchant who enriches his country, gives orders from his office to Surat and Cairo, and contributes to the well-being of the world?"[56]

This vision of commerce, or what in the eighteenth century was called the "commercial society," amounted, however, to far more than the mere exchange of goods.[57] It was also an elevated principle of behavior that seemed to offer to all the peoples of the world greater possibilities for human interaction. The whole language of commerce is suffused with notions of communicability. The word *commercium* in Latin had been applied to all kinds of intercourse between individuals long before it acquired any economic meaning. And we still speak, somewhat coyly, today of "sexual commerce." "Everything in the universe is commerce," wrote Mirabeau. "Because by commerce one must understand all the natural and indispensable relationships of the entire species, which are, and will always be, those between one man and another between one family, one society, one nation and another."[58]

This had been something of a commonplace since antiquity, although not in quite this form. Commerce, in the words of the first-century Jewish philosopher Philo of Alexandria, was the expression of "a natural desire to maintain a social relationship." Any attempt to interfere with this process must, therefore, constitute an offence against humanity. The gods, Seneca had claimed, had distributed their goods unequally over the surface with the sole purpose of compelling humans to communicate with one another. Furthermore, they had been thoughtful enough to provide winds that blew in contrary directions so as to make sailing possible.[59] The same sentiments were expressed with even greater force in the eighteenth century. Nature, or God, enthused the abbé Noël-Antoine Pluche, author of *The Spectacle of Nature,* a survey of natural history for "young people" and one of the most widely read books of the century, had designed the tides so as to allow ships to come into and out of port more easily. (Such a shame, commented Voltaire acidly, that while the Mediterranean has many ports, it has no tides.)

The interaction, ineluctably cosmopolitan, between peoples and nations inevitably, or so it was hoped, "polished" the initially uncouth human personality by smoothing away all its rough edges. "Commerce"—wrote Montesquieu in what was perhaps the most enduring, certainly the most enduringly optimistic, of the accounts of these potential benefits for humankind—"has made known the customs of all the peoples of the world, and spread everywhere." For this reason, it has the power to cure "destructive prejudices; and it is almost a general rule, that wherever the customs are gentle [*douce*] there is commerce; and wherever there is commerce, customs are gentle."[60] "Sweet Commerce" came to be seen as a panacea for the world's ills, a device for encouraging enlightenment within nations and of spreading it around the globe. Even Adam Smith believed firmly that "the communication of knowledge and of all sorts of improvements which an extensive commerce from all countries naturally, or rather necessarily, carries along with it" brought not only prosperity but also peace and harmony—in other words, "civilization." Unsurprisingly, perhaps, it was also looked upon with intense suspicion by all those, most obviously the religious, who had no wish to be relieved of their "destructive prejudices" and had the most to lose from the possibilities of diversity that commerce seemed to offer. "Universal commerce," warned Smith's opponent, the Reverend Alexander Carlyle, who hated it as a force in which he saw the future destruction of the beliefs he served, "propagates opinions as well as commodities."[61]

Commerce, with all that the word implied, offered to link all the peoples of the globe. It was the final instrument of civilization that would eventually make some kind of cosmopolitan future a real possibility. It was the practical manifestation of the "sympathy" that had replaced innate sense, ideas, and judgment as the one defining feature of all that it was to be human. It was this that had made the abbé Raynal's *History* both so controversial and so successful. It had excited the indignation of the enlightened intelligentsia of most of Europe and the United States with its condemnation of European colonization, of slavery, and of the disastrous consequences of the attempts to export Christianity, by force if necessary, to the unsuspecting peoples of the Americas and Asia. But its real novelty lay in the fact that it was an attempt, the first of its kind, to write a history of the world as a truly global system, and because of this it generated an immense enthusiasm for the civilizing power of commerce.[62] The whole of Paris, wrote Diderot in 1769, is "concerned with administration, commerce, agriculture, imports, exports and finance. . . . The abbé Raynal can boast of having been the hero of this change."[63]

III

At the heart of this enthusiasm for the polishing properties of commerce and polite conversation, for civilization in general, there lay, however, an unresolved tension. For as progress, accompanied by higher standards of living, greater respect for others, and the development of the arts and sciences, moved onward, so the very dynamism that had created it in the first place appeared to diminish. Commerce, warned Adam Smith, because it allowed men to give all their attention to "the arts of luxury," had encouraged them to leave the nasty business of fighting, even in defense of themselves, to others. To Smith's mind this had only recently been demonstrated by experience. In 1745, in what the English called the "Second Jacobite Rebellion" or "the Forty-Five," the followers of Charles Edward Stuart, known somewhat mockingly as "Bonnie Prince Charlie" and the "Young Pretender," had raised his standard at Glenfinnan in a bid to restore the Stuart dynasty to the throne of England and Scotland, from which it had been ousted in 1688. With a motley army of some three hundred men collected from those highland clans that had remained loyal to the Stuarts, he marched south toward the border with England. Although the "Young Pretender" succeeded in taking Edinburgh and in terrifying its highly Anglicized population, his forces were finally defeated at Culloden near Inverness on April 16, 1746. In Smith's recollection of the events—he was about nineteen at the time—"Four or 5 thousand naked Highlanders" (the Highlanders were famous for running into battle dressed only in their shirts) had appeared out of the wildernesses of northern Scotland and taken "possession of the improved parts of this country without any opposition from its unwarlike inhabitants." Had there not been a standing army to drive them back, "they would have seized the throne with little difficulty. 200 years ago such an attempt would have roused the spirit of the nation."[64] In 1745, however, the English (or in Smith's case, the lowland Scots) had been so softened by the luxuries of the commercial society in which they now lived that they no longer had any spirit to arouse. Put differently, "civilization" could also become a process of feminization. And the feminine both beckoned and alarmed. It improved and refined, but it also—or so it was feared—weakened.

Modern, polite, commercial, or, as it would eventually come to be called, "bourgeois" (a word that itself describes a city dweller, a "citizen") society, having surrendered its ancient martial values, inevitably ceded considerably more space and influence to women than they had ever enjoyed before. This did not, of course, mean very much by modern western standards. Even such otherwise enlightened men as Diderot, despite the emotional, moral, and intellectual confidence he placed in Sophie Volland, and although he generally attributed women's inferiority to their legal status and to the poor education that most received under the *ancien régime,* was still capable of implying at least that they were somehow less reliable, more devious, more impulsive than men. "What will the women think?" asks "B" at the very end of the *Supplement to Bougainville's Journey*. "Probably the opposite of what they will say," replies "A."[65]

But for all that very few of the major writers of the Enlightenment (Condorcet was perhaps an exception) could be properly classed as feminist, there were many, Diderot and Voltaire (in his better moments) among them, who were prepared to concede that the long-standing assumption that women were intellectually and emotionally (as well as

Marie-Jean-Antoine de Caritat, marquis de Condorcet, eighteenth century, by French school

Denis Diderot, 1767, by Louis-Michel van Loo

Jean-Jacques Rousseau, 1766,
by Allan Ramsay

Charles de Secondat,
Baron de Montesquieu, *c.* 1728,
by Jacques-Antoine Dassier

Voltaire, 1748, marbled bust by Jean-Baptiste Lemoyne

Immanuel Kant, 1791, by Gottlieb Doebler

Portrait of Omai by Joshua Reynolds (1776)

ahitians presenting fruits to Bougainville attended by his officers (1768?)

Jean-Baptiste Le Rond d'Alembert, 1753, by Maurice Quentin de La Tour

David Hume, 1766, by Allan Ramsay

Adam Smith, 1790, by John Kay

Anthony Ashley Cooper, third Earl of Shaftesbury, and an unidentified figure, *c.* 1700–01, by John Closterman

morally and politically) inferior to men had at best been greatly exaggerated and was for the most part based upon delirious fantasies of past ages, no more credible than the existence of the Gorgon.

As the Spanish Benedictine Benito Jerónimo Feijoo, who despite his profession and undoubted faith was in this respects, as in many others, one of the most "enlightened" minds of the early eighteenth century, pointed out sarcastically, all the books written about women over the centuries had been written by men, and "if the women had written them it would be we [the men] who would have ended up underneath." After having examined all the evidence at great length, he came to the conclusion that if women knew less than men and had achieved less than men (although even this was not universally so, and he provided innumerable examples from ancient history of societies in which it was women who had been the philosophers, the scientists, and the rulers), this certainly did not prove that they were less able than men. All it meant was that they had been given less opportunities *by* men. If men, he asked, "dedicated themselves to nothing else but agriculture (as the illustrious Thomas More suggests in his *Utopia*), so that they knew nothing else, would this then be grounds for saying that they were capable of nothing else?"[66] The arguments used for claiming that women were inferior to men and thus denying them equal status with men, as Voltaire and many others had pointed out, were no different from those used to justify the continuing existence of the slavery of Africans. And just as ridding the world of slavery was, as Condorcet put it, a necessary condition of the future evolution of humanity, so too was the emancipation of women. For it was also the case that most of the enlightened, Feijoo among them, also firmly believed that the humanity, the civility, the decency of a society could be measured by the way in which it treated its women. "The rank . . . and condition, in which we find women in any country," wrote William Alexander, the author of a sometimes condescending but also remarkably prescient history of, as he phrased it, "the progress [of women] from slavery to freedom":

> mark out to us with the greatest precision the exact point in the scale of civil society the people of such a country have arrived at;

> and were their history entirely silent on every other subject, and only mentioned the manner in which they treated their women, we would from thence be enabled to form a tolerable judgment of the barbarity, or culture of their manners.[67]

This, at least, is one of the legacies of the Enlightenment that is still with us (or most of us). No one today would describe as "civilized" any people, or culture or law or religion, that refused to extend the same legal rights to women as to men, that sanctioned female infibulation (already considered a mark of barbarism and a cause for concern in the eighteenth century), or that forbade women to drive, denied them an education equal to men, or obliged them to wear disfiguring clothing in public.

In somewhat grudging response to these arguments, women during the eighteenth century came to acquire positions of individual responsibility and to exercise personal freedom in ways they had never achieved before. True, these were generally restricted to the wealthier and the better educated. But then, so too, however we define it, was "Enlightenment." There were the mistresses of the salon, a seventeenth-century creation that figured prominently in (largely French) intellectual life: women like D'Alembert's mother, the novelist Claudine Guérin de Tencin, or the abiding love of D'Alembert's own life, Julie de Lepinasse. There were also those who were literary and scientific figures in their own right: Voltaire's mistress Gabrielle-Émilie, Marquise du Châtelet (whom we have already met), and Condorcet's wife, Sophie de Grouchy, who collaborated widely with her husband and translated Smith's *Theory of Moral Sentiments* (to which she added eight "Letters on Sympathy" of her own) into French.[68] Then there were yet more insistent, more angry voices who were not content to be mere *salonnières,* however influential, however learned—women like Olympe de Gourges, who ended up under the guillotine in 1793 for daring to write a *Declaration of the Rights of Women* to match the *Declaration of the Rights of Man* of 1789 and was denounced for so doing as a "virago" and a "woman-man" who had "forgotten the virtues of her sex."[69]

None of these women, for obvious reasons, had any time for any version of Rousseau's Neolithic nostalgia. Françoise de Graffigny's Inca princess, for all her endorsement of the simple life supposedly led in pre-conquest Peru, is really, as Turgot recognized, only a mouthpiece with which to denounce the iniquities and unjustifiable inequalities inflicted upon women by French society. Women were unequivocally modern, enthusiastically civilized. They could not afford to be otherwise. In the "*cabane*" all that awaited them was Rousseau's illiterate, silent, and tyrannical male. "The more I see of the world," wrote the great pioneer feminist Mary Wollstonecraft at the end of the eighteenth century, "the more I am convinced that civilization is a blessing not sufficiently estimated by those who have not traced its progress; for it not only refines our enjoyments, but produces a variety which enables us to retain the primitive delicacy of our sensations."[70]

And much of this progress could be attributed to the increasing presence of women in what was still a male-dominated world. Now, as Hume described it, men and women "flock into cities; love to receive and communicate knowledge; to show their wit or breeding, their taste in conversation or living, in clothes or furniture. . . . Both sexes meet in an easy and sociable manner; and the tempers of men, as well as their behaviour refine apace." Women, as William Alexander put it, "had been formed with a beauty and tenderness sufficient to soothe us into softer behavior."[71] For the uneasy, suspicious male, however, this soothing into softer behavior was precisely where the danger lay. The strong, rough, "simple" man so beloved of Rousseau could not allow himself to be "refined" or "soothed" in so unguarded a manner. Rousseau, with his longing for the world of crude, unpolished virtue, excoriated the arts and sciences because these, as Hume had seen, threatened the solitude of the "ignorant and barbarous nations" he so admired.[72] For the same reason he generally belittled women, whom he held responsible for most of the moral evils of the world. True, he claimed to be "far from believing that the ascendency of women is an evil in itself." Properly directed, they might even "produce as much good as they do evil today."[73] There were also those who, in civic virtue and military heroism, could be the match of any man. (He even wrote a curious little "Essay on the Important Events of Which Women Have Been the Secret

Cause.") But in general he was convinced that they were passive, feeble, and corrupting, which was why Paris was entirely ruled by them.[74]

But Rousseau was a hysterical misogynist. There were too many obvious benefits to be had from enfeeblement and what Rousseau understood by corruption, in particular when the alternative was a life of "stupid ferocity beneath an animal skin."

The ease of modern life encouraged Condorcet to imagine a time in which "enlightenment linked to genius" had produced a future condition in which "for happier generations a system of laws and education" had been created, "which would render the virtue of courage almost useless."[75] The mistake had always been to suppose that martial valor could ever be a virtue in itself. It had only ever been a means to an end, and now that end was, in most of the civilized world, in the process of vanishing. Like Smith, Condorcet was well aware that naked Highlanders, or some analogues thereof, were forever waiting to burst in upon the calm pastures of the civilized world. It was, as it remains, a terror from our remote historical past. But in the modern world we no longer rely upon citizen militias or "the spirit of the nation" to keep them at bay. We have professional armies to do that. And although so many of the writers of the Enlightenment, Smith and Kant among them, were suspicious of standing armies (which were still a recent innovation) for fear that they might be turned against their own people, they were, perilous though they have sometimes proved to be, an inescapable condition of Enlightenment. As Benjamin Constant—Swiss critic, historian, political theorist, political activist, novelist, gambler, and celebrated lover of perhaps the most famous writer of the day, Germaine de Stäel—felt able to assure his readers in 1813, Europe, "this mass of [nations]," was now "strong enough to have nothing to fear from hordes that are still barbarous. It is sufficiently civilized to find war a burden. Its uniform tendency is towards peace. The warlike tradition [is] a heritage from distant ages."[76] In such a world, martial valor and "the spirit of the nation" were as outmoded as jousting or dueling.

If civilization was inescapably a process of "softening," it was also the outcome of constant progression. And the irony of progress was that it had always gone hand in hand with conflict. Without Kant's "unsociable sociability" there would have been no progress in the sciences or the arts, indeed, no progress at all.[77] It was an idea as old as the Greek poet Hesiod. But in the eighteenth century, as the ancient warrior ethos seemed truly to be slipping into oblivion, it acquired a new urgency. Liberty, and from liberty progress and the constant betterment of humanity, thrived off conflict. Science, learning, the arts—all of these depended upon free communication between peoples, but they could equally only exist in a society that encouraged competition, that recognized the need for debate and for interpretation rather than simply repetition. Civilization, like Enlightenment itself, was an unfinished process. It could have no end. But the prospect of unfinished processes is always unsettling. For they all raise the question: What if this particular process were, somehow, to come to fulfillment? What would it look like? Would we not, in a perfectly civilized, enlightened world, also be facing the prospect of interminable stagnation? In the eighteenth century this unease found its most contentious expression in a debate over the civilization of another place, as remote from Europe and as unlike it—although in quite different ways—as the South Pacific: China.

IV

Most Europeans had tended to assume that, for all its many and obvious failings, its bloody wars, the injustices its nations had perpetrated against one another and the rest of the world, Europe represented the highest level of civility attained by any people on Earth. But did it really? Possibly in terms of the arts and sciences, but what about civil life and those elusive entities "morality" and "virtue" that the theologies of the world had done so very little to illuminate? Certainly there was nowhere in America or Africa where anything resembling a true civilization could be found. Neither were the great Muslim societies, from Turkey to India, for all that they had once dominated half the globe in their own ways, likely contenders. But beyond the Himalayas, at the furthest extremity of the world, lay quite another people, far more alien and yet far more refined, more cultivated, in short, more "civilized," than any other that had previously been encountered.

Information about the great civilizations of the Far East, and in particular about China, had been circulating widely in Europe since the late sixteenth century, due largely to the careful and detailed reports of Jesuit missionaries who had been allowed to establish a base there in 1582. The Jesuits, although they had gone to convert, recognized that here, unlike elsewhere in the world, they were faced with an ancient and highly sophisticated culture. If the Chinese were to be persuaded to accept Christianity, the kinds of simple tricks, the mixture of coercion and accommodation that (apparently at least) had worked in the Americas and certain parts of Africa (and most parts of rural Europe), would not do. The Chinese needed to be convinced of the superiority of what must have seemed to them a bizarre and, with its tales of bloody martyrdom and of a slain and resurrected god, repulsive creed to anything that they knew, and to do that it was clearly necessary to have a more than superficial grasp of their deeply alien but also immensely complex world. The Jesuits had to work from the inside and on the terms dictated to them by the Chinese themselves. The most famous of them, the Italian Matteo Ricci, lived from 1583 until his death in 1610 in China, befriended members of the Chinese intelligentsia, wrote in elegant literary Chinese, and may have been responsible for much of the image of Confucianism that we have today.[78] The detailed accounts that Ricci and his colleagues sent home to Europe were also accompanied by a steady flow of tangible evidence of Chinese skills. Exotic objects, silks, carved woods, bronze ornaments, "japanned" (lacquered) furniture, mahogany tea tables and china cabinets, and above all "china," that is, porcelain, were produced in large quantities, and in all qualities, for the European market. Chinese pagodas became highly fashionable additions to the carefully landscaped gardens of English country houses. Entire villages that their creators imaged to be "Chinese" were built at Drottningholm in Sweden and Tsarskoe Selo in Russia.

The Jesuits, however, were not alone. They had been accompanied by the Franciscans and the Dominicans, both of whom had rather different views on how to convert the unbeliever. In the 1630s a struggle had broken out between the two groups over the meaning and possible source of the Chinese "rites." What has come to be known as the "Rites Controversy" was in essence a debate, on the one hand, over the meaning of what was taken to be the Chinese name, or names, for "God"—such as *Shangdi* ("Lord on High" or "Supreme Ancestor") and *Tian* ("Heaven")—and on the other, about the rituals by which the Chinese honored their ancestors and Confucius. The Jesuits, for the most part, insisted that Chinese "rites" were merely social conventions, civil or political cults, and therefore in no way idolatrous. (After all, as Leibniz pointed out, the cult of Confucius was not so very unlike those encouraged by Christian kings, who similarly believed their rule to be divinely sanctioned.)[79] This meant that the neophyte had no need to abandon them on conversion. The Friars, together with the "Foreign Missions of Paris" and backed by a powerful lobby within the Vatican, maintained that the Chinese conception of God and the means by which it, or he, was known was a violation of Christian monotheism and that the Chinese rites were, in effect, pagan superstitions and therefore had to be expurgated. In the end what was at stake in the dispute was whether it was necessary—since Christianity was not merely the only true religion but also the only possible basis for a proper way of life—for converts to give up not only their former pagan beliefs but also their former non-European ways. Finally the Friars, who, it must be said, although seemingly indifferent to their own best interests, also had the better arguments, won. It *was* impossible to separate Chinese social and moral beliefs from their "religion." Two papal decrees of 1715 and 1742 banned all the "Chinese rites"—and the use of Chinese terms for "God"—and forbade any further debate on the matter.[80] This in effect put an end to the Christian mission to China for over a generation. The whole affair, as Voltaire said of it later, had arisen from the persistent European error of "judging their customs by our own. For we carry our prejudices and spirit of contention along with us, even to the extremities of the earth."

None of this, however, did anything to damage, even among most Christians, the impression of a society that was complex, refined, and technologically as advanced as, if not superior to, anything to be found in Europe. As a wider, if still very haphazard and schematic, knowledge of the great Chinese classics, and in particular of Confucius, became better known, China came to be praised as a place of immense, and immensely ancient, wisdom, made more valuable by having had no prior contact whatsoever with Christianity. When he heard about Confucius (but before he had actually read him), François de La Mothe Le Vayer, poet, occasional libertine, and tutor to Louis XV, declared ecstatically that it was all he could do to prevent himself from crying out *"Sancte Confuci, ora pro nobis"* ("Holy Confucius, pray for us"—an echo of Ficino and Erasmus' famous invocation of Socrates: *Sancte Socrates, ora pro nobis*).[81]

By far the most influential person to promote a—rather more measured—version of this image was, however, Gottfried Wilhelm Leibniz. Leibniz was a polymath—philosopher, mathematician, creator of differential calculus (independently of Newton), and pioneer in the development of mechanical calculators. He had also hoped to find, or fabricate, a universal language so as to bring together all the peoples of the world and wished, as Turgot said of him later, his works "to become a kind of center where all human knowledge would be united."[82] Today he is perhaps best known for his theodicy and for Voltaire's mockery of it—and for his theory of "monads," an attempt to find an explanation for the structure of a universe created by a god that would be superior to, and yet avoid some of the obvious disadvantages of, the theory of atoms. Leibniz took a keen interest in just about everything, and one subject to which he dedicated a great deal of careful study was what might be the implications for Europe of Chinese moral philosophy.

For Leibniz, China was clearly the only other civilization in the world that could match that of Europe. "I consider it a singular plan of the fates," he wrote in the closing decade of the seventeenth century, "that human cultivation and refinement should today be concentrated, as it were, in the two extremes of our continent, in Europe and in Tschina [China] (as they call it), which adorns the Orient as Europe does the opposite edge of the earth." And of these he was by no means certain that Europe could claim to have the upper hand. Locked in an endless embrace across a single vast continent, the Chinese Empire, "which challenges Europe in its cultivated areas and certainly surpasses her in population, vies with us in many . . . ways in equal combat, so that now they win, now we do." More remarkable still for a man who was a firm, if unorthodox, Lutheran was the argument that his God, for whom the Chinese had displayed to date very little sympathy, should have "ordained such an arrangement, so that, as the most cultivated and distant peoples stretch out their arms to each other, those in between may gradually be brought to a better way of life."[83] It was not simply a vision of what only recently has come to be called "Eurasia" (although the recognition that Europe is a peninsula of Asia is as old as Herodotus); it was a vision of a universal "civilizing mission," which would be undertaken not by one dominant power and by force, but by two very different civilizations and by example and persuasion. Leibniz, it is true, was given to flights of fantasy, but this was perhaps the most strikingly ecumenical of them all.

Because China apparently lacked any single dogmatic religious creed, let alone the competing sects that had turned Europe into a killing field for much of the sixteenth and seventeenth centuries, Leibniz also believed that the Chinese had succeeded in preserving what any reasonable person must assume to be God's wishes, where all the other world religions, in particular Christianity, had, in this respect at least, failed. Not that Leibniz had any doubt about the truth of the Gospels, but he could see, as he put it, that "the government of China would be incomparably better than that of God, if God were as the Sectarian Doctors, who attach salvation to the chimeras of their party, depict Him."[84]

He had, he said, nothing against the Church sending missionaries to China, but in its present state Europe had a far more urgent need of "missionaries from the Chinese who might teach us the use and practice of natural religion."[85] For Leibniz, the Chinese were not simply great craftsmen and ingenious designers, they were also a deeply moral people. Ethics was their true strength, and theirs was an ethics that crucially eschewed metaphysical or theological speculation and adhered to education and conversation. "Who would have believed," he asked in apparent wonder, "that there is on earth a people who, though we are in our view so very advanced in every branch of behavior, still surpasses us in understanding the precepts of civil life?" For the sad truth, for every Christian, was that "they surpass us (though it is almost shameful to confess this) in practical philosophy, that is, the precepts of ethics and politics adapted to the present life and use of mortals." "Practical philosophy," he told the Jesuit Joachim Bouvet, "consists . . . in these good orders for education, and for the conversation and sociality of men."[86] If man, he wrote, echoing Hobbes, was indeed "a wolf to man," and if "our folly in heaping woes on ourselves . . . as though they were lacking from elsewhere" was a universal human condition, here at least was one people who had apparently found a way to escape from its more murderous consequences.

The laws of the Chinese were all, as far as he could see, designed to produce the greatest degree of "public tranquility." All classes, from the emperor himself to the lowliest peasant, were bound together by mutual respect and courtesy, so that "scarcely anyone offends another by the smallest word in common conversation. And they barely show evidence of hatred, wrath, or excitement."[87] The Chinese, Voltaire insisted later, were essentially what Europeans had so often tried and so often failed to be: true Stoics. "Their morality," he declared (without, however, knowing very much about it), "is as pure and as severe, and at the same time as humane, as that of Epictetus."[88]

But while Leibniz and Voltaire believed that the Chinese excelled in moral philosophy, they also denied them any real understanding of logic, geometry, metaphysics, astronomy, or the natural sciences. "The Chinese," claimed Leibniz, largely on the basis of what the Jesuits had told him, "are thus seen to be ignorant of that great light of the world demonstration, and they have remained content with a sort of empirical geometry, which our artisans universally possess."[89] What, then, could be more enlightening for humanity than an exchange? "We could," he wrote enthusiastically, "give them our knowledge almost at once and by a kind of infusion, and on our side we could learn from them, also at once, a world of new instructions that, without them, we would not at all obtain in I know not how many centuries."[90] Then at last the arms of the two great civilizations of the world would finally be able to reach out to each other across the vastness of central Asia to form one great global civilization.

Leibniz focused on what he had identified as Chinese moral philosophy and on what he understood to be the Chinese art of government. But he was also concerned with another aspect of Chinese society, which seemed at once both a cause for admiration and an explanation as to why China, in common with all other eastern states, had somehow failed to keep pace with the scientific advances made by the West. For China was a place not only of toiling masses, skilled artisans, and virtuous Confucians; it was also one of the very few societies in the world—on some accounts, the only one—that had remained apparently untroubled by civil war or invasion for centuries.

Already in the sixteenth century Giovanni Botero, a failed Jesuit and highly influential writer on politics (it was he who first used the term "reason of state"), had noted that the Chinese were unique among civilized peoples in having recognized that "there is no greater folly than to lose what you have in order to acquire things from others." For Botero, as for most later sinophiles, the visual symbol of this had been the Great Wall. Having reached the obvious geographical limits of their domains, the Chinese emperors, so the story went, had called a halt. There they had erected a fixed, immutable barrier, as much to keep their overambitious subjects in as to keep their enemies out.

By the eighteenth century, when problems of the decline and demise of imperial power were much on everyone's minds, this image of a society immured behind one of the greatest feats of civil engineering in the history of mankind came to be described, admiringly—at least by some—as the "Immobile Empire." And longevity seemed to imply good government. The Chinese Empire, as Voltaire put it, was "the oldest of the entire world, the best governed doubtless because it was the longest lasting."[91] Only the Chinese, observed the abbé Raynal, offered the prospect of a "history of men"; the rest of the earth being, to his mind, "only an image of the chaos in which all matter was before the creation of the world." Only the Chinese seemed to be exempt from the general law that required that all nations, no matter how powerful, would sooner or later collapse into "broken and dismembered states."[92]

And if the Chinese had remained stable for so long, when the great empires of Europe had failed so dismally to do so, might not China offer a model that the West would do well to emulate?

Many believed that it did. The "Panegyrists of China," as Raynal called them, maintained that China's stability derived from its strict adherence to "nature's laws." Here was a society ruled over by a beneficent emperor and governed by a trained civil service, chosen not—as were the elites of Europe—by accident of birth but by a much-celebrated, and intensely difficult, exam system. The Mandarins, those inscrutable, learned, omniscient beings, unlike their European counterparts, constituted a true meritocracy. In a world in which, little by little, the older aristocracies of land were giving way to professional aristocracies of service, to a "middle class," as it would eventually become, this image had a powerful appeal. In China the wisest held power, and inevitably they worked always in the interests of the community as a whole. Little wonder, then, that China had succeeded in maintaining its stability while the fractious European powers, ruled over by power-hungry despots, had squandered all their resources in fighting among themselves.

The "Detractors of China" took a very different view. One of the earliest, and certainly the most influential, of them was Montesquieu. Montesquieu had a long and abiding fascination for the cultures of Asia. His reflections on the significance of what came to be called "Oriental despotism" and on all that was involved in the civilizing process were to be found in his most famous work, *The Spirit of the Laws.* Written, or for the most part dictated, while its author was steadily going blind, it first appeared, unlicensed but unopposed, in Geneva in 1748. It proved almost as great a success—although with a rather different readership, one supposes—as his *Persian Letters,* which had first appeared anonymously in 1721 and gone through ten editions in less than a year. *The Spirit of the Laws* did not perhaps do quite so well (but then it had none of the somewhat elusive eroticism of the *Letters*), but within two years of its publication Montesquieu told a friend there were twenty-two editions of the work and it was being read all over Europe. "Before Montesquieu," declared the characteristically effusive Jeremy

Bentham, "all was unmixed barbarism."[93] The book had a marked and lasting influence on the founders of the United States. Montesquieu was, James Madison said, "in his particular science what Bacon was in universal science," and by the 1780s he had become the most frequently quoted of modern authors.[94] And although he was both moderate in his (professed) religious convictions and in every sense an aristocrat, Montesquieu also became the most frequently cited author in the pamphlets that accompanied the meeting of the Estates-General in France in May of 1789 and that, before the summer was out, had launched the French Revolution.[95]

Montesquieu was less dogmatic, less assertive, and in some ways more traditional perhaps than many of his contemporaries. "His virtues," said Lord Chesterfield, that expert on polite and civilizing behavior, "did honour to human nature, his writings to justice. A friend to mankind, he asserted their undoubted and inalienable rights with freedom."[96] He fought hard to keep *The Spirit of the Laws* off the papacy's *Index Librorum Prohibitorum* (Index of Prohibited Books)—which perhaps explains some of his more conciliatory references to Christianity and to the Church. He failed in the end, as almost everyone who had anything remotely original to say inevitably did, and by 1751 the book had been condemned for heresy. This, however, did nothing to diminish its popularity, although as the Milanese Cesare Beccaria—who claimed to have been converted to philosophy by reading *The Persian Letters*—complained, it sometimes made it harder to come by.[97] Montesquieu was also, in most senses, a true eclectic, something that earned him high praise from Diderot. When he died, in 1755, Diderot was the only one of his contemporaries to follow his funeral cortège. "It seems," he wrote,

> that in the Republic of Letters we conduct ourselves according to the same cruel policies which prevailed in the ancient democracies, where every citizen who became too powerful was exterminated. I wrote these reflections on Fe.X [February 10] 1755, having just returned from the funeral of one of our greatest men, saddened by the loss which the nation and the world of letters have

> made and profoundly indignant at the persecution which he had to suffer.[98]

The *philosophes,* with the exception of Diderot and D'Alembert, may have turned their backs on him at his death, but when Buffon was asked to list the greatest men of the modern age he named Bacon, Newton, Leibniz, Montesquieu, and (modestly) himself.[99]

The Spirit of the Laws carried an epithet from the Roman poet Ovid, "*Prolem sine matrem,*" "A child without a mother," and to this day it has eluded adequate definition. D'Alembert said of it, shrewdly, that it was "to the study of the laws what Descartes had been for philosophy: it illuminates frequently and fails sometimes, but even in its failings it is instructive for those who know how to read."[100] Long, often rambling, and split up into brief chapters crammed with information on myriad subjects, its main objective was to find the guiding principles that underpinned the laws and customs and the links that existed between them, which in one way or another controlled the lives of all peoples everywhere. "Many things govern the lives of men," Montesquieu wrote, "climate, religion, laws, maxims of government, examples of past things. Customs, manners—as a result, from all of these are formed a general spirit." Today we would call this assembly a "culture."[101] As Dugald Stewart said of it, *The Spirit of the Laws* was the first work to consider in this way "laws as originating chiefly from the circumstances of society." For this reason, Montesquieu had refrained from "bewildering himself" among what Stewart called "the erudition of scholiasts and antiquarians" and had instead borrowed "his lights" from "the most remote and unconnected quarters of the globe."[102] The outcome, as David Hume said of it, somewhat grudgingly, was "a system of political knowledge which abounds in ingenious and brilliant thoughts and is not wanting in solidity."[103] It has been hailed as the first work of comparative sociology, the beginning of modern anthropology, the source of the great twentieth-century German sociologist Max Weber's theory of "ideal types," and the earliest attempt at what in the nineteenth century would be the bid to find through the study of the law a key to the understanding of all human culture.[104] It is also a grand reflection on what a "civilization"—although Montesquieu himself never uses the term—actually is or should be.

Montesquieu identified three possible types of government: republics, monarchies, and despotism. In the first of these—which may be either "democratic" or "aristocratic"—the "people as a body or only a part of the people" exercise sovereign power. In the second, sovereignty is held by "one alone," although in accordance with "fixed and established laws"; in the third, "one alone, without law and without rule, drags everything along by his will and his caprice."[105] To each type of government he ascribed a "principle," which he described as "that which makes it act," and crucially, "the human passions that drive it." In a republic this is virtue; in a monarchy it is "honor"; in a despotism it is "fear."[106] Montesquieu's "republic" combines both democracy and aristocracy, while his "monarchy" is split into what he thinks of as true monarchy and despotism. Not all of this is original. It owes something to the classical distinction between "democracy," the rule of the many; "aristocracy," the rule of the few; and "monarchy," the rule of the one. The idea of a republic as a mixed form of government is a Roman one, and the distinction between a "monarchy" and a "tyranny" we owe to Aristotle. Similar divisions also crop up in the writings of a number of Montesquieu's immediate predecessors and near-contemporaries, including the Neapolitan Paolo Mattia Doria, whom Montesquieu may have visited during his journey through Italy in 1729.[107] But his understanding of "despotism" is largely his own.

All three types of government were to be found throughout human history and through the world. Of all three only the first two were truly legitimate, truly civil, and capable of constituting political societies worth the name. (Montesquieu, on the whole, preferred what he called a "moderated monarchy," the best example of which he assumed, largely on the basis of a reading of the works of Henry St. John, Viscount Bolingbroke, and the time he spent there between 1729 and 1731, to be England.) But, in an image as old as Aeschylus, the most compelling examples of the third were to be found in Asia. Unlike all other regions of the world, where—or so Montesquieu believed (neither Africa nor pre-conquest America have any significant place in his political geography)—"a spirit of Liberty forms itself from age to age and down through the centuries," in Asia "there reigns still a spirit of servitude which has never left it; and in all the histories of that land, one cannot find trace of a single feature which marks out the free spirit." Because there is no temperate zone in Asia, "hot" and "cold" nations face one another, so that "brave, active warrior people are immediately adjacent to effeminate, lazy, and timid peoples." In Europe, by contrast, where the temperate zone is very broad, "strong nations face the strong: those that are adjacent have more or less the same amount of courage."[108] It is for this reason that Asia has always been in the grips of those over-extended empires known to him and to most of his contemporaries as "universal monarchies," whereas in Europe "they have never been able to survive."[109] These, then, were those societies from Ottoman Turkey to Safavid Iran to, as we shall see, Qing China, which, ever since the seventeenth century, had all been lumped together under the name "Oriental despotism."

On Montesquieu's account of it, despotism is a condition in which "there are no laws, so to speak, there are only customs and manners, and if you overturn them, you overturn everything. Laws are established, customs are inspired."[110] One way of construing this would be to say that in truly civil societies, be they republics or monarchies, government is conducted by means of a form of examined conscience. It is constrained by promulgated laws that are of purely human invention, public and not private, subject to constant examination and modification. In a despotism, by contrast, such rules of conduct as do exist are nothing more than the reflection of ancient rites, too sacred, too—as Montesquieu puts it—"inspired" to be open to rational inquiry or possible change, for "when you instruct a beast, you take care not to let him change masters, training, or gait; you stamp his brain with two or three impulses and no more."[111] Government in such a world is inevitably prey to the unbridled passions of single individuals. Sovereignty, which even in the most unmoderated monarchy is always exercised with the consent of the governed, in a despotism becomes a form of ownership. The Asian despot does not rule over his subjects; he literally owns them. While chattel slavery was a condition for many even in many parts of Europe and, with ever-increasing brutality, in Europe's overseas colonies, only in despotisms did there exist what Montesquieu termed "political slavery," the absence of any freedom to act or express oneself independently of the sovereign's will. For this reason, argued Rhedi, one of the minor correspondents in *The Persian Letters,* with the exception of a few towns in Asia Minor and the perhaps more troubling exception of Carthage, republics—always the freest of societies—were unknown in Asia and Africa, which "have always been crushed under despotism."[112] There were examples of this kind of isolated despotic society to be found throughout Asia. But for Montesquieu, the clearest, and the most contentious, was China, and his account of the "Celestial Empire" as the very antithesis of enlightened civil society set off a debate that lasted well into the following century.

Montesquieu knew quite a lot about China. Like most of his generation he had read the Jesuit Jean-Baptiste du Halde's *Description of the Empire of China* and the Jesuit miscellany known as *Edifying and Intriguing Letters Written by Foreign Missions,* which was the main source of information about China available to Europeans. He had also read Commodore—later Admiral—George Anson's detailed account of his visit to China in 1743 in his *A Voyage Around the World* (which contained a scathingly dismissive view of virtually every aspect of Chinese culture), along with a number of collections of travel accounts from various parts of Asia that ever since the sixteenth century had been the staple of most armchair theorists, and he had also had long conversations in Rome in 1729 with the Jesuit Jean-François Foucquet, who had lived in China from 1699 to 1721.

Unlike most of his contemporaries, however, Montesquieu may also have actually met a real, if deracinated and Christianized, Chinese.[113] Known as Arcadio Huang, or "Ouange," he was the son of an imperial assistant to the provinces of Nanking and Shantung who had been converted to Catholicism in 1638, a move that, from his son's account, had brought him and his family a great deal of suffering. Huang had himself been baptized and educated by the French Foreign Missions in China and in 1702 had traveled, under their protection, first to London and then to Rome, so that he could be presented to the Pope as an example of a "literate Chinese Christian," the living proof of the Jesuits' persistent claim that the Chinese were adherents of a religion easily assimilated to Christianity. The missionaries had intended him for ordination, but on reaching Rome he refused because, as he explained in the memoir of his life that he wrote on his deathbed, the hostility toward the Chinese generated by the Rites Controversy "brought back to me all the painful struggles which my parents had had with their family in order to protect their faith." Although he knew that he had been "chosen by Our Saviour for a mission, at the very moment that I declared myself to have been chosen, the idea of the priesthood terrified me."[114] This last-minute defection does not, however, seem to have lost him the support of the missions which, in 1704 or 1705, arranged for his passage to France, where he became the "Chinese Interpreter to the Sun King" and possibly his Keeper of Chinese Books. In April 1713 he married a Mademoiselle Régnier, "of modest income but irreproachable habits," who, he says, helped him to acquire a new French identity. He worked closely with the young *savant* Nicolas Fréret, who was also known to Montesquieu, in the compilation of a Chinese-French dictionary and a Chinese grammar.[115] He died, however, in 1716, before any of this was complete. During the period 1709–13 he may have met and had a number of conversations with Montesquieu, then in his early twenties (although Huang himself makes no mention of them), on various aspects of Chinese culture and society. Whether Montesquieu acquired this information directly or through Fréret we may never know. But what is certain is that it made a lasting impression on him. It transformed what in his mind had been a remote outpost of Asia into the most perfectly detailed empirical model of a despotism that existed.

Montesquieu did a lot to upset Leibniz's benign view of the ethically superior Chinese. He was not convinced that Confucianism was some kind of deism and thought that in fact the Chinese were, "properly speaking, atheists or Spinozists." The flattering image of China so popular in the West was, he believed, an illusion fostered by the not entirely disinterested Jesuits and based upon the mere "appearance of order" that had been achieved by "the continuous exercise of the will of one alone by which they themselves are governed"—in other words, their despotic emperor.[116]

Chinese despotism, however, was in most respects unlike most of the other forms that existed, even within Asia. For unlike the Persians or the Ottomans or the Mongols, who lived in a condition of more or less constant warfare, the Chinese appeared to have maintained their state for centuries, shut off from the outside world and apparently immune to invasion and internal discord. What he called mockingly the "immortality" of the Chinese Empire was for Montesquieu the real mystery. And it provided him with a reflection not merely on China or even on the inner working of despotic governments but in the end on the true nature of civilization.

In reality, China's famous "stability" was largely a myth, perpetrated by ill-informed Europeans. "The marvel which is the duration of the Chinese Empire," he wrote in his *Pensées* (Thoughts), a miscellaneous collection of reflections he kept throughout his life, "fades the closer one gets to it." As he had learned from Huang,

> [This empire] has not always remained the same but has suffered an infinite number of divisions, that this country has had more than three kings at the same time, and that there have even been republics before the coming of Our Lord. The whole world knows that it has twice been invaded by the Tartars and still groans under their tyranny. . . . There is hardly an empire in the world as rife with civil wars as this one; one family succeeds another to the throne incessantly, and the new usurpers chase out the old, and discord and confusion reigns everywhere.

Had the government of China been as wonderful as its European admirers claimed, "the Tartars would not have been able to make themselves masters of it in a day." Such stability as it did possess derived from the fact that it was surrounded on all sides by "petty princes separated from one another, for the most part, by deserts and inaccessible terrain; no people other than the Tartars ever had the power to overthrow the Chinese." The term "Chinese Empire" was, in effect, a misnomer. The term "China" referred to a territory, not to a single polity or even a single culture. If, Montesquieu pointed out, "one were to say that Europe had always been governed by Europeans, or if one were to trace the [modern] Persian Empire to the predecessors of Cyrus, one would find [in Europe and Persia] empires as ancient as that of China."[117]

What was truly significant about China was not its illusory stability but its immobility, and for Montesquieu this was the inescapable consequence of the kind of government its miserable subjects had had to endure for century after century. In China, as in all despotic states, "the authority of the prince is limitless, he combines both secular and ecclesiastical power. . . . The welfare and the lives of his subjects are always at the disposition of the sovereign, exposed as they are to the caprice and the whims and the utterly unlimited will of the tyrant."[118] Since people who are accustomed to bowing before the will of a tyrant become less inclined to do so the farther they are from his reach, it was only to be expected that, in such a vast terrain as China, the conquest of its outlying provinces by "bandit chiefs and Tartars"—the latest had been as recent as 1644—was relatively simple and frequent.[119] The seemingly endless cycle of civil conflicts and the waves of invasions that had swept over China since the thirteenth century had not, however, led to any substantial change in government, as similar events would have done in Europe—hence the appearance of stability. In Europe the conquerors had changed the conquered; in China it seems to have been the other way round. The rough, barbarous Tartars, rather than injecting some of their native vigor into the supine Chinese population, had instead simply appropriated its despotic ways for themselves and, in turn, had become lethargic and unchanging. Nothing, it would seem, could penetrate the carapace of inertia that surrounded the whole of Chinese society as inexorably as its famous wall. Why?

The reason, Montesquieu believed, lay in the spirit in which the Chinese emperors, ever since the fall of the Ming (whom he credited, somewhat inconsistently, with all that was evidently beneficial about Chinese society), had governed. Like all despotic states, China was ruled not so much by laws as by "manners" and "customs."[120] Montesquieu does not always distinguish very precisely between the two. Both are described as "institutions of the nation in general."[121] Customs, however, are generally those long-accepted practices of a community that hold it together on a daily basis. Manners are roughly what we might understand by the word today: the routine social exchanges between individuals, the codes of behavior that all but real savages need in order to negotiate their daily lives. They are superficial and transitory, the first line of contact with strangers. They are by no means unimportant, even in the most civil societies—Montesquieu lived in a world where men still fought duels over breaches of etiquette—but are, in themselves, devoid of ethical content. "In Paris," he wrote, a city of which he was suspicious and somewhat disdainful, "one is stunned by the world; one knows only manners; there is no time to get to know either vice or virtue."[122] As they have nothing to do with vice or virtue, manners are merely conventional, and they vary greatly from culture to culture. After all, as Adam Smith pointed out, that "degree of politeness which . . . would be thought effeminate adulation in Russia would be regarded as rudeness and barbarism at the court of France."[123] Manners were matters of general agreement, in much the same way as aesthetics. For this reason, Montesquieu claimed, "a French beauty is horrible in China, a Chinese one horrible in France."[124] Unlike laws, which reflect a consensus and can, and indeed must, change as circumstances change, neither customs nor manners, which are unexamined, have any reason for existing beyond the fact that they have always existed. In Europe, manners and customs have no significant role to play in the political order. In China, however, manners were not only taught in the schools, as if they were some kind of science—so that one could identify a "man of letters" by the way he bowed—they had been transformed by a cadre of "grave scholars" into the very thing with which, in reality, they were wholly unconnected, namely "principles of morality."[125] This was a conflation of the private and the public of the kind that had once existed in feudal Europe but that had now been entirely abolished.[126] To reinforce these principles, the Chinese emperors, like so many other despotic rulers, had resorted to an even more terrible conflation: that of the sacred and the secular. Religion in China, as in all despotic states, was "fear added to fear."[127] Religion—or at least the kind of religion so important to the survival of despotic regimes—relies upon a sacred text that, like the creed it supposedly upholds, is exempt from change or criticism. So, just as the Arabs had chosen the Qur'an as their "sacred book that acts as a rule," as the Persians (or so Montesquieu thought) had chosen the writings of Zoroaster and the Hindus the Veda, so the Chinese had their "classics" (and he might have added, but perhaps from fear of the consequences did not, the Jews and the Christians have their Bible). In this way "the religious code replaces the civil code and fixes what is arbitrary."[128] The Chinese, however, seemed to have gone one step further than any other "Oriental" despotism, in that their legislators had successfully "confused religion, laws, mores, and manners," thus emptying the concepts of vice and virtue of any real meaning.[129] This was what, in effect, all theocracies did, and theocracies were the direst forms of despotism.

The outcome of all this was to make of the nation one single, indivisible character, so tightly bound together as to be impervious to any change. This was the reason why in China, unlike other places in the world, the conquerors had always become, in the end, sinicized. For whereas it was possible for the "Tartars," who could distinguish among customs, manners, and laws, to change one of these without necessarily changing the others, the Chinese could not. Faced with such resilience, the invader had no option, short of annihilating the entire population or of withdrawing, but to accept them as they were. For the same reason, Montesquieu believed that the missionaries were wasting their time. "It is almost impossible," he declared, "for Christianity ever to be established in China."[130]

In this way China had come to resemble not a society but an immense family, in which he said, echoing a judgment by Plato on the Persians, "everything comes down to reconciling political and civil government with domestic government, the officers of the state with those of the seraglio."[131] It was an image that Chinese philosophy had worked hard to present as the reflection of a perfectly harmonious world. "The Emperors of China," wrote Montesquieu in the collection of notes and jottings he called his *Spicilège,* "are very eager for the people to believe the maxim of the Chinese philosopher that the empire is a family and the emperor its father." But no state could ever actually be a family. It was one of the illusions fostered by despots, who habitually styled themselves, as had the Roman emperors, as "fathers of the *patria.*" In reality, however, although the Chinese emperor, like his Roman counterpart, "loves to cultivate the reputation for clemency," he gives "no more thought to human life than he does to that of a fly." This elaborate deception allowed the emperor, by "referring everything to himself alone," to reduce "the state to its capital, the capital to the court, and the court to his person alone."[132] Since families tend to preserve what is ancient and hallowed at the expense of what is new but potentially disruptive, the outcome had been an excessive veneration of the past, which, as Voltaire put it, "makes in their eyes perfect all that is ancient."[133] The entire society could be seen reflected in that bizarre, rambling structure, the emperor's palace. It was, wrote Montesquieu, "a spider's web, with the emperor like the spider at the center. He cannot move without everyone else moving, and no one else can move without him moving also."[134]

Despotism of this kind, however, could only exist in isolation. Contact with the outside world, exposure to other forms of life, other customs and habits, were an obvious threat. "Such a state," Montesquieu argued, "will be in the best situation when it is able to consider itself alone in the world, when it is surrounded by deserts and separated from the peoples it calls barbarians."[135] It was this that accounted for the obsessive isolationism of the Chinese, the belief that the empire lay at the center of the globe, that they were superior to all other peoples, whom they, as the ancient Greeks had once done, lumped together under a single term that the Europeans rendered as "barbarians." Of all the things that Robinson Crusoe on his brief visit to China (in the second, and now rarely read, part of Daniel Defoe's novel) is made to find "to the last degree ridiculous" is the Chinese "contempt for all the world but themselves."[136]

The flow of conversation, the communication that came from the links that bound the advanced commercial societies to one another, outside influence, the liberty to choose a way of life, the suggestion that beyond the frontiers of one's own nation there might exist ways preferable to one's own: these were the things that all autocratic societies most feared.

China's isolation was reinforced by the Chinese system of writing, which both fascinated and appalled Montesquieu, as it did many Europeans. He appears to have learned from Huang that the Chinese system of writing had 214 radicals that formed the basis of most Chinese characters. Huang gave Montesquieu a number of examples of this, wrote out the Lord's Prayer, and sang him a popular song to demonstrate tonal differences.[137] Montesquieu was clearly not unimpressed by all this dexterity but ultimately came to the conclusion that since the Chinese had never succeeded in devising for themselves what Commodore Anson called "that almost divine invention," the alphabet, they had to spend most of their life learning the symbols necessary for them to be able to read about the rites that "encompassed all the minor activities of life."[138] Thus engrossed, they had neither the resources nor the inclination even to interpret, much less challenge, the received wisdom of past centuries. What science the Chinese had, remarked Diderot with contempt, was thus reduced to little more than "the knowledge of language" and, furthermore, of a language "barely sufficient for daily life."[139]

Many years later, in 1836, the German polymath Wilhelm von Humboldt, who, unlike any of the *philosophes* engaged in the China debate, had some firsthand knowledge of Chinese (and Sanskrit and Malay and Burmese and Javanese and Nahuatl and Basque), made a similar, if more damning, observation. The alphabet, he wrote, was the only certain scientific tool, and "once the mind begins to ascend to *scientific thinking,* a pictographic script simply cannot survive for long." Humboldt, often looked upon as if not the first then certainly one of the earliest modern linguisticians, wondered whether there might not exist an "ascent in stages" through which all languages pass "to an ever *more perfect state.*"[140] If this were indeed the case, then Chinese, which had clearly made the first step out of simple depiction, had singularly failed to devise a true alphabet. Because of this, he concluded, Chinese was a "petrified language."

This observation was not, however, merely linguistic. It was also reflected in the endlessly elaborate courtesies and rituals that marked every aspect of daily life in China. In the opinion of the abbé Gabriel Bonnot de Mably, perhaps the most widely read of the "detractors of China" besides Montesquieu and whose views on citizens' rights were to become one of the ideological sources of the French Revolution, China was a society ruled by "the most puerile of ceremonies." Inhabited by the "the most regimented people on earth and the least capable of thought," its famous meritocracy was selected only on the basis of an exam that never once asked the only important question, "If that which is done, is that which should be done."[141] Trapped thus in a rigid hierarchy, passive before the decrees of the emperor, prevented by their very system of notation from advancing beyond the position in which Confucius had left them in the sixth century BCE, the Chinese had become frozen in time.

On this issue, at least, few were inclined to disagree. Even Voltaire, who on the whole rejected what he called the "vague imputations to be found in *The Spirit of the Laws* against this government, the most ancient in the world," accepted that the Chinese

> were then [at the end of the seventeenth century] and are now, in both philosophy and literature, where we were about two hundred years ago. Their respect for their ancient masters prescribed for them certain boundaries beyond which they dared not pass. . . . The Chinese, who have remained for two thousand years within the terms which they had first attained, have remained mediocre in the sciences, and the first of all the peoples of the world in both morality and civility [*police*], as well as the most ancient.[142]

What Voltaire, like Leibniz, saw as the tranquillity of moral order had been purchased at the price of complicity and inertia. China was, in truth, the very antithesis of a civilization. The Chinese had become fixed in time, looking always back to past authorities, guiding their lives by the teaching of a man who had been dead for over a millennium. Deference to the past, like the deference to the scripts and the laws and the wild and revolting stories that the world's religions have told about themselves, was, said Diderot in defense of Montesquieu's account of China, what "reduces a man of genius to silence or strangles him." It is this that buries a "nation . . . in the barbarity of its religion, its laws, its customs, and its government, in the ignorance of those things that are most important to its true interests, to its power and its commerce, to its splendor and its felicity." Or as Turgot had argued in the plan he drew up for a *Discourse on Universal History* that he never wrote, "what is never perfect [he was referring to reason and justice] ought never to be entirely immobilized . . . as has virtually happened in China." China, for all its morality and the refinement of its crafts, had drained all the passions out of human life. And the passions, declared Turgot, are "the mainsprings of action and consequently of progress; everything which draws men away from their present condition, and everything which puts varied scenes before their eyes, extends the scope of their ideas, enlightens them, stimulates them, and in the long run leads them to the good and the true."[143]

For all its carefully cultivated skills, for all its lacquerwork, its porcelain and its silks, for all its craftsmanship, for all its undoubted human abundance, and despite whatever "morality" Montesquieu had left it, China was, said Diderot, "almost a barbarous country." Or, he added, "what is worse, a half-civilized country." The stubborn attachment of the Chinese to their customs, the indifference of their rulers, and the "law which prevents them from ever leaving the country"—these had created for the Chinese a condition of intellectual and moral paralysis that "must fix [this country] through an indefinite series of centuries in its present condition." For how can you teach "wisdom to someone who believes himself to be all wise? How do you perfect someone who believes himself to be perfect?"[144] Civilization, enlightenment, was, as we have seen time and time again, the outcome of history, of the human being's unique relationship with time, and it was an unfinished process. The Chinese had made the mistake of supposing that there could be an end to human history, and that they were it. The result had been not, as China's admirers had claimed, immobility, but rather stagnation. Kant even believed that the fact that Chinese had remained for centuries untouched by other languages meant that, although the Chinese had become "cultivated," they could never become enlightened and their concepts would always remain limited. Civilization, naturally, relied in large measure on language, and language needed to be cross-fertilized. The great power of Greek, to which all the western world ultimately owed its literary success, lay, he claimed, precisely in the fact that it had been mixed with Celtic, Thracian, Phrygian, and "perhaps Syrian" before it finally became Greek.[145]

China lay at the far extreme of the historical continuum from Tahiti. Yet its peoples faced, in their own way, the same inevitable fate as the Tahitians. For like them, the Chinese were doomed to remain quietly where they were until they were finally overrun by a truly "civilized" power that would bring them back into history, which meant into the modern world. Their immobility had led to their isolation from the entire human race. They had denied the principle that all human beings were meant to communicate with one another, just as they were meant to trade with one another (which the Chinese emperors had expressly forbidden). This attitude of mind, which Diderot called "insularity," the inward gaze of the isolated community, was capable of sanctioning, and ultimately sanctifying, all manner of hideous crimes. In societies that are closed off from the world, observed "B" in Diderot's *Supplement to Bougainville's Journey,*

> women undergo infibulation, which gives rise to so many bizarre customs, at once cruel and unnecessary, for which the justification is lost in the mists of antiquity, leaving the philosophers at their wits' ends to explain them. It appears to be a fairly universal rule that supernatural and divinely inspired practices grow stronger and more durable with time, eventually becoming transformed into civil and national laws, while civil and national institutions become consecrated and degenerate into supernatural and divine precepts.[146]

In this respect, China bore a startling resemblance to Tahiti. Cut off by its deserts and its Great Wall, it too was an island. Like the Tahitians of

Diderot's imagination, the Chinese had for centuries held themselves aloof from the world. True, the Chinese had never practiced infibulation, but footbinding was perhaps almost as bad. Both the simple savage and the overly refined Oriental despot had this in common: neither had chosen to participate in what Diderot called a "regard for the general will of the species."[147] It was, as we have already seen, the capacity for sympathy with others of our kind that, together with our experience of time, is what ultimately defines us as human. In both Tahiti and China sympathy had remained at home, confined by "customs" and "habits." And in both cases time had been arrested. In a true civilization, regarding the "general will of the species" meant recognizing the claims of the entire species, for every true civilization is, necessarily and inescapably, cosmopolitan. Tahiti had, at least, as the "Old Man" had feared, been prepared to welcome the world when the world, in the shape of Bougainville and his crew, had finally arrived. The Chinese, however, having created their own island, had ruthlessly defended it from any possible influence from outside. But sooner or later they too would have to trade their customs and habits for true laws and join the world.

The Tahitians had yet to begin their ascent through the various stages of social human evolution. The Chinese, having reached a highly advanced stage—arguably as advanced as the Europeans, if not more so—had somehow taken a false turn. They had chosen simply to stop, and so long as it remained thus in glittering and belligerent isolation the so-called Celestial Kingdom would only ever be the antithesis of the world, dynamic and cosmopolitan, that Montesquieu and Diderot, D'Alembert and Condorcet, Hume and Smith confidently hoped would one day come about. China provided a warning of what an unduly complacent, overly self-regarding Europe could so easily become. For if all human societies are driven by their very nature to progress from savagery to civilization, they also have a tendency to move beyond the narrow limits of the communities in which they were formed. This, which the Chinese emperors had so skillfully prevented from happening, was to be the final stage in the development of the species.

7

THE GREAT SOCIETY OF MANKIND

I

"IF I KNEW SOMETHING useful to me, and harmful to my family," wrote Montesquieu, "I would reject it from my mind. If I knew something useful to my family, and not to my country, I would try to forget it. If I knew of something useful to my country, and harmful to Europe, or useful to Europe and harmful to Mankind, I would look upon it as a crime."[1] Diderot had defined what he called the "general will of the species" in similar terms. It was, he explained, that "common desire" that creates "the rule binding the common conduct of the individual towards another in the same society, together with the conduct of an individual towards the whole society to which he belongs, and of that society itself towards other societies."[2] Montesquieu expressed this sentiment—for sentiment it was—as an obligation, Diderot as a desire. But both were rephrasing an image as old, at least, as the Stoic philosopher Hierocles of the first to second centuries CE, an image of concentric circles, which moved steadily outward from the individual and the family to the homeland or the *patria,* until finally they reached the whole of humanity.[3] The point of departure was always the self, but the ultimate horizon of loyalty and concern was the species itself. It was an image repeated, in one way or another, by virtually all the thinkers of the Enlightenment.

"Self-love, but serves the virtuous mind to wake," enthused Alexander Pope:

As the small pebble stirs the peaceful lake;
The centre mov'd, a circle strait succeeds,
Another still, and still another spreads;
Friend, parent, neighbour, first it will embrace,
His country next, and next all human race;
Wide and more wide, th'o'erflowings of the mind
Take ev'ry creature in, or ev'ry kind.[4]

Adam Smith arrived at much the same conclusion by a somewhat different route. If, he said, "the wise and virtuous man" was always willing, as Smith assumed he was, to sacrifice his own private interests to those of the "public interests of his own particular order and society," and he recognized that this should in turn, when required, be "sacrificed to the greater interest of the state or sovereignty, of which it is only a subordinate part," then it followed that "he should be equally willing that all those inferior interests should be sacrificed to the greater interests of the universe."[5] Even Edmund Burke, ardent champion of the local, who derided the French Revolution for trafficking in just such abstractions as "humanity and the rights of man," and who held that "to be attached to the subdivision, to love the little platoon we belong to in society is the first principle (the germ as it were) of public affections"—even he believed that this love was also "the first link in a series by which we proceed towards a love of our country and of mankind."[6]

All were voicing the Stoic sense of the necessary interrelatedness of all human beings, of what the Greeks had called *oikeiosis,* or the natural attachment to what is appropriate, or akin to oneself (which we met in chapter 2). Each, too, recognized that these "benevolent sentiments," as Hume calls them, depended upon communication, and each knew that communication, like charity, begins at home. The Chinese were not the only ones to feel the pull of "custom." The human mind, as Hume observed, "is of a very imitative nature." It is so not because we lack imagination as individuals—although some of us, such as, in Hume's opinion, soldiers and priests, clearly do—but because of the natural sympathy we have with our fellow beings. "No quality of human nature is more remarkable," he believed, "both in itself and in its consequences, than that propensity we have to sympathize with others, and to receive by communication their inclinations and sentiments, however different from, or even contrary, to our own."[7] It was, he thought, to this that we owed the "great uniformity we may observe in the humours and turn of thinking of those of the same nation." Most peoples, even the most independent-minded, find it hard to "follow their own reason or inclination" when this conflicts with that of their family or friends. The consequences of a shared sympathy, although generally benign, could also pull in another direction: "Popular sedition, party zeal, a devoted obedience to factious leaders; these are some of the most visible, though less laudable effects of this social sympathy in human nature."[8] The same passions that might lead ultimately, and with the right encouragement, to a cosmopolitan world are also those that are responsible for binding together the members of a religious sect. We are, after all, primarily herd animals, sociable creatures. Isolated from our own kind, we invariably die or go insane. Even Hobbes's first men lived in bands, if not societies. Civil men, as Rousseau had seen more clearly than most, lived resolutely, inescapably, in the opinion of others, and from others they took on what Hume called "a tincture."[9] Little by little, this then built up into "national characters."

At this point, however, most people stopped. The next step, from nation or *patria,* community, or parish to "humanity," was, for many, too great a stretch. Humanity was, as Burke insisted, for most at best an abstraction, its limits as yet unknown, its myriad peoples for the most part unknowable. In Hume's duly skeptical view, although we may have some moral duty to consider the welfare of the species before that of our own "little platoon," in actual fact "the general interest of mankind is better promoted" when every individual concerns himself solely with "the good of his own community" than it is likely to be by any "loose indeterminate views to the good of the species, whence no beneficial action could ever result, for want of a duly limited object, on which they could exert themselves."[10] Most of the inhabitants of early modern Europe, before the arrival of mass communication in the nineteenth century, could not be expected to feel anything, or share anything, with beings whom they did not know personally and in all likelihood would never meet. But they could be persuaded, in particular in times of conflict, to conjure up some sense of affinity with, some loyalty toward, those who spoke the same language, observed the same laws and the same religion, and professed the same ties to what the great nineteenth-century French sociologist Émile Durkheim called that "obscure mystic idea," the nation.[11]

The idea of the nation went through very many mutations before, sometime in the nineteenth century, it became the entity we understand today: roughly—for no description of anything so powerful yet so amorphous can ever be adequate—a single people, often speaking a single language, with a single political affiliation that in time would come to be called a "nationality," binding them to a clearly defined patch of soil: a "Native ground," as Shaftesbury, quoting Ovid, defined it, that "draws all with indefinable sweetness."[12] The remote origins of this conception in western Europe derive from the chaos that overtook the continent as the Roman Empire in the West slowly collapsed during the fifth and sixth centuries into isolated, warring, monarchical states. Under the empire the emperor had been represented as the embodiment of the state. Ever since the days of Augustus, the true founder of the "Principate" that had replaced the Roman Republic and initiated the rule of the Caesars, the emperor had assumed the title of "Father of the Patria" (*pater patriae*), and his rule depended upon what was termed the *patria potestas*—the power of the *patria*. From then on, the peoples of the Roman world were to be their grateful, obedient children. The Roman Empire, as the great nineteenth-century English jurist Henry Sumner Maine remarked in 1861, had been conceived by its rulers as one vast, imaginary jural kinship group. "The Patria Potestas of the Romans," Maine wrote,

> which is necessarily our type of the primeval paternal authority, is equally difficult to understand as an institution of civilised life, whether we consider its incidence on the person or its effects on property.
>
> Yet if this was itself remarkable more remarkable still was the diffusion of the Potestas over the whole of a civilisation from which it had once disappeared. . . . Every African or Spaniard, every Gaul, Briton, or Jew, who received this honour by gift, purchase, or inheritance, placed himself under the Roman Law of Persons, and [all] . . . were on the ordinary footing of a Roman filius familias [son of the family].[13]

For most of these supposed children, the presence of their putative father was too remote to have much imaginative appeal and became increasingly so over time as the Empire expanded and fragmented. The petty kings of medieval Europe, however, were very close indeed, and the feudal system that cast the world into a strict hierarchy from monarch to peasant made them seem closer still.

For each of these petty kingships the nation came to be identified with the person of the monarch him- (and only very rarely her-) self. The medieval monarch famously had two bodies, one natural, the other political; while the sovereign himself was clearly no more than a mere mortal, the sovereignty he exercised, the kingdom that he literally embodied, was immortal. In the old times, reflected nostalgically the fourteenth-century jurist Baldus de Ubaldis, when the Roman Empire was at its height, they used to say that the emperor's "material and visible crown" consisted of a diadem but that he also had an "invisible" crown that had been placed on his head by God alone.[14] And that crown did not die. You might, as the English did in 1649 and the French in 1792, succeed in killing a king. But monarchy was an altogether more durable creation. Oliver Cromwell is famously supposed to have said to Algernon Sidney on the eve of the execution of Charles I: "I tell you we will cut off his head with the crown on it."[15] He did not. Charles I lost his head, but the monarchy, ultimately, survived.

The French kings, in particular, took this very much to heart. As Jacques-Bénigne Bossuet, one of the most influential theorists of absolute kingship of the seventeenth century, sternly informed the son of Louis XIV, the "Sun King": "The state is in the person of the prince." Louis, who of all the monarchs of Europe most embodied the ideal of divine personal rule, never actually told the *parlement* of Paris in April 1655, "*L'état c'est moi*"—"I am the state"—as he is so often believed to have done. But he might well have, and he certainly said many things that came very close: "When one works for the state," for instance, "one works for oneself." There is also a story that the great comic playwright Jean-Baptiste Poquelin, best known by his stage name Molière, was one day called into the royal presence when the king was eating supper. Louis, who was Molière's patron, pointed to a chair and said, "France is eating chicken. Sit and eat chicken with France."

The king was not only literally the personification of the nation, he was also the closest thing there was on earth to a God, albeit a mortal one.[16] The divination, or quasi divination, of rulers is of course an ancient and widespread practice. Its origins in the West go back to Alexander the Great's claim to have been recognized by Zeus as his son and his subsequent importation of the trappings of ancient Persian monarchy—the robes, the diadem, and the customs of prostration and veneration—into Greece and from thence into Europe more widely. The Roman emperors, in their turn, all claimed to be divine, even if they had to wait until after death for deification. Their *imperium* was not, as it had been for the Roman senate under the Republic, a merely mundane right to rule; it was a quasi-mystical power reserved to them alone. With the final triumph of Christianity none of this was any longer possible. But the Christian emperors and the petty kings of Europe who claimed to be their successors did their best to deck themselves out with semidivine trappings and claimed, if not to be gods, then to derive their powers from God alone. Like God, they recognized no superiors on Earth (except in some cases the pope), and they exercised sovereignty over their peoples absolutely, as God was supposed to do. If God was the father in heaven, the monarch was the father on earth and the love he had for the kingdoms was, explained Bossuet, "confounded with the love he has for his family."[17] Accession, therefore, would seem to bring about a metamorphosis in the very person of the monarch himself. "By the Law of Nature," explained James I of England (and VI of Scotland), who was an unusually literate monarch, "the King became a natural Father of all his Lieges at his Coronation."[18] Kings ruled like God the Father, and, as far as they were able, they looked like God, or at least they did their best to look as much like God as their subjects imagined God to look. "Kings are justly called Gods," said James, "for that they exercise a manner or resemblance of divine power on Earth: For if you will consider the Attributes of God, you shall see how they agree in the person of a King."[19] The king was the most devout of his subjects, who were themselves the chosen people of the "New Alliance" (between God and man); and he became himself an object of devotion, second only to, and only slightly below, the deity.[20] This made any opposition to the royal will not merely treason but also heresy. As the French jurist Cardin Le Bret expressed it succinctly in 1632, "When one insults the king one insults God himself."[21]

This image of the divinely sanctioned monarch and of the semisacral nation over which he ruled was, if anything, greatly enhanced after the end of the Thirty Years' War. The doctrine of *cuius regio eius religio,* which had, in effect, banished religion as a source of conflict between nations, had also greatly enhanced the semisacred standing of the monarch. As the aura of the priesthood diminished, so that of kingship increased. It was one of the prices Europeans were compelled to pay for relative stability and a virtual end to religious conflict. Inexorably, King, God, and Nation became a single entity. This brought with it not only greater political stability and freedom from internal conflict; it brought, too, greater limitations upon political expression and greater restrictions upon political participation by anyone who was not the king or a member of his immediate entourage—what the *ideologue* Constantin-François Volney in 1791 called "that class of civil and sacred tyrants."[22] The king became, in effect, in the terms by which the emperor Justinian in the sixth century had defined the Roman emperor, someone who was "unfettered by laws" and for whom the law was always the expression of his "frank good will." Ultimately, sovereignty was always a matter of the law: who made it, by whom it was interpreted, and how it was enforced. The king's "sovereignty" was inalienable or, as Le Bret phrased it, "indivisible as a point in geometry." For the absolutist states of seventeenth-century Europe, the monarch was now no longer, as his predecessors had been, a magistrate, albeit the supreme magistrate, but—as the Roman emperors had been—a judge. As a consequence, the power of what were known as the "lesser magistrates" in the various parliaments, estates, cortes, and assemblies of Europe steadily diminished, until in many cases they were abolished altogether. When Louis XII of France dismissed the Estates-General in 1614, they would not meet again until 1789.

England was something of an exception. Not only did the monarchy lose much of its aura of sanctity, together with a great deal of its real power, during the civil wars of the seventeenth century, but those wars brought with them a new conception of political authority. This claimed that all civil society is not based upon divine degree and maintained by divine sanction but is in fact the consequence of a contract—what came to be known as the "social contract"—between the monarch and the people. The two main authors of this theory were Thomas Hobbes and John Locke. There are considerable and significant differences between them, and it is Locke's understanding of the nature of the contract—in part because it had such a marked influence on the founders of the United States—that has become the most enduringly influential. But both were initially a response to the political crises created first by the English Civil Wars of 1642–51 and then the so-called Exclusion Crisis from 1678 until 1681, which finally resulted, in 1688, in what has ever since been known as the "Glorious Revolution," a relatively bloodless coup in which Parliament "excluded" the Catholic and would-be absolutist king James II and replaced him with the Protestant and less dictatorially inclined William of Orange and his consort, Queen Mary. The Glorious Revolution, in the words of one who lived through it at close quarters, had snuffed out the previous regime "like a farthing candle" and opened the way "not to mending the Government but to melting it down and making all new."[23] Although it would be well over a century—and after it had been sanctified, so to speak, first by the American and then by the French Revolution—before it became widely accepted, the idea of a contract between ruler and ruled is today everywhere, except in the world's few remaining theocratic monarchies, the basis of all credible accounts of the origins and sources of political power.

Hobbes's objective had been to strengthen the authority of the state so as to eliminate the possibility of any future civil war. Locke's had been to restrict the power of would-be absolute monarchs. But the insistence of both that society was not an outpouring of the natural order, much less the creation of divine decree, but the result of an agreement among men seriously undermined the idea of the sovereign as an object of reverence. The sovereign's subjects might, as Hobbes put it, "in his presence . . . shine no more than the Stars in the presence of the Sun."[24] But he owed this refulgence solely to the power that had been invested in him by that "Multitude of men [who] do Agree, and *Covenant, every one, with every one,* that to whatsoever *Man,* or *Assembly of Men,* shall be given by the major part, the *Right to Present* the Person of them all, (that is, to be their *Representative*)."[25] Hobbes's sovereign, and Locke's, did not even need to be a single person. Sovereignty could just as easily be vested in an "Assembly of Men" as in a man. A republic could enjoy as much legitimacy as any monarchy (an argument that did not endear Hobbes to the restored Charles II), and it would shine just as brightly. And although kings might be able to pass themselves off as the fathers of their nations and as God's anointed legatees on Earth, assemblies could not. As the American political philosopher Michael Walzer once wryly observed, no matter how you imagine God, he does not look like a committee.

There was also another sense in which the monarch had been transformed into the instrument of his electors. Hobbes makes no real distinction between the state and what Hegel would later call "civil society." But as Durkheim pointed out in a remarkable series of lectures he gave on Hobbes in Bordeaux in 1895, crucially for Hobbes, the

> state and society are not two absolutely distinct realities, but two aspects of the same reality. The state is nothing more than the representative of the community; it is the organization, nothing more, and it is not, therefore, created by the native superiority of certain individuals who impose themselves on the others by virtue of their natural superiority.[26]

The sovereign holds the people in "awe," but because the sovereign *is* the state and because the state is the "organizing principle," in Durkheim's terms, of the society at large, he does not demand, as an *individual,* nor can he possibly expect, the kind of worship that European monarchs habitually demanded (and expected). Locke, who does distinguish between the state and civil society, was even less inclined to venerate kingship. His *Two Treatises on Government* had initially been written as a refutation of Sir Robert Filmer's *Patriarca,* possibly the most entrenched defense of patriarchal kingship ever written in England, and whereas Hobbes's "multitude" enters into a covenant with its chosen sovereign—and a covenant is something that cannot be broken by either party—in Locke's account men enter into a true contract, subject, like all contracts, to constant reevaluation. And whereas for Hobbes the relationship between sovereign and subject is one of submission, for Locke it is one of *trust,* which is why, for Locke, it was "evident that Absolute Monarchy, which by some men is counted the only Government in the world, is indeed inconsistent with Civil Society."[27] Of any persons, he stated bluntly, who "tell us that monarchy is *jure divino* [by divine right] . . . 'tis to be suspected that they have forgot what country they are born in, under what laws they live, and certainly cannot but feel obliged to declare Magna Carta to be downright heresy."[28]

The idea, however formulated, that society was based upon a contract, a covenant, or, as Rousseau would later conceive it, a *pact* among pre-social human beings for their own perceived ends and not an order imposed by the divinity in a shimmering likeness of the Kingdom of Heaven meant, as David Hume said, that the state had "no other object or purpose but the distribution of justice, without which there can be no peace among [men], nor safety nor mutual intercourse. We are, therefore, to look upon all the vast apparatus of government, as having ultimately no other object or purpose but the distribution of justice."[29]

Increasingly during the eighteenth century, the image by which the rulers of Europe chose to represent themselves began to shift from the semidivine absolute monarch, father of the nation, father of the people, to—in the term adopted by Frederick the Great of Prussia—the "first servant of the state." This, as we shall see, was something on which Frederick's most distinguished subject, Immanuel Kant, was to lay great emphasis. For as Kant put it, "A government established on the principle of benevolence towards the people, like that of a father towards his children—that is, a paternalistic government . . . is the greatest despotism thinkable." It was one in which subjects are treated like children, who depend upon the sovereign to tell them not only how to behave but also when and how to be happy and who are consequently deprived of any sense of what might be good or harmful to them.[30] From Frederick to Peter Leopold, Grand Duke of Tuscany, to Charles III of Spain to Catherine the Great of Russia, the "enlightened despots" of Europe, as they came to be called in the late nineteenth century, steadily distanced themselves from the archaic image and the archaic practices of the patriarchal monarchy upheld by their predecessors. The new monarchs, if never quite the "servants" of the state, nevertheless saw themselves as administrators, keepers of the public good, whose task was no longer the enhancement of their own personal glory but the continuing welfare of their subjects. Peter Leopold, for instance, was the first ruler to approve the composition of a written constitution, possibly the most remarkable legal document of the century, which, had it ever been made law, would have severely restricted his own powers. Peter, however, left Italy in 1790 to become Holy Roman Emperor, and his celebrated constitution passed into oblivion. But he made provisions for state-run hospitals, greatly improved legal protection for the mentally insane, and made vaccination against smallpox widely available. On November 30, 1786, he also abolished the death penalty and banned the use of judicial torture. This made Tuscany the first modern state to put a permanent end to capital punishment, and November 30 is today celebrated around the world as "Cities for Life Day."

The men with whom these new monarchs surrounded themselves were also increasingly members not of the older military aristocracy but of a new rising professional class of "civil" servants. They were men like the Count of Floridablanca, first secretary of state to Charles III of Spain, who had been born José Moñino, the son of a local notary, and who had himself painted by Goya not in armor, not on horseback, but surrounded by artists and scientists, or Gaspar de Jovellanos, Spanish minister for justice in 1797, who chose to have himself painted, also by Goya, with his head resting on his hand in the traditional pose of the philosopher and surrounded not by the symbols of power but by books. Such men were professionals who, unlike the previous generation of government servants, had risen on their merit and wished to have this fact recorded for posterity.

For most of the writers of the Enlightenment, this was a marked improvement on the style of government pursued by most of the kings of Europe. Voltaire had a long correspondence with Frederick the Great and translated the king's *Anti-Machiavel* into French. Diderot assisted Catherine, at her invitation, to reform the Russian legal code and, from 1774 until his death in 1784, received a pension from her, ostensibly as her librarian. But for all that most remained wary of absolutism or despotism in all of its many guises. However enlightened these monarchs might be, they were still absolute, still despots. They still believed their power to be above the law, and as Diderot bluntly told Catherine, "There is no true sovereign except the nation; there can be no true legislator except the people."[31]

Even if the monarch could be detached from the monarchy, the nation itself remained eternal, undying. If anything, contract theory, by placing the sources of authority entirely in the hands of the people, had only served to increase its emotive power. This "nation," as Edmund Burke said of it, "is not an idea only of local extent and individual momentary aggregation, but it is an idea of continuity, which extends in time as well as in numbers, and in space."[32] Despite his passion for reverence, aristocracy, and most of the trimmings of absolute monarchy, Burke lived, like all of his generation, in the shadow of the mystique of 1688 and was, therefore, quite prepared to accept that "society is indeed a contract." Only this contract was not, he said bitingly, a mere arrangement born of convenience, as so many of the French seemed to suppose—not "a partnership agreement in a trade of pepper and coffee, calico or tobacco"; it was instead a partnership between those who are living and those who are dead and those who are to be born. It was a clause "in the great primeval contract of eternal society."[33]

Already toward the end of the seventeenth century a new understanding of the possible relationship between the people and their sovereign had begun to enter the political vocabularies of Europe. It was one that very much downplayed the standing and the role of the monarch and that tended to substitute the word *patria*—"homeland"—for "nation." The idea of the *patria* had, of course, occupied a highly significant place in the ancient Roman conception of loyalty. The *patria* embodied not merely—perhaps not even—a place but a cluster of moral virtues, of family alliances, of duties and rights, and it was infused with something far more evasive, and potentially more divisive, than mere duty: love. For Cicero, its most eloquent and most often-cited champion, love of *patria* overruled even the love of family and children, because, in his view, the *patria* "has on its own embraced the affections of all of us."[34] Such love was also closely associated with ideas of reverence; reverence for one's ancestors, whose lingering presence defined the *patria;* and—although the ancients never asked for love for their singularly unlovable deities—reverence for the gods. After the collapse of the Empire that it had helped to sustain, the conception of *patria* fell steadily out of use. The word itself became progressively demystified, until it came to refer merely to one's place of birth, the Latin equivalent of the French *pays* or the German *Heimat*. The alliance, reverence, and love that the *patria* had demanded had then been vested wholly in the person of the king. You were no longer called upon to love your father-*land,* only your father. Something resembling ancient patriotism survived only in those areas of Europe, the Italian communes and republics, where there were no kings. The Church, which took a very different view of paternity, persisted with the old usage, but transferred the notion of the terrestrial *patria* to the Kingdom of Heaven and the celestial city of Jerusalem as the Christian's true *patria*. It was the Church that, by moving the classical ideal of the *civitas* and the *polis* to the other world, had preserved the term *patria,* and all the many shades of meaning it had acquired, for the time when a new, secularized Europe would need it. By the early eighteenth century, that time had arrived.[35]

II

On November 15, 1715, Henri-François d'Aguesseau, the Lord Chancellor of France (and Diderot's patron), dressed in the scarlet robes of his office and, with all the symbols of the majesty of kingship, entered a courtroom in the Palais de Justice in Paris. There, beneath the image of the *fleur-de-lis,* the heraldic emblem of the kings of France, and surrounded by the magistrates of the Paris *parlement,* the highest court in the land, he delivered a speech on "love of country." The *patrie,* he declared, meant love of the common good, not love of the monarch, and it was constituted by the "body of citizens who enjoyed perfect equality" and perfect "fraternity." He also, as Voltaire and others would do later, equated this with republicanism. In republics, he went on, "every citizen from the earliest age, practically from birth, grows used to serving the state as his own. This perfect equality, and the kind of civil fraternity which makes all citizens like a single family, interests them all equally in the fortunes and misfortunes of the *patrie.*"

D'Aguesseau was no revolutionary, despite attempts by later generations to make him into a forerunner of the "incorruptible" Maximilien Robespierre. His oration was a moral exhortation rather than a demand for change, and it was certainly not directed against the monarchy, of which he remained a loyal, if not uncritical, servant.[36] He was the embodiment of the "good magistrate, virtuous, impartial and incorruptible."[37] His appeal to something beyond the nation of which Louis XIV believed himself to be the embodiment was part of a shifting political language, one that was intended to lead not to the narrow sectarianism of Robespierre's "virtuous republic" but to the new, enlightened embrace of something far larger. And it was intended to transform the perception not only of the state but also of the entire nation—indeed, of the entire species.

For men like D'Aguesseau—and he was certainly not alone—the *patrie* and the nation involved two quite different ways of understanding the relationship between the monarch and his people. Both demanded love, but love of two very distinct kinds. The true subject loved the monarch, but this, as Jean Bodin—possibly the first political theorist to use the term *sovereignty*—had stressed in the sixteenth century, was, like traditional paternal love, always something due. The subject was also expected to love the nation, but only because it was the reflection of the person of the monarch. It is important to remember that all of this talk of the monarch as a father and the people as his obedient children was based not so much upon a loose and evocative analogy as on certain precise distinctions in Roman family law. And in ancient Rome the father had the power of life and death over his children.

Love of the *patria* was something quite different. Although the literature of absolutism is filled with constant reminders that the Latin word *patria* derived from *pater*—"father"—the kind of fatherhood represented by the Republic was more often seen as an extension not of the father but of the family.[38] "The philosopher knows that this word [*patrie*] comes from the Latin *pater,*" wrote Louis chevalier de Jaucourt, distinguished physician and author of a life of Leibniz (and of an introduction to an edition of his *Theodicy*), in the entry he composed on *patrie* for the *Encyclopédie,* "which represents a father and children, and consequently that it expresses the meaning we attach to that of family, of society, of a free state, of which we are members, and whose laws assure our liberties and our well-being." Unlike the nation, the *patria* was a community, a group. You owed it your love and your life, but you were also a part of it. You were, crucially, a citizen, not a subject. As Jaucourt put it: "There is no *patrie* under the yoke of despotism. The love that we bear it leads to goodness of morals, and goodness of morals leads to love of the *patrie*." Under a free government, he added, patriotism was "not a chimerical duty" but a "real obligation."[39] The Greeks had defeated the Persians at the Battle of Salamis, where they had been heavily outnumbered—claimed the editor of the *Historical and Critical Dictionary of Customs* in 1772—not because of any cunning on the part of the Athenian general Themistocles but because "on one side was heard the voice of an imperious master driving his slaves to battle, while, on the other, the name of *patrie* that inspired free men."[40] It was a new spin on a commonplace whose origins can be found in the Greek historian Herodotus' interpretation of the titanic clash in the fifth century BCE between the mighty Persian Empire and the tiny, scattered, fractious but democratic Greek city-states as a struggle between free men living under what he called *isonomia*—"equality before the law"—and the enslaved hordes under the lash of the Persian "Great King," Xerxes.[41] The Greeks were a people; the subjects of Xerxes only a mob. "Absolute power," as Shaftesbury phrased it, "annuls the public. And where there is no public or constitution there is in reality no mother country or nation."[42] It could be said that for most of the self-styled patriots of the eighteenth century, the *patria* was not a place at all but a projection of the mind and that patriotic love did not necessarily imply a recognition of the sovereignty of the nation or of the sovereign who embodied it.[43]

This concept of the *patria,* then, became a kind of unsituated version of the Greek *polis* and the Roman *civitas,* which, although it did not necessarily imply a republican government, relied heavily upon some kind of loosely conceived republican sentiment. When the Latin term *res publica* was generally understood, as it clearly was by D'Aguesseau, in its original meaning as "the public thing" or, as the English called it, the "commonwealth," it described a particular kind of society, rather than a specific constitution, a society upheld by what Montesquieu called "political virtue" (and of which, for him, the clearest embodiment was in fact the "moderate monarchy" that existed in England). *Political* virtue was not to be confused with the traditional Aristotelian (and Christian) moral virtues. It did not determine the relationship of individuals either to themselves or to one another. It governed only the relationship of individuals to the larger social and political spheres to which they belonged as citizens. It amounted, in Montesquieu's view, to a form of self-renunciation. But it did not demand charity or courage or fortitude. All it demanded was a certain kind of love. "One can define this virtue," he wrote, "as love of the laws and of the homeland [*patrie*]. This love requires continuing preference of the public interest over one's own, producing all the individual virtues; they are only that preference."[44] Furthermore, political virtue was conceived as a sentiment and not, as Montesquieu put it, "the consequence of knowledge." True, the virtuous citizens had to be able to distinguish good laws from bad, but they did not require any special knowledge to do that; they did not need to understand precisely what a republic actually was, or how its institutions operated, nor did they—as the ancients would, in fact, have assumed that they did—have to be actively involved in it, in order to love it; for the "last man in the state can have this sentiment as can the first."[45] Or, as Kant phrased it, the sole government fit for "human beings who are capable of right" is a patriotic one, and truly patriotic government "derives its name from *patria,* not from *pater*."[46]

This kind of identification with the *patria* was crucially not, however, to be confused with the ancient (and in certain respects also with Rousseau's) vision of a society based upon what Robespierre understood by "virtue." To do so was to deploy the language of love of *patria* for very different ends, and crucially, it was to conflate the two conceptions of virtue that Montesquieu wished to keep apart. For Montesquieu, the virtuous citizen did not need to be a virtuous person. But for Rousseau and for Robespierre, the "virtuous republic" was a kind of secularized version of St. Augustine's City of God, which, in Robespierre's words, would substitute "morality for egoism, honesty for love of honor, principles for conventions, duties for decorum, the empire of reason for the tyranny of fashion." And in his view (although not in Rousseau's), such a dramatic transformation of the entire political, moral, and psychological structure of society could only be brought about though terror, "without which virtue has no power."[47] Once this virtuous republic had been established, the virtue of the mere individual, together with his or her individual political will, vanished with it. It was only this belief that could make any sense of the old adage "my country right or wrong," for in the virtuous republic the individual had no identity independently of the mass: he *was* his country. For Montesquieu, such a position would have been merely an abdication of individual moral responsibility. No one "loved" a tyranny. No one willingly died for it, whether it was his country or not. Even Rousseau (although he was deeply inconsistent on the subject) was prepared to concede as much. A child, on opening its eyes, he wrote in 1772, in the comments on the government of Poland he prepared at the request of the Polish patriot Count Michael Wielhorski, should see "the *patrie,* and until death should see nothing but her." Yet "the love of his *patrie,*" which "every true republican imbibes with his mother's milk," he added, echoing Jaucourt, was a devotion to "laws and liberty" and should, therefore, never be confused with a blind obedience to moral demands.[48]

This is, broadly speaking, what has come to be called modern civic patriotism. It was benign, generous, outward-looking, and, in principle at least, excluded no one, and it was precisely this kind of patriotism that some eighteenth-century Frenchmen thought that they could see in England (or at least among the most enlightened Englishmen). "Indeed the French are almost excessive," wrote Edward Gibbon in 1763 of his experience of the best of the Paris salons. "From being unjustly esteemed a set of pirates and Barbarians, we are now by more agreeable injustice looked upon as a nation of Philosophers and Patriots. I wish we would consider this opinion, as an encouragement to deserve a Character, which I am afraid, we have not yet deserved."[49]

The patriotism that the French now seemed to find in the English, undeserved though it probably was, was inescapably linked to what for some time had been widely perceived as the nation's dedication to "liberty" and its hard-won parliamentary constitution in which, as Montesquieu famously expressed it, a "republic hides under the form of monarchy."[50] Montesquieu knew a great deal about England. He had lived in London from 1729 to 1731, for the most part a distinguished aristocrat among fellow aristocrats. He seems to have been widely liked. He was elected to the Royal Society in 1731, attended many of its meetings, and by all accounts became a close friend of the Society's secretary at the time, Martin Folkes, a notorious freethinker, of whom Montesquieu once said that he was the only perfect person he had ever met. He even joined the Freemasons. He was also influenced by the mercurial politician Henry St. John, Viscount Bolingbroke, a Francophile who had lived in France from 1715 until 1725 and in 1719 had married Marie-Claire de Marcilly, marquise de Villette. England, claimed Bolingbroke, had been "given the fairest opportunities, as well as the justest reasons, for completing the scheme of liberty and improving it to perfection." The country was, he believed, the embodiment of what he imagined to have been Roman Republican liberty, and it was to that that all (English) men gave their loyalty and their love. Even the king was a "patriot" in that, as his people owed their allegiance to the *patria,* he owed his not to God, who had played no part in his election, but to his people. Admittedly, this "Patriot King" was, said Bolingbroke, who had a strongly Lockean understanding of the social contract, "the most uncommon of all phenomenon in the physical or moral world," but only such a person "will make one, and but one, distinction between his rights and those of his people: he looks on his to be a trust, and theirs a property."[51] Only under such a king will a people be truly free, and only here in "Great Britain, as far as waters roll and winds can waft them," sits a "Patriot King at the head of his people."[52] As the Anglo-Irish poet and playwright Oliver Goldsmith makes his imaginary Chinese visitor and "Citizen of the World" Lien Chi Altangi declare, with approval (and surprise): "An Englishman is taught to love his king as a friend, but to acknowledge no other master than the laws which [he] himself has contributed to enact."[53]

The monarchs of continental Europe saw in "liberty" little more than the threat of usurpation. The English venerated it as a virtue. "We are free," boasted the *Daily Courant*—the first English daily newspaper—on June 13, 1734, in that ostentatiously self-congratulatory language characteristic of modern tabloids, "from Religious Disturbances which distract almost every other nation. Our liberties and our Properties are perfectly secure." By and large this was—if inflated—true. The liberty might have been more limited and constrained than the *Daily Courant* was prepared to admit, and it could, at times, be reduced to little more than a political shibboleth. But the word itself was not, as it was in France before 1789 and was to be again after the restoration, in 1814, of the Bourbon king Louis XVIII, a synonym for unfettered licentiousness. English liberty, or at least the English perception of it, was also obvious to outsiders. The people will tell you, remarked one Swiss visitor to England, César de Saussure, in 1729, that "there is no country in the world where such perfect freedom may be enjoyed as in England."[54] On the whole, Saussure seems to have agreed with them. Such high-minded sentiments did not, however, exclude a narrower exceptionalism that, already by the early eighteenth century, was beginning to acquire some of the ugly racial tones that it would adopt wholeheartedly in the following century.[55] And even if the English were more liberty-loving than (most of) their European neighbors and subsequently passed on a part of this self-esteem to their former American colonists, it was still a liberty for national consumption alone. When it came to the "liberty" of others, the English could be the most ferocious upholders of the most despotic of friendly regimes (another characteristic, one is tempted to argue, that her former American colonists have taken very much to heart). In early 1799 the people of Naples, aided by the French and led by members of what was called the *popolo civile*—the "civil people," lawyers, intellectuals, and enlightened aristocrats—rose in revolt against their bloated King Ferdinand IV and, for a few brief months, transformed their terminally corrupt, priest-ridden monarchy into a republic. On June 28 the hero of the hour, Admiral Horatio Nelson, helped to crush the uprising, violated the promise of an amnesty he had made to the leaders of the revolt, and hanged them at his yardarms in full view of a roaring, monarchist, and staunchly Catholic mob, while his celebrated mistress Emma Hamilton stood by his side and shrieked for blood. Thus perished the short-lived "Parthenopean Republic." It was, as one of Nelson's secretaries is said to have written at the time, "the most horrid villainy in order to place on his throne the most stupid of kings."[56] Albion, as Napoleon famously remarked, was always nothing if not perfidious.

Although it might have been Roman in inspiration, this brand of patriotism implied a very different kind of duty from the obligation summed up in that famous exhortation of the Roman poet Horace: *Dulce et decorum est pro patria mori* (It is sweet and seemly to die for the *patria*). Dying might indeed, in the last instance, be necessary. But for the English the modern *patria* was not, as the Roman Republic had been, a war machine. It was an instrument of civilization. Enlightened Germans took the same view. "What was called 'love of the fatherland,'" wrote Christoph Wieland—whom we last met clutching his "maculature" and wondering what the meaning of "Enlightenment" was—"by the proud citizens of that city [Rome] that believed it was founded to rule the world" was not true patriotism. It was, in his view, a kind of republican "enthusiasm," which rested merely upon the assertion that the "prosperity, fame, or the size of one's country" were grounds for "preferential treatment and the oppression of other states."[57]

If what Shaftesbury called this "natural passion for society and a country" were to have any purchase on the mind, it had, he believed, to be "something moral and social," something that could be described as "the intercourse of minds, the free use of our reason and the exercise of mutual love and friendship." It had also to allow for self-criticism, something sovereign authorities rarely encouraged. The love of his country, said Shaftesbury, did not prevent him from acknowledging that the English were "the latest barbarous, the last civilized or polished people of Europe."[58] For Shaftesbury, as for all enlightened minds, beyond the horizons of the *patria* there always lay humanity itself, and the former, however dear, however "sweet," should never be loved at the expense of the latter. Patriotism, as the German epicurean Louis de Beausobre expressed it in 1762, should never be confused "with that blind love of our nation, a love that seems inseparable from a decided disdain for other nations."[59] Even Herder, who speaks constantly of the "Fatherland," and for whom the *patria* most clearly was a place, who believed that peoples had been irreversibly separated from one another by nature, and who in general despised what he saw as the soggy French (and Kantian) ideals of cosmopolitanism, firmly rejected the idea of the kind of blind obedience to the state conjured up by the sordid phrase "my country right or wrong." We all, he believed, have a duty as citizens to steer the fatherland—which disconcertingly he envisages as a ship—in the right direction. Most important of all, since the very word *father,* in Herder's opinion, possessed a "moral tendency," the ideal of the fatherland "links the human species in a chain of continuing members who are to each other brothers, sisters, betrothed, friends, children, parents." Patriots of one fatherland do not fight the patriots of other fatherlands. "*Fatherlands* do not move against each other in that way: they lie peacefully beside each other, and support each other as families. *Fatherlands against fatherlands* in a combat of blood is the worst barbarism in the human language."[60]

This is very close to what the German political theorist Dorf Steinberger in the 1970s called "constitutional patriotism," the identification not with a place or a religion or a language, or even a culture—all those things which for Herder had made up "the people," the *Volk*—but with the constitution adopted and defended by a particular group of peoples and therefore, in theory at least, extendable to all peoples. It was, he believed, precisely this love of just laws and common liberties that, from Aristotle to the late eighteenth century, had been understood by *patriotism,* and it was this, rather than some form of resurgent nationalism, that the postwar Federal Republic of Germany should attempt to revive. The idea was taken up by Jürgen Habermas in 1986 and has since become the topic of heated contemporary debate, in particular in the context of the evolution of the European Union, for which there exists no territory or language or ethical group, no one "little platoon" upon which would-be patriots could attach their affections.[61]

But there was a darker side to all this talk of love and liberty. The true patriot ought to give his love exclusively to a particular kind of society, and if that society was not the one into which he happened to have been born, then he should work to make it so. "Our first concern as a lover of our country," wrote Richard Price, Unitarian and champion of the American cause during the American Revolution, "must be to enlighten it," even possibly at the cost of taking up arms against it—a view that, together with his republican sympathies, led Edmund Burke to describe him as a man of "wicked principles" with a "black heart."[62] And if that failed, the true patriot should be prepared, however painful it might be, to take himself off into exile. He ought even be prepared to transfer his allegiance, as Tom Paine had done, moving from England to America, then to France and back to America again, until such time as he found a *patria* to match his ideals. *Ubi libertas, ibi patria,* as the saying went: "Where there is liberty, there is my country."

In sober reality, however, the distance between this idealized, abstract conception of the *patria* and the concrete reality of the nation was never so great as it was often made out to be; while patriotism bound individuals together into something larger and, arguably, more uplifting than the family, it also threatened to isolate the members of one nation from those of all others. Most, and the more prevalent, forms of patriotism, like all kinds of sectarianism, were, for all the language of love and inclusion in which they were cloaked, based ultimately on narrow self-interest, and anyone who claimed otherwise was deluding himself, dressing up a self-regarding passion in the borrowed garments of universal benevolence.

While the "love of our country" is clearly "our duty," warned Price, it certainly should not be taken to "imply any conviction of the superior value of it to other countries, or any particular preference of its laws and constitutions of government." Such, however, he lamented, "is a common delusion," which derives from the human inclination to overvalue "everything related to us." In this, patriotism became indistinguishable from tribalism. "What has the love of country hitherto been among mankind?" Price asked.

> What has it been but a love of domination, a desire for conquest, and a thirst for grandeur and glory, by extending territory and by enslaving surrounding countries? What has it been but a blind and narrow principle producing in every country a contempt of other countries, and forming men into combinations and factions against their common rights and liberties?

This virtue, he concluded, which has "too often been cried up as . . . of the first rank," was sadly often nothing more than the principle "which governs clans of Indians and tribes of Arabs."[63]

Tribalism not only isolated groups from one another, it inevitably generated hostilities between them. You cannot claim to believe yourself to be superior to the rest of the world without, at some point, coming into conflict with others who share the same delusions about themselves. The man who acts justly at home, observed Smith, who prefers to give rather than take, is nevertheless regarded "as a fool and an idiot, who does not understand his business" if he extends his charitable inclinations beyond the limits of his own society. What Smith—who spoke of "ferocious" patriots—called the "impartial spectator" is, in all dealings between different peoples, located at a great distance, while the "partial spectator" is always very much at hand. "We do not," regretted Smith, "love our country merely as a part of the great society of mankind," which is how it should be loved; "we love it for its own sake, and independently of any such consideration."[64] We love what is near because our human imagination is generally limited to what we know. What Smith called our "effectual good offices" can, he said, "very seldom be extended to any wider society than that of our country."[65] In some cases this could even be desirable, for, in his view, one of the more lamentable consequences of this broad love of an impersonal humanity was that it all too easily gave birth to what he nicely called those "whining and melancholy moralists" (we are all familiar with them) whose "artificial commiseration" demanded that, so long as so much of the earth is infested with human suffering, no one has a right to his own pleasure or prosperity, and who were only, in effect, creating new miseries where none need have existed. For in the end, "to what purpose should we trouble ourselves about the world in the moon"?[66] Had patriotism really derived from "a love of mankind," then a Briton should have more concern for the French, since the population of France was three times that of Britain. Yet anyone who actively favored the prosperity of the French over the British "would not be thought a good citizen of Great Britain."[67]

Human beings naturally cling to their own, and they cling equally fiercely to what they know. All, however seemingly benign they might appear, are, with a few enlightened exceptions, everywhere suspicious of difference. The contempt that one nation feels for another, observed

Helvétius, "depends invariably on the apparent differences in customs and habits." "Every nation, convinced that it alone knows what wisdom is, despises the folly of all the others."[68] Only we have just laws, it cries, we alone have a perfect constitution, we are exceptional, and so on.

Wishing greatness for one's own country, therefore, all too often meant wishing for the destruction of all others. Benito Jerónimo Feijoo was certain that love of country must be an essentially ennobling sentiment. But in searching through all the literature of antiquity, he had found, "at every step, millions of victims sacrificed to this idol." "What war," he asked, "has ever been started without this invaluable pretext? What campaign has there ever been which has not been bathed in blood and whose corpses have not had conferred upon them by posterity the honorable funeral inscription that they lost their lives for the *patria*?"[69] To behave otherwise, to think otherwise, was to be branded as unpatriotic. To love one's country did not imply abandoning the love one felt for one's family or oneself—least of all for oneself—although, as Lucius Junius Brutus, the semilegendary founder of the Roman Republic who put his two sons to death for treason, discovered, it might sometimes impose difficult choices. But to prove his devotion, said Voltaire, the "good patriot," like Brutus, was necessarily driven to "be an enemy of the rest of mankind." And the man "who wished that his *patria* were neither greater nor smaller, nor richer nor poorer [than all others]," would not be a patriot at all. He would instead be "a citizen of the universe."[70]

Kant would have agreed with him. All those who belong to such narrow communities, he told the students of his course on the "Metaphysics of Morals" in 1793,

> Separatists and sectarians of every kind, clubbists, lodge-brothers [Freemasons], Herrnhuters [the Moravian Brotherhood, a Protestant sect], and Pietists, are likewise destroyers of general goodwill and philanthropy; in brief, a society may be aiming at a narrower bond, in regard to morals, politics, or religion—its members' adherence to their sect and the *esprit de corps* founded on

> this, make for an indifferentism towards the human race which inhibits the dissemination of general human good-will and prevents any communal participation for everyone.[71]

Patriotism, or what the revolutionary and abolitionist, the abbé Henri Grégoire, in 1792 called "exclusive patriotism," required "forgetting the links which bound all peoples to one another."[72]

There was yet another potentially deleterious consequence of the call for patriotic love. For forgetting the links that bind us to others beyond the frontiers of the *patria* was not always entirely voluntary. There was always the lure of distant lands, the nagging fear that life elsewhere might be better, more exciting, more satisfying. No one, after all, is in a position to choose his or her *patria*. And although patriotism may have been, initially at least, a "natural sentiment," in that the true *patria* is an extension of oneself and of one's family, it was never a consistently reliable one. Not everyone, therefore, could be depended upon to share in it equally. But in the interests of the unity of purpose without which no *patria* could last for long, those who did not had, all too often, to be compelled to conform, or as Rousseau famously (or infamously) phrased it, since love of the *patria* was the only true liberty, they had to be "forced to be free." In Plato's ideal state of "Magnesia," only those who had served the state for twenty years—a very long time in terms of the average life expectancy of ancient Greece—were allowed to leave, and their duty was to travel the world and then return home to report to the "Nocturnal Council," which sat guard over the morals and laws of the state, how much better life was in Magnesia than anything that they had seen outside. These were the true patriots, like the antihero of Louis-Charles Fougeret de Monbron's libertine novel *The Cosmopolitan, or Citizen of the World,* of 1753, who returns home to discover that, in the end, the "greatest benefit I have derived from my travels and my excursions is to have learnt how to hate with reason what before I only hated by instinct."[73]

Plato's ideal was clearly unworkable, although other would-be ideal states, like the Soviet Union and Maoist China, have tried to put into practice not-dissimilar policies. Since Utopia is not a place one could have any reason for wishing to leave, leaving should not be an option. But if most states are not in a position to oblige their citizens to stay firmly at home, every one of them has tried by other means—by swearing allegiance to flags and anthems, by serving in armed forces—to confine their loyalties to one place, one society, one state.

In such a world, what Diderot mockingly called "good citizens" were merely those who thought that all knowledge should be shut up within the border of the nation, because knowledge constitutes "a part of their superiority over other nations." They would sacrifice the happiness (*bonheur*) of centuries to come, and of the entire species, "for their own narrow interests which occupy but one point on the globe and last but an instant." For such peoples, it "would seem that the word *humanity* is a word without meaning."[74] It was on this, he added, that "the fame, pride, and seeming courage of the martyrs was founded." For by this account there was little to choose between the sect and the *patria.* Just as the Christian martyr suffered joyfully for opinions that were, as Michel de Montaigne had protested centuries earlier in a tone of uncomprehending disgust, "borrowed from others, unknown and not understood," so the patriot would sacrifice himself voluntarily for empty symbols, for differences in customs and beliefs that were not of his own choosing.[75] "The patriot," as Alexander Pope put it succinctly, was "a fool in any age."[76]

III

The great Roman orator Cato the Elder was said to have finished every speech with the sentence "It is my opinion, likewise, that Carthage ought to be destroyed." It was an obsessive but not unintelligible claim. Cato had begun his career as a young soldier in the Second Punic War between Rome and the Carthaginian Empire, Rome's only rival in the Mediterranean, which dominated most of the North African littoral and southern Spain. The Carthaginians had sworn to bring about the destruction of Rome, and in 216 BCE, at Cannae, the great Carthaginian general Hannibal, with his massive armies and terrifying, if not always very effective, war elephants, had come very close to doing just that. In stark contrast to Cato, however, Publius Cornelius Scipio, who had also served in the Second Punic War and would eventually perish at the hands of the Carthaginians, is said to have ended all his speeches with the words "It is my opinion likewise that Carthage ought to be saved." For Adam Smith, Cato and Scipio were perfect examples of two quite distinct brands of patriotism. Cato represented the "natural expression of the savage patriotism of a strong but coarse mind"; Scipio, however, "was the liberal expression of a more enlarged and enlightened mind." To take pleasure in the "internal happiness and prosperity" of other peoples, even if they had been your enemies, as he supposed that Scipio had done, would, Smith believed, lead inevitably to "real improvements of the world we live in. Mankind are benefitted, human nature is ennobled by them." Every nation, he concluded, should therefore not only seek to improve the lot of its own citizens but also, from "the love of mankind, to promote, instead of obstructing the excellence of its neighbours."[77] Love of humanity might, in fact, come after—sometimes a long way after—the love we feel for our kin, and even for our immediate neighbors and our *patria,* but it should always take priority as a duty. We are bound to others, no matter how remote or alien, by ties that are more compelling that any man-made law. "There is no civil nor religious law," as Diderot told Hume, "that has broken, nor can break the bond of fraternity which nature has established between men."[78] If the true *patria* was, as so many insisted, only worthy of our love because it was the source of liberty, a place, like the true *polis,* of "human flourishing," then there was a strong sense in which our love for it could not be confined within its borders. True patriotism, said Christoph Wieland, had to be compatible with "cosmopolitan principles," for "only a true cosmopolitan can be a good citizen, only he can do the great work to which we have been called, to cultivate, enlighten, and ennoble the human race."[79]

What Kant called the true "cosmopolites" and the "cosmotheroi" (students of the world) were not being asked to sacrifice their love of family, or of *patria;* much less were they being asked to subsume their identity into anything quite so amorphous as the "cosmos."[80] These true "cosmopolites" were moved only by their "inclination to promote the well-being of the entire world," which derived initially from the sense of loyalty that originated in a love for those of one's own country. But what they had always to keep their eyes fixed upon was the wider horizon of humankind itself. It was what Kant, significantly, called "global patriotism."

If today we (or at least many of us) accept the idea of giving aid to distant peoples whom we have never met and whose lives we can only with great difficulty imagine and will never impinge on our own, we do so largely because of Smith's "effectual good offices." It is unlikely that anyone in Europe before the eighteenth century would have regarded the request that he or she should have great concern for the sufferings of Africans or Asians as anything other than extraordinary, if not actually offensive. If, as Smith observed, neither the French nor the British were very likely to "bear any sort of envy to the prosperity of China or Japan," neither were they likely to extend their "good will towards such distant countries . . . with much effect."[81] But Smith was writing precisely at a time when the extension of goodwill toward even the most remote and alien of peoples was, indeed, coming to seem not only a recognizable sentiment but even a moral obligation.

The precept of charity had always been an obligation for all Christians, as it was for all Muslims. But charity of this sort not only began at home—it very largely remained there. It was, after all, for the Christian, a *theological* virtue and as such was of more immediate value to the giver, to whom, in the words of St. Thomas Aquinas, it "brings life to those who are spiritually dead," than to the receiver.[82] True, the Christian is also enjoined to "love others truly, for their own sakes rather than our own."[83] But these others are also neighbors, and it is unlikely that Aquinas would have expected anyone to accept as his neighbor someone who was not a member of his own community. Love of this kind is related to friendship, and whereas you might feel some distant bond with "humanity," however defined, you can only be friends with individuals, individuals who are known to you. For most Europeans, Africans and Asians, American Indians and Tahitians, indeed any people who were not their own, simply lay beyond their imaginative reach. The theater-going public of Paris, complained Diderot, could weep its heart out over the fate of Phaedra but never gave a single thought to the plight of African slaves. Phaedra might have been merely a character in a play by Racine, but while they were watching her suffer, the good Parisian bourgeoisie looked upon her as one of their own. The African, by contrast, whom they had never seen and in all probability would never see, even on the stage, was merely a remote and distant "other."

The kinds of sentiments that would eventually make an appeal to individuals in the name of a common humanity, if they were to be in any way intelligible, were always, like enlightenment itself, confined to the few. Montesquieu, Smith, Diderot, and Hume were all—in the original meaning of the word—aristocrats, and the kind of detachment from national sympathies and allegiances they advocated is a profoundly aristocratic sentiment. I do not mean by "aristocratic" that they were bearers of titles. Although some, such as Montesquieu, Turgot, Condorcet, and Holbach, were, many more were not. Diderot was the son of a cutler from Langres (although by all accounts a highly successful one), Hume and Smith were both sons of advocates, and Rousseau's father had been a clockmaker. I mean that they belonged to what the Greeks called the *aristoi,* a word that means simply "the best"—a self-appointed elite whose members were marked, not as traditional aristocracies were, by rank or wealth but by their intellectual gifts, their open-mindedness, their benevolence toward their fellow beings (as they would see it), and their generosity. They were linked by ties of friendship and sometimes by membership of secret and not-so-secret societies, Masonic lodges, academies.[84] And naturally, those of them who could frequented the great literary salons of Paris, where, in Diderot's words, "one can find the true cosmopolitan."[85] They belonged to an informal network sometimes known as the "Republic of Letters"—a term that seems to have been first used in this context by Pierre Bayle for the title of his journal *News from the Republic of Letters* in 1684—a secular version of the clerisies that had previously united Christian intellectuals, although their common language was now more often French than Latin. They translated one another, wrote ceaselessly to one another across the whole length of Europe, from Edinburgh to Naples, and sometimes—as with the ill-fated journey of Rousseau to Edinburgh to see Hume in 1766—even stayed with one another. They made up an international intellectual elite, much like the kind constituted by the higher echelons of the academic world today. (Unlike the members of that coterie, however, many of the greatest of them had little direct contact with the universities.)

These men and women abhorred the narrow limits set by nations or communities and deplored the sectarian violence, the lack of common concern for the welfare of those from whom nothing could be gained, which the more traditional form of "patriotism" all too often involved. They looked with mounting horror at the rapaciousness with which the European powers, France and Britain in particular, sought to exploit what they saw as defenseless peoples in the pursuit of narrow concerns with personal wealth and aggrandizement. They were also, of course, "philosophers," and the philosopher, wrote the Neapolitan Gaetano Filangieri—author of a highly ambitious and influential attempt, after the example of the "immortal Montesquieu," to make jurisprudence into a systematic science—"is a citizen of all ages and places" who takes the "whole world for his disciple."[86] Writers such as Montesquieu and Hume were "intellectual leaders," said Bolingbroke, who had known both, who "engross almost the whole reason of the species, who are born to instruct, to guide and to preserve; who are designed to be the tutors and the guardians of human kind." They were those who, he hoped, would one day come to replace "that pack of anchorites and enthusiasts [the saints], with whose names the calendar is crowded and disgraced."[87] As Diderot wrote to Hume, of whom he seems to have been particularly fond, "you belong to all nations. . . . I flatter myself that I am, like you, a citizen of that great city, the world."[88] They were a new secular priesthood for a new cosmopolitan, enlightened world.

The cosmopolitanism that all these men and women embraced was the political expression of the unity of the species that the "sciences of man" had been created to describe. Like so many of our more important philosophical concepts, "cosmopolitanism" also has its origins in the ancient world, and what the ancients had to say about it has for long been an integral part of its history. Much of that history, however, from the philosopher Diogenes the Cynic himself, who supposedly coined the term, to Diderot, Hume, Montesquieu, and Voltaire, largely represented a dislike of entrenched customs and local ties and a corresponding disposition to treat all of humanity as equals and as equally interesting and instructive. Cosmopolitans knew what they did not like: nationalism, tribalism, jingoism, xenophobia, sectarianism in all its guises. But they offered few suggestions as to how these things might be abolished in favor of some wider, more equitable world. They made no plans for a constitution for the "great city, the world" of which they were all nominally citizens. Neither did Diogenes. He too merely rejected. His celebrated remark "I am a citizen of the world" had been intended as a calculated insult. (He was a master of insult, a man who lived in a barrel in the marketplace, denounced all aspects of conventionally civilized life—marriage, family, politics, sexual or any other kind of physical restraint, all forms of social distinction, even the city itself—who urinated on the people who insulted him, defecated in the theater, and masturbated in public.) He knew that for the curious Athenians who had asked to what city he belonged, the answer that his city was the world was literally meaningless. What Diogenes manifestly was *not* offering was any alternative to the *polis*.

The Athenians have not been alone. The term "citizen of the world" is itself, and was intended to be, nearly an oxymoron, at best a misnomer. As Michael Walzer has pointed out, the "cosmos"—the world—is not something one can very easily be a citizen *of*. "No one has ever offered me citizenship," he protested, "or described the naturalization process . . . or given me an account of its decision procedures . . . or provided me with a list of the benefits and obligations of citizenship, or shown me the world's calendar and the common celebrations and commemorations of its citizens."[89] This may seem somewhat literal-minded. Calendars and celebrations and commemorations are, one might argue, precisely the stuff of the narrow understanding of patriotism that the Enlightenment was seeking to overcome. But he has a point. Citizenship demands the existence of a *civitas* or a *polis*. To claim allegiance to anything else can all too often seem to be a way of evading more immediate attachments and the obligations they carry with them. Love of the human species could easily be construed, in Rousseau's harsh denunciation of it, as the brainchild of "those pretended cosmopolites who . . . boast of loving all the world in order to enjoy the privilege of loving no one."[90] The only thing one could love that was any larger than the family circle was the *patria,* and even that, in Rousseau's view, had ideally to be bound by the limits to which the human voice would carry. (Athens, he believed, had been just such a state, but then, in Rousseau's estimation, the ancients, more manly than the moderns, had also had more powerful voices.) Jingoism was for Rousseau a form of ideological cement. "Every patriot is hard on foreigners," he wrote, "they are but men [as distinct from citizens], and they are nothing in his eyes." There might exist a "few great Cosmopolitan Souls who cross the imaginary barriers which separate Peoples and, following the example of the sovereign being that created them, embrace the whole of mankind in their benevolence."[91] But for the most part, the professed cosmopolitan was merely someone who sought to evade his stern obligations to love and die for the *patria*. "Have nothing to do with those cosmopolitans who wish to find at a distance in their books, the duties they do not deign to fulfil among themselves," he advised the future architects of his ideal state. "Such a philosopher loves the Tartars so as not to have to love his neighbors."[92]

Rousseau was to be followed by a long line of detractors, ending in Nazi Germany and Stalinist Russia, who saw in "cosmopolitans" only unreliable, "rootless," fickle drifters—the term was most frequently and most cruelly used to describe the Jews, possibly the only people in the history of the world to have had their cosmopolitanism forced upon them. The self-proclaimed "citizens of the world" of the eighteenth century, however, were anything but rootless. Diderot, in particular, had a strong dislike of most forms of travel (reinforced by his melancholy experience of Catherine the Great's Moscow) and an abiding anxiety that prolonged traveling might make "nomadic savages" of us all. What Diderot, Hume, and Montesquieu understood by "citizen of the world" was a disposition to treat all of humanity as equals and as equally interesting and instructive. But if it were to do that, if it were to escape the kinds of criticism Rousseau had leveled at it, the cosmopolis could not for long remain merely a benevolent landscape of the mind. If the new science of man that had been so painstakingly constructed out of the philosophical history of humankind pointed finally to the coming together of all mankind, then it could not concern itself solely with the well-being of individuals.[93] Eventually "cosmopolis," like the *polis* it derived from, had to be a concrete political community. Once, that is, our love has moved from the family to the *patria,* that "love" has in effect become, as Montesquieu himself had described it, a political "sentiment." And if we are to love the cosmos as we love the *patria,* because of its liberty and its laws, then it has to have some laws to love. But no such place as a law-governed political community that might be called a "cosmopolis" had ever existed, either in the eighteenth century or—even within the much narrower definition of the "world" then available—in antiquity. (In Oliver Goldsmith's imagination it existed in China, but that was only because it allowed him to poke fun at the parochialism of the English.)

With one troubling exception. Cosmopolitanism, as we have seen, has its roots in what Montesquieu, in *The Spirit of the Laws,* called "the Stoic sect." That sect alone, he wrote, "knew how to make citizens; it alone was capable of making great men; it alone made great emperors. . . . Born for society, they all believed that their destiny was to work for it . . . it seemed that only the happiness of others could increase their own."[94] The allusion to emperors was more than casual. A look at the ancient sources of cosmopolitanism show, indeed, just how closely linked the idea of a cosmopolitan world was, in fact, to empire.

The founder of Stoicism, Zeno of Citium, is said to have told his followers: "We should all live not in cities and demes [tribal groups], each distinguished by separate rules of justice, but should regard all men as members of the same tribe and fellow citizens; and . . . there should be one life and order [*koinos*] as of a single flock feeding together on a common pasture." Over the centuries this remark has been much quoted in defense of a cosmopolitan world. But the context from which it comes is rarely mentioned. That is perhaps because Zeno's words have survived for us only because they were recorded by the first-century Greco-Roman philosopher and biographer Plutarch, and Plutarch bothered to repeat them only because he saw Alexander the Great as embodying Zeno's "dream or, as it were, shadowy picture, of a well-ordered and philosophical community."[95] For Plutarch, cosmopolitanism did not so much mean making each man a citizen of the world as it meant making the world into a single body of citizens. If all humanity was to be one, then humanity should belong to one community, one city, one *polis*. For Zeno (possibly) and for Plutarch certainly, that city had been Alexander's empire. For the Romans it could clearly only be Rome, or, more precisely, the Roman *civitas*. One of the most engaging, sympathetic, and eloquent Stoic cosmopolitans, perhaps the last significant one, had after all been a Roman emperor, Marcus Aurelius—of whom John Stuart Mill said that he "preserved throughout his life the most unblemished justice, but what was less to be expected from his Stoic breeding, the tenderest heart."[96] In a series of notes "To Myself"—written in Greek—which have come down to us under the title of *The Meditations of Marcus Aurelius,* he reflected, "As the Emperor Antoninus, Rome is my city and my country; but as a man, I am a citizen of the world. . . . Asia and Europe are mere corners of the globe, the Great Ocean, a mere drop of water, Mount Athos is a grain of sand in the universe. The present instant of time is only a point compared to eternity."[97]

Imperial Rome, at least under the Antonines, the "Five Good Emperors" as they have come to be known, from Nerva (reigned 96–98 CE) to Marcus Aurelius (161–180) himself, could indeed have been said to have brought peace, posterity, order, and justice to most, if not quite all, of what it thought of as the "world." Centuries later Edward Gibbon, looking back from well beyond the disasters that were soon to befall this Eden, declared, "If a man were called upon to fix the period in the history of the world, during which the condition of the human race was the most happy and prosperous, he would, without hesitation, name that which elapsed from the death of Domitian [96 CE] to the accession of Commodus [180 CE]." It was, he added, a time when "the Roman Empire comprehended the fairest part of the earth and the most civilized portion of mankind."[98]

The Christians, who embraced another type of cosmopolitanism, had similarly seen in the Roman Empire the embodiment of their own aspirations. God, it was said, had chosen Rome to unite the cosmos so that the birth of Christ might reach into, if not quite every part of it, then certainly most of what the Greeks called the *oikoumene,* the "inhabited world." For the pagan Pliny it had been the numen of the gods that had been responsible for Rome's bid to "give humanity to man." For the Christians it had been the will—*voluntas*—of their God.

"God taught nations everywhere," wrote the fourth-century Christian panegyrist Aurelius Prudentius,

> to bow their heads beneath the same laws and all to become Roman. . . . A common law made them equals, bound them by a single name, and brought them, though conquered, into bonds of brotherhood. We live in every conceivable region scarcely different than if a single city and fatherland enclosed fellow citizens with a single wall.[99]

Things in the eighteenth century, however, looked very different. The ecumenical vision of Rome had come and gone. Its place had been taken by the European overseas empires, the creation of seaborne adventurers, those "birds of prey," in the words of Edmund Burke, who swoop down "wave upon wave . . . [with] nothing before the eyes of the natives but an endless hopeless prospect of new flights . . . with appetites continually renewing for a food that is continually wanting."[100] The writers of the Enlightenment had nothing but suspicion for empires, even an enlightened cosmopolitan one, as the Roman Empire was once imagined to have been. Their time had come and gone. Today, argued Montesquieu, anything resembling the Roman Empire would be "morally impossible."[101] But if there were to be some political shape to the vague cosmopolitan yearnings of the majority of the thinkers of the Enlightenment, and this were not to be merely another form of empire, or, as it was often called in the eighteenth century, a "universal monarchy," what could it be?

8

THE VAST COMMONWEALTH OF NATURE

I

ONE OF THE FIRST to attempt an answer to Montesquieu's question was Christian Wolff, professor of mathematics and "natural philosophy" at the University of Halle, in the German state of Brandenburg-Prussia. Leibniz's most gifted and influential admirer, known to his contemporaries as "our German Newton," Wolff wrote widely on a range of subjects, and like Leibniz, like all the significant figures of the Enlightenment, he was convinced that it was possible to apply rigorous scientific methods to the understanding of mankind. He was also one of the earliest German philosophers to write extensively, although not exclusively, in German rather than Latin or French and to attempt, as Kant was also to do, to create a specifically German philosophical language. He believed not only that German should acquire, as French had done, its own philosophical idiom but also that philosophy itself should not be merely "the pursuit of the knowledge of the truth" but should offer a practical guide for ordinary people in their everyday lives. "A person should learn philosophy," he wrote, in the preface to his aptly named *German Logic,* not so as to be able to wallow in "the vicious taste of the schools for idle disputation and wrangling, but in order to [enjoy its] usefulness in future life." Later in life he began a correspondence with Voltaire's brilliant mistress, the Marquise du Châtelet, whom he came to see as his "Apostle to the French" in his bid to put an end to the "not very useful principles of the present-day English" and to replace them with his own. In 1741 one of Wolff's followers, Johann Heinrich Formey, published a popular "philosophical" novel called *The Beautiful Wolffian,* whose heroine was clearly modeled on Madame du Châtelet.[1]

Wolff is best remembered today for two closely related things: his project for an ideal world state and his tumultuous defense of Chinese "morality." In 1705, at the start of what was to prove to be a brilliant, if troubled, academic career, Wolff began a correspondence with Leibniz about China, which led to what was to become a lasting interest in Chinese thought. Like Leibniz, Wolff was convinced that the Chinese had understood how to regulate their lives in ways that the Europeans could only hope to emulate. He also seems to have believed that the writings of Confucius in particular held the secret of what he called broadly "natural morality," a morality that all human beings were capable of discovering for themselves by reason alone, independently of divine revelation. Although this scandalized and infuriated the Christians of the day, it was not in itself a revolutionary claim. Even for the most unbending Christian, a good deal of everyday morality (and most of our understanding of the dictates of nature) we owe to reason, not revelation or faith. But to attribute such morality to a people who were not merely not Christian but who were also widely regarded in Europe—when they were thought of at all—as "atheists and Spinozists" was outrageous. It was particularly offensive to the group of highly conservative Pietist theologians who effectively controlled the University of Halle. To make matters worse, Wolff, unlike the theologians, was very popular with the students and made little effort to hide from them his contempt for the bigotry of his colleagues.

On July 12, 1721, he delivered a public oration, "On the Practical

Philosophy of the Chinese," before an audience of over a thousand people made up of the entire faculty and student body of the university. China, he enthused, had the longest continual historical record of any people on Earth. The Chinese had created a system of "practical philosophy" based upon reason and nature, which had taught them the grounds for duty and virtue without the assistance of a belief in any kind of divinity.[2] Although Wolff insisted that none of this was in contradiction to Christian doctrine, that Chinese philosophy was practical and philosophical and not theological, his enemies, in particular the theologian Joachim Lange, denounced him as impious.

Leibniz's outspoken and potentially scandalous comparison between virtuous Chinese and squabbling, unprincipled Christians had caused him no harm. Hanover, where Leibniz lived from 1676 until his death, was a relatively tolerant state, and Leibniz himself, who had been the correspondent and adviser to the Electress Sophia of Hanover, her daughter Sophia Charlotte, and the Queen of Prussia and was the Privy Counsellor of Justice, was clearly permitted a freedom of expression denied to a mere professor. Wolff, in nearby Brandenburg-Prussia, was not so lucky. After more than two years of repeated slurs against him as a champion of atheism and "Spinozism" and an endless stream of defamatory tracts, none of which persuaded him to change his position, the theologians finally appealed directly to the king, insinuating slyly that if Wolff's arguments were to be accepted, no soldier would be under any obligation to obey his officers if to do so were in any way in conflict with his conscience. Friedrich Wilhelm I—the "soldier-king"—was a nervous and intensely conservative monarch, easily alarmed by anything represented as an attack upon the established order and, by implication, upon himself. On November 8, 1723, by secret royal edict, Wolff was stripped of his position and given forty-eight hours to leave Prussian territory "under pain of death by strangulation."[3]

The treatment of Wolff became one of the most hotly debated intellectual scandals of the century, and over two hundred books and pamphlets arguing for and against him had already appeared by 1737. "This Wolff," wrote Voltaire, giving his own particular spin on the story, "attracted to Halle thousands of scholars from every nation. In the same university there was a theologian named Lange who attracted no one." In despair at "shivering alone in his cold auditorium," Lange plotted to get rid of Wolff, and "as was the custom among his peers, he accused him of not believing in God." Since a number of writers from Europe who knew nothing about China had called the Chinese "atheists," and since Wolff had high praise for Chinese philosophers, Lange had managed to persuade the university authorities that "Wolff must therefore be an atheist." "Envy and hate," Voltaire concluded archly, "never produce the best syllogisms." Wolff's dismissal, Voltaire claimed, had deprived "the king of 300,000 ecus a year that the influence of this philosopher had attracted to the kingdom." This, he hoped, might be a lesson to kings that in future "they should not always listen to calumny, and sacrifice a great man to the fury of a dolt."[4]

Wolff belonged firmly in the camp of the "panegyrists of China," and like most, including Leibniz, whom he followed quite closely, was less interested in Chinese culture itself than he was in the possibility of a universal morality that derived its authority from the idea of shared, universal humanity, rather than scripture or divine command. It was this, not his lavish praise of Confucius, that had made it possible for Lange to argue that for Wolff no human being, not even a soldier, had an obligation to obey laws that ran counter to the common good of the human race. Lange may have been, and probably was, simply a disappointed, resentful bigot. But the more perceptive of Wolff's opponents had seen that he had laid the grounds for a far more decisive dismissal of the role of God in human affairs than any of his (German) predecessors.[5] The most exhaustive demonstration of this was the massive eight-volume Latin treatise on the natural law, *The Law of Nature, Treated According to a Scientific Method,* published between 1740 and 1748, followed in 1750 by a further volume on *The Law of Nations, Treated According to a Scientific Method.* In both Wolff offered what he believed to be a fully scientific account of a law linking all human beings by admitting "as true only what is inferred as necessary consequences from previous conclusions." His method, he claimed, required only "truth without coloring or childish devices." This remark was aimed explicitly at "the mass of jurists" who, in Wolff's view, worked backward from "their preconceived opinions" to the reasons by which they might have arrived at them.[6] But it could as easily have been directed at the theologians.

Wolff agreed with Hobbes, as had both Grotius and Pufendorf, that all states were necessarily human creations and that in the current international order all had the same relationship to one another as "individual free persons living in a state of nature."[7] Where Wolff disagreed with all three was in their assumption that the original contract between isolated individuals that had resulted in the creation of civil society must necessarily have erased all the original bonds that had previously held mankind together. Wolff's criticism of Hobbes, like Leibniz's—to which it owes a great deal—is that without these ties of affectivity, without precisely the "sympathy" that in one way or another all the writers of the Enlightenment identified as the necessary element in any kind of social bond, it would have been impossible for individuals to have created societies in the first place. In politics, as in ethics, we must all, Wolff insisted, look upon others "as if they were one person with us"—we must, and in fact we do, since our mere survival depends upon it.[8] In Wolff's view, Hobbes's account of the origins of society was so absurdly limited as to resemble a satire on the human condition. The creation of nations, although purely an act of human volition (on this at least Hobbes was right), must have been dictated by some kind of natural instinct—there being nothing else on which it could have been based. The relationship among nations, therefore, could only be the outcome of the same affective bonds, the same moral obligations—the same level of benevolence—as had once existed between individuals. If every individual treated all others "as if they were one person with us," then it was clear that "every nation owes to every other nation that which it owes to itself." From this Wolff argued that "society, which nature has established among individuals, still exists among nations, and consequently, after states have been established in accordance with the law of nature, and nations have arisen thereby, nature herself also must be said to have established society among all nations and bound them to preserve society."[9] And if this were true, then it could only be an absurdity to suppose, as Hobbes had done (and Rousseau would do later), that the emergence of mankind from the state of nature and the creation of "particular societies" had done away with "that great society which nature has established among men." For "just as in the human body individual organs do not cease to be organs of the whole human body, because certain ones taken together constitute one organ; so likewise individual men do not cease to be members of that great society which is made up of the whole human race, because several have formed together a certain particular society."

Now, if we assume this (rather strained) analogy to hold true, then it must follow that, just as individual communities are able to constitute themselves as states, so humanity as a whole must also possess the ability to constitute itself as something that at least resembles a state. This is, in part, a continuation of the Stoic ideal of what Cicero had called the "republic of all the world" and Leibniz a "great society"—a shadowy congregation of persons, united only by reason and a shared humanity. Wolff, however, grafted onto this a far more ambitious project for what he called the *civitas maxima,* or "supreme state": a society or commonwealth based upon the consent of all persons everywhere, "as if they had signed a contract"—in the same way that the founders of the first civil societies were believed to have done. Such a contract, although clearly only imaginary, was at least morally binding. It was based, just as Hobbes had understood the first covenants between individuals to have been, on "a kind of democratic form of government" emanating from the will of the majority. It could be said to be the political manifestation of what Wolff elsewhere called "the harmony of the manifold."[10] What exact constitutional shape this megastate would take Wolff does not say, although he does equip it with a ruler—or "rector"—whose task is to impose "what nations ought to consider as law amongst themselves."

This placed Wolff in the same predicament all would-be international legislators have faced since the sixteenth and seventeenth centuries. Obviously the whole world cannot be consulted directly on what all its peoples ought to consider to be "the laws amongst themselves";

therefore someone has to decide for them what those laws should be. Wolff was driven back on the claim that such laws are those that all nations "are bound to agree upon if following the leadership of nature they use right reason," and in practice this could only amount to "what has been approved by the more civilized nations."[11] Grotius, faced with a similar problem, had used a similar argument. The problem was that it left unstated what those nations were and what exactly was meant, in this context, by "civilized." "Who will determine if a nation is civilized or barbarian?" asked the eclectic German jurist and philosopher Christian Thomasius in 1705:

> For all peoples are equal amongst themselves, and this latter term [civilized] has its origins in the arrogance of the Greeks and the Romans, and among those nations who imitate them and who stupidly despise all other nations. The customs of the so-called civilized nations can be very much crueller than those of the Barbarians, as one can see from the treatment of Protestants by a Catholic prince.[12]

What Wolff, and subsequently all the eighteenth-century advocates of legal cosmopolitanism, wished to avoid was precisely the conclusion to which the English historian of the law of nations, Robert Ward, came in 1795, that "we expected too much when we contended for the *universality* of the duties laid down by the Codes of the Laws of Nations . . . however desirable such universality might be." Like many later international jurists, he had come to believe that "what is commonly called the Law of Nations . . . is not the Law of *all* Nations, but only of particular classes of them; and thus there may be a *different* Law of Nations for *different* parts of the globe."[13] For Wolff, as for Grotius and Pufendorf before him, such pluralism was unthinkable. So long as the law of nations was tied to the natural law, so long as it was held to be universally applicable, its content would have to be found in the actual practices of actual states. But in this case, the "most civilized nations" whose laws were held to be the standard for all others turned out to be the nations of Europe. And if that were the case, how could such laws possibly be called universal? It was a dilemma that was to haunt most subsequent attempts to imagine a future "Cosmopolis."

The "Supreme State" was, as Wolff readily admitted, in the legal sense of the term a "fiction." The victim of the impressionable "soldier-king" was unlikely to have imagined that anything as ecumenical as a world state could possibly emerge from out of the factious, quarrelsome states of Europe as they existed in the second half of the eighteenth century—let alone one that included, as the *civitas maxima* would have had to do—the Ottoman Empire, China, Mughal India, and all the other myriad nations, "barbarous" and "civilized," from across the globe. The construction of a real universal state—whatever form it might take—would require both human agency and the kind of goodwill that most humans, in particular those in positions of power, self-evidently lacked. The *civitas maxima,* like Rousseau's state of nature, had never actually existed and in all probability would never exist; such were the prevailing passions and inconsistencies of the human will. The point was, once again, that it could exist, if only in the mind of the philosopher. It offered the reader a means of judging what might be done to attain something that, although obviously and necessarily imperfect, was at least a reflection of supposedly universal human instincts.

Wolff's treatise, unlike his spectacular dismissal from Halle, did not, it must be said, attract much attention outside the academy. By the mid-eighteenth century his philosophy, "dogmatic, not critical," as Kant later said of it, had come to seem dusty and old-fashioned.[14] But one of those who read him with great care and who was to exercise considerable influence, directly and indirectly, on the development of the future understanding of international law and international relations, was the Swiss diplomat Emer de Vattel.[15] Vattel was born in 1714 in Neuchâtel, an anomalous part of the Swiss confederacy, a country, he said, "of which liberty is the soul, the treasure, and the fundamental law." Prior to 1757 he had a peripatetic and not entirely distinguished career, much of it plagued by ill health, poverty, and the broken promises of the powerful. Like Wolff, he began as a follower of Pufendorf and

Leibniz, and one of his earliest works was a lengthy defense of Leibniz against the charges of atheism. He spent the years between 1743 and 1757, while serving in a somewhat obscure capacity for the Elector Friedrich August II of Saxony, studying Wolff and writing dissertations on the role of natural law, some not very good poems, and, significantly, a series of unilluminating dialogues between Diogenes, Alexander the Great, and Marcus Aurelius, and between Henri IV of France and the duc de Sully, author of the so-called Gran Design of about 1640, the first project for a united federal Europe, which by reordering the current balance of powers would create a "Very Christian Republic" and by so doing bring perpetual peace to the continent.[16] In 1755 Vattel had also written a review of Rousseau's *Discourse on the Origin of Inequality,* whose view of pre-civil men as isolated individuals devoid of any natural inclination to sociability he found simply incredible. If nature, he said, echoing Aristotle, had made "Beavers, Bees, Ants and other animals" sociable, how could she have failed to make men so as well?[17]

In 1757 he published in Neuchâtel (although the title page says "London 1758") the book that was to make him famous throughout Europe and beyond: *The Law of Nations or Principles of the Law of Nature, Applied to the Conduct and Affairs of Nations and Sovereigns*. This secured him a position as a member of the Privy Council of Saxony and the elector's chief adviser on foreign affairs. It was translated into English in 1760 and became the standard textbook on international law throughout most of Europe. It was read by Jefferson, Washington, and Benjamin Franklin, who, in thanking Charles William Frederic Dumas in December 1775 for the copy he had sent him, remarked that it "came to us in good season, when the circumstances of a rising state make it necessary frequently to consult the law of nations."[18]

Vattel had begun by attempting to synthesize Wolff's findings on the natural law and to distill from them something that might be an improvement on what he saw as the revolutionary but still highly imperfect systems of Grotius and Pufendorf. What he was after was what he called "a natural law of nations," and when he heard that Wolff was writing a definitive account of the law of nations, he was convinced that this might provide him with the means to finding it. He therefore "impatiently waited for Monsieur Wolff's production." When *The Law of Nations, Treated According to a Scientific Method* finally arrived, however, he was sadly disillusioned. It was, he complained, not only dependent on the "sixteen or seventeen quarto volumes which preceded it" but was also written "in the manner and even the formal method of geometrical works." This made it not only "dry, and in many respects incomplete," it also rendered it "nearly useless to those very persons in whom the knowledge and taste of the true principles of the law of nations are most important and most desirable"—diplomats, that is, like himself.[19]

The single most important aspect of Wolff's overall argument he found most unsatisfactory, although it was also clearly highly suggestive, was precisely Wolff's conception of a "supreme state." As Vattel pointed out, the origins of the *civitas maxima* could not possibly be found in a rule of nature, since human societies were, it was now universally accepted (except among theologians), purely artificial creations. What Vattel called the "ties of the universal society which nature has established among men" were based "solely on the quality of mankind" *qua* species. They could not, therefore, be linked in any sense to a particular kind of social order. Nature might oblige us to recognize others when we meet them on, for instance, the high seas, it might oblige us to observe the laws of hospitality, but it could not constitute anything like a *civitas,* a state, unless it were also bound together by a commonly accepted body of laws and something resembling a common language. And these things clearly did not exist outside civil society. But what did, what was the most salient characteristic of the "universal society which nature has established among men" was, once again, the urge and the duty to assist one another, that "sympathy" or *pitié* that so many of the *philosophes* of the Enlightenment had seen as the sole enduring definition of the human species. It was this, combined with the corresponding urge to communicate, that, Vattel believed, might finally draw all the nations of the world together, not into a "Supreme State," but into some kind of cosmopolitan world order.

Vattel's own extensive reading of the prolonged debate over the nature of the state of nature and the evidence collected from the various parts of the globe all suggested that human beings had only become aggressive, hostile, and suspicious of one another once they had come together as nations. (On this point, at least, he agreed with Rousseau.) It was not fear or the relentless pursuit of power, as Hobbes had claimed, but natural sociability that had first persuaded men to unite together into civil societies, and it was necessity that had slowly induced them to create nations. Ever since then, however, these nations had existed in a state of permanent hostility to one another. This suggested that Rousseau had been right after all in claiming that in the process of nation building human beings had lost all those sentimental attachments to one another that defined them as individuals. Yet, as Wolff had seen, this was unlikely to be true. The condition of incessant conflict and belligerence in which all nations currently found themselves could only be described as an unnatural, inhuman one. If that were the case, then what could now be used to mobilize the natural affinity we all feel for one another, so as to reunite all the peoples of the world into some kind of union, however vague, without at the same time demanding either that every individual retreat back into the state of nature (an impossible task, as even Rousseau knew) or renounce any attachment to the nation? The short answer was, once again, commerce. Vattel looked upon commerce, as did most of the thinkers of the Enlightenment, as the final stage of the civilizing process and the sole effective means of refining human relationships.[20]

There was, however, more to it than that. Nations, once they began to trade with one another, not only became more polished, more civilized, and less belligerent, they also inevitably, whatever they might actually think of one another, became mutually dependent. As Montesquieu (whom Vattel had also read with care) observed, this had already happened in Europe, which, through commerce, had now become "one nation made up of many," France and Britain were dependent upon "the opulence of Poland and Muscovy" in much the same way that any one of the separate provinces of any single nation might be dependent upon all the others.[21] For Vattel, too, Europe, through commerce and skillful diplomacy, had been made into "a kind of republic whose independent members are all linked by common interests." And what applied to Europe would surely one day apply to the entire world.[22] It was an irreversible process that had been going on ever since those two "greatest and most important" events in human history—the discovery of America and that of the sea route to India. Inexorably, the world had grown increasingly globalized, until by the second half of the eighteenth century no one part of the earth could hope to remain for very long aloof from what happened to the inhabitants of the rest of it. What this new globalized world singularly lacked, however, was anything resembling a single body of laws that could offer it any degree of political cohesion. Wolff's and Vattel's search for a scientifically grounded set of premises for a universal law on which all reasonable, rational human beings could agree, no matter what their religious beliefs or national allegiances might be, was the continuation and constant revision of the project that Samuel Pufendorf had begun in 1672. It was also to be the final manifestation of the Enlightenment's "science of man."

Lifted up by the vision of a world of peacefully competitive commercial states, Vattel launched into an enthusiastic endorsement of the future modern cosmopolis. At some as yet uncertain future date, he wrote,

> The nations of the world would communicate their goods and their Enlightenment [*lumières*]. A profound peace would reign over the earth, and would enrich it with its precious fruits. Industry, sciences, and the arts would be as much concerned with our well-being as with our needs. There would be no more violent means for resolving such differences which might arise. They would all be solved by moderation, justice, and equity. The world would seem like one great republic. Man would live everywhere as brothers, and each one would be a citizen of the universe.[23]

The difficulty with this is that commerce was, as we have seen, recognized as being the final stage of mankind's social evolution. If commerce—however broadly understood—was to be the means of bringing together all the peoples of the world, then, as with Wolff's "supreme state," it could only be achieved in a world in which all peoples were, more or less, at the same level of civilization. Only when "the voice of nature" had reached all "the civilized peoples of the world" would they finally come to realize that all men are brothers, and only then, when "that happy time arrives, will [they] begin to behave as such."[24] Until that day arrived the modern cosmopolis would have to remain an illusion, constantly derailed by human passions and interests.

Vattel's image of a universal, harmonious world order held together by the bonds of commerce was to exercise considerable influence over subsequent attempts to envisage a future in which the desire for a worldwide community would finally triumph over the narrow sectarian interests of individual states. Neither were Wolff and Vattel alone in sensing the need for an ecumenical vision that would reach out beyond the limits of the slowly evolving nation-states, so as to consolidate the lessons already learned from the massive expansion of world trade since the seventeenth century and at the same time place some voluntary limit upon the destructive forces that had followed in their wake.

II

Cosmopolitanism was clearly not only a means of rendering human life more satisfying: it was, and remains, possibly the only way to persuade human beings to live together in harmony with one another or, to put it differently, to stop killing one another. For if it was, as the Stoics had claimed, love that bound men to their families, and to their *patria,* and ultimately to humanity, it was, as Hobbes had noted, indisputably hatred, or at best suspicion and fear, that separated one nation from another. The hope, the desire, that warfare could one day be brought to an end had long been an ambition of pacifists of one kind or another, ever since a doctrinally pacifist religion had inexplicably seized control of one of the world's most remarkable war-making machines, the Roman Empire, in the second century CE. Few Christian pacifists, however, were prepared to argue, like the Dutch humanist Desiderius Erasmus in the fifteenth century, that "war was not a necessary part of the natural or divine order." The vast majority looked upon war as one of the wages of sin, a consequence of the disobedience of Adam, and thus inevitable if not desirable. It might be contained, it might reasonably be limited to the seemingly perpetual struggle with Islam, but a universal peace would only descend upon the entire earth when the Second Coming was at hand, and then the earth itself would be at an end. The universalizing, cosmopolitan initiatives for bringing about world peace with which the eighteenth century is strewn were, by contrast, staunchly secular. To be sure, some endorsed the view that warfare, if not exactly a punishment for sin, was certainly the consequence of moral turpitude and could, therefore, only be eradicated once humans had learned how to live truly moral, which also implied truly cooperative, lives. But they had little doubt that with sufficient will—and sufficient time—this could be achieved. Sometime in the late seventeenth century it became possible for the first time to think seriously that one day humankind might live not merely in a state of reduced hostilities but actually in a condition of "perpetual peace." As Henry Sumner Maine observed in 1888, on looking back over two centuries of international law and many many more of international war, "war appears to be as old as mankind, but peace is a modern invention."[25]

It would, however, be misleading to call most eighteenth-century advocates of world peace "pacifists." They did not necessarily see conflict as an evil in itself. They did not believe that there were no conditions under which war would be perfectly justified. They believed instead in the possibility of eliminating all human conflict through mutual accord. There were a large number of proposals as to how to bring this about, some of which were narrowly practical, many more hopelessly visionary. One of the earliest, Eméric Crucé's *New Cyneas* of 1624, had laid out plans for a permanent peace conference to be held in Venice, a convenient gateway, geographically and culturally, between Christianity and Islam, the two warring power blocs of the early modern world. All the nations of the world, including the Ottomans, would be represented. The pope would be the president and the sultan his deputy. There was to be a common currency and free trade—a kind of early outline, as some have seen it, of the European Union, extended eastward to include Europe's oldest and, in the mid-seventeenth century, still its most deadly enemy. Others ranged from the pragmatic, if improbable, to the fantastical. They included William Penn's *An Essay Towards the Present and Future Peace of Europe* of 1693; the *Declaration for a Lasting Peace in Europe* by the "Old Pretender" (known to his followers as King James III of England and VIII of Scotland) of 1722; Voltaire's "Perpetual Peace" (which we have already met); the *Scheme of a "Perpetual Diet" for Establishing the Public Tranquillity* of 1736 (which was more of a proposal for conquering the Ottoman Empire) by Giulio Alberoni, skilled social climber and cardinal in the service of Philip V of Spain; the *Project for Perpetual Peace Between the Sovereigns of Europe and their Neighbors* by a former galley slave, Pierre-André Gargaz, which so impressed Benjamin Franklin that in 1782 he printed it on the press he had set up on his estate at Plassy outside Paris; and Jeremy Bentham's *A Plan for a Universal and Perpetual Peace* of 1789, which called for the dissolution of the European overseas empires, which he denounced as "violations of common sense" and "bungling imitations of miserable [Greco-Roman] originals."[26]

One was also outlandishly extravagant. In June 1790 the wealthy Prussian Jean-Baptiste du Val-de-Grâce, Baron de Cloots, calling himself "Anarcharsis" after a legendary Scythian prince and known somewhat derisively during the French Revolution as "the orator of mankind" and the "citizen of Humanity," turned up at the meeting of the National Assembly at the head of a delegation of thirty-six foreigners he had gathered together for the occasion. This motley gang, he declared, were the representatives of the human race (although most of them looked suspiciously European), which had now subscribed to the articles set down in the "Declaration of the Rights of Man and Citizen" of 1789. It made him an instant celebrity. He was elected to the National Convention, spent part of his not-inconsiderable fortune on equipping the French army, became president of the Committee on Foreign Affairs, and was even elected president of the Jacobin Club in November 1793. But despite his support for the execution of Louis XVI (he thought that it might be a good idea to execute the King of Prussia as well) and his defense of the necessity for what he called "salutary terror," he, like so many other ardent revolutionaries, finally fell foul of

Robespierre and the Committee of Public Safety. He was guillotined in March 1794, after first having bowed in all directions so as to pay his last respects to humanity everywhere. One of Cloots's crimes, paradoxically, had been his unrestrained onslaught against the Church, which even Robespierre had found too extreme. But the most serious, in Robespierre's eyes, was his cosmopolitanism. Starting from the dubious proposition that it was "easier for a large state to be just than a small one" and that a world in which there was a plurality of states was doomed to remain marooned forever in the state of nature, Cloots drew up a plan for what he called the "Whole Republic of Man." Its members were all to be bound by the "Bill of Human Rights," but they would all enjoy cultural autonomy. The exact limits of this Republic were left vague, but in effect it was to be an extension of the "country formerly called France, but which should now be renamed *The Universal Republic.*" Its capital was to be in Paris, which would now be the "world metropolis through Peace," just as Rome had once been through war. But, he declared, "I demand the suppression of the name French. . . . All humans want to belong to the universal republic, but not all peoples want to be French." (Needless to say, this too was something that Robespierre found hard to swallow.)[27]

Cloots's proposal ran into the problem that so many such projects had encountered: despite his insistence that the French stop calling themselves French, it read far more like a blueprint for a universal empire ruled by one nation than a "Whole Republic of Man." It might unite the entire world, it might bring about peace, but it could only do so at the expense of all those who had little wish to submerge themselves in a French-led "Universal Republic." But then, in Cloots's view, those poor souls had been so abused by their tyrannical rulers that they could no longer see where their true interests lay. It was, therefore, up to the (renamed) French to enlighten them. Cloots's plan fell along with his head. But much of it was taken up, both as an ideology and as a practice, by Napoleon, who had probably never read it.

Most of these projects owed rather more than their titles to a bulky, ponderous work by Charles-Irénée Castel, abbé de St. Pierre, *A Project for Establishing a Perpetual Everlasting Peace in Europe,* written in 1713, a text whose influence, attenuated but perceptible, has carried down through the centuries, via the pioneer socialist Henri de Saint-Simon in the nineteenth century to Jean Monnet, architect of the European Coal and Steel Community of 1952 and consequently of the European Union—a term that St. Pierre seems to have been the first to use. St. Pierre was in many respects a remarkable, and remarkably prescient, man. A diplomat who had been a negotiator of the Treaty of Utrecht in 1712–13 and had been expelled from the Académie française in 1718 for denouncing the rule of its patron, Louis XIV, he devised plans for a graded tax system—virtually unthinkable in the early eighteenth century—and for free education for all, both men and women.[28] His *Project* envisaged a future European federation drawn together through the beneficial effects of trade, bound by a "treaty of European Union" but ruled not as individual states are, by a single sovereign, but by a council, or diet, on which the princes of every member state would sit. This, St. Pierre believed, would eliminate warfare from the continent forever, bring the greatest happiness to the greatest number, and finally demonstrate to princes that their true interests lay not in conflict but in what he called *bienfaisance*—or that *bienfaisance* (a word he appears to have been the first to use, or "beneficence," we owe to others, and which was, once again, an expression of the "sympathy" that all human beings were supposed, as individuals, to share with one another. He also believed that such a Union would bring an end to what Hume called "the jealousy of trade," that "narrow and malignant opinion" that led all states that had made "some advances in commerce . . . to look on the progress of their neighbors with a suspicious eye, to consider all trading nations as their rivals, and to suppose that it is impossible for them to flourish, but at their expense."[29] And when that happened commerce would finally become "universal, free, equal, certain, and perpetual amongst all nations."

St. Pierre hoped that one day it would be possible to extend this federation to Asia, Africa, and America, but he reflected that any such proposal at this date would make his plan seem absurdly unrealistic. Even without attempting to embrace the entire world, the *Project* was duly mocked by most of those who read it. Voltaire dismissed it as "a chimera that could no more exist among princes than it could among elephants and rhinoceroses, or wolves and dogs."[30] Leibniz, ironical as ever, remarked that it reminded him of a "device in a cemetery with the words: *Pax perpetua* [perpetual peace]; for the dead do not fight any longer: but the living are of another humour; and the most powerful do not respect tribunals at all."[31] But it is a measure of its influence and its widespread diffusion that the likes of Voltaire and Leibniz—and, as we shall shortly see, Kant—took so much trouble over it. Most of the other such projects came and went with hardly a mention.[32]

St. Pierre himself died in 1743, but two decades later he found an unexpected, somewhat reluctant, and on the face of it highly unsuitable editor in Rousseau. In 1756 the brilliant, wealthy *salonnière* Louise-Marie Dupin de Chenonceau, a pacifist and, in her own way, a feminist, to whose son Rousseau had acted for a while as tutor and who had known St. Pierre in her youth, at the suggestion of the abbé Gabriel Bonnot de Mably asked Rousseau to compile an edition of his works. Rousseau, who described himself, with characteristic false modesty but not inaccurately, as a man "who found the trouble of thinking too wearying and preferred . . . to clarify and dust off the ideas of another than to create his own," accepted. Despite his hostility toward most kinds of universalizing sentiments, Rousseau had a certain sympathy for St. Pierre's overall ambitions, if not exactly for the *Project* itself, and he hoped that St. Pierre's manuscripts would turn out to contain innumerable "treasures." Instead, when he examined the hefty collection with which he had been entrusted, all he found were copies of the abbé's printed works and "one or two other pieces which had not seen the light of day," together with a number of "political works which revealed only superficial views, and useful but impractical projects." Sadly, he came to the conclusion that the "high opinion" the abbé had had of "modern understanding, had led him to adopt the false principle of perfectible reason." St. Pierre was clearly "the honor of his century and of his species," but he had "gone from mistake to mistake in all his systems, through wishing to make all men like him, rather than taking them as they are, and will continue to be." Rousseau therefore decided to provide his readers first with an edition of St. Pierre's works, as he had been asked, and then, sometime later, when these "had made their impact," publish his own reflections on them.[33]

Like many similar projects, Rousseau's edition came to nothing. All he managed to complete was a draft of an introduction, a handful of suggestive jottings, and an extract from the *Project*. He also wrote a brief "Judgment" on the work, which he claimed to be a demonstration in the "general and particular utility" of "moral truth."[34] He acknowledged, however, that many would toss it aside, as they would any such utopian project, as mere "vain speculation." He himself disagreed with the idea that a federation could achieve peace (historically, as he pointed out, most had been created for the purposes of war). Neither did he believe that commerce encouraged harmony and cooperation; in reality, it only increased the sources for competition between states and thus the grounds for war. In the end Rousseau came to the conclusion that the kind of federation of states St. Pierre had conjured up out of his overly optimistic imagination would require a situation in which "the sum of particular interests did not overpower the common interest and . . . each one sees in the good of all, the greatest good which he could hope for himself."[35] The only possible way to bring that about would, in his view, be a revolution. And if that were the case, then "who among us would dare to say whether the European League were more to be feared than desired?"[36]

III

It was Immanuel Kant who finally provided the answer to this question. In the wake of the Peace of Basel on April 5, 1795—which ended the War of the First Coalition between the monarchical states of Europe, including Prussia and Revolutionary France; ceded to France all territory west of the Rhine; and allowed Russia, Austria, and Prussia to carve up Poland among them—Kant set out his own project for ending warfare. He called it *Toward Perpetual Peace, a Philosophical Project*. In 1795 Kant was seventy-one years old and widely admired throughout Europe. His three great Critiques, the *Critique of Pure Reason* of 1781, the *Critique of Practical Reason* of 1788, and the *Critique of the Power of Judgment* of 1790, together with *The Groundwork of the Metaphysics of Morals* of 1785, had, in Kant's own terms, brought about a "Copernican Revolution" in philosophy. They would certainly make him famous as the most dauntingly difficult (Herder said of the *Critique of Pure Reason* that it was a "tough nut to crack," obscured by "all this heavy gossamer") but also perhaps the most important, the most ambitious, European philosopher since Aristotle.

Although he deplored the sufferings caused by warfare and the conditions under which it was generally waged, and although he frequently described warfare as, with the possible exception of despotism, the greatest evil ever to have afflicted mankind, and denied that it could ever be a legitimate means of settling a dispute, Kant was not in the conventional sense a pacifist. War had sometimes served mankind well in the past and might continue to serve it well, under certain very specific conditions, in the future. It had been war that had driven the first men out of their original habitats and across the globe.[37] Without war humans would, like all other animals, still be huddling together on the small patch of land where they had first emerged. How else could one explain the presence of human settlements around the Arctic Ocean or in the Altay Mountains or in Patagonia? It had been warfare, "however great an evil it might be," that had motivated "the transition from the brutish state of nature into a state of civil society."[38] At a later stage it had been war, all wars, which "amount to attempts . . . not in the intentions of humanity, but indeed in the intentions of nature," that had compelled more socialized humans to establish relationships between states and create new ones.[39] Man is the only animal that, "to the extent that he is able, works towards the destruction of his own species."[40] And it is war, and fear of future war, that demands "even of the heads of states" a certain "*respect for humanity*." China, which because of its location "has no powerful enemy to fear," had for this very reason been stripped of "every trace of freedom."[41] China, as we have seen, was the paradigmatic proof that stagnation would always, ultimately, be the price to pay for security. War is an instrument of what Kant calls "culture" (*Kultur*), the willful social and moral improvement of the human species, which alone makes it finally fit to "pursue any ends whatsoever." It was, after all, the "Saracens, the Crusades, and the conquest of Constantinople" that, between them, had "spread science, taste, and learning to the West."[42] Thus, "only after culture has been perfected (God alone knows when this will be) would a lasting peace be salutary for us, and only through such culture would it become possible."[43]

War, then, "is a deeply concealed, perhaps intentional attempt of the most supreme wisdom, if not to establish then at least to prepare lawfulness along with the freedom of states and thereby the unity of a morally grounded system of states."[44] Freedom, and from freedom progress, is only possible for man in the face of persistent anxiety. Without war the whole of mankind would have remained like those happy but ineffectual Tahitians who could not give any adequate explanation as to why they bothered to live at all. In the end, however, it is warfare that drives man, inexorably and despite himself, and if only to avoid the actual destruction of the species, toward the development of the "universal *cosmopolitan condition.*" For Kant that existence was not merely the solution to a problem. It was the final end of human existence, "the end . . . which nature has as its aim" and the "womb in which all original predispositions of the human species will be developed."[45]

Toward Perpetual Peace, then, is a contribution to an as yet unfinished project—the project of Enlightenment itself—a project that we humans are clearly not yet able to complete, which is, indeed, almost certainly not yet "salutary" for us, but which, given our very nature, we cannot but try to realize. Hence the very uncertainty of Kant's title.[46] It is a proposal, a mere "project" that will lead "toward" a condition that can only be realized in the future. Perhaps for that reason it is written, unpromisingly, in the form of a series of articles—and Kant's lengthy reflections on the meaning of each one—for a hypothetical universal peace treaty. It is a treaty unlike any that had hitherto existed but, in Kant's mind, the only one that could ensure the future and inescapably cosmopolitan development of the human race. Its conclusions were to have a powerful and widespread, if also diffuse, influence well beyond the confines of professional philosophy. It has left its mark on many later generations, and its presence can still be seen not only in contemporary discussions over global governance and global justice but also in the creation of the universal institutions intended to sustain them, in the League of Nations, the United Nations, and perhaps most closely of all, the European Union.

As St. Pierre had acidly observed, the sovereign powers of Europe, as they were currently constituted, were no different from "the little kings of Africa, the unhappy Caciques, or the little sovereigns of America." There existed among them nothing that could be described as a "sufficiently powerful and permanent society." The closest they had come was the Swiss Federation or the states of the Netherlands. As a consequence, all the other powers were ceaselessly driven to war to resolve their differences.[47] Kant agreed. Every treaty organization that the states of Europe had used to bind themselves—including the one concluded at Basel—had been nothing other than a "mere truce, a suspension of hostilities, not *peace,*" since none of them had ever aimed at a stable, permanent condition.[48] St. Pierre's project may have been illusory and without any practical value, since all such proposals have always been "ridiculed by great statesmen, and even more by heads of state, as pedantic, childish, and academic ideas," but that, in Kant's view, was probably only because St. Pierre had believed that "its execution was too near."[49] His basic claim, however, that perpetual peace, within Europe or beyond, could only be brought about by some kind of federation, was inescapable. So, too, was the implication that this was not merely a solution to a problem but a crucial, possibly the final, stage in the history of humankind.

If humans were to be persuaded to create a federation of this kind, then, as with everything else that was merely human, they had to make it for themselves. And in Kant's opinion they had to begin somewhere other than the law of nations as it was currently understood. Like Pufendorf, Wolff, and Vattel before him, Kant looked upon civil societies as "moral persons," which could not, therefore, by their very nature, be owned by anyone, any more than individuals could. "For the state," he wrote, "is not (like the ground on which it resides) a belonging *(patrimonium)*. It is society of human beings that no one other than itself can command or dispose of."[50] Most of the princes of modern Europe, however, persisted in behaving as if their states were merely some private patrimony, which they could sell, bequeath, and even marry off to one another. For them, going to war was therefore "the simplest thing in the world," because war "will not force [the prince] to make the slightest sacrifice so far as his banquets, hunts, pleasure palaces, and court festivals are concerned." War was merely another form of hunting, "a kind of pleasure party," and, Kant added with heavy sarcasm, the prince could happily "leave the justification of war, for the sake of propriety, to the diplomatic corps, which is always ready to provide it."[51] Clearly, no agreement for a universal perpetual peace could ever be concluded among such people.

Humankind, he reflected, had lost touch with instinct but had not yet learned how to live according to the law of reason.[52] In the current state of affairs, all the nations of the world continued to exist in the same relationship with one another, "like lawless savages," as single individuals had once done in the state of nature. For this reason alone, they "already wrong one another by being near one another."[53] Such a condition (and on this Kant agreed with Hobbes) was one of war, "even if there is no actual war or continuous fighting," and was so far removed from any possible moral condition that "it cannot even be said that one people may do wrong to another."[54] Savages "prefer the freedom of folly to the freedom of reason" and would rather suffer incessant strife than submit to any kind of legal restraint. Civilized beings, however, rightly look upon this kind of behavior as "barbarism, coarseness, and brutish debasement of humanity." Yet when it came to their relations with other nations, these very same people, rather than hastening "to abandon so degrading a condition," persisted in waging wars across the globe, and they did so, in Kant's opinion, merely because every ruler believed his glory to consist in "his power to order thousands of people to immolate themselves for a cause which does not truly concern them, while he need not incur any danger whatsoever." Here, in the "unrestricted relations which obtain between the various nations" of the world, the "depravity" of human nature was on full display, "without disguises." The sole difference, said Kant with heavy-handed mockery, between the American Indians and the Europeans on this score, was that while the former "have been eaten up by their enemies," the latter had made a strategic decision to use theirs to increase "the number of their subjects, and so too the multitude of their instruments for even more extensive wars, by means of them."[55] More economical, perhaps, but hardly more commendable.

All those who had in the past sought a solution to this problem, Grotius, Pufendorf, Vattel, "and the rest," whom Kant lumped together as the "sorry comforters of mankind," had, of course, all come to similar conclusions. The remedies they had offered, however, had all been expressed in terms of a common international law, a "law of nations," and that law had, in Kant's view, been "simply an Idea" and a useless one at that, because no legal code could possibly have any force in a world in which "states are not subject to a common external constraint." The "law of nations" not only had no binding force, it also had no obvious content. Indeed, "it is difficult even to form a concept of this or to think of law in this lawless condition . . . without contradicting oneself."[56] It was all very well for Holbach, from his retreat in the rue Royale, to claim airily that "the law of nations ought to be nothing other than the moral [law] applied to all the nations of the earth."[57] But no one, even within Europe, could ever decide what should be included in the term *moral,* much less how this could be transformed into any remotely compelling law. In the world as it is (or was in the eighteenth century; things are now a little different), the "law of nations," as Adam Smith had noted, was "frequently violated without that bringing any considerable dishonour upon the violator," since all any ruler really ever cared for was the judgment of his own fellow citizens, and not very many cared even for that.[58]

In Kant's view, what these "sorry comforters" had all failed to see was that no law could possibly exist between nations until they chose to exit from the state of nature in which they currently found themselves. To the already familiar categories of law—the domestic or civil law and the law of nations—Kant added a third of his own devising, what he famously called the "cosmopolitan right" (*ius cosmopoliticum* or *Weltbürgerrecht*).[59] And it was this, not the now largely discredited *ius gentium,* that would govern the future relations between individuals and states. For the only possible solution to the current condition of unstructured barbarism was for all the states of the world to form "a general league of nations, establish a public legislation, define a public authority to appropriate national prerogatives, and thereby make possible a universal peace." It would, in other words, be a universal, cosmopolitan existence.[60]

The analogy between the individual and the nation, however, could be taken only so far. The great beauty of the contract theory of government was that, no matter what form it took—Hobbesian covenant, Lockean contract, or Rousseauian pact—it assumed that humans could exit, by their own volition, from their original lawless condition and create civil societies, without having to alter their identities as individuals. It was also, even in its most qualified (Lockean) form, binding on both parties so long as both parties continued to observe the terms of the original agreement. The same, however, could not be said of nations. The only contracts that had ever existed between them were treaties, or cease-fires, what Kant called a "peace pact *(pactum pacis)*," and these had only ever put an end to a "current war . . . but not a condition of war, of always finding pretexts for a new war."[61] If these unsatisfactory arrangements were to be replaced by anything more binding, if the nations themselves were to emerge from the state of nature, as nations, they would have first to change their political identities radically. In this respect, then, the sorry comforters had all been looking in the wrong place. St. Pierre and Rousseau had been looking in the right place, but even Rousseau had failed to see the implication of his own claim that nothing resembling St. Pierre's project could come into existence unless each state created a form of government in which "the sum of particular interests did not overpower the common interest." For what this raised was what form such a state would take, and that had been the question that had dogged political thinking since antiquity.

Kant's answer was what he famously called a "representative republic." This he defined as a society in which no individual should be constrained by any external—that is, purely human—law (what Kant called "the moral law within me" was clearly another matter), other than "those to which I could have given my consent."[62] Kant dismissed the idea that society could literally have been the outcome of some kind of contract between the people and their sovereign as a simple fiction. Any argument that it was anything else would "first have to prove from history that some nation whose rights and obligations have been passed down to us, did in fact perform such an act, and handed down some authentic record or legal instrument, orally or in writing, before we could regard ourselves as bound by a pre-existing civil constitution." And "savages draw up no record of their submission to the law."[63] The exception would seem to be the United States, which, in the Declaration of Independence and the Constitution, does possess such documents, one reason why they have always had such a hallowed place in the nation's image of itself. But then the United States was not founded by "savages" and was, at the date of its founding, the only state since ancient Athens to have been created largely *ex nihilo* out of a political theory, or rather a medley of political theories. No European nation, however, until the French Republic of 1792 and the Batavian Republic of 1795, had been created in this way, and therefore no such founding charters existed for any of them. The true force of the social contract, however, lay not in its historical plausibility but in the fact that it was, in a phrase Kant uses frequently, "a *mere idea* of reason,"

> yet one which has unquestionable practical reality. Namely this idea obliges every legislator to pass laws in such a way that they *would have been able* to arise from the united will of an entire people and to regard every subject, insofar as he wishes to be a citizen, as though he had given his assent to this will. For that is the touchstone of the lawfulness of any public law.[64]

Such a contract might never have existed in any one nation, but it could and certainly should have; for once the idea that God was the source of political power had been stripped away, there could be no legitimate political authority other than one derived from consent. This made of all citizens "co-legislating members of a state (not merely as means but also as ends in themselves)."[65] And only a republic could provide the conditions under which this would be possible. Only a republican constitution would be able, in this way, to give "complete justice to the rights of man." Many, however, had argued that such a state was an impossible fantasy, since only angels possess such powers of cooperation and mutual understanding. Only angels are ever that *good*. But Kant insisted that his republic had nothing to with the good or evil principles in man. It could just as easily be created by a "nation of devils" (assuming devils to be, like most men, rational self-interested creatures) as by human beings. No moral superiority was required; all that was needed was a "mechanism of nature" that would balance out the conflicts that always arose between individuals without eradicating the naturally "self-seeking energies" of the human.[66] In Kant's view, only a republic in which all the citizens were represented by one means or another (and Kant is never very explicit about what these might be) could achieve this. Only in such a society is man, "even if he is not good in himself . . . nevertheless compelled to be a good citizen." It is also the only one that "offers a prospect of attaining the desired result, i.e. Perpetual Peace," since only then would the citizens be in a position to "give their free assent, through their representatives, not only to the waging of war in general, but also to each particular declaration of war."[67] Great powers, Kant observed, are "never shamed before the judgment of the masses, but only before one another." In a representative republic, however, it is these common masses (or at least their representatives) who have to decide whether to declare war or not, and since their honor is not at stake, they have nothing to be ashamed of in front of other powers, great or small.[68] For them, going to war inevitably means only "taking upon themselves all the hardships of war" and "to make the cup of troubles overflow," assuming the "burden of debt that embitters peace itself, and that can never be paid off because of new wars always impending."[69] And they are likely to do that only if they are certain there can be no solution other than war.

This—although Kant does not describe it quite like that—would be the truly modern state, one that had turned its back upon the archaic military cultures that had benefited the autocratic rulers of preceding centuries, in which, as Bernard Mandeville had slyly suggested, honor and embarrassment were the prime motives for war.[70] Furthermore, since the citizens of a republic must necessarily take responsibility for their own lives, only the republic could provide the conditions required for the creation of a true civilization. Only in a republic would humanity finally be released from the "leading-reins" that had kept it in perpetual infancy since the beginning of history. Then there would be a clear answer to Christian Thomasius' question "Who will determine if a nation is civilized or barbarian?" The civilized nations would be those that had chosen to become "representative republics"; the barbarians, those that had not.

What Kant meant by the term *republic* has been a subject of much debate. He has been hailed as the father of "democratic peace theory," the—ultimately unfalsifiable and empirically unsustainable—claim that democracies do not make war on one another, and he has been viewed as the originator of the argument best expressed by Woodrow Wilson's famous phrase, that the world should "be made safe for democracy."[71] Yet Kant is adamant that his concept of representative republicanism should *not* be confused with democracy. Like many political theorists, from Aristotle to Kant's contemporary, James Madison, he was fearful of what Madison called the "common interest or passion" of the *demos,* the people. True democracy could all too easily become mob rule, a form of tyranny no different from, and often far worse than, the tyranny of ruthless individuals. "Hence it is that such democracies have ever been spectacles of turbulence and contention," wrote Madison, as he pondered what form the Constitution of the United States should take, "have ever been incompatible with personal security or the rights of property; and have in general been as short in life as they have been violent in their deaths."[72] Kant was even more sharply dismissive. "Democracy," he wrote, "in the truest sense of the word, is necessarily a despotism, because it establishes an executive power through which all the citizens may make decisions about (and indeed against) the single individual without his consent." Even the "enlightened despotism" of Frederick II of Prussia would be preferable, since he at least "*said* that he was merely the highest servant of the state," whereas in a democracy "everyone . . . wants to be a ruler."

This does not, however, disqualify Kant as a democratic theorist in the sense in which the troubled, abused, and much-misdescribed term *democracy* is understood today (any more than it does Madison). For what Kant here calls a democracy, "in the strict sense of the word" (and what Madison called "a pure democracy"), was what he referred to as the government in "the so-called 'republics' of antiquity."[73] It was what Benjamin Constant, who had also been a close and critical reader of Kant, called "ancient liberty." In 1819 Constant delivered a now-celebrated speech to the Athénée royal in Paris, an institution with strong Masonic connections, in which he drew a stark distinction between ancient liberty and its modern counterpart. His objective, in the aftermath of the Terror and the Napoleonic Wars, was to detach the idea of liberty from that of political virtue, which had been the inspiration behind Rousseau's entire political program and about which he was particularly scathing. For the liberty of the democracies of the ancient world, he said, had "consisted in exercising [power] collectively and directly" in every aspect of public and private life, and this "collective freedom" had resulted in "the complete subjection of the individual to the authority of the community." In this way, the individual, although "almost always sovereign in public affairs, was a slave in his private relations." By contrast, "modern liberty" was essentially private, pleasure-seeking, and utilitarian. In a modern republic the people had complete freedom over their own private affairs so as to be able to pursue the "peaceful enjoyment of private independence." But they exercised public authority only indirectly, through "some influence on the administration of the government, either by electing all or particular officials, or through representations, petitions, demands to which the authorities are more or less compelled to pay heed."[74]

This, broadly speaking, was also Kant's position (although he would have had little sympathy for Constant's claim that all that modern man wished for was to be left in peace to pursue his own private pleasures). The true republic is founded upon the freedom of every individual (as an individual), the "dependence of everyone upon a common legislation," and full equality for all before the law. The sovereign acts on behalf of the people, whom he represents. Who actually does the representing is a matter for debate, although Kant claims to believe, on rather shaky grounds, that the smaller the number of people actually in government, the more representative it is likely to be.[75] What matters is not the form of government but the source of political power and the degree to which every individual is able to exercise his or her control over it.[76]

Kant's "representative republic," then, does indeed look remarkably like a modern "liberal democracy." For that, too, is certainly not any kind of democracy the Athenians—or Rousseau—would have recognized as such. Of the three forms of government imagined in antiquity and that, with minor variations, are with us still—monarchy (the rule of the one), aristocracy (the rule of the "best"), and democracy (the rule of the many)—modern "liberal democracies" are, as the modern French political philosopher Bernard Manin has argued, in fact, aristocracies.[77] They are, of course, no longer dominated—as they were in Europe until very recently—by elites based on lineage and land, if only because land is no longer a source of great wealth and power. They are no longer dynastic. But their political classes are made up of exactly what Aristotle would have recognized as "the best," the richest, most powerful, and (sometimes) best educated. Those who have hailed Kant as the first of the modern liberals, and the first to claim that modern liberal democracy was bound eventually to become the form of government that all enlightened and civilized peoples would one day embrace, are not far wrong.[78]

Transforming the despotic, authoritarian monarchies of the late eighteenth century into representative republics would, for Kant, however, be only the first step toward perpetual peace. Once this had been achieved (and Kant offers no suggestions as to how it would be done in practice), these newly formed republican states would acquire a moral obligation to unite together, to create "a league of a special kind which can be called a *pacific league (foedus pacificum)*."[79] For without what he calls this "*cosmopolitan* whole" and "given the obstacle presented by the lust for honor, by the thirst for power and greed, primarily among those who have it in their power to oppose even the possibility of this project," war is, and will always continue to be, inevitable.[80] Although he does not say so, only the kind of political transformation Kant was demanding from all the peoples of the world in the name of one simple, self-evident, and self-evidently self-interested calculation would resolve the dilemma of just where the content of the law of nations was to come from, if, that is, it were to be anything more than one particular set of laws observed by one specific group of peoples. The "pacific league," although it could never be created through force, nevertheless placed an obligation upon all the peoples of the world, civilized and uncivilized alike. Certainly, since no such heterogeneous group of peoples would ever be likely to act simultaneously, some one nation would have to show the way. But once "one powerful and enlightened people can form itself into a republic (which by its nature must be inclined to seek perpetual peace), this would provide a focal point of federative union for other states."[81] It was not threat or coercion but imitation that would finally alter the political institutions of the world, since all humans, given enough time, are clearly able to see what will be of most benefit to them. Slowly thereafter all the states of the world would follow suit. All would become republics and, abandoning their "savage (lawless) freedom," would "accommodate themselves to public coercive laws, and so form an (always growing) state of nations (*civitas gentium*) that would finally encompass all the nations of the earth."[82] Only within such a "confederation of peoples" would it be possible for each individual "to be at once both a citizen of a nation and a full member of the society of the citizens of the world," and this, he added, "is the most sublime idea which a man may conceive of his destiny." The image he had before him was not a "world state," such as Wolff's would have been, dominated ultimately by the laws, if not by the armies, of "the most civilized nations," nor anything resembling Cloots's "Universal Republic." For both of these would, sooner or later, have turned into a "Universal Monarchy," and for Kant that, by the mere fact of its size, if nothing else, could only ever become the "graveyard of freedom" and a "soulless despotism."[83] Like Herder, with whom he agreed on little else, Kant believed that nature would always find a way to frustrate what Herder bitingly described as the despot's dream of cramming "all the four quarters of the globe . . . into the belly of a wooden horse."[84] Kant saw empires as unnatural creations, humans having been divided into distinct peoples (if not races), distinguished by what were for him the key markers of cultural identity, religion, and language. Any attempt to eliminate these, and "all freedom would necessarily expire, and together with it, virtue, taste, and science (which follow upon freedom)." Finally the laws themselves would gradually lose their force, until the whole enterprise collapsed back into a collection of small, belligerent states, where it had originally been conceived. And then these "begin the same game all over again, so that war (that scourge of the human race)" continues unabated. Yet even war itself was not so "incurable an evil" as "the grave of universal despotism."[85]

The new cosmopolitan order would be something quite different. Kant used many different terms to describe this—a "league of peoples," "an international state," a "universal union of states," a federation, a confederation, a partnership—and, it must be said, is inconsistent even in his use of the same term.[86] But whatever else it might be, it would be a peaceful, consensual body, and all those who joined it would do so because they perceived it to be in their particular interests, and they would do so of their own volition. The effect would be not to erase those differences which had hitherto been the cause of war, but with "increasing culture and the gradual approach of human beings to greater agreement in principles," it would finally result not, as all empires had, in the "weakening of all forces" but in "their equilibrium in liveliest competition."[87]

The model to which Kant returned most often was that of the leagues of the Greek city-states, free associations of neighboring cities formed originally to protect a sacred shrine or sanctuary, and in particular the Delian League, which exercised the right to wage "sacred war" on those members of the league that transgressed its laws.[88] The model had become increasingly popular throughout the eighteenth century. James Madison believed that it offered a "very instructive analogy to the present confederation of the United States." (He also warned, however—which Kant did not—that "it happened but too often . . . that the deputies of the strongest cities awed and corrupted those of the weaker; and that judgement went in favour of the most powerful party." The Delian League had, after all, eventually become the "Athenian Empire.")[89]

No matter what form it might finally take or when it comes about—and there was no doubt in Kant's mind that it one day would—any type of international association among peoples will ultimately be more than a merely practical arrangement for suppressing warfare, much as that was to be applauded. It would also, for Kant, be the instantiation of what he calls humanity's "cosmopolitan right." This is not, he insists, a philanthropic principle. It is a right. And if there was any single "systematic thing in the history of human behavior," it was that "one idea led all the others, that is, the idea of their right."[90] It is the right that each people has to enjoy a peaceful relationship and to communicate with all others, for the desire for communication with one's fellow beings was for Kant, as it was for most of the writers of the Enlightenment, a primal human drive. Because humanity, he wrote, "means on the one hand the universal *feeling of participation,* and on the other the capacity for being able to *communicate* one's innermost self universally, which properties, taken together, constitute the sociability that is appropriate to humankind, by means of which it distinguishes itself from the limitations of animals."[91]

From this original and—since it is one of the things that distinguishes us from other animals—innate drive derives the "condition of hospitality," and it is on this that the "cosmopolitan right" is grounded.[92] Hospitality, as we have seen, had for centuries been looked upon as a semisacred right of association. For Kant, too, hospitality was a natural inclination and, like the *ius cosmopoliticum,* not mere "philanthropy" but the *right* that all persons possessed, as persons, "to try to establish community with all and, to this end, to visit all regions of the world," for "all men are entitled to present themselves in the society of others by virtue of the right to communal possession of the earth's surface."[93] Only under such conditions would it be "possible for [strangers] to enter into relations with the native inhabitants," since societies cannot flourish in isolation from one another, much less in contempt of one another. It had been, Kant had argued, precisely the tendency of the Greeks to isolate themselves from the rest of humanity, whom they then lumped together as "barbarians," that had been "the prime cause contributing to the downfall of their states."[94] This did not, however, apply to the innocent victims of "the *inhospitable* behavior of civilized, especially commercial, states of our part of the world [in] the injustice which they show in *visiting* foreign lands and peoples (which with them is tantamount to *conquering* them)." The Chinese, together with the Japanese, whom Kant generally reviled for isolating themselves from the rest of humanity, having "given such guests a try," were in this instance perfectly within their rights to place severe limitations on the activities of European trading companies.

But despite this still inhospitable behavior, which, as he pointed out, in the end benefited no one, Kant remained convinced that even in his own day the conditions of international trade had resulted in a state in which "the community of the nations of the earth has now gone so far that a violation of rights in one place of the earth is felt in all," and as a consequence it had become possible for the enlightened, at least, to look forward to the possibility of a future cosmopolitan world as something more than a simple fantasy.[95] From this, Kant hoped that a greater understanding between peoples would result, to the point where they might "enter into peaceful mutual relations which may eventually be regulated by public laws, thus bringing the human race nearer and nearer to a cosmopolitan existence." The "community of nations" is one of mutual assistance and care. It is still divided into people living together in distinct political communities (the *ius cosmopoliticum* must render the *ius gentium*—however defined—redundant, but it could never eliminate the civil law). But the old Westphalian system, in which each state exercised absolute and undivided sovereignty over its own affairs, would be gone forever.[96] For any truly cosmopolitan order, however defined, would require the division of sovereign power between states, or what today is called "liberal international sovereignty."

This "universal *cosmopolitan condition*" would be the "womb in which all the original predispositions of the human species will be developed."[97] The citizens of this "perfect state constitution" were not, however, to be mere rootless unattached beings. They were to be patriots, in the true meaning of the term; they would recognize the worth of others without surrendering their own particular identities; they would recognize themselves in others, learn their languages, and respect their beliefs—provided, of course, that these did not conflict with the rights of humanity. The cosmopolitan society would seem to have it all ways.

All of this, however, still lay in the future. Kant was not about to make the mistake St. Pierre had been ridiculed for making. His objective had always been to obtain what he calls "a history of future times, i.e. a predictive history."[98] For although animals, if left to themselves, reach their "complete destiny" as individuals, humans can only do so as a species, and they can, therefore, get there only "through *progress* in a series of innumerably many generations." Neither was he prepared to hazard a guess as to just how long this process might take—although at one point he seems to have believed that it might be "thousands of years."[99] The "complete destiny" of man always remains a distant but attainable goal, yet while the human race may experience many setbacks on its long journey through time, and although "the *tendency* to this final end can often be hindered, it can never be completely reversed."[100] The "cosmopolitan right" was an idea, a "dream of perfection," but like all such ideas it should not abandoned, as Kant had said of the Platonic republic, "under the very wretched and harmful pretext of its impracticability."[101] So long as we are free—morally and intellectually—we can only go on hoping that some kind of cosmopolitan world will be achieved. More pressingly, perhaps, the very fact that we are able to imagine such a state makes it our duty "to work toward this (not merely chimerical) end."[102] Were we to accept that no such future state was possible, that where we now find ourselves is the end of history, then, and only then, might we be forgiven for agreeing with "Rousseau's preference for the savage state." For Rousseau's conjectural history of mankind was flawed in that it had precisely left out "the last stage which our species has yet to surmount," without the hope for which there might be said to be little to recommend the present condition of the civilized world.[103] And although Kant was certain that it would be a long time before we reached this final goal, there would always be signs along the way. The mere fact that states persisted in using the word *right* in justifying their hostilities toward one another, even if in practice this was "superfluous pedantry," was, he believed, evidence that behind their openly aggressive and uncivilized behavior there lurked an uneasy sense of moral obligation toward fellow human beings. And this alone "proves that there is to be found in the human being a still greater, though at present dormant, moral disposition to eventually become master of the evil principle within him (which he cannot deny), and also to hope for this from others."[104] And one of the clearest outward signs of the apparent progress of the human will was what he called, in 1798, in the last work he ever published, "The revolution of a gifted people which we have seen unfolding in our day."[105]

IV

Many educated Europeans at the time had had similarly enthusiastic reactions to the early phases of the French Revolution. "O times," wrote William Wordsworth in 1805, looking back on his youth (he had been nineteen in 1789),

> *In which the meagre, stale, forbidding ways*
> *Of custom, law, and statute, took at once*
> *The attraction of a country in romance!*
> *When Reason seemed the most to assert her rights*
> *When most intent on making of herself*
> *A prime enchantress—to assist the work,*
> *Which then was going forward in her name!*[106]

And not only was Reason clearly asserting her rights in the streets of Paris; so, too, were those attachments that human beings were supposed to feel toward one another. France in the first years of the Revolution seemed to many who visited it to be a new kind of cosmopolitan society, where only the stubborn adherents of the old order and the old religion could fail to feel at home. "Is it really true that I am in Paris?" asked the linguist Joachim Campe in 1789.

> I could have embraced the first people who met us. They seemed no longer French, and we had for the moment ceased to be Branden-

> burgers and Brunswickers. All national differences and prejudices seemed to have melted away. They had regained their long-lost rights, and we felt that we were men. . . . Laugh as you will! I felt as if the whole French nation had entered into brotherhood with me.[107]

The Revolution had restored to an entire people the sense of its own dignity that generations of kings and priests had denied it. It had created, self-consciously, a people, a *patria,* in which even the dispossessed could take personal pride. And it had harnessed this concept of nationhood to the idea of rights that the individual might claim, not merely as Frenchmen but also as "men." (Although not, as yet, as women—not that this would have troubled Kant.)

The full meaning of the Revolution had been visible to all. Some welcomed it, hoping that it would soon spread throughout Europe. Others reviled it. But only Kant saw—or thought he saw—its full political and moral significance. As Karl Marx said of him later, what he had written was, in effect, "the German political theory of the French Revolution." On learning of the fall of the Bastille on July 14, 1789, he is said for the first time in his adult life to have abandoned his daily walk (Kant was a man of fixed habits) so that he could read every newspaper available. His friend and biographer Reinhold Bernhard Jachmann described him as being so eager to know of every critical event as soon as it happened that he "would have walked miles to the post-office to collect [the papers]; and we could give him no greater pleasure than to bring him the latest and most authentic news from France." He was a man whose "knowledge of the world and of men, permitted him to anticipate in the progress of events; every incident which retarded or accelerated that progress was followed by him with the keenest interest." He even acquired a reputation as something of a prophet, and in the words of Thomas De Quincey's later admiring biographical sketch, "threw out many conjectures, and what were then accounted paradoxical anticipations, especially in regard to military operations, which were as punctually fulfilled."[108] And when, in 1792, he heard of the creation of the Republic, he is said to have declared, "Lord let your servant depart in peace, for I have lived to see this remarkable day."

The French revolutionaries, still beleaguered within a staunchly monarchist Europe and eager for foreign support wherever they could find it, responded in kind. It was widely rumored, on the basis of an article in the most popular of the Königsberg newspapers, the *Königsberger Zeitung,* that Emmanuel-Joseph Sieyès, one of the most influential, and more moderate, theorists of the Revolution (who subsequently helped Napoleon to seize power in November 1799), had asked Kant for his help in drafting a new French constitution. Rumors then began to circulate throughout Europe that Kant was about to become the lawmaker to the new republic. *Toward Perpetual Peace,* which, in contrast with Kant's other works was relatively easy to digest and by the standards of the day had already become something of a best seller in German, was rapidly translated into French and published in Königsberg and Paris simultaneously.[109] It was greeted with understandable enthusiasm by the revolutionary journal *Le Moniteur:* "The celebrated Kant . . . has lent the power of his name to the cause of the republican Constitution. Six hundred leagues away from Paris, a philosopher professes republicanism, not of France but of the whole world."[110] In January 1796 the Directory (the five-man executive council that had taken power after the fall of Robespierre and the end of the Terror) sent an envoy, Charles Théremin, to persuade Kant to place his considerable international reputation at the service of the Republic, because its members claimed to believe that "the study of this philosophy by the French would be a complement of the Revolution" and that "Europe had now reached the state that it could only be governed by philosophers."[111] Kant refused the offer on the grounds that he could not become involved in the internal affairs of another nation. Always wary of how his unpredictable sovereign would react, he had no desire, at his advanced age, to leave Königsberg and no desire to become embroiled in the business of practical politics. His republic, and the "cosmopolitan right," were both, as he says again and again, constructs of reason. His business was to think them. It was up to others to make them happen.

Anyone familiar with Kant's earlier writings, however, would have found this enthusiasm for revolution somewhat puzzling. In 1784 he had denied that any revolution could ever bring about a "true reform in one's way of thinking" but would only ever result in the substitution of new prejudices for old ones, a position he repeated with few qualifications in 1793.[112] His position, however, is perhaps not so inconsistent as it might at first appear. For what seems to have troubled him most about what he described as the "revolts by which Switzerland, the United Netherlands, and Great Britain attained their much-acclaimed constitutions" is that the violent transition from one constitution to another by means of rebellion can only ever be achieved by the people acting not "as *commonwealth,* rather only as a mob," and the outcome can only be "a state of anarchy . . . with all the horrors it brings with it." Switzerland, the United Netherlands, and Great Britain turned out to be successful, but had they not, "the reader of the history of those uprisings would see in the execution of their now so celebrated initiators nothing other than the deserved punishment of persons guilty of high treason."[113] And no new constitution born out of anarchy can ever be truly representative of the entire polity. For what for Kant was crucial for the legitimacy of any constitution was what he called the "law of continuity" (*lex continuo*) because it is precisely that which separates civil society from the lawless condition of the state of nature. On his apparent reading of the events of May 1789, however, no disruption of the *lex continuo* had in fact occurred. It was Louis XVI himself who, by calling the Estates-General in an attempt to resolve a financial crisis, had voluntarily, if inadvertently, surrendered the "supreme authority" within the French state to the people, and "the consequence was that the monarch's sovereignty wholly disappeared (it was not merely suspended) and passed to the people." Once anything like this has happened a situation is created in which "the united people does not merely represent the sovereign: it is itself the sovereign."[114] On Kant's understanding, therefore, there had never existed a moment during the entire course of the Revolution in which "the entire juridical condition [of the state] was nullified" and that would subsequently have made any attempt to bring about change through the "violent overthrow of an already existing defective constitution" undesirable.[115] The *Declaration of the Rights of Man* and the formal declaration of the Republic in September 1792 had not constituted a "revolution" in this sense; they had been the legal instruments for the creation of a regime that could be cast not only as a liberation from the corrosive and unrepresentative rule of kings but also as an attempt by an enlightened people to build for themselves a new cosmopolitan future.

For Kant, it seemed as if the Revolution had arisen not from simple anger or popular discontent (like so many of the ultimately inconsequential uprisings that had preceded it), nor from some brand of religious fanaticism, but had instead been brought about by what he called "metaphysics." Here, he believed, was evidence of something that had hitherto been unheard of: that ideas could be responsible for changes in the real world.[116] It was a confirmation of his claim that any state in which "power belongs not to human beings but to the law" could not be derived "from the experience of those, who have hitherto found it most to their advantage" but only "*a priori* by reason from the ideal of a rightful association of human beings under public laws as such"; for this "a metaphysics is certainly required."[117]

Kant's attitude toward the Revolution, even his public silence on the extremes of the Terror, was, Jachmann believed, driven by his intense desire to see "the realization of his ideal," not out of any personal vanity but from "the impersonal sympathy of a citizen of the world and of an independent philosopher who observes the construction of a state on the basis of reason, exactly in the same way as a scientist observes an experiment destined to confirm his hypothesis."[118]

"We have our revolts in the mind," remarked the German Romantic poet Heinrich Heine, who loathed Kant, "and the French in the world of matter: we were as excited over the destruction of the old dogmatism, as they over the storming of the Bastille."[119] But in the opinion of most of those who saw in the Revolution something akin to Wordsworth's new dawn for humankind, "not in Utopia, subterranean fields, or some secreted island" but in "the world of all of us," the two had gone, inextricably, hand in hand.

Jachmann's analogy with the natural scientist, however, was not quite right. The Revolution had not gone so far as to confirm Kant's vision of a future world of allied republics. What it had done was to provide a sign that such a world might one day be possible. "Even one single example," Kant had written, "can be sufficient sign in the course of events that it [a republican constitution] must happen one day. One cannot foresee that it will be accomplished, but only that [men] will try it so often that it must eventually be realized."[120] What the Revolution had shown him was that certain individuals, at least, were capable of being moved to the point of acting on ideas that were more than simply hedonistic and that were directed toward the common rather than the individual good.[121] In reply to Moses Mendelssohn's view that, while individuals may progress, mankind "maintains in all periods of time roughly the same level of morality, the same measure of religion and irreligion, of virtue and vice, of happiness and misery," Kant had reaffirmed his conviction that "since the human race is constantly advancing with respect to culture (as its natural end), it is also to be conceived as progressing toward what is better with respect to the moral end of its existence." Whatever limitations he might himself have been guilty of—and he was certain that he was "not so good in the moral character required of me"—Kant was nevertheless convinced that "for all practical purposes human progress is possible." This "hope for better times" had always driven the better part of mankind—the enlightened and civilized part—to attempt to "do something useful for the common good." No scientist had ever given up on the hope that something that had not worked once might not be made to work again. Hot-air balloons—a novelty in Kant's day—were for him proof enough of this. They did not always work. But eventually, with perseverance, the balloonist would rise from the ground and drift majestically away over the rooftops. And as for the sadly fashionable idea that mankind was growing ever more decadent, he was convinced that this was simply an illusion based on the fact that "as our standards are forever improving, so the judgments we pass on our own day are inescapably harsher than they were in the past."[122] And the French Revolution was clearly a sign that such a future was possible. It might, he conceded, in the end turn out to have been so costly, so "filled with misery and atrocities," that "a sensible man, were he boldly to hope to execute it successfully the second time, would never resolve to make the experiment at such a cost." But what mattered for Kant, what made the Revolution an outward indication of something far larger than itself, was the "wishful participation which borders closely on enthusiasm" that was to be found "in the hearts of all spectators." And as, for Kant, "genuine enthusiasm [as opposed to the fanatical religiosity that usually went under that name] always moves only toward what is ideal and, indeed, to what is purely moral, such as the concept of right," this, he believed, could "have no other cause than a moral disposition in the human race."[123]

Kant's "cosmopolitan right," the vision of a humanity moving steadily toward a cosmopolitan future free of strife and hostility in which all humans might pursue their own individual ends without somehow endangering those of others was—or was intended to be—the inescapable conclusion of the Enlightenment project. Was it not reasonable to expect, asked Condorcet, of what he saw, by the shaded light of his candle, as a bright shimmering world that lay just ahead, "that the human race would perfect itself by the new discoveries in the arts and sciences, and consequently by securing through them the means to acquire personal well-being and communal prosperity; be it in the progress in the principle of conduct, and in practical morality; be it finally in the real perfection of intellectual, moral, and physical faculties?" His answer, like Kant's, was that "the experience of the past, from the observation of the progress which science and civilization have made up until now, in the analysis of the forward march of the human mind and of the development of its faculties," was at least sufficient to believe "that nature has set no limits to our hope."[124] Now all that the future would hold was ever-increasing understanding, ever-expanding enlightenment, which would "have no limit other than the lifespan of the universe."[125]

Kant has left his mark on almost all thinking about the possibility of some future world order, from his own day to this. All the international institutions, from the creation of the League of Nations in 1919, of the United Nations in 1945, to that of the European Union between the Treaty of Rome in 1957 and the Treaty of Lisbon in 2009, bear some trace of the idea that, although we are still very far from achieving anything resembling a cosmopolitan existence, we have indeed reached the stage at which "a violation of rights in one part of the world is felt everywhere." The UN, wrote the idiosyncratic Alfred Zimmern, a classicist and key policy maker during the First World War, who exercised a powerful influence on its ideological formation, was "the *res-publica* with which it is our duty to concern ourselves" and that "extends to the ends of the earth."[126] It was to be, in time, the expression of Kant's "cosmopolitan right." Even Mikhail Gorbachev cited *Toward Perpetual Peace* in his speech accepting the Nobel Peace Prize in 1990.

In 1948, on the 150th anniversary of the publication of *Toward Perpetual Peace,* the great German émigré legal scholar and political scientist (who had been involved in the drafting of the postwar German constitution) Carl Joachim Friedrich wrote a book called *Inevitable Peace* to mark the occasion. He was not, he said, himself a Kantian, yet the events of the intervening century and a half had allowed him to see, cautiously to be sure and with many qualifications, that "the philosophy of man's history was combined with the idea of freedom and self-realization in a critical rationalism which enables us to resolve some of the most persistent ideological conflicts of our time."[127]

Now, more than half a century later, as old ideologies have failed and new, yet more irrational ones have come to take their place, we cannot be so confident. The League of Nations passed rapidly into oblivion. The UN is frequently accused of being corrupt, inept, ineffectual, and far from impartial. And, at the time of writing (2012), the EU is facing the first major crisis of its brief existence, from which many—although not I—think that it may not emerge intact. Yet for all that, it is also becoming increasingly evident that, to quote Habermas, states have become "increasingly enmeshed in the horizontal networks of a global society."[128] And if there is any kind of future still in Friedrich's belief, it will be not to Kant alone that it will owe its inspiration but to the entire Enlightenment ambition to create a historically grounded human science that would one day lead to the creation of a universal civilization capable of making all individuals independent, autonomous, freed of dictates from above and below, self-knowing, and dependent solely upon one another for survival.

CONCLUSION: ENLIGHTENMENT AND ITS ENEMIES

I

FOR KANT, the French Revolution had been a turning point in world history, the evidence that his long-held belief in the ineluctable progress of mankind toward a republican, cosmopolitan existence was demonstrably true. For others, however, in particular for those who had lived through the Revolution and its aftermath, the lessons to be drawn were very different. The Revolution of 1789, when the French had briefly created a constitutional monarchy, had, said Richard Price, been the moment when the seed that "Montesquieu, Fenelon, Turgot, etc." had sown in France had "taken root and is now growing up to a glorious harvest. To the information they conveyed by their writings we owe those revolutions in which every friend of mankind is now exulting."[1] Those revolutions that had forced the king to defer to the Estates-General and then led to a new constitution in 1791 had been the true children of the Enlightenment. Subsequent events, however—the trial and execution of the king and queen and the creation of the so-called Reign of Terror—cast a very different light on the whole process. Between 1793 and 1794 the "Committee of Public Safety," dominated by the "incorruptible" Maximilien Robespierre and the very young demagogue Louis-Antoine-Léon Saint-Just, attempted to transform France not merely into a republic but into what Robespierre called "a Virtuous Republic," one that would "substitute morality for egoism, honesty for love of honor, principles for conventions, duties for decorum, the empire of reason for the tyranny of fashion." And such a republic, in Robespierre's view, could only be created through terror, "without which virtue has no power."[2] Thousands, and not only aristocrats and other more obvious "enemies of the Revolution" but even its intended beneficiaries, like the unfortunate seamstress Mary Angelica Plaisant, who was overheard to say that she did not give a "a fig for the nation," lost their heads to Dr. Joseph-Ignace Guillotin's new humane instrument of execution, the "National Razor," in order to protect the purity of the new republic.[3]

The Terror wholly altered the subsequent perception of the Revolution and demonstrated to what lengths "licentiousness" as opposed to "liberty"—as James Madison had expressed it—would inevitably lead.[4] What he called the "possibility of setting law on the throne," wrote the German poet Friedrich Schiller in 1794, in bitter resignation, had been nothing but a "vain hope." Now, with the Revolution in effect dissolved into a form of autocracy, the whole world had turned on the one hand "to the savage state, on the other to complete lethargy. In other words, to the two extremes of human depravity, and both united in a single epoch!"[5]

Behind this catastrophe it was easy for many to see the influence of the more radical figures of the Enlightenment. The destruction of "the system," which had originally only been an intellectual project, had eventually brought down the entire edifice of society, without ever having suggested very clearly what would take its place. Kant had been right. The Revolution was proof that "metaphysics" could alter the course of human affairs. And it had been a disaster. The French constitution, said the conservative Hanoverian statesman August Wilhelm Rehberg—described by Jachmann as "the finest mind" among all Kant's students, derided by Fichte as a German Sophist—differed from all other constitutions "which had ever been established, including that of the United States of North America," in having been dreamt up out of nothing by "savants and men of state seized by Ideas."[6] This was not meant as praise. In Rehberg's view, constitutions grew up over time; they were the product of experience and reflection, not of "metaphysics," and while "the laws of nature and of reason" are fixed and immutable, those of "human understanding" are, and must be, constantly changing.[7] Like Edmund Burke, with whom he has always been closely linked, Rehberg deplored the ways in which the savants of the Revolution—whom he identified as Montesquieu, Rousseau, Voltaire, the abbé Mably, and Raynal—had manipulated the "metaphysics of politics" so as to eliminate every memory of all past "constitutions, customary rights, and conditions" so that they might finally be able to "play with citizens as if they were pieces on a chess board."[8] The result had been inescapable: destruction, chaos, and bloodshed.

But for all this postrevolutionary angst, in particular in Germany, the "Enlightenment" had, in fact, always been identified with reform rather than revolution. None of the *philosophes,* not even the most radical, not even Rousseau, had openly proposed armed insurrection as a means of bringing about his idealized state, although, like many before him, Rousseau was also highly ambiguous about quite how he did think it would come into being. Most of the major figures of the French Enlightenment were already dead by 1789, but many had been aware, as early as the 1760s, that some cataclysm was on its way, which at least some of them looked upon as both inevitable and desirable. "Everything I observe is sowing the seeds of a revolution," Voltaire had written in 1764, "that will inevitably come to pass, but which I will not have the pleasure of witnessing." There is some truth in the Catholic reactionary Louis-Gabriel-Ambroise de Bonald's sneer that Voltaire, Rousseau, D'Alembert, Helvétius, "and other writers of the same period," were responsible for advocating such radical transformations in society that, had they ever been put into practice, "they would have detested, and to which, sooner or later they would have fallen victim."[9]

Rousseau, politically the most extreme of the *philosophes,* was the most obvious target for the anti-Revolutionaries. Robespierre may have been the architect of the Terror, wrote the German poet Heinrich Heine in 1833, but Robespierre had merely been "the bloody hand that drew from the womb of time the body whose soul Rousseau had created."[10] Rousseau, in particular, had become something of a patron saint for the new Republic. During the Revolution passages from his one major, and potentially most inflammatory, political work, *The Social Contract,* had been read aloud to enthusiastic, if also no doubt mystified, crowds, and streets had been named after both it and him. In 1794 his body had been disinterred and taken to the Panthéon, along with a copy of *The Social Contract* on a velvet cushion. "Ah," wrote Robespierre after the event, "if he had witnessed this revolution which has carried him to the Panthéon, who can doubt that his generous soul would have embraced with rapture the cause of justice and equality."[11]

But it was not only Rousseau who was at fault. For many, in particular those who had experienced both the Revolution and the Napoleonic Wars that followed, the entire Revolutionary process, from the storming of the Bastille to the restoration of the Bourbon monarchy in 1815, had been the inescapable, and wholly deplorable, consequence of the Enlightenment insistence that mankind had, in Kant's formulation, to rid itself of all those "dogmas and formulas, those mechanical instruments for rational use (or rather misuse) of [mankind's] natural endowments," which were "the ball and chain of an everlasting permanent minority."[12] In the subsequent retelling, the whole Enlightenment project had been directly responsible for the collapse of the *ancien régime.* "If we see a man," remarked the immensely influential historian and literary critic Hippolyte Taine in 1875, "whose constitution is a little weak, but who otherwise appears to be healthy and of untroubled habits, drink what is evidently a new potion, and then fall suddenly to the ground, slavering at the mouth, delirious and in convulsions," we would need no complex analysis to tell us that what he had drunk was a poison. Such had been French society in the eighteenth century. And the poison was the philosophy of the Enlightenment. "Today," complained Kant's pupil Johann Heinrich Hirsch in 1794, as the Terror came finally to an end, "heresy, freethinking, Jacobinism, and the rejection of authority, however respectable, are all called enlightenment. Today enlightenment is treason."[13] He was speaking of Germany, but much the same sentiments were echoed over most of Europe and would grow deeper as the Napoleonic Wars unfolded across the continent. "Enlightenment," the "Rights of Man," "Republicanism," and "Cosmopolitanism" all became identified in the minds of the cautious, conservative elites of Europe with the destructive power of Revolution. As late as 1910, with Napoleon's final defeat nearly a century in the past, Sir Gerard Lowther, the British ambassador to Istanbul, wrote home to warn his masters in Whitehall that the "Young Turks," officially known as the Party of Union and Progress, who were set on creating a new modern Turkish nation out of the crumbling ruins of the Ottoman Sultanate, saw themselves as "the vanguard of awakened Asia" and were now bent on "imitating the French revolution and its godless and leveling methods."[14]

The most eloquent, most powerful, and perhaps most perceptive of those who believed that they could see an unbroken line reaching from the Enlightenment to the Terror and thence to the collapse of all established order, all religion, all civilization, was Joseph de Maistre. De Maistre was a diplomat from the northern Italian kingdom of Savoy, although he wrote mostly about France and looked upon the French nation as something close to a chosen people. He spent the years between 1803 and 1817 as ambassador to the court of Tsar Alexander I at St. Petersburg, where he composed *The Evenings of St. Petersburg, or Dialogues on the Temporal Government of Providence,* the most ferocious, uncompromising, and sometimes far-fetched of all the counterrevolutionary, counter-Enlightenment writings of the nineteenth century. For De Maistre, not only was monarchy, supported by a hereditary aristocracy, the only legitimate form of government, he even hoped one day to see a theocracy established across Europe under the supreme jurisdiction of the papacy. "A fierce absolutist," the literary critic Émile Faguet called him, "a furious theocrat, and intransigent legitimist, apostle of a monstrous Trinity composed of Pope, King, and Hangman."[15]

De Maistre was certainly an extremist. But he was no mere demagogue, and in his own way he understood better than many what the project of the Enlightenment had really been. For him it was self-evident that the members of the detestable "philosophic sect" had been "the principal authors of the Revolution."[16] But not because they had ever actually advocated revolution. Their abiding sin had been to take as their subject "man and his environment," so that "everything that might be said about his soul, about his origins, about his destiny was only secondary, and should all be derived not from revelation but from the observations which they had provided."[17] It had been the likes of Voltaire who had made the Revolution, and the atrocities it had perpetrated, possible by unmasking centuries of divinely sanctioned restraint. Voltaire, "whom blind enthusiasts have placed in the Panthéon," was, in De Maistre's view, "perhaps more guilty of the judgment of the Divinity than [Jean-Paul] Marat, for he may have made Marat, and he certainly did more evil than Marat."[18] It had been the "philosophers" who had sought to destroy religion by tearing it down from the exalted place it had occupied in what he called "France's great century," the seventeenth. In the "age of the Sun King," he wrote, "religion, valor, and science had been put into equilibrium." The age that had followed, the "age of philosophy," the "age of reason" and of light, had, in De Maistre's view, been nothing less than "a war to the death" between Christianity and what he referred to contemptuously as "philosophism," in which, if only for a brief while, he hoped, "philosophism" had won.[19] The architects of the Revolution, and of the Terror that had followed, had merely reaped the whirlwind. In his view, individual humans were incapable of the untutored responsibility the *philosophes* had urged upon them. Hobbes had been right. Man is a wolf to man, worse, in fact. For the wolf is equipped with certain innate instincts of restraint. Not so man. "He kills to obtain food and kills to clothe himself. He kills to protect himself and he kills in order to attack. He kills in order to defend himself; he kills in order to instruct himself, and to amuse himself. He kills in order to kill."[20] The only force that can control him is society, and society is not something built by a "science of man." It is imposed from above, created slowly over time, through reverence and obedience. What keeps men in check is not mutual understanding, nor anything so remote from any individual's actual experience as love of one's own kind or mutual benevolence. It is awe. And awe is enforced by religion, by custom, by habit—by what Voltaire and his whole crew had dubbed "prejudice." It was these things that, when clustered together, formed individual nations; it was these, and these alone, that had made the savage beast, that "deformed child, robust and ferocious, on whom the flame of intelligence casts only a pale and intermittent light," into a civil being.[21] Once out of nature, "man," that gross abstraction that had been the Enlightenment's cherished object, simply vanished. "I have seen Frenchmen, Italians, Russians, etc.," De Maistre remarked sardonically. "I know, too, thanks to Montesquieu, that one can be a Persian. But as for man, I declare I have never met him in my life." Nature, he added, was a lady to whom he had never been introduced.[22]

The cosmopolitanism so beloved of the Enlightenment, if only because no one individual could possibly have any understanding of or direct acquaintance with "humanity," was an arid abstraction, a desire to shed the obligations to family, heart, and nation; it was mere high-demanding rhetoric, which could only ever lead, if taken seriously, as it had been in France, to the collapse of all social, political, and religious order. The entire objective of the Enlightenment, in the opinion of Edmund Burke, could be summarized in a single sentence: "Benevolence to the whole species, and want of feeling for every individual with whom the professors come in contact, form the character of the new philosophy."[23] It was a common complaint. Almost every major Enlightenment figure was subjected to a measure of the same treatment, some with more justification than others. "Friend of men," sneered the nineteenth-century English historian of the French Revolution Thomas Carlyle of the Marquis de Mirabeau, who had helped to have his own son incarcerated, "and enemy of almost every man he had to do with."[24]

II

These outbursts were not, however, merely instinctive reactions to the horrors unleashed by the Revolution. They were also the elaboration of arguments that predated the Revolution and that, initially at least, had been a direct response to Kant's view of Enlightenment and Kant's cosmopolitanism. In 1784, the same year in which Kant published his famous essay "What Is Enlightenment?," Johann Georg Hamann wrote a brief, tortured essay entitled "Metacritique on the Purism of Reason." Hamann, the "magus of the north," of whom Hegel said that he was "not only . . . original . . . but *an* Original" and whose writings "do not so much *have* a particular style, as they *are* style," was something of a crank (whom Goethe, although he thought him the "brightest head of his time," once shrewdly compared to Vico). Despite remaining an impoverished, independent scholar for almost his entire life, he exercised a great influence on the early Romantic movement in Germany.[25] He was also perhaps Kant's most dogged, and often most perceptive, critic.[26] Despite his often tortuous, elusive, and erratic prose, his critique of Kant was fundamentally a simple and telling one. The "enlightenment of our century," or at least Kant's version of it, was, Hamann thought, "a mere northern light," pale and insubstantial, "from which can be prophesied no cosmopolitan chiliasm except in a night-cap and by the stove."[27] Kant's entire enterprise had been based upon a simple illusion, what Hamann called "the partly misunderstood, partly failed attempt to make reason independent of all tradition and custom, and belief in them." The only position from which any human being could examine the entire process of human understanding would be from what is now known as the "standpoint of Providence." And that, clearly, was simply not available to mere mortals. Even identifying "pure reason," as Kant had sought to do, was an absurdly impossible objective, because "the entire faculty of thought is founded upon language," and language is shaped and conditioned by its own past. It has, Hamann stated categorically, "no credential but *tradition* and *usage*." In other words, it is precisely language, the very language in which Kant had attempted to carry out his critique, which is "*the center of reason's misunderstanding with itself.*"[28] Since no individual can ever free him- (or her-) self from the languages in which he or she frames an understanding of the world, no fully "objective" account of the world can ever be possible. "Truth," as Richard Rorty has phrased it, "cannot be out there—cannot exist independently of the human mind—because sentences cannot so exist, or be out there. The world is out there, but descriptions of the world are not."[29] For Hamann, this meant that the only possible kind of knowledge available to human beings was to be found precisely in the traditions and customs that Kant was urging the enlightened person to "dare" to shed.

Hamann was a Lutheran Pietist who believed that he had been rescued from depression by reading the Bible. He believed in its literal truth and in every person's obligation to believe in it. But his argument is not that we must all agree to be bound by traditions and customs and by the dictates of those who, in Kant's words, would "do our thinking for us," because they are the expression of God's—or even nature's—law. Neither does he insist that customs, habits, and unexamined opinions must in some sense be right simply because they have been accepted by so many people for so long. What he is arguing is that our customs, our habits or beliefs—our "prejudices," if you will—are simply all that there is. "Dogmas and formulas" were not, as Kant claimed, forms of blindness. They are simply all our world is made of. Without them we are nothing, adrift, persons without identity or purpose. Anyone so rash as to discard them would stumble into the light, only to find himself lacking all direction, unable to move, unable to act, not knowing where he was or where he should go. In this condition it was little wonder that this disoriented being should have launched himself with unrestrained enthusiasm into the kind of atrocities that had followed the Revolution of 1789. Enlightened man, said Friedrich Karl von Moser, jurist, polemicist, and for a while minister in the government of Hesse-Darmstadt, would find that his seemingly heroic gesture had in fact taken from him "what he requires for comfort, light, support, and peace in the current state of education of this earthly life" and that all he had been given in exchange was "more than he can use, employ, and manage according to his powers of intellect and understanding" so that sooner or later his only recourse would be to "make his own arbitrary natural law" and bring upon himself the "ruin of all civil society." This Enlightenment, concluded Moser, "begins with philosophy and ends with scalping and cannibalism."[30] Many conservatives, then and since, have expressed—rather less eloquently for the most part—similar sentiments.

One person on whom Hamann's thinking exercised a lifelong fascination was Gottfried von Herder, Hamann's close friend and the first person to whom he had sent a copy of "Metacritique." Today Herder is seen as the main philosophical voice behind the Sturm und Drang ("Storm and Stress") movement, a forerunner of German Romanticism, which at one time included both Goethe and Schiller. Like Hamann, he had begun not only as a devoted pupil of Kant but also—which Hamann had never been—as a keen supporter of the French Enlightenment. He also shared its same broad objectives: "to collect accurate data from . . . the whole economy of the human race" and to incorporate it into a unified "science of man," as his French and British counterparts were doing.[31] It remained his lifelong project. But the conclusions to which he came were, in the end, to be very different from those of Diderot, Hume, or Condorcet—and of Kant himself.

The "human science" of the Enlightenment had led inevitably to a cosmopolitan, universalizing vision of the human world that, as we have seen, was also an expression of something, however hard to pin down, called "civilization." This allowed for a wide degree of diversity, but it also demanded a high degree of reciprocity. If, as in Christian Wolff's phrase, we—whoever we may be—must treat all others—whoever they may be—"as if they were one person with us," there can be no retreat into self-defining, self-sealing "communities," no demand for the respect of "traditions" or customs when these violate the natural and individual rights—and frequently the bodies—of individuals, no matter how much they themselves might be willing to submit to their own debasement: no "honor" killings, no enforced polygamy, no female infibulation.

Herder's view was very different. In his opinion, man in the state of nature, Rousseau's "phantom . . . natural man," had obviously never existed.[32] For far from being individual, autonomous, moral beings, humans are, in fact, naturally sociable, their characters and identities shaped only by the societies in which they have evolved. All the past ages that lay between the supposedly uncorrupted primitive state of humankind and today, those ages that Voltaire and his like had condemned as characterized by "*barbarism, miserable state authority, supersti-*

tion and *stupidity, lack of ethics* and *tastelessness*" (Herder was fond of italics), had in truth been responsible for the creation of all the conditions of human life. The monasteries and the feudal estates, the knights, the kings, and courtiers of the Gothic age, were not simply a catalogue of human errors: they were the building materials without which "poor civilly administered Europe" would have been—"*a wasteland.*"[33]

Each people—each *Volk*—was the product of a collective past. It was an indivisible entity, created by language and, above all, culture and marked by its own art, its own music and poetry, and, crucially for Herder, its own religion. And all those things had grown up slowly over time. All his experience, all his studies had persuaded him that "the history of the world is necessarily a chain of socialness and plastic tradition."[34] All you had to do was look around you to see that "nature has not established her borders between remote lands in vain." The peoples who inhabited them were each inescapably "confined to their own world"—so confined, indeed, that communication between them would seem to be virtually impossible. The European could therefore have "no idea of the boiling passion and imagination which glow in the Negro's breast; and the Hindu has no conception of the relentless desires that chase the European from one end of the world to another."[35] Every people has its own way of being human and cannot exchange it with that of any other. This is why the colonist (a particularly heinous breed of man) will, sooner or later, find himself the victim of triumphant nature. Where, Herder asked, "are the conquests, the factories, and invasions of former times?" The answer was not hard to find. Even as the rapacious Europeans were still trampling across the face of the earth, he could look confidently forward to a time when the "still breath of climate has dissipated and consumed them, and it was not difficult for the native to give the finishing strokes to the rotten tree."[36]

Even happiness, which had for so long been taken to be, together with pain, the common experience of all humans, was for Herder equally contingent, equally fragmentary, and equally linked to a particular culture, a particular place. Herder did not agree with Kant that happiness was merely a "shadowy image" of something much more fundamental to the human condition.[37] But he also refused to accept the idea that it was so central to the nature of humanity that it had to be, for every human being everywhere, the same. "The ideal of happiness," he wrote, "itself *changes* with every situation and point of the compass," for what else is it but "the satisfaction of wants, the attainment of goals, and the gentle satisfaction of needs"? Rather than being integral to the human condition, it grows "out of the land, the time, and the place." And as for all those nice tales of endless progression, that "pet idea," as he called it, that everything in human existence was leading to "*more virtue* and *happiness of individual human beings,*" that were being peddled by the Kants, the Diderots, and the Condorcets, well, these too were only "novels, novels that no one believes, at least not the true pupil of history and the human heart."[38]

For all this, however, it is a mistake to see in Herder merely the "father of German nationalism" (or of nationalism in general), as he has so often been described. Something of an antirationalist he certainly was, but that does not mean that he was the kind of ignorant, unthinking, sentimentalist usually identified as a "nationalist." He was in most respects a liberal, a republican, and an egalitarian, to a far greater degree indeed than Kant. For Herder, cultures may have been isolated and incommensurable, but, with a few exceptions, this did not make them of unequal worth. Indeed, comparison between them was, he thought, probably futile. Not that Herder's relativism, as it has been presented, was irreproachable. He took, for instance, a very dim view of the Chinese, those "people endowed by nature with small eyes, snub noses, flat foreheads, scant beards, large ears, and protruding bellies," but such racism—and it is hard to see it as anything else—is rare in his work and unassociated with any wider theory of racial difference.[39] By and large he looked upon the physical differences, skin color, cranial configuration, size, and so on, which Kant, and subsequently all the racial theorists of the nineteenth century, saw as the distinguishing features of individual races, as utterly insignificant. Some people were white, some were black, some red, some yellow. There must clearly exist a natural reason for these distinctions—the most obvious, in his view, being climate. But nothing of any intellectual or moral significance could be derived from it. "The Negro," as he put it, "has as much right to consider the white man a degenerate, a born albino freak, as the white man considers him a beast, a black animal." No natural history of humanity of the kind Herder aspired to write could be based upon what he referred to as—in dismissive allusion to Kant—"the so-called races [*Rasen*]" of mankind.[40]

For Herder, Kantian cosmopolitanism was a vain, foolish objective, doomed to collapse into yet another expression of the "universal monarchy" Kant himself had so feared, precisely because it was an attempt to weld together what nature had intended to keep apart. All peoples are essentially incommensurable with one another (which also makes nonsense of any common moral standard for all of them) and should all be treated as equally valid in their difference. What we call "ethnocentrism" was for Herder absurd, as absurd as the delusions of the "madman of Piraeus," who believed that all inventions must be Greek simply because those were the only ones he knew. "The Negro, the [native] American, the Mongol," he wrote,

> has gifts, talents, pre-formed dispositions which the European does not have. Perhaps the sum is equal only in different proportions and compensations. We can be certain that what in the *human type* was able to develop on our round earth has developed or will develop—for who could prevent it from doing so? The original form, the *prototype of humanity,* hence lies not in a single nation or single region of the earth; it is the abstracted concept from all exemplars of human nature in both hemispheres. The *Cherokee* and the *Huswana,* the *Mongol* and the *Gonaqua,* are as much letters in the great word of our species as the most civilized Englishman or Frenchmen.[41]

It was foolish, criminal, for these civilized Englishmen and Frenchmen to wish to impose themselves and their much-vaunted scientific achievements upon the entire world. "Steer thy frigate to Otaheite," he told Bougainville and Cook contemptuously, "bid thy cannon roar along the shores of the New Hebrides, still you are not superior in skill to the inhabitants of the South Sea islands who guides with art the boat he has constructed with his own hands."[42] Not superior, but certainly very different. And if that is the case, if no one can really know what it is like to be an African or an Indian except Africans and Indians, if all cultures are hermetic, divided by nature, then there can be no grounds on which they can be evaluated (or judged). But then neither can there be—and this is what separates Herder most sharply from his enlightened predecessors—any reason for caring very much about them either. And if, as Herder believed, the main passion that any *Volk* inspires in another is most likely to be "*jealousy, feeling of honor in their race* and their *superiority,*" then there is also no reason to suppose that conflict and hatred will ever vanish from the world.

Herder himself may not have been any very obvious kind of proto-nationalist, or proto-"communitarian," for that matter. But his view of humankind as divided into distinct nations, each with a separate, unchangeable culture, lent considerable force to the idea that human identity was made up of precisely those traditions and customs and the languages that derived from them, which, according at least to Hamann, Kant had attempted to dispense with in his construction of the fully free, fully mature person. Take it but one step further and it becomes possible to argue either that there is no such thing as a "human nature" or that it is largely irrelevant. This was not Herder's view. He had, indeed, a very clear conception of the common humanity linking all peoples. But that did not prevent later generations, down to the Nazis and the ideologues of apartheid, from claiming him as an ancestor.

For Herder's nineteenth-century successors, the Enlightenment came increasingly to be seen not as a moment of liberation but as a period of restraint and limitation, of the narrowing of the grand horizons that only the power of the imagination and the force of the passions could bring about. By equating "Enlightenment" largely with Kant, it became possible to represent it as a movement wholly concerned with the triumph of "reason" and therefore as the purveyor of an undifferentiated, absolutist, bloodless concept of humanity. For the Romantics, nature, which the Enlightenment had tried to restrain through "civilization" (a word that in German had, by the end of the eighteenth century, come to imply simple technological domination), became an indomitable stream that ran through all humankind and that made of man, in Herder's words, "the organ of the sense of his God in all living things of creation."[43] Once a vision of freedom, of self-determination, the Enlightenment was now rendered as a form of enslavement. Once "aristocratic," it now came to be seen as—worst of all things—"bourgeois," and "petty-bourgeois" at that. No longer the hope of any kind of "philosophical sect," it now became a religion of shopkeepers. "The great destroyer," Heinrich Heine called Kant, whose "petty-bourgeois" values, paradoxically, shared so much with those of Robespierre:

> Both had the same prosaic honesty. Both possessed the same talent of suspicion, only that in the one it manifested itself against thought and was called criticism, whilst in the other it was directed against mankind and was styled republican virtue. . . . Nature had destined them for weighing out coffee and sugar, but fate decided that they should weigh out other things, and in the scales of the one it laid a king, in the scales of the other a God. . . . And they both gave the correct weight![44]

From Herder and Heine, through Hegel and on to Martin Heidegger, the founding father of "postmodernism," a vision of the Enlightenment emerged that was as cold, toneless, monotonous, and calculating as the bourgeois who had supposedly embraced it. It had tried to crush out of all human life difference, heroism, and desire. It had replaced passion with politeness and wisdom with wit. It had also, with even greater and more determined ferocity, tried to eliminate religion, leaving only what Hegel called this "stain of unsatisfied longing."[45] And in its place all that remained was the empty sentimentality of the pious—pure feeling, in Hegel's term—while thought, for its part, had gone on to deal only with "pure thinghood." In the place of a once-rich potential for human expression, in which feeling and thought had been complementary, all the Enlightenment had to offer was the endlessly barren plains of the cosmopolitan world and the insatiable demands of the "empire of reason."[46]

At worst it had allowed itself to be transformed into the kind of universalism that Anacharsis Cloots had urged upon the National Assembly in the name of "the Country formerly called France," a distortion most clearly embodied, in both theory and practice, by Napoleon. From his final captivity, marooned on the rocky island of St. Helena, Napoleon apparently told his secretary Emmanuel de Las Cases, in November 1807, that his "great design" had been to bring together the "the agglomeration, the concentration of the same geographical peoples" of Europe that "revolutions and politics had broken down" and to make of them "one and the same national body," over which would reign one indivisible "unity of laws, of principles, of opinions, sentiments, views, and interests."

Napoleon was nothing if not an opportunist, and even with the possibility of any return to power—and France—firmly behind him, he might still have been hoping to save for himself an honorable place in history. But if he did have any coherent or consistent political objective, it might indeed have been to create a pan-European state under French sovereignty, exercised, if possible, in the different regions by members of his own family. The "sisterhood of republics" of which the new Europe was to be composed was ultimately to have only one president (or in Napoleon's case, an emperor), a single code of laws—the famous Code Napoléon—a new, rational system of weights and measures (the metric system), a single educational system, even a new calendar—and all of these were to be French. For "what people," he wrote to his feckless brother Jérôme, whom he had made king of Westphalia, "having enjoyed the benefits of a wise and liberal administration" such as his, would ever wish to return to the "arbitrary government" under which it had previously lived? Or as he is reported as saying rather more brutally elsewhere, "What is good for the French is good for everyone."[47] The philosophy of the Enlightenment, which, as Horkheimer and Adorno put it, had "put the fear of death into infamy in the eighteenth century," had chosen in the end "to serve that very infamy under Napoleon."[48]

III

Any direct causal link between the Enlightenment, the Revolution, and the Revolutionary Wars that followed, although apparently obvious, is, however, a spurious one. Had the Enlightenment in fact been a precursor to the Revolution and to Napoleon, had it been the intellectual instrument that had allowed Saint-Just to believe that he could create the world anew, then—perhaps paradoxically—it would not today be of much lasting importance. The Revolution transformed European society and made a lasting impact, directly and indirectly, on the shaping of the modern world. But not because it succeeded in bringing into being anything resembling what the English philosopher Bernard Williams called "Saint-Just's illusion," the illusion that time could be reversed, that the virtues that had supposedly sustained the Roman Republic could be revived in modern France.[49] The liberals of the post-Revolutionary era, Alexis de Tocqueville, Benjamin Constant, and John Stuart Mill, saw the Revolution—for all its admitted excesses, for all that it had finally collapsed into the brief but bloody reign of Napoleon—as a necessary evil that had ultimately cleared the way for the liberal-democratic order that ultimately came to replace the *ancien régime* throughout Europe. It had, as Tocqueville said of it in 1858, "regulated, coordinated, and legalized the effects of a great cause."[50] That "great cause" was the cause of what today we might call loosely "liberal democracy," which, for all the suffering the West has undergone in the succeeding centuries (not to mention what the rest of the world has suffered at the hands of the West), is still very much the political system under which most of us now live. And it, too, was a child of the Enlightenment.

The rise of post-Napoleonic liberalism, however, was also closely associated with another movement, which later came to be called "liberal nationalism" and which emerged in those states—Italy, Poland, Greece—that after the end of the Napoleonic Wars had found themselves still under the yoke of one or another of the Great Powers. "Liberal nationalism," as its name implies, was not, as later forms of nationalism would be, the ugly assertion of national superiority, the cries of angry and ignorant people that "my country is the best," that culminated in Nazism and Fascism. It was, rather, an ecumenical reformulation of the civic patriotism on which so much of Enlightenment cosmopolitanism had itself been based.

The final defeat of Napoleon at the Battle of Waterloo on June 18, 1815, had ended the French Empire in Europe, but it had also strengthened those imperial states, Britain, Austria, Russia, and Prussia, that had contributed to his downfall. "Twenty-two years of war," wrote Giuseppe Mazzini in 1849, "had worn out Europe." When the "long-cherished peace" finally arrived, "those who had brought it were praised, no matter who they were. Blessed by victory, the old dynasties resumed their interrupted domination." On September 25, 1815, Prussia, Russia, and Austria formed the "Holy Alliance," whose objective was to restore, as far as possible, the pre-Revolutionary balance of power throughout mainland Europe. For those smaller nations, in particular the Italians and the Poles, that found themselves under the rule of one of these Great Powers, this was a massive disappointment. To them, the Alliance seemed to be anything but holy. It had, said Mazzini, undone the centuries-old division between Church and State that the Enlightenment had struggled so hard to reinforce and had ushered in a new age in which "dualism [between Church and State] of the Christian age seemed to fade into a pact of mutual love." Henceforth, these new "masters of the world had united against the future." Rather than to maintain the peace among otherwise benign Christian states, as they claimed, the true objective of this "league of unlawful powers" was to crush any kind of "progressive principle." For the Great Powers had seen very clearly that the defeat of Napoleon had not been the ultimate destruction of the principles of the Revolution, much less of the Enlightenment, and that sooner or later a new threat to their continuing authority would arise. Therefore they had made certain that every time any "oppressed or diminished nation" attempted to assert its own identity or "freely determine its own future," the so-called Holy Alliance would descend upon it "to prevent progress and protect the oppressors."[51] The Europe whose disappearance De Maistre had so lamented, with its kings, its clergy, and its hangmen (not that they had ever left), would seem to have returned—at least for a while.

Mazzini was the intellectual architect of Italian unity, an impassioned reader of Vico and Herder, a man who was known and admired throughout Europe by such dissimilar figures as John Stuart Mill and

Friedrich Nietzsche, who described him as one of the most heroic and noble characters of the age, a veritable *Übermensch*.[52] He was, said the Russian radical thinker Alexander Herzen, the "shining star" of the democratic revolutions of 1848.[53] Although he saw himself as a practical politician, a man of action, concerned with the creation of realizable ideals, and in 1849 became, for a few months, one of the triumvirs of the short-lived Roman Republic, Mazzini spent most of his adult life in poverty and in exile. He was a patriot and a nationalist (although he himself never used that word and only ever spoke of "nationality"). His voice was clearer, more powerful than many others and less embittered, despite his personal sufferings, and less grandiloquent than those of the German philosophers Johann Gottlieb Fichte and August Wilhelm Schlegel, whom he so admired. But he was also, like them, fiercely critical of all the varieties of sectarianism that had taken root in Europe in the wake of the Napoleonic Wars.[54] Mazzini had understood, as the new masters of Europe perhaps had not, that although they might have snuffed out Bonapartism and the more extreme ideals of the Revolution, what they had failed to destroy, what they would never be able to destroy, was this new, liberal ideal of the nation. It had been not the "brute force of kings," wrote Mazzini, that had brought down Napoleon, but the very idea of the nation that he had "offended with his arrogance." The new post-Revolutionary nation, as Mazzini saw it, sought to merge the earlier conception of the *patria* as a devotion to "laws and liberty" with a quasi-mystical sense of its own identity as a people. The nation-state was, as Hegel said of it, a "wholly spiritual entity" and a "spirit in its substantial rationality, and immediate actuality, and . . . therefore the immediate power on earth."[55]

Unlike the idea of the "nation" that had served to shore up the power of the monarchs of medieval Europe, Hegel's nation was, like the Enlightenment image of the *patria,* wholly detached from both the divinity and the ruler. It was composed solely of its people. For Hegel, human identity itself was an expression of what he called a *Volksgeist,* a "spirit of the people," which manifests itself in the institutions, the beliefs—in the culture, in the broadest sense of the term—of every nation. His ideal, unsurprisingly, was the ancient Greek *polis,* a community that resembles a living organism, in which the distinction between means and ends is finally transcended in that everything becomes simultaneously both an end and a means.[56] In the post-Revolutionary world, this devotion to the nation meant, in effect, becoming a part, an active part, of something larger than oneself. If subjection to a monarch had been a species of subservience, however willingly entered into, the new citizenship was a union of one with the whole. And it was only through this union that true freedom could be achieved. Patriotism, said Hegel, was "in essence that disposition, which in the normal conditions and circumstances of life, habitually knows that the community is the substantial basis and end." It is a disposition, a form of trust that "my substantial and particular interest" as an individual "is preserved and contained in the interests and end of another (in this case the state), and in the latter's relation to me as an individual. As a result, this other immediately ceases to be an other for me, and in my consciousness of this, I am free."[57] Freedom was always the final objective, and freedom could only ever have been achieved not, as the misguided advocates of Enlightenment had supposed, by individuals struggling alone in a cosmopolitan world shorn of all meaningful local attachments but only as part of something larger, grander, more imposing, and more enduring than the self. For those like Mazzini—although he criticized Hegel for what he saw as the latter's "adoration of force" and his exaggeration of the claims of the state—this new nation was the only means by which the scattered peoples of Europe might throw off the yoke of the "Holy Alliance."

The objective of the new concept of nationality was rejuvenation, and every effort at rejuvenation, wrote Mazzini, had as its ultimate objective the reconciliation of "country [*patrie*] and humanity." In its final form this would result in what he called the "blending" together of very diverse peoples. This, however, remained, as it had for Kant, a still-remote possibility, and no one should attempt to "superimpose [on the present] a world whose time has not yet come." All that could be hoped for humanity in the near future was "harmonization," and in the Europe that had emerged, fragmented and discordant, from out of the devastation of the Napoleonic Wars, that could only be undertaken by the nation. To those who would argue that the nation is a "manifestation of the past, a medieval concept that has caused much bloodshed and continues to fractionalize God's thinking on earth," his reply was that the new "nationality" was to be no "bitter war on individualism." It was not intended to foster a new sectarianism. "Ours is not a national project," he claimed, "but an international one."[58] He denounced the triple pillars of race, language, and climate on which so much exceptionalism had previously rested.[59] Much less was this to be the revival of what De Maistre had hoped for: a fierce alliance between Church and Monarch, with the nation as nothing but the extended shadow of its ruler. And when he was told by "honorable men, motivated by the best intentions," that "we no longer believe in the nation: we believe in humanity; we are Cosmopolitans," Mazzini's reply was that it was cosmopolitanism that was a "somewhat outdated idea" and something "much more vague and difficult to realize than that of Nationality." Cosmopolitanism, as his "honorable men" understood it, had become a "barren sentiment of reaction against a past which is forever dead in our own hearts."[60] Of course, he said, we are all cosmopolitans, if all that means is the approval of a general sense of benevolence and obligation toward our fellow beings and "the destruction of all barriers that separate the Peoples and provide them with opposite interests." But this is hardly enough. In the world in which he lived, cosmopolitan well-meaning was powerless. For the trouble with the cosmopolitan was that ultimately all he was concerned with was individuals. He stands, said Mazzini, in his own understanding of the Stoic circles, "at the center of an immense circle that extends itself around him, and whose limits are beyond his grasp." He is not so much wrong as ineffectual. He does what he can to the best of his abilities, but in the end all that that amounts to is charity and "mere almsgiving," and that was hardly likely to provide an adequate solution to "the social problems that occupy our attention today." The alternative had only ever been a shrunken version of Marcus Aurelius' vision of the cosmos, in which the cosmopolitans "end up placing their own county, even their own town, at the center of their theoretical edifice." In other words, their vision became, once again, what Kant had most feared: the cosmopolitan ideal expressed as universal empire, or what Mazzini tellingly called "Napoleonic" nationalities. These, however, are no longer—"thank God"—in the position to impose themselves by force of arms, any more than they are able to do so—as France, Britain, Belgium, and Germany were still trying to do in the world beyond Europe—by "the pretentious coda of permanent exclusive moral and intellectual leadership."[61] Mazzini, like Kant (whom, at least on this issue, he may never have read), believed that as more and more of the new nations that would emerge from the collapse of the post-Napoleonic world formed themselves into what Kant would have recognized as "representative republics," then they might one day be able to unite into a "United States of Europe."[62]

IV

Since Mazzini's day the "United States of Europe" has come close to being (almost) a reality; certainly, a European federation has emerged with many of the institutions that he had hoped to see (and many that he could not even have imagined), and it is still a Europe of nations. "Liberal nationalism," however, has suffered some crushing ideological blows. In Europe it degenerated into various varieties of racism, which helped to sustain the period of national empire-building in the second half of the nineteenth century and then met some kind of nemesis in Fascism and National Socialism in the middle of the twentieth. Since 1945 very few people in the West have dared to call themselves "nationalists." Americans, of both the North and the South, are generally less bashful about worshipping the trappings of their nations, its flags and national anthems, its sports, its ever-elusive "values," than Europeans. But although they, especially those on the right, like to think that their country is better than all others, they generally prefer to be thought of as patriots rather than nationalists. Elsewhere, in the Middle East, the Balkans, colonial Africa and Asia, and Ireland, nationalism became, as it had for the Italians, the Greeks, and the Poles in the nineteenth century, a means of freeing indigenous peoples from the rule, direct or indirect, of foreign imperial overlords. But, with few exceptions, the experiments of these postimperial states with nationalism have not been happy ones. Nationalism, like Marxism, was a homegrown European creed, and it did not travel well. Little wonder that the more extreme Islamic political movements, after years of unfortunate experiments with nationalism, have turned their back on it, as they have on Marxism, as just another manifestation of what in Iran is called "Westoxification."[63] In Islam there are not nations, just one people under God.

In Europe and the United States today there is another, still narrower, form of localism, often called—although the definitions are vague and the implications broad—"communitarianism," which, like nationalism, often sets itself up in opposition to the Enlightenment. A community may be many things. It may be identical with the nation, or it may be, and usually is, something far smaller. It may even be a diaspora—emigrants from another nation or region of the world—nesting within a nation. In the United States, which is a state composed very largely of quite recent immigrants, these communities are often given hyphenated names so as to emphasize their difference from the nation itself. Just as its Creole founders dubbed themselves "English-" or "British-Americans," so now there are "Hispanic-Americans," "Asian-Americans," "Italian-Americans," and so on. Or a community might be far smaller: a class, for instance, or an ethnicity, a culture, or even a parish or village, and all those older groupings that nationalists had hoped, vainly, to subsume within the nation itself. Communitarians inevitably have much in common with nineteenth-century nationalists. Their vision of the community draws much of its inspiration from similar sources, in particular from Hegel and Herder.[64] (It is not incidental that the philosopher Charles Taylor—one of the most subtle and allusive of them—wrote his first major work on Hegel and that he has been instrumental in the current revival of interest in Herder.) Like the old nationalists, communitarians would argue that while Enlightenment cosmopolitanism might have much in theory to recommend it, the claims on which it is based are airy and vague, filled only with nice feelings and pious sentiments. In any real world inhabited by real human beings, they can only be hopelessly ineffective and possibly, like most forms of imprecision, potentially lethal. Worse, they are also, in a profound sense, simply wrong. For humans delude themselves into believing that they are the creators of the social and political worlds they inhabit. In fact they are their creatures. Communitarians believe that, in the German philosopher Martin Heidegger's striking image, we have been "thrown" into the world and therefore have no choice over where we happen to have landed. All of the communities in which humans live, however simple or complex they may be, have evolved over very long periods of time. All can—or at least should—recognize one another as human and respect one another's chosen ways of doing things. There may indeed exist a single "human nature," just as we now know that there exists only one human "race," but that only means that we no longer have—if we ever did—any grounds for enslaving or seeking to exterminate or even to "improve" entire peoples. This belief in a common humanity may even go so far as to imply that "others" should be eligible for the same political rights as "us," but it certainly does not mean that we can share our identity or our moral world (at best a dicey concept) with anyone beyond our immediate social environment. Insofar as the individual has a moral identity, he or she does so only because, and by means of, the community to which he or she belongs.

Some thirty years ago the British philosopher Alasdair MacIntyre wrote a powerful and influential book called *After Virtue*. It begins with a vision of an alternative future. Imagine, he asked his readers, if all knowledge of the natural sciences were to be wiped out. A series of natural disasters has occurred. The general public, in search of someone to blame, turns on the scientists. "Widespread riots occur, laboratories are burnt down, physicists are lynched, books and instruments are destroyed." Then imagine what it would be like to try to reconstruct those sciences from the scattered fragments that remained, from "instruments whose uses has been forgotten; half-chapters from books, single pages from articles, not always fully legible because torn and charred." For centuries, perhaps, until the entire process of scientific reasoning had been reconstructed, no one would know that what they were doing was not science at all, because the "contexts which would be needed to make sense of what they are doing have been lost." This is what the Enlightenment did. It did not, however, destroy the natural sciences. It destroyed morality. Like the inhabitants of this futuristic nightmare who have lost all contact with the natural sciences, "we have—very largely, if not entirely—lost our comprehension, both theoretical or practical, of morality."[65] And what is worse, *we do not know it*. The solution, the way to recover our lost morality, to undo the consequences of the Enlightenment, was, MacIntyre believed, to resurrect the old Aristotelian conception of "virtue" and with it to rebuild our moral worlds in something resembling the image of medieval monastic communities.

MacIntyre's position is extreme and his account of the Enlightenment historically eccentric (although it makes perfect sense in terms of his own argument against it). It was, he claims, almost wholly northern European ("Spaniards, Italians, Gaelic and Slavonic speaking peoples do not belong to it"); it was as much musical as philosophical—its greatest exponents were Kant and Mozart—and the French, who were "the most backward of Enlightened nations," are largely excluded from it. Its outcome and its epitaph was *Either/Or,* a work written in 1842 by the Danish philosopher-theologian Søren Kierkegaard.[66] But, despite these peculiarities, some version of MacIntyre's argument—diluted, shorn of most of its historical narrative, and, often also philosophically impoverished—has become a commonplace. The Enlightenment has separated us from our moral roots. By insisting that morality was a question of individual choice, that each person had, in Kant's terms, a moral law within him, the Enlightenment has produced a culture devoid of direction and purpose. It has done so because the Enlightenment was fundamentally wrong about morality—and not only about morality, but about everything to do with our social and ethical being—in short, about our lives. These things do not come to us from within but from without. They are dictated to us, and they make sense only in the context of the communities to which we belong. It is, therefore, absurd to believe that such essentially diverse creatures could ever be brought to agree upon so difficult an issue as how best to live their lives in the absence of some kind of community to give them real meaning. Without the guidelines of tradition, without, some would add (MacIntyre among them), the systems of religious belief that all human societies share, humans are lost. The Enlightenment, by insisting that what should be of concern to all of us was some greater cosmopolitan world, had made the thought of community almost untenable. It had been a false move, and we—in the western world at least—have been suffering for it ever since.

The Enlightenment had insisted, in MacIntyre's words, that "every point of view, whatever its source, could be brought into rational debate with every other" and that "such rational debate could always, if adequately conducted, have a conclusive outcome." Like Hamann, he believed that those claims were inevitably vain, since the standard by which any "rational debate" would have to be conducted could only be established by some prior "theoretical or conceptual scheme," and such schemes do not exist independently of the ways of life, the beliefs, the customs and habits of those who belong to them. In other words, "rationality" itself—like Herder's concept of "happiness"—is not a universal category.[67] What looks like rational argument to an American may seem mere gibberish to an Iranian, or, more pertinently, what might seem unquestionably obvious to an educated atheist might seem merely incomprehensible to an uneducated believer. Furthermore, man, as MacIntyre put it, is not only a rational creature, he is also a storytelling one, a *Homo fabulans*. His moral sensibilities are essentially narrative ones, and the stories he tells are not about "humanity" or the cosmos, because although both may, in some sense, be said to have stories, none of them are very pertinent or compelling ones. Why should anyone in a modern western nation really care about the activities of hunter-gatherer societies or for that matter about the goings-on of the Chinese or the Nuer? They might make for interesting reading. We might admire or pity them. But they can tell us nothing about how we should live our own lives. What we really care about are the stories about our own kind. This is why history and genealogy are so clearly important for all of us, for every nation, every "community," is the creature of a single story, more often than not arrived at by more or less conscious omission, distortion, and fabrication. This is why nationalists are so keen that national histories should be taught in schools. It is precisely because of their roles in such nationalist narratives that Magna Carta, the American Declaration of Independence (and the Constitution), and the French *Declaration of the Rights of Man and the Citizen* occupy such a prominent place not only in official histories but also in the popular imagination of their respective nations—even if, as is generally the case, very few of their citizens have the least idea of what is in them. All religions, all political systems are likewise stories. Some of these may be true, others are clearly false. We often have no certain means of knowing. What matters is that we believe them. For MacIntyre, one of the people who had seen this most clearly was Giambattista Vico. "For it was Vico," he claimed, somewhat disingenuously, who had been the first to see that "the subject matters of moral philosophy . . . are nowhere to be found except as embodied in the historical lives of particular social groups."[68] For MacIntyre, for all communitarians generally, as for Hegel, "the community is the substantial basis and end." Outside the community there can exist no grounds for making any kind of moral, social, anthropological, or religious judgment about anything that may be found within. What the writers of the Enlightenment habitually referred to as those "prejudices" that, in Holbach's view, were "the true cause of the evils which afflict [humanity] from every direction" were in fact the customs and the shared beliefs of which the ethical life of the community was built.[69] As Edmund Burke, always certain of the good sense of his fellow countrymen, had explained to the French, the English, "instead of exploding general prejudices," employ their sagacity to discover the latent wisdom that prevails in them. "If they find what they seek, and they seldom fail, they think it more wise to continue the prejudice, with the reason involved, than to cast away the coat of prejudice and leave nothing but the naked reason." In origin, *prejudice* is a Roman legal term—a "prejudgment"—that was required concerning the status of a case before it could be brought to trial. It could, therefore, be said to be what the twentieth-century German philosopher Hans-Georg Gadamer, another with communitarian sympathies, calls the historical "fore-structuring" of knowledge, which we all need if we are to make any sense of the world we live in, against precisely "enlightenment and its critique of religion."[70] For without such "fore-structuring" no one has any point of reference, any place from which to begin to make the kind of judgments required to live even the most rigorously "examined"—to use Socrates' favorite term—life.

What I am, the moral life that I lead, all that I venerate or abhor, comes to me, in MacIntyre's words, from "this particular social life inhabited by me." This does not mean that, given the opportunity, I might not find other "similar forms of social life in other communities" that were just as congenial. What it does mean is that, "deprived of the life of [my] community, I would have no reason to be moral"[71]—although by what means I would find lives in communities other than my own "congenial," if the attachment to a community is, by definition, not something of my own choosing, is not clear. I may choose to go and live in, say, France rather than the United Kingdom because, having seen how the French live, I find living in Paris more congenial than living in London. But that does not make me, in any sense that MacIntyre would accept, part of the community called "France." Presumably I would, therefore, have no more reason for being "moral" in the France to which I cannot fully belong in any but a formal legal sense than in the United Kingdom to which I no longer belong. Or at least, my compulsion to live a "moral" life in either place could not be said to come to me from "this particular social life inhabited by me." This, in MacIntyre's eyes, must surely make me a rootless, and thus necessarily amoral, cosmopolitan.

This understanding of human association also extends to what is unquestionably the most central aspect of social life in any community: justice and the law. For in a world conceived in the way MacIntyre, and many other communitarians, conceive it, justice cannot possibly be "global," because justice, too, can only ever be a matter of agreement among the members of the tribe, community, nation, and so on to which it applies. MacIntyre's conception of humans as storytelling animals, and of human social lives as structured by narratives, is also the source of Jean-François Lyotard's critique of what he calls the "cosmopolitical." (Lyotard was not himself a communitarian. Communitarians seem to be confined to the English-speaking world. But communitarianism shares some common ground with postmodernism, as MacIntyre implicitly recognizes.) "The *Volk,*" Lyotard wrote—using the language that Herder had first introduced into philosophy—"shuts itself up in the *Heim* [home] and identifies itself though narratives."[72] Lyotard illustrates this claim with an example—an extreme one, perhaps—of a Central American people called the Cashinahua. The Cashinahua, apparently, think of themselves as the only "true-men." The stories that they tell themselves, their "savage" narratives, as Lyotard calls them, are therefore only ever about themselves. They are, as he puts it, resolutely "anti-cosmopolitical." "Traditions," Lyotard tells us, "are mutually opaque. Contact between two communities is immediately a conflict, since the names and narratives of the one community are exclusive of the names and narratives of the other." There is no place where conflict can ever be resolved, no tribunal "before which it can be presented, argued, and decided," because any such tribunal would already have to be "universal, human, having an international law at its disposal, etc.," and such things for Lyotard simply do not exist. They are the deluded creations of the Enlightenment, the main prop of its "meta-narrative," which postmodernism has finally and triumphantly overcome.[73] Locked in their world of incommunicable "savage" narratives, the Cashinahua, it would seem, are true postmoderns by virtue of being perfect premoderns. They possess, indeed, many of the attributes that Rousseau gave to his savages, or Diderot to his fictional Tahitians. Any talk of consensus beyond the borders of the community is, in Lyotard's view, an "outmoded and suspect value." Justice can only ever be highly localized and arranged like a game "agreed on by its present players and subject to eventual cancellation." And since there can exist no tribunal to establish the value (and the force) of even the most temporary contract between these different consensuses, each group must remain forever locked within its own world, defined by its own customs and its own languages. When confronted with child marriage, slavery, castration, all I can do is stand aside and say, "I have no language with which I can describe, let alone judge, such behavior." For Lyotard, we all in fact live as the Cashinahua do, only we refuse to recognize it. The postmodernists speak of language, the communitarians (and the multiculturalists, who also share the same basic premises) of "stories," of "culture." But in the end they come to very much the same conclusions.

What is other, then, is simply other. There can be no universal position on anything. There can, of course, exist conversations between different "Spheres of Justice," to use Michael Walzer's term, because "every language," as Lyotard says with unwarranted confidence, "is translatable." But there is no possibility of a true law between nations, because any such law must necessarily be dependent upon a wholly impossible consensus. The Indian caste system, for instance, so apparently and blatantly unjust to contemporary secular sensibilities, would, argues Walzer, be entirely just if it were accepted as such by all those who are affected by it. (In fact it is not—or so he says—so the question does not arise.)[74] We can no more free ourselves from our language or from the cultural expectations of the community into which we were "thrown" than we can from our own skins. And if all that we do—and, more important, think—is given to us and there is no place outside the community from which it might be judged, it is hard to see how it can ever change. The true communitarian cannot, therefore, adequately explain how slavery, forced marriages, bearbaiting, or public executions ever came to be considered distasteful.

For MacIntyre, and for many others, these "particular social groups" can also only be made intelligible, can only hope to survive and command the respect and loyalty they require, if they are based on a religion. This is not because the claims put forward by most religions, and the myths on which they are based, are necessarily true. (Although MacIntyre himself, as a practicing Catholic, must surely think that Christianity at least is true.) It is because religion is ultimately, as Hegel recognized, the supreme cement that binds the community together. It is not, of course, the only one. Communities can find a common identity in any number of things, the concept of race being the most insidious. But religion has often proved to be the appeal of last resort. It defies questioning. It demands only observance and is clearly capable of generating passionate loyalties. There are also many who will argue with Pope Benedict XVI that, leaving aside the attractions (or likelihood) of an afterlife, above every positive law there must always be a higher law whose source can only ultimately be a divinity. Otherwise why should anyone choose to observe it? It is the old argument, best expressed in Dostoyevsky's famous observation "Now assume there is no God or immortality of the soul. Now tell me, why should I live righteously and do good deeds if I am to die entirely on earth? . . . And if that is so, why shouldn't I (as long as I can rely on my cleverness and agility to avoid being caught by the law) cut another man's throat, rob, and steal?"[75] Spinoza and Pierre Bayle thought that they had found an answer in the seventeenth century, but it was never one that would have persuaded anyone who, like Benedict XVI, clearly does not believe in the possibility of any kind of purely secular legal or political morality.

For many communitarians, the ultimate blame for all that they most deplore about the world they actually inhabit can only be found in the baleful influence of Enlightenment universalism. They are not, like some of their more extreme Christian or Muslim counterparts, hostile to modern science. They do not generally believe in the subjugation of women to men or the sanctity of the marriage between "one woman and one man." They are not generally racists or homophobes. But what they believe in is a world made collectively, not individually, a world where change must be slow and looked upon always with suspicion, a world that, however liberal and outward-looking its champions might themselves be, is all too likely to become, in reality, insular, claustrophobic, ignorant, and intolerant.

The outcome might indeed be something close to the nightmare dreamed up by the contemporary American philosopher and psychologist Daniel Dennett: "The Enlightenment is long gone: the creeping secularization of modern societies that has been anticipated for two centuries is evaporating before our eyes . . . religion soon resumes something like the dominant social and moral role it had before the rise of modern science in the seventeenth century . . . populations come to be even more divided among Christianity, Islam, Judaism, Hinduism. . . . Eventually one major faith sweeps the planet."[76]

There may indeed be, as Dennett assumes there are, many who look eagerly forward to a future in some revivified version of the Middle Ages, with the added benefits of antibiotics and running water. Benedict XVI may look back nostalgically upon a world in which theology was still the "mother of sciences," the dominant "magisterium," and still had the last say; in which the Church was still the most powerful international institution in the (western) world and secularism a slightly freakish anomaly. Charles Taylor may sincerely believe that we are now entering a post-secular age. But the attempt to reinvigorate religion though rational argument as the solution to the perceived crisis of modernity (or postmodernity) is no more likely to be persuasive in the twenty-first century than it was in the late nineteenth. It is unlikely that Christianity, on the retreat since the seventeenth century and long accustomed to dissimulation and compromise, will be able to make much significant impact on the modern world. Islam, however, is quite a different matter. It is Muslim extremists of one shade or another—and for all the perhaps misplaced optimism that greeted the "Arab Spring," there is little sign at the time of writing that their power and influence is in decline—who have gone furthest in replacing the political tenets of western modernism by an ethics of belief. It was, not surprisingly, a "colleague from Tehran" who told Habermas that "the comparative study of cultures and religious sociology surely suggests that European secularization was the odd one out among the various developments—and that it ought to be corrected." Nor is it remarkable that the pope, when told of this, should have replied that it was an observation that "seems to me not devoid of significance."[77] But who in the West, apart from the pope and a few on the fringe of the Christian right in the United States, would really wish to see a world ruled by theocracies, of whatever confession? Even Benedict XVI is fully aware of the dangers that exist in what he calls the "pathologies of religion."[78] Charles Taylor, who has done more than most to build a bridge between an enlightened sensibility and the possibility of undogmatic religious belief, has warned against the dangers of "mainline narratives of simple cost-free supersession, whether narrated by Christians or by protagonists of the Enlightenment."[79] He is right to do so, but his own warning can leave us in no doubt as to where the ultimate line of demarcation falls.

Furthermore, the "religion" that is on the increase today is not anything over which Benedict XVI could hope to exercise much control. It is chaotic, chiliastic, intuitive, pathological, and for the most part utterly devoid of any theological content. It has also turned its back upon its founders. The Christians who crowd the "megachurches" of the United States know who Christ was, or was believed to have been; they may even have some sketchy notion of some of his teaching; but they have probably never even heard of St. Paul—the true founder of the Christian Church—and have certainly never encountered any of the Church Fathers. Their faith is, indeed, a reflection of those "pathologies of religion" that Benedict rightly fears. It is what Hume would have called "enthusiasm." It may well be true that, as some have argued, because of this the gap between "the core values held by the more religious and secular societies," which has led to atrocities from Amsterdam to Benghazi, will continue to increase.[80] It is also certainly the case that although there are many secular societies, there are still, as there were in Hume's day, very few self-confessed unbelievers in the world. In 2007 they accounted for only 11 percent of the world's population. But that 11 percent was, predictably perhaps, located among the wealthiest and the best-educated regions of the world. Religion is most prevalent in areas that are poor and whose populations are under-educated. But even here it would seem to be, broadly, on the decline.[81] Even in the United States—always the "outlier" in matters of religion—the number of people prepared to define themselves as "religious" appears to be decreasing.[82] Many in the "developing" world feel themselves—as Muslims have for so long, and not unreasonably—to be at the mercy of foreign predators, who are often seen as not only "western" but also "godless."[83] For these people, religion, like "community," has become not only a refuge but also an ideology of protest. The brand—or brands—of Islam that seem to be gaining ground in the countries affected by the "Arab Spring" are nothing like as heterodox as the various brands of the new Christianity. But like them, they are essentially cries of protest. And when the very real injustices and deprivations which they are cries of protests against have died away—assuming that they ever do—then the religious "enthusiasm" will die away too. At present, at least, it seems unlikely that the dire prediction the English philosopher John Gray made in 2007 that "the violence of faith looks set to shape the coming century" will in fact be fulfilled.[84]

V

What so many of these opponents of Enlightenment have failed even to ask is why the world of virtue and moral authority that had apparently served our ancestors so well should have been overturned in the first place. Why, in other words, did the Enlightenment happen at all? It cannot simply be explained away, as the De Maistres and the Burkes had hoped, as the murderous revenge of disinherited minorities suddenly—and inexplicably—grown powerful. I have tried to offer an answer, not in terms of a conflict between "reason" and belief, between science and religion, but rather in terms of the historical failure of Christianity to continue to provide the kind of intellectual, and consequently moral, certainty that it had once done. By the mid-seventeenth century the entire structure on which all monotheistic beliefs rest, that the universe had been the creation of a divinity who continues to dictate every aspect of its being, had come to seem to many Europeans as threadbare as paganism had once seemed to Plato and Aristotle. In origin, all except the strictly theological aspects of Christianity—all that it could salvage from its Judaic origins—everything that relates to the human, and to life on earth—derived exclusively from ancient pagan sources manipulated by a powerful and often brilliantly imaginative clerical elite. Hence the description of it as "Hellenized Judaism."[85] What the Enlightenment did was to replace this Christianized vision of the human condition with a more appealing, less dogmatic account, derived initially from the same attempt to reshape the most powerful of the ancient philosophical schools.

Those who claim that "the Enlightenment has failed"—by which they always also mean that modernity has failed—generally have in mind some caricature of a project to reduce all human life to a set of simple rational calculations. If all the Enlightenment had amounted to had been "promoting autonomous human reason and according to science a privileged status in relation to all other forms of understanding" (in John Gray's words), then indeed it most surely would have failed.[86] But, as we have seen, it was far, far more than that. It was about creating a field of values, political, social, and moral, based upon a detached and scrupulous understanding—as far as the human mind is capable—of what it means to be human. And today most educated people, at least in the West, broadly accept the conclusions to which it led. Most generally believe that it is possible to improve, through knowledge and science, the world in which we live. Because they believe this, they also believe that there exists a "human nature"—although few today would employ such a term—that is much the same everywhere; that what counts as justice for the Germans must count as justice for the Hausa; and that what every man can claim as his own can be claimed by every woman. They hold, that is, that although cultures are important and difference must be respected, this can be so only when cultures conform to some minimal ethical standards that every rational being could be brought to understand. They believe that although most rights come to us courtesy of the states to which we belong, there are others to which we are all entitled by virtue of our humanity.[87] We are owed them whether we be Mexican or Malagasy, male or female, black or white, Christian, Muslim, or Hindu. We are owed them merely and solely because we belong to the species *Homo sapiens sapiens,* with all that that necessarily implies.

Most educated people also believe in the possibility of some form of "global" justice or at the very least in the possibility of a true law among all nations. In general they would agree with Kant that the only truly human world is one that every individual would choose to create for him- or herself if they did not know beforehand what position they would occupy within it. It is for this reason, if for no other, that they also believe that the only possible just society must necessarily be a secular one. They do not wish to deny others the right to believe in their gods. What they are not prepared to accept, however, is that the laws by which humans order their lives can be anything other than human, intelligible, and changeable. To borrow the words of Richard Rorty, they believe that "getting rid of our sense of being responsible to something other than, and larger than, our fellow human beings is a good idea."[88]

It was the Enlightenment that made it possible for us to think, in this way, beyond the narrow worlds into which we are born, to think globally. It was the Enlightenment that made it possible for anyone to imagine that any nation had any kind of responsibility for the welfare of any other. Today the economically advanced nations of the world send billions of dollars in financial aid to the less privileged peoples of the "developing world." It is never enough, many will say, and they may well be right. And the motives are often murky. The hope that cash might help the donor nations to exercise a degree of "soft power" in potentially unstable parts of the world is clearly one of them; the belief that some of the beneficiaries might one day evolve into profitable trading partners another. But there is also a broader, more imprecise sense that because the peoples of these countries are poor and suffering, and because they are, like us, humans, we owe it to them to help. (It cannot be for many other reasons that the contribution to world aid made by Denmark, which wields no power "hard" or "soft" in the developing world, in percentage terms far exceeds that of the United States.) Without the Enlightenment this, too, could hardly have occurred.[89]

The Enlightenment was, however, a moment of transformation and consolidation, not a moment of revolution. This is one of the reasons why both the Romantics and their heirs, the Marxists and the neo-Marxists, so despised it. But in its intention to transform the most significant, most lasting insights available to the western philosophical tradition in such a way as to make them usable in a world from which God had been finally and irrevocably removed; by insisting on the changing, unfinished nature of all human action; by insisting, indeed, on its own unfinished nature, the Enlightenment quite simply created the modern world. It is, indeed, impossible to imagine any aspect of contemporary life in the West without it.

But let me try. Let me play a version of Alasdair MacIntyre's game of "what if."

What if, to begin with, the Protestant Reformation had never taken place?

Luther, who was burned as a heretic in 1521, has gone down in history as nothing more than yet another troublesome friar hankering after the purity of the early Church. Christianity, although rarely ever at peace, remains united. The discovery of America has led to some flutters of uncertainty within the universities, but any thought that it might present a challenge to the traditional view of the laws of nature or God have been successfully repressed. There have been no French Wars of Religion, no English Civil Wars. The Revolt of the Netherlands, lacking ideological cohesion and foreign aid, has been swiftly suppressed. There has been no Thirty Years' War. Spain continues to be the richest, most powerful nation in Europe and remains locked in an unending struggle with France. Copernicus and Galileo, Bacon, Descartes, and Mersenne succeed in creating a new kind of Renaissance, which flourishes for a while under moderately tolerant regimes. Thomas Hobbes, however, although he enjoys some small success as a mathematician, eventually follows his father into the Church and dies, like him, an embittered alcoholic. John Locke is an obscure doctor at Christ Church, Oxford, renowned only for the silver tap he succeeded in inserting into the Earl of Shaftesbury's lower intestine without killing him in the process. Newton achieves recognition as a gifted astrologer and competent administrator and some notoriety as a somewhat heterodox theologian. By the end of the century the "Scientific Renaissance," as it later came to be called, has been silenced, the heliocentric theory and Descartes's atomism between them having proved too much for the Church to tolerate. The next generation has nothing to build on. The "mighty Light which spreads itself over the world," which Shaftesbury had seen in 1706 and which he believed must ensure that "it . . . is impossible but Letters and Knowledge must advance in greater Proportion than ever," is instead a steadily darkening cloud.[90] Western Christendom drops behind its centuries-old antagonist to the east, the Ottoman Empire. In 1683 Vienna falls to the armies of Sultan Mehmed IV. Russia, or "Muscovy," as it still calls itself, backward and divided, is easily defeated and overrun in January 1699. Spain and France still control the western Mediterranean and dominate most of northern Europe. But threatened by the seemingly irresistible Ottoman armies, they become increasingly theocratic and resistant to any innovation, from mechanical clocks to vaccination, which, they fear, might offend their ever-unpredictable God. The *Encyclopédie* is nothing more than an uninspiring French translation of Chambers's *Cyclopaedia*. Diderot manages a certain literary fame but dies in prison in the Château de Vincennes in 1749. Rousseau lives, and dies, a penny-grubbing musical critic. His novel *Julie, or the New Héloïse* enjoys moderate underground success but is then burned in Paris by the public executioner. David Hume, after an early attempt to revolutionize philosophy that is swiftly silenced by the "zealots," lives as the librarian at St. Aloysius' College in Glasgow and writes a popular history of the kings of England. Voltaire achieves both fame and popularity as a playwright and poet but is finally forced to seek refuge in Switzerland, which has preserved a degree of independence and a reputation for toleration, where, to his horror, he is soon joined by Rousseau. Bougainville never leaves France, and Banks eventually becomes a dyspeptic Lincolnshire squire with a passion for horticulture. Vico is elected to a chair in theology at the University of Naples, and Kant lectures on a variety of topics to listless students in Königsberg, renowned only for his short essay "On the Beautiful and the Sublime." Lacking any capacity for scientific or social innovation, the European powers not already under Ottoman control steadily decline until finally, in May 1789, Sultan Selim III marches into Paris. Within a few years what the English ecclesiastical historian Edward Gibbon had predicted in 1776 has come true, and "the interpretation of the Koran is now taught in the schools of Oxford and her pupils demonstrate to a circumcised people the sanctity and truth of the Revelation of Mahomet."[91] United in one massive religious and political community, which reaches from the Himalayas to the coasts of Scotland, the Ottoman Empire survives into the twentieth century. In size it has outstripped ancient Rome, but, as in ancient Rome, the only changes that have occurred within its frontiers in nearly half a millennium have been literary and architectural. In all other respects, like Rome, it firmly imagines itself to be the final end of history and has therefore no need to examine the ideals and assumptions on which it is based.[92] Ever obedient to God, his Prophet, and his laws, it continues on its unbroken course. Having long since given up any aspiration to influence the future course of events, everyone waits for something to arrive from outside. As for the Romans—or perhaps they are Byzantines, as in Constantine Cafavy's allusive poem "Waiting for the Barbarians"—for these imaginary Europeans only a crude barbarous people from beyond the borders of the empire can offer "a kind of solution." But the barbarians never come and may, in fact, no longer exist at all.[93]

An utterly implausible flight of fancy? An illusion? Perhaps, but something not wholly dissimilar did, in fact, befall the Islamic world. During the reigns of the Caliphs al-Mansûr (712–75) and his successors Hârûn-al Rashîd (786–809) and al-Ma'mûn (813–33), an entire school of Hellenizing philosophers, jurists, and doctors grew up: men like the surgeon Abul Qasim Al-Zahravi, known as "Albucasis"; the mathematician and astronomer Muhammad ibn Mûsâ al-Khwârizmî, after whom a crater on the far side of the moon is now named; Abû or Ibn Sînâ, called "Avicenna" in the West, the author of a vast treatise that brought together all the medical knowledge of the ancient Greek world then available, from Aristotle, Hippocrates, and Galen; Muhammad ibn Ahmad al-Biruni, physician, astronomer, mathematician, physicist, chemist, geographer, and historian, who in 1018 made calculations, using instruments he had created himself, of the radius and circumference of the Earth that vary by as little as 15 and 200 kilometers from today's estimates. The best known in the West, however, was Abû al-Walîd Muhammad ibn Rushd, or "Averroës" as he was called by his Latin readers, who was so highly regarded in the Christian world that he became known simply as "The Commentator" (just as Aristotle was known as "The Philosopher")—which is how he appears, peering over the shoulder of Aristotle, in Raphael's great fresco *The School of Athens* in the Sistine Chapel. But Averroës was not only the greatest of the Arab Muslim scholars and perhaps the most influential of all Muslim philosophers, he was also the last. In the late twelfth century the Muslim clergy began a concerted onslaught on translation from the Greek and against all forms of learning that did not derive from either the Qur'an itself or from the sayings of the Prophet. When Averroës died in 1198, in exile in Morocco, a victim of this war against "philosophy" and its adherents throughout the Islamic world, the "Arab Renaissance" died with him. Islamic power, Sunni and Shia, under Mongol, Turcoman, Safavid, and Sassanid rulers remained dominant within western and central Asia for another four hundred years, during much of which time the Ottomans gobbled up large tracts of eastern Europe. But inside the Muslim world there was little of importance that separated the twelfth century from the seventeenth. Certain of its own superiority, Islam ultimately repulsed any attempt to bring about any kind of change, in particular if it arrived, or seemed to have arrived, from the West.

In this case, however, the barbarians did arrive, first in the shape of the Austrians, then the Russians, who inflicted a humiliating peace treaty on the Ottomans at Karlowitz in the Voivodina on January 26, 1699, and then the French. The European powers nibbled unceasingly away at the frontiers of the Ottoman Empire, until finally, in the early nineteenth century, the sultans, desperate to preserve what still remained to them, began slowly to adopt western technologies, western education, western laws, and, in 1876, to the dismay of the clergy, a European-style constitution and even a parliament, if only a somewhat toothless one. In 1919, having chosen the wrong side in the First World War, the Ottoman Empire, with the exception of Turkey itself, was dismantled and parceled out among the victorious allies.

Without the Enlightenment, Europe's history could well have followed a similar trajectory. For it is not only the science of human understanding itself that we owe to the Enlightenment; it is, as I have argued, also the ways in which we all, in the West, live our political and social lives. "Citizenship," the concept that undergirds all modern western political creeds, has its origins in Greece and Rome, but the modern understanding of the word, and all that it implies, is a creation of the Enlightenment. Modern liberal democracy—the kind of political system that, for better and sometimes for worse, governs most modern societies—is a creation of the Enlightenment, refined and institutionalized during the course of the nineteenth century. And although the idea of a law of nations is an ancient one, the modern understanding of what that might mean in a world of ever-expanding nation-states we owe to the Enlightenment. It was, after all, one of its last, if often most idiosyncratic, representatives, Jeremy Bentham, who coined the term "international law."

Other crucial aspects of modern societies are, admittedly, far older, far more deeply embedded. The most hallowed, perhaps, is the claim that all political and social life should be governed by the rule of law. And not just any law but one made and administered by humans, not gods—one that is therefore susceptible to change and alteration. You do not need to be enamored of the Enlightenment and all it stands for to believe in that. Only a modern-day De Maistre (such as the recent U.S. Attorney General John Ashcroft, who once told an audience at the Bob Jones University that "we have no king but Jesus" and that the separation of Church and State was "a wall of religious oppression") would wish to see what no Christian society has ever been: a fusion of Church and State.[94] Happily, however, there are very few of them.

It is still far from clear what will finally shape the twenty-first century. But one thing does seem certain: that although the central Enlightenment belief in a common humanity, the awareness of belonging to some world larger than the community, family, parish, or *patria,* may still be shakily primitive and incomplete, it is also indubitably a great deal more present in all our lives—whoever "we" might be—than it was even fifty years ago. "Global governance," "Constitutional Patriotism," globalization, multiculturalism are not only topics of debate; they are also, in many parts of the world, realities. Cosmopolitanism, expressed as a firm belief in the possibility of a truly international system of laws, has been the animating principle behind both the League of Nations and the United Nations and is the main assumption that underlies the Universal Declaration of Human Rights. "No longer is it credible for a state to turn its back on international law, alleging a bias towards European values and influence," warned the United Nations' "Report of the Commission on Global Governance" in 1995, significantly entitled *Our Global Neighbourhood*. Such a law may be of European origin, at least as it is currently understood (for similar concepts certainly do exist in many other places in the world), but this cannot now be used as a reason for invalidating it. There now exists, the report claimed, a "global civic ethic" based on "a set of core values that can unite people of all cultural, political, religious, or philosophical backgrounds."[95] This may have been unduly optimistic in 1995, with the war in Bosnia-Herzegovina barely over, and might seem even more so today. But for all that, Habermas is surely right to believe that we "have long since begun the transition from classical international law to what Kant saw as a 'cosmopolitan condition' " and that, "normatively speaking," there cannot be "any coherent alternative to such a development."[96] As evidence we have some—admittedly somewhat ramshackle, often ineffective—cosmopolitan institutions, not utterly unlike the kind that Kant had hoped for: the United Nations, the International Court of Justice, the International Criminal Court, the International Labor Organization, the International Maritime Organization. We have transnational economic institutions and any number of formal and informal channels of communication between states and between individuals. And of course we have had, since 1948, a "Universal Declaration of Human Rights," which, vague though its statements sometimes are—there are a number to which even the most conscientious western countries do not subscribe—has indubitably been influential in shaping foreign policy in the West since at least the late 1970s. Together with the associated ideal of the "dignity of man," they constitute what Habermas has called a "realistic utopia."[97] Then there is at least one confederacy, the European Union, that fulfills many of the conditions of Kant's "League of Nations." True, it is confined to Europe, although it is a "Europe" whose understanding of itself, together with its own borders, is constantly expanding, so that one day it may (and certainly should) come to include what for centuries was its oldest enemy, Turkey. In too many respects it also still exists only in embryo, as it passes through the first real crisis of its short existence. But it provides a model, even as it evolves, that may well one day come to provide an alternative for the gradually faltering nation-state.

The realists may claim, as realists invariably do, that most of these institutions (the EU aside) are only fora in which people merely talk. But talking counts, and states today spend a great deal more time doing it than they ever have in the past. Then, on another level, few of us in the West can, or would probably want to, live out our lives unaffected by the lives of often radically different others. The world of communicating beings that Kant saw as providing the necessary basis for any future cosmopolitan world may still be some way off. But it is far closer today than it was in, say, 1945.

None of this was achieved, and nothing in the future will ever be achieved, by shutting ourselves up in communities, by measuring out our lives by the horizons of what our fathers and our forefathers have set down for us, or by regulating our actions, and our desires, according to the dictates of those who have appointed themselves to be the representatives on earth of a highly improbable divinity. Much of what modern civilization has achieved we obviously owe to many factors, from increased medical knowledge to information technologies to vastly improved methods of transport, which although they are an indirect legacy of the Enlightenment and the revolutions in science and technology that both preceded and followed it, have no immediate or direct connection to its ideals. But our ability even to frame our understanding of the world in terms of something larger than our own small patch of ground, our own culture, family, or religion, clearly does. And in that, we are all, inescapably, the heirs of the architects of the Enlightenment "science of man." For this, then, if for no other reason, the Enlightenment still matters.

NOTES

All Greek and Latin sources have been cited in the traditional manner, without reference to any particular edition. In the case of modern works for which there exist large numbers of editions, I have, where possible, used book, chapter, or paragraph numbers instead of page numbers. In some cases I have singled out a particular edition. Wherever possible I have used the most accessible and reliable English translation for works in languages other than English, although I have sometimes made changes of my own. Where no English-language edition is cited, the translation is my own. In the case of the works of Immanuel Kant, I have generally followed the wording of the Cambridge Edition. I have also provided the standard references to the edition of the Royal Prussian Academy of Sciences (*Kants gesammelte Schriften, Herausgegeben von der königlich preussischen Akademie der Wissenschaften*), known as "the Akademie edition" (and given here as "AK"), by volume and page number. The only exception is the *Critique of Pure Reason,* which is cited, as is customary, by the page numbers from the first (A) and second (B) editions.

Introduction

1. Keith Baker, *Condorcet from Natural Philosophy to Social Mathematics* (Chicago and London: University of Chicago Press, 1975).
2. On Condorcet and the Revolution, see Bronislaw Baczko, *Job mon ami. Promesses du bonheur et fatalité du mal* (Paris: Gallimard, 1997), 354–75.
3. As told in Simon Schama, *Citizens: A Chronicle of the French Revolution* (London: Penguin Books, 1989), 722. A more mundane version of the story has him ar-

rested by agents of the Revolutionary Committee after he was unable to produce any papers to prove that he was, as he claimed to be, one Pierre Simon.

4. *Reflections on the Revolution in France,* ed. J.C.D. Clark (Stanford, Calif.: Stanford University Press, 2001), 190.
5. *Considerations on France,* trans. Richard A. Lebrun (Cambridge: Cambridge University Press, 1994), 29.
6. Quoted in Alain Pons, "Introduction," *Esquisse d'un tableau historique des progrès de l'esprit humain,* ed. Alain Pons (Paris: Flammarion, 1988), 57.
7. Quoted in Emma Rothschild, *Economic Sentiments: Adam Smith, Condorcet, and the Enlightenment* (Cambridge, Mass., and London: Harvard University Press, 2001), 189.
8. "Discours prononcé dans l'Académie française . . . a la réception de M. le marquis de Condorcet," in *Œuvres complètes de Condorcet* (Paris, 1804), X, 101.
9. *Esquisse d'un tableau historique des progrès de l'esprit humain,* 265–69.
10. According to Plutarch, Socrates had also claimed: "I am not an Athenian, nor a Greek, but a Citizen of the World." But the context of the remark, in a wider discussion on banishment, and the absence of any other similar claims by Socrates makes it hard to interpret.
11. See Mary Kaldor, *Global Civil Society: An Answer to War* (Cambridge: Polity Press, 2003); and Daniel Archibugi and David Held, eds., *Cosmopolitan Democracy: An Agenda for a New World Order* (Cambridge: Polity Press, 1995).
12. *Cosmopolitanism: Ethics in a World of Strangers* (New York and London: W. W. Norton & Co., 2006), xiv.
13. The texts are printed in Norbert Hinske, ed., *Was ist Aufklärung? Beitragäge aus der Berlinischen Monatsschrift* (Darmstadt, 1977). On Germany, see H. Stuke, "Aufklärung," in Otto Brunner, W. Conze, and R. Kosselleck, eds., *Geschichtliche Grundbegriffe, Historisches Lexikon zur politisch-sozialen Sprache in Deutschland* (Stuttgart, 1972–), I, 244. See also H. B. Nisbet, "Was ist Aufklärung? The Concept of Enlightenment in Eighteenth-century Germany," *Journal of European Studies* 12 (1992): 77–95.
14. "A Couple of Gold Nuggets from the . . . Wastepaper, or Six Answers to Six Questions," in James Schmidt, ed., *What Is Enlightenment? Eighteenth-Century Answers and Twentieth-Century Questions* (Berkeley and Los Angeles: University of California Press, 1996), 2, 78–79.
15. "On the Question: What Is Enlightenment?" in ibid., 53–77.
16. "Thoughts on Enlightenment," in ibid., 65.
17. "On Freedom of Thought and the Press: For Princes, Ministers and Writers," in ibid., 87–99.
18. All cited in Rothschild, *Economic Sentiments,* 15.
19. *The Philosophy of the Enlightenment,* trans. Fritz C. A. Koelln and James P. Pettegrove (Princeton, N.J.: Princeton University Press, 1951), xv.
20. James Boswell, *Journal of a Tour to the Hebrides with Samuel Johnson, 1733,* ed. Frederick A. Pottle and Charles H. Bennet (New York: McGraw-Hill, 1961), 189.
21. These various historical approaches are all summarized, and dissected, by Dan

Edelstein, *The Enlightenment: A Genealogy* (Chicago: University of Chicago Press, 2010), 7–28.

22. This is the basic thesis of Venturi's magnum opus, *Settencento riformatore* (Turin: Einaudi, 1969–80).
23. *The Structural Transformation of the Public Sphere: An Enquiry into a Category of Bourgeois Society,* trans. T. Burgher (Cambridge, Mass.: Harvard University Press, 1989).
24. These various approaches to the Enlightenment are summarized and discussed by John Robertson in *The Case for Enlightenment: Scotland and Naples, 1680–1760* (Cambridge: Cambridge University Press, 2005), 1–44, and in Jonathan Israel, *Democratic Enlightenment: Philosophy, Revolution, and Human Rights, 1750–1790* (Oxford: Oxford University Press, 2011).
25. *An Answer to the Question: "What Is Enlightenment?"* in *Practical Philosophy,* trans. and ed. Mary J. Gregor (Cambridge: Cambridge University Press, 1996), 21: AK 8: 40.
26. *Reflexionen zur Anthropologie,* no. 1524, AK 16: 898–99.
27. *Critique of Pure Reason,* trans. and ed. Paul Guyer and Allen W. Wood (Cambridge: Cambridge University Press, 1998), 397: A317/B373–74.
28. "Qu'est-ce que les Lumières?" in *Dits et écrits 1954–1988* (Paris: Gallimard, 1994), IV, 562.
29. *Essai sur les éléments de philosophie ou sur les principes des connaissances humaines* [1759] (Paris: Fayard, 1989), 19.
30. *Critique of Pure Reason,* 100: A, xii.
31. *Système de la Nature*, in *Œuvres philosophiques complètes,* ed. Jean-Pierre Jackson (Paris: Editions Alive, 1999), II, 165.
32. *Esquisse d'un tableau historique des progrès de l'esprit humain,* 74.
33. "A Couple of Gold Nuggets from the . . . Wastepaper, or Six Answers to Six Questions," in Schmidt, *What Is Enlightenment?* 80–81.
34. For a more detailed discussion, see pp. 396–400.
35. *Treatise on the Origin of Language,* in *Philosophical Writings,* trans. and ed. Michael N. Forster (Cambridge: Cambridge University Press, 2002), 151–52. William Robertson was a Scottish historian and Isaac Iselin a Swiss one.
36. *Dialectic of Enlightenment,* trans. John Cumming (New York: Herder & Herder, 1972), 3, 12. See also the excellent account in Yvonne Sherratt, *Continental Philosophy of Social Science: Hermeneutics, Genealogy and Critical Theory from Greece to the Twenty-first Century* (Cambridge: Cambridge University Press, 2006), 203–9.
37. *Dialectic of Enlightenment,* 86–89.
38. *Nuremberg Trial Proceedings,* vol. 18, Tuesday, July 9, 1946, The Avalon Project, Yale Law School, http://avalon.law.yale.edu/imt/07-09-46.asp.
39. *Enlightenment's Wake: Politics and Culture at the Close of the Modern Age* (London and New York: Routledge, 1997).
40. See the comments by James Schmidt, *What is Enlightenment?* 63n1.
41. *An Answer to the Question: "What Is Enlightenment?"* in *Practical Philosophy* 17: AK 8: 35–36.

42. For an excellent account of what he interprets as two "Enlightenments," see Michael L. Frazer, *The Enlightenment of Sympathy: Justice and Moral Sentiments in the Eighteenth Century and Today* (Oxford: Oxford University Press, 2010).
43. See pp. 149–50.
44. *The Post-Modern Condition: A Report on Knowledge,* trans. Geoff Bennington and Brian Massumi (Manchester: Manchester University Press, 1984), xiii.

Chapter 1

1. *De la démocratie en Amérique* (Paris: Gallimard, 1961), II, 15–16.
2. *Essai sur les éléments de philosophie ou sur les principes des connaissances humaines,* 9–12. See also Ernst Cassirer, *The Philosophy of the Enlightenment,* 3–4, who begins his magisterial account with some of the same passage.
3. "Discours prononcé dans l'Académie française . . . a la réception de M. le marquis de Condorcet," in *Œuvres complètes de Condorcet,* X, 101–5.
4. See Frank Manuel, *The Religion of Isaac Newton* (Oxford: Oxford University Press, 1974).
5. *Essai sur les éléments de philosophie ou sur les principes des connaissances humaines,* 57.
6. *Discours preliminaire de l'Encyclopédie*, in *Œuvres complètes de D'Alembert* (Paris, 1821–22), I, 67.
7. Quoted in Quentin Skinner, "Thomas Hobbes: Rhetoric and the Construction of Morality," Dawes Hicks Lecture on Philosophy, *Proceedings of the British Academy* 76 (1991), 1–61.
8. *Leviathan,* ed. Richard Tuck (Cambridge: Cambridge University Press, 1991), 461–62 (III, XLVI, 36).
9. F.W.J. von Schelling, *On the History of Modern Philosophy,* trans. Andrew Bowie (Cambridge: Cambridge University Press, 1994), 42.
10. *Essai sur les moeurs et l'esprit des nations,* ed. R. Pomeau (Paris: Classiques Garnier, 1990), II, 245.
11. Ibid., 217.
12. Steven Pinker, *The Better Angels of Our Nature: Why Violence Has Declined* (New York: Viking, 2011), 142.
13. Paul Hazard, *La Pensée européenne du XVIIIe siècle* (Paris: Librairie Arthème Fayard, 1963), 395.
14. Quoted in Theodore K. Rabb, *The Struggle for Stability in Early-Modern Europe* (New York: Oxford University Press, 1975), 81.
15. See Benjamin Straumann, "The Peace of Westphalia as a Secular Constitution," *Constellations* 15 (2008): 173–88.
16. *On Liberty,* in *On Liberty and Other Writings,* ed. Stefan Collini (Cambridge: Cambridge University Press, 1989), 11. On negative toleration, see Raymond Geuss, *History and Illusion in Politics* (Cambridge: Cambridge University Press, 2001), 73–84.
17. "*Letter to the* Edinburgh Review," in *Essays on Philosophical Subjects*, ed. I. S. Ross (Oxford: The Clarendon Press, 1980), 243.
18. *Leviathan,* 85 (I, XII, 12).

19. *First Tract on Government,* in *Political Essays,* ed. Mark Goldie (Cambridge: Cambridge University Press, 1997), 48–49.
20. *The Theory of Moral Sentiments,* ed. D. D. Raphael and A. L. Macfie (Oxford: Clarendon Press, 1976), 318 (VII, iii, 2, 2).
21. *An Essay Concerning Human Understanding,* ed. Peter H. Nidditch (Oxford: Clarendon Press, 1975), 66 (I, III, 2).
22. Quoted in Anthony Pagden, *European Encounters with the New World: From Renaissance to Romanticism* (New Haven, Conn., and London: Yale University Press, 1993), 89–90.
23. *An Anatomie of the World: The First Anniversary,* lines 205–8, 213–18.
24. *Second Meditation* 7.25.
25. See Michael Oakeshott, "Introduction to *Leviathan,*" in *Rationalism in Politics and Other Essays* (Indianapolis: Liberty Fund, 1991), 268.
26. "Droit naturel," in *Political Writings,* ed. John Hope Mason and Robert Wokler (Cambridge: Cambridge University Press), 17.
27. *Digest* I, I, 1, 3–4.
28. The best, and most succinct, general account of this complex history is still Alexander Passerin d'Entrèves, *Natural Law: An Introduction to Legal Philosophy,* re-edition with an introduction by Cary J. Nederman (New Brunswick and London: Transaction Publishers, 1994 [1950]).
29. *Summa contra gentiles* II, 68; Arthur O. Lovejoy, *The Great Chain of Being* (Cambridge, Mass.: Harvard University Press, 1936), 79–80.
30. This is explained with great lucidity and brilliance in Annabel S. Brett, *Changes of State: Nature and the Limits of the City in Early-Modern Natural Law* (Princeton, N.J.: Princeton University Press, 2011), 72–73.
31. *Summa theologiae* Ia, 2ae, q.91, art.1 and 2; q. 93, a.1.
32. *Institutes* II, I,1,
33. *De legibus ac deo legislatore* II. xix, 4.
34. For an exhaustive analysis of the various ways in which the *ius gentium* was understood, see the discussion in Brett, *Changes of State,* 75–89.
35. On the eccelesiasticization of Aristotle, see Ernst Kantorowicz, *The King's Two Bodies: A Study in Medieval Political Theology* (Princeton: Princeton University Press, 1957), 210–11.
36. See pp. 108–10.
37. See Ernest Bloch, *Natural Law and Human Dignity* (Cambridge, Mass.: MIT Press, 1986), 25–35.
38. Walter Ullmann, "Some Observations on the Mediaeval Evaluation of the 'Homo naturalis' and the 'Christianus,' " in *L'Homme et son destin d'après les penseurs du Moyen Age. Actes du premier congrès international de philosophie médiévale* (Louvain–Paris, 1960), 145–51.
39. *Inferno* iv, 36–39.
40. *An Enquiry Concerning Human Understanding,* in *Enquiries Concerning the Human Understanding and the Principles of Morals,* ed. L. A. Selby-Bigge (Oxford: Clarendon Press, 1970), 22n1.
41. *Comentarios a la Secunda Secundae de Santo Tomás,* ed. Vicente Beltrán de Heredia (Salamanca: Universidad de Salamanca, 1932–52), III, 11.

42. *Natural Law,* trans. T. M. Knox (Philadelphia: University of Pennsylvania Press, 1975), 59f.
43. All these examples are given by Francisco de Vitoria.
44. *An Essay Concerning Human Understanding,* 102 (I, IV, 25).
45. *Three Essays on Religion,* in *The Collected Works of John Stuart Mill* (London: Routledge, 1963–91), X, 373–402.
46. *The Complete Essays,* trans. M. A. Screech (London: Penguin Books, 1987), 127–29.
47. "On the Cannibals," in ibid., 231, 240–41, 235–36.
48. *Dictionnaire philosophique,* ed. Alain Pons (Paris: Gallimard, 1994), 66–67.
49. "On Habit: And on Never Easily Changing a Traditional Law," in *The Complete Essays,* 30. La Mettrie's comment is in *Anti-Seneca or the Sovereign Good* in *Machine Man and Other Writings,* trans. and ed. Ann Thomson (Cambridge: Cambridge University Press, 1996), 129.
50. *An Essay Concerning Human Understanding,* 66 (I, III, 2).
51. *The Elements of Law, Natural and Political,* ed. Ferdinand Tönnies, 2d ed. (London: Frank Cass, 1969), 188–89 (2, 10, 8).
52. "Thou shalt not avenge, nor bear any grudge against the children of thy people, but thou shalt love thy neighbor as thyself: I am the LORD," Leviticus 19:18. "So in everything, do to others what you would have them do to you, for this sums up the Law and the Prophets," Matthew 7:12.
53. *Discours sur l'origine et les fondements de l'inégalité,* in *Œuvres complètes,* ed. Bernard Gagnebin and Marcel Raymond (Paris: Bibliothèque de la Pléiade, 1959–95), III, 118.
54. *Émile ou l'éducation,* in *Œuvres complètes,* IV, 836.
55. *De Cive, On the Citizen,* trans. and ed. Richard Tuck and Michael Silverthorne (Cambridge: Cambridge University Press, 1998), 22 (1.1).
56. Ibid., 25 (1, 7).
57. *Leviathan,* 70 (I, XI).
58. See Richard Tuck, "The 'Modern' Theory of Natural Law," in *The Languages of Political Theory in Early-Modern Europe,* ed. Anthony Pagden (Cambridge: Cambridge University Press, 1987), 99–119.
59. "Defence of Seneca and Plutarch," in *The Complete Essays,* 821.
60. *De Cive,* 27 (1, 7).
61. *Leviathan,* 91 (1, XIV). See also the observations in Brett, *Changes of State,* 109.
62. Ibid., 100–9 (1, XV). Hobbes's method of argument is remarkably similar, in fact, to that of his despised scholastic opponents, although the presuppositions from which he begins, and the conclusions at which he arrives, are very different. Like them, he ends up by claiming that the law of nature can be summed up in the commandment "Do unto others as you would have others do unto you," although he, characteristically, phrases this as a negative command: "Do not that to another, which thou wouldest not have done to thy selfe."
63. *De iure belli ac pacis,* I, 40.
64. Ibid., I, 13.
65. Judith N. Shklar, "Subversive Genealogies," in *Political Thought and Political Thinkers* (Chicago and London: University of Chicago Press, 1998), 132–60.

66. *Leviathan,* 89 (I, XIII, 62).
67. Ibid., 9 (Introduction).
68. Ibid., 77 (I, XII, 12).
69. Ibid., 121 (II, XVIII).
70. "On the Common Saying: 'This may be true in theory, but it is of no use in practice,'" in *Practical Philosophy,* 302: AK 8:804.
71. "Sensus Communis, an Essay on the Freedom of Wit and Humour," in *Characteristics of Men, Manners, Opinions, Times,* ed. Lawrence E. Klein (Cambridge: Cambridge University Press, 1999), 42.
72. "Reflections upon Laughter," in *Philosophical Writings* (London: J. M. Dent, 1994), 46.
73. "Hobbisme," from the *Encyclopédie,* in *Political Writings,* 27.

Chapter 2

1. Francisco de Vitoria, "On the American Indians," 3, 1, in *Political Writings,* ed. Anthony Pagden and Jeremy Lawrance (Cambridge: Cambridge University Press, 1991), 279.
2. Anthony Pagden, "Human Rights, Natural Rights and Europe's Imperial Legacy," *Political Theory* 31 (2003): 171–99.
3. See, for instance, Jürgen Habermas, *Theorie und Praxis. Sozialphilosophische Studien* (Frankfurt am Main: Suhrkamp, 1978), 78–79.
4. *An Enquiry Concerning the Principles of Morals,* in *Enquiries Concerning the Human Understanding and the Principles of Morals,* 298.
5. *An Inquiry into the Human Mind on the Principles of Common Sense,* ed. Derek R. Brookes (Edinburgh: Edinburgh University Press, 1997 [1764]), 210–11. Tityrus, who thought that Rome was merely a larger version of his own home, appears in the first of Virgil's *Eclogues*.
6. Ibid., 21.
7. Quoted in E. C. Mossner, *The Life of David Hume* (Oxford: Oxford University Press, 1980), 136.
8. *Discours préliminaire de l'Encyclopédie*, in *Œuvres complètes de D'Alembert,* I, 17–99: 67.
9. *Mémoire A. M. de Mably*, in *Œuvres complètes,* IV, 31. The same words are repeated in *Pour l'éducation de Sainte-Marie,* in ibid., 51.
10. I owe this information to Theodore Christov.
11. *Elementa jursiprudentiae universalis,* I Def, Iv, 1.
12. *De iure naturae et gentium libri octo,* VII, ii, 13.
13. "Inaugural Lecture on the Social Nature of Man" [1730], in *Two Texts on Human Nature,* ed. Thomas Meitner (Cambridge: Cambridge University Press, 1993), 135.
14. *De iure naturae et gentium,* III, 2, 1. A slightly different version of the same passage appears in *On the Duty of Man and Citizen According to Natural Law,* ed. James Tully (Cambridge: Cambridge University Press, 1991), 61.
15. "Fragments politiques," in *Œuvres complètes,* III, 554.

16. Quoted in Samuel Pufendorf, *On the Duty of Man and Citizen According to Natural Law,* xxvii–xxviii.
17. "Morality According to Prof. Kant: Lectures on Baumgarten's Practical Philosophy," in Immanuel Kant, *Lectures on Ethics,* ed. Peter Heath and J. B. Schneewind (Cambridge: Cambridge University Press, 1997), 240: AK 29:621.
18. *Letter to Menoeceus,* 128.
19. *An Enquiry Concerning the Principles of Morals,* 298–99 (Appendix II). Hume's views on Stoicism, however, were not much more flattering. It was, he said, only "a more refined system of selfishness" that would "reason us out of all virtue as well as social enjoyment" (p. 40 and cf. p. 101).
20. *Praktische Philosophie Herder* (1794), AK 27: I, 15; *Esquisse d'un tableau historique des progrès de l'esprit humain,* 148.
21. *De Finibus,* III. 63.
22. Article "Éclectisme" from the *Encyclopédie,* in *Œuvres,* ed. Laurent Versini (Paris: Robert Laffont, 1994), I, 300.
23. In fact Smith himself made very little use of this image. His idea of the interrelatedness of all human activities, however, does have clearly Stoic origins. On the "invisible hand," see Rothschild, *Economic Sentiments,* 116–56.
24. *An Enquiry Concerning the Principles of Morals,* 217 (V, 1).
25. *An Essay Concerning Human Understanding,* 7 ("Epistle to the Reader"). For the context of the discussion, see Maurice Cranston, *John Locke: A Biography* (Oxford: Oxford University Press, 1985), 140–41.
26. *Discours preliminaire de l'Encyclopédie,* in *Œuvres complètes de D'Alembert,* I, 70.
27. Paul Hazard, *La Pensée européenne du XVIIIe siècle* (Paris: Librairie Arthème Fayard, 1963), 49.
28. *An Essay Concerning Human Understanding,* 10 ("Epistle to the Reader").
29. Ibid., 42 (I, I, 2).
30. Ibid., 67 (1, 3, 3).
31. G. W. Leibniz, *New Essays on Human Understanding,* trans. and ed. Peter Remnant and Jonathan Bennett (Cambridge: Cambridge University Press, 1981), 49, 70.
32. *An Enquiry Concerning the Human Understanding,* 22.
33. *Life, Unpublished Letters, and Philosophical Regimen of Anthony, Earl of Shaftesbury,* ed. Benjamin Rand (London: S. Sonnenschein & Co., 1900), 414. That the entire tradition of innateness from the Stoics to the scholastics was indeed Locke's prime target is much more obvious from the collection of texts known as *Essays on the Law of Nature,* which were in fact lectures, originally delivered by Locke in his capacity as Censor of Moral Philosophy at Christ Church, Oxford, in 1663–64, and which, in certain respects, constitute a first draft of portions of the *Essay*. Here the title of Chapter II of the *Essay*, "No Innate Principles in the Mind" is phrased as a question and an answer: "Is the Law of Nature inscribed in the Minds of Men? No." It is also the case that since here Locke was writing in Latin, the vocabulary he uses is much closer to that of the scholastics. The "principles" discussed in the *Essay* are, for instance, described as they are by the scholastics as *praeceptae*.
34. In *Œuvres,* I, 473. He was not alone, Condillac, Helvétius, and Holbach, among

others, had all come to similar conclusions. See Jørn Schøsler, *John Locke et les philosophes français: la critique des idées innées en France au dix-huitième siècle* (Oxford: Voltaire Foundation, 1997), who briefly summarizes the arguments of a number of them.

35. *An Essay Concerning Human Understanding,* 104 (II, 1). In fact Locke misrepresented the views of the "Schoolmen" on this issue. They did not suppose that their precepts or ideas, although innate, were active until the child reached the "age of reason," which was generally held to be eight years of age.
36. Ibid., 295–317 (II, 23). A very elegant account of this is given in Roy Porter, *The Creation of the Modern World: The Untold Story of the British Enlightenment* (New York and London: W. W. Norton, 2000), 63–64.
37. *Sir Isaac Newton's Mathematical Principles of Natural Philosophy and his System of the World,* ed. Florian Cajori (Berkeley: University of California Press, 1946), 398.
38. *An Essay Concerning Human Understanding,* 45–46 (I, I, 5). See also Ian Hacking, *The Emergence of Probability: A Philosophical Study of Early Ideas About Probability, Induction and Statistical Inference* (Cambridge: Cambridge University Press, 1975).
39. *An Essay Concerning Human Understanding,* 46–47 (I, I, 6–7).
40. Ibid., 159 (II, 11, 10).
41. *Correspondance,* ed. Theodore Besterman (Geneva: Institut et Musée Voltaire, 1953–77), VI, 227.
42. *Œuvres,* 1, 467.
43. "Reflections upon Laughter," in *Philosophical Writings,* 46.
44. *Life, Unpublished Letters, and Philosophical Regimen,* 403–5.
45. *Second Characters or the Language of Forms,* ed. Benjamin Rand (Cambridge: Cambridge University Press, 1914), 106–7.
46. Quoted in Jonathan I. Israel, *Radical Enlightenment: Philosophy and the Making of Modernity, 1650–1750* (Oxford: Oxford University Press, 2001), 348.
47. *An Essay Concerning Human Understanding,* 72 (I, III, 10); cf. 78 (I, III, 18) and 353–4 (II, 28, 10–11).
48. *A Treatise on Human Nature,* ed. L. A. Selby-Bigge and P. H. Nidditch (Oxford: Clarendon Press, 1978), 183.
49. *Enquiries Concerning the Human Understanding,* 300.
50. "A Letter Concerning Enthusiasm," in *Characteristics of Men, Manners, Opinions,* 9.
51. Letter of Nov. 1768 to Kant, in Immanuel Kant, in *Correspondence,* trans. and ed. Arnulf Zweig (Cambridge: Cambridge University Press, 1999), 98, and "Fragments on Recent German Literature" [1767–68], in *Philosophical Writings,* 47.
52. On the influence of Shaftesbury's aesthetics, see Paul Guyer, *Kant and the Experience of Freedom: Essays on Aesthetics and Morality* (Cambridge: Cambridge University Press, 1993), 48–55. On Stäudlin, see T. J. Hochstrasser, *Natural Law Theories in the Early Enlightenment* (Cambridge: Cambridge University Press, 2000), 210.
53. "Schöngeister," in "How Philosophy Can Become More Universal and Useful for the Benefit of the People" [1765], in *Philosophical Writings,* 6.
54. *A Methodical System of Universal Laws,* trans. George Turnbull, ed. Thomas Ahnert and Peter Schröder (Indianapolis: Liberty Fund, 2008 [1741]), 578.

55. "How Philosophy Can Become More Universal and Useful for the Benefit of the People," 6–7.
56. *A Treatise on Human Nature,* xvii, 646. Adam Smith gives a similar list, with the addition of Hobbes and Clarke, all of whom are said, "according to their different and inconsistent systems," to have added something "to that stock of observations with which the world has been furnished before them." "Letter to the *Edinburgh Review,*" in *Essays on Philosophical Subjects,* ed. I. S. Ross (Oxford: Clarendon Press, 1980), 250.
57. "An Inquiry Concerning Virtue or Merit," in *Characteristics of Men, Manners, Opinions, Times,* 170.
58. "Sensus Communis, an Essay on the Freedom of Wit and Humour," in ibid., 51.
59. In ibid., 325.
60. *An Essay on the Nature and the Conduct of the Passions and Affections with Illustrations on the Moral Sense,* ed. Aaron Garrett (Indianapolis: Liberty Fund, 2002 [1728]), 148.
61. Diderot, *Histoire des deux Indes,* in *Œuvres,* III, 685. On this text, see pp. 201–02.
62. See Frazer, *The Enlightenment of Sympathy,* 18–19.
63. An Inquiry Concerning Virtue or Merit, in *Characteristics of Men, Manners, Opinions, Times,* 178.
64. Ibid., 173; see also Charles Taylor, "Self-Interpreting Animals," in *Philosophy and the Human Sciences: Philosophical Papers* (Cambridge: Cambridge University Press, 1985), I, 46.
65. *A Treatise on Human Nature,* 386.
66. It is also not so very hard to see what Kant was getting at when he accused Shaftesbury of being an Epicurean—much though it astonished Moses Mendelssohn. Ernst Cassirer, *Kant's Life and Thought,* trans. James Haden (New Haven, Conn., and London: Yale University Press, 1981), 236–37.
67. *Theory of Moral Sentiments,* ed. D. D. Raphael and A. L. Macfie (Oxford: Clarendon Press, 1976), 10–11, which he took, wrongly, to be based on a notion of propriety. See note 50.
68. Ibid., 9.
69. Ibid., 11–12, emphasis added.
70. "Of National Characters," in *Essays Moral, Political, and Literary,* ed. Eugene F. Miller (Indianapolis: Liberty Fund, 1985), 202.
71. *La logica per gli giovanetti. Classici italiani di economia politica* (Milan, 1835), CCCLVIII, 23, 454. In 1758 Genovesi was elected to a newly created chair in "Commerce and Mechanics"—in effect, political economy—the first of its kind in Europe. On Genovesi and Hume, see Robertson, *The Case for Enlightenment,* 373–76, although he is not concerned with this issue.
72. *An Enquiry Concerning the Principles of Morals,* 222 (v, II).
73. "Letter to the Edinburgh Review," in *Essays on Philosophical Subjects,* 198.
74. *Émile,* in *Œuvres complètes,* IV, 314. On the ties between Hobbes and Rousseau, see Richard Tuck, *The Rights of War and Peace: Political Thought and the International Order from Grotius to Kant* (Oxford: Oxford University Press, 1999), 197–200.
75. *Discours sur l'origine de inégalité,* in *Œuvres complètes,* III, 153–55.

76. "Lettre de J. J. Rousseau a M. de Voltaire" (Aug. 18, 1756), in *Œuvres complètes,* IV, 1072.
77. See E. J. Hundert, *The Enlightenment's Fable: Bernard Mandeville and the Discovery of Society* (Cambridge: Cambridge University Press, 1994), 237–49.
78. "Letter to the Edinburgh Review," in *Essays on Philosophical Subjects,* 250.
79. *Discours sur l'origine de inégalité,* in *Œuvres complètes,* III, 153–55.
80. *Anthropologie structurale deux* (Paris: Plon, 1973), 48.
81. *Theory of Moral Sentiments,* 10.
82. *A Treatise on Human Nature,* 457, 415.
83. "Droit naturel," in *Political Writings,* 20.
84. *Volonté generale.* Not to be confused with Rousseau's use of the same term, which, although similarly all-embracing, is limited to the collective will of the members of only one society bound together by a contract (or *pacte*).
85. "Discours prononcé dans l'Académie française . . . a la réception de M. le marquis de Condorcet," in *Œuvres complètes de Condorcet,* X, 103.

Chapter 3

1. "Philosophie," in *Œuvres,* I, 464.
2. "Hobbisme," in *Political Writings,* 28.
3. Ibid. Hobbes's remark to Selden is quoted in Alex Schulman, *The Secular Contract: The Politics of Enlightenment* (New York and London: Continuum Books, 2011), 25.
4. *Dictionnaire philosophique,* ed. Alain Pons (Paris: Gallimard, 1994), 78, "Athée, Athéisme."
5. *An Essay Concerning Human Understanding,* 10 ("Epistle to the Reader").
6. See Frank Manuel, *The Religion of Isaac Newton* (Oxford: Oxford University Press, 1974).
7. See Anthony Pagden, "The Search for Order: The 'School of Salamanca' and the *ius naturae,*" in *The Uncertainties of Empire* (Aldershot: Variorum, 1994), III, 164.
8. *Du Contrat social,* in *Œuvres complètes,* III, 463.
9. *An Account of Denmark as It Was in the Year 1692* (London, 1694), b3r.
10. Quoted in Reinhart Koselleck, *Critique and Crisis: Enlightenment and the Pathogenesis of Modern Society* (Oxford, New York, and Hamburg: Berg, 1988), 140.
11. Quoted in David Bell, *The Cult of the Nation in France: Inventing Nationalism, 1680–1800* (Cambridge, Mass.: Harvard University Press, 2001), 30.
12. *An Answer to the Question: "What Is Enlightenment?"* in *Practical Philosophy,* 21: AK 8: 41.
13. See David Carrithers, "The Enlightenment Science of Society," in *Inventing Human Science: Eighteenth-Century Domains,* ed. Christopher Fox, Roy Porter, and Robert Wokler (Berkeley, Los Angeles, and London: University of California Press, 1995), 232–70.
14. *Essai sur les éléments de philosophie ou sur les principes des connaissances humaines* (Paris: Fayard, 1986), 58.
15. Corinthians 3:11.

16. "The Diversity of Goods," in *Philosophy and the Human Sciences: Philosophical Papers* (Cambridge: Cambridge University Press, 1985), II, 232.
17. See J. B. Scheenwind, *The Invention of Autonomy: A History of Modern Moral Philosophy* (Cambridge: Cambridge University Press, 1998), 480.
18. *Addition aux pensées philosophiques,* in *Œuvres,* I, 47.
19. For an account of these sessions, see René Pomeau, *La Religion de Voltaire* (Paris: Librairie Nizet, 1956), 159–84. On her death Châtelet left a five-volume commentary on the Old and New Testaments. See Ira O. Wade, *Voltaire and Madame du Châtelet: An Essay on the Intellectual Activity at Cirey* (Princeton, N.J.: Princeton University Press, 1941).
20. *Histoire de l'établissement du christianisme* (1777), in *Œuvres complètes de Voltaire* (Paris, 1880), XXXI, 59.
21. *Dictionnaire philosophique,* 164–65, "Christianisme."
22. Ibid., 422, "Paul."
23. *Histoire critique de Jésus Christ,* Préface, in *Œuvres philosophiques complètes,* II, 657.
24. Ibid., 726–35.
25. "De la paix perpétuelle par le docteur Goodheart," in *L'Evangile du Jour* (London, 1770), 13–14, 26.
26. *Dieu et les hommes,* cited in Frank Manuel, *The Changing of the Gods* (Hanover and London: University Press of New England, 1983), 63.
27. *Dictionnaire philosophique,* 193, "Christianisme."
28. All of these reflections come from the *Sermon des cinquante* ("Sermon of the fifty"), which Voltaire probably wrote in 1750–52 when he was the somewhat unwilling guest of Frederick II of Prussia. The translations I have used come from Peter Gay, *Deism: An Anthology* (Princeton, N.J.: D. Van Nostrand & Co., 1968), 143–58.
29. "De la paix perpétuelle par le docteur Goodheart," in *L'Evangile du Jour,* 39.
30. The best-known formulation of the "watchmaker god" is that of William Paley in 1802, although the analogy had been made by Bernard de Fontenelle as early as 1686.
31. *Physics,* 267b, 18–26.
32. *Metaphysics,* 1072b, 213–29.
33. *Système de la nature* (II. 3), in *Œuvres philosophiques complètes,* II, 429.
34. *Dictionnaire philosophique,* 423, "Péché original."
35. *Essais de théodicée, sur la bonté de dieu, la liberté de l'homme et l'origine du mal* (Paris: Garnier-Flammarion, 1969), 370.
36. *Theory of Moral Sentiments,* 235–36 (VI, ii, 3–6).
37. *Correspondence of Adam Smith,* ed. Ernest Campbell Mossner and Ian Simpson Ross (Oxford: Clarendon Press, 1977), 34.
38. *Histoire de l'établissement du christianisme,* in *Œuvres complètes de Voltaire,* 113.
39. *Dictionnaire philosophique,* 490, "Théiste."
40. Quoted in Lawrence E. Klein, *Shaftesbury and the Culture of Politeness: Moral Discourse and Cultural Politics in Early Eighteenth-Century England* (Cambridge: Cambridge University Press, 1994), 158.
41. "The Moralists, a Philosophical Rhapsody," in *Characteristics of Men, Manners, Opinions, Times,* 243. Shaftesbury is here speaking in the voice of "Philocles."

42. *Dictionnaire philosophique,* 367, "Lois (Des)." The passage is also quoted in J. B. Schneewind, *The Invention of Autonomy,* 461; on Voltaire's religious beliefs, see 460–62.
43. *Dictionnaire philosophique,* 491, "Théiste."
44. *An Inquiry into the Origin of Honour, and the Usefulness of Christianity in War* (London, 1732), 27–28.
45. *Du Contrat social,* in *Œuvres complètes,* III, 467–68.
46. Ibid., 385–86.
47. *Esquisse d'un tableau historique des progrès de l'esprit humain,* 172.
48. *Le fanatisme, ou Mahomet le prophète, Tragédie en cinq actes* (first performed in Lille in April 1741), Act I, scene 5.
49. Quoted in Maurice Cranston, *Philosophers and Pamphleteers: Political Theorists of the Enlightenment* (Oxford: Oxford University Press, 1986), 44.
50. *Histoire des deux Indes,* in *Œuvres,* III, 613.
51. Quoted by Peter Gay, *The Enlightenment: An Interpretation* (New York: Knopf, 1966), II, 28.
52. *Histoire des deux Indes,* in *Œuvres,* III, 614.
53. Quoted in Émile Benveniste, "Civilisation: contribution a l'histoire du mot," in *Problèmes de linguistique générale* (Paris: Gallimard, 1976), 338.
54. On Bayle, see Elizabeth Labrousse, *Pierre Bayle* (The Hague: Martinus Nijhoff, 1963); Israel, *Radical Enlightenment;* and Cassirer, *The Philosophy of the Enlightenment,* 201–9.
55. Jonathan Israel, *Enlightenment Contested: Philosophy, Modernity, and the Emancipation of Man, 1670–1752* (Oxford: Oxford University Press, 2006), 88–92; see also H. T. Mason, *Pierre Bayle and Voltaire* (Oxford: Oxford University Press, 1963).
56. *A Treatise on Human Nature,* 240–41 (I, iv–v).
57. *Machine Man,* in Thomson, *Machine Man and Other Writings,* 22–23.
58. *The System of Epicurus,* in ibid., 110.
59. *History of Western Philosophy* (London: George Allen & Unwin, 1946), 521.
60. Quoted in J.C.A. Gaskin, "Hume on Religion," in *The Cambridge Companion to Hume,* ed. David Fate Norton (Cambridge: Cambridge University Press, 1993), 333.
61. *L'Ingénu* [1767], in *Romans et contes,* ed. René Gros (Paris: Classiques Garnier, 1954), 279.
62. "De l'abus de la critique en matière de la religion," in *Œuvres complètes de D'Alembert,* I, 552.
63. "Réflexions philosophiques," in *Œuvres complètes,* ed. Roger Caillois (Paris: Bibliothèque de la Pléiade, 1949), I, 1177.
64. Letter to Sophie Volland, Oct. 30, 1759, in *Correspondance de Denis Diderot,* ed. Georges Roth (Paris: Les Editions de Minuit, 1955–70), II, 299.
65. Letter to C. de Beaumont, in *Œuvres complètes,* IV, 960.
66. *Jugement sur Émile,* in *Œuvres complètes de D'Alembert,* IV, 463.
67. *Émile,* in *Œuvres complètes,* IV, 589; see also John McManners's brilliant evocation of the sufferings of poor Jean-Jacques in *Death in the Enlightenment: Changing Attitudes to Death in Eighteenth-Century France* (Oxford: Oxford University Press, 1985), 172–75.

68. *De la suffisance de la religion naturelle,* in *Œuvres,* I, 57.
69. Ibid., 55.
70. "My Own Life," in *Natural History of Religion,* ed. J.C.A. Gaskin (Oxford: Oxford University Press, 1992), 9.
71. Letter to Sophie Volland, Oct. 6, 1765, in *Œuvres,* V, 537. A slightly different version is given in Mossner, *The Life of David Hume,* 483.
72. *Mémoires inédites de l'abbé Morellet: précédés d'un éloge historique de l'abbé Morellet par M. Leémontey* (Paris, 1823), 113–15; and Mossner, *The Life of David Hume,* 484. For a more extensive account, see Alan Charles Kors, *D'Holbach's Coterie: An Enlightenment in Paris* (Princeton, N.J.: Princeton University Press, 1976).
73. Letter to Horace Walpole, Nov. 1766, in *The Letters of David Hume,* ed. J.Y.T. Greig (Oxford: Clarendon Press, 1932), II, 10.
74. Porter, *The Creation of the Modern World,* 104, 127.
75. See, for example, J.G.A. Pocock's ongoing opus magnum, *Barbarism and Religion* (Cambridge: Cambridge University Press, 1999–), four volumes to date.
76. *Reflections on the Revolution in France,* 254–55.
77. Letter of Mar. 18, 1776. In *The Autobiography of Edward Gibbon,* ed. Lord Sheffield (Oxford: Oxford University Press, 1950), 181.
78. *Lettres philosophiques,* ed. René Pomeau (Paris: Flammarion, 1964), 42.
79. Ibid., 47.
80. Letter to Sophie Volland, Oct. 6, 1765, in *Œuvres,* V, 537.
81. *Theory of Moral Sentiments,* 214 (VI, 1, 8).
82. All quoted in Rothschild, *Economic Sentiments,* 54.
83. Recorded by an anonymous member of Smith's circle who wrote under the pen name "Amicus," from "The Bee, or Literary Weekly Intelligencer" (May 11, 1781), in *Lectures on Rhetoric and Belles Lettres,* ed. J. Bryce (Oxford: Clarendon Press, 1983), 228.
84. For an analysis of the language of "enthusiasm," see Michael Heyd, *"Be Sober and Reasonable": The Critique of Enthusiasm in the Seventeenth and Early Eighteenth Centuries* (Leiden: E. J. Brill, 1995).
85. "Of Superstition and Enthusiasm," in *Essays Moral, Political, and Literary,* 74; see also John Passmore, "Enthusiasm, Fanaticism, and David Hume," in *The "Science of Man" in the Scottish Enlightenment: Hume, Reid, and Their Contemporaries,* ed. Peter Jones (Edinburgh: Edinburgh University Press, 1989), 85–107.
86. "A Letter Concerning Enthusiasm to my Lord ******," in *Characteristics of Men, Manners, Opinions, Times,* 10–18.
87. *De la démocratie en Amérique,* II, 37–47 (I, V).
88. "Letter to Dr. Joseph Priestley" [1803], in *Writings* (New York: Library of America, 1984), 1121.
89. Quoted in Gordon S. Wood, *Empire of Liberty: A History of the Early Republic* (Oxford: Oxford University Press, 2009), 577.
90. *Writings,* 285.
91. See the wonderful account of his demise in Darrin McMahon, *The Pursuit of Happiness: A History from the Greeks to the Present* (London: Penguin Books, 2007), 222–23.
92. *Essai sur les règnes de Claude et de Néron,* in *Œuvres,* I, 1119.

93. *Anti-Seneca or the Sovereign Good,* in Thomson, *Machine Man and Other Writings,* 119.
94. Schneewind, *The Invention of Autonomy,* 462–65.
95. "De l'abus de la critique en matière de la religion," in *Œuvres complètes de D'Alembert,* I, 553.
96. Passmore, "Enthusiasm, Fanaticism, and David Hume," 86.
97. What follows is heavily dependent upon J.C.A. Gaskin, *Hume's Philosophy of Religion* (New York: Macmillan, 1980) and "Hume on Religion," in *The Cambridge Companion to Hume,* 313–44.
98. Letter to William Strachan, Nov. 9, 1776, in *Correspondence of Adam Smith.*
99. *An Enquiry Concerning Human Understanding,* 110 (X, 1).
100. Mossner, *The Life of David Hume,* 100–101.
101. *An Enquiry Concerning Human Understanding,* 115 (X, 1).
102. Ibid., 130–31.
103. Ibid., 10.
104. Ibid., 135.
105. *Lettre sur les aveugles,* in *Œuvres,* I, 167–68.
106. *Dialogues Concerning Natural Religion,* ed. J.C.A. Gaskin (Oxford: Oxford University Press, 1993), 64.
107. Ibid., 60, 45. Hume also uses the term *anthropomorphism* in ibid., 61.
108. *An Essay on the Nature and Conduct of the Passions and Affections with Illustrations on Moral Sense,* 116.
109. *Persian Letters,* trans. C. J. Betts (New York: Viking-Penguin, 1973), 124 (Letter 59).
110. *Dialogues Concerning Natural Religion,* 63.
111. Ibid., 111.
112. "Of the Immortality of the Soul," in *Essays Moral, Political, and Literary.*
113. *A Treatise on Human Nature,* 316 (II, xi).
114. Ibid., 318 (II, xi).
115. *An Enquiry Concerning Human Understanding,* 135 (XI).
116. *Dialogues Concerning Natural Religion,* 123–24.
117. "Of Suicide," in *Essays Moral, Political, and Literary,* 587.
118. *Dialogues Concerning Natural Religion,* 122.
119. Judith N. Shklar, *Freedom and Independence: A Study of Hegel's "Phenomenology of Mind"* (Cambridge: Cambridge University Press, 1976), 172.
120. *Natural History of Religion,* 134; "On Superstition and Enthusiasm," in *Essays Moral, Political, and Literary,* 74.
121. *Natural History of Religion,* 130.
122. *Rocks of Ages: Science and Religion in the Fullness of Life* (New York: Ballantine Books, 1999).
123. "Of Superstition and Enthusiasm," in *Essays Moral, Political, and Literary,* 71–72.
124. *Essai sur les éléments de philosophie ou sur les principes des connaissances humaines,* 19–27.
125. Ibid., 57.

Chapter 4

1. *Essai sur les éléments de philosophie ou sur les principes des connaissances humaines,* 19–20, emphasis added.
2. Ibid., 25–26.
3. *Idée d'un système général de la Nature,* in *Œuvres philosophiques* (The Hague: Martinus Nijhoff, 1975), II, 215. See also Israel, *Enlightenment Contested,* 499–504.
4. *Discours sur l'origine et les fondements de l'inégalité,* in *Œuvres complètes,* III, 123. See pp. 206–07.
5. *Sketches of the History of Man* [1788], ed. James A. Harris (Indianapolis: Liberty Fund, 2007), III, 714.
6. Quoted in Mossner, *The Life of David Hume,* 113.
7. "My Own Life," in *Principal Writings on Religion,* ed. Gaskin, 3–4.
8. Quoted in Mossner, *The Life of David Hume,* 112.
9. "Of Essay Writing," in *Essays Moral, Political, and Literary,* 533–36.
10. *Œuvres,* V, 575.
11. *A Fragment on Government* (1776), ed. J. H. Burns and H.L.A. Hart (Cambridge: Cambridge University Press, 1988), 51n2.
12. *A Treatise on Human Nature,* xvi (Introduction).
13. Not to be confused with the Lockean distinction between primary and secondary qualities. For Locke, "secondary qualities"—for instance the warmth derived from fire—"in truth are nothing in the Objects themselves, but Powers to produce various Sensations in us by their primary Qualities." *An Essay Concerning Human Understanding,* 10–11 (II, VIII). Hume, like Berkeley and Holbach, maintained that the distinction was a spurious one.
14. *A Treatise on Human Nature,* 13 (I, IV).
15. Ibid., xvii–xviii (Introduction). See pp. 80–81.
16. *Essay on Man,* Epistle I, line 4; Epistle II, lines 1–2.
17. *A Treatise on Human Nature,* xviii (Introduction).
18. *Essai sur les éléments de philosophie,* 27.
19. *The Letters of David Hume,* I, 16.
20. "Soliloquy, or Advice to an Author," in *Characteristics of Men, Manners, Opinions, Times,* 131–32.
21. "Discours prononcé dans l'Académie française . . . a la réception de M. le marquis de Condorcet," in *Œuvres complètes de Condorcet,* X, 100.
22. *An Enquiry Concerning the Human Understanding,* 83–84 (VIII, 1).
23. *A Treatise on Human Nature,* xvi (Introduction).
24. See A. Child, *Making and Knowing in Hobbes, Vico, Dewey* (Berkeley and Los Angeles: University of California Press, 1953); and Giulio Severino, *Principi e modificazioni in Vico* (Genoa: Il Melangolo, 1981), 17–25.
25. Emphasis added. Vico's *New Science* (*Scienza nuova*) went through three editions, each one significantly different from the last. The most important, however, are the first (1725) and the third (1744). I have used the standard paragraph numbers to the third edition—hereafter *NS*—and the first—hereafter *NS* 1. Where possible I have used the translations in Vico, *Selected Writings,* ed. and trans. Leon Pompa (Cambridge: Cambridge University Press, 1982). The account of the

verum ipsum factum principle is in *NS* 331 (and cf. *NS* 349 and 374). Vico's descriptions of the nature of his project, or as he calls them, his "discoveries," are to be found in *NS,* 386–99, and *NS* 1, 519–26.

26. Described in Robertson, *The Case for Enlightenment,* 201–3.
27. *NS* 347. In his *Autobiography* Vico lists Grotius together with Plato, Tacitus, and Bacon as the main sources of his inspiration: "Vita di Giambattista Vico," in *G. B. Vico Opere,* ed. F. Nicolini (Bari: 1911–41), V, 38–39.
28. Jules Michelet, *Discours sur le système et la vie de Vico* [1827], in *Œuvres complètes,* ed. Paul Viallaneix, 8 vols. (Paris, 1971–82), I, 283–350; on Vico as a veiled Spinozist, see Gino Bedani, *Vico Revisited: Orthodoxy, Naturalism and Science in the* Scienza Nuova (Oxford, Hamburg, and Munich: Berg, 1989), and more recently, Israel, *Radical Enlightenment,* 669, and *Enlightenment Contested,* 526–37.
29. On Hobbes having taught "English to speak philosophy" in the tone of "the sane and moderate savant beset on all sides by fanaticism and stupidity," see Quentin Skinner, *Reason and Rhetoric in the Philosophy of Hobbes* (Cambridge: Cambridge University Press, 1996), 436.
30. "Letters for the Advancement of Humanity (1793–97)—Tenth Collection," in Herder, *Philosophical Writings,* 393. For a different kind of comparison between Hume and Vico, see Robertson, *The Case for Enlightenment,* 316–24.
31. *Truth and Method* [*Wahrheit und Methode,* 1965] (London: Sheen & Ward, 1975), 20–21.
32. *Essai sur les éléments de philosophie,* 57; cf. Bernard Mandeville, "The Word Moral, without doubt, comes from *Mos* and signifies everything that relates to Manners," *An Inquiry into the Origin of Honour, and the Usefulness of Christianity in War* (London, 1732), iii.
33. "Of National Characters," in *Essays Moral, Political, and Literary,* 198.
34. *An Enquiry Concerning the Human Understanding,* 46–47 (V, 1).
35. *A Treatise on Human Nature,* xix (Introduction).
36. Kant's project, however, was quite different. Although he remarks that "the German word Sitten, like the Latin mores, mean only manners and customs," in the *Metaphysik der Sitten* of 1797, he is explicitly concerned with "the doctrine of morals" or *Sittenlehre. The Metaphysics of Morals,* in *Practical Philosophy,* trans. and ed. Gregor, 372: AK 6: 216. "Man does not derive instructions from observing himself and his animal nature or from perceiving the ways of the world, what happens and how we behave. . . . Instead reason commands how we are to act even though no example of this could be found, and it takes no account of the advantages we can thereby gain, which only experience could teach us."
37. *A Treatise on Human Nature,* xvi (Introduction).
38. *De civitate dei,* XIV, I. And cf. XII, 22, where the need to create this "feeling of kinship" is given as the reason for the creation of Eve.
39. "Of the Populousness of Ancient Nations," in *Essays Moral, Political, and Literary,* 378.
40. *Essai sur les éléments de philosophie ou sur les principes des connaissances humaines,* 63.
41. *An Enquiry Concerning the Human Understanding,* 83, 84 (VIII, 1).
42. "Of the Populousness of Ancient Nations," in *Essays Moral, Political, and Literary,* 378.

43. *An Enquiry Concerning the Human Understanding,* 84–85 (VIII, 1).
44. "A Dialogue," in *An Enquiry Concerning the Principles of Morals,* 327–28.
45. Benjamin Isaac, for instance, has argued for the existence of something he calls "proto-racism" in antiquity. See *The Invention of Racism in Classical Antiquity* (Princeton, N.J.: Princeton University Press, 2004) and the essays in Miriam Eliav-Feldon et al., eds., *The Origins of Racism in the West* (Cambridge: Cambridge University Press, 2009).
46. See Judith Shklar, "Jean D'Alembert and the Rehabilitation of History," in *Political Thought and Political Thinkers,* 301, and *De l'Esprit des lois,* XVII, 3–2.
47. *De l'Esprit* (Paris: Fayard, 1988), 319.
48. *A Treatise on Human Nature,* 316–17 (II, xi).
49. "Of National Characters," in *Essays Moral, Political, and Literary,* 204.
50. "Essai sur les causes qui peuvent affecter les esprits et les caractères," in *Œuvres complètes,* II, 61–62.
51. *A Treatise on Human Nature,* 316–17 (II, xi).
52. "On National Characters," in *Essays Moral, Political, and Literary,* 208n10. The original essay was written in 1748, the note was added to the edition of 1753, and in the edition of 1777, published the year after Hume's death, the phrase "and in general all other species of men (for there are four or five different kinds)" was deleted. See Colin Kidd, *The Forging of Races: Race and Scripture in the Protestant Atlantic World* (Cambridge: Cambridge University Press, 2006), 93–95.
53. *Émile ou de l'éducation,* in *Œuvres complètes,* IV, 267.
54. *On the Use of Teleological Principles in Philosophy,* trans. Günter Zöller, in *Anthropology, History, and Education,* ed. Günter Zöller and Robert B. Louden (Cambridge: Cambridge University Press, 2007), 209: AK 8: 174.
55. *Observations on the Feeling of the Beautiful and the Sublime,* trans. Paul Guyer, in ibid., 59: AK 2: 253. See Pauline Kleingeld, *Kant and Cosmopolitanism: The Philosophical Ideal of World Citizenship* (Cambridge: Cambridge University Press, 2012), 96–117; and Sankar Muthu, *Enlightenment Against Empire* (Princeton, N.J.: Princeton University Press, 2003), 183.
56. John H. Zamato, *Kant, Herder: The Birth of Anthropology* (Chicago and London: University of Chicago Press, 2002), 304–5; and Thomas McCarthy, *Race, Empire, and the Idea of Human Development* (Cambridge: Cambridge University Press, 2009), 42–68.
57. "On the Different Races of Human Beings," trans. Holly Wilson and Günter Zöller, in *Anthropology, History, and Education,* 86: AK 2: 431.
58. Kleingeld, *Kant and Cosmopolitanism,* 111–17.
59. *Sketches of the History of Man,* I, 41–42.
60. *Histoire des deux Indes,* in *Œuvres,* III, 737–44.
61. *Du Contrat social,* 1, II, in *Œuvres complètes,* III, 353.
62. *Examen critique des voyages dans l'Amérique septentrionale de M. le m.s. de Chastellux* (London, 1786), 104.
63. *Examen de cette question: quel sera pour les colonies de l'Amérique le résultat de la Révolution française, de la guerre qui en est la suite, et de la paix que doit le terminer?* (London, 1797), 5–6.

64. "A Discourse on the Love of Our Country," in *Political Writings,* ed. D. O. Thomas (Cambridge: Cambridge University Press, 1991), 184.
65. "Le Rêve de D'Alembert," in *Œuvres,* 1, 631. On this passage, see Charles Taylor, *A Secular Age* (Cambridge, Mass.: Harvard University Press, 2007), 327.
66. "Principes philosophiques sur la matière et le mouvement," in *Œuvres,* I, 681–82; see Jean Starobinski, *Action et Réaction. Vie et aventures d'un couple* (Paris: Seuil, 1999), 53–97.
67. Jacques Roger, *Buffon: un philosophe au Jardin du Roi* (Paris, 1989) and *Les Sciences de la vie dans la pensée francaise au XVIIIème siècle* (Paris, 1963).
68. Cited in Otis Fellows, "Buffon and Rousseau: Aspects of a Relationship," *Proceedings of the Modern Languages Association* 75 (1960), 184–96.
69. "Letter to the Edinburgh Review," in *Essays on Philosophical Subjects,* 248.
70. Quoted in Jean Starobinski, "Rousseau et Buffon," in *Jean Jacques Rousseau: la transparence et l'obstacle* (Paris: Gallimard, 1971), 383. Formey was also the author of *La Belle Wolfienne*. See p. 330.
71. "De la nature de l'homme," in *De l'homme,* ed. Michèle Duchet (Paris: François Maspero, 1971), 39–41.
72. *Histoire naturelle,* in *Œuvres complètes de Buffon avec la nomenclature linnéenne et la classification de Cuvier. Revues sur l'édition de l'Imprimerie royale et annotées par M. Flourens* (Paris, 1853–55), II, 336–38.
73. Starobinski, "Rousseau et Buffon," 388.
74. Michèle Duchet, *Anthropologie et histoire au siècle des lumières* (Paris: François Maspero, 1971), 240–41.
75. Antonello Gerbi, *La disputa del Nuovo Mondo. Storia di una polemica, 1750–1900* (Milan: Riccardo Ricciardi, 1983).
76. Keith Thomson, "Jefferson, Buffon, and the Moose," *American Scientist* 98 (2010).
77. *Philosophical Review of the Successive Advances of the Human Mind,* in *Turgot on Progress, Sociology and Economics,* trans. and ed. Ronald L. Meek (Cambridge: Cambridge University Press, 1973), 42.
78. *An Enquiry Concerning the Human Understanding,* 84–85 (VIII, 1). For Hume's use of history, see Andrew Sabl, *Hume's Politics: Coordination and Crisis in the History of England* (Princeton, N.J.: Princeton University Press, 2012).
79. *The Philosophy of the Enlightenment,* 197; cf. Peter Reill, *The German Enlightenment and the Rise of Historicism* (Berkeley: University of California Press, 1975).
80. For the relationships between Voltaire, Robertson, Hume, and Gibbon, see Karen O'Brien, *Narratives of Enlightenment: Cosmopolitan History from Voltaire to Gibbon* (Cambridge: Cambridge University Press, 1997).
81. See Shklar, "Jean D'Alembert and the Rehabilitation of History," in *Political Thought and Political Thinkers,* 301.
82. *Essai sur l'étude de la littérature,* ed. Robert Mankin (Oxford: Voltaire Foundation, 2010), 126–27. See also Pocock, *Barbarism and Religion,* II, *The Narratives of Civil Government,* 23.
83. Quoted in Cassirer, *Philosophy of the Enlightenment,* 216.
84. Quoted in Bruce P. Lenman, "'From Savage to Scot' via the French and the

Spaniards: Principal Robertson's Spanish Sources," in *William Robertson and the Expansion of Empire,* ed. Stewart J. Brown (Cambridge: Cambridge University Press, 1997), 204.

85. *The History of England: From the Invasion of Julius Caesar to the Revolution in 1688* (Indianapolis: Liberty Fund, 1983–85), I, 2.
86. "Older Critical Forestlet" (1767–68), in Herder, *Philosophical Writings,* 265–66.
87. *NS* 7. Vico's descriptions of the nature of his project, or as he calls it, his "discoveries," are to be found in *NS* 386–99. Cassirer said of *New Science* that it was "the first to point the way to a philosophy of history in the eighteenth century," *The Philosophy of the Enlightenment,* 209.
88. "Fragment sur l'histoire générale," in *Essai sur les moeurs et l'esprit des nations,* ed. R. Pomeau (Paris: Classiques Garnier, 1990), II, 951–94.
89. "Supplément a l'Essai sur les moeurs," in ibid., 906.
90. Pocock, *Barbarism and Religion,* II, 72–162.
91. Quoted in Cassirer, *Philosophy of the Enlightenment,* 216.
92. Donald Kelley, *Faces of History: Historical Inquiry from Herodotus to Herder* (New Haven, Conn., and London: Yale University Press, 1998), 266.
93. "Account of the Life and Writings of Adam Smith LL.D," in *Essays on Philosophical Subjects,* 292.
94. *De l'Esprit des lois,* "Preface."
95. Ibid., I, 1.
96. *Between Facts and Norms: Contributions to a Discourse Theory of Law and Democracy,* trans. William Rehg (Cambridge, Mass.: MIT Press, 1996), 46.
97. On Kant's conception of the imagination as "entering into the direct service of reason," see Guyer, *Kant and the Experience of Freedom,* 215–16.
98. *Idea for a Universal History with a Cosmopolitan Aim,* trans. Allen W. Wood, in *Anthropology, History, and Education,* 108–9: AK 8: 17–18.
99. *The Conflict of the Faculties,* trans. Mary J. Gregor and Robert Anchor, in *Religion and Rational Theology,* trans. and ed. Allen W. Wood and George di Giovanni (Cambridge: Cambridge University Press, 1996), 297: AK 7: 79.
100. *Idea for a Universal History with a Cosmopolitan Aim,* trans. Allen W. Wood, in *Anthropology, History, and Education,* 109: AK 8: 18.
101. *Conjectural Beginning of Human History,* trans. Allen W. Wood, in ibid., 163: AK 8: 109.
102. Quoted in Schneewind, *The Invention of Autonomy,* 491.
103. *Conjectural Beginning of Human History,* in *Anthropology, History, and Education,* 163: AK 8: 109.
104. *Esquisse d'un tableau historique des progrès de l'esprit humain,* 80.
105. *Conjectural Beginning of Human History,* in *Anthropology, History, and Education,* 169: AK 8: 115.
106. *Discours sur l'origine et les fondements de l'inégalité,* 135; see also Shklar, "Subversive Genealogies," in *Political Thought and Political Thinkers,* 132–60.
107. *Conjectural Beginning of Human History,* in *Anthropology, History, and Education,* 166: AK 8: 112–13.
108. "From the Lectures of Professor Kant. Königsberg, Winter Semester, 1784–85,

Georg Ludwig Collins (on Baumgarten)," in *Lectures on Ethics,* 155–62: AK 27: 384–92.

109. *Critique of the Power of Judgment,* trans. and ed. Paul Guyer and Eric Mathews (Cambridge: Cambridge University Press, 2000), 297–98: AK 5: 430–31.
110. *The Idea for a Universal History with a Cosmopolitan Aim*, in *Anthropology, History, and Education,* 111: AK 8: 20–21.
111. *De Cive*, 22 (1, 1).
112. *Discours sur l'origine et les fondements de l'inégalité,* in *Œuvres complètes,* III, 169–70.
113. Ibid., 193; see also the observations of Tzvetan Todorov, *La Vie commune. Essai d'anthropologie générale* (Paris: Seuil, 1995), 25–29.
114. *Discours sur l'origine et les fondements de l'inégalité,* in *Œuvres complètes,* III, 197.
115. *The Idea for a Universal History with a Cosmopolitan Aim,* in *Anthropology, History, and Education,* 111: AK 8: 21.
116. Ibid., 113: AK 8: 22.
117. *An Answer to the Question: "What Is Enlightenment?"* in *Practical Philosophy,* 19–20: AK 8: 38–9.
118. *Nicomachean Ethics,* 109.
119. *Epodes,* XVI, 43–44.
120. *Critique of the Power of Judgment,* 297: AK 5: 430.
121. "Review of Herder's Ideas on the Philosophy of Mankind," trans. Allen W. Wood in *Anthropology, History, and Education,* 141: AK 8: 65.
122. *Critique of the Power of Judgment,* 250: AK 5: 378.
123. "Review of Herder's Ideas on the Philosophy of Mankind," in *Anthropology, History, and Education,* 141–42: AK 8: 65.
124. *Conjectural Beginning of Human History,* in *Anthropology, History, and Education,* 174: AK 8: 122.
125. Ibid., 168: AK 8: 155.
126. *Critique of the Power of Judgment,* 299: AK 5: 432.
127. *The Idea for a Universal History with a Cosmopolitan Aim,* in *Anthropology, History, and Education,* 110: AK 8: 19.
128. *The Conflict of the Faculties,* in *Religion and Rational Theology,* 300: AK 7: 83.
129. *Esquisse d'un tableau historique des progrès de l'esprit humain,* 80.
130. *The Conflict of the Faculties*, in *Religion and Rational Theology,* 297: AK 7: 80.
131. *Du Contrat social*, in *Œuvres complètes,* III, 351.
132. *Pensée,* 1266. Cf. *L'Esprit de lois,* I, ii.
133. *Leviathan,* 89 (1, XIII, 63).
134. Kinch Hoekstra, "Hobbes on the Natural Condition of Humankind," in *The Cambridge Companion to Hobbes's Leviathan,* ed. Patricia Springborg (Cambridge: Cambridge University Press, 2007), 109–27.
135. *Caesarinus Fürstenerius*, in *The Political Writings of Leibniz,* ed. Patrick Riley (Cambridge: Cambridge University Press 1972), 113–14.
136. "Second Treatise of Government," in Locke's *Two Treatises of Government,* ed. Peter Laslett (Cambridge: Cambridge University Press, 1960), 298 (III, 19).
137. *Discours sur l'origine et les fondements de l'inégalité,* in *Œuvres complètes,* III, 132.
138. *NS* 127.

139. *NS* 113–14.
140. "Report dated 1766," in *Lectures on Jurisprudence,* ed. R. L. Meek et al. (Oxford: Oxford University Press, 1980), 398.
141. *An Essay on the History of Civil Society,* ed. Fania Oz-Salzberger (Cambridge: Cambridge University Press, 1995), 75.
142. Ibid., 12, 9.
143. *Théorie des loix civiles, ou principes fondamentaux de la société* (London, 1767), 221.
144. Ibid., 208–9.
145. *An Enquiry Concerning the Principles of Morals,* 189n1 (III.1). Hume also pointed out that the image of the state of nature as a state of war "was not first started by Mr. Hobbes, as is commonly imagined." Plato had rejected just such an idea in The Republic, and Cicero, "on the contrary, supposes it certain and universally acknowledged."
146. *Leviathan,* I, xii (p. 89).
147. *Discours sur l'origine et les fondements de l'inégalité,* in *Œuvres complètes,* III, 132–33. Judith N. Shklar, *Men and Citizens: A Study of Rousseau's Social Theory* (Cambridge: Cambridge University Press, 1969), 2.
148. *Discours sur l'origine et les fondements de l'inégalité,* in *Œuvres complètes,* III, 220–21n.
149. *Histoire naturelle,* in *Œuvres complètes,* II, 200–1.
150. *L'Antiquité dévoilée par ses usages* (Amsterdam, 1772), I, 8. Boulanger was apparently echoing Vico, although there is no evidence that he had ever read him. See Vicenzo Ferrone, *I profeti dell'Illuminismo* (Rome: Laterza, 2000), 263–64.

Chapter 5

1. Quoted in Muthu, *Enlightenment Against Empire,* 72.
2. For its influence, and a detailed account of the publishing history, see Jonathan Israel, *Democratic Enlightenment: Philosophy, Revolution, and Human Rights,* 1750–1790 (Oxford: Oxford University Press, 2011), 413–22.
3. Maurice Tourneaux, ed., *Correspondance littéraire, philosophique et critique par Grimm, Diderot, Raynal, Meister etc.* (Paris, 1877), IX, 487–88. On Raynal's association with Choiseul and the Bureau des colonies, see Michèle Duchet, *Anthropologie et histoire au siècle des lumières. Buffon, Voltaire, Helvétius, Diderot* (Paris, 1971), 126.
4. Quoted in Pierre-Victor, baron de Malouet, *Mémoires de Malouet publiés par son petit-fils le baron Malouet,* 2 vols. (Paris, 1868), I, 180.
5. "Lettre apologétique de l'abbé Raynal a M. Grimm," in Diderot, *Œuvres philosophiques,* ed. Paul Vernier (Paris: Garnier, 1956), 640.
6. *Histoire des deux Indes,* in *Œuvres,* III, 682.
7. For Diderot's views on travel, see Anthony Pagden, *European Encounters with the New World* (New Haven, Conn., and London: Yale University Press, 1993), 156–62.
8. *Législation orientale* (Amsterdam, 1778), 181.
9. Ibid., iii–v; see also Jennifer Pitts, "Empire and Legal Universalism in the Eighteenth Century," *American Historical Review* 117 (2012): 92–121.

10. Quoted by Girolamo Imbruglia, "Tra Anquetil-Duperron e L'Histoire des deux Indes. Libertà, dispotismo e feudalismo," *Rivista Storica Italiana* 106 (1994): 141.
11. Letter to Michael Ainsworth, in *Life, Unpublished Letters, and Philosophical Regimen of Anthony, Earl of Shaftesbury,* 403–5. On Shaftesbury's views on diversity, see Daniel Carey, *Locke, Shaftesbury, and Hutcheson: Contesting Diversity in the Enlightenment and Beyond* (Cambridge: Cambridge University Press, 2006), 98–149.
12. *Discours sur l'origine et les fondements de l'inégalité,* in *Œuvres Complètes,* III, 212.
13. *Émile ou l'éducation,* in *Œuvres complètes,* IV, 827.
14. "Soliloquy, or Advice to an Author," in *Characteristics of Men, Manners, Opinions, Times,* 155, 154n.
15. Francis Hutcheson, *An Inquiry into the Original of Our Ideas of Beauty and Virtue* (3rd ed., London, 1729), 205–7.
16. *Discours sur l'origine et les fondements de l'inégalité,* in *Œuvres Complètes,* III, 212.
17. Harry Liebersohn, *The Travelers' World: Europe to the Pacific* (Cambridge, Mass., and London: Harvard University Press, 2006), 202–5.
18. *Determination of the Concept of a Human Race,* trans. Holly Wilson and Günter Zöller, in *Anthropology, History, and Education,* 145: AK 8: 91.
19. *A Voyage to the Cape of Good Hope, Towards the Arctic Polar Circle and Around the World* (London, 1785), iii. On Kant's dispute with Forster, see Kleingeld, *Kant and Cosmopolitanism,* 92–123.
20. *Discours sur l'origine et les fondements de l'inégalité,* in *Œuvres Complètes,* III, 213–14.
21. The most detailed account of the society is Jean-Luc Chappey, *La Société des observateurs de l'homme (1799–1804). Des anthropologues au temps de Bonaparte* (Paris: Société des études robespierristes, 2005).
22. B. Kilborne, "Anthropological Thought in the Wake of the French Revolution: La Société des observateurs de l'homme," *European Journal of Sociology* 23 (1982): 73–91.
23. Jean Copans and Jean Jamin, eds., *Aux origines de l'anthropologie française. Les mémoires de la Société des observateurs de l'homme en l'an VIII* (Paris: Le Sycomore, 1978), 129–32.
24. Neil Safier, *Measuring the New World: Enlightenment Science and South America* (Chicago and London: University of Chicago Press, 2008).
25. "Memoir from the King to serve as instructions to Mr De Bougainville . . . concerning the operations he will be undertaking," in *The Pacific Journal of Louis-Antoine de Bougainville, 1767–1768,* trans. and ed. John Dunmore (London: Hakluyt Society, 2002), xiv.
26. Quoted in Bernard Smith, *European Vision and the South Pacific* (New Haven, Conn., and London: Yale University Press, 1985), 129–30.
27. *Mémoires de l'Amérique septentrionale,* in *Œuvres complètes,* ed. Réal Ouellet (avec la collaboration d'Alain Beaulieu) (Montréal: Les Presses de l'Université de Montréal, 1990), I, 669–75.
28. Ibid., 657.
29. "Judgment of the Works of the Earl of Shaftesbury," in *Political Writings,* ed. and trans. Patrick Wiley (Cambridge: Cambridge University Press, 1972), 196; see

also R. Ouellet, "Lahontan: les dernières années de sa vie/ses rapports avec Leibniz," *Revue d'histoire littéraire de la France* 87 (1987): 121–29.

30. *Observations on the Feeling of the Beautiful, and the Sublime,* in *Anthropology, History and Education,* 60: AK 2: 253.
31. *Notes on the State of Virginia,* in *Writings,* 188.
32. Quoted in Sergio Moravia, *Il pensiero degli idéologues. Scienza e filosofia in Francia (1780–1815)* (Florence: La Nuova Italia Editrice, 1974), 539.
33. *Histoire des navigations aux terres australes* (Paris, 1756), 79.
34. For the possible influence of De Brosses, see Nicholas Thomas, *Cook: The Extraordinary Voyages of Captain James Cook* (New York: Walker & Co., 2003), 16–17.
35. *Supplément au voyage de Bougainville,* in *Political Writings,* 36.
36. *Voyage autour du monde par la frégate la Boudeuse et la flûte l'Étoile; en 1766, 1767, 1768 et 1769,* ed. Michel Bideaux and Sonia Faessel (Paris: Presse de l'Université de Paris-Sorbonne, 2001), 57.
37. Ibid., 201–3.
38. Ibid., 224–25.
39. Ibid., 203–6.
40. *Observations de Mr. de la Condamine sur l'insulaire de Polynésie, amené de l'isle de Tayti en France par Mr. de Bougainville,* printed in Philippe Despoix, *Le Monde mesuré. Dispositifs de l'exploration à l'âge des Lumières* (Geneva: Droz, 2005), 172–75.
41. "Salon de 1761," in *Œuvres,* IV, 205.
42. *Voyage autour du monde,* 221.
43. *The* Endeavour *Journal of Joseph Banks, 1768–1771,* ed. J. C. Beaglehole (Sydney: Angus & Robertson, 1962), I, 252.
44. "Thoughts on the Manners of Otaheite," in ibid., II, 330.
45. See the discussion in Thomas, *Cook,* 156–59.
46. *The Endeavour Journal of Joseph Banks,* I, 281–82.
47. "Journal de Charles-Othon de Nassau-Siegen," in *Bougainville et ses compagnons autour du monde 1766–1769, Journaux de navigation,* ed. Étienne Taillemite (Paris: Imprimerie Nationale, 2006), II, 396.
48. Quoted in Thomas, *Cook,* xxvi.
49. Quoted in Pamela Cheek, *Sexual Antipodes: Enlightenment Globalization and the Placing of Sex* (Stanford, Calif.: Stanford University Press, 2003), 142; see also 139–64.
50. Quoted in Thomas, *Cook,* 156.
51. Quoted in Smith, *European Vision and the South Pacific,* 46.
52. For a balanced account, see Thomas, *Cook,* 153–59.
53. See Jean Meyer, "Le Contexte des grands voyages d'exploration du XVIIIe. Siècle," in *L'Importance de l'exploration maritime au siècle des Lumières: a propos du voyage de Bougainville,* ed. M. Mollat and E. Taillemite (Paris: Editions du Centre national de la recherche scientifique, 1982), 28–35.
54. Jean Étienne Martin-Allanic, *Bougainville, navigateur et les découvertes de son temps* (Paris: Presses universitaires de France, 1964), 890.
55. *Voyage autour du monde,* 234.
56. Ibid., 237.

57. Ibid., 161–62.
58. See Georges Benrekassa, "Dit et non dit idéologique; à propos du *Supplément au voyage de Bougainville,*" *Dix-huitième siècle* 5 (1973): 29–40.
59. *Alzire, ou les Américains, tragédie* (Paris, 1736), 15.
60. "On the Cannibals," in *The Complete Essays,* 233.
61. *Relation abrégée d'un voyage fait dans l'intérieur de l'Amérique méridionale* (Maastricht, 1778), 52–53.
62. *Treatise on the Origin of Languages,* in *Philosophical Writings,* 117.
63. *Briefe die neueste Literatur betreffend* (New York: G. Olms, 1974), 19, 43–44. His example is the Greenlanders.
64. *Discours sur l'origine et les fondements de l'inégalité,* in *Œuvres complètes,* III, 149.
65. *Dissertation sur les différents moyens dont les hommes se sont servis pour exprimer leurs idées,* in *Œuvres de Mr. de Maupertuis* (Lyons, 1756), III, 444.
66. *Voyage autour du monde,* 161.
67. Prince Hoare, *Memoirs of Granville Sharp, Esq.* (London, 1820), 148–52, quoted in part in Faramerz Dabhoiwala, *The Origins of Sex: A History of the First Sexual Revolution* (London: Allen Lane, 2012), 227. For eighteenth-century views on polygamy, see ibid., 25–31.
68. James Boswell, *Life of Johnson,* ed. R. W. Chapman (Oxford: Oxford University Press, 1953), 723.
69. Recorded in *Blackwood's Magazine* 13 (Jan. 1823): 129, from "The Edinburgh Review and Phrenological Journal."
70. *The Journals of Captain James Cook on his Voyages of Discovery,* ed. J. C. Bagehole (Cambridge: Hakluyt Society, 1955–68), III, *The Voyage of the* Resolution *and* Discovery, *1776–1789,* 239–59.
71. Quoted in Daniel O'Quinn, *Staging Governance: Theatrical Imperialism in London, 1770–1800* (Baltimore: Johns Hopkins University Press, 2005), 86.
72. *Mémoires historiques et philosophiques sur la vie et les œuvres de Denis Diderot* (Paris, 1821), 291. See Girolamo Imbruglia, "Dopo *L'encyclopédie.* Diderot e la saggezza dell'immaginazione," *Studi settecenteschi* 11–12 (1988–89): 305–58.
73. "Salon de 1767," in *Salons,* ed. Jean Seznec and Jean Adhemar (Oxford: Oxford University Press, 1957–67), III, 148.
74. *Supplément au voyage de Bougainville,* in *Political Writings,* 74.
75. Ibid., 48–49.
76. *Eléments de physiologie,* in Denis Diderot, *Œuvres complètes,* ed. Jules Assevat and Maurice Tourneaux (Paris, 1875–77), VIII, 352.
77. *Supplément au voyage de Bougainville,* in *Political Writings,* 71.
78. See pp. 156–57 above.
79. John Dunmore, *Monsieur Baret: The First Woman around the World, 1766–68* (Greenhithe, U.K.: Heritage Press, 2002).
80. *Voyage autour du monde,* 259–60.
81. "Journal de François Vivez, chirurgien sur *L'Etoile,*" in *Bougainville et ses compagnons autour du monde, 1766–1769,* II, 243.
82. "Observations sur le Nakaz," in *Œuvres,* III, 564.
83. *De l'Esprit des lois,* Preface.
84. *Bougainville et ses compagnons autour du monde, 1766–1769,* II, 81.

85. *Supplément au voyage de Bougainville*, in *Political Writings,* 50–53.
86. *Lectures on Pedagogy,* trans. Robert B. Louden, in *Anthropology, History, and Education,* 448: AK 9: 454.
87. *Supplément au voyage de Bougainville,* in *Political Writings,* 63.
88. *Réfutation suivie d'ouvrage de Helvétius intitulé l'homme,* in *Œuvres,* 1, 903.
89. "Addresse a mon ami Mr Grimm," in *Salon de 1767,* in *Salons,* III, 61, 125.
90. *Supplément au voyage de Bougainville,* in *Political Writings,* 41–42.
91. *The Task,* Book I, lines 633–48.

Chapter 6

1. Letter to Sophie Volland, Oct. 30, 1759, *Correspondance de Denis Diderot,* II, 299.
2. *Réfutation suivie de l'ouvrage d'Helvétius intitulé L'homme,* in *Œuvres,* I, 786.
3. On the "Brahmanes," or Gymnosophists, see Diderot's article in the *Encyclopédie,* in *Œuvres,* I, 282–83.
4. Letter to Pierre-Étienne Falconet, Sept. 6, 1768, in *Correspondance,* ed. Besterman, 848.
5. "Court essai sur le caractère de l'homme sauvage," in *Histoire des deux Indes,* in *Œuvres,* III, 599.
6. On the history of the word, see Jean Starobinski, "Le Mot civilisation," in *Le Remède dans le mal. Critique et legitimation de l'artifice à l'âge des Lumières* (Paris: Gallimard, 1989), 11–59.
7. "Civilization," in *Essays on Politics and Society,* ed. J. M. Robson, *Collected Works of John Stuart Mill,* vol. 18 (Toronto: Toronto University Press, 1977), 119.
8. Brett, *Changes of State,* 2–3.
9. *L'Ami des hommes, ou Traité de la population* (Paris, 1756), 136; and Starobinski, "Le Mot civilisation," 14.
10. In the opinion of Edward Glaeser, *The Triumph of the City: How Our Greatest Invention Makes Us Richer, Smarter, Greener, Healthier, and Happier* (New York: Penguin, 2011). See also Paul Romer, quoted in *The New York Times,* Feb. 16, 2011, B1; and Steven Pinker, *The Better Angels of Our Nature: Why Violence Has Declined* (New York: Viking, 2011), 179.
11. *Essai sur les moeurs et l'esprit des nations,* I, 22–23.
12. Francescantonio Grimaldi, *Riflessioni sopra l'inegualianza tra gli uomini* [1779–80], ed. Franco Venturi (Milan and Naples: Riccardo Riccardi, 1958), V, 562. See Robertson, *The Case for Enlightenment,* 397–99.
13. See Istvan Hont and Michael Ignatieff, "Needs and Justice in the *Wealth of Nations:* An Introductory Essay," in *Wealth and Virtue: The Shaping of Political Economy in the Scottish Enlightenment,* ed. Hont and Ignatieff (Cambridge: Cambridge University Press, 1987), 253–76.
14. *An Inquiry into the Nature and Causes of the Wealth of Nations* [1776], ed. W. B. Todd (Oxford: Clarendon Press, 1976), 24 [1, i].
15. *Œuvres de Turgot,* ed. Gustave Schelle (Paris: Librairie Félix Alcan, 1913), I, 243–45.
16. "Civilization," in *Essays on Politics and Society,* 120.

17. *Anthropology from a Pragmatic Point of View,* trans. Robert B. Louden, in *Anthropology, History, and Education,* 422: AK 7: 326–27.
18. "Review of J. G. Herder's Ideas for the Philosophy of the History of Humanity," in *Anthropology, History, and Education,* AK 8: 65, and *Reflexionen zur Anthropologie,* no. 1500, AK 15: 785.
19. See Ronald L. Meek, *Social Science and the Ignoble Savage* (Cambridge: Cambridge University Press, 1976).
20. See "The Language of Sociability and Commerce: Samuel Pufendorf and the Theoretical Foundations of the 'Four-Stages' Theory," in Istvan Hont, *Jealousy of Trade: International Competition and the Nation-State in Historical Perspective* (Cambridge, Mass., and London: Harvard University Press, 2005), 159–84.
21. *De l'Esprit des lois,* XVIII, 11.
22. "Civilization," in *Essays on Politics and Society,* 122.
23. On savage indolence, see Pocock, *Barbarism and Religion,* IV, 79–96.
24. *Religion Within the Boundaries of Mere Reason,* trans. George di Giovanni, in *Religion and Rational Theology,* 56: AKA 6: 33.
25. *Toward Perpetual Peace: A Philosophical Project,* trans. Mary J. Gregor, in *Practical Philosophy,* 333: AKA 8: 364.
26. "Report of 1762–3," in *Lectures on Jurisprudence,* 14–15.
27. *An Inquiry into the Nature and Causes of the Wealth of Nations,* 715 (II, 2).
28. Pocock, *Barbarism and Religion,* IV, 100–1.
29. *Esquisse d'un tableau historique des progrès de l'esprit humain,* 98.
30. Émile Benveniste, *Indo-European Language and Society*, trans. Elizabeth Palmer (London: Faber and Faber, 1973), 71–83.
31. *Histoire des deux Indes,* in *Œuvres,* III, 684–85; see also Jimmy Klausen, "Of Hobbes and Hospitality in Diderot's *Supplement to the Voyage of Bougainville,*" in *Polity* 37 (2005): 186–92.
32. *Conjectural Beginning of Human History,* in *Anthropology, History, and Education,* 164: AK 8: 111n.
33. *Essay on the Origin of Language Which Treats of Melody and Musical Imitation,* trans. John H. Moran, in *On the Origin of Language* (Chicago: University of Chicago Press, 1966), 31–47, 31n2. See Jean Starobinski, "Rousseau et l'origine des langues," in *Jean-Jacques Rousseau: La Transparence et l'obstacle*, 356–79.
34. *Esquisse d'un tableau historique des progrès de l'esprit humain,* 93.
35. *Philosophical Review of the Successive Advances of the Human Mind,* in *Turgot on Progress, Sociology, and Economics,* 41.
36. *De l'Esprit des lois,* XVIII, 13.
37. "Report of 1762–3," in *Lectures on Jurisprudence,* 331–32; see also Hont, *Jealousy of Trade,* 161.
38. *Esquisse d'un tableau historique des progrès de l'esprit humain,* 97.
39. "The Second Treatise of Government," 306 (V, 28).
40. *Discours sur l'origine et les fondements de l'inégalité,* 163.
41. Ibid., 170, quoting *An Essay Concerning Human Understanding,* II, III, 18. Locke's point, however, is about the relationship between names and ideas and has nothing to do with the foundation of civil society.
42. *Esquisse d'un tableau historique des progrès de l'esprit humain,* 106, 111.

43. *Plan of the Discourses on Universal History,* in *Turgot on Progress, Sociology, and Economics,* 69.
44. *Conjectural Beginning of Human History*, in *Anthropology, History, and Education,* 172–73: AK 8: 120.
45. *Sur les femmes,* in *Œuvres,* I, 957.
46. *Discours sur les sciences et les arts,* in *Œuvres complètes,* III, 7.
47. "The Second Treatise of Government," 311–12 (V, 36–37).
48. Ibid., 319 (V, 47).
49. The story of Aristippus is told in the preface to the sixth book of the Roman architect Vitruvius' *De architectura*. It also provides the title of the remarkable book by Clarence J. Glacken, *Traces on the Rhodian Shore: Nature and Culture in Western Thought from Ancient Times to the Eighteenth Century* (Berkeley and Los Ageless: University of California Press, 1967).
50. *De l'Esprit des lois,* XVIII, 15.
51. *An Inquiry into the Nature and Causes of the Wealth of Nations,* 13 (I, 1).
52. Guillaume-Thomas-François Raynal, *Histoire philosophique et politique des établissements et du commerce des Européens dans les deux Indes,* ed. Anthony Strugnell et al. (Paris: Centre international d'études du XVIIIe siècle, 2010), I, 23; and *An Inquiry into the Nature and Causes of the Wealth of Nations,* 626–27 (IV, vii).
53. *Le Spectateur américain, ou remarques générales sur l'Amérique septentrionale . . . Suivi de recherches philosophiques sur la découverte de l'Amérique* (Amsterdam, 1784), 11.
54. *An Inquiry into the Nature and Causes of the Wealth of Nations,* 626 (IV, vii).
55. *Histoire des deux Indes,* in *Œuvres,* III, 689.
56. *Lettres philosophiques,* 67.
57. On the vocabulary of commerce and on the French understanding of its global significance, see Anoush Terjanian, *Commerce and Its Discontents in Eighteenth-Century French Political Thought* (Cambridge: Cambridge University Press, 2012).
58. *L'Ami des hommes, ou traité de la population,* III, 5.
59. Anthony Pagden, "Commerce and Conquest: Hugo Grotius and Serafim de Freitas on the Freedom of the Seas," *Mare Liberum* 20 (2000): 33–55.
60. *De l'Esprit des lois,* XX, 1.
61. Quoted in Rothschild, *Economic Sentiments,* 17.
62. For Raynal's objective, see Pocock, *Barbarism and Religion,* IV, 230–33.
63. In "Salon de 1769," *Œuvres,* IV, 872–84.
64. "Report dated 1766," in *Lectures on Jurisprudence,* 540–42; see also Christopher J. Berry, *The Idea of Luxury: A Conceptual and Historical Investigation* (Cambridge: Cambridge University Press, 1994), 170–73.
65. *Supplément au voyage de Bougainville,* in *Political Writings,* 42.
66. *Teatro crítico universal. Discursos varios en todo género de materias, para desengaño de errores comunes* (Madrid, 1726), I, 350–51.
67. *The History of Women from the Earliest Antiquity to the Present Time* [1779] (London, 1782), I, 151–53. See Dabhoiwala, *The Origins of Sex,* 183–84.
68. See Evelyn Forget, "Cultivating Sympathy: Sophie Condorcet's Letters on Sympathy," *Journal of the History of Economic Thought* 23 (2001): 39–337.

69. Joan Wallach Scott, *Only Paradoxes to Offer: French Feminists and the Rights of Man* (Cambridge, Mass.: Harvard University Press, 1996), 19–56.
70. Quoted in Sylvana Tomaselli, "Civilization, Patriotism and Enlightened Histories of Women," in *Women, Gender and Enlightenment,* ed. Sarah Knott and Barbara Taylor (London: Palgrave Macmillan, 2005), 117–35.
71. *The History of Women from the Earliest Antiquity to the Present Time,* I, 152.
72. "Of Refinement in the Arts," in *Essays Moral, Political, and Literary,* 271; see also Rothschild, *Economic Sentiments,* 21.
73. *Discours sur les sciences et les arts,* in *Œuvres complètes,* III, 21n.
74. Shklar, *Men and Citizens,* 144–45.
75. "Discours prononcé dans l'Académie française . . . a la réception de M. le marquis de Condorcet," in *Œuvres complètes de Condorcet,* X, 103; see also Rothschild, *Economic Sentiments,* 235.
76. *The Spirit of Conquest and Usurpation and Their Relation to European Civilization,* in *Political Writings,* ed. Biancamaria Fontana (Cambridge: Cambridge University Press), 53.
77. *Idea for a Universal History with a Cosmopolitan Aim,* in *Anthropology, History, and Education,* 111: AK 8: 820–21.
78. Lionel Jensen, *Manufacturing Confucianism: Chinese Tradition and Universal Civilization* (Durham, N.C.: Duke University Press, 1997). On Ricci's life and mission, see Michele Fontana, *Matteo Ricci. Un gesuita alla corte dei Ming* (Milano: Mondadori, 2005).
79. "On the Civil Cult of Confucius," in Gottfried Wilhelm Leibniz, *Writings on China,* ed. and trans. Daniel J. Cook and Henry Rosemont Jr. (Chicago and La Salle: Open Court, 1994), 61.
80. See D. E. Mungello, *The Great Encounter of China and the West, 1500–1800* (Lanham, Md.: Rowman and Littlefield, 1999), 59–82, and the essays in Mungello, ed., *The Chinese Rites Controversy: Its History and Meaning* (Nettetal: Steyler Verlag, 1994).
81. As reported by Paul Hazard, *The European Mind, 1680–1715* (Cleveland and New York, Meridian Books, 1963), 23.
82. *Plan of the Discourses on Universal History,* in *Turgot on Progress, Sociology, and Economics,* 96.
83. Preface to the *Novissima sinica,* in Leibniz, *Writings on China,* 45–46.
84. Quoted in Franklin Perkins, "Virtue, Reason, and Cultural Exchange: Leibniz's Praise of Chinese Morality," *Journal of the History of Ideas* 63 (2002): 447–64, 460.
85. Preface to the *Novissima sinica,* 51.
86. Quoted in Perkins, "Virtue, Reason, and Cultural Exchange," 455.
87. Preface to the *Novissima sinica,* 46–47.
88. *Essai sur les moeurs et l'esprit des nations,* I, 220. Epictetus was a first- to second-century Greek Stoic who taught that the proper response to moral error was education, not punishment.
89. Preface to the *Novissima sinica,* 2–3.
90. Quoted in Franklin Perkins, *Leibniz and China: A Commerce of Light* (Cambridge: Cambridge University Press, 2004), 122.

91. *Essai sur les moeurs et l'esprit des nations,* II, 903–4.
92. *Histoire philosophique et politique des établissements et du commerce des Européens dans les deux Indes,* I, 102.
93. *A Fragment on Government,* 14n.
94. Judith N. Shklar, *Montesquieu* (Oxford: Oxford University Press, 1987), 122.
95. Ibid., 111.
96. Quoted by D'Alembert in "Éloge de Montesquieu," in *Œuvres complètes de D'Alembert,* III, 456n.
97. Letter to André Morellet, Jan. 26, 1766, in Cesare Beccaria, *Opere. Carteggio,* ed. Carlo Capra et al. (Milan: Mediobanca, 1994), IV, 222.
98. "Éclectisme," from the *Encyclopédie,* in *Œuvres,* I, 339.
99. Shklar, *Montesquieu,* 10.
100. "Éloge de Montesquieu," in *Œuvres complètes de D'Alembert,* III, 452.
101. *De l'Esprit des lois,* XIX, 4.
102. "Account of the Life and Writings of Adam Smith LL.D.," in Adam Smith, *Essays on Philosophical Subjects,* 295.
103. *An Enquiry Concerning the Principles of Morals,* 196–97, (III, 2), although he added, as an afterthought, that Montesquieu's supposition "that all right be founded on rapports or relations" was irreconcilable "with true philosophy."
104. See Cassirer, *The Philosophy of the Enlightenment,* 209–10.
105. *De l'Esprit des lois,* II, 1.
106. Ibid., III, 1–2.
107. See Michael Curtis, *Orientalism and Islam: European Thinkers on Oriental Despotism in the Middle East and India* (Cambridge: Cambridge University Press, 2009), 72–102.
108. *De l'Esprit des lois,* XVII, 3.
109. *Réflexions sur la monarchie universelle,* in *Œuvres complètes,* II, 23–24.
110. *De l'Esprit des lois,* XIX, 12.
111. Ibid., V, 14.
112. *Persian Letters,* 234, Letter 131.
113. From the *Geographica,* a manuscript collection of writings on various parts of the world, discovered after World War II in Montesquieu's chateau at La Brède by the English Scholar Robert Shackleton. There is some doubt, however, as to whether the text known as "Some remarks on China that I have taken from a conversation which I had with M. Ouanges" is, in fact, by Montesquieu or by someone better informed about China than Montesquieu, possibly Nicolas Fréret, secretary to the Académie des inscriptions, who knew Montesquieu. See the introduction to *Geographica,* in *Œuvres complètes de Montesquieu* (Oxford: Voltaire Foundation, Istituto italiano per gli studi filosofici, 2007), 16, 109–12, and the account in Jonathan D. Spence, *The Chan's Great Continent: China in Western Minds* (New York and London: W. W. Norton & Co., 1998), 88–94.
114. Danielle Elisseeff, *Moi, Arcade interprète chinois du Roi-Soleil* (Paris: Arthaud, 1985), 37–40.
115. Danielle Elisseeff, *Nicolas Fréret (1688–1749). Réflexions d'un humaniste du XVIIIe siècle sur la Chine* (Paris: Collège de France, 1978), 37–51.
116. *De l'Esprit des lois,* VIII, 21.

117. *Geographica,* in *Œuvres complètes de Montesquieu,* 124. This is repeated with a slightly different wording in *Pensée,* 234.
118. *Geographica*, in *Œuvres complètes de Montesquieu,* 124.
119. *Pensées,* 271.
120. *De l'Esprit des lois,* XIX, 4.
121. Ibid., XIX, 14.
122. *Pensées,* 1079.
123. *Theory of Moral Sentiments,* 204 (V, 2, 7).
124. *Pensées,* 272.
125. *De l'Esprit des lois,* XIX, 13.
126. Ibid., XXVI 15–17; see also Shklar, *Montesquieu,* 70–74.
127. *De l'Esprit des lois,* V, 14.
128. Ibid., XII, 29.
129. Ibid., XIX, 17.
130. Ibid., XIX, 18.
131. Cf. *Laws* 697c, 712e–713a.
132. *De l'Esprit des lois,* VIII, 6, 21.
133. *Essai sur les moeurs et l'esprit des nations,* I, 215.
134. *Spicilège,* 483. The word is Montesquieu's own translation of the Latin term *spicilegium,* meaning a collection of notes or unpublished documents.
135. *De l'Esprit des lois,* V, 14.
136. Quoted in Spence, *The Chan's Great Continent,* 69.
137. Ibid., 89.
138. Quoted in ibid., 55.
139. *Histoire des deux Indes,* in *Œuvres,* III, 657–58.
140. *On Language: On the Diversity of Human Language Construction and Its Influence on the Mental Development of the Human Species,* ed. Michael Losonsky, trans. Peter Heath (Cambridge: Cambridge University Press, 1999), 232–33; on Humboldt's place in the development of modern linguistics, see Steven Pinker, *The Language Instinct: How the Mind Creates Language* (New York: Morrow, 1994), 84.
141. *Doutes proposés aux philosophes économistes sur l'ordre naturel et essentiel des sociétés politiques* (The Hague, 1768), 132–37.
142. *Essai sur les moeurs et l'esprit des nations,* I, 216, 231.
143. *Plan of the Discourses on Universal History*, in *Turgot on Progress, Sociology, and Economics,* 70.
144. *Histoire des deux Indes,* 657.
145. *Reflexionen zur Anthropologie,* no. 1455a, AK 16: 637.
146. *Supplément au voyage de Bougainville*, in *Political Writings,* 38. "B" is here referring not to Tahiti but to "Lancer's Island," Akiaki, in the Tuamoto Archipelago.
147. "Droit naturel," in *Political Writings,* 20.

Chapter 7

1. *Pensées,* 350.
2. "Droit naturel," in *Political Writings,* 20.

3. See Martha Nussbaum (with respondents), *For Love of Country: Debating the Limits of Patriotism,* ed. Joshua Cohen (Boston: Beacon Press, 1996), 9.
4. *Essay on Man,* IV, 363–10.
5. *Theory of Moral Sentiments,* 235 (VI, ii, 3, 1).
6. *Reflections on the Revolution in France,* and quoted in Appiah, *Cosmopolitanism,* 152.
7. "Of National Characters," in *Essays Moral, Political, and Literary,* 202.
8. *An Enquiry Concerning the Principles of Morals,* 224 (V, II).
9. *A Treatise on Human Nature,* 317; see also Sharon R. Krause, *Civil Passions: Moral Sentiment and Democratic Deliberation* (Princeton, N.J.: Princeton University Press, 2008), 79–83.
10. *An Enquiry Concerning the Principles of Morals,* 225n (V, II).
11. Quoted in Marcel Detienne, *Les Grecs et nous* (Paris: Perrin, 2005), 13.
12. "Miscellany III," in *Characteristics of Men, Manners, Opinions, Times,* 400.
13. Henry Sumner Maine, *Ancient Law* (London: Dent, 1917 [1861]), 82, 85.
14. Kantorowicz, *The King's Two Bodies,* 336–37.
15. Quoted in Michael Walzer, ed., *Regicide and Revolution: Speeches at the Trial of Louis XVI* (Cambridge: Cambridge University Press, 1974), 4.
16. *Leviathan,* 120 (II, 17).
17. Quoted in Walzer, ed., *Regicide and Revolution,* 25.
18. "The Trew Law of Free Monarchies," in King James VI and I, *Political Writings,* ed. Johann Sommerville (Cambridge: Cambridge University Press, 1994), 65.
19. "A Speech to the Lord and Commons of the Parliament . . . March 21, 1609," in ibid., 181; also quoted in Walzer, ed., *Regicide and Revolution,* 15; for a succinct and brilliantly perceptive account of the theory of divine right, see pp. 14–34.
20. Colette Beaune, *Naissance de la nation France* (Paris: Gallimard, 1985), 208–10.
21. Quoted in Liah Greenfeld, *Nationalism: Five Roads to Modernity* (Cambridge, Mass.: Harvard University Press, 1992), 14.
22. *Les Ruines, ou Méditations sur les révolutions des empires,* in *Œuvres,* ed. Anne and Henry Deneys (Paris: Fayard, 1989), 267.
23. Letter from Lady Mordaunt to John Locke, quoted in *Locke's Two Treatises of Government,* 45. For a detailed account of the impact of the Glorious Revolution on not only Britain, but the whole of Europe, see Steven Pincus, *1688: The First Modern Revolution* (New Haven, Conn., and London: Yale University Press, 2009).
24. *Leviathan,* 128 (II, 18).
25. Ibid., 121 (II, 18).
26. *Hobbes à l'agrégation,* ed. Jean-François Bert (Paris: Editions EHESS, 2011), 42.
27. "Second Treatise of Government," in *Locke's Two Treatises of Government,* 344 (VII, 90).
28. *An Essay on Toleration,* in *Political Essays,* 135–36.
29. "Of the Origin of Government," in *Essays Moral, Political, and Literary,* 37.
30. "On the Common Saying: 'This may be true in theory, but it is of no use in practice,'" in *Practical Philosophy,* 291: AK 8: 290; and *Reflexionen zur Rechtsphilosophie,* no. 7979, AK 19: 570. In the *Metaphysics of Morals* he speaks of the "fatherland" as made up of those born "in an intellectual and from the perspective of rights . . . of one common mother (the republic)" and constituting "a family (*gens, natio*)," *Practical Philosophy* 482: AK 6: 343.

31. "Observation sur les Nakaz," in *Œuvres,* III, 507.
32. Edmund Burke, "Speech on the State of Representation of Commons in Parliament," in *Writings and Speeches,* ed. J. F. Taylor (New York: Little, Brown, 1901), VII, 94–95.
33. *Reflections on the Revolution in France,* 261.
34. *De Officis,* I, 57. The term Cicero uses here, however, is *caritas,* not *amor*. See the comments on this in Maurizio Viroli, *For Love of Country: An Essay on Patriotism and Nationalism* (Oxford: Clarendon Press, 1995), 22–23.
35. As explained in Kantorowicz, *The King's Two Bodies,* 232–35.
36. See David Bell, *The Cult of the Nation in France,* 51–54, who provides a brilliant evocation of the setting, and an analysis, of the oration.
37. Marisa Linton, *The Politics of Virtue in Enlightenment France* (Basingstoke, U.K.: Palgrave, 2001), 159.
38. See Peter Campbell, "The Language of Patriotism in France, 1750–1770," *e-France,* 1 (2007): 14, and "The Politics of Patriotism in France (1770–1788)," *French History* 24, 4 (2010): 550–75.
39. Quoted in Campbell, "The Politics of Patriotism in France (1770–1788)," 552. Jaucourt then goes on to paraphrase Montesquieu.
40. Quoted in Greenfeld, *Nationalism,* 163.
41. Anthony Pagden, *Worlds at War: The 2,500-Year Struggle Between East and West* (New York: Random House, 2008), 3–39.
42. "Miscellany III," in *Characteristics of Men, Manners, Opinions, Times,* 400n10; see also Viroli, *For Love of Country,* 57–60.
43. For the distinction in France between *patrie* and *nation,* see Campbell, "The Politics of Patriotism in France (1770–1788)," 558.
44. *De l'Esprit des lois,* IV, 5.
45. Ibid., V, 2.
46. *Reflexionen zur Rechtsphilosophie,* no. 7979, AK 19: 570.
47. Quoted in Ruth Scurr, *Fatal Purity: Robespierre and the French Revolution* (London: Chatto & Windus, 2006), 275.
48. *Considérations sur le gouvernement de Pologne,* in *Œuvres complètes,* III, 966.
49. Quoted in Pocock, *Barbarism and Religion,* I, 241.
50. *De l'Esprit des lois,* V, 19.
51. *The Idea of a Patriot King,* in Bolingbroke, *Political Writings,* ed. David Armitage (Cambridge: Cambridge University Press, 1997), 221, 245.
52. Ibid., 294.
53. *Letters from a Citizen of the World to His Friends in the East* (Bungy [London], 1820), I, 19.
54. Quoted in Roy Porter, *The Creation of the Modern World,* 42–44.
55. See Colin Kidd, *British Identities Before Nationalism: Ethnicity and Nationhood in the Atlantic World, 1600–1800* (Cambridge: Cambridge University Press, 1999).
56. Quoted in Vincenzo Cuoco, *Saggio storico sulla rivoluzione di Napoli* [1801], ed. Antonino de Francesco (Paris: Les Belles Lettres, 2004), 202. He does not cite his source.
57. Quoted in Kleingeld, *Kant and Cosmopolitanism,* 25.
58. "Miscellany III," in *Characteristics of Men, Manners, Opinions, Times,* 401–3.

59. Quoted in Campbell, "The Language of Patriotism in France, 1750–1770," 4–5.
60. *Letters for the Advancement of Humanity* (1793–97), in Herder, *Philosophical Writings,* 378–79.
61. Described and analyzed in Jan-Werner Müller, *Constitutional Patriotism* (Princeton, N.J.: Princeton University Press, 2007), 16–22.
62. "A Discourse on the Love of Our Country," in *Political Writings,* ed. D. O. Thomas (Cambridge: Cambridge University Press, 1991), 178. Burke's comments are in "Letter to Philip Francis," Feb. 20, 1790, in *Further Reflections on the Revolution in France,* ed. Daniel E. Ritchie (Indianapolis: Liberty Fund, 1992), 181.
63. "A Discourse on the Love of Our Country," 178–79.
64. *Theory of Moral Sentiments,* 154–55, (III, 3, 42).
65. Ibid., 235 (VI, 2, 3.1).
66. Ibid., 140 (III, 3, 10).
67. Ibid., 229 (III, 2, 4).
68. *De l'Esprit,* 196–97.
69. *Teatro crítico universal,* III, 223–24.
70. *Dictionnaire philosophique,* 419–20, "Patrie."
71. "Kant on the Metaphysics of Morals: Vigilantius' Lecture Notes," in *Lectures on Ethics,* 406: AK 27: 674.
72. Quoted in Marc Belissa, "Introduction," in *Cosmopolitismes, patriotismes. Europe et Amériques, 1773–1802,* ed. Marc Belissa and Bernard Cottret (Rennes: Les Perséides, 2005), 9.
73. *Le Cosmopolite ou le citoyen du monde* (London, 1761), 3, 43–44.
74. "Encyclopédie," in *Œuvres,* 428.
75. "Defence of Seneca and Plutarch," in *The Complete Essays,* 821.
76. *Epilogue to the Satires,* Dialogue, 1, I, 41.
77. *Theory of Moral Sentiments,* 228–30 (VI, ii, 3–5).
78. Letter of Nov. 24, 1767, *Œuvres,* V, 810.
79. *Gespräch unter vier Augen,* in *Werke,* ed. J. G. Gruber (Berlin 1824–27), 42, 127–28.
80. "Kant on the Metaphysics of Morals: Vigilantius' Lecture Notes," in *Lectures on Ethics,* 406: AK 27: 674.
81. *Theory of Moral Sentiments,* 229–30, 154–55 (VI, ii, 2.5–6).
82. *Disputatio de caritate,* I ad 24.
83. *De Duobus praeceptis caritatis,* 5.
84. See Margaret C. Jacob, *Strangers Nowhere in the World: The Rise of Cosmopolitanism in Early-Modern Europe* (Philadelphia: University of Pennsylvania Press, 2006).
85. Salon of 1765, quoted in Paul Hazard, "Cosmopolite," in *Mélanges d'histoire littéraire générale et comparée offerts à Fernand Baldensperger* (Paris: Librairie Ancienne Honoré Champion, 1930), 360. He was speaking explicitly of Holbach's house in the Rue Royale.
86. *La scienza della legislazione,* ed. Vincenzo Ferrone et al. (Venice: Centro di Studi sull'Iluminismo europeo "Giovanni Stiffoni," 2003), I, 19.
87. "On the Spirit of Patriotism," in *Political Writings,* 193–94.

88. Letter of 22 Feb. 1768, *Œuvres,* V, 812.
89. "Spheres of Affection," in Nussbaum (with respondents), *For Love of Country,* 125.
90. *Du Contrat social* (1e version) I, II, in *Œuvres Complètes,* III, 287. This passage was dropped from the final version.
91. *Discours sur l'origine et les fondements de l'inégalité,* in *Œuvres complètes,* III, 178.
92. *Émile ou l'education,* in *Œuvres Complètes,* IV, 249.
93. Cf. John Rawls, *The Law of Peoples* (Cambridge, Mass.: Harvard University Press, 1999), 119. "The ultimate concern of a cosmopolitan view is the well-being of individuals not the justice of societies."
94. *De l'Esprit des lois,* XXIV, 10.
95. *On the Fortune of Alexander,* 329. See pp. 326–27.
96. *On Liberty,* in *On Liberty and Other Writings,* ed. Stefan Collini (Cambridge: Cambridge University Press, 1998), 28.
97. *The Meditations of the Emperor Marcus Aurelius Antoninus,* VI, 50, 58.
98. *Decline and Fall of the Roman Empire,* ed. David Womersley (London: Penguin, 1994), 103 (ch. III).
99. Quoted in Clifford Ando, *Imperial Ideology and Provincial Loyalty in the Roman Empire* (Berkeley, Los Angeles, and London: University of California Press, 2000), 63.
100. Quoted in Uday Singh Mehta, *Liberalism and Empire: A Study in Nineteenth-Century British Liberal Thought* (Chicago: University of Chicago Press, 1999), 139–40.
101. "Réflexions sur la monarchie universelle en Europe," in *Œuvres complètes,* II, 19.

Chapter 8

1. Israel, *Radical Enlightenment,* 85.
2. See Israel, *Enlightenment Contested,* 654–56.
3. Donald F. Lach, "The Sinophilism of Christian Wolff (1679–1754)," in *Discovering China: European Interpretations in the Enlightenment,* ed. Julia Ching and Willard G. Oxtoby (Rochester, N.Y.: University of Rochester Press, 1992), 118–30; and Robert Louden, "'What Does Heaven Say?': Christian Wolff and Western Interpretations of Confucian Ethics," in *Confucius and the Analects: New Essays,* ed. Bryan W. Van Norden (New York: Oxford University Press, 2002), 73–93.
4. *Dictionnaire philosophique,* 160–61, "Chine (de la)."
5. On this see T. J. Hochstrasser, *Natural Law Theories in the Early Enlightenment* (Cambridge: Cambridge University Press, 2000), 150–86.
6. *Jus gentium methodo scientifica pertractatum* (Oxford: Clarendon Press, 1934), II, 9–7.
7. Ibid., II, 9. See Tuck, *The Rights of War and Peace,* 187–91.
8. Georg Cavallar, *The Rights of Strangers: Theories of International Hospitality, the Global Community, and Political Justice Since Victoria* (Aldershot, U.K.: Ashgate, 2002), 211.
9. *Jus gentium methodo scientifica pertractatum,* II, 11. On Wolff's distinction between

what he calls "pure" natural law and the consensual "will of nations," see Martii Koskenniemi, *From Apology to Utopia: The Structure of International Legal Argument* (Cambridge: Cambridge University Press, 2005), 108–12.

10. Quoted in Scheenwind, *The Invention of Autonomy,* 436.
11. *Jus gentium methodo scientifica pertractatum,* II, 17.
12. *Fundamenta juris naturae et gentium ex sensu communi deducta* (Halle, 1718), 161 (LXXII). On Thomasius, see Hochstrasser, *Natural Law Theories in the Early Enlightenment,* 111–49. The last remark is a reference to the revocation of the Edict of Nantes of 1685.
13. *An Enquiry into the Foundations of the Laws of Nations in Europe from the Time of the Greeks and Romans to the Age of Grotius* (London, 1795), 1, xiii–xiv, and 169; see also Pitts, "Empire and Legal Universalism in the Eighteenth Century."
14. *Reflexionen zur Metaphysik,* no. 4866: AK 18: 14.
15. See, in general, Emmanuelle Jouannet, *Emer de Vattel et l'émergence doctrinale du droit international classique* (Paris: Pedone, 1998).
16. *Poliergie ou mélange du littérature et de poésies* (Amsterdam [in fact Paris], 1757), I, 21–126.
17. "Réflexions sur le Discours de M. Rousseau touchant l'origine de l'inégalité parmi les hommes," in *Mélanges de littérature, de morale et de politique* (Neuchâtel, 1760), 82.
18. See David Armitage, *The Declaration of Independence: A Global History* (Cambridge, Mass.: Harvard University Press, 2008), 38–41.
19. *Le Droit de gens, et les devoirs des citoyens, ou principes de la loi naturelle* (Nimes, 1793), I, "Preface," 12–13. See also Koskenniemi, *From Apology to Utopia,* 112–22.
20. *Le Droit de gens, et les devoirs des citoyens,* I, 147–50; see also Tuck, *The Rights of War and Peace,* 191–96.
21. "Réflexions sur la monarchie universelle en Europe," in *Œuvres complètes,* II, 34.
22. Ibid., II, 22.
23. *Le Droit de gens, et les devoirs des citoyens,* I, 149–50.
24. Ibid., I, 153.
25. *International Law* (London: John Murray, 1888), 8.
26. Jeremy Bentham, *Principles of International Law,* in *The Works of Jeremy Bentham* (Edinburgh, 1843), 11, 546, 557. For selections from all of these, see Esref Asku, ed., *Early Notions of Global Governance: Selected Eighteenth-Century Proposals for "Perpetual Peace"* (Cardiff: University of Wales Press, 2008).
27. Kleingeld, *Kant and Cosmopolitanism,* 40–43. See also the comments in Tuck, *The Rights of War and Peace,* 223–24.
28. See Merle J. Perkins, *The Moral and Political Philosophy of the Abbé de Saint-Pierre* (Geneva: Droz, 1959).
29. "Of the Jealousy of Trade," in *Essays Moral, Political, and Literary,* 327–28.
30. "De la paix perpétuelle par le docteur Goodheart," in *L'Évangile du Jour,* 2.
31. "On the Works of the Abbé de St. Pierre" (1715), in *Political Writings,* 183.
32. On the arguments of the proposal and its relationship to Kant's *Toward Perpetual Peace,* see Massimo Mori, *La pace e la ragione Kant e le relazioni internazionali: diritto, politica, storia* (Bologna: Il Mulino, 2004), 23–35.

33. *Les Confessions,* in *Œuvres complètes*, I, 408, 422–23.
34. "Jugement sur le projet de paix perpétuelle," in *Œuvres complètes,* III, 591.
35. Ibid., 594–95.
36. Ibid., 600.
37. *Toward Perpetual Peace: A Philosophical Project,* trans. Mary J. Gregor, in *Practical Philosophy,* 333: AK 8: 363.
38. Ibid., 334: AK 8: 364–65 and *Anthropology from a Pragmatic Point of View,* in *Anthropology, History, and Education,* 425: AK 7: 330.
39. *Idea for a Universal History with a Cosmopolitan Aim,* in ibid., 144–45: AK 8: 24–25.
40. *Critique of the Power of Judgment,* 298: AK 5: 430.
41. *Conjectural Beginning of Human History,* in ibid., 173: AK 8: 121.
42. *Reflexionen zur anthropologie,* no. 1521, AK 16: 892. It was a widespread belief at the time that the destruction of Byzantium had led to a transfer of Greek culture to western Europe that had in turn led to the Renaissance.
43. *Conjectural Beginning of Human History,* in *Anthropology, History, and Education,* 173: AK 8: 121.
44. *Critique of the Power of Judgment,* 300: AK 5: 432–33.
45. *Idea for a Universal History with a Cosmopolitan Aim,* in *Anthropology, History, and Education,* 118: AK 8: 28. On the role of war in Kant's theory of historical evolution, see Yirmiahu Yovel, *Kant and the Philosophy of History* (Princeton, N.J.: Princeton University Press, 1980), 151–54; and Pierre Hassner, "Les concepts de guerre et de paix chez Kant," *Revue française de science politique* 11 (1961): 642–70.
46. *Zu ewigen Frieden: Ein philosophischer Entwurf.* "Zu" can mean both "to" and "toward."
47. *Project pour rendre la paix perpétuelle en Europe* (Paris: Fayard, 1986), 22–23.
48. *Toward Perpetual Peace*, in *Practical Philosophy,* 317: AK 8: 343.
49. *Idea for a Universal History with Cosmopolitan Aim*, in *Anthropology, History, and Education,* 114–15: AK 8: 24; see also "On the Common Saying: 'This may be true in theory, but it is of no use in practice,' " in *Practical Philosophy,* 309: AK 8: 313.
50. *Toward Perpetual Peace*, in *Practical Philosophy,* 318: AK 8: 344.
51. Ibid., 324: AK 8: 351.
52. *Reflexionen zur Anthropologie,* no. 1524, AK 16: 898–99.
53. *Toward Perpetual Peace,* in *Practical Philosophy,* 326: AK 8: 354.
54. *The Metaphysics of Morals,* in *Practical Philosophy,* 456: AK 6: 313; and "Kant on the Metaphysics of Morals: Vigilantius' Lecture Notes," in *Lectures on Ethics,* 340: AK 27: 591.
55. *Toward Perpetual Peace,* in *Practical Philosophy,* 326: AK 8: 354–55.
56. *The Metaphysics of Morals,* in *Practical Philosophy,* 485: AK 6: 347.
57. *La Politique naturelle,* in *Œuvres philosophiques complètes,* III, 589.
58. *Theory of Moral Sentiments,* 155 (III, 3, 42).
59. On Kant's three categories of *lex,* see Sharon B. Byrd and Joachim Hruschka, "Lex iusti, lex iuridica und lex iustitiae in Kants *Rechtslehre,*" *Archiv für Rechts und Sozialphilosophie* 91 (2005): 484–500.

60. "Kant on the Metaphysics of Morals: Vigilantius' Lecture Notes," in *Lectures on Ethics,* 339: AK 27: 591.
61. *Toward Perpetual Peace,* in *Practical Philosophy,* 327: AK 8: 356.
62. Ibid., 323n: AK 8: 350. And see Arthur Ripstein, *Force and Freedom: Kant's Legal and Political Philosophy* (Cambridge, Mass.: Harvard University Press, 2009), 182–231.
63. *The Metaphysics of Morals,* in *Practical Philosophy,* 480: AK 6: 339.
64. "On the Common Saying: 'This may be true in theory, but it is of no use in practice,'" in ibid., 296–97: AK 8: 297.
65. *The Metaphysics of Morals,* in ibid., 484: AK 6: 346.
66. *Toward Perpetual Peace,* in ibid., 335: AK 8: 366.
67. *The Metaphysics of Morals,* in ibid., 584: AK 6: 345–46.
68. *Toward Perpetual Peace,* in ibid., 342: AK 8: 375.
69. Ibid., 323–24: AK 8: 351.
70. This is the final conclusion of *An Inquiry into the Origin of Honour, and the Usefulness of Christianity in War* (1732): a deep sense of honour, and belief in the Christian God, are powerful devices for persuading people to kill one another.
71. Zeev Maôz and Bruce Russett, "Normative and Structural Causes of Democratic Peace, 1946–1986," *American Political Science Review* 87 (1993): 624–38; and Otfried Höffe, *Kant's Cosmopolitan Theory of Law and Peace,* trans. Alexandra Newton (Cambridge: Cambridge University Press, 2006), 177–81.
72. *Federalist* X, in James Madison, Alexander Hamilton, and John Jay, *The Federalist Papers,* ed. Isaac Kramnick (London and New York: Penguin, 1987), 126.
73. *Toward Perpetual Peace,* in *Practical Philosophy,* 324: AK 8: 352.
74. "The Liberty of the Ancients Compared with That of the Moderns," in *Political Writings,* 310–11.
75. *Toward Perpetual Peace,* in *Practical Philosophy,* 325: AK 8: 353.
76. On Kant's use of counterfactual reasoning in his account of representation, see Nadia Urbinati, *Representative Democracy: Principles and Genealogy* (Chicago: Chicago University Press, 2006), 120–30.
77. *The Principles of Representative Government* (Cambridge: Cambridge University Press, 1997), and see Nadia Urbinati, *Representative Democracy: Principles and Genealogy,* 1–6.
78. See in particular, Michael W. Doyle, "Kant, Liberal Legacies, and Foreign Affairs," *Philosophy and Public Affairs* 12 (1983): 205–353.
79. *Toward Perpetual Peace,* in *Practical Philosophy,* 327: AK 8: 356.
80. *Critique of the Power of Judgment,* 300: AK 5: 432.
81. *Toward Perpetual Peace,* in *Practical Philosophy,* 327: AK 8: 356.
82. Ibid., 328: AK 8: 357.
83. Ibid., 336: AK 8: 367, and on size, *The Metaphysics of Morals,* in *Practical Philosophy,* 487: AK 6: 350. See Ripstein, *Force and Freedom,* 226–27; on Kant's anti-imperialism, see Muthu, *Enlightenment Against Empire,* 120–72.
84. *Outlines of a Philosophy of the History of Man* [*Ideen zur Philosophie der Geschichte der Menschheit*], trans. T. Churchill (London, 1800), 224.
85. *Religion Within the Boundaries of Mere Reason,* trans. George di Giovanni, in *Reli-*

gion and Rational Theology, 81: AK 6: 35. On human diversity, see the remarks in the *loser Blätter,* AK 23: 167–69.

86. On Kant's uses of these terms, see Andrew Hurrell, "Kant and the Kantian Paradigm in International Relations," *Review of International Studies* 16 (1990): 183–205. On Kant's shifting views on the desirability of the world state (*Völkerstaat*) as opposed to a world federation (*Völkerbund*), see Mori, *La pace e la ragione Kant e le relazioni internazionali,* 103–14.
87. *Toward Perpetual Peace,* in *Practical Philosophy,* 336: AK 8: 367.
88. *The Metaphysics of Morals,* in ibid., 483: AK 6: 344; *Idea for a Universal History with a Cosmopolitan Aim,* in *Anthropology, History and Education,* 114: AK 8: 24.
89. *Federalist XVIII,* in Madison, Hamilton, and Jay, *The Federalist Papers,* 160.
90. *Reflexionen zur Anthropologie,* no. 1420: AK 16: 618.
91. *Critique of the Power of Judgment,* 229: AK 5: 355.
92. For a more extensive discussion, see Kleingeld, *Kant and Cosmopolitanism,* 74–86.
93. On what Kant understands by this, see ibid., 81–82.
94. "Kant on the Metaphysics of Morals: Vigilantius' Lecture Notes," in *Lectures on Ethics,* 406: AK 27: 674, and see Seyla Benhabib, with Jeremy Waldron, Bonnie Honig, and Will Kymlicka, *Another Cosmopolitanism,* ed. Robert Post (Oxford: Oxford Unversity Press, 2006), 22–24.
95. *Toward Perpetual Peace,* in *Practical Philosophy,* 329–31: AK 8: 359–60.
96. Benhabib, with Waldron, Honig, and Kymlicka, *Another Cosmopolitanism,* 23; see also Jeremy Waldron's response to Benhabib's insistence on the importance for Kant of "state-sized political communities," ibid., 89.
97. *Idea for a Universal History with a Cosmopolitan Aim,* in *Anthropology, History, and Education,* 116–18: AK 8: 27; see also Kleingeld, *Kant and Cosmopolitanism,* 76.
98. *The Conflict of the Faculties,* in *Religion and Rational Theology,* 297: AK 7: 79, and see pp. 194–95.
99. Pauline Kleingeld, "Approaching Perpetual Peace: Kant's Defence of a League of States and His Ideal of a World Federation," *European Journal of Philosophy* 12 (2004): 304–25.
100. *Anthropology from a Pragmatic Point of View,* in *Anthropology, History, and Education,* 419: AK 7: 324.
101. *Critique of Pure Reason,* 397: A 316/B 372. Cf. *The Conflict of the Faculties,* in *Religion and Rational Theology,* 307: AK 7: 93.
102. *Toward Perpetual Peace,* in *Practical Philosophy,* 337: AK 8: 368.
103. *Idea for a Universal History with a Cosmopolitan Aim,* in *Anthropology, History, and Education,* 116: AK 8: 26.
104. *Toward Perpetual Peace,* in *Practical Philosophy,* 327: AK 8: 355.
105. *The Conflict of the Faculties,* in *Religion and Rational Theology,* 303: AK 7: 86–87.
106. *The Prelude,* 109–16.
107. Quoted in G. P. Gooch, *Germany and the French Revolution* (New York: Russell & Russell, 1966), 41–43.
108. "Last Days of Immanuel Kant" [1827], in *Last Days of Immanuel Kant and Other Writings* (Edinburgh: 1871), 112.

109. François Azouvi and Dominique Bourel, *De Königsberg à Paris. La Réception de Kant en France (1788–1804)* (Paris: Vrin, 1991), 69.
110. "13 nivôse an IV" (Jan. 3, 1796), quoted in Alexis Philonenko, "Kant et le problème de la paix," in *Essais sur la philosophie de la guerre* (Paris: Vrin, 1976), 27.
111. Quoted in Jacques Droz, *L'Allemagne et la révolution française* (Paris: Presses Universitaire de France, 1949), 160; and Gareth Stedman Jones, "Kant, the French Revolution and the Definition of Republic," in *The Invention of the Modern Republic,* ed. Biancamaria Fontana, (Cambridge: Cambridge University Press, 1994), 154–72.
112. *An Answer to the Question: "What Is Enlightenment?"* in *Practical Philosophy,* 18: AK 8: 36; "On the Common Saying: 'This may be true in theory, but it is of no use in practice,'" in *Practical Philosophy,* 298: AK 8: 299, "any insurrection that breaks out into a rebellion, is the highest and most punishable crime within a commonwealth because it destroys its foundations."
113. "On the Common Saying: 'This may be true in theory, but it is of no use in practice,'" in *Practical Philosophy,* 300: AK 8: 301n. In each of the three cases he cites, however, what he calls the "uprising" was in fact initiated not by a "mob" but by a duly convened representative assembly.
114. *The Metaphysics of Morals,* in *Practical Philosophy,* 481: AK 6: 341–42. He makes a similar observation in the *Reflexionen zur Rechtsphilosophie,* no. 8055, AK 19: 595–96. "In France the National Assembly was able to change the constitution even though it had only been convened to put the nation's finances in order. They [its members] became, in effect, the representatives of the assembly of the people after the king had allowed them to pass decrees by virtue of full powers which were ill-defined."
115. *The Metaphysics of Morals,* in *Practical Philosophy,* 491–92: AK 6: 355; see also Lewis W. Beck, "Kant and the Right of Revolution," in *Immanuel Kant: Critical Perspectives,* ed. Ruth F. Chadwick (London and New York: Routledge, 1992), III, 399–41.
116. *Vorarbeiten zu Über den Gemeinspruch: das mag in der Theorie richtig sein, taugt aber nicht für die Praxis,* AK 23: 127.
117. *The Metaphysics of Morals,* in *Practical Philosophy,* 491–92: AK 6: 355.
118. Quoted in Droz, *L'Allemagne et la révolution française,* 156. See also Frederick C. Beiser, *Enlightenment, Revolution, and Romanticism: The Genesis of Modern German Political Thought, 1790–1800* (Cambridge, Mass.: Harvard University Press, 1992).
119. *Religion and Philosophy in Germany: A Fragment,* trans. John Snodgrass (Boston: Beacon Press, 1959), 106.
120. *Reflexionen zur Rechtsphilosophie,* no. 8077, AK 19: 609.
121. Georges Vlachos, *La Pensée politique de Kant* (Paris: Presses Universitaires de France, 1962), 553–54.
122. "On the Common Saying: 'This may be true in theory, but it is of no use in practice,'" in *Practical Philosophy,* 305–7: AK 8: 307–10. The quotation from Mendelssohn is from his *Jerusalem: A Treatise on Ecclesiastical Authority and Judaism* (1783).
123. *The Conflict of the Faculties,* in *Religion and Rational Theology,* 303: AK 7: 86–87.

124. *Esquisse d'un tableau historique des progrès de l'éprit humain,* 266–67.
125. Quoted in David Williams, *Condorcet and Modernity* (Cambridge: Cambridge University Press, 2004), 92.
126. Quoted in Jeanne Morefield, *Covenants Without Sword: Idealist Liberalism and the Spirit of Empire* (Princeton, N.J., and Oxford: Princeton University Press, 2005), 99. On Zimmern's role in the creation of the League of Nations and subsequently of the United Nations, see Mark Mazower, *No Enchanted Palace: The End of Empire and the Ideological Origins of the United Nations* (Princeton, N.J., and Oxford: Princeton University Press, 2009), 66–103.
127. *Inevitable Peace* (Cambridge, Mass.: Harvard University Press, 1948), 239.
128. On Kant's juggling of these different conceptions of sovereignty, see Jürgen Habermas, *The Divided West,* ed. and trans. Ciaran Cronin (Cambridge: Polity Press, 2006), 115–16.

Conclusion

1. "A Discourse on the Love of Our Country," in *Political Writings,* 177.
2. Quoted in Scurr, *Fatal Purity,* 275.
3. Ibid., 2.
4. Quoted in Gordon Wood, *Empire of Liberty,* 177.
5. *On the Aesthetic Education of Man,* trans. E. M. Wilkinson and L. A. Willoughby (Oxford: Oxford University Press, 1982), 25.
6. *Untersuchungen über die französische Revolution* (Hanover, 1793), xi. Jachmann's comments on Rehberg are in a letter to Kant, Oct. 14, 1790, *Correspondence,* 368, AK11: 225, not that Rehberg was in any formal sense a pupil of Kant's.
7. Ibid., 12.
8. Ibid., 92.
9. "De la politique et de la morale" (Jan. 1806), in *Mélanges littéraires politiques et philosophiques, Œuvres complètes* (Paris, 1838), X/2, 162.
10. *Religion and Philosophy in Germany: A Fragment,* trans. John Snodgrass (Boston: Beacon Press, 1959), 106.
11. Quoted in Maurice Cranston, *The Solitary Self: Jean-Jacques Rousseau in Exile and Adversity* (Chicago: University of Chicago Press, 1977), 189.
12. *An Answer to the Question: "What Is Enlightenment?"* in *Practical Philosophy,* 17: AK 8: 35.
13. "On the Influence of Enlightenment on Revolutions," in Schmidt, *What Is Enlightenment?,* 217.
14. Quoted in Elie Kedourie, *Arabic Political Memoirs and Other Studies* (London: Frank Cass, 1974), 260.
15. Quoted in Isaiah Berlin, "Joseph de Maistre and the Origins of Fascism," in *The Crooked Timber of Humanity: Chapters in the History of Ideas* (New York: Alfred A. Knopf, 1991), 94.
16. *Considerations on France,* 10n3.
17. *Les Origines de la France contemporaine* (Paris, 1899), I, 265–77.
18. *Considerations on France,* 9–11, also quoted in Darrin M. McMahon, *Enemies of*

Enlightenment: The French Counter-Enlightenment and the Making of Modernity (Oxford: Oxford University Press, 2001), 99.

19. Ibid., 102.
20. *Les Soirées de Saint-Pétersbourg, ou entretiens sur le gouvernement temporal de la providence,* in *Œuvres complètes de Joseph de Maistre* (Lyon and Paris, 1884–87), V, 22.
21. Ibid., IV, 84.
22. Quoted in Isaiah Berlin, *Against the Current: Essays in the History of Ideas* (London and New York: Penguin Books, 1982), 139.
23. "A Letter to a Member of the National Assembly," in *Further Reflections on the Revolution in France,* 48.
24. Quoted in Appiah, *Cosmopolitanism,* xvi.
25. *Hegel on Hamann,* trans. Lise Marie Anderson (Evanston, Ill.: Northwestern University Press, 2008), 7.
26. See Robert Alan Sparling, *Johann Georg Hamann and the Enlightenment Project* (Toronto: Toronto University Press, 2011).
27. "Letter to Christian Jacob Krause," in Schmidt, *What Is Enlightenment?* 147.
28. *Metacritique on the Purism of Reason,* in ibid., 155.
29. "The Contingency of Languages," in *Contingency, Irony, and Solidarity* (Cambridge: Cambridge University Press, 1989), 5.
30. "True and False Political Enlightenment" [1792], in Schmidt, *What Is Enlightenment?,* 212–16.
31. *Treatise on the Origin of Language,* in *Herder: Philosophical Writings,* 164. See Johan H. Zamito, *Kant, Herder: The Birth of Anthropology,* 344–45.
32. *Treatise on the Origin of Language,* in *Herder: Philosophical Writings,* 151–52.
33. *This, Too, a Philosophy of History,* in ibid., 307–12.
34. *Outlines of a Philosophy of the History of Man* [*Ideen zur Philosophie der Geschichte der Menschheit*], trans. T. Churchill (London, 1800), 288.
35. Ibid., 221.
36. Ibid., 189.
37. See pp. 398–99.
38. *This, Too, a Philosophy of History,* in *Herder: Philosophical Writings,* 298.
39. "Reflections on the Philosophy of History," in *On World History: An Anthology,* ed. Hans Adler and Ernst A. Menze (Armonk, N.Y., and London: M. E. Sharpe, 1997), 232.
40. "Letters for the Advancement of Humanity (1793–97)—Tenth Collection," in *Herder: Philosophical Writings,* 393–94. For a discussion of Herder's allusion to Kant's essay, *On the Different Races of Man,* see ibid., 393–94n33.
41. Ibid., 395. The "Huswana" are unidentified. The "Gonaqua" are a tribe of the Khoikhoi, of Southwest Africa.
42. *Outlines of a Philosophy of the History of Man,* 241.
43. Charles Taylor, *Sources of the Self: The Making of the Modern Identity* (Cambridge: Cambridge University Press, 1989), 369.
44. *Religion and Philosophy in Germany,* 58.
45. Shklar, *Freedom and Independence,* 171.
46. See Lewis P. Hinchman, *Hegel's Critique of the Enlightenment* (Tampa: University of Florida Press, 1984), 185–215.

47. Napoleon to Las Cases, Nov. 11, 1816. Las Cases was not a reliable witness, but Napoleon had made a similar statement to the Corps législatif on Feb. 15, 1805. Biancamaria Fontana, "The Napoleonic Empire and the Europe of Nations," in *The Idea of Europe: From Antiquity to the European Union,* ed. Anthony Pagden (Cambridge: Cambridge University Press, 2002), 122–23.
48. *Dialectic of Enlightenment,* p. xii.
49. "Saint-Just's Illusion," in *Making Sense of Humanity and Other Philosophical Papers, 1982–1992* (Cambridge: Cambridge University Press, 1995).
50. *L'Ancien régime et la révolution,* ed. François Mélonio (Paris: Flammarion, 1988), 84.
51. "Towards a Holy Alliance of Peoples" (1849, written in Italian), in *A Cosmopolitanism of Nations: Giuseppe Mazzini's Writings on Democracy, Nation Building and International Relations,* ed. and trans. Stefano Recchia and Nadia Urbinati (Princeton, N.J.: Princeton University Press, 2009), 117–19.
52. Denis Mack Smith, *Mazzini* (New Haven, Conn., and London: Yale University Press, 1994), 215.
53. Quoted in Stefano Recchia and Nadia Urbinati, "Introduction: Giuseppe Mazzini's International Political Thought," in *A Cosmopolitanism of Nations,* 1.
54. Viroli, *For Love of Country,* 144–45.
55. *Elements of the Philosophy of Right,* trans. H. B. Nisbet (Cambridge: Cambridge University Press, 1991), 367, 368 (331, 335).
56. Charles Taylor, *Hegel* (Cambridge: Cambridge University Press, 1975), 387–88.
57. *Elements of the Philosophy of Right,* 288–89 (268).
58. "From a Revolutionary Alliance to the United States of Europe" (1850, originally written in Italian), in *A Cosmopolitanism of Nations,* 134.
59. "Humanity and Country" (1839, originally written in French), in ibid., 53–57.
60. "Nationality and Cosmopolitanism" (1847, originally written in English), in ibid., 58.
61. Ibid., 59.
62. "From a Revolutionary Alliance to the United States of Europe," 132–35.
63. James P. Piscatori, *Islam in a World of Nation States* (Cambridge: Cambridge University Press, 1986), 22.
64. See Amy Gutman, "Communitarian Critics of Liberalism," *Philosophy and Public Affairs* 14 (1985): 308–22.
65. *After Virtue: A Study in Moral Theory* (Notre Dame, Ind.: University of Notre Dame Press, 1981), 1–2.
66. Ibid., 37–38.
67. *Three Rival Versions of Moral Enquiry: Encyclopaedia, Genealogy, and Tradition* (Notre Dame, Ind.: University of Notre Dame Press, 1990), 172–73.
68. *Religion and Philosophy in Germany,* 265.
69. *Essai sur les préjugés,* in *Œuvres philosophiques complètes,* II, 12.
70. *Truth and Method,* 234ff. The concepts of fore-structure, fore-warning, etc. are taken from Heidegger. Gadamer makes a passing allusion to Burke and must have been aware of the passage I have quoted.
71. "Is Patriotism a Virtue?" in *Theorizing Citizenship,* ed. Ronald Beiner (New York: State University of New York Press, 1995), 216–17.

72. *The Differend: Phrases in Dispute,* trans. Georges Van Den Abbeele (Minneapolis: University of Minnesota Press, 1988), 151.
73. Ibid., 157.
74. *Spheres of Justice: A Defense of Pluralism and Equality* (New York: Basic Books, 1983), 314–15.
75. Letter to N. L. Ozmidov, 1878, in *Selected Letters of Fyodor Dostoyevsky,* trans. Andrew R. MacAndrew (New Brunswick, N.J.: Rutgers University Press, 1987), 446.
76. *Breaking the Spell: Religion as a Natural Phenomenon* (New York: Penguin Books, 2007), 35–36.
77. Jürgen Habermas and Joseph Ratzinger, *The Dialectics of Secularization: On Reason and Religion* (San Francisco: Ignatius Press, 2005), 37, 75.
78. Ibid., 77. To be fair to Benedict, what he is asking for is not a total surrender to the claims of religion but rather, in the spirit, as he claims of the Church Fathers, a world "purified and structured by religion."
79. *A Secular Age* (Cambridge, Mass.: Harvard University Press, 2007), 772.
80. Pippa Norris and Ronald Ingelhart, *Sacred and Secular: Religion and Politics Worldwide* (Cambridge: Cambridge University Press, 2004), 241.
81. Ibid. For a discussion of this and of its global significance, see Roberto Farneti, "Cleavage Lines in Global Politics: Left and Right, East and West, Earth and Heaven," *Journal of Political Ideologies* 17 (2012): 127–45.
82. According to the "The Global Index of Religiosity and Atheism," the number of Americans who say they are "religious" dropped from 73 percent in 2005 (the last time the poll was conducted) to 60 percent, and the number who say they are atheists rose, from 1 percent to 5 percent. As reported in the Huffington Post, December 5, 2012.
83. See Cesare Merlini, "A Post-Secular World?," *Survival* 53 (2011): 117–30.
84. *Black Mass: Apocalyptic Religion and the Death of Utopia* (London and New York: Allen Lane, 2007), 210.
85. See pp. 29–30 above.
86. John Gray, *Enlightenment's Wake: Politics and Culture at the Close of the Modern Age* (London and New York; Routledge, 1997), 145.
87. On the Enlightenment origins of human rights, see Lynn Hunt, *Inventing Human Rights: A History* (New York: W. W. Norton, 2007).
88. "The Continuity Between the Enlightenment and 'Postmodernism,'" in *What's Left of Enlightenment?,* ed. Keith Michael Baker and Peter Hans Reill (Stanford, Calif.: Stanford University Press, 2002), 20.
89. See pp. 20–21.
90. *The Life, Unpublished Letters, and Philosophical Regimen of Anthony, Earl of Shaftesbury,* 353, and quoted in Roy Porter, *The Creation of the Modern World,* 3.
91. *Decline and Fall of the Roman Empire,* LII, 16. Gibbon's predication, however, was about what might have become of Europe if an invading Arab army under the command of 'Abd Rahman, the governor of Al-Andalus, had not been defeated at Poitiers in southern France in October 732.
92. On the reasons for Rome's failure to progress beyond the intellectual state it had arrived at in the first century, see Aldo Schiavone, *The End of the Past: Ancient*

Rome and the Modern West, trans. Margaret J. Schneider (Cambridge, Mass., and London: Harvard University Press, 2000).

93. *What are we waiting for, assembled in the forum?*
The barbarians are due here today.
Why isn't anything happening in the senate?
Why do the senators sit there without legislating?

Because the barbarians are coming today.
What laws can the senators make now?
Once the barbarians are here, they'll do the legislating.
Why did our emperor get up so early,
and why is he sitting at the city's main gate
on his throne, in state, wearing the crown?

Because the barbarians are coming today
and the emperor is waiting to receive their leader.
He has even prepared a scroll to give him,
replete with titles, with imposing names.
Why have our two consuls and praetors come out today
wearing their embroidered, their scarlet togas?
Why have they put on bracelets with so many amethysts,
and rings sparkling with magnificent emeralds?
Why are they carrying elegant canes
beautifully worked in silver and gold?

Because the barbarians are coming today
and things like that dazzle the barbarians.
Why don't our distinguished orators come forward as usual
to make their speeches, say what they have to say?

Because the barbarians are coming today
and they're bored by rhetoric and public speaking.
Why this sudden restlessness, this confusion?
(How serious people's faces have become.)
Why are the streets and squares emptying so rapidly,
everyone going home so lost in thought?

Because night has fallen and the barbarians have not come.
And some who have just returned from the border say
there are no barbarians any longer.
And now, what's going to happen to us without barbarians?
They were, those people, a kind of solution.

(Translated from the Greek by Edmund Keeley.)
In a similar vein John Gray has argued—admittedly some little time ago—that we live "amid the dim ruins of the Enlightenment project, which was the ruling

project of the modern period," from which only a new input from outside, probably from Asia, can now save us: *Enlightenment's Wake,* 145.

94. Quoted in Garry Wills, "A Country Ruled by Faith," *New York Review of Books* 53, 18 (Nov. 16, 2006), 8.
95. *Our Global Neighborhood: Report of the Commission on Global Governance of 1995* (Oxford: Oxford University Press, 1995). The report was issued in preparation for the World Conference on Global Governance of 1998.
96. *The Divided West,* 19.
97. *Zur Verfassung Europas. Ein Essay* (Berlin: Suhrkamp, 2011).

BIBLIOGRAPHY

Alexander, William. *The History of Women from the Earliest Antiquity to the Present Time.* London, 1782 [1779].

Ando, Clifford. *Imperial Ideology and Provincial Loyalty in the Roman Empire.* Berkeley, Los Angeles, and London: University of California Press, 2000.

Anquetil-Duperron, Abraham Hyacinthe. *Législation orientale.* Amsterdam, 1778.

Appiah, Anthony Kwame. *Cosmopolitanism: Ethics in a World of Strangers.* New York and London: W. W. Norton & Co., 2006.

Archibugi, Daniele, and David Held, eds. *Cosmopolitan Democracy: An Agenda for a New World Order.* Cambridge: Polity Press, 1995.

Armitage, David. *The Declaration of Independence: A Global History.* Cambridge, Mass.: Harvard University Press, 2008.

Asku, Esref, ed. *Early Notions of Global Governance: Selected Eighteenth-Century Proposals for "Perpetual Peace."* Cardiff: University of Wales Press, 2008.

Azouvi, François, and Dominique Bourel. *De Königsberg à Paris. La réception de Kant en France (1788–1804).* Paris: Vrin, 1991.

Baczko, Bronislaw. *Job mon ami. Promesses du bonheur et fatalité du mal.* Paris: Gallimard, 1997.

Baker, Keith. *Condorcet: From Natural Philosophy to Social Mathematics.* Chicago and London: University of Chicago Press, 1975.

Baker, Keith, and Peter Hans Reill, eds. *What's Left of Enlightenment?* Stanford, Calif.: Stanford University Press, 2002.

Banks, Joseph. *The* Endeavour *Journal of Joseph Banks, 1768–1771.* Ed. J. C. Beaglehole. Sydney: Angus & Robertson, 1962.

Bayly, C. A. *The Birth of the Modern World, 1780–1914.* Malden and Oxford: Blackwell, 2004.

Beaune, Colette. *Naissance de la nation France.* Paris: Gallimard, 1985.

Beck, Lewis W. "Kant and the Right of Revolution." In *Immanuel Kant: Critical Perspectives,* ed. Ruth F. Chadwick, III, 399–41. London and New York: Routledge, 1992.

Bedani, Gino. *Vico Revisited: Orthodoxy, Naturalism and Science in the* Scienza Nuova. Oxford, Hamburg, and Munich: Berg, 1989.

Beiser, Frederick C. *Enlightenment, Revolution, and Romanticism: The Genesis of Modern German Political Thought, 1790–1800.* Cambridge, Mass.: Harvard University Press, 1992.

Belissa, Marc, and Bernard Cottret, eds. *Cosmopolitismes, patriotismes. Europe et Amériques, 1773–1802.* Rennes: Les Perséides, 2005.

Bell, David. *The Cult of the Nation in France: Inventing Nationalism, 1680–1800.* Cambridge, Mass.: Harvard University Press, 2001.

Benhabib, Seyla, with Jeremy Waldron, Bonnie Honig, and Will Kymlicka. *Another Cosmopolitanism.* Ed. Robert Post. Oxford: Oxford University Press, 2006.

Benrekassa, Georges. "Dit et non dit idéologique; à propos du *Supplément au voyage de Bougainville.*" *Dix-huitième siècle* 5 (1973): 29–40.

Bentham, Jeremy. *The Works of Jeremy Bentham.* Edinburgh, 1843.

———. *A Fragment on Government.* Ed. J. H. Burns and H.L.A. Hart. Cambridge: Cambridge University Press, 1988.

Benveniste, Émile. *Problèmes de linguistique générale.* Paris: Gallimard, 1966.

———. *Indo-European Language and Society.* trans. Elizabeth Palmer. London: Faber and Faber, 1973.

Berlin, Isaiah. *Against the Current: Essays in the History of Ideas.* London and New York: Penguin Books, 1982.

———. *The Crooked Timber of Humanity: Chapters in the History of Ideas.* New York: Alfred A. Knopf, 1991.

Berry, Christopher J. *The Idea of Luxury: A Conceptual and Historical Investigation.* Cambridge: Cambridge University Press, 1994.

Bloch, Ernest. *Natural Law and Human Dignity.* Cambridge, Mass.: MIT Press, 1986.

Bolingbroke, Henry St. John, Viscount. *Bolingbroke, Political Writings.* Ed. David Armitage. Cambridge: Cambridge University Press, 1997.

Bonald, Louis-Gabriel-Ambroise de. *Œuvres complètes.* Paris, 1838.

Boswell, James. *Life of Johnson.* Ed. R. W. Chapman. Oxford: Oxford University Press, 1953.

———. *Journal of a Tour to the Hebrides with Samuel Johnson, 1733.* Ed. Frederick A. Pottle and Charles H. Bennet. New York: McGraw-Hill, 1961.

Bougainville, Louis-Antoine de. *Voyage autour du monde par la frégate la Boudeuse et la flûte l'Étoile; en 1766, 1767, 1768 et 1769.* Ed. Michel Bideaux and Sonia Faessel. Paris: Presse de l'Université de Paris-Sorbonne, 2001.

———. *The Pacific Journal of Louis-Antoine de Bougainville, 1767–1768.* Trans. and ed. John Dunmore. London: Hakluyt Society, 2002.

Boulainvilliers, Henri de. *Œuvres philosophiques.* The Hague: Martinus Nijhoff, 1975.

Boulanger, Nicolas-Antoine. *L'Antiquité dévoilée par ses usages.* Amsterdam, 1772.

Brett, Annabel S. *Changes of State: Nature and the Limits of the City in Early-Modern Natural Law.* Princeton: Princeton University Press, 2011.

Brissot de Warville, Jacques-Pierre. *Examen critique des voyages dans l'Amérique septentrionale de M. le m.s de Chastellux.* London, 1786.

Brown, Stewart J., ed. *William Robertson and the Expansion of Empire.* Cambridge: Cambridge University Press, 1997.

Buffon, Georges-Louis Leclerc de. *Œuvres complètes de Buffon avec la nomenclature linnéenne et la classification de Cuvier. Revues sur l'édition de l'Imprimerie royale et annotées par M. Flourens.* Paris, 1853–55.

———. *De l'homme*. Ed. Michèle Duchet. Paris: François Maspero, 1971.

Burke, Edmund. *Writings and Speeches*. Ed. J. F. Taylor. New York: Little, Brown, 1901.

———. *Further Reflections on the Revolution in France*. Ed. Daniel E. Ritchie. Indianapolis: Liberty Fund, 1992.

———. *Reflections on the Revolution in France*. Ed. J.C.D. Clark. Stanford, Calif.: Stanford University Press, 2001.

Byrd, Sharon B., and Joachim Hruschka. "*Lex iusti, lex iuridica und lex iustitiae* in Kants *Rechtslehre*." *Archiv für Rechts und Sozialphilosophie* 91 (2005): 484–500.

Campbell, Peter. "The Language of Patriotism in France, 1750–1770." *e-France*, I (2007), 14.

———. "The Politics of Patriotism in France (1770–1788)." *French History* 24, 4 (2010): 550–75.

Carey, Daniel. *Locke, Shaftesbury, and Hutcheson: Contesting Diversity in the Enlightenment and Beyond.* Cambridge: Cambridge University Press, 2006.

Carrithers, David. "The Enlightenment Science of Society." In *Inventing Human Science: Eighteenth-Century Domains,* ed. Christopher Fox, Roy Porter, and Robert Wokler, 232–70. Berkeley, Los Angeles, and London: University of California Press, 1995.

Cassirer, Ernst. *The Philosophy of the Enlightenment*. Trans. Fritz C. A. Koelln and James P. Pettegrove. Princeton, N.J.: Princeton University Press, 1951.

———. *Kant's Life and Thought*. Trans. James Haden. New Haven, Conn., and London: Yale University Press, 1981.

Cavallar, Georg. *The Rights of Strangers: Theories of International Hospitality, the Global Community and Political Justice Since Victoria.* Aldershot, U.K.: Ashgate, 2002.

Chappey, Jean-Luc. *La Société des observateurs de l'homme (1799–1804). Des anthropologues au temps de Bonaparte.* Paris: Société des études robespierristes, 2005.

Cheek, Pamela. *Sexual Antipodes: Enlightenment, Globalization and the Placing of Sex.* Stanford, Calif.: Stanford University Press, 2003.

Child, A. *Making and Knowing in Hobbes, Vico, Dewey.* Berkeley and Los Angeles: University of California Press, 1953.

Commission on Global Governance. *Our Global Neighbourhood: Report of the Commission on Global Governance of 1995.* Oxford: Oxford University Press, 1995.

Condorcet, Marie Jean Antoine Nicolas de Caritat, Marquis de. *Œuvres complètes de Condorcet.* Paris, 1804.

———. *Esquisse d'un tableau historique des progrès de l'esprit humain*. Ed. Alain Pons. Paris: Flammarion, 1988.

———. *Essai sur les éléments de philosophie ou sur les principes des connaissances humaines.* Paris: Fayard, 1989.

Constant, Benjamin. *Political Writings*. Ed. Biancamaria Fontana. Cambridge: Cambridge University Press, 1988.

Cook, James. *The Journals of Captain James Cook on His Voyages of Discovery*. Ed. J. C. Beagle. Cambridge: Hakluyt Society, 1955–68.

Copans, Jean, and Jean Jamin, eds. *Aux Origines de l'anthropologie française. Les Mémoires de la Société des observateurs de l'homme en l'an VIII.* Paris: Le Sycomore, 1978.

Cranston, Maurice. *John Locke: A Biography.* Oxford: Oxford University Press, 1985.

———. *Philosophers and Pamphleteers: Political Theorists of the Enlightenment.* Oxford: Oxford University Press, 1986.

Cuoco, Vincenzo. *Saggio storico sulla rivoluzione di Napoli.* Ed. Antonino de Francesco. Paris: Les Belles Lettres, 2004 [1801].

Curtis, Michael. *Orientalism and Islam: European Thinkers on Oriental Despotism in the Middle East and India.* Cambridge: Cambridge University Press, 2009.

Dabhoiwala, Faramerz. *The Origins of Sex: A History of the First Sexual Revolution.* London: Allen Lane, 2012.

D'Alembert, Jean-Baptiste Le Rond. *Œuvres complètes de D'Alembert.* Paris, 1821–22.

———. *Essai sur les éléments de philosophie ou, sur les principes des connaissances humaines.* Ed. Catherine Kintzler. Paris: Fayard, 1986.

Daniel, Norman. *Islam, Europe, and Empire.* Edinburgh: Edinburgh University Press, 1966.

De Brosses, Charles. *Histoire des navigations aux terres australes.* Paris, 1756.

De Maistre, Joseph. *Œuvres complètes de Joseph de Maistre.* Lyon and Paris, 1884–7.

———. *Les Origines de la France contemporaine.* Paris, 1899.

———. *Considerations on France*. Trans. Richard A. Lebrun. Cambridge: Cambridge University Press, 1994.

Dennett, Daniel C. *Breaking the Spell: Religion as a Natural Phenomenon*. New York: Penguin Books, 2007.

De Quincey, Thomas. "Last Days of Immanuel Kant." In *Last Days of Immanuel Kant and Other Writings.* Edinburgh: 1871 [1827].

Despoix, Philippe, *Le Monde mesuré. Dispositifs de l'exploration à l'âge de Lumières.* Geneva: Droz, 2005.

Detienne, Marcel. *Les Grecs et nous.* Paris: Perrin, 2005.

Diderot, Denis. *Œuvres complètes*. Ed. Jules Assevat and Maurice Tourneaux. Paris, 1875–77.

———. *Œuvres philosophiques*. Ed. Paul Vernier. Paris: Garnier, 1956.

———. *Correspondance de Denis Diderot*. Ed. Georges Roth. Paris: Les Editions de Minuit, 1955–70.

———. *Salons*. Ed. Jean Seznec and Jean Adhemar. Oxford: Oxford University Press, 1957–67.

———. *Political Writings*. Ed. John Hope Mason and Robert Wokler. Cambridge: Cambridge University Press, 1992.

———. *Œuvres*. Ed. Laurent Versini. Paris: Robert Laffont, 1994.

Dostoyevsky, Fyodor. *Selected Letters of Fyodor Dostoyevsky*. Trans. Andrew R. MacAndrew. New Brunswick: Rutgers University Press, 1987.

Doyle, Michael W. "Kant, Liberal Legacies and Foreign Affairs." *Philosophy and Public Affairs* 12 (1983): 205–353.

Droz, Jacques. *L'Allemagne et la révolution française.* Paris: Presses Universitaires de France, 1949.

Duchet, Michèle. *Anthropologie et histoire au siècle des Lumières.* Paris, François Maspero, 1971.

Dunmore, John. *Monsieur Baret: The First Woman Around the World, 1766–68.* Greenhithe, U.K.: Heritage Press, 2002.

Durkheim, Émile. *Hobbes à l'agrégation.* Ed. Jean-François Bert. Paris: Editions EHESS, 2011.

Edelstein, Dan. *The Enlightenment: A Genealogy.* Chicago: University of Chicago Press, 2010.

Eliav-Feldon, Miriam, et al., eds. *The Origins of Racism in the West.* Cambridge: Cambridge University Press, 2009.

Elisseeff, Danielle. *Nicolas Fréret (1688–1749). Réflexions d'un humaniste du XVIIIe siècle sur la Chine.* Paris: Collège de France, 1978.

———. *Moi, Arcade interprète chinois du Roi-Soleil.* Paris: Arthaud, 1985.

Farneti, Roberto. "Cleavage Lines in Global Politics: Left and Right, East and West, Earth and Heaven." *Journal of Political Ideologies* 17 (2012): 127–45.

Feijoo, Benito Jerónimo. *Teatro crítico universal. Discursos varios en todo género de materias, para desengaño de errores comunes.* Madrid, 1726.

Fellows, Otis. "Buffon and Rousseau: Aspects of a Relationship." *Proceedings of the Modern Languages Association* 75 (1960): 184–96.

Ferguson, Adam. *An Essay on the History of Civil Society*. Ed. Fania Oz-Salzberger. Cambridge: Cambridge University Press, 1995.

Ferrone, Vincenzo. *Scienza, natura, religione. Mondo newtoniano e cultura italiana nel primo settecento.* Naples: Jovene, 1982.

———. *I profeti dell'Illuminismo*. Rome: Laterza, 2000.

Filangieri, Gaetano. *La scienza della legislazione*. Ed. Vincenzo Ferrone et al. Venice: Centro di Studi sull'Iluminismo Europeo "Giovanni Stiffoni," 2003.

Fontana, Biancamaria. "The Napoleonic Empire and the Europe of Nations." In *The Idea of Europe: From Antiquity to the European Union,* ed. Anthony Pagden, 122–23. Cambridge: Cambridge University Press, 2002.

Fontana, Michele. *Matteo Ricci. Un gesuita alla corte dei Ming.* Milan: Mondadori, 2005.

Forget, Evelyn. "Cultivating Sympathy: Sophie Condorcet's Letters on Sympathy." *Journal of the History of Economic Thought* 23 (2001): 319–37.

Forster, Georg. *A Voyage to the Cape of Good Hope, Towards the Arctic Polar Circle and Around the World.* London, 1785.

Foucault, Michel. "Qu'est-ce que les Lumières?" In *Dits et écrits 1954–1988.* Paris: Gallimard, 1994, IV, 562–69.

Fougeret de Monbron, Louis-Charles. *Le Cosmopolite ou le citoyen du monde.* London, 1761.

Frazer, Michael L. *The Enlightenment of Sympathy: Justice and Moral Sentiments in the Eighteenth Century and Today.* Oxford: Oxford University Press, 2010.

Friedrich, Carl Joachim. *Inevitable Peace.* Cambridge, Mass.: Harvard University Press, 1948.

Gadamer, Hans-Georg. *Truth and Method.* [*Warheit und Methode*, 1965.] London: Sheen & Ward, 1975.

Gaskin, J. C. A. *Hume's Philosophy of Religion.* New York: Macmillan, 1980.

———. "Hume on Religion." In *The Cambridge Companion to Hume,* ed. David Fate Norton, 313–44. Cambridge: Cambridge University Press, 1993.

Gat, Azar. *War in Human Civilization.* Oxford: Oxford University Press, 2008.

Gay, Peter. *The Enlightenment: An Interpretation.* New York: Knopf, 1966.

———. *Deism: An Anthology.* Princeton: D. Van Nostrand & Co., 1968.

Genovesi, Antonio. *La logica per gli giovanetti. Classici italiani di economia politica.* Milan, 1835.

Gerbi, Antonello. *La disputa del Nuovo Mondo. Storia di una polemica, 1750–1900.* Milan: Riccardo Ricciardi, 1983.

Geuss, Raymond. *History and Illusion in Politics.* Cambridge: Cambridge University Press, 2001.

Gibbon, Edward. *The Autobiography of Edward Gibbon*. Ed. Lord Sheffield. Oxford: Oxford University Press, 1950.

———. *Decline and Fall of the Roman Empire*. Ed. David Womersley. London: Penguin, 1994.

———. *Essai sur l'étude de la littérature*. Ed. Robert Mankin. Oxford: Voltaire Foundation, 2010.

Glacken, Clarence J. *Traces on the Rhodian Shore: Nature and Culture in Western Thought from Ancient Times to the Eighteenth Century.* Berkeley and Los Angeles: University of California Press, 1967.

Glaeser, Edward. *The Triumph of the City: How Our Greatest Invention Makes Us Richer, Smarter, Greener, Healthier, and Happier.* New York: Penguin, 2011.

Goldsmith, Oliver. *Letters from a Citizen of the World to His Friends in the East.* Bungy [London], 1820.

Gooch, G. P. *Germany and the French Revolution.* New York: Russell & Russell, 1966.

Gould, Stephen Jay. *Rocks of Ages: Science and Religion in the Fullness of Life.* New York: Ballantine Books, 1999.

Gray, John. *Enlightenment's Wake: Politics and Culture at the Close of the Modern Age.* London and New York: Routledge, 1997.

———. *Black Mass: Apocalyptic Religion and the Death of Utopia.* London and New York: Allen Lane, 2007.

Greenfeld, Liah. *Nationalism: Five Roads to Modernity.* Cambridge, Mass.: Harvard University Press, 1992.

Grimaldi, Francescantonio. *Riflessioni sopra l'inegualianza tra gli uomini* [1779–80]. Ed. Franco Venturi. Milan and Naples: Riccardo Riccardi, 1958.

Gutman, Amy. "Communitarian Critics of Liberalism." *Philosophy and Public Affairs* 14 (1985): 308–22.

Guyer, Paul. *Kant and the Experience of Freedom: Essays on Aesthetics and Morality.* Cambridge: Cambridge University Press, 1993.

Habermas, Jürgen. *Theorie und Praxis. Sozialphilosophische Studien.* Frankfurt am Main: Suhrkamp, 1978.

———. *The Structural Transformation of the Public Sphere: An Enquiry into a Category of Bourgeois Society*. Trans. T. Burgher. Cambridge, Mass.: Harvard University Press, 1989.

———. *Between Facts and Norms: Contributions to a Discourse Theory of Law and Democracy*. Trans. William Rehg. Cambridge, Mass.: MIT Press, 1996.

———. *The Divided West*. Ed. and trans. Ciaran Cronin. Cambridge: Polity Press, 2006.

Habermas, Jürgen, and Joseph Ratzinger. *The Dialectics of Secularization: On Reason and Religion.* San Francisco: Ignatius Press, 2005.

Hacking, Ian. *The Emergence of Probability: A Philosophical Study of Early Ideas About Probability, Induction, and Statistical Inference.* Cambridge: Cambridge University Press, 1975.

Hassner, Pierre. "Les Concepts de guerre et de paix chez Kant." *Revue française de science politique* 11 (1961): 642–70.

Hazard, Paul. "Cosmopolite." In *Mélanges d'histoire littéraire générale et comparée offerts à Fernand Baldensperger.* Paris: Librairie Ancienne Honoré Champion, 1930.

———. *The European Mind, 1680–1715.* Cleveland and New York: Meridian Books, 1963.

———. *La Pensée européenne du XVIIIe siècle.* Paris: Fayard, 1963.

Hegel, Georg Wilhelm Friedrich. *Natural Law*. Trans. T. M. Knox. Philadelphia: University of Pennsylvania Press, 1975.

———. *Elements of the Philosophy of Right.* Trans. H. B. Nisbet. Cambridge: Cambridge University Press, 1991.

———. *Hegel on Hamann*. Trans. Lise Marie Anderson. Evanston, Ill.: Northwestern University Press, 2008.

Heine, Heinrich. *Religion and Philosophy in Germany: A Fragment*. Trans. John Snodgrass. Boston: Beacon Press, 1959.

Heineccius, Johann Gottlieb. *A Methodical System of Universal Laws*. Trans. George Turnbull. Ed. Thomas Ahnert and Peter Schröder. Indianapolis: Liberty Fund, 2008 [1741].

Helvétius, Claude-Adrien. *De l'esprit.* Paris: Fayard, 1988.

Herder, Johann Gottfried von. *Outlines of a Philosophy of the History of Man* [*Ideen zur Philosophie der Geschichte der Menschheit*]. Trans. T. Churchill. London, 1800.

———. *On World History: An Anthology*. Ed. Hans Adler and Ernst A. Menze Armonk. New York and London: M. E. Sharpe, 1997.

———. *Philosophical Writings*. Trans. and ed. Michael N. Forster. Cambridge: Cambridge University Press, 2002.

Heyd, Michael. *"Be Sober and Reasonable": The Critique of Enthusiasm in the Seventeenth and Early Eighteenth Centuries.* Leiden: E. J. Brill, 1995.

Hinchman, Lewis P. *Hegel's Critique of the Enlightenment.* Tampa, Fla.: University of Florida Press, 1984.

Hinske, Norbert, ed. *Was ist Aufklärung? Beitragäge aus der Berlinischen Monatsschrift.* Darmstadt: Wissenschaftliche Buchgesellschaft, 1977.

Hoare, Prince. *Memoirs of Granville Sharp, Esq.* London, 1820.

Hobbes, Thomas. *The Elements of Law, Natural and Political*. Ed. Ferdinand Tönnies. 2d ed. London: Frank Cass & Co., 1969.

———. *Leviathan*. Ed. Richard Tuck. Cambridge: Cambridge University Press, 1991.

———. *De Cive: On the Citizen*. Trans. and ed. Richard Tuck and Michael Silverthorne. Cambridge: Cambridge University Press, 1998.

Hochstrasser, T. J. *Natural Law Theories in the Early Enlightenment.* Cambridge: Cambridge University Press, 2000.

Hoekstra, Kinch. "Hobbes on the Natural Condition of Humankind." In *The Cambridge Companion to Hobbes's* Leviathan. Ed. Patricia Springborg, 109–27. Cambridge: Cambridge University Press, 2007.

Höffe, Otfried. *Kant's Cosmopolitan Theory of Law and Peace*. Trans. Alexandra Newton. Cambridge: Cambridge University Press, 2006.

Holbach, Paul-Henri Thiry, Baron de. *Œuvres philosophiques complètes*. Ed. Jean-Pierre Jackson. Paris: Editions ALIVE, 1999.

Hont, Istvan. *Jealousy of Trade: International Competition and the Nation-State in Historical Perspective.* Cambridge, Mass., and London: Harvard University Press, 2005.

Hont, Istvan, and Michael Ignatieff, eds. *Wealth and Virtue: The Shaping of Political Economy in the Scottish Enlightenment.* Cambridge: Cambridge University Press, 1987.

Horkheimer, Max, and Theodor Adorno. *Dialectic of Enlightenment*. Trans. John Cumming. New York: Herder & Herder, 1972.

Humboldt, Wilhelm von. *On Language: On the Diversity of Human Language Construction and Its Influence on the Mental Development of the Human Species*. Ed. Michael Losonsky. Trans. Peter Heath. Cambridge: Cambridge University Press, 1999.

Hume, David. *The Letters of David Hume*. Ed. J.Y.T. Greig. Oxford: Clarendon Press, 1932.

———. *Enquiries Concerning the Human Understanding and the Principles of Morals*. Ed. L. A. Selby-Bigge. Oxford: Clarendon Press, 1970.

———. *A Treatise on Human Nature*. Ed. L. A. Selby-Bigge and P. H. Nidditch. Oxford: Clarendon Press, 1978.

———. *The History of England: From the Invasion of Julius Caesar to the Revolution in 1688.* Indianapolis: Liberty Fund, 1983–85.

———. *Essays Moral, Political, and Literary*. Ed. Eugene F. Miller. Indianapolis: Liberty Fund, 1985.

———. *Natural History of Religion*. Ed. J.C.A. Gaskin. Oxford: Oxford University Press, 1992.

———. *Dialogues Concerning Natural Religion*. Ed. J.C.A. Gaskin. Oxford: Oxford University Press, 1993.

Hundert, E. J. *The Enlightenment's Fable: Bernard Mandeville and the Discovery of Society.* Cambridge: Cambridge University Press, 1994.

Hurrell, Andrew. "Kant and the Kantian Paradigm in International Relations." *Review of International Studies* 16 (1990): 183–205.

Hutcheson, Francis. *An Inquiry into the Original of Our Ideas of Beauty and Virtue.* 3d. ed. London, 1729.

———. *Two Texts on Human Nature*. Ed. Thomas Meitner. Cambridge: Cambridge University Press, 1993.

———. *Philosophical Writings.* London: J. M. Dent, 1994.

———. *An Essay on the Nature and Conduct of the Passions and Affections, with Illustrations on Moral Sense*. Ed. Aaron Garrett. Indianapolis: Liberty Fund, 2002.

Imbruglia, Girolamo. "Dopo l'Encyclopédie. Diderot e la saggezza dell'immaginazione." *Studi settecenteschi* 11–12 (1988–89): 305–58.

Isaac, Benjamin. *The Invention of Racism in Classical Antiquity.* Princeton, N.J.: Princeton University Press, 2004.

Israel, Jonathan I. *Radical Enlightenment: Philosophy and the Making of Modernity, 1650–1750.* Oxford: Oxford University Press, 2001.

———. *Enlightenment Contested: Philosophy, Modernity and the Emancipation of Man, 1670–1752.* Oxford: Oxford University Press, 2006.

———. *Democratic Enlightenment: Philosophy, Revolution, and Human Rights, 1750–1790.* Oxford: Oxford University Press, 2011.

Jacob, Margaret C. *Strangers Nowhere in the World: The Rise of Cosmopolitanism in Early-Modern Europe.* Philadelphia: University of Pennsylvania Press, 2006.

James VI and I. *Political Writings*. Ed. Johann Sommerville. Cambridge: Cambridge University Press, 1994.

Jefferson, Thomas. *Writings.* New York: Library of America, 1984.

Jensen, Lionel. *Manufacturing Confucianism: Chinese Tradition and Universal Civilization.* Durham, N.C.: Duke University Press, 1997.

Jones, Gareth Stedman. "Kant, the French Revolution and the Definition of Republic." In *The Invention of the Modern Republic.* Ed. Biancamaria Fontana. Cambridge: Cambridge University Press, 1994, 154–72.

Jouannet, Emmanuelle. *Emer de Vattel et l'émergence doctrinale du droit international classique.* Paris: Pedone, 1998.

Kaldor, Mary. *Global Civil Society: An Answer to War.* Cambridge: Polity Press. 2003.

Kames, Henry Home. *Lord Kames, Sketches of the History of Man*. Ed. James A. Harris. Indianapolis: Liberty Fund, 2007.

Kant, Immanuel. *Kants gesammelte Schriften, Herausgegeben von der königlich preussische Akademie der Wissenschaften.* Berlin: Walter de Gruyter, 1902–.

———. *Practical Philosophy*. Trans. and ed. Mary J. Gregor. Cambridge: Cambridge University Press, 1996.

———. *Religion and Rational Theology*. Trans. and ed. Allen W. Wood and George di Giovanni. Cambridge: Cambridge University Press, 1996.

———. *Lectures on Ethics.* Ed. Peter Heath and J. B. Schneewind. Cambridge: Cambridge University Press, 1997.

———. *Critique of Pure Reason*. Trans. and ed. Paul Guyer and Allen W. Wood. Cambridge: Cambridge University Press, 1998.

———. *Correspondence.* Trans. and ed. Arnulf Zweig. Cambridge: Cambridge University Press, 1999.

———. *Critique of the Power of Judgment.* Trans. and ed. Paul Guyer and Eric Mathews. Cambridge: Cambridge University Press, 2000.

———. *Anthropology, History, and Education*. Ed. Günter Zöller and Robert B. Louden. Cambridge: Cambridge University Press, 2007.

Kantorowicz, Ernst. *The King's Two Bodies: A Study in Medieval Political Theology.* Princeton, N.J.: Princeton University Press, 1957.

Kelley, Donald. *Faces of History: Historical Inquiry from Herodotus to Herder.* New Haven, Conn., and London: Yale University Press, 1998.

Kidd, Colin. *British Identities Before Nationalism: Ethnicity and Nationhood in the Atlantic World, 1600–1800.* Cambridge: Cambridge University Press, 1999.

———. *The Forging of Races: Race and Scripture in the Protestant Atlantic World.* Cambridge: Cambridge University Press, 2006.

Kilborne, B. "Anthropological Thought in the Wake of the French Revolution: La Société des observateurs de l'homme." *European Journal of Sociology* 23 (1982): 73–91.

Klausen, Jimmy. "Of Hobbes and Hospitality in Diderot's Supplement to the Voyage of Bougainville." *Polity* 37 (2005): 186–92.

Klein, Lawrence E. *Shaftesbury and the Culture of Politeness: Moral Discourse and Cultural Politics in Early Eighteenth-Century England* (Cambridge: Cambridge University Press, 1994).

Kleingeld, Pauline. "Approaching Perpetual Peace: Kant's Defence of a League of States and his Ideal of a World Federation." *European Journal of Philosophy* 12 (2004): 304–25.

———. *Kant and Cosmopolitanism: The Philosophical Ideal of World Citizenship.* Cambridge: Cambridge University Press, 2012.

Kors, Alan Charles. *D'Holbach's Coterie: An Enlightenment in Paris.* Princeton: Princeton University Press, 1976.

Koselleck, Reinhart. *Critique and Crisis: Enlightenment and the Pathogenesis of Modern Society.* Oxford, New York, and Hamburg: Berg, 1988.

Koskenniemi, Martii. *From Apology to Utopia: The Structure of International Legal Argument.* Cambridge: Cambridge University Press, 2005.

Krause, Sharon R. *Civil Passions: Moral Sentiment and Democratic Deliberation.* Princeton: Princeton University Press, 2008.

Labrousse, Elizabeth. *Pierre Bayle.* The Hague: Martinus Nijhoff, 1963.

Lach, Donald F. "The Sinophilism of Christian Wolff (1679–1754)." In *Discovering China: European Interpretations in the Enlightenment.* Ed. Julia Ching and Willard G. Oxtoby, V.K. Rochester. University of Rochester Press, 1992, 118–30.

La Condamine, Charles-Marie de. *Relation abrégée d'un voyage fait dans l'intérieur de l'Amérique méridionale.* Maastricht, 1778.

Lahontan, Louis-Armand de Lom d'Arce, Baron de. *Œuvres complètes*. Ed. Réal Ouellet (avec la collaboration d'Alain Beaulieu). Montréal: Les Presses de l'Université de Montréal, 1990.

La Mettrie, Lucien Offray de. *Machine Man and Other Writings*. Ed. and trans. Ann Thomson. Cambridge: Cambridge University Press, 1996.

Leibniz, Gottfried Wilhelm. *Essais de théodicée, sur la bonté de dieu, la liberté de l'homme et l'origine du mal.* Paris: Garnier-Flammarion, 1969.

———. *The Political Writings of Leibniz*. Ed. Patrick Riley. Cambridge: Cambridge University Press, 1972.

———. *New Essays on Human Understanding*. Trans. and ed. Peter Remnant and Jonathan Bennett. Cambridge: Cambridge University Press, 1981.

———. *Writings on China*. Ed. and trans. Daniel J. Cook and Henry Rosemont Jr. Chicago and La Salle: Open Court, 1994.

Lévi-Strauss, Claude. *Anthropologie structurale deux.* Paris: Plon, 1973.

Liebersohn, Harry. *The Travelers' World: Europe to the Pacific.* Cambridge, Mass., and London: Harvard University Press, 2006.

Linguet, Simon-Nicholas Henri. *Théorie des loix civiles, ou principes fondamentaux de la société.* London, 1767.

Linton, Marisa. *The Politics of Virtue in Enlightenment France.* Basingstoke, U.K.: Palgrave, 2001.

Locke, John. *Locke's Two Treatises of Government.* Ed. Peter Laslett. Cambridge: Cambridge University Press, 1960.

———. *An Essay Concerning Human Understanding.* Ed. Peter H. Nidditch. Oxford: Clarendon Press, 1975.

———. *Political Essays.* Ed. Mark Goldie. Cambridge: Cambridge University Press, 1997.

Louden, Robert. "'What Does Heaven Say?': Christian Wolff and Western Interpretations of Confucian Ethics." In *Confucius and the Analects: New Essays.* Ed. Bryan W. Van Norden, 73–93. New York: Oxford University Press, 2002.

Lovejoy, Arthur O. *The Great Chain of Being.* Cambridge, Mass.: Harvard University Press, 1936.

Lyotard, Jean-François. *The Post-Modern Condition: A Report on Knowledge.* Trans. Geoff Bennington and Brian Massumi. Manchester: Manchester University Press, 1984.

———. *The Differend: Phrases in Dispute.* Trans. Georges Van Den Abbeele. Minneapolis: University of Minnesota Press, 1988.

Mably, Gabriel Bonnot de. *Doutes proposés aux philosophes économistes sur l'ordre naturel et essentiel des sociétés politiques.* The Hague, 1768.

MacIntyre, Alasdair. *After Virtue: A Study in Moral Theory.* Notre Dame, Ind.: University of Notre Dame Press, 1981.

———. *Three Rival Versions of Moral Enquiry: Encyclopaedia, Genealogy and Tradition.* Notre Dame, Ind.: University of Notre Dame Press, 1990.

———. "Is Patriotism a Virtue?" In *Theorizing Citizenship.* Ed. Ronald Beiner. New York: State University of New York Press, 1995, 216–28.

Madison, James, Alexander Hamilton, and John Jay. *The Federalist Papers.* Ed. Isaac Kramnick. London and New York: Penguin Books, 1987.

Maine, Henry Sumner. *International Law.* London, 1888.

———. *Ancient Law.* London: Dent, 1917 [1861].

Malouet, Pierre-Victor, Baron de. *Examen de cette question: quel sera pour les colonies de l'Amérique le résultat de la révolution française, de la guerre qui en est la suite, et de la paix que doit le terminer?* London, 1797.

———. *Mémoires de Malouet publiés par son petit-fils le baron Malouet.* 2 vols. Paris, 1868.

Mandeville, Bernard. *An Inquiry into the Origin of Honour, and the Usefulness of Christianity in War.* London, 1732.

Mandrillon, Joseph. *Le Spectateur américain, ou remarques générales sur l'Amérique septentrionale . . . Suivi de recherches philosophiques sur la découverte de l'Amérique.* Amsterdam, 1784.

Manin, Bernard. *The Principles of Representative Government.* Cambridge: Cambridge University Press, 1997.

Manuel, Frank. *The Religion of Isaac Newton.* Oxford: Oxford University Press, 1974.

———. *The Changing of the Gods.* Hanover and London: University Press of New England, 1983.

Maôz, Zeev, and Bruce Russett. "Normative and Structural Causes of Democratic Peace, 1946–1986." *American Political Science Review* 87 (1993): 624–38.

Martin-Allanic, Jean Étienne. *Bougainville, navigateur et les découvertes de son temps.* Paris: Presses Universitaires de France, 1964.

Mason, H. T. *Pierre Bayle and Voltaire.* Oxford: Oxford University Press, 1963.

Maupertuis, Pierre Louis Moreau de. *Œuvres de Mr. de Maupertuis.* Lyons, 1756.

Mazower, Mark. *No Enchanted Palace: The End of Empire and the Ideological Origins of the United Nations.* Princeton, N.J., and Oxford: Princeton University Press, 2009.

Mazzini, Giuseppe. *A Cosmopolitanism of Nations: Giuseppe Mazzini's Writings on Democracy, Nation Building, and International Relations*. Ed. and trans. Stefano Recchia and Nadia Urbinati. Princeton, N.J.: Princeton University Press, 2009.

McCarthy, Thomas. *Race, Empire and the Idea of Human Development.* Cambridge: Cambridge University Press, 2009.

McMahon, Darrin M. *Enemies of Enlightenment: The French Counter-Enlightenment and the Making of Modernity.* Oxford: Oxford University Press, 2001.

———. *The Pursuit of Happiness: A History from the Greeks to the Present.* London: Penguin, 2007.

McManners, John. *Death in the Enlightenment: Changing Attitudes to Death in Eighteenth-Century France.* Oxford: Oxford University Press, 1985.

Meek, Ronald L. *Social Science and the Ignoble Savage.* Cambridge: Cambridge University Press, 1976.

Mehta, Uday Singh. *Liberalism and Empire: A Study in Nineteenth-Century British Liberal Thought.* Chicago: University of Chicago Press, 1999.

Mendelssohn, Moses (Friedrich Nicolia, Gotthold Ephraim Lessing). *Briefe die neueste Literatur betreffend.* New York: G. Olms, 1974, 19, 43–4.

Merlini, Cesare, "A Post-Secular World?" *Survival* 53 (2011): 117–30.

Michelet, Jules. *Œuvres complètes*. Ed. Paul Viallaneix. Paris: Flammarion, 1971–82.

Mill, John Stuart. *The Collected Works of John Stuart Mill.* London: Routledge, 1963–91.

———. *Essays on Politics and Society*. In *The Collected Works of John Stuart Mill,* vol. 18. Ed. J. M. Robson. Toronto: Toronto University Press, 1977.

———. *On Liberty and Other Writings*. Ed. Stefan Collini. Cambridge: Cambridge University Press, 1989.

Mirabeau, Victor de Riquetti, Marquis de. *L'Ami des hommes, ou Traité de la population.* Paris, 1756.

Molesworth, Sir Robert. *An Account of Denmark as It Was in the Year 1692.* London, 1694.

Mollat, M., and E. Taillemite, eds. *L'Importance de l'exploration maritime au siècle des Lumières: à propos du voyage de Bougainville.* Paris: Éditions du Centre national de la recherche scientifique, 1982.

Montaigne, Michel de. *The Complete Essays*. Trans. M. A. Screech. London: Penguin, 1987.

Montesquieu, Charles-Louis de Secondat, Baron de. *Œuvres complètes*. Ed. Roger Caillois. Paris: Bibliothèque de la Pléiade, 1949.

———. *Persian Letters*. Trans. C. J. Betts. New York: Viking-Penguin, 1973.

———. *Œuvres complètes de Montesquieu.* Oxford: Voltaire Foundation and Istituto italiano per gli studi filosofici, 2007.

Moravia, Sergio. *Il pensiero degli idéologues. Scienza e filosofia en Francia (1780–1815).* Florence: La Nuova Italia Editrice, 1974.

Morefield, Jeanne. *Covenants Without Swords: Idealist Liberalism and the Spirit of Empire.* Princeton, N.J., and Oxford: Princeton University Press, 2005.

Morellet, André. *Mémoires (inédits) de l'abbé Morellet: précédés d'un éloge historique de l'abbé Morellet par M. Leémontey.* Paris, 1823.

Mori, Massimo. *La pace e la ragione. Kant e le relazioni internazionali: diritto, politica, storia.* Bologna: Il Mulino, 2004.

Mossner, E. C. *The Life of David Hume.* Oxford: Oxford University Press, 1980.

Müller, Jan-Werner. *Constitutional Patriotism.* Princeton, N.J.: Princeton University Press, 2007.

Mungello, D. E., ed. *The Chinese Rites Controversy: Its History and Meaning.* Nettetal, Germany: Steyler Verlag, 1994.

———. *The Great Encounter of China and the West, 1500–1800.* Lanham, Md.: Rowman & Littlefield, 1999.

Muthu, Sankar. *Enlightenment Against Empire.* Princeton, N.J.: Princeton University Press, 2003.

Naigeon, Jacques-André. *Mémoires historiques et philosophiques sur la vie et les œuvres de Denis Diderot.* Paris, 1821.

Newton, Isaac. *Sir Isaac Newton's Mathematical Principles of Natural Philosophy and His System of the World.* Ed. Florian Cajori. Berkeley: University of California Press, 1946.

Nisbet, H. B. "Was ist Aufklärung? The Concept of Enlightenment in Eighteenth-Century Germany." *Journal of European Studies* 12 (1992): 77–95.

Norris, Pippa, and Ronald Ingelhart. *Sacred and Secular: Religion and Politics Worldwide.* Cambridge: Cambridge University Press, 2004.

Nussbaum, Martha (with respondents). *For Love of Country: Debating the Limits of Patriotism.* Ed. Joshua Cohen. Boston: Beacon Press, 1996.

Oakeshott, Michael. *Rationalism in Politics and Other Essays.* Indianapolis: Liberty Fund, 1991.

O'Brien, Karen. *Narratives of Enlightenment: Cosmopolitan History from Voltaire to Gibbon.* Cambridge: Cambridge University Press, 1997.

O'Quinn, Daniel. *Staging Governance: Theatrical Imperialism in London, 1770–1800.* Baltimore: Johns Hopkins University Press, 2005.

Ouellet, R. "Lahontan: les dernières années de sa vie/ses rapports avec Leibniz." *Revue d'histoire littéraire de la France* 87 (1987): 121–29.

Pagden, Anthony. *European Encounters with the New World: From Renaissance to Romanticism.* New Haven, Conn., and London: Yale University Press, 1993.

———. *The Uncertainties of Empire.* Aldershot, U.K.: Variorum, 1994.

———. "Commerce and Conquest: Hugo Grotius and Serafim de Freitas on the Freedom of the Seas." *Mare Liberum* 20 (2000): 33–55.

———. "Human Rights, Natural Rights and Europe's Imperial Legacy." *Political Theory* 31 (2003): 171–99.

———. *Worlds at War: The 2,500-Year Struggle Between East and West.* New York: Random House, 2008.

Passerin d'Entrèves, Alexander. *Natural Law: An Introduction to Legal Philosophy.* Re-edition with an introduction by Cary J. Nederman. New Brunswick and London: Transaction Publishers, 1994 [1950].

Passmore, John. "Enthusiasm, Fanaticism and David Hume." In *The "Science of Man" in the Scottish Enlightenment: Hume, Reid and their Contemporaries,* ed. Peter Jones, 85–107. Edinburgh: Edinburgh University Press, 1989.

Perkins, Franklin. "Virtue, Reason and Cultural Exchange: Leibniz's Praise of Chinese Morality." *Journal of the History of Ideas* 63 (2002): 447–64, 460.

———. *Leibniz and China: A Commerce of Light.* Cambridge: Cambridge University Press, 2004.

Perkins, Merle J. *The Moral and Political Philosophy of the Abbé de Saint-Pierre.* Geneva: Droz, 1959.

Philonenko, Alexis. "Kant et le problème de la paix." In *Essais sur la philosophie de la guerre*. Paris: Vrin, 1976, 26–46.

Pincus, Steven. *1688: The First Modern Revolution*. New Haven, Conn., and London: Yale University Press, 2009.

Pinker, Steven. *The Language Instinct: How the Mind Creates Language.* New York: Morrow, 1994.

———. *The Better Angels of Our Nature: Why Violence Has Declined.* New York: Viking, 2011.

Piscatori, James P. *Islam in a World of Nation States.* Cambridge: Cambridge University Press, 1986.

Pitts, Jennifer. "Empire and Legal Universalism in the Eighteenth Century." *American Historical Review* 117 (2012): 92–121.

Pocock, J.G.A. *Barbarism and Religion.* Cambridge: Cambridge University Press, 1999–.

Pomeau, René. *La Religion de Voltaire.* Paris: Librairie Nizet, 1956.

Porter, Roy. *The Creation of the Modern World: The Untold Story of the British Enlightenment.* New York and London: W. W. Norton, 2000.

Price, Richard. *Political Writings*. Ed. D. O. Thomas. Cambridge: Cambridge University Press, 1991.

Pufendorf, Samuel. *On the Duty of Man and Citizen According to Natural Law*. Ed. James Tully. Cambridge: Cambridge University Press, 1991.

Rabb, Theodore K. *The Struggle for Stability in Early-Modern Europe.* New York: Oxford University Press, 1975.

Rawls, John. *The Law of Peoples.* Cambridge, Mass.: Harvard University Press, 1999.

Raynal, Guillaume-Thomas-François. *Histoire philosophique et politique des établissements et du commerce des Européens dans les deux Indes*. Ed. Anthony Strugnell et al. Paris: Centre international d'études du XVIIIe siècle, 2010.

Rehberg, August Wilhelm. *Untersuchungen über die französische Revolution.* Hannover, 1793.

Reid, Thomas. *An Inquiry into the Human Mind on the Principles of Common Sense.* Ed. Derek R. Brookes. Edinburgh: Edinburgh University Press, 1997 [1764].

Reill, Peter. *The German Enlightenment and the Rise of Historicism.* Berkeley: University of California Press, 1975.

Ripstein, Arthur. *Force and Freedom: Kant's Legal and Political Philosophy.* Cambridge, Mass.: Harvard University Press, 2009.

Robertson, John. *The Case for Enlightenment: Scotland and Naples, 1680–1760*. Cambridge: Cambridge University Press, 2005.

Roger, Jacques. *Buffon: un philosophe au Jardin du Roi.* Paris: Fayard, 1989.

———. *Les Sciences de la vie dans la pensée française au XVIIIe siècle.* Paris: A. Colin, 1963.

Rorty, Richard. *Contingency, Irony, and Solidarity.* Cambridge: Cambridge University Press, 1989.

Rothschild, Emma. *Economic Sentiments: Adam Smith, Condorcet and the Enlightenment.* Cambridge, Mass., and London: Harvard University Press, 2001.

Rousseau, Jean-Jacques. *Œuvres complètes.* Ed. Bernard Gagnebin and Marcel Raymond. Paris: Bibliothèque de la pléiade, 1959–95.

———. *Essay on the Origin of Language Which Treats of Melody and Musical Imitation.* Trans. John H. Moran. In *On the Origin of Language.* Chicago: University of Chicago Press, 1966.

Russell, Bertrand. *History of Western Philosophy.* London: George Allen & Unwin, 1946.

Sabl, Andrew. *Hume's Politics: Coordination and Crisis in the History of England.* Princeton, N.J.: Princeton University Press, in press.

Safier, Neil. *Measuring the New World: Enlightenment Science and South America.* Chicago and London: University of Chicago Press, 2008.

Saint-Pierre, Charles-Irénée Castel, abbé de. *Project pour rendre la paix perpétuelle en Europe.* Paris: Fayard, 1986.

Schama, Simon. *Citizens: A Chronicle of the French Revolution.* London: Penguin, 1989.

Scheenwind, J. B. *The Invention of Autonomy: A History of Modern Moral Philosophy.* Cambridge: Cambridge University Press, 1998.

Schelling, F.W.J. von. *On the History of Modern Philosophy*. Trans. Andrew Bowie. Cambridge: Cambridge University Press, 1994.

Schiller, Friedrich. *On the Aesthetic Education of Man*. Trans. E. M. Wilkinson and L. A. Willoughby. Oxford: Oxford University Press, 1982.

Schmidt, James, ed. *What Is Enlightenment? Eighteenth-Century Answers and Twentieth-Century Questions.* Berkeley and Los Angeles: University of California Press, 1996.

Schøsler, Jørn. *John Locke et les philosophes français: la critique des idées innées en France au dix-huitième siècle.* Oxford: Voltaire Foundation, 1997.

Schulman, Alex. *The Secular Contract: The Politics of Enlightenment.* New York and London: Continuum Books, 2011.

Scott, Joan Wallach. *Only Paradoxes to Offer: French Feminists and the Rights of Man.* Cambridge, Mass.: Harvard University Press, 1996.

Scurr, Ruth. *Fatal Purity: Robespierre and the French Revolution.* London: Chatto & Windus, 2006.

Severino, Giulio. *Principi e modificazioni in Vico.* Genoa: Il Melangolo, 1981.

Shaftesbury, Anthony Ashley Cooper, Third Earl of Shaftesbury. *Life, Unpublished Letters, and Philosophical Regimen of Anthony, Earl of Shaftesbury*. Ed. Benjamin Rand. London: S. Sonnenschein & Co., 1900.

———. *Second Characters or the Language of Forms*. Ed. Benjamin Rand. Cambridge: Cambridge University Press, 1914.

———. *Characteristics of Men, Manners, Opinions, Times*. Ed. Lawrence E. Klein. Cambridge: Cambridge University Press, 1999.

Sherratt, Yvonne. *Continental Philosophy of Social Science: Hermeneutics, Genealogy and*

Critical Theory from Greece to the Twenty-first Century. Cambridge: Cambridge University Press, 2006.

Shklar, Judith N. *Men and Citizens: A Study of Rousseau's Social Theory.* Cambridge: Cambridge University Press, 1969.

———. *Freedom and Independence: A Study of Hegel's "Phenomenology of Mind."* Cambridge: Cambridge University Press, 1976.

———. *Montesquieu.* Oxford: Oxford University Press, 1987.

———. *Political Thought and Political Thinkers.* Chicago and London: University of Chicago Press, 1998.

Skinner, Quentin. "Thomas Hobbes: Rhetoric and the Construction of Morality." Dawes Hicks Lecture on Philosophy. *Proceedings of the British Academy* 76 (1991): 1–61.

———. *Reason and Rhetoric in the Philosophy of Hobbes.* Cambridge: Cambridge University Press, 1996.

Smith, Adam. *An Inquiry into the Nature and Causes of the Wealth of Nations.* Ed. W. B. Todd. Oxford: Clarendon Press, 1976.

———. *The Theory of Moral Sentiments.* Ed. D. D. Raphael and A. L. Macfie. Oxford: Clarendon Press, 1976.

———. *Correspondence of Adam Smith.* Ed. Ernest Campbell Mossner and Ian Simpson Ross. Oxford: Clarendon Press, 1977.

———. *Essays on Philosophical Subjects.* Ed. I. S. Ross. Oxford: Clarendon Press, 1980.

———. *Lectures on Jurisprudence.* Ed. R. L. Meek et al. Oxford: Oxford University Press, 1980.

———. *Lectures on Rhetoric and Belles Lettres.* Ed. J. Bryce. Oxford: Clarendon Press, 1983.

Smith, Bernard. *European Vision and the South Pacific.* New Haven, Conn., and London: Yale University Press, 1985.

Smith, Denis Mack. *Mazzini.* New Haven, Conn., and London: Yale University Press, 1994.

Sparling, Robert Alan. *Johann Georg Hamann and the Enlightenment Project.* Toronto: Toronto University Press, 2011.

Spence, Jonathan D. *The Chan's Great Continent: China in Western Minds.* New York and London: W. W. Norton & Co., 1998.

Starobinski, Jean. *Jean-Jacques Rousseau: La Transparence et l'obstacle.* Paris: Gallimard, 1971.

———. "Le Mot civilisation." In *Le Remède dans le mal. Critique et légitimation de l'artifice à l'âge des Lumières.* Paris: Gallimard, 1989.

———. *Action et réaction. Vie et aventures d'un couple.* Paris: Seuil, 1999.

Straumann, Benjamin. "The Peace of Westphalia as a Secular Constitution." *Constellations* 15 (2008): 173–88.

Stuke, H. "Aufklärung." In *Geschichtliche Grundbegriffe, historisches Lexikon zur politisch-sozialen Sprache in Deutschland.* Ed. Otto Brunner, W. Conze, and R. Koselleck. Stuttgart: Klett-Cotta, 1972–.

Taillemite, Étienne, ed. *Bougainville et ses compagnons autour du monde 1766–1769, Journaux de Navigation.* Paris: Imprimerie nationale, 2006.

Taylor, Charles. *Hegel.* Cambridge: Cambridge University Press, 1975.

———. *Philosophy and the Human Sciences: Philosophical Papers.* Cambridge: Cambridge University Press, 1985.
———. *Sources of the Self: The Making of the Modern Identity.* Cambridge: Cambridge University Press, 1989.
———. *A Secular Age.* Cambridge, Mass.: Harvard University Press, 2007.
Terjanian, Anoush. *Commerce and Its Discontents in Eighteenth-Century French Political Thought.* Cambridge: Cambridge University Press, 2012.
Thomas, Nicholas. *Cook: The Extraordinary Voyages of Captain James Cook.* New York: Walker & Co., 2003.
Thomasius, Christian. *Fundamenta juris naturae et gentium ex sensu communi deducta.* Halle, 1718.
Tocqueville, Alexis de. *De la démocratie en Amérique.* Paris: Gallimard, 1961.
———. *L'Ancien régime et la révolution.* Ed. François Mélonio. Paris: Flammarion, 1988.
Todorov, Tzvetan. *La Vie commune. Essai d'anthropologie générale.* Paris: Seuil, 1995.
Tomaselli, Sylvana. "Civilization, Patriotism and Enlightened Histories of Women." In *Women, Gender and Enlightenment.* Ed. Sarah Knott and Barbara Taylor. London: Palgrave Macmillan, 2005, 117–35.
Tourneaux, Maurice. *Correspondance littéraire, philosophique et critique par Grimm, Diderot, Raynal, Meister, etc.* Paris, 1877.
Tuck, Richard. "The 'Modern' Theory of Natural Law." In *The Languages of Political Theory in Early-Modern Europe.* Ed. Anthony Pagden. Cambridge: Cambridge University Press, 1987, 99–119.
———. *The Rights of War and Peace: Political Thought and the International Order from Grotius to Kant.* Oxford: Oxford University Press, 1999.
Turgot, Anne-Robert-Jacques. *Œuvres de Turgot*. Ed. Gustave Schelle. Paris: Librairie Félix Alcan, 1913.
———. *Turgot on Progress, Sociology, and Economics*. Trans. and ed. Ronald L. Meek. Cambridge: Cambridge University Press, 1973.
Ullmann, Walter. "Some Observations on the Mediaeval Evaluation of the 'Homo naturalis' and the 'Christianus.' " In *L'Homme et son destin d'après les penseurs du Moyen Age. Actes du premier congrès international de philosophie médiévale*, 145–51. Louvain and Paris: Nauwelaerts, 1960.
Urbinati, Nadia, *Representative Democracy: Principles and Genealogy*. Chicago: University of Chicago Press, 2006, 120–30.
Vattel, Emer de. *Poliergie ou mélange du littérature de poésies.* "Amsterdam" [in fact Paris], 1757.
———. *Mélanges de littérature, de morale et de politique.* Neuchâtel, 1760.
———. *Le Droit de gens, et les devoirs des citoyens, ou Principes de la loi naturelle.* Nimes, 1793.
Venturi, Franco. *Settecento riformatore.* Turin: Einaudi, 1969–80.
Vico, Giambattista. *Vico Opere*. Ed. Fausto Nicolini. Bari: Laterza, 1911–41.
———. *Vico Selected Writings*. Ed. and trans. Leon Pompa. Cambridge: Cambridge University Press, 1982.
Viroli, Maurizio. *For Love of Country: An Essay on Patriotism and Nationalism.* Oxford: Clarendon Press, 1995.

Vitoria, Francisco de. *Comentarios a la Secunda Secundae de Santo Tomás*. Ed. Vicente Beltrán de Heredia. Salamanca: Universidad de Salamanca, 1932–52.

———. *Political Writings*. Ed. Anthony Pagden and Jeremy Lawrance. Cambridge: Cambridge University Press, 1991.

Vlachos, Georges. *La Pensée politique de Kant.* Paris: Presses Universitaires de France, 1962.

Volney, Constantin-François. *Les Ruines, ou Méditations sur les révolutions des empires*. In *Œuvres.* Ed. Anne et Henry Deneys. Paris: Fayard, 1989, 267.

Voltaire (François-Marie Arouet). *Alzire, ou les Américains, tragédie.* Paris, 1736.

———. *L'Evangile du jour.* London, 1770.

———. *Œuvres complètes de Voltaire.* Paris, 1880.

———. *Correspondance*. Ed. Theodore Besterman. Geneva: Institut et musée Voltaire, 1953–77.

———. *Romans et contes*. Ed. René Gros. Paris: Classiques Garnier, 1954.

———. *Lettres philosophiques*. Ed. René Pomeau. Paris: Flammarion, 1964.

———. *Essai sur les moeurs et l'esprit des nations*. Ed. R. Pomeau. Paris: Classiques Garnier, 1990.

———. *Dictionnaire philosophique*. Ed. Alain Pons. Paris: Gallimard, 1994.

Wade, Ira O. *Voltaire and Madame du Châtelet: An Essay on the Intellectual Activity at Cirey.* Princeton, N.J.: Princeton University Press, 1941.

Walzer, Michael, ed. *Regicide and Revolution: Speeches at the Trial of Louis XVI.* Cambridge: Cambridge University Press, 1974.

———. *Spheres of Justice: A Defense of Pluralism and Equality.* New York: Basic Books, 1983.

Ward, Robert. *An Enquiry into the Foundations of the Laws of Nations in Europe from the Time of the Greeks and Romans to the Age of Grotius.* London, 1795.

Wieland, Christoph. *Werke*. Ed. J. G. Gruber. Berlin, 1824–27.

Williams, Bernard. *Making Sense of Humanity and Other Philosophical Papers, 1982–1992.* Cambridge: Cambridge University Press, 1995.

Williams, David. *Condorcet and Modernity.* Cambridge: Cambridge University Press, 2004.

Wolff, Christian. *Jus gentium methodo scientifica pertractatum.* Oxford: Clarendon Press, 1934.

Wood, Gordon S. *Empire of Liberty: A History of the Early Republic.* Oxford: Oxford University Press, 2009.

Yovel, Yirmiahu. *Kant and the Philosophy of History.* Princeton, N.J.: Princeton University Press, 1980.

Zamato, John H. *Kant, Herder: The Birth of Anthropology.* Chicago and London: University of Chicago Press, 2002.

INDEX

ABOUT THE AUTHOR

Anthony Pagden is distinguished professor of political science and history at the University of California, Los Angeles. He was educated in Chile, Spain, and France, and at Oxford. He has been the reader in intellectual history at Cambridge, a fellow of King's College, a visiting professor at Harvard, and Harry C. Black Professor of History at Johns Hopkins University. He is the author of many prize-winning books, including *Peoples and Empires: A Short History of European Migration, Exploration, and Conquest, from Greece to the Present; European Encounters with the New World: From Renaissance to Romanticism; The Fall of Natural Man: The American Indian and the Origins of Comparative Enthnology;* and *Worlds at War: The 2,500-Year Struggle Between East and West.* Pagden contributes regularly to such publications as *The New York Times, Los Angeles Times, The National Interest,* and *The New Republic.*